HANDBOOK ON UNDERGRADUATE CURRICULUM

PREPARED FOR THE CARNEGIE COUNCIL
ON POLICY STUDIES IN HIGHER EDUCATION

Arthur Levine

HANDBOOK ON UNDERGRADUATE CURRICULUM

 Jossey-Bass Publishers

San Francisco • Washington • London • 1978

HANDBOOK ON UNDERGRADUATE CURRICULUM
Arthur Levine

Copyright © 1978 by: The Carnegie Foundation
for the Advancement of Teaching

Jossey-Bass, Inc., Publishers
433 California Street
San Francisco, California 94104

Jossey-Bass Limited
28 Banner Street
London EC1Y 8QE

The Carnegie Council on Policy Studies in Higher Education,
2150 Shattuck Avenue, Berkeley, California 94704, has sponsored
preparation of this report as part of a continuing effort to
obtain and present information for public discussion. The views
expressed are not necessarily shared by all members of the Council.

Copies are available from Jossey-Bass, San Francisco,
for the United States and Possessions, and for Canada,
Australia, New Zealand, and Japan.
Copies for the rest of the world are available from
Jossey-Bass, London.

Library of Congress Catalogue Card Number LC 78-50893

International Standard Book Number ISBN 0-87589-376-7

Manufactured in the United States of America

DESIGN BY WILLI BAUM

FIRST EDITION

Code 7818

The Carnegie Council Series

The Federal Role in Postsecondary
Education: Unfinished Business,
1975–1980
*The Carnegie Council on Policy
Studies in Higher Education*

Low or No Tuition: The Feasibil-
ity of a National Policy for the
First Two Years of College
*The Carnegie Council on Policy
Studies in Higher Education*

More Than Survival: Prospects for
Higher Education in a Period
of Uncertainty
*The Carnegie Foundation for the
Advancement of Teaching*

Managing Multicampus Systems:
Effective Administration in an
Unsteady State
Eugene C. Lee, Frank M. Bowen

Making Affirmative Action Work
in Higher Education: An Analysis
of Institutional and Federal Policies with Recommendations
*The Carnegie Council on Policy
Studies in Higher Education*

Challenges Past, Challenges
Present: An Analysis of
American Higher Education
Since 1930
David D. Henry

Presidents Confront Reality: From
Edifice Complex to University
Without Walls
*Lyman A. Glenny, John R. Shea,
Janet H. Ruyle, Kathryn H. Freschi*

The States and Higher Education:
A Proud Past and a Vital Future
*The Carnegie Foundation for the
Advancement of Teaching*

Progress and Problems in Medical
and Dental Education: Federal
Support Versus Federal Control
*The Carnegie Council on Policy
Studies in Higher Education*

Educational Leaves for Employees: European Experience
for American Consideration
*Konrad von Moltke,
Norbert Schneevoigt*

Contents

Foreword

The undergraduate curriculum has been a subject of major concern to both the Carnegie Council on Policy Studies in Higher Education and The Carnegie Foundation for the Advancement of Teaching ever since the Council was established in 1974. This concern derives from our observation that the curriculum has undergone considerable change in the past decade, partly in response to student protests in the 1960s and partly in response to new labor market situations in the 1970s that have raised questions about the match between what is learned in college and what is needed by students after they graduate. But there has also been an impressive amount of change taking place in the composition and capacities of student bodies and in the social concerns that animate students, faculty members, and the public alike. Prospectively, the period ahead is one of essentially no growth for higher education but of fundamental social changes. Many colleges and universities, including Harvard, Columbia, Stanford, to name but a few, are already giving serious attention to curricular reform and many others may be expected to do so in the near future.

As a contribution to these deliberations and developments that we expect to take place in the coming years, The Carnegie Foundation for the Advancement of Teaching and the Carnegie Council on Policy Studies in Higher Education are issuing three related documents on the American undergraduate curriculum. First, The Carnegie Foundation offered a commentary on this subject, *Missions of the College Curriculum,* in December 1977. Second, the Carnegie Council, which participated in the development of the

Foundation's commentary, commissioned Frederick Rudolph, Mark Hopkins Professor of History at Williams College, to write a comprehensive review of the development of the college curriculum in America. The result of his work, the excellent *Curriculum: A History of the American Undergraduate Course of Study Since 1636*, also appeared in December 1977. *The Handbook on Undergraduate Curriculum*, prepared for the Council by Arthur Levine, is the final work in our curriculum trilogy.

This volume is intended as a resource book. It is one that curriculum planners and students of the curriculum will want to read from cover to cover; but it is also designed as a reference for administrators, faculty members, students, trustees, and others involved with undergraduate education.

This handbook, like its companion commentary, was made possible by the efforts of many persons who served as guides and consultants on the various campuses visited during its preparation. We deeply appreciate their contributions to our work. We wish also to express our thanks to the members of special advisory groups and the other individuals who met with us to discuss the curricular issues addressed here and who reviewed drafts of the manuscript and gave us many helpful suggestions. Their names, along with those of our staff who have been closely associated with the preparation of the handbook, are found in Appendix C.

We particularly wish to express our appreciation to Arthur Levine for his dedicated and meticulous efforts in making this enormously comprehensive work possible.

CLARK KERR
Chairperson
Carnegie Council on Policy Studies
in Higher Education

Preface

Each week at the Brandeis Educational Policy Committee someone would insist that the future of the university rested on our dropping a given requirement or adding a proposed program. And each week we traded anecdotes and guesses about the effects of the proposals. The most compelling arguments were based on the experience of a relative or a friend or a friend of a relative at another school where the proposal or something like it had been adopted. Through the magic of parliamentary procedure, we were able to resolve the same issue at several consecutive meetings with any number of different conclusions. Everybody had an equal chance to win, and everybody did one week or another. But when a proposal went to the faculty for final approval, we all stood behind it. The faculty then repeated the same discussions that we had had and voted in their own way, basing their votes on their own feelings and their own anecdotes. And the resolutions that came out of the faculty meetings became educational policy.

John Weingart and I wrote this account of our experiences in helping to make educational policy at Brandeis University in the late 1960s (A. Levine and J. Weingart, *Reform of Undergraduate Education,* San Francisco: Jossey-Bass, 1973, pp. ix–x). The description was by no means unique to Brandeis; in fact, it mirrored well the way curriculum was developed at most other American colleges and universities.

Since the 1960s, there have been changes in educational policy: The subject of curriculum debate has shifted from a concern with adding programs and dropping requirements to one of adding requirements and dropping programs. And the motivation for curriculum debate has shifted from student unrest to steady-state economic woes and the continuing post-Watergate moral crisis. But the basic process of making educational policy is still the same.

The purpose of this *Handbook on Undergraduate Curriculum* is to bring information to bear on educational decision making—from the classroom level to the institutional level—and for producers of educational services as well as consumers of these services. The *Handbook* is divided into two parts: the first consists of basic information about American college curricula; the second puts this information in philosophical, chronological, institutional, and cultural perspective. Part One, entitled "Undergraduate Curriculum Today," consists of nine chapters on "General Education," "The Major or Concentration," "Basic and Advanced Skills and Knowledge," "Tests and Grades," "Education and Work," "Advising," "Credits and Degree," "Methods of Instruction," and "The Structure of Academic Time." These are the elements that make up the undergraduate curriculum. Together with the extracurriculum (the noncredit and nonclassroom activities available to students through recreational, social, and cultural activities sponsored by colleges or by college-related organizations) and the hidden curriculum (learning that is informally and sometimes inadvertently acquired by students in interactions with fellow students and faculty members and inferred from the rules and traditions of an institution) they constitute a college education. Each chapter in Part One discusses three points regarding each curriculum element—first, its definition and history; second, its current state; and third, popular criticisms and proposals of the current state.

Part One is primarily descriptive, dealing with normative practices, their history, their strengths, their weaknesses, and their alternatives. In it, I have tried to avoid inflicting upon the reader my personal preferences and visions of what undergraduate education should be, even in the face of almost irresistible temptation, nearly overwhelming desire, and weakening will power. For example, the discussion of popular criticisms and proposals in each chapter describes the range of policy alternatives that have been suggested to solve particular problems rather than the solutions I personally favor. Offering a policy analysis and recommendations on undergraduate education is the rationale for *Missions of the College Curriculum: A Contemporary Review with Suggestions,* by The Carnegie Foundation for the Advancement of Teaching—another book in the curriculum trilogy from the Carnegie Council on Policy Studies in Higher Education that Clark Kerr discusses in his Foreword.

Several research projects of the Carnegie Council on Policy Studies in Higher Education and its predecessor, the Carnegie Commission on Higher Education are referred to throughout Part One. They are "Carnegie Surveys, 1969–70"; "Carnegie Surveys 1975–76"; "Catalog Study, 1976"; and "Reflections of an Itinerant Interviewer." Each warrants explanation here.

The "Carnegie Surveys 1969–70" were conducted under the auspices of the Carnegie Commission on Higher Education with the cooperation of the American Council on Education and support from the U.S. Office of Education. They probed the opinions and experiences of 60,000 faculty, 70,000 undergraduates, and 30,000 graduate students. The technical details of the survey and the survey questionnaire can be found in Martin Trow (Ed.), *Teachers and Students: Aspects of American Higher Education,* New York: McGraw-Hill, 1975.

The "Carnegie Surveys, 1975–76" were conducted by the Carnegie Council on Policy Studies in Higher Education and involved 25,000 faculty members, 25,000 undergraduates, and 25,000 graduate students. The questions used in these surveys and their technical details will be discussed in a forthcoming book by Judy Roizen, Oliver Fulton, and Martin Trow.

The 1976 "Catalog Study" was a Carnegie Council staff analysis of 1975 catalogs from a representative sample of 270 two- and four-year colleges and universities (listed in Appendix B), based on the nine-category Carnegie institutional typology discussed in the Introduction. This study examined stated curricular policies in a cross section of programs in six areas: the arts and sciences, business, education, engineering, health sciences, and trade and technical arts.

"Reflections of an Itinerant Interviewer" is an unpublished report that I prepared for the Carnegie Council summarizing current curriculum trends based on field visits to 19 diverse postsecondary institutions.

Part Two, entitled "A Comparative and Historical Perspective on Undergraduate Curriculum," adds breadth to Part One. Chapter 10 compares and contrasts the visions of the university and the undergraduate curriculum of seven modern philosophers of education—Newman, Dewey, Whitehead, Veblen, Flexner, Hutchins, and Kerr. Chapter 11 presents more recent, radical, or recently rejected curriculum proposals from 21 additional authors, ranging from Daniel Bell to Ivan Illich. Chapter 12 moves from philosophy to action. It describes 12 highlights in the development of the American college curriculum between 1900 and 1964—bright spots that are commonly referred to when people discuss undergraduate education, including the Honors Program at Swarthmore and the Harvard report on *General Education in a Free Society*. Chapter 13 discusses 13 highlights of the present, including the creation of the University of California, Santa Cruz, and the development of the competency-based curriculum at Sterling College. Based on Chapters 12 and 13, Chapter 14 analyzes the "Characteristics of Curriculum Change," with particular reference to strategies for curriculum change, stages of change, participants in change, and elements of successful change. Chapter 15 then puts the American undergraduate curriculum in perspective via an examination of the curricula of seven other nations—the People's Republic of China, France, the Federal Republic of Germany, Great Britain, Japan, Sweden, and the Union of Soviet Socialist Republics. Finally, Chapter 16 provides a concluding overview and chronology of the history of undergraduate education from 532 B.C. to the present, divided into two sections—"Antecedents of American Higher Education" and "The American Experience." This chapter is supplemented by Appendix A, a documentary history of the American undergraduate curriculum. Each of the chapters concludes with its own partially annotated bibliography, for handy use as a self-contained resource, but a glossary of technical and foreign terms for the entire volume follows Chapter 16. In Part Two, I have taken slightly more liberty than in Part One in selecting and emphasizing those trends and events that seem to me of critical importance in dealing with today's curricular problems.

Like most books, this handbook could not have been written without the help of many generous people. In this case, the number is so large that a separate appendix, Appendix C, is necessary to list their names. I especially wish to thank JB Hefferlin who labored long and painstakingly on the manuscript, giving generously of his energy and wisdom and the Carnegie Council and its staff who deserve particular mention here because their efforts were truly prodigious. For a year and a half, Clark Kerr and the other members of the Council read, commented on, made suggestions, and carried all over the country outlines, partial drafts, and full drafts of this book, which came increasingly to resemble the Manhattan telephone directory in size. The associate director of the Council, Verne Stadtman, who gave me the opportunity to write this volume, read, reread again and again, commented on, and finally edited these pages; he debated ideas with me, offered insights that found their way into the manuscript, disputed passages that found their way out of the manuscript, and in general kept me honest. Claudia White, our assistant, raced more deadlines than she'd care to remember typing draft after draft of this book, handled countless administrative duties associated with the volume, consistently offered useful advice, and did it all with good humor and grace. Nanette Sand, the Carnegie Council librarian, managed to find literature on almost any subject I inquired about regardless of how abstruse the topic and how long out of print the work. Jeanne Marengo performed a lion's share of work in the final months of turning this manuscript into a book, and Marian Gade provided a helping hand throughout. I thank them all very much.

Berkeley, California   ARTHUR LEVINE
February 1978

The Author

ARTHUR LEVINE is a senior fellow at the Carnegie Council on Policy Studies in Higher Education. He earned his bachelor's degree in biology at Brandeis University (1970) and his doctor's degree in sociology and in higher education at the State University of New York, Buffalo (1976). He is the author of *Undergraduate Curriculum Evaluation* (with J. Weingart, 1972) and of *Reform of Undergraduate Education* (with J. Weingart, 1973), which received the American Council on Education Book of the Year Award in 1974.

Introduction

There is no such thing as *the* undergraduate curriculum in America. There are more than 3,000 colleges and universities in this country, and each has a curriculum that is in some ways unique.

This situation would seem to make it impossible to discuss undergraduate curricula, but fortunately things are not quite that bad. American colleges and universities fall naturally into groups or clusters, and in these groups curricular similarities are greatly increased and their differences are reduced to manageable or comprehensible levels. This volume divides American colleges and universities into groups based on a 1970 Carnegie Commission on Higher Education typology with nine categories (see Carnegie Commission on Higher Education, 1973). This introduction explains the nine types and illustrates differences among them in their curricula, their faculty, and students.

Types of Institutions

RESEARCH UNIVERSITIES

1. Research universities I. These 50 universities are leaders in terms of federal financial support for at least two academic years from 1968–69 to 1970–71, provided they awarded at least 50 Ph.D.s in 1969–70. Examples include the University of California, Berkeley; Cornell University; Duke University; the University of Illinois, Urbana; The Johns Hopkins University; the University of Michigan; Ohio State University; and Yale University. In this book, they frequently are called the "most research-oriented universities" to emphasize their most distinctive attribute.

2. Research Universities II. These institutions are either on the list of the 100 leading institutions in terms of federal financial support in two of the above-mentioned three academic years, provided they awarded at least 50 Ph.D.s in 1960–70, or are listed among the top 50 in terms of total Ph.D.s awarded between 1960 and 1970. Examples include the University of Connecticut, George Washington University, Indiana University, Louisiana State University, the State University of New York at Buffalo, and West Virginia University.

DOCTORATE-GRANTING UNIVERSITIES

3. Doctorate-Granting Universities I. These universities awarded 40 or more Ph.D.s in 1969–70 or received at least $3 million in total federal financial support in either 1969–70 or 1970–71. Examples include Brigham Young University; the University of California, Riverside; Dartmouth University; Kent State University; and the University of New Hampshire.

4. Doctorate-Granting Universities II. These institutions awarded at least ten Ph.D.s in 1969–70 or are universities with several promising new programs. Examples include Bowling Green State University; Clark University; Memphis State University; the University of Nevada, Reno; and the New School for Social Research.

COMPREHENSIVE UNIVERSITIES AND COLLEGES

5. Comprehensive Universities and Colleges I. These colleges and universities offer a liberal arts program and at least two professional courses of study, such as engineering and business. All of them have either no doctoral program or else an extremely limited one; most award master's degrees. Enrollments are 2,000 or more. Examples include Arkansas State University, Bob Jones University, Canisius College, Federal City College, Gonzaga University, and Skidmore College.

6. Comprehensive Universities and Colleges II. These colleges and universities offer a liberal arts program and at least one professional course of study. Enrollments begin at 1,000 to 1,500. In the past, many of these institutions were teacher colleges. Examples include

Delaware State College; Emerson College; the University of Minnesota, Morris; and Saint Norbert College.

LIBERAL ARTS COLLEGES

7. *Liberal Arts Colleges I.* These colleges have a strong liberal arts tradition and modest, if any, occupational programs. They scored five or better on the Astin Selectivity Index (a measure based on average student scores on the Scholastic Aptitude Test, American College Test, and National Merit Scholarship Qualifying Test) or were among the 200 leading baccalaureate-granting institutions in terms of numbers of their graduates having received Ph.D.s at 40 leading doctorate-granting institutions from 1920 to 1966. Examples include Amherst College, Bennington College, Colorado College, Grinnell College, Hamilton College, Pomona College, Reed College, and Swarthmore College. In this book, they are generally denoted as "selective" or the "most selective liberal arts colleges."

8. *Liberal Arts Colleges II.* These are all the remaining liberal arts schools. Examples include Curry College, Lone Mountain College, Loretto Heights College, Lyndon State College, Ottawa University, and Spring Hill College. They are referred to in later chapters as the "less selective liberal arts colleges."

TWO-YEAR COLLEGES

9. The ninth and final type consists of two-year colleges, such as Dixie College, Flathead Valley Community College, Grand Rapids Junior College, LaGuardia Community College, and Rhode Island Junior College. In later pages these colleges are sometimes called "community and junior colleges."[1]

These nine Carnegie types represent very different kinds of institutions. They differ in regard to faculty, students, and curriculum character. Consider some faculty and student differences before reviewing the concomitant curriculum differences.

Faculty Characteristics

Teaching staffs at these nine types of institutions vary widely with respect to size, research credentials, research interest, concern

[1]The Carnegie typology was recently updated and some changes were made in the definitions of the nine colleges and university types. See Carnegie Council on Policy Studies in Higher Education, 1978.

with undergraduate academic problems, and quality of teaching performance. These differences among types are illustrated in Table A.

Table A shows a 25-fold variation in faculty size between the largest type of institutions and the smallest. The median department size varies fivefold, meaning that the largest institutions have five times the number of departments of the smallest. The number of faculty and the size of departments decrease systematically by type among universities and four-year institutions, with research universities I the largest and baccalaureate-granting institutions the smallest. Two-year colleges employ more faculty than solely baccalaureate-granting institutions.

Students at larger institutions have an opportunity to study with more faculty, but they do not rate their teaching as well as other undergraduates. Students are more satisfied with teaching and believe faculty to be most interested in their academic problems at smaller colleges—liberal arts colleges I, liberal arts colleges II, and two-year colleges. Even so, the majority of undergraduates at all types of institutions rate their teaching satisfactory.

This situation exists despite wide variation in faculty interest and training for teaching. With the exception of liberal arts colleges I, whose mission is in great measure training students for graduate school, the interest of faculty in teaching over research increases progressively from type to type—from 46 percent in research universities I to 94 percent in two-year colleges. Publication rates and percentage of faculty with Ph.D.s vary in the same fashion. Teaching is rated worst at institutions where faculty have the most Ph.D.s, the highest rate of publication, and the greatest interest in research. Teaching is rated quite highly, though not the best, at the institutions where faculty have the fewest Ph.D.s, the highest rate of nonpublication, and the least interest in research.

Undergraduate Characteristics

The student body at the nine types of colleges and universities differ in size, sex, race, age, residential status, degree aspirations, high school achievement, parents' education, transfer rate, and competitiveness, as shown in Table B. The largest university has 23 times the number of undergraduate students of the smallest col-

Table A. Characteristics of faculty at different institutions by Carnegie type

	Research universities		Doctorate-granting universities		Comprehensive universities & colleges		Liberal arts colleges		Two-year colleges
	I	II	I	II	I	II	I	II	
Average number of FTE faculty	1,605	992	678	623	297	236	76	64	141
Median department size	21–25	16–20	16–20	11–15	11–15	11–15	6–7	4–5	6–7
Percentage of faculty with Ph.D.	66	63	64	57	48	45	57	38	10
Percentage of faculty more interested in teaching than research	46	56	61	68	82	86	82	91	94
Percentage of faculty without professional publications in last two years	18	23	28	36	52	58	53	69	82
Percentage of students believing "most faculty at my college are strongly interested in the academic problems of undergraduates"	38	44	52	44	53	57	81	70	65
Percentage of students satisfied with teaching at their college	65	64	71	65	68	69	85	76	76

Source: Catalog Study, 1976; and Carnegie Surveys, 1975–76.

Table B. Characteristics of undergraduates at different institutions by Carnegie type

	Research universities		Doctorate-granting universities		Comprehensive universities & colleges		Liberal arts colleges		Two-year colleges
	I	II	I	II	I	II	I	II	
Median number of FTE undergraduates	11,000 to 13,500	15,000 to 17,500	7,500 to 10,000	11,000	4,000 to 5,500	1,500 to 2,200	750 to 1,000	750 to 1,000	1,200 to 1,400
Percentage of women undergraduates	43	47	43	52	50	56	66	56	50
Percentage of nonwhite undergraduates	9	12	10	6	16	15	8	18	20
Percentage of undergraduates above 24 years of age	11	11	18	11	19	19	4	15	45
Median percentage of residential students	41–50	31–40	31–40	21–30	31–40	41–50	71–80	61–70	0
Percentage of students aspiring to a bachelor's degree or less	29	37	39	40	43	37	26	40	61

Table B. (continued)

	Research universities		Doctorate-granting universities		Comprehensive universities & colleges		Liberal arts colleges		Two-year colleges
	I	II	I	II	I	II	I	II	
Percentage of students with A– average or better in high school	49	41	35	33	27	25	43	29	17
Percentage of students with C+ average or less in high school	9	12	15	14	20	17	8	20	31
Median fathers' education	college graduate	some college	some college	some college	high school graduate	high school graduate	college graduate	high school graduate	high school graduate
Percentage of students who attended more than one college	32	31	40	33	34	32	20	29	36
Percentage of faculty stating "students in my department are very competitive"	65	56	55	49	47	39	41	43	44

Source: Catalog Study, 1976; and Carnegie Surveys, 1975–76.

lege, and the average research university II enrolls more than 15 times as many undergraduates as the average liberal arts college. Students at smaller colleges tend to be less competitive than their counterparts at larger universities. Other undergraduate characteristics seem less determined by institutional size than by college and university type.

The two-year college is a magnet for new or nontraditional students. It has the largest proportion of nonresidential students, older students, nonwhite students, and low academic achievers in terms of high school grade-point average and degree aspirations. The counterpart for the traditional student is the most selective liberal arts college (liberal arts college I) and the most research-oriented university (research university I). They enroll the largest proportion of young, white, high academic achievers whose fathers graduated from college. Interestingly, the major difference between the two types is that research universities I enroll the least women and liberal arts college I enroll the most. This is so because selective liberal arts colleges are more likely than any other type of institution to be single sex colleges—particularly women's colleges.

Curriculum Characteristics

Tables C, D, and E deal with curriculum or curriculum-related concerns. Table C illustrates the range of subjects taught at the nine types of institutions. Subjects are divided into four areas—arts and science studies, professional studies, occupational/technical studies, and "new" subjects—those current topics that have only recently entered the undergraduate curriculum in substantial fashion. For three of the four areas, common or exemplary courses of study have been selected and the proportion of institutions of each type offering classes on the topic are compared. This was not necessary for arts and science studies (consisting of courses of study such as biology, psychology, and English), because nearly all of the colleges offer them in substantially the same form. In fact, with the exception of the arts and sciences, this table shows significant differences in subject matter emphasis among the nine types of colleges and universities. Professional studies are most common in doctorate-granting universities and least common in liberal arts colleges I. Occupational/technical programs are found most frequently in two-year colleges and least frequently in liberal arts colleges I and research universities I. New subjects are offered most often in research universities I and least often in liberal arts colleges II.

Table D compares the number of courses offered and the ratio of courses to full-time-equivalent faculty (a summary measure of full-time and part-time faculty) at the nine types of institutions. As might have been expected, the institutions with the most faculty and students offer the most courses—both undergraduate and graduate. Thus, the university with the most courses has nearly ten times as many as the institution with the fewest—making quite a difference for its students in terms of the diversity of courses available to them.

What is especially interesting in Table D is not this expected difference in number of courses but instead the considerable differences among institutions in the ratio of courses to faculty members. Institutions with the largest number of courses—research universities I—have the lowest ratio of courses to faculty, while the four-year institutions with the smallest number of courses—liberal arts colleges I and II—have the largest ratio. For example, research universities I offer less than three courses per faculty member while liberal arts colleges I and II list nearly eight. Eight courses are a lot of subjects to teach, far more than most faculty are equipped to teach well. As a consequence, liberal arts faculty members may be required to broaden their teaching abilities significantly beyond their graduate training or else teach subjects in which they are not expert. At best, this difference in course/faculty ratios is the difference between having faculty who teach expert specialties and having faculty with broad expertise; at worst, it is the difference between myopic specialists and unqualified generalists.

Student perceptions of the academic ethos of the different colleges and universities are compared in Table E—in particular, the percentage of students comparing their colleges with high school, expressing satisfaction with college, indicating that college wastefully duplicated parts of high school, and feeling impersonally treated.

Students compare college with high school with increasing frequency as institutions (except liberal arts colleges I) decrease in size, award less advanced degrees, and engage in less research. Im-

Table C. Percentage of institutions offering undergraduate programs in selected subjects by Carnegie type

	Research universities		Doctorate-granting universities		Comprehensive universities & colleges		Liberal arts colleges		Two-year colleges
	I	II	I	II	I	II	I	II	
ARTS AND SCIENCE	100	100	100	100	100	100	100	100	98
PROFESSIONAL STUDIES									
Business	66	77	91	95	91	83	46	94	93
Education	77	81	82	95	66	92	76	91	67
Engineering	91	73	77	50	37	13	5	6	55
Forestry	5	23	18	0	7	4	5	6	27
Health science	38	45	46	55	60	4	9	24	65
Home economics	14	50	45	60	40	29	5	9	32
OCCUPATIONAL/TECHNICAL STUDIES									
Law enforcement	0	23	36	50	31	42	9	15	60
Medical technology	14	36	55	55	47	46	14	29	25
Secretarial science	0	18	18	20	24	46	5	21	73
Trade/technical	5	10	9	40	29	8	0	3	68
NEW SUBJECTS									
Environmental studies	36	64	45	60	24	25	28	41	18
Ethnic studies	77	55	45	50	29	21	23	9	23
Urban studies	50	41	18	35	16	29	28	32	12
Women's studies	23	14	9	20	7	8	18	0	7

Source: Catalog Study, 1976.

Table D. Relationship between the average number of courses and faculty at different institutions by Carnegie type

	Research universities		Doctorate-granting universities		Comprehensive universities & colleges		Liberal arts colleges		Two-year colleges
	I	II	I	II	I	II	I	II	
Number of courses offered									
Undergraduates	2,385	2,285	1,835	1,767	1,226	874	579	501	463
Graduate	2,132	1,754	1,043	916	298	108	12	3	0
Total	4,517	4,039	2,878	2,683	1,524	982	591	504	463
Course/faculty ratio									
Undergraduate	1.5	2.3	2.7	2.8	4.1	3.7	7.6	7.8	3.3
Graduate	1.3	1.8	1.5	1.5	1.0	.4	.2	.1	0
Total	2.8	4.1	4.2	4.3	5.1	4.1	7.8	7.9	3.3

Source: Catalog Study, 1976.

Table E. Academic ethos of different institutions by Carnegie type

	Research universities		Doctorate-granting universities		Comprehensive universities & colleges		Liberal arts colleges		Two-year colleges
	I	II	I	II	I	II	I	II	
Percentage of undergraduates stating "my college is much like high school"	12	15	13	16	24	26	20	31	39
Percentage of undergraduates indicating "part of my undergraduate education was a wasteful repetition of high school"	37	40	38	42	40	41	22	37	36
Percentage of undergraduates satisfied with college	71	69	77	68	69	69	80	70	74
Percentage of undergraduates believing most students are treated like "numbers in a book"	65	60	50	59	45	36	9	18	33

Source: Carnegie Surveys, 1975–76.

personal treatment or being treated like a number in a book has exactly the opposite relationship (with three exceptions—doctorate-granting universities II, liberal arts colleges I, and two-year colleges). Satisfaction with college and wasteful duplication of high school studies have no relationship to college similarity with high school or impersonal treatment. With the exception of liberal arts colleges I, all institutions are comparable in satisfaction and duplication. This may be indicative of either a sorting process whereby students with differing college expectations and varying backgrounds choose institutions of varying types, or a process of adaptation whereby institutions mold themselves to the students they admit.

Throughout this volume the curricula of American colleges and universities will be discussed in six ways: (1) in terms of these nine Carnegie types, (2) in terms of five aggregations of the nine types—"research universities," "doctorate-granting universities," "comprehensive universities and colleges," "liberal arts colleges," and "two-year colleges"; (3) in terms of four-year institutions and two-year institutions; (4) in terms of arts and science colleges and professional/technical colleges (a composite of work-related programs, consisting of five fields—business, education, engineering, health sciences, and technical arts); (5) in terms of varying degrees awarded; and (6) in terms of the more than 3,000 American colleges and universities combined.

References

Carnegie Commission on Higher Education. *A Classification of Institutions of Higher Education.* Berkeley, Calif., 1973.

Carnegie Council on Policy Studies in Higher Education. *A Classification of Institutions of Higher Education: Revised Edition.* Berkeley, Calif., 1978.

HANDBOOK ON UNDERGRADUATE CURRICULUM

PREPARED FOR THE CARNEGIE COUNCIL
ON POLICY STUDIES IN HIGHER EDUCATION

Part One

Undergraduate Curriculum Today

1

General Education

Question: What part of undergraduate education was recently described as "a disaster area" that "has been on the defensive and losing ground for more than 100 years" by The Carnegie Foundation for the Advancement of Teaching (1977)?

Answer: General education, the portion of college study most entering students encounter first.

Definition and History

General education is the breadth component of the undergraduate curriculum and is usually defined on an institutionwide or college-wide basis. It generally involves study in several subject areas and frequently aims to provide a common undergraduate experience for all students at a particular institution. It has been variously described as the necessary prerequisite for specialized study (A. S. Packard, in Thomas, 1962, p. 11); "a corrective to the overemphasis of specialization" (A. Meiklejohn, in Thomas, 1962, p. 68); the necessary rudiments for common discourse (Levine and Weingart, 1973, p. 50); the universals of human culture (Hutchins, 1967, p. 59); an integrative experience underlining the unity of knowledge (J. Dewey, in Thomas, 1962, p. 53); knowledge of the world around us (A. C. True, in Thomas, 1962, p. 77); preparation for participation in a democratic society (President's Commission on Higher Education for Democracy, in Hofstadter and Smith, 1961.

p. 989); learning common to all students (W. Wilson, in Thomas, 1962, p. 5); "a number of general courses in wholly unrelated fields" (A. L. Lowell, in Thomas, 1962, p. 59); a combination of ideology, tradition, contraspecialization, and integration (Bell, 1968, pp. 51–52), an antidote to barbarism (J. Ortega y Gasset, in McGrath, 1976, p. 25); a means for achieving human potential (A. MacLeish, in Thomas, 1962, pp. 73–74); "the discipline and the furniture of the mind" (1828 Yale Report, in Hofstadter and Smith, 1961, p. 275); knowledge necessary for a satisfying private life (J. S. Mill, in McGrath, 1976, pp. 20–21); education encouraging personal and moral development (Taylor, 1962, Chapters 8–9); "first principles" (Thomas, 1962, p. 50); a body of knowledge and methods of inquiry (A. L. Lowell, in Thomas, 1962, pp. 49–50); and liberal education (Harvard Committee, 1945). *Liberal education* is perhaps the most commonly used synonym, but this term, like general education, has been interpreted in many ways by many people. The Carnegie Council defines it as education rooted in the concerns of civilization and our common heritage, and others define it even more broadly to include any form of education that liberates students in body, mind, or soul.

The many different and occasionally conflicting definitions and purposes attributed to general education are largely a consequence of its historical evolution. Colonial colleges offered a four-year general education curriculum which commonly included a small number of subjects—12 in the original Harvard curriculum, as Appendix A indicates. The state of knowledge at the time made it possible to teach the broad-ranging curriculum in a comprehensive fashion, enabling students to acquire both breadth and depth of knowledge as a result of their general education study. Fully prescribed general education programs, like that required of all students during the colonial period, have come to be called *core general education programs.*

When new subjects such as modern language, science, and technical studies were added to the colonial curriculum in the late eighteenth and nineteenth centuries, some educators rose to defend the common core curriculum. In fact, the earliest known reference to "general education" was a product of this movement. A. S. Packard of Bowdoin College used the term in an 1829 article defending the common elements of the curriculum in the *North American Review* (in Thomas, 1962, p. 11) only one year after the Yale Report's historical defense of the classic curriculum (discussed in Chapter 16 and Appendix A). During the early and middle nineteenth century, general education was praised for training the mind (mental discipline), establishing a necessary and solid foundation for the professions, developing student character and morality, offering an antidote to barbarism, and providing a liberal education. The mental discipline theory has long since been disproved (Brubacher and Rudy, 1976, p. 291).

As the nineteenth century progressed, the college curriculum expanded even further. One result was the free elective system that was popular during the last three decades of the nineteenth century and the first decade of the twentieth century. This system, in its purest form, required of students no prescribed courses; students could freely elect whatever courses they desired. As a remedy for several of the perceived abuses of free electives—such as overspecialization by students, the erosion of common elements in a college education, the lack of a sequential introduction to advanced work, and fragmentation of knowledge into specialty areas—a second general education movement began at the end of the nineteenth century.

Two new forms of general education developed as part of this movement. In 1909, A. Lawrence Lowell, president of Harvard University, created the general education "distribution" requirement. Harvard students were required to take six of 16 year-long courses required for graduation in three fields outside of their major. General education distribution requirements usually specify the subject areas or groups of courses that students are required to study. What distinguishes the distribution requirement from the core program is that there is more choice for the student and less prescription by the institution.

The other invention was the survey course, a synoptic in a broad academic field. The rationale for such courses was that the proliferation of knowledge made it otherwise impossible for students to attain a global world view. The first survey course was created by President Alexander Meiklejohn of Amherst College in 1914. The freshman course, entitled "Social and Economic Institutions," was designed to serve as an introduction to the arts and sciences; to provide students with "the facts of the human situation" and "a showing of intellectual method"; and to offer instruction in ethics, logic, history, economics, law, and government (Thomas, 1962, pp. 66–67). Columbia University's famed "Contemporary Civilization" course (discussed in Chapter 12) was established five years later. Over the years the realm of the survey course has been expanded to include overview and introductory courses in academic departments or disciplines such as sociology, biology, and art.

During the 1920s and 1930s, a number of well-known general education programs were created. (Case studies on each can be found in Chapter 12.) The work-study curriculum at Antioch College proved in part to be a general education endeavor; it acquainted usually well-heeled freshmen and sophomores with a slice of life, usually outside their major areas, that the often sheltered student had not previously seen and would never experience again after earning a degree.

General education programs were established at the University of Chicago and St. John's College that reinstituted the core curriculum in the spirit of the colonial college. St. John's did so by basing its program entirely on approximately 100 classical works—the "Great Books" (current list can be found in Appendix A).

Another form of general education involved the creation of thematic general education subunits within larger institutions. The best known of these programs was Alexander Meiklejohn's Experimental College at the University of Wisconsin, a two-year, lower-division, self-contained college offering a unified core general education curriculum focusing on the development of Western civilization. For five years beginning in 1927, Meiklejohn's college was a supplement to the Wisconsin general education program, but even at its peak it enrolled only 155 students.

World War II gave renewed impetus to the general education movement. In 1945, Harvard's influential *General Education in a Free Society* was published. The "Redbook," as it was called, proposed a core general education program for Harvard undergraduates. (Chapter 12 and Appendix A offer detailed information.) In the same year, a study by the Amherst College Committee on Long Range Planning reached a similar conclusion. And, as Appendix A shows, in 1947 President Truman's Commission on Higher Education underlined the need for general education in America. Each of these reports and many of the immediate post–World War II general education curriculum developments stressed the need for a well-informed citizenry in a democratic society.

One innovation that did not emphasize this theme was a pedagogical technique introduced by Nathan Pusey at Lawrence College in 1945. It was a small class concerned with general education and writing for freshmen. The course, not surprisingly called "the freshman seminar," became popular in colleges around the country during the late 1960s. Its senior counterpart, intended as a capstone to general education, had been inaugurated at Reed College some 21 years earlier.

Since World War II, changes in general education have involved the mounting of courses dealing with new subjects, such as non-Western culture at Eckerd College; new alignments of older subjects, such as "Twentieth Century Physics and Its Philosophical Implications" at Brandeis University; problem-based courses, such as "Human Survival in Global Perspective" at Antioch College; and courses emphasizing methods of inquiry rather than any particular subject matter, such as "Modes of Thought" at Brown University. There also has been experimentation with alternatives to courses as ways of satisfying general education requirements at institutions such as Metropolitan State University, which will be discussed later, and more concern has been given to affective and personal development, as at Duke University where several "Small Group Learning Experiences" are required of all students.

In very recent years, interest in general education once again has increased. As Chapters 11 and 12 note, for example, both Harvard and Princeton universities have just completed major studies of general education. The revival of interest in the topic has been premised in many institutions upon a desire to reinstitute the coherence felt to be currently lacking in undergraduate education, to create common elements in a curriculum which has grown more individualized and diverse, and to provide moral training to young people in a time when moral scandals have repeatedly rocked the nation.

Philosophies of General Education

General education programs have been based on a variety of philosophies of education. Four of the most common are perennialism, essentialism, progressivism, and reconstructionism.

Perennialism is founded on the assumption that the substance of education is perennial or everlasting. Perennialists view the ability to reason as the characteristic which distinguishes human beings from other animals and believe that education should be concerned principally with training the rational faculties. Perennialists also believe that people are everywhere alike and that education should be the same for everyone. As a result, perennialist education or the training of the rational faculties is based upon the study of immutable and universal truths, which are thought to be best acquired by study of the "Great Books." The people and writings most closely associated with this philosophy are Robert Hutchins, author of *The Higher Learning in America* (1967) (see Chapter 10); Mark Van Doren, author of *Liberal Education* (1943); Mortimer Adler, editor of the 54-volume *Great Books of the Western World* (1952); and the founders of the St. John's College program, Stringfellow Barr and Scott Buchanan. The "Great Books" program at St. John's in Santa Fe, New Mexico, and Annapolis, Maryland (discussed in Chapter 12 and Appendix A), is the best-known perennialist curriculum in higher education.

Essentialism holds that education should be based upon an essential or prescribed body of knowledge dealing with the heritage of humankind. The subject matter tends to be abstract or conceptual rather than applied or practical. There is no one essentialist curriculum. However, all essentialist curricula are teacher centered, utilize tried-and-true forms of pedagogy and learning, and are premised on the assumption that learning is hard work that is often done unwillingly by students. This brand of philosophy is reflected in the work of Arthur Bestor and the 1945 Harvard committee on general education as illustrated in Chapter 12 and Appendix A. Many common core general education programs are based on the essentialist philosophy.

Progressivism is based on life experience. Perennialism and essentialism might be more aptly described as preparation for life.

The more practical progressive philosophy is student centered, which is to say that student interest determines the direction of education. The instructor is viewed as an expert and adviser whose job is to guide the student. The progressive curriculum is problem oriented rather than subject matter based. Progressives believe that the methods of critical thought are life-long skills while bodies of knowledge are continually changing. John Dewey and William Kilpatrick (discussed in Chapter 10) are perhaps the best known of the progressive philosophers. The progressives were responsible for the development of courses stressing methods of inquiry or modes of thought, survey courses, and the progressive curricula of colleges such as Bennington (profiled in Chapter 12) and Sarah Lawrence.

Reconstructionism accepts the progressive design of education but adds an additional ingredient—an emphasis on reconstructing society. George Counts and Theodore Brameld are spokesmen of this school. Brookwood Labor College, an institution committed to educating workers and expanding the union movement during the 1920s and 1930s, and Maharishi International University, a school seeking to change the world through transcendental meditation, are examples of colleges with curricula based on reconstructionist philosophies.

The State of General Education

Types of General Education

General education at American colleges and universities falls into three categories: core curricula, distribution requirements, and free electives (no required program).

CORE CURRICULA

Core general education programs are common, tightly knit, yet broad and often interdisciplinary series of courses usually required of all students. The general education program prescribed in the Harvard Redbook and described in Chapter 12 is an example of a core curriculum. Originally three common general education courses were to be required of all Harvard students—one each in the humanities and social sciences and one of two alternatives in the sciences. Some core general education programs are not divided into course units, as was the case in Meiklejohn's Experimental College at the University of Wisconsin, Joseph Tussman's Experimental College Program at the University of California, Berkeley, and St. John's College in Annapolis (all described in Chapters 12 and 13). General education core programs can be based on any of the educational philosophies previously discussed.

The core curriculum is found at approximately 10 percent of American colleges—7 percent of colleges of arts and sciences and 14 percent of professional/technical colleges (Catalog Study, 1976). They are best suited to homogeneous student bodies. With heterogeneous students, the core curriculum runs the risk of duplicating the previous learning of the most advanced students and being too rigorous for the least well-prepared students. The growing acceptance of advanced placement courses in high schools, the College Level Examination Program, and credit for prior learning in college, which enables students to receive credit and/or placement out of introductory college courses, has tended to undermine the common character of core curricula, as Chapter 9 demonstrates. St. John's College, with its four-year Great Books core program (discussed in Chapter 12) has avoided these two dilemmas by permitting neither credit nor placement for work completed outside the college and by admitting a homogeneous student body.

Nonetheless, 47 percent of college and university faculty favor the common core as a general education requirement (Carnegie Surveys, 1975–76). And several colleges, including Antioch College and the Massachusetts Institute of Technology, have adopted optional core curricula in recent years. Antioch initiated a core program in 1975 that attempts to integrate the freshman year experience. Each of the four sections of the core course is taught by four faculty from the three academic divisions (humanities, science, and social science) and the Center for Cooperative Education. The course is organized around broad topics such as "Human Survival in Global Perspective" and "World Views and Ways of Knowing." It satisfies all freshman general education requirements and ties the required work or cooperative experience to the freshman's academic courses. Students in the core are urged to take additional courses from a list of offerings that supplement their core sections.

The adoption of the core was attributed to the lack of integrity of the previous general education distribution requirement, the inadequacy of Antioch's advising system, the politically divided nature of the campus, which necessitated some common effort to reunite the college, and the increasing isolation of the work program from the academic core. The first three rationales, in less dramatic form, are also among the principal reasons that Harvard's dean of the faculty, Henry Rosovsky, formed a task force in 1975 to examine the possibility of designing a core curriculum for that institution, as noted in Chapter 12.

The MIT program, "Concourse," which enrolled 51 students in 1975–76, is an example of the core curriculum utilized as an alternative to the traditional or dominant mode of general education. Like the Antioch core, Concourse is organized around a broad interdisciplinary theme. That theme provides the context for integrating all of the subjects freshmen normally study at MIT. Concourse consists of two types of classes. In "techniques of disciplines" classes, students learn typical freshman skills such as calculus, and in "general meetings," the skills are applied and enriched. Concourse meets three hours a day, five days a week.

DISTRIBUTION REQUIREMENTS

Distribution requirements are designed to ensure that each student takes a minimum number of courses or credits in specified academic areas. For instance, at the University of California, Santa Cruz, each student is required to take a total of six courses: two each in the humanities, social sciences, and natural sciences. There are four forms of distribution requirements: prescribed distribution requirements, minimally prescribed or "smorgasbord" distribution requirements, recommended distribution guidelines, and a small group of programs which can best be described only as "other."

Prescribed Distribution Requirements. Of all forms of general education, prescribed distribution requirements are the most common. Eighty-five percent of all colleges have this type of general education program (Catalog Study, 1976), and the distribution requirement is the form of general education program favored by 46 percent of all faculty. It is, however, inconsistent with the perennialist and essentialist philosophies of education, which specify a core body of knowledge that all students or all students in a particular culture must master.

Prescribed distribution requirements involve combinations of specified courses, student course options from short preselected lists, and a limited number of electives in designated areas. The general education program at the Residential College of the University of Michigan is an example of prescribed distribution. Students are required to take a freshman seminar, an arts practicum, foreign language to the level of reading comprehension, three courses in the social sciences, three courses in the humanities, and three courses in the natural sciences. Approximately 60 percent of colleges and universities have distribution requirements with some specified courses. Forty-eight percent of colleges of arts and sciences and 74 percent of professional/technical colleges have such requirements (Catalog Study, 1976).

Minimally Prescribed or "Smorgasbord" Distribution Requirements. Smorgasbord distributions generally require few if any specified courses. The emphasis is on areas that must be studied. Bennington College has such a program. Students are required to take one course in any four of the college's eight academic divisions. In practice, this requirement can be satisfied with four arts and humanities courses. Approximately 24 percent of colleges and universities have smorgasbord distribution requirements. Thirty-five percent of colleges of arts and sciences and 11 percent of professional and technical colleges have such requirements (Catalog Study, 1976).

Recommended Distribution Guidelines. Recommended distribution guidelines are generally the same as smorgasbord distribution requirements except that they are not required. The student is given the option of satisfying the requirements or ignoring them. For instance, Trinity College of Hartford, Connecticut, recommends that students take courses in four areas: language and other symbolic systems, human interaction with the natural world, human social institutions, and forms of culture. Levine and Weingart

(1973, p. 28) found that students at Trinity "had no interest in the guidelines and almost no one indicated using them at all." Nonetheless a majority of Trinity students indicated distributing their courses well across the curriculum. Less than 3 percent of institutions of higher education employ recommended distribution guidelines; few if any professional/technical schools and 5 percent of arts and sciences colleges have them (Catalog Study, 1976).

Other Distribution Requirements. New forms of general education distribution requirements referred to previously as "other" have also been developed. Among the most novel of these are the programs of Sterling College and Hampshire College. They differ from traditional distribution requirements in procedure rather than substance. Sterling College (described in Chapter 13) has a competency- or outcome-based general education program. Students are required to demonstrate attainment in eight general education areas: Christian heritage, values, acquisition and use of knowledge, art and aesthetics, physical and social environment, verbal communication, physical and recreational activity, and groups. With regard to arts and aesthetics, for instance, the student must "comprehend the artistic and aesthetic dimensions of culture." To do that the student is required to demonstrate (1) an understanding of some aspects of his or her cultural heritage and the contributions to it by the arts and artists, (2) an understanding of the way an artist works in a particular medium, (3) some knowledge of aesthetic experience, and (4) an awareness of aesthetic values and a capacity to make discriminating judgments of his or her own. Students are required to demonstrate their abilities to a faculty committee via courses, independent study, standardized tests, and/or field experience. Students most often choose the traditional courses as the vehicle for demonstrating competence.

Hampshire College (also described in Chapter 13) requires that all students pass comprehensive examinations in natural sciences and mathematics, social sciences, language and communication, and humanities and arts. There are no course requirements. Every Hampshire student, with the aid of a faculty committee of his or her own choosing, develops an examination—usually a paper—which will demonstrate mastery of the modes of thought in each academic area. Each student forms four separate committees.

FREE ELECTIVES

In a free elective curriculum, no general education program is specified by the college. The student can create a general education based on whatever courses he or she selects. The student may also neglect general education. Amherst College and Brown University offer students free elective programs. Free electives, like distribution requirements, are inconsistent with the philosophies of essentialist and perennialist education. No general education requirement is favored by 6 percent of college and university faculty (Carnegie Surveys. 1975–76) and is found at 2 percent of higher education institutions. It is more common at arts and sciences colleges (3 percent) than professional schools (.2 percent) (Catalog Study, 1976). Levine and Weingart (1973, pp. 28–29) report that students tend to specialize earlier when there are no or minimal general education requirements. They also note that under such conditions students generally sample fields outside their major but that "nonscientists tend not to take science courses, and a sizable number of humanities students take little more than humanities."

The three states of general education—core curricula, distribution requirements, and free electives—represent a continuum. There is a sizable and still-growing body of literature that indicates that colleges tend to move across the continuum from core curricula to free electives and back in a pendular fashion. Recently colleges have tended to move from cores toward free electives. In a 1975 study of eight selected core general education programs varying in age from five years to more than fifty years, Levine (1976, p. 14) found that one program had evolved into a free elective curriculum and seven into distribution requirements, five of which were of the smorgasbord variety. Levine and Weingart (1973, p. 26) documented this pattern among colleges with distribution requirements. They discovered a common movement from prescribed distribution requirements to smorgasbord distributions. The most wide-ranging study of this type was that of Blackburn and others (1976, p. 37). In this study of curriculum change in 270 colleges and universities between 1967 and 1974, they found a two-stage movement among institutions altering their general education programs from prescribed courses to distribution requirements and from distribution requirements to free electives.

The Amount of General Education in an Undergraduate Program

The quantity of general education required of undergraduates varies for different academic degrees, subject areas, and types of colleges and universities. It also varies widely within the same degrees, subject areas, and types of institutions. Table 1 shows the percentage (in deciles) of undergraduate education that colleges and universities require in general education to complete the associate of arts (A.A.), associate of science (A.S.), associate of applied science (A.A.S.), bachelor of arts (B.A.), and bachelor of science (B.S.) degrees. The associate's degrees normally require two years of study and the bachelor's degrees usually require four years.

Table 1 indicates that the quantity of general education required to earn degrees varies as much as it possibly could. Both the associate of arts and the associate of science degrees require between 0 percent general education and 100 percent general education. The range of required general education is smaller for the

Table 1. Percentage of colleges and universities requiring varying amounts of general education by degree type

Percentage of program consisting of general education	Degree type				
	A.A.	A.S.	A.A.S.	B.A.	B.S.
0	.8	1.1	4.2	2.5	.7
1–10		5.3	20.8	.7	2.0
11–20	4.8	9.6	20.8	5.4	11.7
21–30	12.1	16.0	25.0	18.7	25.6
31–40	10.5	16.0	12.5	40.3	34.4
41–50	11.3	11.7	12.5	24.1	20.0
51–60	8.1	9.6		6.8	4.0
61–70	16.1	7.4	4.2	.7	1.6
71–80	2.4	2.1		.7	
81–90	18.5	5.3			
91–100	15.3	16.0			

Source: Catalog Study, 1976.

bachelor's degrees but still quite large, with the bachelor of arts varying from 0 percent to as much as 80 percent general education.

Table 1 also shows variation between the different degrees. The variation is greatest among the associate's degrees. The most common percentage (mode) of the undergraduate program required in general education for the A.A. was 81–90 percent, which deviates sharply from the 21–30 percent of the A.A.S. Differences between bachelor's degrees are considerably less.

Tables 2 and 3 show the variation in the amount of general education required by institutional type and by subject area. Table 2 shows the percentage of five different types of colleges and universities (research universities, other doctorate-granting universities, comprehensive universities, liberal arts colleges, and community colleges) requiring varying amounts of general education

Table 2. Percentage of institutions requiring varying amounts of general education in their arts and science colleges by institutional type

Percentage of program consisting of general education		Institutional type			
	Research univer- sities[a]	Other doctorate- granting univer- sities[a]	Compre- hensive univer- sities[a]	Liberal arts colleges[a]	Community and junior colleges[b]
0	2.5	2.4		8.6	3.4
1–10	2.5	2.4			1.1
11–20	2.5	1.2	3.1	1.2	2.3
21–30	18.8	17.0	15.3	26.0	5.7
31–40	41.3	23.2	46.6	32.1	6.9
41–50	27.5	39.0	26.0	19.8	16.1
51–60	5.0	8.5	5.3	11.1	13.8
61–70		4.9	3.1	1.2	12.6
71–80		1.2	.8		3.4
81–90					4.6
91–100					29.9

[a] Four-year programs only.

[b] Two-year programs only.

Source: Catalog Study, 1976.

(in deciles) to earn a degree in their colleges of arts and sciences. Table 3 provides the same information for professional and technical colleges, an aggregation of the practices of colleges of business, education, engineering, health sciences, and trade and technical arts.

Examination of Tables 2 and 3 reveals the same types of variation discussed with regard to Table 1. A comparison of Tables 2 and 3, however, shows that arts and sciences colleges consistently require more general education than professional schools. This difference disappears in practice because colleges of arts and sciences generally permit students to satisfy approximately one-fourth to one-third of their general education requirements by taking courses in their major area.

Though the amount of general education that colleges and

Table 3. Percentage of institutions requiring varying amounts of general education in their professional/technical colleges by institutional type[a]

	Institutional type			
Percentage of program consisting of general education	Research universities[b]	Other doctorate-granting universities[b]	Comprehensive universities[b]	Community and junior colleges[c]
0	1.7	2.8		6.8
1–10	20.0	9.2	8.5	3.4
11–20	30.8	24.6	19.7	15.3
21–30	30.8	34.4	47.0	23.7
31–40	14.2	26.8	23.1	23.7
41–50	1.7	4.2	1.7	10.2
51–60	.8			6.8
61–70				3.4
71–80				3.4
81–90				1.7
91–100				1.7

[a] Liberal arts colleges are not included in Table 3 because they are by definition solely arts and science colleges.

[b] Four-year programs only.

[c] Two-year programs only.

Source: Catalog Study, 1976.

universities require ranges from all to nothing, there have been clearly observable overall trends. Institutions of higher education now require less general education than in previous years. This was the finding of a study by Blackburn and others (1976) of a representative cross section of American colleges and universities consisting of 270 institutions. Blackburn and others (1976, p. 11) reported a decline between 1967 and 1974 in the mean proportion of general education required in four-year arts and sciences institutions from 43.1 percent to 33.5 percent of the undergraduate program and at two-year arts and sciences institutions from 58.7 percent to 53.8 percent (p. 11). This Blackburn finding represents a marked contrast with that of Dressel and DeLisle (1969, p. 30), which indicated no change in the amount of general education required between 1957 and 1967 at similar colleges.

Components of General Education

Three types of course—introductory disciplinary, advanced disciplinary, and interdisciplinary—form the most frequent components of general education programs. The *introductory disciplinary course,* an overview of a discipline such as introduction to biology, business, sociology, art, or education, is the most common element of all. Ninety-four percent of college and university general education programs include such courses (Catalog Study, 1976).

Advanced disciplinary courses, which can be defined as specialized courses within a discipline, are almost as widely used. Classes such as "European and American Sculpture," "Cytology," and "Effects of Early Environmental Deprivation" are examples. Eighty-eight percent of general education programs, including those of community and junior colleges, permit requirements to be satisfied by this type of course (Catalog Study, 1976). It is surprising to find that 60 percent of all community and junior colleges utilize advanced disciplinary courses; such schools are normally thought of as lower-division institutions while these courses are usually classified as upper-division offerings.

Interdisciplinary courses, which join two or more disciplines, are also a frequent general education offering. Fifty-eight percent of general education programs include interdisciplinary classes (Catalog Study, 1976). Examples of such courses are "Aztec Civilization" at Brandeis University, which deals with the art and architecture, social and political organization, education, literature, poetry, religion, philosophy, law, science, medicine, and history of the Aztec people; "History of Biology and Medicine" at Brown University; and "Science, Technology, and Society" at the University of Tulsa. Thirty-nine percent of undergraduates have had at least a few such courses (Carnegie Surveys, 1975–76). Sixty-two percent of faculty regard interdisciplinary courses as at least as effective in encouraging students to acquire a variety of perspectives as breadth requirements (Carnegie Surveys, 1975–76). Nonetheless, faculty have difficulty teaching such courses because their training is usually in a single discipline and because interdisciplinary courses are frequently team taught, which requires a good deal of joint effort and knowledge of an unfamiliar field from faculty who are used to teaching alone in a single discipline (Levine and Weingart, 1973, Chapter 3).

No other form of instruction besides these three types of course can be described as a staple in general education programs, although three others play a small role.

Freshman seminars have been praised for giving students an opportunity in their freshman year to meet a faculty member who frequently serves as the students' adviser; providing students with a bird's eye view of the basic elements of scholarship in an area of their own and a faculty member's interest; and allowing faculty members to experiment with new pedagogies. Their small size makes them a costly endeavor for colleges, however (Levine and Weingart, 1973, pp. 29–38); and they are found in only 6 percent of the programs—more commonly at arts and sciences colleges (8 percent) than professional/technical schools (4 percent) (Catalog Study, 1976). Only 20 percent of undergraduates have had one, but another 23 percent wish they had had one (Carnegie Surveys, 1975–76).

Senior seminars, courses designed to cap the general education experience by application of different student majors to a common problem, are found in 3 percent of general education programs. They are far more common in arts and sciences colleges (4 percent) than professional/technical colleges (1 percent) (Catalog Study, 1976).

Finally, *great books courses* constitute only 1 percent of all general education courses.

Content of General Education[1]

The content of general education varies from college to college. Some subjects are required in most general education programs; others are required in only a few. The content of general education includes advanced learning skills, field distribution subjects, and general understanding courses.

Advanced learning skills—English composition, mathematics through geometry and two years of algebra, one year of foreign language, and physical education—are tools that students generally need to sustain college-level study. Advanced learning skills require students to have a firm base in the three R's and other basic skills. English composition is the most common general education requirement in two- and four-year colleges and universities, and in arts and sciences and technical/professional colleges combined. It is specifically required in 76 percent of the general education programs and can be used to satisfy distribution requirements in another 14 percent of the programs. Mathematics is required in 48 percent of general education programs and is a means of satisfying distribution requirements in another 33 percent of the programs. Foreign language is a requirement in 24 percent of general education programs and a distribution subject in 39 percent of the programs. Physical education is specifically required in 56 percent of general education programs and satisfies distribution requirements in another 9 percent of the programs.

Field distribution subjects involve no specified courses, but indicate one or more of three broad areas—humanities, natural science, or social science—in which the student must take courses or credits. Social science is a requirement in 81 percent of the general education curricula and satisfies distribution requirements in another 9 percent. Natural science is a requirement in 71 percent of the programs and a distribution area in 13 percent. Humanities is required in 70 percent of the programs and fulfills distribution requirements in 11 percent more.

General understanding courses, intended to give students both a broad and basic undergraduate learning experience, are required in a large number of colleges, though not a majority. Fine arts, gov-

[1]All of the data in this section are drawn from the Carnegie Council Catalog Study, 1976.

ernment and institutions, and religion are the most common courses in this category. Fine arts is required in 20 percent of the curricula and fulfills distribution requirements in 59 percent. Government and institutions is a specific requirement in 18 percent of general education programs and a distribution subject in 63 percent of the programs. Religion is primarily a requirement at sectarian institutions. Seventeen percent of all general education programs require religion and 19 percent permit religion to satisfy distribution requirements.

The content of general education appears to fluctuate with time. For example, in a study of curriculum change in the arts and sciences between 1947 and 1967, Dressel and DeLisle (1969, p. 30) found that mathematics and foreign language increased as general education requirements, but a similar study by Blackburn and others (1976, pp. 15–16) reported a decline in these two subjects as requirements between 1967 and 1974. Both studies noted declines in the requirement of physical education and English composition. With regard to field distribution requirements, Dressel and DeLisle (1969, pp. 25–26) reported a constant level of natural science, social science, and humanities requirements in the curriculum, while Blackburn and others (1976, p. 15) reported a subsequent decline.

Concerns and Proposals

Certain aspects of general education have been regularly criticized. Some of the criticisms are just, and in several instances proposals have been advanced or even implemented to remedy the deficiencies. Some of the criticisms are unjust and are occasionally based upon misinformation. The merits and demerits of common criticisms are examined in the following pages.

Criticism 1: General education is a good idea in theory, but fails in practice.

Several difficulties seem to plague many if not most general education programs. They include the following (Levine, 1976, pp. 24–25):

- Rewards and incentives to faculty for participation in general education are meager.

- General education teaching, even in nonuniversity settings, often serves as an adverse factor in faculty promotion or tenure because general education involves service outside the discipline, because general education teaching demands a disproportionate amount of faculty time which could be used for other more positively perceived activities such as publication or committee work, and because the average faculty member does not excel at general education teaching, causing a blot on his or her teaching record.
- The training and experience of most faculty members does not prepare them well for broad, cooperative, interdisciplinary teaching.
- The turnover rate for faculty in general education is high, and participation is sometimes involuntary.
- Academic disciplines or departments have not utilized their most able and most senior faculty and/or graduate students to teach general education.
- Academic disciplines have often transformed general education courses into department introductions or the first course in the major which is an effective way to recruit student concentrators.

These problems do not exist at all colleges. St. John's College is an example of an institution without any of the six problems. However, proposals for improvement at other colleges that are experiencing these problems include:

- Hiring faculty with abilities and interests more attuned to general education teaching. In this regard, the Carnegie Commission (1971, pp. 16–18) recommended the establishment of doctor of arts graduate programs which would stress teaching in contrast to the research orientation of current Ph.D. programs. This proposal finds support from at least a modest majority of faculty (51 percent) who believe that undergraduate education would be improved if there were less emphasis on specialized training and more on liberal education (Carnegie Surveys, 1975–76). Only 31 percent of undergraduates agree with the faculty assessment (Carnegie Surveys, 1975–76).
- Separating general education teaching from the functions of academic departments or disciplines. This proposal has been

tried many times with mixed results. At the University of Chicago the establishment of a general education college separate from the university (described in Chapter 12) caused the faculty at the college to be treated as second-class citizens within the university. In contrast, separation of the college faculty from the graduate school at the Claremont University Center has resulted in undergraduate colleges with vital and diverse missions. At institutions where graduate school activities are more prestigious than undergraduate teaching, this strategy is unlikely to work.

- Reformulating the rewards system to encourage general education teaching (Mayhew, 1976).
- Improving general education teaching through faculty and instructional development (Gaff, 1975).
- Creating general education courses that link departmentally offered mini-courses (short-term courses) on the same topics, such as ethics of the discipline or research methods (Smith, 1977).

Criticism 2: General education programs are unpopular with students.

It is possible that students are not satisfied with the general education programs that they are required to take, but they do want general education. Ninety-seven percent of the students questioned in the 1976 Carnegie Council survey of undergraduates indicated that "a well-rounded general education" was an essential or fairly important element of a college education for them. There has been no change in student opinion on this question since the survey was administered in 1969.

Criticism 3: The student clientele of American colleges and universities is too heterogeneous to permit common general education programs.

Nationally, higher education has a highly diverse student body, but there are many institutions with student bodies sufficiently homogeneous to offer a common general education program if they so wished. However, this is not true for a large number of institutions, and there is nothing basic to general education which requires that it be the same throughout the country or even within a single institution. In fact, several large institutions have responded to their inability to offer a single general education program by offering several that correspond to different student needs. The University of Pennsylvania, for instance, offers four different general education programs to the students in its College of Arts and Sciences.

Criticism 4: General education is of little economic value to the student who is forced to study it.

There are many who would challenge this statement with the claim that liberal education is the best long-run economic value to students (Bowen, 1977, pp. 33–37). Rather than debating the issue, it is appropriate to note that there is nothing intrinsic to general education that requires it to be impractical or unworldly. Indeed, Earl Cheit (1975) has proposed a fusing of professional and liberal arts endeavors. This has to some extent been accomplished in curricula like the Antioch College cooperative or work-study program (described in Chapter 12), which provides both a vocational experience and general education, and by the creation of courses like those recommended by Martin Meyerson (1974, pp. 177–178), including philosophy of law, social psychology of health, and aesthetics of engineering.

Criticism 5: General education programs are weak in educational and philosophical integrity.

This criticism is founded upon the gradual drift of general education programs from core curricula to free electives which was described earlier. This process is often more the result of political negotiation than educational philosophy (Levine and Weingart, 1973, p. x). Such reasoning is certainly borne out in the case studies of the contemporary civilization curriculum at Columbia University and general education at Harvard University in Chapter 12 of this volume.

Lack of integrity is not a fair indictment of all general education programs, however. Meiklejohn's Experimental College at the University of Wisconsin, Tussman's Experimental College Program at the University of California, Berkeley, the Great Books program at St. John's College, the general education college at the University of Chicago, and the General College at the University of Minnesota (all described in Chapters 12 and 13) were notable for their sound philosophical foundations. In fact, several general education proposals formulated since World War II have been applauded nationally for the cogency of their educational vision. Among them are the proposals of the Harvard Redbook committee (outlined in Chapter 12), the Magaziner-Maxwell report at Brown University (described in Chapter 13), and Daniel Bell's *The Reforming of General Education* (1968) at Columbia University (discussed in Chapter 11), and Philip Phenix's *Realms of Meaning* (1964) (summarized in Chapter 11).

Criticism 6: General education is poorly timed.

This criticism has been voiced in two ways. The first is to say that general education is more appropriate to older adults than to 18- to 22-year-olds whose most immediate need is gainful employment. One response to this has been to say that society cannot afford to give jobs to people who are unaware of the ethical dilemmas and social implications of their jobs in the world around them. Another, which is not inconsistent with the first, is the response of The Carnegie Foundation for the Advancement of Teaching (1977, p. 204) which suggested a possible reduction in the amount of time students spend in college, combined with the introduction of "deferred electives" that will be available to the student later in life.

The second way in which the criticism of poor timing has been raised is in calling for general education to become the province of secondary schools rather than colleges. For instance, the Carnegie Commission (1973, p. 20) proposed that "more responsibility for general education . . . be assumed by high schools." It is frequently pointed out that several functions of general education, such as education for citizenship, are important for all people, not just those who attend college. There is also evidence of duplication in college and high school studies, particularly in the area of general education. Blanchard (1971) reported an average duplication of two-thirds of a year of course work. In 1976, 38 percent of undergraduate students agreed that part of their undergraduate education was a wasteful duplication of work already covered in high school (Carnegie Surveys, 1975–76). A less radical proposal than transferring all general education instruction to the high school is that colleges and secondary schools work together to ensure better articulation in programming (Carnegie Commission, 1973, p. 103).

*   *   *

For a commentary on general education, see Chapter 8, "General Education: An Idea in Distress," in The Carnegie Foundation for the Advancement of Teaching, *Missions of the College Curriculum: A Contemporary Review with Suggestions* (1977).

References

Adler, M. and Hutchins, R. *Great Books of the Western World.* Chicago: Encyclopaedia Britannica, 1952.

Bell, D. *The Reforming of General Education: The Columbia College Experience in Its National Setting.* Garden City, N.Y.: Anchor Books, 1968.
This book is discussed in Chapter 11.

Blackburn, R., Armstrong, E., Conrad, C., Didham, J., and McKune, T. *Changing Practices in Undergraduate Education.* Berkeley, Calif.: Carnegie Council on Policy Studies in Higher Education, 1976.
This monograph examines continuities and changes in the constitution of American undergraduate education between 1967 and 1974, with emphasis on general education, electives, and majors via a study of 270 colleges and universities.

Blanchard, B. E. *Curriculum Articulation Between the College of Liberal Arts and the Secondary School: A National Survey.* Chicago: DePaul University, 1971.

Bowen, H. *Investment in Learning: The Individual and Social Value of American Higher Education.* San Francisco: Jossey-Bass, 1977.

Bowen, W. G. *Report of the President.* Princeton, N.J.: Princeton University, May 1977.
This interesting report discusses the evolution and meaning of the term *liberal education* with particular reference to how it is accomplished at Princeton.

Brubacher, J. S., and Rudy, W. *Higher Education in Transition: A History of American Colleges and Universities, 1636–1976.* (3rd ed.) New York: Harper & Row, 1976.

Carnegie Commission on Higher Education. *Less Time, More Options: Education Beyond the High School.* New York: McGraw-Hill, 1971.

Carnegie Commission on Higher Education. *Continuity and Discontinuity: Higher Education and the Schools.* New York: McGraw-Hill, 1973.

The Carnegie Foundation for the Advancement of Teaching. *Missions of the College Curriculum: A Contemporary Review with Suggestions.* San Francisco: Jossey-Bass, 1977.
This volume is discussed in Chapter 11.

Carnegie Surveys, 1975–76.
This study is discussed in the Preface.

Catalog Study, 1976.
This project is discussed in the Preface.

Cheit, E. F. *The Useful Arts and the Liberal Tradition*. New York: McGraw-Hill, 1975.

Dressel, P., and DeLisle, F. *Undergraduate Curriculum Trends*. Washington, D.C.: American Council on Education, 1969.

These authors studied changes in the nature of the undergraduate curriculum between 1957 and 1967 at 322 four-year arts and sciences colleges.

Gaff, J. G. *Toward Faculty Renewal: Advances in Faculty, Instructional, and Organizational Development*. San Francisco: Jossey-Bass, 1975.

Harvard Committee. *General Education in a Free Society*. Cambridge, Mass.: Harvard University Press, 1945.

This report is excerpted in Appendix A.

Hoftstadter, R., and Smith, W. *American Higher Education: A Documentary History*. 2 vols. Chicago: University of Chicago Press, 1961.

Hutchins, R. M. *The Higher Learning in America*. New Haven, Conn.: Yale University Press, 1967.

The educational philosophy of Robert M. Hutchins is discussed in Chapter 10.

Levine, A. "Reflections of an Itinerant Interviewer: A Sketch of Undergraduate Curriculum Trends." A report prepared for the Carnegie Council on Policy Studies in Higher Education. Berkeley, Calif., June 1976 (mimeographed).

Levine, A., and Weingart, J. *Reform of Undergraduate Education*. San Francisco: Jossey-Bass, 1973.

This book, which includes a chapter on general education, describes the nature of and examines the successes and failures associated with eight undergraduate curriculum practices at 26 colleges and universities.

McGrath, E. J. *General Education and the Plight of Modern Man*. Indianapolis, Ind.: The Lilly Endowment, Inc., 1976.

In this book McGrath combines essays growing out of many years of thought about general education with discussions of landmark and promising general education programs.

Magaziner, I., and Maxwell, E. "Draft of a Working Paper for Education at Brown University." An unpublished report, Brown University, 1966.

This report is discussed in Chapter 13.

Mayhew, L. B. *How Colleges Change: Approaches to Academic Reform*. Stanford, Calif.: ERIC Clearinghouse on Information Resources, Stanford Center for Research and Development in Teaching, 1976.

Meyerson, M. "Civilizing Education: Uniting Liberal and Professional Learning." *Daedalus*, Fall 1974, *1*, 173–179.

Phenix, P. H. *Realms of Meaning*. New York: McGraw-Hill, 1964.

This volume is discussed in Chapter 11.

Smith, H. L. "Toward a New Synthesis in the Postdisciplinary Era." Presentation at the 32nd National Conference on Higher Education. Chicago, Ill., May 20–23, 1977.

Taylor, H. *Students Without Teachers: The Crisis in the University*. New York: McGraw-Hill, 1962.

Thomas, R. *The Search for a Common Learning: General Education, 1800–1960*. New York: McGraw-Hill, 1962.

This volume traces the historical development of general education from 1800 to 1960 and examines the general education programs of 18 colleges and universities.

Van Doren, M. *Liberal Education*. Boston: Beacon Press, 1943.

2

The Major or Concentration

The major or concentration is the dominant feature of under-graduate education today and, according to The Carnegie Foundation for the Advancement of Teaching (1977), probably the most successful part. It is also the most important element of college studies to many faculty and students. Ironically this prominence, prosperity, and popularity have been consistently criticized for weakening and undermining much of the rest of the under-graduate curriculum.

Definition and History

The major or concentration, which usually consists of a number of courses in one field or in two or more related fields, is the depth component of the undergraduate curriculum. It is intended to provide students with a body of knowledge, methods of study, and practice appropriate to a subject or subject area. A possible exception to this design is the competency-based major, which is rooted in outcomes rather than in courses and, at least theoretically, may involve taking no courses at all (see Chapter 9).

Three alternative purposes for the major identified by W. H. Cowley (in Payton, 1961, p. 57) are nonpreparatory specialization, preparatory specialization, and occupational specialization. Non-preparatory specialization is study involving learning for its own sake rather than preparation for a career; preparatory specialization is preprofessional education leading to medical school, law school, graduate school, or the like; and occupational specialization leads directly to a career in areas such as education, business, or engineering.

The topic of the major is most often selected by the student from among a number of formally organized concentrations offered by a college or university. At some institutions, however, the student may create his or her own major, or may build a concentration by combining the elements of several existing majors. A minimum number of courses or credits for the major is frequently established on a collegewide or institutionwide basis; but the general design of the major—including the determination of additional credits or courses required beyond the institutional minimum, the content of the courses, the number of courses offered, the sequencing of courses, which courses are required, which courses are elective, the character of comprehensive examinations or theses, and the rules for granting credit—are almost always determined by faculty with expertise in the major area, usually members of a department, particularly for single subject majors.

The modern major evolved from the group system, which involved broad-based fields of study, such as science, philosophy, and history/political science. Students took their courses, which varied from being largely or completely prescribed at some colleges to being fully or almost fully elective at others, in the group they chose for specialization. Probably the earliest form of this curriculum in the United States was that of the University of Virginia, which in 1825 offered students a choice of eight fully prescribed programs ranging from ancient languages to anatomy and medicine. A curriculum using the name *group system* was adopted at Cornell University in 1868 by President Andrew Dickson White, who borrowed the idea from Daniel Coit Gilman, who was then at Yale's Sheffield School. As majors became increasingly specialized, the character of the group system changed. It became the basis for general education distribution requirements. That is, students were increasingly asked to take courses from among the broadly defined areas rather than required to specialize in one. But the group or broad-based major is still an option at many schools.

The term *major* appears to have been used for the first time in The John Hopkins University catalog of 1877–78. The term *minor* denoting an abbreviated major, was introduced in that catalog as well. Johns Hopkins undergraduates were required to show "marked proficiency" in two of the university's six academic departments. The major involved two years of study and the minor required one year of study. Specifically, the Johns Hopkins catalog stated that "the major course must be followed in any subjects which the candidate offers as one of his two chief departments of work; the minor course must be followed in those subjects taken as subsidiary" (in Payton, 1961, p. 58).

Phillip Payton (1961) identifies two possible sources for the terms *major* and *minor*. One is the German university, which required students to complete a *hauptfach* (major) and *nebenfach* (minor) for the doctorate. Johns Hopkins adopted the same system for its own doctoral programs, so it was quite possible that the terms subsequently diffused to the undergraduate college.

The other possibility is that the terms were introduced by classicist Charles D'Urban Morris, who was head of the undergraduate division at Johns Hopkins. Payton suggests that Morris could have learned the terms from the classical grammar of Priscian which was divided into magnus, or major, and minor works. Priscian's writings were used at both the University of Paris and at Oxford University, where Morris went to graduate school and later taught. The terms *major* and *minor* were also used to describe portions of the classical curriculum, such as the major logic and minor logic or major ethics and minor ethics at Cambridge University in the seventeenth century and in American colleges between the late eighteenth and nineteenth centuries.

During the last two decades of the nineteenth century and the first decade of the twentieth century, when the free elective curriculum was at the height of its popularity, the major-minor system became increasingly common, probably because it represented an acceptable compromise between election and prescription. In 1881, the major-minor curriculum was adopted at the University of Indiana by David Starr Jordan, who is credited with giving the concept national visibility. When Jordan became president of Stanford ten years later, he took the program with him. By 1905, major-minor requirements were found from coast to coast, from the College of William and Mary in Virginia to the University of California.

In 1909, A. Lawrence Lowell of Harvard used the term *concentration* to identify the depth component of the curriculum in contrast to *distribution* or the breadth component.

State of the Major or Concentration

The Amount of the Major in the Undergraduate Curriculum

Most colleges (89 percent) have a major requirement. Such requirements are more common in professional/technical colleges (business, education, engineering, health sciences, and trade/technical) than arts and sciences colleges (96 percent versus 85 percent). They are also more common in four-year undergraduate programs than in two-year undergraduate programs (97 percent versus 48 percent) (Catalog Study, 1976).

The amount of the undergraduate curriculum devoted to the major varies by degree program and subject area. It differs little in the various types of colleges and universities, however. Table 4 shows the percentage of undergraduate programs by degree type (associate of arts, associate of science, associate of applied science, bachelor of arts, bachelor of science) that require varying amounts (in deciles) of the curriculum to be devoted to the major.

Among the associate degrees, the associate of arts generally requires the least amount of major study and the associate of

Table 4. Percentage of undergraduate programs requiring varying amounts of the undergraduate curriculum for the major by degree type

Percentage of time spent on major	Degree				
	A.A.	*A.S.*	*A.A.S.*	*B.A.*	*B.S.*
1–10					
11–20	2	3		4	3
21–30	23	7		36	17
31–40	23	6	7	32	18
41–50	18	20	9	17	19
51–60	8	14	9	7	18
61–70	13	18	26	3	13
71–80	7	12	21	1	9
81–90	4	15	19		3
91–100	2	6	9		

Note: Only programs requiring a major or, at some two-year institutions, a specialization leading to a major at a four-year institution are included. Bachelor's and associate's degrees should not be compared since the associate's degree is usually two years in duration and the bachelor's degree is typically four years.

Source: Catalog Study, 1976.

applied science the most. The opposite is true for general education programs (see Chapter 1). The median or halfway point for
the A.A. is 41–50 percent, the median for the A.S. is 60–61 percent, the median for the A.A.S. is 61–70 percent. The amount of
major required varies at least as widely within degrees as between
degrees, as was the case in general education programs.

Among bachelor's degrees, the bachelor of arts (median,
31–40 percent) generally requires less time for the major than the
bachelor of science (median, 41–50 percent). Like the associate's
degrees, variation within bachelor's degrees is at least as great as
between them.

Table 5 shows the variation in the amount of time that must
be spent on the major in eight different subject areas (humanities,
social science, science, business, education, engineering, health science, trade and technical arts) in four-year undergraduate programs. Table 6 offers the same information for two-year programs.

Tables 5 and 6 show that occupational areas (business, education, engineering, health sciences, and trade and technical arts)

**Table 5. Percentage of bachelor's degree programs in eight different subject
areas requiring varying amounts (in deciles) of the undergraduate curriculum
to be spent on the major**

Percentage of time spent on major	Subjects							
	Human- ities	Social science	Science	Busi- ness	Educa- tion	Engi- neering	Health science	Trade and technical arts
1–10								
11–20	5	9	2	1	2		1	
21–30	39	49	21	18	18	7	4	5
31–40	39	26	28	30	18	7	8	
41–50	12	12	29	22	23	6	17	5
51–60	2	2	14	20	25	12	19	23
61–70	2	2	5	9	12	24	25	23
71–80	1		1	1	3	24	24	27
81–90						20	2	18
91–100						1		

Source: Catalog Study, 1976.

generally require more time for the major than the arts and sciences subjects (humanities, social sciences, and science). Among the arts and sciences courses, the natural sciences (median, 21–40 percent) tend to require the longest time for majors. The social sciences (median, 21–30 percent) require the least in four-year programs. Among occupational programs, engineering, health sciences, and trade and technical arts require the greatest amount of concentration. The median amount of major for each is 61–70 percent of the undergraduate program. Again it should be pointed out that the variation within each of the eight subject areas in the amount of time required for the major is quite large—and at least as great as the variation between the subject areas. Dressel and De-Lisle (1969) also noted wide variations within majors in a 1967 study of arts and sciences concentrations.

In contrast, the amount of time spent on the major at different types of institutions (research universities, doctorate-granting institutions, comprehensive colleges and universities, liberal arts colleges, and community and junior colleges) is quite comparable.

Table 6. Percentage of associate's degree programs in eight different subject areas requiring varying amounts (in deciles) of the undergraduate curriculum to be spent on the major

Percentage of time spent on major	Subjects							
	Human- ities	Social science	Science	Busi- ness	Educa- tion	Engi- neering	Health science	Trade and technical arts
1–10								
11–20	12			2	4			2
21–30	24	26	23	13	12	9	4	9
31–40	24	32	15	11	40	3	5	2
41–50	29	13	18	23	8	13	8	22
51–60	6	16	15	11	4	6	13	7
61–70	6	13	13	17	12	20	20	20
71–80			13	11	12	22	17	11
81–90			3	8	8	19	25	15
91–100				5		3	9	11

Source: Catalog Study, 1976.

Table 7. Percentage of different types of colleges and universities requiring varying amounts (in deciles) of the undergraduate curriculum to be spent on the major

Percentage of degree program required for major	*Types of colleges and universities*				
	Research univer-sities	Doctorate-granting univer-sities	Compre-hensive colleges	Liberal arts colleges	Community colleges
1–10					
11–20	2	5	7	7	5
21–30	28	44	36	37	23
31–40	29	27	33	35	23
41–50	23	16	18	17	22
51–60	8	6	5	4	14
61–70	7	29	2		7
71–80	3				6
81–90					
91–100					

Source: Catalog Study, 1976.

When the five types of institutions are compared with regard to arts and sciences majors (the one area of concentration common to all), the median amount of the undergraduate curriculum spent on the major is 31–40 percent for each (Catalog Study, 1976). This is illustrated in Table 7.

The amount of time higher education institutions require for major study appears not to have changed over the past few years. Blackburn and others (1976) examined major requirements in arts and sciences programs between 1967 and 1974 and concluded: "There has been essentially no change in the number of courses individual majors require and in the fraction of the total degree requirements a major represents (about one-third)" (p. 34).

Types of Majors

More than half of all four-year undergraduate programs (53 percent) and more than two-thirds of all two-year undergraduate programs (67 percent) offer students a choice of major options (Catalog Study, 1976). The options include disciplinary majors; interdisciplinary, field, and joint majors; double and major-minor concentrations; student-created majors; and no major. Few, if any schools offer all of the options.

DISCIPLINARY MAJORS

The disciplinary major is the most common form of concentration. It can be defined as a concentration in an area having a unique body of knowledge and method of inquiry. English, biology, and sociology are examples of disciplinary majors. The disciplinary major is not the same as the departmental major. Although all or nearly all disciplinary majors, including the past three examples, are usually administered by departments, some colleges and universities also have departments that combine two or more disciplines—for example, American studies and medieval civilization. The majors offered by these departments are departmental majors, but they are not unidisciplinary.

Disciplinary majors are offered in 99 percent of the bachelor's degree programs. In 46 percent of the programs the disciplinary major is required, and in 53 percent of the programs it is optional. Such majors are found in approximately three-fourths (76 percent) of all community and junior colleges (Catalog Study, 1976). In 23 percent of the colleges it is specifically required, and in 53 percent of the colleges it is optional. Seventy percent of all students choose the disciplinary major. They choose it least frequently at community and junior colleges (62 percent) and most frequently at research and doctorate-granting universities (73–76 percent) (Carnegie Surveys, 1975–76). Some disciplines offer more than one major with tracks for both graduate-school-bound and non-graduate-school-bound students. There has been continuing criticism of the disciplines for not offering a sufficient number of non-graduate-school track majors (Bell, 1968).

INTERDISCIPLINARY, FIELD, AND JOINT MAJORS

Interdisciplinary, field, and joint majors involve combinations of two or more disciplines. The interdisciplinary major, also called the interdepartmental or divisional major, can be defined as any formally established or institutionalized concentration linking two or more disciplines. Field and joint majors are forms of the interdisciplinary major. Examples of established interdisciplinary majors include American studies, applied mathematics/psychology, modernization, urban studies, arts and aesthetics, social psychology, and environmental studies. Simon's Rock in Great Barrington, Massachusetts, requires that all bachelor's degree students complete one of eight interdisciplinary majors, while Brown University makes available 24 interdisciplinary majors as alternatives to disciplinary or student-created majors, which are also offered.

Field majors, also called subject-field majors, are broad-based concentrations composed of several disciplines in related fields. Natural sciences, social sciences, fine arts, and humanities are examples of such concentrations. Yale University offers at least three field majors in its special majors program.

For the joint major, the student constructs a concentration with the participation and consent of two departments and generally fulfills most of the requirements of both departments. The joint major is permitted at several universities, such as the University of California, Santa Cruz.

Interdisciplinary majors of all kinds are found in 53 percent of programs leading to the bachelor's degree and 43 percent of programs leading to associate's degrees. They are required in fewer than 1 percent of the programs conbined (Catalog Study, 1976). Interdisciplinary majors are selected by 6.4 percent of undergraduates. They are selected most frequently at the most distinguished research universities and liberal arts colleges (9 percent). They are least often selected at two-year colleges (6 percent) (Carnegie Surveys, 1975–76). Critics have attacked the interdisciplinary major for lacking the coherence and rigor of a discipline. Defenders have not only denied the charges but also assert that the interdisciplinary major is better at integrating different fields of knowledge and modes of inquiry than the disciplinary major.

DOUBLE AND MAJOR-MINOR CONCENTRATIONS

The double major and major-minor are examples of multiple concentrations. The double major simply involves completing the requirements of two majors. It is a formal option at 30 percent of all four-year colleges (Catalog Study, 1976). Fifteen percent of all undergraduates choose the double major option (Carnegie Surveys, 1975–76). The double major is selected least at doctorate-granting universities (13 percent) and most at the more selective liberal arts colleges (19 percent).

The major-minor involves completing one major and a shorter-term concentration in another area. The shorter-term concentration or minor generally involves a course of study equivalent to about one-half of a major. The minor is required in 6 percent of bachelor's degree programs and 6 percent of associate's degree programs. It is a specific option at an additional 38 percent of four-year undergraduate programs and 6 percent of two-year programs (Carnegie Surveys, 1975–76). Ten years ago Dressel and De-Lisle (1969, p. 28) found the minor to be a requirement or suggested option at more than half of American four-year arts and sciences colleges.

Today's economy and tight job market have encouraged some students to take a second major or minor as career insurance. Indeed, 17 percent of the students responding to the 1976 Carnegie Council undergraduate survey indicated they had made such curricular choices because of the country's economic situation. Some colleges and universities are creating minors for liberal arts students in subjects likely to increase their employment opportunities after graduation. For instance, the College of Letters and Science at the University of California, Berkeley, is developing a four-course sequence in administration and management.

STUDENT-CREATED MAJORS

The student-created major involves the construction of a concentration by the student and approval of the program by a designated university officer or committee. Examples of such majors at Brown University include astronomy, immunology, studies in the causality of social movements, health delivery systems, existentialism, and ancient art and culture. None of these majors are otherwise available in the formal Brown curriculum. The student-created major is an option in 16 percent of all four-year undergraduate programs and is required in less than 1 percent of such programs (Catalog Study, 1976). It is neither a requirement nor a formal option at community and junior colleges, but a greater percentage of community and junior college students (12 percent) than students in other colleges have such majors. The reason for this apparent paradox is that many community and junior colleges either require or permit a student not to major. As a result the student is able to put together informally a major of his or her own choice. Nationally, only 7 percent of all undergraduates choose the self-created major. It is done least frequently by students in the most research-oriented universities (4 percent) (Carnegie Surveys, 1975–76).

The student-created major has been criticized for being inappropriate in the basic sciences, where study requires sequencing and prerequisites, and for lacking the coherence and rigor of established majors. However, Levine and Weingart (1973, p. 69) found that faculty who worked with student-created majors were enthusiastic about the concept and satisfied with all or most of the programs they were involved with. They went on to say that "most faculty considered the programs at least as coherent as departmental majors" (p. 69). Levine and Weingart further hypothesized that the option was not used more often because students and faculty were not aware of it, because the major is a lonely experience for the student who is "in effect in a program by himself [and] must forfeit some of the services normally provided as part of a departmental . . . major," because of the red tape involved in getting such majors approved, and because the option is of interest to a very few aggressive students with well-thought-out learning needs not easily satisfied by the traditional array of majors (pp. 70–71).

NO MAJORS

Some colleges, such as Sarah Lawrence, require no major. Less than 1 percent of all four-year undergraduate programs require no major, and an additional 2 percent offer that possibility as an option. A nonmajor is also sometimes inadvertently offered to students through the student-created major. For instance, students have designed majors such as serendipity and prelaw. Among community and junior colleges, 8 percent do not offer majors and 45 percent offer the student the option of not majoring (Catalog Study, 1976). Two and a half percent of undergraduates choose not to major. This choice is most common at community and junior colleges (6.5 percent) and least common at the most research-oriented universities (.2 percent) (Carnegie Surveys, 1975–76).

Variety and Number of Majors

There are great differences in undergraduate majors. The most obvious difference is in the wide variation in subject matter. Some schools offer no majors; others offer more than 90 in their larger colleges (Catalog Study, 1976). This is shown in Table 8.

The median number of majors offered in different types of colleges and universities (research universities, doctorate-granting universities, comprehensive colleges, liberal arts colleges, and community and junior colleges) is comparable. Arts and sciences colleges offer a greater number of majors (median 26–30 majors) than professional/technical schools (median 6–10 majors), however. And large colleges and universities have more majors than smaller colleges (see Introduction). For instance, no liberal arts college offers more than 40 majors, while the largest arts and sciences school in one comprehensive college offers more than 90 majors (Catalog Study, 1976).

Another source of variation in major content is the number of

Table 8. Percentage of two- and four-year programs offering varying numbers of established majors

Number of formal majors offered	Percentage of degree programs
0	1.6
1–5	22.8
6–10	15.9
11–15	12.3
16–20	11.8
21–25	7.0
26–30	8.5
31–35	5.5
36–40	4.9
41–45	4.0
46–50	1.2
51–55	1.0
56–60	1.0
61–65	.4
66–70	.6
71–75	.1
76–80	.1
81–85	
86–90	.3
More than 90	.1

Source: Catalog Study, 1976.

Table 9. Number of courses offered in the major at percentages of different types of institutions, by Carnegie classification

Number of courses offered	Research universities	Doctorate-granting universities	Comprehensive colleges	Liberal arts colleges	Community colleges
0	1.3	.8	2.0	2.7	.9
1–5		.8	2.0	.5	8.9
6–10	1.3	2.3	3.0	5.0	18.8
11–15	.8	1.6	7.9	18.3	15.6
16–20	2.9	4.3	7.9	16.9	16.1
21–30	5.4	9.8	22.8	29.7	10.3
31–40	10.4	14.1	16.8	15.1	12.1
41–50	11.7	12.9	14.9	7.3	8.0
51–60	12.9	11.7	6.2	1.8	4.5
61–70	9.6	8.6	4.2	.9	1.8
71–80	5.8	8.2	2.5	1.4	1.3
81–90	9.2	5.1	2.7	.5	.4
91–100	5.8	4.3	1.0		
101–125	5.4	4.1	2.0		.9
126–150	4.6	3.9	2.0		.4
151–175	1.7	1.9	.5		
176–200	1.3	1.6	.5		
201–225	1.7	.8	.5		
226–250	.8	.8	.5		
More than 250	7.5	1.6	.2		

Source: Catalog Study, 1976.

courses an institution offers in the area of concentration. As shown in Table 9, some colleges offer no courses in certain majors; instead they have cooperative arrangements that permit their students to take courses at other schools. This is most common in the health sciences. In contrast a number of universities offer more than 250 courses in one major subject (Catalog Study, 1976).

The number of courses available in the major differs significantly across school types. Research universities offer a median of 61–70 courses per major, doctorate-granting universities offer a median of 51–60 courses per major, comprehensive colleges and universities offer a median of 31–40 courses per major, liberal arts colleges offer a median of 21–30 courses per major, and community and junior colleges offer a median of 16–20 courses per major (Catalog Study, 1976). This is also shown in Table 9.

The number of courses available to the student for his major is even greater than indicated in Table 9 because a number of concentrations, particularly disciplinary majors, require courses outside the area of concentration but in related or tool skill subjects. These are called cognate courses. The biology major at Marquette University, for instance, requires seven courses in chemistry, physics, and mathematics. This is not unusual.

The course content of the undergraduate major was recently studied by Jonathan Warren of the Educational Testing Service. He examined student transcripts in nine different fields at a variety of institutions and found: "The transcripts from one institution tended to be similar, although occasionally a transcript was more like those from other institutions. Even in chemistry, where the curriculum is fairly standard across most institutions, this similarity by institution was most common. Transcripts showing similar course patterns could be grouped into clusters that identified three or four types of programs in each field" (Warren, 1975, p. 142). In history, for example, Warren discovered several types of major programs. The majors differed in the geographic area emphasized, in the amount of historiography and philosophy of history studied, in the breadth and depth with which the field was covered, in the time frame emphasized, and in the use of electives for in-major or out-of-major study.

Warren's research illustrates the thesis with which this discussion began. There are great differences in undergraduate majors. The differences grow larger if one adds to the brew student-created majors and interdisciplinary majors. However, the vast majority of students elect traditional disciplinary majors like those Warren studied. Warren shows that these majors are similar for students in the same college, and the variations in some majors for students at different colleges appear to be of only three or four types rather than being infinite. Moreover, the differences appear to be functional and at least partially a result of the rationale for which the student studies the major subject. For instance, Warren speculates that the emphasis on historiography or philosophy of history may occur in the majors of persons preparing for graduate school.

Students and Their Majors

The major is not only an important area of the curriculum to undergraduates, but also in general a source of satisfaction to them. Ninety-six and a half percent of the students responding to the 1976 Carnegie Council undergraduate survey stated that getting "a detailed grasp of a special field" was either essential or fairly important to them. When asked in the same survey for an overall evaluation of their major studies, 69.8 percent of the already concentrating juniors and seniors were satisfied or very satisfied with the majors, 21 percent of the students were on the fence, and 9.2 percent were dissatisfied or very dissatisfied with their majors.

Nonetheless, almost half (43.2 percent) of all upper-division students have changed their majors at least once. Change of major is most common at research universities (48–49 percent of the students) and least common at selective liberal arts colleges (30 percent of the students). The reason for changes in majors are many. However, 13 percent of all undergraduates attribute their changes specifically to the current economic situation (Carnegie Surveys, 1975–76).

Another common rationale for changes in majors often cited is specialization early in the college career. Most schools require the students to select a major formally by the end of the sophomore year or prior to the beginning of the junior year. However, some schools such as Harvard College require students to declare a major at the end of the freshman year. Major choices are rarely binding, however. With varying amounts of difficulty, students can change majors later. It is generally easiest to change to a social science major, which usually requires the least number of courses and little in the way of prerequisites (courses specified as requirements for more advanced courses) or sequencing (which involves courses that build upon one another and must as a result be taken in a particular order). The sociology major at Brandeis University, for instance, requires eight courses in sociology and two additional courses in other social sciences. This major can be completed in one year, so that a student could theoretically decide to major in sociology in his or her senior year.

However, some majors, particularly those in the natural sciences, performing arts, and many professional/technical areas encourage their students to begin taking major courses as early as the first day of college. Because some concentrations, such as biology, require many courses and specify prerequisites, cognates, and sequences of study, failure to begin the major in the freshman year often means attending summer school or late graduation for the average student.

College admission is another factor in early choice of major. Students must make some preliminary choice of major prior to applying to college in order to direct their applications to arts and sciences colleges, agricultural colleges, engineering colleges, colleges of education, colleges of business, and so forth. In addition, many colleges ask students to make a tentative major choice at the time of application in order to avoid mismatching student admittees with the institution's distribution of faculty and physical resources.

Practices that unnecessarily force early decisions about a major have been criticized for fostering premature specialization—causing students to choose a major before they are ready to do so or to select a major before they have had an opportunity to sample a sufficient number of fields to make a reasoned decision. Premature specialization and the need for early choice of major is frequently blamed for students' unhappiness or boredom with their majors, discouraging students from taking general education courses, and overemphasis by students on the major. Levine and Weingart (1973, p. 28) describe the declaration of the major as "a clear demarcation point: most students who have a major are no longer distributing their courses [in areas outside the major], while students who are uncertain about the major distribute because it is a way to find a major."

Today, when the student selects a major, he or she spends more time on it than was the case in previous years. Blackburn and others (1976), who found no change in the amount of course work colleges and universities required for the major between 1967 and 1974, discovered a decline in the proportion of the undergraduate curriculum required in general education and an increase in the amount of the curriculum available for election. They report a 22 percent decline in general education, which was transformed into a comparable increase in electives. However, the authors found "a much greater share of the elective time spent in the division of specialization than in breadth study" (p. 35). For instance, at the colleges and universities with the largest increase in electives, Blackburn and others noted an increase in the proportion of major study from 44 percent to 58 percent of the undergraduate program. This means that when institutions of higher education seek to increase the flexibility of their general education programs by substituting electives for some of the general education requirements, they are usually increasing the amount of time that will be spent in depth study at the cost of breadth study. In addition, this means that undergraduates are voluntarily putting more time into their majors than is being demanded of them by departmental or institutional requirements. It is speculated that the rationale for this is the tight job market.

Other features of the major that change with time are the subjects that students pick or enrollment patterns. For example, Glenny and others (1976) examined enrollment changes in the major from 1968 to 1974 at 1,227 colleges and universities. At least half of the institutions reported increases in enrollments in two-year vocational/technical programs, health sciences, business, biological sciences, social sciences, fine arts, and agriculture (p. 21). At least one-quarter of the institutions reported declines in enrollment in the foreign languages, engineering, education, humanities, and physical sciences (p. 21). This situation was not the case in previous years and will probably not be the case in future years. For example, enrollment in the humanities was up 28 percent between 1966 and 1972, and enrollment rises are expected by 45 percent of the institutions in the Glenny sample in engineering and 30 percent of the sample in the physical sciences in the period from 1974 to 1980 (pp. 20, 22). This indicates that enrollment patterns fluctuate within major fields over time.

This is not true for all majors, however. Some are fads and quickly decline in enrollments without experiencing significant gains in subsequent years. That has been the fate of some geographical area studies majors. Other concentrations, like the foreign languages, decline without a major increase for several years. Some majors in developing undergraduate fields, such as the health sciences, appear to be growing in enrollment without an end in sight. Still other majors that have not been particularly popular, such as medieval studies, suddenly come into vogue and attract large numbers of concentrators.

The rationale most frequently attributed to changing enrollment patterns is the job market. In fact, vocational/professional majors are increasing in popularity relative to traditional liberal arts majors. Glenny and others (1976) also examined changes of enrollment in six liberal arts fields and seven vocational/professional fields at 1,227 colleges and universities. Twenty-seven percent of the institutions experienced enrollment increases in more than one-half of the liberal arts fields and 52 percent experienced increases in more than half of the vocational/professional fields (p. 27). Some vocational/technical majors are so popular that students are on waiting lists to be admitted. (This is discussed more fully in Chapter 5.)

The job market, then, is part of the explanation for enrollment shifts, but it is not the whole explanation. Many students choose majors with knowledge that the job prospects in the area are less than good. For instance, 46 percent of the juniors and seniors responding to the 1976 Carnegie Council undergraduate survey rated the job prospects for students in their major for the next ten years as fair, poor, or very poor.

Student personality is also a factor in major choice. Feldman and Newcomb (1969) state that "students pursuing different majors tend to have distinctive characteristics" (p. 193). For example, students of high socioeconomic status are likely to choose majors in social sciences, arts and humanities, and government, while students of low socioeconomic status are likely to choose majors in engineering and education (p. 153). Men are likely to choose majors in engineering, physical sciences, prelaw, premedicine, and business, while women are most likely to select majors in education, humanities and fine arts, social sciences, and biological sciences (p. 153). Students scoring high on measures of political-economic and social liberalism are most likely to major in the social sciences and students scoring low are most likely to major in engineering (p. 162).

Feldman and Newcomb (1969) also report that "preexisting differences in characteristics typical of students initially choosing different curricula tend to become more pronounced following experience in those major fields" (p. 193). They attribute this accentuation to faculty and peer group influence and find it to occur more often in large universities than small colleges. Their rationale is that the major or department is more likely to be the student's "home" at the large university than at the small college.

Faculty and the Major

The major is widely recognized as the best working element of the undergraduate curriculum. Part of the reason for this is that faculty training and teaching interests are well tuned to the specialty instruction that is required for this part of the curriculum.

With regard to training, most faculty have spent at least a year pursuing a field of concentration beyond the level of the bachelor's degree. Ninety-four percent have earned a graduate degree. Forty-eight percent have Ph.D.s and 28 percent are working on Ph.D.s (Carnegie Surveys, 1975–76).

With regard to teaching, a majority of college and university faculty (53 percent) prefer teaching students majoring in or intending to major in their own fields to those with other interests. This is true for more than half of all faculty at all types of colleges and universities except the most selective liberal arts colleges, where 59 percent say they prefer teaching nonmajors (Carnegie Surveys, 1975–76). This is likely to be a result of more catholic faculty selection by elite liberal arts colleges as well as the need for faculty to teach in courses covering a wider swatch of their discipline.

Almost half of all faculty (48 percent) also prefer teaching courses that focus on limited specialties to those which cover wide varieties of material (Carnegie Surveys, 1975–76). Faculty are more partial to limited specialties at the most research-oriented universities (51 percent) and least partial to such courses at the most selective liberal arts colleges (35 percent).

Concerns and Proposals

In the following pages, the validity of six common criticisms is examined.

Criticism 1: Majors vary in quality and substance within as well as between schools.

This criticism is not concerned with diversity in majors. There is no proof, for example, that the student-created major is better or worse than the formally established disciplinary major. This criticism is concerned with the fact that a major can be simply a collection of courses lacking depth or cohesion. Furthermore, some departments specify only a number of courses or credits required for the major without reference to content. The history department at the University of Pennsylvania, for instance, requires 12 courses on unspecified topics and as many as three of the courses can be outside the department. This criticism is also concerned with the fact that majors can be too narrow in their formulation, dealing strictly with subspecialty areas and lacking in the breadth that may be appropriate to undergraduate studies. There is no evidence, however, that lack of coherence or narrow specialization in the major is common.

Nonetheless, the competency-based major has been recommended as a means of abating both problems. By placing emphasis on outcomes rather than process or courses that go into the major, it has been suggested that the competency-based major provides minimal institutionwide and concentrationwide standards of quality and substance.

Other frequent recommendations are that colleges and universities offer students better academic advising in the major (Levine and Weingart, 1973); that colleges and universities not require the major, as incoherent concentrations may simply result if students try to avoid the concentration requirement (Taylor, 1971); and that colleges and universities offer students a wide choice of majors, so that students do not have to skirt the rules of established concentrations in order to build a major that satisfies their needs (Levine and Weingart, 1973).

Criticism 2: Students spend too much time on the major.

Robert Hutchins, who believed that a college education should deal only with general education, would readily agree with this criticism. Thorstein Veblen, who thought of a college education as a probationary period in scholarship, would have disagreed. In fact, he might have amended the statement to read, "students spend too little time on the major."

Regardless of philosophy, however, the situation is this: "The overall course-taking pattern for the degree . . . shows a significant increase in depth and a corresponding diminution of breadth" in the period between 1967 and 1974 (Blackburn and others, 1976, p. 35). In arts and sciences colleges, where it was shown earlier that major requirements are far lower than for professional/technical schools, Blackburn and others discovered that between electives and major requirements students were spending an average of 44 percent to 58 percent of their studies on the major (p. 32). The more electives available, the more time students spent in concentration (p. 31). Yet, 41 percent of the undergraduates feel that degree requirements prevent them from taking as many courses in their major as they would like. This attitude is most common at community and junior colleges (44 percent), which have relatively the heaviest general education requirements, and least common at excellent liberal arts colleges (31 percent), which stress general education in their student recruiting (Carnegie Surveys, 1975–76).

Those unhappy with this situation have recommended limits on the number of courses a student can take in the major areas. At Mills College, for instance, a student cannot take more than 50 percent of his or her courses in the major area. Another suggestion revolves about individualized group advising, in which every student is required periodically to seek advice and explain his or her academic plans to an advising committee chosen by the student. This is done at the University of Alabama's New College, as noted in Chapter 6. A final proposal offers in-service orientation to students regarding the demands of employers and graduate or professional schools. It is often contended that students choose heavy concentrations because they incorrectly believe that it is expected of them by employers or graduate schools.

Criticism 3: Majors prepare students primarily for graduate school.

This criticism exaggerates the situation. Many majors, particularly those offered in vocational/technical programs, are not designed for students planning to attend graduate school. However, a large number of majors, especially in the arts and sciences, are. Daniel Bell (1968, p. 299) observed at Columbia College that "each department sees its major mainly as a preparation for graduate work in that subject." Such major training is certainly not functional for all students since only 43 percent of the students responding to the 1976 Carnegie Council undergraduate survey indicated they would certainly or probably attend graduate or professional school. And many of those who do attend graduate or professional school will do so in a subject area other than their undergraduate major.

As a result Bell (1968, p. 299) proposed "double tracks" in each major; that is, majors with broad backgrounds for students who are not planning to attend graduate school and more detailed majors for students with graduate school plans.

Criticism 4: Liberal arts concentrators are at a disadvantage in the job market.

In addressing this criticism, it is important to remember that Cowley (in Payton, 1961) identified three purposes for specialization, one of which was nonoccupational (specialization for the sake of learning) and another preprofessional (specialization for professional school). With regard to the third purpose—occupational preparation—underemployment and unemployment face students majoring in liberal arts subjects more frequently than students concentrating in other subjects (College Placement Council, 1975). As a result some colleges supplement or are planning to supplement their liberal arts majors with the skills necessary to land a first job. The supplements include practical minors in areas such as management and administration (University of California, Berkeley), internship experiences (Scripps College), career planning and counseling classes (Allegheny State College), and applied courses in a major area—such as energy and environmental management in chemistry (Flathead Valley Community College). A few colleges have responded to the problem by significantly reducing their number of liberal arts majors in favor of occupational majors. Earl Cheit (1975, p. 137) reports that San Bernardino College, established as a liberal arts institution, now focuses on work-related programs.

Criticism 5: Majors and faculty specialization deleteriously dominate the undergraduate curriculum.

This criticism is considered valid in many quarters. Jacques Barzun believed it to be the case:

> Consider the forces at work. First, it seems desirable to have the great scholar teach undergraduates, and he naturally teaches them as if they were future scholars in his own line, as professionals. Then, the young themselves want to get on as quickly as possible, and in the last two years of college they elect a major which relates directly to the future profession.... An even stronger influence is that of the young teachers, all Ph.D.s who need to establish themselves. This they can do only in one way: by showing productivity in research.... Accordingly, these junior scholars decline to teach anything not related to their own specialties. As one of them said to me, they "do not want to teach secondhand subjects." Firsthand subjects are necessarily narrow, and what is worse, they are treated as if everyone in the class were to become a professional, a duplicate of his own teacher [in Bell, 1968, p. 56].

Levine and Weingart (1973), like Barzun, believe that the major and specialization dominate the college. They observe: "With the dilution of general education, concentration has become the prime focus of the undergraduate college.... It was only natural that, by default, concentration filled the gap, since colleges are organized and faculty are trained according to specialty" (p. 64).

This point of view is also accepted by almost half of America's college and university faculty. Forty-nine percent of faculty agree that the typical undergraduate curriculum has suffered from the specialization of faculty members (Carnegie Surveys, 1975–76).

Proposals designed to mitigate the influence of the major and specialties in the undergraduate curriculum are common in many quarters. Two such proposals, discussed in more detail in Chapter 1, are to reshape faculty rewards to stress nonspecialty performance, and to train and recruit faculty knowledgeable in more than one specialty area.

Another frequently suggested improvement is to organize faculty in ways that decrease the stress on specialization. Today, most colleges and universities organize faculty into academic departments or specialty areas. The idea of the department was imported from Germany. The first academic departments in this county were established at the University of Virginia and Harvard University in 1825. The invention of the semiautonomous academic departments commonly found on most campuses is credited to Daniel Coit Gilman. As early as 1880 Cornell and Johns Hopkins had such departments. The idea was popularized at Harvard and many other colleges in the 1890s.

However, some colleges and universities have avoided departmental or specialty organization. Hampshire College and Bennington College organize their faculty into divisions or groups of related disciplines such as mathematics and science, humanities and arts, and social sciences. Divisions tend to work best when the number of faculty is small. As faculty size increases to more than a few individuals in any specialty area, de facto departments commonly coalesce. The University of California, Santa Cruz, organizes its faculty into disciplinary units called boards of study and interdisciplinary units called colleges. Every faculty member belongs to a college and board of studies. Over the years the boards of study have grown increasingly dominant relative to the colleges. The reasons advanced for this include the growth of graduate programs at Santa Cruz, the nature of the faculty recruited, the character of faculty as a species, and the University of California reward system (discussed further in Chapter 13). The University of Wisconsin at Green Bay, an institution with an environmental mission, organizes its faculty into interdisciplinary, problem-centered units such as urban analysis, science and environmental change, modernization processes, and population. An initial difficulty facing Green Bay was reluctance on the part of the faculty to be separated from colleagues in similar specialties.

Criticism 6: Neighboring colleges commonly duplicate most of each other's majors while failing to include in their curricula other desirable subject fields.

This criticism is based on the intention of most colleges and universities to be full-service institutions. As a result they usually offer the same basic core of subjects, causing significant duplication of academic programs and the systematic absence of certain majors from the curricula of nearly all colleges. To provide for the lacking subjects, the Carnegie Council has recommended that colleges form consortia to share the costs of instruction in esoteric teaching areas, in courses with relatively low enrollments, and in programs requiring large capital expenses. Certain consortia, such as the Claremont Colleges and the Worcester consortium, have also managed to reduce the overlap in the core areas.

* * *

For a commentary on the major and concentration, see Chapter 9, "The Major—A Success Story," in The Carnegie Foundation for the Advancement of Teaching, *Missions of the College Curriculum: A Contemporary Review with Suggestions* (1977).

References

Bell, D. *The Reforming of General Education: The Columbia College Experience in Its National Setting.* Garden City, N.Y.: Anchor Books, 1968.
   This book is discussed in Chapter 11.
Blackburn, R., Armstrong, E., Conrad, C., Didham, J., and McKune, T. *Changing Practices in Undergraduate Education.* Berkeley, Calif.: Carnegie Council on Policy Studies in Higher Education, 1976.
   Blackburn and others examine changes in the nature of the major between 1967 and 1974 at 270 two- and four-year colleges and universities.
The Carnegie Foundation for the Advancement of Teaching. *Missions of the College Curriculum: A Contemporary Review with Suggestions.* San Francisco: Jossey-Bass, 1977.
   This volume is discussed in Chapter 11.
Carnegie Surveys, 1975–76.
   This study is described in the Preface.
Catalog Study, 1976.
   This research is discussed in the Preface.
Cheit, E. F. *The Useful Arts and the Liberal Tradition.* New York: McGraw-Hill, 1975.
College Placement Council, Inc. *Four Year Liberal Arts Graduates: Their Utilization in Business, Industry, and Government—The Problem and Some Solutions.* Bethlehem, Penn., 1975.
Dressel, P. *The Undergraduate Curriculum in Higher Education.* New York: Center for Applied Research in Education, Inc., 1966.
Dressel, P., and DeLisle, F. *Undergraduate Curriculum Trends.* Washington, D.C.: American Council on Education, 1969.
Feldman, K. A., and Newcomb, T. M. *The Impact of College on Students.* Vol. 1. San Francisco: Jossey-Bass, 1969.
Glenny, L. A., Shea, J. R., Ruyle, J. H., and Freschi, K. H. *Presidents Confront Reality: From Edifice Complex to University Without Walls.* San Francisco: Jossey-Bass, 1976.

Levine, A., and Weingart, J. *Reform of Undergraduate Education.* San Francisco: Jossey-Bass, 1973.

One chapter in this book discusses variations in the major and their consequences at 26 colleges and universities. Another chapter discusses alternatives to faculty organization by department.

McHenry, D. E., and Associates. *Academic Departments: Problems, Variations, and Alternatives.* San Francisco: Jossey-Bass, 1977.

Payton, P. "Origins of the Terms 'Major' and 'Minor' in American Higher Education." *History of Education Quarterly,* 1961, 1 (2), 57–63.

Taylor, H. *How to Change Colleges: Notes on Radical Reform.* New York: Holt, Rinehart and Winston, 1971.

Warren, J. R. "Alternatives to Degrees." In D. W. Vermilye (Ed.), *Learner-Centered Reform: Current Issues in Higher Education 1975.* San Francisco: Jossey-Bass, 1975.

3

Basic and Advanced Skills and Knowledge

For the past few years, declines in student test scores and abilities among the three R's and more advanced subjects have been popular discussion topics in forums varying from the local PTA to the cover of *Newsweek*. The declines are real and colleges and universities are spending increasing amounts of time trying to overcome them through enhanced basic and advanced skills instruction.

Definition and History

Basic skills are the abilities and *basic knowledge* is the information a student needs to embark upon college study. Colleges differ in the kinds of skills and knowledge they regard as basic or entrance level. Proficiency in the three R's (reading, writing, and arithmetic) and study skills are considered essential for all college work; however, some colleges also require students to have *advanced skills and knowledge* in foreign language, geometry, advanced algebra, English composition, and even swimming. Colleges also differ in the level of skills and knowledge within a subject they feel necessary for undergraduate study. For instance, the University of California, Berkeley, requires prospective students to complete two years of high school mathematics, but Amherst College requires three years, and the California Institute of Technology requires four.

Not all students enter college with the basic skills or knowledge necessary to function at their institution. The instruction provided to bring them up to required basic skills or knowledge levels is called compensatory education. Because colleges vary in what they label basic skills and knowledge, they also vary in what they call compensatory education. Richard Richardson illustrates this in the field of mathematics: "Anything below the level of Calculus I is remedial at Lehigh University. At Moravian College, two miles away, there is less emphasis on the sciences and anything less than college algebra and trigonometry is remedial. At Kutztown State College, 20 miles from Moravian, the initial mathematics course is called Fundamentals of Mathematics, and is at least a step below the entering level of mathematics at Moravian" (The Carnegie Foundation for the Advancement of Teaching, 1977, p. 207).

The terms *remedial* and *developmental* education are frequently used as synonyms for *compensatory* education, but there are important differences. Remedial education implies improvement of student skills and knowledge for the purpose of entering a program for which the student was previously ineligible. Its emphasis is upon correcting weaknesses. Compensatory or developmental education emphasizes the building of new strengths—the enhancement of skills, knowledge, and attitudes that may not necessarily be needed to qualify students for more advanced academic programs (Cross, 1976, pp. 30–31). Compensatory education in particular seeks by enrichment to overcome deprivations associated with the home, family, and earlier study. Of the three terms, *compensatory* will be used throughout this volume except when historically inappropriate.

Skills and knowledge requirements of one sort or another have been with us for a long time. At Harvard in 1640, students were required to speak and read Latin and to know Greek grammar in order to be admitted. These were the skills and knowledge necessary to study the classical curriculum of the day described in Appendix A. More than 100 years passed before arithmetic was first required by a college; Yale took this step in 1745. By 1870 the arithmetic requirement was upgraded to include more sophisticated branches of mathematics; and history, science, geography, foreign language, and English were required by various American colleges (Brubacher and Rudy, 1976, pp. 12, 242). (The changes were a response to the expansion of the classical curriculum that is described in Chapter 16.)

In order to find students with the required background skills and knowledge, the early colleges developed relationships with preparatory schools. Harvard, for instance, established a feeder arrangement with Boston Latin School, Cambridge Latin School, and Roxbury Latin School (Sizer, 1964, p. 36). In time, such relationships permitted the participating colleges to upgrade their programs by dropping some of the more elementary courses to the preparatory school level. For instance, at Yale in 1720 geometry was a senior-year course, in 1743 it was a sophomore course, in 1825 it was a freshman course, and in 1855 geometry was a requirement for admission (Brubacher and Rudy, 1976, p. 12).

Curricular upgrading and arrangements with preparatory schools or high schools were not possible for most colleges, however, because secondary schools were few, their location was primarily urban, and most students prepared for college under the tutelage of private tutors, ministers, and parents. As a result most colleges were forced to reduce entrance requirements to a level students could attain at common (elementary) schools or to introduce their own preparatory divisions. The University of Missouri eliminated entrance requirements during the second half of the nineteenth century, admitting any student who applied and paid the necessary fees. It was not until about the time of World War I that this university was able to raise requirements to the equivalent of a high school education (Brubacher and Rudy, 1976, (p. 85).

An alternative remedy—establishing a preparatory division—was also prevalent. In 1870, there were only five states in the country (Connecticut, Massachusetts, New Hampshire, New Jersey, and Rhode Island, all located in the secondary school rich Northeast) where none of the colleges were engaged in preparatory work. Outside of these five states, 12 colleges avoided preparatory divisions (Rudolph, 1962, pp. 281–282).

Preparatory students, who were often barely teenagers, lived in college dormitories, attended classes in college buildings, and were subject to the same discipline as the older students (Proctor, 1956, p. 22). Their age made them enormously unpopular with college teachers and students in spite of the fact that "there were usually more students in the preparatory department than in the 'regular' college classes" (Brubacher and Rudy, 1976, p. 156). As late as 1894 such students still comprised over 40 percent of the entering students in American colleges (Sizer, 1964, p. 36).

The proliferation of high schools in the late nineteenth and early twentieth centuries gradually reduced the need for preparatory divisions. Nonetheless, in 1915, 350 colleges still offered such programs (Brubacher and Rudy, 1976, p. 243); and most colleges still admitted students who had failed to meet their entrance requirements, owing to intense competition for students, institutional financial need, and wide variation in college and secondary school requirements. For these reasons more than half of the Harvard, Yale, and Princeton freshmen in 1907 had not satisfied their college's admission requirements (p. 244). To remedy this problem, a new type of course, the remedial course, was created at Wellesley College in 1894 to bring students up to grade level in deficient areas.

K. Patricia Cross (1976), in examining the evolution of compensatory education, found the original remedial courses to be voluntary how-to-study classes, offered as a service by the dean of students office and dealing with subjects such as note taking, good study habits, test taking, and health. These courses were premised on the assumption that student deficiencies were based upon immaturity and lack of discipline rather than lack of ability or poor training.

In the late 1930s and 1940s, remedial reading instruction was initiated, often as a supplement to the how-to-study course. Diagnostic tests and small-group instruction were used in the remedial programs, but evaluation of program success was usually absent and when present was generally poor. During this period, prior training was thought the primary cause of student deficiency.

In the 1950s and early 1960s, remedial education focused upon high-ability students performing poorly academically. In the mid-1960s, colleges became more interested in low-academic-ability students. The remedial efforts of the period included intensive mathematics and English courses; counseling; and U.S. government-supported programs such as Upward Bound, created in 1965, and Special Services to Disadvantaged Students, established in 1968, which were designed to provide students with compensatory instruction, counseling, and support services. The causes for academic deficiencies were thought to be low academic ability, psychological-motivational blocks to learning, and sociocultural factors.

In the 1970s, colleges that cater to students low in academic skills and information shifted from remedial to compensatory education (Cross, 1976). This shift involved the use of tutors and laboratory technicians in addition to counselors and faculty members. It also involved the creation of individualized programs, mastery learning, learning laboratories, and programs specifically designed for low achievers. Today, all of the causes for lower-than-average basic skills noted previously are recognized, but compensatory programs are based on the assumption that education should maximize the talents and skills of each student rather than seeking solely to bring student skills up to a prespecified level that can be classified as "nondeficient."

State of Basic and Advanced Skills and Knowledge

Student Achievement in Basic and Advanced Skills and Knowledge

READING AND WRITING

The National Assessment of Educational Progress (NAEP) has surveyed the educational attainment of a cross section of American 17-year-olds, generally high school seniors. With regard to reading, which is thought to be an excellent predictor of academic performance particularly for community college students (Henard and Stenning, 1976), NAEP concluded: "Many 17-year-olds can read and understand the literal meaning of information presented in short, straightforward materials. However, if the amount of material to be read is increased, the proportion of readers able to answer literal questions about the material drops off. Long selections with unusual subject matter or vocabulary are clearly the most difficult type of material to read either literally or inferentially" (Mullis and others, 1977, p. 94). NAEP studies of reading were conducted in 1971 and 1975, and over this four-year period, there was little change in student ability and no change in study skills or literal comprehension. However, there was a small but significant decline in inferential comprehension among female students and students whose parents were educated beyond high school (Mullis and others, 1977, p. 114).

NAEP also examined student writing ability. Results of the examination indicated that: "Over half of the 17-year-olds have learned to write competently in a variety of situations—some can even write with sophistication. On the other hand, about 10% do not have a basic command of writing skills. Another third have not learned how to amplify or develop an idea in order to communicate it clearly and fully. Many do not carry their explanations far enough; others elaborate extensively on their statements, but the details are not presented logically" (Mullis and others, 1977, p. 98). NAEP writing surveys, which involved descriptive essay assignments, were conducted in 1969 and 1974. In 1974 the mean quality of the papers declined significantly from 1969; there were fewer average essays and more poor ones. They used simpler vocabulary, contained fewer complex sentences, had more run-on sentences, and included a greater number of incoherent paragraphs (26 percent versus 15 percent) (p. 114).

Declines in student verbal performance have also been reported by the two national college testing services—the College Entrance Examination Board (CEEB) and the American College Testing Program (ACT). The CEEB's Scholastic Aptitude Test (SAT), which was taken by 71 percent of 1976 freshmen (Astin and others, 1976, p. 36), tests verbal and mathematics ability and assigns scores between 200 and 800. Average scores on the verbal test, concerned with reading comprehension, vocabulary, and verbal reasoning, have declined year after year from a high of 478 in 1962–63 to a low of 429 in 1976–77.[1] The American College Testing Program battery in English, mathematics, science, and social studies was taken by 51 percent of 1976 freshmen (Mullis and others, 1977). Its verbal examination (ACT-English) measures grammar, punctuation, sentence structure, diction, logic, and organization on a scale from 1 to 36. Between 1964–65 and 1973–74, these scores declined from 18.7 to 17.5.[2]

The test findings are reflected in student perceptions of their reading and writing skills as well. Only 31 percent of 1976 college

---

[1] Based on a telephone conversation with the Educational Testing Service, August 25, 1977. All future references to this will be cited as ETS, 1977.

[2] Based on a 10 percent random sample. This information was obtained through the American College Testing Program, December 17, 1976. Hereafter it will be cited as ACTP, 1976.

freshmen believed their high school prepared them very well in reading and composition and only 18 percent rated their preparation in study habits as very good (Mullis and others, 1977, p. 49). Among all students, those at two-year colleges rated their preparation poorest—but they also had taken fewer writing-skills courses than other students. Thus 33 percent of them did not take English composition in their junior or senior year of high school, in contrast to 18 percent of the students at research universities. Students at other types of schools fell in between (Carnegie Surveys, 1975–76).

After entering college, a number of students discover that they are not as well prepared as their peers in reading and writing skills. Twenty-five percent feel they are not as well prepared to write essays and papers, 13 percent believe themselves less well prepared to read and comprehend English, and 25 percent sense they are less well prepared to research papers on their own (Carnegie Surveys, 1975–76). Students at community colleges most frequently believe they are underprepared.

The students' sense of being underprepared is shared by their professors. At Harvard a senior faculty member in English reported that students "show less facility in reading and do not know grammar." At Columbia University an instructor reported that students "can't write and won't read." At Ohio State University placement tests show that 30 percent of the freshmen lack college-level writing skills. At the University of California, Berkeley, 40 to 65 percent of the incoming freshmen take compensatory English. At Sterling College, a sectarian liberal arts institution, more than one-half of the entering students have difficulty with texts written at the freshman level (The Carnegie Foundation for the Advancement of Teaching, 1977, pp. 209–210).

MATHEMATICS

The National Assessment of Educational Progress also examined the mathematics skills and knowledge of 17-year-olds. NAEP found that: "Most 17-year-olds have mastered the basic arithmetic operations. They are familiar with basic facts and terminology of geometry. More students can multiply fractions than can add them. The majority can solve straightforward word problems that call for addition, subtraction, or multiplication of whole numbers. The majority of 17-year-olds do not understand probability, but they can compute a simple average. When asked to find solutions to problems that involve more than one step, few of the 17-year-olds are successful" (Mullis and others, 1977, p. 82).

NAEP offers no information about changes in recent years as its mathematics retest has not yet been completed. However, both the College Board and the American College Testing Program report declines in mathematics aptitude test scores. Both examinations deal with five basic operations: (1) addition, subtraction, multiplication, and division; (2) properties of numbers; (3) averages; (4) basic algebra, not as advanced as quadratic equations; and (5) elementary geometry. Between 1962–63 and 1976–77, SAT mathematics scores declined continuously from 502 to 470 (ETS, 1977). Between 1964–65 and 1975–76, scores on the mathematics portions of the ACT dropped from 19.6 to 17.5 (ACTP, 1976).

Consistent with these declines, less than one-third of 1976 college freshmen (29 percent) thought they had been prepared well by the high schools in mathematics (Astin and others, 1976, p. 49). While in high school, most college students had taken geometry (79 percent) and a second year of algebra (66 percent). But geometry had been taken least often by students at two-year colleges (63 percent) and at nonselective liberal arts colleges (78 percent), in contrast to between 85 percent and 94 percent of the undergraduates at other types of institutions (Carnegie Surveys, 1975–76).

A large proportion of students intend to continue with mathematics in college. Forty-seven percent of undergraduates have taken or plan to take college algebra, which is considered a compensatory course at some selective colleges; 40 percent have taken or plan to take statistics; and 37 percent have taken or plan to take calculus. The group expectations fail to tell the whole story, however. Approximately one-third of all undergraduates (33 percent) felt less well prepared than their classmates to work in mathematics or statistics. At two-year colleges and nonselective liberal arts institutions, only 12 percent and 17 percent of the students respectively have taken calculus in college versus 54 percent at research universities (Carnegie Surveys, 1975–76). This is not surprising because many community colleges have reported their students to be weak in arithmetic, algebra, and geometry. For instance, the General College at the University of Minnesota, an open admission, two-year college, found only 10 percent of its students capable of studying college algebra or trigonometry at the time of entrance (Levine, 1976, p. 9).

NATURAL SCIENCE

The most recent NAEP study of achievement by 17-year-olds in the natural sciences concluded: "The majority of 17-year-olds know a number of facts about a variety of science topics. They know basic facts about disease, nutrition, the human body, plants and animals. In addition they know some generally useful science-related facts. They have difficulty with earth science and astronomy—for example, only about half can use an apparatus to demonstrate the daily cycle of the earth. Seventeen-year-olds are basically unfamiliar with concepts from physics and chemistry" (Mullis and others, 1977, p. 85). Between 1969 and 1973, NAEP found a 3 percent decline in the proportion of 17-year-olds who knew the answer to a typical science question (p. 113). Over the same period, the American College Testing Program natural science scores indicated a change in the opposite direction. Average scores based on the test which asks questions on short readings in biology, chemistry, physics, geology, astronomy, and general sciences rose from 20.0 in 1968–69 to 20.8 in 1975–76 (ACTP, 1976).

There is no reason to believe the results of the ACT and NAEP tests inconsistent. NAEP examined the science knowledge of a cross section of 17-year-olds; ACT focused on the interpretation of science readings by college aspirants of comparable ages. NAEP science score declines are surprising because college-bound youth rate science education as the second strongest element of the secondary school program. Thirty-three percent of 1976 college freshmen felt their high schools prepared them very well in science (Astin and others, 1976, p. 49). Eighty-three to 90 percent of students at all types of four-year colleges and universities had taken a year or more of science in high school. At two-year colleges, 70 percent did so (Carnegie Surveys, 1975–76).

After entering college, about one-fourth of all undergraduates (26 percent) find they are not as well prepared as their classmates in the natural sciences. Nonetheless most have taken or plan to take a year or more of physical science (53 percent) or biological science (51 percent) in college (Carnegie Surveys, 1975–76). The enthusiasm for the subject is at least in part externally motivated; as Chapter 1 noted, most colleges have general education requirements in the sciences and mathematics that students must satisfy to graduate.

SOCIAL SCIENCE

The National Assessment of Educational Progress conducted a more general examination of the subject of citizenship and social studies. It found that 17-year-olds did not perform as well on social studies knowledge items as they did on skill questions. For instance, most knew that senators are elected, the Supreme Court rules on the constitutionality of laws, and the president is not a lawmaker. However, when asked how Congress could stop the president from making war, half said Congress could declare the law unconstitutional. Seventeen-year-olds were found to have a basic knowledge of the courts, not to understand basic economic concepts such as the causes of poverty, and to have difficulty applying their knowledge of geography (Mullis and others, 1977, pp. 90–92).

NAEP has as yet no comparative data on 17-year-olds' performance in the social studies. However, the American College Testing Program reported a sharper decline in scores on its social studies reading test—involving reading passages in European and ancient history, government and American history, current social issues, sociology, and economics—than in any of its other three examinations: from an average of 20.6 in 1964–65 to 17.5 in 1975–76 (ACTP, 1976).

Basic instruction in social studies is an integral part of most high school courses, and in this area freshmen feel they are best equipped for college. Forty percent of 1976 freshmen said their high school education prepared them very well in history and social science (Astin and others, 1976, p. 49).

LITERATURE

The information available on student achievement in literature is meager. All that is avaialble is the 1970–71 National Assessment of Education Progress (NAEP) findings. NAEP reported: "17-year-olds can read and understand certain elements of literary language. They know what can be gained from reading literature and say that literature should be taught in all schools. They are familiar with a variety of literary works and characters. A survey of reading habits indicates that 17-year-olds do not read extensively outside of school or read a wide variety of literature; almost all report that they do some reading on their own—mostly popular novels. However, when asked to discuss a literary work, either orally or in writing, less than one-third of the 17-year-olds are able to find meanings or evaluate the work with much reflection or understanding" (Mullis and others, 1977, p. 96). This is despite the fact that literature of one sort or another is a staple in precollege instruction.

FOREIGN LANGUAGE

There is no data on how well students perform in foreign language, considered an advanced learning skill, or how performance has changed in recent years. It is known, however, that students feel they are ill prepared for college language study. Only 15 percent of 1976 college freshmen said their high school programs prepared them very well in foreign languages (Astin and others, 1976, p. 41).

College students believe they are ill prepared even though 72 percent have had at least a year of foreign language study in secondary school. This percentage varies dramatically at different types of colleges and universities, being lowest at community colleges (58 percent) and highest at selective liberal arts colleges (95 percent). Between these two poles are research universities (86 percent), doctorate-granting universities (81 percent), comprehensive colleges (76 percent), and nonselective liberal arts colleges (73 percent) (Carnegie Surveys, 1975–76).

A far smaller percentage of undergraduates (39 percent) plan to take or have taken additional foreign language study in college. In general the students with the most foreign language experience in high school are most likely to take foreign language in college. For example, 69 percent of the students at selective liberal arts colleges have taken or plan to take a year or more of foreign language in college versus 33 percent at two-year institutions (Carnegie Surveys, 1975–76). Wide variations in institutions' general education requirements (illustrated in Chapter 1) also explain these differences in foreign language enrollments.

Undergraduate Education in Basic and Advanced Skills and Knowledge

Nearly all American colleges and universities offer one form or another of skills and knowledge education. Their efforts are of three types: (1) supplements to the traditional curriculum, (2) skills and knowledge courses, and (3) learning centers. Many colleges use combinations of the three.

SUPPLEMENTS TO THE TRADITIONAL CURRICULUM

Supplements to the traditional curriculum consist of practices intended to enrich the skills and knowledge content of the regular undergraduate programs without changing it. Supplements include testing programs, common communication systems, counseling, and tutoring. Basic and advanced skills and knowledge tests are of two types—diagnostic entrance tests and graduation tests. Diagnostic entrance tests are designed to gauge student achievement for the purpose of directing students to the appropriate campus learning resources. Graduation tests examine whether students have achieved the minimum basic skills and knowledge required to earn a degree. The testing program at the University of Minnesota's General College includes both. The diagnostic test has two parts—the School and College Ability Test, produced by the Educational Testing Service, consisting of verbal and mathematics examinations; and an internally-produced Entrance Comprehensive Examination, which deals with organizational ability, arithmetic, and algebra. On the basis of their performance on the diagnostic battery, students are directed to skills courses, a learning center, and/or counseling. The General College graduation test focuses on ability in reading comprehension, organizational ability, quantitative theory, inference, and several more advanced subjects. A minimum score on the examination qualifies a student who has accumulated a sufficient number of credits to earn an associate's degree. The records of students who receive lesser scores are reviewed and, when appropriate, alternatives such as papers and oral examinations are offered.

Common communication systems are employed only in the area of writing skills. They involve the use, throughout an entire institution, of one set of symbols to correct English usage on student tests and papers. The symbols are used in all courses to provide common and enhanced levels of feedback on writing skills. Pomona College, which has such a system, provides a writing skills handbook and symbol guide for all faculty and students.

Academic, personal, vocational, and special group (minorities, women, and so forth) counseling are part of basic skills and knowledge education at many colleges. All four types of counseling are used in the Special Services for Disadvantaged Students in College program, which was created by the Higher Education Amendments of 1968 and is intended to provide compensatory and support services for students who are enrolled or accepted for enrollment in institutions of higher education. (Advising and counseling are discussed more fully in Chapter 6.)

Tutoring is one-on-one or small-group instruction outside of formal classes. Tutoring has three functions in compensatory skills and knowledge instruction (Roueche and Kirk, 1973, p. 67): It provides supportive teaching immediately after the student has made a mistake; it helps to reduce student anxiety over failure or slowness in learning by providing crisis teaching; and it offers individualized and diagnostic teaching. Faculty, students, university staff, and community resource people have been used as tutors. Eight percent of 1976 freshmen either needed or expected to need tutoring in some classes (Astin and others, 1976, p. 60).

BASIC SKILLS AND KNOWLEDGE COURSES

Most colleges offer skills and knowledge courses on topics ranging from English composition to reading, writing, and arithmetic. The courses vary in length from a few weeks, as is the case with a noncredit speed-reading course at Brandeis University, to four years, as is the case with the core English composition course at St. Joseph's College. Basic skills and knowledge courses are more common at two-year institutions than four-year colleges and universities; advanced skill courses such as English composition are more common at arts and sciences colleges than professional/technical colleges (business, education, engineering, health science, and trade/technical arts); and basic skills courses in the three R's are more common in professional/technical colleges than arts and sciences colleges. This is shown in Table 10.

Table 10. Skills courses offered in arts and sciences and professional/technical[a]
colleges at two- and four-year institutions (in percentages)

	Two-year colleges		Four-year colleges and universities	
	Arts and sciences	Professional/ technical	Arts and sciences	Professional/ technical
English composition	97	90	82	65
Noncredit courses in reading, basic writing, and arithmetic	52	51	48	58
Credit courses for reading, basic writing, and arithmetic	78	90	39	50

[a]An aggregation of practices at business, education, engineering, health science, and trade/technical colleges.

Source: Catalog Study, 1976.

Table 10 also shows that credit is offered for courses in the three R's at the vast majority of two-year institutions. In fact, courses for credit are more common than noncredit courses at these schools. In contrast, while approximately half of the four-year colleges and universities offer credit courses in the three R's, slightly more offer noncredit courses.

Course policy in basic skills varies from college to college, however. This is shown in Table 11 for five different types of institutions of higher education (research universities, doctorate-granting universities, comprehensive colleges and universities, liberal arts colleges, and two-year colleges).

Table 11 shows that a majority (67 percent or more) of each of the five types of colleges offer some form of skills courses, but liberal arts colleges offer both credit and noncredit courses in the three R's far less than any other type of institution. Only 18 percent of liberal arts colleges offer credit for reading, basic writing, and arithmetic courses, while fully 54 percent of research universities and 83 percent of community and junior colleges do so.

Not all reading, basic writing, and arithmetic courses are labeled compensatory by the institutions offering them. For example, Miami-Dade Community College, which offers four courses in

**Table 11. Skills courses offered at different types of colleges and universities
(in percentages)**

	Research universities	Doctorate-granting universities	Comprehensive colleges & universities	Liberal arts colleges	Two-year colleges
English composition	67	77	71	77	94
Noncredit course in reading, basic writing, and arithmetic	54	51	45	25	52
Credit course in reading, basic writing, and arithmetic	54	51	47	18	83

Source: Catalog Study, 1976.

reading, like many similar colleges, calls none of its classes compensatory. But at colleges that do classify some of their courses in the three R's as compensatory, 13 percent of their undergraduates take one or more such courses on a noncredit basis and 16 percent take one or more for credit. Noncredit compensatory courses are taken most frequently by students at community colleges (17 percent) and least frequently by students at research universities (7 percent). Credit-bearing compensatory courses are taken most often by students at comprehensive colleges (18 percent) and nonselective liberal arts colleges (18 percent) and least by students at research universities (10 percent) (Carnegie Surveys, 1975–76).

More undergraduates wish to take such courses, however. Twenty-one percent of the students responding to the 1976 Carnegie Council undergraduate survey indicated that they would like to have had a compensatory basic skills course for credit and 14 percent would like to have had a noncredit compensatory course. Students want such courses most often at community colleges (24 percent credit and 17 percent noncredit) and nonselective liberal arts colleges (22 percent credit and 17 percent noncredit). The courses are desired least by students at the most selective liberal arts colleges (14 percent credit and 13 percent noncredit) and most at research-oriented universities (15 percent credit and 11 percent noncredit) (Carnegie Surveys, 1975–76).

LEARNING CENTERS

Learning centers are individualized, walk-in, basic skills resource centers for students. They frequently deal with basic skills in mathematics, English, writing, spelling, reading, vocabulary, test taking, and study skills. Advanced skills such as foreign language and algebra are also occasionally included. Learning centers can be staffed by faculty, paraprofessionals, peer tutors, and professional counselors. They may utilize a variety of instructional methods, including diagnostic and achievement tests, workbooks, audio-visual casettes, programmed texts, seminars, small-group sessions, and other pedagogical techniques. (The use of libraries as learning centers is discussed in Chapter 8.)

Learning centers are found at 60 percent of two-year institutions and 43 percent of four-year colleges and universities. They are more common at professional/technical schools (52 percent) than arts and sciences colleges (37 percent) (Catalog Study, 1976).

Unfortunately, center use is sometimes considered a stigma by students. For this reason, as well as the lack of credit associated with many of their activities, attendance is often low or sporadic, particularly among non-minority students. Burnout is also high among staff because the work load is very heavy and frequently unsatisfying.

Concerns and Proposals

The state of basic and advanced skills and knowledge is a perennial topic of discussion and dismay. Some current criticisms are listed below. The basis for these criticisms is explained and their validity is examined. When the criticism seems valid, proposals for improvement are discussed.

Criticism 1: Declining scores on basic skills and knowledge tests by undergraduates are due to flaws in the tests rather than changes in student performance.

Changes in test scores can be a result of flaws in the testing procedure, changes in the people taking the test, or both. Flaws in the testing procedure can be of two basic types—errors in validity (a test does not measure what it is supposed to measure) or errors in reliability (a test fails to produce the same results consistently). But the likelihood that the many tests which have reported declines in basic skills and knowledge among Americans are all invalid or unreliable is small. For instance, the College Entrance Examination Board formed a blue-ribbon advisory panel to examine the reasons for the declines on the Scholastic Aptitude Test (SAT). The panel found no evidence of reduced validity in the SAT; in fact, it found an increase in the predictive validity of the tests (Advisory Panel on the Scholastic Aptitude Test Score Decline, 1977, p. 44). A reliability error in the scaling of the test was discovered, but the error was in an unexpected direction: It reduced the amount of score decline rather than exaggerating it. ("Research into the SAT Score Decline: A Progress Report," 1975, pp. 4–5).

It is quite likely then that the decline is a result of changes in the people taking the tests. The College Entrance Examination Board's advisory panel attributed two-thirds to three-quarters of the decline between 1963 and 1970 and one-quarter of the decline since 1970 to changes in the applicant pool. During that period there was a steady rise in the proportion of low-scoring minority and educationally disadvantaged students taking the test (Advisory Panel on the Scholastic Aptitude Test Score Decline, 1977, p. 45). This explains the increase in the number of low scores but not the dramatic reduction of high scores. The panel believed those declines to be the result of a combination of factors, including television and other media, which result in less attention to school and homework; increased societal permissiveness (grade inflation, automatic grade-to-grade promotions, easier school textbooks, tolerance of more absenteeism, reduced homework loads, lower standards for admission to college, and compensatory courses in college); broken homes; lowered student learning motivation; national discord between 1972 and 1975; and changes in secondary school preparation of students, including an increase in elective courses and a reduction in common requirements, particularly in the area of English and verbal skills (Advisory Panel on the Scholastic Aptitude Test Score Decline, 1977, pp. 46–48).

Even before the panel report, there was ample evidence on the latter cause. Harnischfeger and Wiley (1975, p. 98) reported a general drop in enrollments in academic courses at secondary schools, particularly in algebra, first-year foreign languages, chemistry, and physics. McCurdy and Speich (1976b) also found a substitution of elective courses for required academic courses in high school. They also noted that basic skills and knowledge declines were occurring most often in the subjects in which requirements have been reduced and electives have grown.

In the hunt for causes of score declines, several hypothesized factors have been shown to have no effect. These include changes in the number of times students took the tests, bad diet, birth control pills, declines in Latin enrollments, drug taking, reduced IQ, and busing (Howe, 1976, p. 3; McCurdy and Speich, 1976b). Many changes in the nature of the high school teacher are also ruled out, as teachers are better educated than in the past, their salaries are higher, and student-to-faculty ratios are lower (Harnischfeger and Wiley, 1975).

Criticism 2: Skill declines are due to college open admissions practices, which permit unqualified students to attend higher education.

This is false. Even the very selective ivy league colleges are experiencing skill declines. The declines are a nationwide event, independent of race, socioeconomic status, or particular sections of the country (McCurdy and Speich, 1976a).

It is true, however, that the United States has made a conscious commitment to universal access to postsecondary education for all Americans. One of the consequences of this commitment is that students are now entering higher education who lack the skills and knowledge mastery of their predecessors. A variety of techniques have been suggested or tried to upgrade the skills of these students prior to college. The techniques include (1) more rigorous precollege basic and advanced skills and knowledge education through high school graduation tests, cooperative high school–college skill programs, and increased college admissions requirements; (2) early identification of students needing skills assistance; and (3) community centers for skills and knowledge enrichment.

The need for *more rigorous precollege basic skills and knowledge education* has resulted in the introduction of high school graduation tests or competency requirements in 33 states. Many of the states, including Arizona, California, New York, and Virginia, require that students prove they can read, write, and perform basic mathematical computations in order to graduate from high school. Arizona, for instance, requires a ninth-grade proficiency in the three R's.

Cooperative high school–college skills programs are exemplified by the Bay Area Writing Program in the San Francisco bay region. In 1972, the University of California, Berkeley, began to invite teachers from feeder high schools to campus during the summer to work with university writing specialists. In 1976, the writing scores of students in the project schools jumped 50 points in contrast to an average increase of 13 points for students at non-project schools. In the same year, the percentage of graduates from participating schools in need of compensatory English at the university dropped 24 percent.

Increased college admissions requirements are also illustrated by the University of California, Berkeley, which has toughened its admission standards to encourage high school students to take more basic and advanced skill and knowledge courses before enrolling on campus. Berkeley will no longer accept journalism, drama, and speech as substitutes for high school English.

Early identification of students in need of assistance—the second major approach to upgrading skills and knowledge—has resulted in the development both of diagnostic tests and special programs. The state of Nebraska, for example, uses diagnostic tests to measure elementary and secondary school student achievement in the three R's. Students must satisfy the minimal performance levels established for their grade levels. Those who are unable to achieve grade-level performance are provided with basic skills instruction to bring them up to level. Students may take the test as many times as necessary for them to pass. At the national level, the Educational Testing Service is developing a comparable battery of examinations, the Basic Skills Assessment Program. The first tests were administered in May 1977. And the College Entrance Examination Board in December 1977, added a 30-minute objective, short-answer examination on standard written English to its Scholastic Aptitude Test in order to provide high schools and colleges with an assessment of the accomplishment and needs of their students in writing skills.

Among special programs there are both national projects and individual college endeavors to provide skills instruction. Talent Search and Upward Bound are the best known of the national programs. Talent Search was created by the Higher Education Act of 1965. Its purpose is to encourage and assist students with cultural and financial need to learn about educational career options and available financial aid resources. Upward Bound, which was a product of the 1964 Economic Opportunity Act, is designed to prepare for college those students who have academic potential but are lacking in motivation and personal and academic skills. Many of the Upward Bound projects, which are usually campus based, utilize summer residential terms for intensive basic skills instruction in reading, writing, mathematics, and science; guidance and counseling on education and career opportunities; and comprehensive counseling and enrichment programs aimed at developing creative thinking and positive atitudes toward education.

An example of an individual college program with aims similar to Upward Bound is the Middle College, opened in 1974 by La Guardia Community College in Queens, New York. Attempting to bridge the gap between secondary school and college for urban youth, the Middle College offers a five-year program that includes three years of high school and two years of community college. Built around a basic skills and knowledge curriculum, it is based on the assumption that the earliest possible start on skills development provides the greatest hope for reducing dropout and underachievement (Lieberman, 1975).

Educational opportunity centers constitute the third major technique for skills enhancement. Recommended by the Carnegie Commission on Higher Education (1970) and created by the Education Amendments of 1972, these centers are designed for locales with high concentrations of low-income people. They offer information about financial and academic assistance available for postsecondary education; aid potential students in applying for postsecondary admission; and give counseling, tutoring, and other support services needed by students in college.

Criticism 3: Compensatory education has a very low success rate.

The truth of this criticism depends upon how one defines compensatory. Some label all education as compensatory because formal education invariably involves a knowledgeable individual remedying a knowledge deficiency on the part of another person. If compensatory is so defined, the contention that compensatory education has a very low success rate is incorrect.

On the other hand, if compensatory education is defined as education designed to bring deficient students up to college-level achievement in basic skills and knowledge, the assertion is true. After reviewing the literature on remedial and compensatory education, Roueche and Kirk (1973, p. 7) concluded that "remedial courses and programs at two-year colleges, and in all of higher education for that matter, have largely been ineffective in remedying student deficiencies." However, they found that some programs are much more successful than others. The factors associated with successful programs were the following (Roueche and Kirk, 1973, Chapter 7):

1. Only volunteer faculty are used.
2. Remedial or compensatory education is organized into a separate division with its own staff and administration.
3. The compensatory curriculum is germane to student interest.
4. Courses carry credit toward graduation or certification.
5. Grading policies and practices are nonpunitive.
6. Instruction is individualized and self-paced.
7. Counseling is an integral part of the programs and of value to students.
8. The transition from compensatory education to "real" college studies is not abrupt.
9. Students who could make use of the program are identified and actively recruited.
10. The college's noncompensatory offerings are comprehensive.

Cross (1976, p. 42) noted two additional factors associated with successful compensatory programs: (1) Skills training is integrated into other college experiences, and (2) cognitive skills are integrated with the social and emotional development of the student.

* * *

For a commentary on basic skills and knowledge, see Chapter 11, "Basic Skill—Where Does College Begin?" in The Carnegie Foundation for the Advancement of Teaching, *Missions of the College Curriculum: A Contemporary Review with Suggestions* (1977).

References

"About Test Scores—SAT Scores." *Education Recaps* (ETS, Princeton, N.J.), October 1976, 16 (2).

Advisory Panel on the Scholastic Aptitude Test Score Declines. *On Further Examination.* New York: College Entrance Examination Board, 1977.
This volume contains the final report and conclusions of the College Board blue ribbon panel.

Astin, A. W., King, M. R., and Richardson, G. T. *The American Freshmen: National Norms for Fall 1976.* Los Angeles: Cooperative Institutional Research Programs of the American Council on Education and the University of California, Los Angeles, 1976.

Brubacher, J. S., and Rudy, W. *Higher Education in Transition: A History of American Colleges and Universities, 1636–1976.* (3rd ed.) New York: Harper & Row, 1976.

Carnegie Commission on Higher Education. *A Chance to Learn: An Action Agenda for Equal Opportunity in Higher Education.* New York: McGraw-Hill, 1970.

The Carnegie Foundation for the Advancement of Teaching. *Missions of the College Curriculum: A Contemporary Review with Suggestions.* San Francisco: Jossey-Bass, 1977.
This report is discussed in Chapter 11.

Carnegie Surveys, 1975–76.
This project is described in the Preface.

Catalog Study, 1976.
This project is described in the Preface.

Cleary, T. A., and McCandless, S. A. *College Board Statistics.* Charts presented at the annual meeting of the American Education Research Association. San Francisco, Calif., April 19–23, 1976.

Cross, K. P. *Accent on Learning: Improving Instruction and Reshaping the Curriculum.* San Francisco: Jossey-Bass, 1976.
This book is discussed in Chapter 11.

Eddy, E. D., Jr. *College for Our Land and Times: The Land-Grant Idea in American Education.* New York: Harper & Row, 1957.

Harnischfeger, A., and Wiley, D. E. *Achievement Test Score Decline: Do We Need to Worry?* Chicago: CEMREL, Inc., 1975.
This book is the most comprehensive treatment of the problem and its causes yet written.

Henard, K. F., and Stenning, W. F. *Life Change and Reading Achievement as Predictors of Academic Performance for Selected Community College Freshmen.* Paper presented at the annual meeting of the American Education Research Association. San Francisco, Calif., April 19–23, 1976.

Howe, H., II, *San Francisco Chronicle,* Oct. 27, 1976, p. 3.

Levine, A. "Reflections of an Itinerant Interviewer: A Sketch of Undergraduate Curriculum Trends." A technical monograph prepared for the Carnegie Council on Policy Studies in Higher Education. Berkeley, Calif., June 1976 (mimeographed).

Lieberman, J. *The Middle College High School: A Model for Remediation.* Paper presented at a Symposium of the International Reading Association. New York, May 14, 1975.

McCurdy, J., and Speich, D. "Drop in Student Skills Unequaled in History." *Los Angeles Times*, Aug. 15, 1976a.

McCurdy, J., and Speich, D. "School Standards Also Decline, Fewer Basics, More Electives Lead to Drop in Student Scores." *Los Angeles Times*, Aug. 16, 1976b.

McCurdy, J., and Speich, D. "Answers to Decline of Student Skills Unsought." *Los Angeles Times*, Aug. 17, 1976c.

This three-article series by McCurdy and Speich examines in readable fashion the degree of decline in student basic skills achievement, probable reasons for its occurrence, and some possible solutions.

Mullis, I. V. S., Oldefendt, S. J., and Phillips, D. L. *What Students Know and Can Do: Profiles of Three Age Groups.* Denver: Education Commission of the States (National Assessment of Educational Progress), 1977.

This monograph summarizes the eight years of research by the National Assessment of Educational Progress regarding continuities and change in the knowledge and skills of young people aged 9, 13, and 17 in areas such as writing, reading, literature, music, science, citizenship, social studies, and mathematics.

Munday, L. A. *Declining Admissions Test Scores.* Iowa City: The Research and Development Division of ACT, 1976.

Proctor, S. "Life of a 'Prep'." *Journal of History of Education*, 1956, 8 (1), 22–23.

"Research into the SAT Score Decline: A Progress Report." *College Board News*, 1975, 4 (1), 4–5.

Roueche, J. E., and Kirk, R. W. *Catching Up: Remedial Education.* San Francisco: Jossey-Bass, 1973.

Rudolph, F. *The American College and University: A History.* New York: Knopf, 1962.

Scully, M. G. "Drop in Aptitude-Test Scores is Largest on Record." *The Chronicle of Higher Education*, 1975, 11 (1), 1.

Sizer, T. *Secondary Schools at the Turn of the Century.* New Haven, Conn.: Yale University Press, 1964.

"Social Factors, Not SAT, Responsible for Score Decline, CEEB Panel Reports." *Higher Education Daily*, Aug. 24, 1977, pp. 1–2.

4

Tests and Grades

Definition and History

Tests are the means of measuring student ability or attainment, and grades are the valuation of student performance. Grades may be based strictly on test results or can include other factors as well.

Both testing and grading have long been associated with higher education.[1] By 1646, Harvard had entrance and graduation tests. The entrance tests, which were one-day affairs, were at first vague and general, but soon became rigid and specific. The graduation tests required students to read and translate from Latin editions of the Old and New Testaments. Both examinations were oral, public, and conducted by outside examining committees composed of "literary gentlemen of good moral standing." In practice, neither the entrance nor the graduation examination was terribly rigorous.

Students also engaged in informal exercises, which were distinguished from tests in that they had no apparent influence on academic progress. These exercises, as noted in Chapter 8, included recitation, declamation, and disputation.

This system of tests and exercises persisted until the nineteenth century, when dissatisfaction with the poor quality of examination procedures peaked. The first known student rebellion against tests occurred at Yale in 1762, when students refused to be

[1]Most of the historical discussion in this chapter is based on Mary Smallwood's book, *Examination and Grading Systems in Early American Universities* (1935). As a result, this chapter considers the history of grading largely from the experience of five institutions—Harvard University, University of Michigan, Mount Holyoke College, College of William and Mary, and Yale University.

examined for graduation. In 1804–05, Yale initiated daily quizzes which had no bearing on graduation and a Yale student introduced a new word in the lexicon, *cram,* as in "cram for a test." In 1815, Yale began yearly tests of all four classes. In 1830, the annual oral examinations became written biennial examinations. Examinations were given at the end of the sophomore and senior years and covered the two preceding years of work. Until this time, written examinations had not been used because they were too costly.

In 1869, Harvard permitted use of laboratory or experimental tests in the sciences. In 1870, the Harvard faculty voted to use written rather than oral examinations as the primary means of testing. A year later, the idea of unscheduled tests was proposed in a memo to the Harvard faculty.

In 1882, the University of Michigan took a significant step that was duplicated on most campuses within a few years. It ended common examinations for entire classes and introduced in-course examinations at the discretion of the instructor. The step was a natural and essential adjustment to the elective curriculum and the diminishing number of courses common to all students. In addition, faculty and outside examiners were getting along poorly because each sought to control the educational process. Furthermore, with written examinations available as a permanent record of achievement, it became unnecessary to have unbiased outsiders observe the procedure. And finally, as faculty grew increasingly specialized, examining committees with the necessary experience were becoming difficult to assemble.

By the end of the nineteenth century, faculties experimented with blind tests (examinations in which the grader does not know the test taker's identity), semiannual and more frequent examinations, and dissertations or papers. After the turn of the century, the standardized college entrance examination (1901), the mental aptitude test (1904), the mathematical reasoning test (1908), the multiple-choice test (1926), and the vocational interest test (1927) appeared. In the 1920s and 1930s, Swarthmore College and the University of Chicago reintroduced external examinations, and Chicago tied college graduation solely to passing 14 comprehensive examinations (see Chapter 12). During World War II, the simulation test, which involves examination of learning in a fabricated real-world setting, was developed.

Formal grading dates back to approximately 1785, when Yale introduced a four-category grading system—*optimi*, second *optimi*, *inferiores (boni)*, and *pejores*. Until that time, colleges used a crude pass-fail system for admission and graduation testing. At Harvard, graduation and class lists were originally based on family social position rather than academic criteria. There were honors such as valedictorian and salutatorian and lists of the top scholars, but the basis for selecting students for these early honors is unknown.

In 1813, Yale adopted another grading procedure which utilized a one-to-four scale, much like today's grade-point system. Two was the average grade. In 1814, Yale grades varied from 1.0 to 3.21.

In 1817, the University of Michigan began operation with a grading system based on descriptive adjectives. In that year the College of William and Mary sent letters to parents describing student performance along these lines: "Mr. _____. He has improved very much of late but during a considerable part of the course was exceedingly inattentive" (Smallwood, 1935, p. 45).

Between 1830 and 1840, Harvard used in succession two numerical grading systems which ranged from 1 to 20 and 1 to 100. The number of students obtaining each grade was posted. By 1850, William and Mary also used the 1-to-100 scale but still sent letters to parents. The letters included overall averages, subject grades, comments on deportment, and attendance reports.

Pass-fail grading was formally adopted at the University of Michigan in 1851. Michigan graded tests 1 to 100 and a score of 50 was passing. Based on the test scores, students received grades of pass, fail, or conditioned (conditional pass).

Percentage grading was introduced at Harvard in 1877. Students were graded from 1 to 100 percent depending upon their mastery of test material. Based upon their grades, students were divided into six divisions: division 1 (90 percent or better), division 2 (75–89 percent), division 3 (60–74 percent), division 4 (50–59 percent), division 5 (40–49 percent), and division 6 (below 40 percent).

The wide divergence in grading practices caused the New England Conference of Colleges to suggest uniform grading policies in 1878. Harvard responded by reducing its six divisions to five, called A (90–100 percent), B (80–89 percent), C (70–79 percent), D (other passing scores), and E (failing). The first three divisions were considered honors designations.

No radical revision in the Harvard grading system was suggested until 1895, when a three-category grading system—failed, passed, and passed with honors, with pluses and minuses—was proposed. This is now called modified pass-fail grading. In the same year, the University of Michigan developed the now often-used "incomplete," a nebulous area between pass and fail indicating the student requires additional work to receive a grade. In 1898, Mount Holyoke College changed the failing grade E to the familar F. Holyoke grading included teachers' written evaluations of student performance.

In 1915, Reed College introduced covert grades. Students were graded but in order to reduce the importance of grades in motivating learning, students were not told what grades they had received. In 1937, St. John's College adopted oral evaluation sessions which were attended by each student and his or her teachers. And in 1970, Hampshire College introduced the dossier—a non-graded transcript—listing student educational activities and containing faculty and student evaluations and examples of student work.

State of Tests and Grades

Characteristics of Tests

Tests can be standardized (generally externally prepared examinations with explicit instructions for administration and scoring, and accompanied by information about normative scores of representative populations of test takers), or they can be nonstandardized or constructed at the institutions where they are administered, generally by a teacher. This chapter is concerned chiefly with teacher-constructed examinations.[2]

---

[2]The reader interested in standardized tests should consult Oscar K. Buros' *Mental Measurement Yearbook(s)* (1938, 1941, 1959, 1965, 1972). Each edition discusses a variety of examinations and their strengths and weaknesses. Several standardized tests are discussed elsewhere in this handbook. The College Entrance Examination Board Scholastic Aptitude Test and the American College Testing Program battery are described in Chapter 3, while the College Level Examination Program, Advanced Placement Program, College Proficiency Examination Program, and the New York State Regents External Degree tests are discussed in Chapter 9.

Tests can measure achievement (student accomplishment or attainment in a subject area such as mathematics or foreign language) or aptitude (readiness or disposition toward a particular form of learning such as specific vocation or college study). Aptitude tests are usually standardized. This chapter focuses on achievement tests.

Tests can also be written, oral, or performed. They can be time based (limited to a prespecified amount of time) or time free. They can be supervised (in-class examinations) or unsupervised (take-home examinations). They can be course based or noncourse based. They may be announced in advance or unannounced. They can be student designed (as is the case with papers), faculty designed (as is the case with quizzes), or both (as is the case with Hampshire College comprehensive examinations discussed in Chapters 9 and 13). They can be administered to one student at a time or to an entire class or group. They can offer students a choice among fixed answers (as is the case with a true-false test), or they can be open-ended (as is the case with an essay test). They can be open book (students can bring resource materials to the test) or closed book (students are not permitted resources). And they can rely upon one or many evaluators.

Despite all of these differences, there are two characteristics that are common to all quality examinations—validity and reliability. A test is valid if it measures what it is intended to measure. A test is reliable if it produces the same results consistently.

Valid tests are characterized by (1) full and balanced coverage of the field being examined; (2) objective answers that most experts in the field would acknowledge as correct; and (3) a good correspondence between the behavior required to respond to test questions and the purpose or objective for formulating the test questions. Reliable tests are characterized by (1) requiring all students to answer the same questions; (2) administration under the same conditions for all test takers; (3) being evaluated in an impartial and consistent fashion; and (4) utilizing multiple observations of performance (a number of test questions) (Chauncey and Dobbin, 1964, p. 62).

Types of Teacher-Constructed Tests

Teacher-created achievement tests include both course-based

examinations and noncourse-based examinations. Course-based tests are most commonly short-answer tests, essay tests, or papers, but may be oral tests, simulation tests, or performance tests. They are used as quizzes, periodic examinations, midterms, or final examinations in individual courses.

Noncourse-based examinations assess the skills and knowledge accumulated in several courses, rather than any particular course. Their two principal types are the comprehensive examination, which tests students in broad areas such as general education or major studies, and the senior thesis or project, usually undertaken by upper-division students in an area related to their major.

COURSE-BASED TESTS

Short-Answer Tests. Short-answer tests take many forms. The most common are the multiple-choice test, the true-false test, and the fill-in test.

Multiple-choice tests consist of a series of questions and several possible answers to each question. The test taker is asked to select the correct answer from among the fixed alternatives. For example:

> In 1885, who was the president of Harvard University?
>   a. Noah Porter
>   b. Charles W. Eliot
>   c. Woodrow Wilson
>   d. A. Lawrence Lowell
>   e. Derek Bok

The advantages of multiple-choice tests are that (1) they are fast and easy to administer; (2) the odds of success at guessing answers are lower than true-false tests; (3) they are easy to grade; (4) they can be returned quickly in large classes; and (5) they are useful in testing facts, dates, and definitions. The disadvantages of multiple-choice tests are that (1) they are poor at testing conceptual learning, integration of knowledge, and complex skills; (2) they reward clever guessing; (3) they are time consuming to construct and the product is often poor; (4) finding four or more plausible answers for each question is frequently difficult; (5) they can be confusing or misleading owing to extraneous information or cues in the questions; and (6) they are inefficient in contrast to other short-answer tests because they require much reading, which serves to limit the number of questions that can be asked in a fixed period of time.

David Payne (1968, pp. 64–72), who examined the errors that people make in constructing several types of tests, offers 15 useful suggestions for writing multiple-choice tests.

- Each item should be stated as a direct question, not as an incomplete statement to be filled in with the fixed alternatives. Incomplete statements are often weak or ambiguous.
- The question should be a clear, definite, explicit, and singular problem.
- To reduce reading time, the question should include any words that would otherwise have to be repeated in each alternative answer.
- Questions and answers should be simply stated; all nonfunctional words should be eliminated.
- Interrelated items that provide clues in answering questions should be avoided.
- Questions and answers should avoid negatives.
- The correct answer should not be systematically different from other options. For example, novices sometimes construct correct answers which are more elaborate or lengthy to insure accuracy.
- Answers should be presented in some logical order if possible.
- Answers should be mutually exclusive.
- All possible answers should be plausible and attractive.
- The answer "none of the above" should be avoided whenever possible.
- The possible answers should be grammatically parallel with one another and the question.
- Irrelevant cues in questions or answers that aid the student, such as common wording, should be avoided.
- In testing for knowledge of a term, it is better to present the term in the question and the definition in the answers.
- Use "objective" questions and answers such that most experts would agree about the best or correct answer.

True-false tests consist of declarative sentences, such as "Charles W. Eliot was president of Harvard University in 1885," which the test taker must rate as true or false. A variation on this format requires the test taker to state why false statments are incorrect. The advantages of true-false tests are: (1) They are efficient because an examination may include a large number of questions that cover a wide range of subjects; (2) they are easy to administer and grade; (3) they can be returned promptly; and (4) they are useful in testing factual knowledge. The disadvantages of true-false tests are: (1) They reward guessing because the test taker has a 50 percent chance of choosing the correct answer to any question without knowledge of the subject; (2) they may encourage false learning because students assimilate the incorrect statements; (3) they encourage response sets or answers to test items based on the form of question rather than the content; (4) they are very hard to construct because minor word flaws or ambiguous wording can easily change a true statement into a false statement; (5) the need for an absolute true-false judgment makes this testing technique tenuous for new frontiers of knowledge; and (6) they cannot be used to examine integration of knowledge, conceptual learning, or advanced skills.

Payne's suggestions for improving true-false tests include the following (1968, pp. 59–63):

- Avoid words that offer students cues to questions. Statements using words such as *no, all, always, never,* and *none* are usually false while statements using the words *may, might, can,* and *generally* are usually true (p. 59).
- Base true-false items on statements that are absolutely true or false, without exceptions or qualifications.
- Avoid double negatives entirely and negatively stated items when possible.
- Use quantitative and precise language (for example, 30 percent) in preference to qualitative language (for example, some).
- Avoid lifting statements directly from textbooks; they frequently lose their meaning when taken out of context.
- Avoid making true statements consistently longer than false statements.

- Avoid unfamiliar or esoteric language.
- Avoid complex sentences with many dependent clauses.
- Place the crucial elements of long or complex items at the end of a statement. The first part of such items should be used to set up the problem for the test taker.

Fill-in tests ask the test taker to complete one or more blanks in a statement. For example: "The president of Harvard University in 1885 was _____." The advantages of this type of test are: (1) It does not rely upon a limited list of answers that aids students in guessing; (2) it can be easily constructed, administered, and graded; (3) it can be returned quickly; (4) it is efficient; and (5) it is a good means of testing factual knowledge. The disadvantages of the fill-in test are: (1) It is not objective—correct but unanticipated answers are common; (2) items are frequently ambiguous; (3) items are often memory based; (4) a course cannot usually be fully covered with a fill-in test; and (5) it is suited only for examining student command of facts.

Payne (1968, pp. 54–56) offers the following suggestions for preparing fill-in tests:

- Require short, definite, clear-cut, and explicit answers. For example, "In 1885, Charles W. Eliot's job title was _____" is better than "In 1885, Charles W. Eliot was _____."
- Avoid items containing multiple blanks, as they can mutilate or make a statement unintelligible.
- Give equal credit to each answer if a blank may be filled in with several correct answers.
- Tell students in advance if grading will take spelling into account.
- When testing for comprehension of a term or concept, it is better to provide the term and ask for the definition than vice versa.
- Place blanks at the end of an item if possible.
- Minimize the use of textbook statements which test only students' memory rather than subject matter comprehension.
- State specifically the terms in which the answer should be given. For example, the answer "Cambridge" is more likely to be ob-

tained by asking, "In what city did President Eliot work?" than
"Where did President Eliot work?"

- Direct questions are preferable to sentence fill-ins.
- Avoid extraneous clues to the answer, such as blanks of differing
  sizes or pronouns establishing gender.

Essay Tests. The essay test asks one or more questions that must be
answered with a descriptive, analytic, or interpretive composition.
Its advantages and disadvantages are almost the reverse of short-
answer tests. With regard to advantages, (1) the essay examination
is easy to construct; (2) it is optimal for testing depth of knowledge
(unlike short-answer tests, which are optimal for testing breadth
of knowledge); (3) it permits students to be creative; (4) it tests
higher-order skills—such as writing and the ability to analyze,
synthesize, apply, and organize knowledge—in addition to knowledge acquisition, which is examined on short-answer tests; and (5)
it is less amenable to in-class cheating than short-answer tests. The
disadvantages of the essay test are that (1) it may require no more
than regurgitating a text or lecture; (2) it can be graded in a
mechanical manner, based simply on covering certain prespecified
points, which penalizes unusual or creative answers; (3) it punishes
students who are weak in basic writing skills; (4) it is subjective to
the extent that assessment will vary among different readers and
often even for the same reader at different times; (5) it is time consuming to grade, which delays test return; and (6) by concentrating
on depth, it generally does not cover the breadth of a course; this
may hurt the student who is weak in one area and strong in others,
while rewarding the student strong in the essay areas and weak in
the rest of the course.

There is evidence that students prepare for essay tests and
short-answer tests in very different ways. In a study reported by
Ohmer Milton (1972, pp. 50–51), 100 students were asked to read
materials that they had not seen before. Each was told tht he or she
would later be examined by an essay test, true-false test, multiple-
choice test, or fill-in test. The students were asked how they studied
for their tests, and the notes they made as well as the materials they
studied were collected for examination. Student reports indicated
that essay-test preparation involved attempting to obtain a general
picture of the material to be learned while the short-answer test

preparation involved memorizing details. This was verified in the examination of the study materials. Short-answer test students underlined more than the essay students, and essay students used summaries and maps more often than short-answer students.

Essay-test preparation may also be a more effective means of learning than short-answer test preparation. Milton (1972, pp. 51–52) cites a study similar to the one just described, except that the students were given both short-answer and essay tests despite their preparation for only one. All of the students who prepared for essay tests performed adequately on the short-answer test. Only 23 percent of the students who prepared for the short-answer test performed adequately on the essay. When the short-answer test was readministered a week later to both groups, the students who prepared for the essay tests did much better than the students who originally prepared for the short-answer tests.

Payne (1968, p. 90) offers 15 suggestions to faculty for writing, evaluating, and using essay examinations:

- Limit the problem which the essay question poses so that the meaning of the question will not be equivocal.
- Use words the student will understand.
- Ask enough questions to sample a course broadly but bear in mind time limits.
- Use essay questions for the purpose of writing, organizing, and handling complicated ideas.
- Prepare questions that require much thought rather than much writing.
- Determine in advance the weighting of the different components of the expected answers.
- Score each question without knowledge of the writer's identity. Use several scorers and read each test several times if possible.
- Require all test takers to answer all of the questions on the test rather than offering optional questions.
- Base questions on materials directly relevant to the course.
- Examine past questions to see how students performed and as a basis for planning new questions.
- Make gross assessments of the quality of answers as the first step in grading.
- Word questions simply to avoid confusion and ambiguity.

- Avoid evaluating papers on the basis of external factors.
- Avoid a generalized estimate of an entire test's worth by grading each question separately.
- Avoid one-question tests.

Papers. Papers vary from one- or two-page writing assignments to term projects. They offer many of the advantages of the essay test, and have strengths of their own. These strengths and advantages are: (1) They test students on higher-order skills such as writing, problem solving, analysis, interpretation, and synthesis of knowledge; (2) they test students on the depth of their knowledge; (3) they test research skills; (4) they are student centered, enabling the student to show his or her attainments and abilities in the best possible light; and (5) they are not based on performance on a single day or a few hours. The disadvantages of papers are: (1) They are time consuming to grade, which causes delay in returning them; (2) they rarely cover the breadth of a course fully; (3) they are amenable to cheating, as papers are unsupervised and assigned far in advance of due dates; (4) they emphasize areas of student strength and may fail to discover weaknesses; (5) they penalize students weak in writing or research skills; (6) they may encourage students to concentrate on paper preparation rather than the course for which it is assigned; and (7) evaluation is subjective.

Three other types of tests—orals, simulations, and performances—are less frequently used to examine course-related learning.

Oral Tests. The oral test is generally a face-to-face, question-and-answer session between a student and his or her teacher, though it can involve a student and a panel of faculty members. St. John's College uses both formats. At the end of each semester, seminar leaders conduct oral examinations with the voluntary participation of any other interested faculty. Students are questioned on the books they read during the previous term with emphasis upon their critical and interpretive opinions.

The advantages of the oral examination are that (1) it increases student-faculty interaction; (2) it drastically reduces the likelihood of students misunderstanding test questions; (3) it permits follow-up questions; (4) it can be used to test breadth, depth, and whatever skills the teacher is concerned about; and (5) it provides immediate feedback to students. The disadvantages of this testing procedure are that (1) it may favor more verbal and confident students; (2) it is time consuming; (3) it may be the most anxiety-provoking type of examination; (4) it is hard to keep test questions secret because all students do not take the examinations at the same time; (5) it is a difficult examination for students to prepare for; (6) it is impossible to compare student performance reliably unless the examinations are tape recorded; (7) it relies upon subjective evaluation; and (8) it often results in varying test conditions and test questions for different students.

Simulation and Performance Tests. Simulation tests are used to measure the application of skills and knowledge in a simulated or specially constructed testing situation. They are particularly popular in nontraditional programs that award course credit for experiential learning. Performance tests are used primarily in skill subjects such as student teaching, performing arts, and laboratories, where students are asked to demonstrate their abilities before one or more experts. They differ from simulation tests in not allowing for role playing or use of a fabricated setting.

NONCOURSE EXAMINATIONS

Comprehensive Examinations. Comprehensive examinations are the oldest type of test. They are written and/or oral examinations covering material taught in more than one course and are administered to all the members of a college class, much like the entrance and graduation tests at seventeenth-century Harvard. Comprehensive examinations are used at 24 percent of four-year arts and sciences colleges and 10 percent of four-year professional/technical colleges. They are less common at two-year institutions, where 2 percent of the arts and sciences colleges and none of the professional/technical colleges employ them (Catalog Study, 1976).

The use of comprehensive examinations has roller-coasted over the past 20 years. In 1957, Dressel and DeLisle found in a study of 322 four-year arts and sciences colleges that 33 percent used comprehensive examinations. Ten years later, the percentage increased to 40 percent (Dressel and DeLisle, 1969, p. 39). By 1975, there was a 16 percentage point drop.

Different colleges use comprehensive tests in different ways. At some institutions (St. John's College; General College, University of Minnesota) they are administered as a test of general education or lower-division achievement at the end of the sophomore year; at others (Bennington, Bard) they form a sophomore-year qualifying test for the major; at at least one college (Reed) they constitute junior-year tests in the majors which students take to qualify for the senior-year thesis; and at many colleges (University of California, Santa Cruz; Reed; Simon's Rock) they are used as senior-year tests of major achievement. Hampshire College requires students to pass six comprehensives—four in general education and two in the major—but they can be taken by students at any time, (as noted in Chapters 9 and 13). Several colleges tie their comprehensives to an essay prepared specifically for the examination (St. John's) or a required senior thesis (Reed). And at least one college (Swarthmore) uses external examiners for its "honors" comprehensive testing (see Chapter 12).

Associated with the comprehensive examination are a number of strengths: (1) It forces students to integrate and synthesize knowledge from more than one course, which the typical undergraduate program does not call upon them to do; (2) it builds a period of review and introspection into a college education; (3) it provides students with an otherwise absent general assessment of their performance by faculty; and (4) it is usually popular (at least in theory) with faculty at colleges using the examinations. There are weaknesses too: (1) The enormity of the comprehensive examination provokes student anxiety; (2) the examinations are generally ritualistic because very few students fail them; (3) comprehensive examination standards vary widely among the academic departments that administer them; and (4) the examinations are generally unpopular with students.

Senior Thesis or Project. The senior thesis or project is more common than the comprehensive examination. Forty-one percent of four-year arts and sciences colleges and 19 percent of professional/ technical programs employ them. They are not found at two-year institutions (Catalog Study, 1976). Senior theses and projects may involve laboratory research, translation of a foreign work, performances or shows in the arts, critical papers, or research papers.

In recent years the number of colleges with senior-project options or requirements has skyrocketed. In 1957, Dressel and DeLisle found senior theses or projects at 8 percent of the arts and sciences colleges they studied. Ten years later the percentage increased to 15 percent (Dressel and DeLisle, 1969, p. 39). By 1975, the number of institutions with senior theses or projects had nearly tripled (Catalog Study, 1976).

The advantages of the senior thesis or project are: (1) It provides students with an opportunity for sustained independent study; (2) it gives students a chance to complete a scholarly or creative work of their own; (3) it gives students a sense of accomplishment (most projects are successful); and (4) it is very positively regarded by faculty and students. The disadvantages of the thesis or project are that (1) it requires much faculty time; (2) it penalizes students who are weak in research skills, writing skills, or ability to pursue independent study; (3) it may duplicate work that some students will pursue in graduate school; (4) it makes undergraduate study more specialized; (5) it often serves as a substitute for one course per term in the senior year that students might prefer to take; (6) it forces some students to continue to work in a concentration in which they are no longer interested at colleges where a thesis is required (such as Reed) rather than optional (such as Brandeis); and (7) it can become a routine exercise at a college where students have much prior experience with independent study (such as New College, Florida).

Characteristics of Grades

Grades or grading systems differ from one another in purpose, standards, and audience. With regard to purpose, grades can be either formative or summative. Formative evaluation is a nonfinal assessment designed to identify strengths and weaknesses in student performance. Its emphasis is upon improvement of student achievement. Summative evaluation is a terminal assessment intended to provide a final or overall judgment of student performance. Its emphasis is upon describing how well the student succeeded.

With regard to standards, grading can be either absolute or relative. Absolute grading, also called "criterion-referenced" grading, involves measuring all students by common, fixed standards or specified criteria. For example, a passing grade on a test may be based strictly on answering one-half of the questions correctly, or a D grade in a music class might be based on playing the violin as badly as Jack Benny pretended to—not on the proportion of students who surpass these criteria. In contrast, relative grading (also called "norm-referenced" grading) relies on sliding standards, such as the performance of all members of a class on an examination ("grading on the curve") or on students' differential academic potential. For example, when grading is based on academic potential, a higher grade may be awarded to a student performing less well than a classmate because he or she was performing at top potential while the other student was not.

With regard to audience, grading systems can be targeted either at students or at others. That is, grades may be used to inform a student candidly how he or she performed, or they can be used to tell others—such as parents, graduate schools, employers, financial aid sources, and at one time draft boards—about student performance. Students and others have very different informational needs.

Types of Grading

At least ten types of grading, including numerical, letter, and pass-fail grading, are currently used in American colleges and universities.

NUMERICAL GRADING

Numerical grading, generally relying upon a 1-100 scale, is found at 3 percent of four-year arts and sciences colleges, at 2 percent of two-year arts and sciences schools, and in less than 1 percent of professional/technical programs. When numerical grading is used, it is required in all or nearly all courses (Catalog Study, 1976).

Numerical grading offers the user several advantages: (1) It employs a common and familiar set of symbols; (2) it is easy to use; (3) it does not require as much faculty time as several other grading methods; (4) it makes record keeping easy; (5) it makes possible a single, impersonal computation of average or overall student performance; and (6) it is not a liability in applying to graduate or professional school. The disadvantages are that (1) it is subjective—grading standards, purpose, and audience vary from grader to grader; (2) it is unidimensional, in that it conveys only a gross sense of student performance; (3) it is low in fidelity—reconstruction of student performance based on a grade is virtually impossible; and (4) it has too many categories to be meaningful.

LETTER GRADES

Letter grades come in two forms: traditional, and modified.

Traditional Letter Grades. Traditional letter grades are the familiar A, B, C, D, and F, with or without pluses and minuses. They are used at 88 percent of four-year arts and sciences colleges and 99 percent of four-year professional/technical colleges. At two-year institutions, they are found in 75 percent of the arts and sciences colleges and 79 percent of professional/technical colleges (Catalog Study, 1976).

Modified Letter Grades. Modifications of the traditional letter grades include such variations as no F grade or no D grade. Such modifications are used at 10 percent of four-year arts and sciences colleges and 4 percent of four-year professional/technical colleges. They are found at 22 percent of two-year arts and sciences colleges and 21 percent of two-year professional/technical colleges (Catalog Study, 1976).

Among institutions using modified letter grades Brown University employs an A, B, C, "no-credit" grading system, eliminating both Ds and Fs; and until recently both Stanford and Yale had A, B, C, F grading systems, eliminating D's. Brown substituted "no credit" for F with the hope of emphasizing learning rather than penalizing people for failing to learn. When students receive no credit for a course, which is usually a consequence of failing the course or dropping it, no record of the course appears on their transcripts. But the use of "no credit" in lieu of F makes little difference because, as will be discussed later in this chapter, few students fail courses today. Brown also eliminated the D grade, which is generally thought of as indicating acceptable but unsatisfactory work, owing to its unsavory and soiled reputation. But with its demise, the Brown faculty lost a handy device often used to shield students who do not deserve passing grades. Thus Stanford and Yale universities recently reinstituted the D to their grading system when they discovered that almost all former D grades were becoming C's.

At schools using either traditional or modified letter grading, grades are generally required in all or nearly all classes. The use of modified letter grades is, however, occasionally restricted: either limited to freshman or sophomore classes, for example; permitted only in selected courses such as internships; or used only in classes where faculty members and students choose this option (Catalog Study, 1976).

The advantages and disadvantages of letter grades are quite similar to those of numerical grades. The only differences on the positive side are that letter grades offer a common grading currency; faculty and students are familiar with them because they are so widely used; and the number of grading categories employed are small enough to be manageable. On the negative side, the widespread use of letter grades creates illusions of comparability at different colleges and puts pressure on colleges not to use other grading systems.

PASS-FAIL GRADING

Pass–fail grading also involves traditional and modified forms.

Traditional Pass-Fail Grading. Traditional pass-fail consists of only two grades, which may be called credit–no credit, satisfactory–unsatisfactory, or pass–no credit, instead of pass–fail. When failure is designated as "no credit," it is not usually recorded on student transcripts.

Traditional pass-fail is used at 35 percent of two-year arts and sciences colleges and 39 percent of two-year professional/technical colleges. It is employed more frequently at four-year institutions. Seventy-seven percent of arts and sciences colleges and 83 percent of professional/technical colleges at four-year institutions have traditional pass-fail grading.

Very few colleges require traditional pass-fail in all or most of their courses. Some require it in freshman courses, sophomore courses, or in a few special programs such as off-campus study. At most schools it is optional. Common options include permitting students or faculty members to designate any course to be graded pass-fail; allowing students to choose a limited number of courses outside of their major to be graded pass-fail; or letting students choose a limited number of courses outside their major and general education to be graded pass-fail (Catalog Study, 1976).

Modified Pass-Fail Grading. Modified pass-fail grading is of two principal types—three-point pass-fail and four-point pass-fail.

Three-point pass-fail grading systems rate students as either honors, pass, or fail. The "honors" designation creates some problems in that the rules for awarding honors are generally vague. Some faculty award it rarely, reserving it for exceptional scholarship or work distinctly above average, while others treat it simply as an A. At Prescott College, which used three-point pass-fail grading prior to closing, there were complaints that the pass grade was devalued to the equivalent of C by outsiders and that the "almost" honors student went entirely unrecognized. There was, as a result, some thought given to requiring fixed percentages of honors, pass, and fail grades in each course. The idea was not adopted because it was thought inimical to the purpose of pass-fail grading.

Four-point pass-fail eliminates many of the problems of three-point pass-fail by adding a second honors designation—honors, high pass, pass, and fail. The pass grade is further devalued, however. In practice, this system, which was used until recently at Yale, is exactly the same as an A, B, C, F grading system.

Modified pass-fail grading is used at very few colleges. It is found at 2 percent of two-year arts and sciences colleges and 3 percent of two-year professional/technical colleges. At four-year institutions, it is used in 1 percent of arts and sciences colleges and 2 percent of professional/technical colleges. Colleges with modified pass-fail grading require it in all or almost all of their courses (Catalog Study, 1976).

Pass-fail grading of all types is used by slightly under half of all undergraduates. By the time students have reached their senior year, 1 percent have taken all their courses pass-fail and 45 percent have taken some of their courses pass-fail. The majority of seniors (54 percent) have never taken a pass-fail course, which is interesting because only about one-third of nontakers (34 percent) were prohibited from doing so by their college (Carnegie Surveys, 1975–76). This means that 36 percent of all seniors had the opportunity to take courses pass-fail and declined to use the option.

Undergraduates (freshmen through seniors) enroll in pass-fail courses most frequently at the most research-oriented universities (58 percent) and at selective liberal arts colleges (52 percent). They do so least at community and junior colleges (22 percent), in part because pass-fail grading is much less available at such schools. Students who take courses pass-fail do so much more frequently outside their major (39 percent) than within their majors (11 percent) (Carnegie Surveys, 1975–76).

The effort students expend on pass-fail courses versus letter or numerically graded courses varies considerably. The majority of undergraduates who have experienced pass-fail grading (56 percent) believe they work just as hard in pass-fail courses as they do in letter or numerically graded courses. But more students say they work "less hard" (34 percent) than "harder" (10 percent) (Carnegie Surveys, 1975–76). This is supported by a 1970 study conducted by Mathew Sgan of pass-fail behavior at Brandeis University. Sgan found that students taking courses on a pass-fail basis earned significantly lower grades than students taking courses for grades. Brandeis faculty are not aware of which students are taking their courses for a grade and which are not, so they submit grades for all students.

Students are more inclined to work "less hard" in pass-fail courses in partial pass-fail grading systems (only some courses are pass-fail) than fully pass-fail systems (all courses are pass-fail). This is so because partial pass-fail establishes a dual economy based on accumulating grades and passes. High grades, which are more difficult to earn, are decidedly more valuable than passes. Accordingly, students put more effort into the graded courses. As a result, partial pass-fail systems, which generally prohibit students from taking pass-fail courses in the major, also encourage students to work harder in their specialty studies than in their nonspecialty studies. In fact, this disparity may be heightened. Sgan (1970) found that students at Brandeis tended to use courses graded pass-fail to satisfy general education requirements.

The advantages of pass-fail grading are that (1) it reduces the anxiety and pressure students feel; (2) it enables students to follow their own learning interests without jeopardizing their overall grades, particularly when their interests deviate from the syllabus of a course they are taking; (3) it is easy to use; (4) it takes little faculty time; (5) it encourages some students to do more work; and (6) it is easy to keep record of. The disadvantages of pass-fail grading are that (1) it provides students with very little information about their performance; (2) it fails to distinguish between students of varying ability, except in the case of modified pass-fail grading; (3) it encourages some students to do less work; (4) it may encourage increased specialization; (5) it does not reduce pressure or anxiety for the failing student; (6) it is low in fidelity; (7) it may diminish student chances for admission or financial assistance in graduate school (this will be discussed later in the chapter); and (8) unless it is used for all courses, pass-fail may be used to artificially inflate the grade-point averages of students who take one less demanding course each term so that more time can be spent on getting better grades in other courses.

WRITTEN EVALUATIONS

Written evaluations, which vary from lists of adjectives with check boxes to blank sheets of paper to be imaginatively filled in by faculty, are frequently used as supplements to other forms of grading—particularly to pass-fail grading, which is low in information content. This is not true at schools like Hampshire College, however. Hampshire has a dossier system, which includes a record of student learning activities, faculty evaluations, student self-evaluations, examples of student work, and perhaps a few grades. The quality of the dossiers vary from student to student and faculty evaluation to faculty evaluation.

Written evaluations are used by 4 percent of four-year arts and sciences colleges and 2 percent of two-year arts and sciences colleges. They are not found at professional/technical colleges. When used, written evaluations are generally required in all or nearly all courses, but in some cases they are required in only a few selected programs, such as freshman seminars, or they are optional—faculty or student may designate which courses are to be so evaluated (Catalog Study, 1976).

The advantages of written evaluations are that (1) if thoughtfully written, they can provide students with much information about their academic performance; (2) they can be geared to the individual student; (3) they can be based on many factors; (4) they encourage faculty to observe individual students; (5) they are an excellent supplement to other grading devices; and (6) they are high in fidelity. The disadvantages of written evaluations are that (1) they vary widely in quality—from a single sentence such as "82 or B-," to "a fine line separated the student and me, and one day we crossed it," to a several-page, single-spaced analysis of student performance; (2) they are hard to write, particularly in large lecture classes; (3) they require much faculty time to prepare; (4) they take up much administrative file space; (5) they are subjective; (6) they have varying standards, purposes, and audiences; (7) they lack uniform symbols by which to compare students; (8) they are often characterized by politeness and lack of candor, particularly if intended for an external audience such as graduate schools; (9) they can be crueler than impersonal grading systems; and (10) they may diminish student chances for academic and financial aid at graduate and professional schools if they are used alone.

ORAL EVALUATIONS

Oral evaluations are formal, face-to-face assessments of student performance. While 3 percent of four-year arts and sciences colleges use them, oral evaluations are rarely, if ever, found at two-year institutions or four-year professional/technical colleges (Catalog Study, 1976). Oral evaluation is always a supplement to other grading mechanisms that an institution employs.

St. John's College is an example of an institution that makes oral evaluations of students at the end of each semester. The evaluation session, called the "Don Rag," brings together a student and all his or her teachers. Each of the teachers reports on the student's work during the past semester and the student is invited to evaluate him or herself. The sessions are used for diagnosis and prescription, not for reporting grades. (The Haverford Freshman Inquiry, another oral evaluation session, is discussed in Chapter 6.)

Oral evaluations have the same advantages and disadvantages of written evaluations plus a few of their own. The additional advantages are that (1) they force shy students to meet with their instructors and (2) they force faculty to be more conscientious than they are with written evaluations because the one-sentence assessment is unacceptable. The additional disadvantages are that (1) they sometimes duplicate informal oral evaluations at small colleges; (2) they are sometimes even more polite, formal, and lacking in candor than the written evaluation because they are face-to-face; and (3) they are even more time consuming than the written evaluation.

SELF-EVALUATION

Self-evaluation is assessment by the learner. One percent of four-year arts and sciences colleges have an official policy of permitting self-evaluation. It is not formally used at other types of institutions (Catalog Study, 1976). When officially sanctioned by an institution, self-evaluation is a supplement to faculty evaluation, as is the case at Hampshire College. However, on occasion, it is selected by a course instructor as the only means of assessment for his class even in institutions where it is not officially sanctioned.

The advantages of self-evaluation are that (1) it allows students to control their own education; and (2) it encourages self-motivated learning. The disadvantages are that (1) it results in inflated grades as there is great temptation for students to give themselves high marks; (2) it is not widely accepted by graduate schools and employers; (3) it is unfair to students at institutions where self-evaluation is used only in an occasional class without notation on the transcript; and (4) it denies students expert feedback on academic performance when used alone.

COVERT GRADING

Covert grading involves evaluating students but not informing them of their grades. Reed College used covert grades until 1974, when the Buckley Amendment to the Family Rights and Privacy Act gave students the freedom to see their educational records. Reed cannot now deny students access to their records, but it makes no effort to disseminate grades on its own.

The advantages of this form of grading are that (1) it reduces tension for many students; and (2) it focuses attention upon learning rather than getting good grades. The disadvantages are that (1) it is difficult to keep grades secret and many students learn their grades; (2) it does not eliminate the negative quality of grades—it just covers them up; (3) it increases tension for some students; (4) it is sometimes called "hypocritical" for labeling grades as pernicious but continuing to use them; and (5) it may encourage students to plan their major field and postgraduate study poorly owing to lack of information.

OTHER TYPES

Several other types of grading systems, including mastery, peer, and blanket grading, are not used anywhere on an institutionwide basis (Catalog Study, 1976).

Mastery Grading. Mastery grading is a variation on several of the grading methods mentioned earlier based upon changes in instructional design. It may use letter, numerical, or pass-fail grading. Mastery learning is associated with criteria or objective-based learning, which requires an instructor to develop an explicit set of course objectives. The objectives are translated into a sequence of short learning units, called modules. Students are required to master the skills and knowledge in each module in order to go onto the next. The instructor designates specific levels of achievement or mastery that students must attain. Grades vary according to the number of modules students satisfactorily complete or the quality of student performance on each module. Students are free to study in their own fashion and at their own pace, and to take examinations when they feel they are ready for them. Students who meet minimum standards for a module may go onto the next, or they may try to improve their performance on that module. (Two forms of mastery learning—self-paced instruction and competency-based education—are discussed in Chapters 8 and 9.)

The advantages of mastery grading are: (1) It focuses on educational successes, not failure; (2) it is based on prespecified criteria; (3) it reduces subjectivity; (4) it is high in fidelity; (5) it is multidimensional; and (6) it is performance based. The disadvantages are that (1) it can only be employed in restructured courses and sometimes only by retrained faculty and (2) it offers students little freedom in setting course goals.

Peer Grading. Peer grading is evaluation of each student by the other members of the class. The advantages of this type of assessment are that (1) it increases the number of opinions offered students and (2) it makes learning a cooperative endeavor. The disadvantages are that (1) it is based on nonexpert opinions and (2) it may depend upon spurious or irrelevant criteria for evaluation.

Blanket Grading. Blanket grading is the practice of giving all students in a class the same grade. In practice it works in exactly the same fashion as pass–no credit grading. It even has the same advantages, but it offers additional disadvantages: (1) It is intellectually dishonest; and (2) it strips grades of all meaning.

Concerns and Proposals

Criticism 1: Tests and grades yield little useful information and their use is detrimental to undergraduate education.

This criticism is frequently based on the low correlation between grades and adult achievement. After reviewing 46 studies of grading and life achievement, Hoyt concluded "present evidence strongly suggests that college grades bear little or no relationship to any measures of adult accomplishment" (in Milton, 1972, p. 48). But Robert Reinhold (1977) reported that grades are better predictors of performance than Scholastic Aptitude Tests (SAT) scores. The SAT is generally thought of as a valid and reliable test of collegiate aptitude. SAT scores correlate fairly well with college grades at first, but deteriorate as predictors in the later years.

Critics also cite grade inflation—the artificial bloating of student averages—as evidence of the meaninglessness of grades. The Office of Institutional Research at the University of California,

Berkeley, found in a study of 50 universities that between the early 1960s and early 1970s the percentage of A grades awarded more than doubled, rising from 16 percent to 37 percent, while the precentage of C grades dropped from 37 percent to 21 percent. At 16 of these same institutions, the mean grade-point average—an overall or summary average in which grades of A are equal to four points and grades of F are equal to zero points—rose from 2.47 to 2.94 (Suslow, 1976). The 1976 Carnegie Council undergraduate survey found comparable grade inflation across the country, with the national grade-point average exactly that reported in the Berkeley study—2.94 or B. On the basis of such higher averages, critics have charged that grades cannot adequately discriminate among students of differing ability. In fact, 78 percent of the faculty responding to the 1975 Carnegie Council faculty survey said that grade inflation is becoming a serious problem. The same percentage felt grading standards to be less rigorous today than in the past.

This change in rigor is the basis of another criticism. Grading is said to be unreliable, meaning that grades are not constant over time or among faculty. Faculty use them differently; they employ varying standards, base grades on differing purposes, and target grades to different audiences. The result is that grades vary widely from department to department (Cohen, 1970; Crawford, 1930; Bass, 1951) as well as from faculty member to faculty member (Levine and Weingart, 1973; Kirby, 1962).

Grades are also criticized for being invalid. They are said to be based on extraneous criteria such as good looks, socioeconomic status, and misperceptions passed on from teacher to teacher (Rosenthal and Jacobson, 1969; Kirschenbaum and others, 1971). Almost half of the undergraduates (48 percent) believe their grades understate the true quality of their work (Carnegie Surveys, 1975–76).

Other critics say that regardless of the possible validity of grades, they are detrimental to learning. Grading and testing are said to encourage cheating. Nine percent of undergraduates feel some forms of cheating are necessary to get the grades they want (Carnegie Surveys, 1975–76).

An allied criticism is that grading and testing cause students much anxiety. Fifty-two percent of the undergraduates responding to the 1976 Carnegie survey said they were under a great deal of pressure to get high grades, in contrast to only 11 percent who reported that they really did not care what grades they got. As a result it is certain that the majority of undergraduates are quite concerned with their grades and most are anxious about doing well, even if it has not been demonstrated that the anxiety they feel is destructive.

Grading and tests are further criticized for encouraging students to "psych out" the system rather than learn. Almost half of all undergraduates believe this to be true. Forty-eight percent agree that many students at their college are successful by "beating the system" rather than by studying. In fact, 44 percent of undergraduates offer a more serious indictment. They say it is difficult both to get good grades and to really learn something (Carnegie Surveys, 1975–76).

Other detrimental effects attributed to grades and tests are that (1) they put emphasis on activities that can be easily measured; (2) they determine student sense of self-worth; (3) grades become more important than learning; (4) tests and grades divide students and teachers; (5) they stifle creativity; (6) they divide students; and (7) they cover up problems such as poor teaching by giving some students lower grades.

The counterarguments advanced are that (1) many of the problems attributed to grades and tests are not a natural consequence of grading or testing as such but instead only of abuses of grading and testing and as a result can be controlled; (2) no one would benefit from letting students glide passively through their education without evaluation ("the real world is not like that"); (3) some students actively desire the external motivation associated with tests and grades; and (4) the information obtained through tests and grading, which is crucial for both students and others, is unobtainable in any other fashion. In fact, only 19 percent of faculty members and 32 percent of college students believe undergraduate education would improve if grades were abolished. Moreover, the majority of undergraduates (57 percent) are satisfied with the methods of grading or evaluation used at their college. Only 22 percent of undergraduates are dissatisfied (Carnegie Surveys, 1975–76). Finally, the defenders of tests and grades state that studies relating grades to life achievement are trivial because life achievement is based on many factors other than ability. They point out that tests like the SAT correlate well with early college grade-point averages and that high school grades are a satisfactory predictor of college grades (Reinhold, 1977, p. 18; Monroe, 1950, pp. 711–715).

The wide diversity of opinion about grading and testing has yielded a wide diversity of proposals for reform. They include the following:

- Eliminate tests and grades (Taylor, 1971).
- Eliminate the incorrect use of tests. Use tests only when necessary and as they are supposed to be used, following guidelines like those offered by David Payne (1968), which were discussed earlier in the chapter, and interpeting the results of tests in a limited fashion.
- Introduce short mastery checklists in all courses in lieu of grading (Elbow, in Milton, 1972, p. 64).
- Offer students multiple grading options. Brown University permits students to choose letter grading, pass-fail grading, and written evaluations.
- Use different grading mechanisms for internal and external consumption. Prescott College used pass-fail and written evaluations internally to increase feedback to students and modified pass-fail grading for external consumption.
- Eliminate the incorrect use of grades. To end grade inflation, a number of ideas have been suggested or introduced, ranging from the use of normative or curved grading in all classes (Reed College) to the elimination of grading on the curve (Raimi, in Milton, 1972, p. 64); and including (1) circulating faculty members' grade distributions to their colleagues (University of California, Berkeley); (2) introducing a new honors letter grade (Scriven, in The Carnegie Foundation for the Advancement of Teaching, 1977); (3) augmenting transcripts to indicate grade averages and number of students in a class as well as the student's

grade in that class (University of California, Berkeley); (4) developing in-service seminars for faculty training in grading (The Carnegie Foundation for the Advancement of Teaching, 1977); and (5) stating explicit institutionwide standards for awarding grades (Reed College).

To end other types of grading abuse, proposals and measures that have been tried include the introduction of seminars to teach faculty and graduate students about measurement theory (The Carnegie Foundation for the Advancement of Teaching, 1977); the creation of an academic grievance committee to handle grading complaints (Milton and Edgerly, 1976); the establishment within each college of a separate examining division composed of test experts (University of Chicago); the use of visiting examiners from other colleges (Swarthmore College); and the hiring of test consultants to work with faculty on course objectives and evaluation procedures (Sterling College). The disadvantages of working with faculty through seminars or consultants is that the procedure involves a long-term strategy for reform that faculty might reject. The disadvantages of separating testing from instruction (as at Chicago and Swarthmore) is that is is not feasible unless a small number of common examinations are planned. All of the proposals with the exception of the grievance committee have the additional disadvantage of being expensive.

Criticism 2: Nontraditional (nonletter or nonnumerical grades are a liability to students in applying to graduate and professional schools.

This statement is correct but exaggerated. Schoemer and others (1973) surveyed the 288 members of the Council of Graduate Schools regarding the effect of nontraditional grades upon graduate admission and financial aid. They found that "once a student records 10 percent or more nontraditional grades, his chances for admission and financial aid are jeopardized." But Levine and Weingart (1973) reported that transcripts without letter or numerical grades do not hurt excellent students who can show their ability via graduate and professional school admission tests and excellent faculty recommendations. Such transcripts seriously disadvantage the borderline student, especially in applying to professional schools that are increasingly calling for easily coded and computerized grades. Even professional schools at universities that use nontraditional grades of the undergraduate level have sometimes refused to admit or even consider graduates of their own undergraduate programs for this reason.

As a consequence some colleges have compromised with professional schools. For example, the University of California, Santa Cruz, which has a pass-fail grading system, permits students the option of electing letter grades in basic science courses as a concession to medical school applicants. Haverford College, before ending its freshman year pass-fail grading altogether, occasionally permitted students to send major grades earned during the pass-fail freshman and sophomore years to graduate schools (Levine and Weingart, 1973, p. 125).

Other colleges, like Metropolitan State University, which sends students primarily to local graduate schools, have made efforts to contact the relevant graduate institutions, alert them to their nontraditional education system, and seek their advice. Metropolitan State now claims to have minimal problems in getting its graduates into graduate schools. Hampshire College has attempted to do the same thing on a national scale, and administrators say it is working well, although there are still occasional snags with professional schools.

In conclusion, nontraditional grades are not an asset in applying to graduate school, and the maximum liability associated with such grades falls upon the mediocre student aspiring to professional school. However, colleges can reduce this degree of liability.

*   *   *

For a commentary on grading see Appendix D, "Evaluating Student Work," in The Carnegie Foundation for the Advancement of Teaching, *Missions of the College Curriculum: A Contemporary Review with Suggestions* (1977).

References

Bass, B. M. "Interuniversity Variations in Grading Practices." *Journal of Educational Psychology,* 1951, *42,* 366–368.

Brubacher, J. S., and Rudy, W. *Higher Education in Transition: A History of American Colleges and Universities, 1636–1976.* (3rd ed.) New York: Harper & Row, 1976.

Buros, O. K. *Mental Measurements Yearbook.* Highland Park, N.J.: Gryphon Press, 1938, 1941, 1959, 1965, 1972.

The Carnegie Foundation for the Advancement of Teaching. *Missions of the College Curriculum: A Contemporary Review with Suggestions.* San Francisco: Jossey-Bass, 1977.

This report is discussed in Chapter 11.

Carnegie Surveys, 1975–76.

This project is described in the Preface.

Catalog Study, 1976.

This research is discussed in the Preface.

Chauncey, H., and Dobbin, J. E. *Testing: Its Place in Education Today.* New York: Harper & Row, 1964.

Cohen, J. "Examination of Departmental Grading Practices, 1964–65 to 1969–70." Unpublished manuscript, 1970.

Crawford, A. B. "Rubber Micrometers." *School and Society,* 1930, *32,* 223–240.

Dressel, P., and DeLisle, F. *Undergraduate Curriculum Trends.* Washington, D.C.: American Council on Education, 1969.

Kirby, B. C. "Three Error Sources in College Grades." *Journal of Experimental Education,* 1962, *31,* 213–218.

Kirschenbaum, H., Simon, S. B., and Napier, R. W. *Wad-Ja-Get: The Grading Game in American Education.* New York: Hart Publishing Company, 1971.

Levine, A., and Weingart, J. *Reform of Undergraduate Education.* San Francisco: Jossey-Bass, 1973.

Milton, O. *Alternatives to the Traditional: How Professors Teach and How Students Learn.* San Francisco: Jossey-Bass, 1972.

This volume offers the reader an interesting collection of research findings on learning, and portions of the chapter entitled "Symbol Scramble" are particularly germane to testing and grading.

Milton, O., and Edgerly, J. W. *The Tests and Grading of Students.* New Rochelle, N.Y.: Change Publications, 1976.

This 62-page monograph offers good perspective on the whys, wheres, and hows of grading and testing.

Monroe, W. S. *Encyclopedia of Education Research.* New York: Macmillan, 1950.

Payne, D. *The Specification and Measurement of Learning Outcomes.* Waltham, Mass.: Blaisdell Publishing, 1968.

This book discusses the general and practical theory of educational measurement and the specification of learning outcomes. There are chapters on constructing and scoring short-answer and essay tests, analyzing various aspects of examinations, using standardized tests, and assigning grades. All chapters conclude with a suggested reading list.

Reinhold, R. "What the Test Scores Do and Don't Say About a Child." *New York Times,* May 1, 1977, p. 18.

Rosenthal, R., and Jacobson, L. *Pygmalion in the Classroom: Self-Fulfilling Prophecies and Teacher Expectations.* New York: Holt, Rinehart and Winston, 1969.

Schoemer, J., Thomas, J. R. and Bragonier, W. H. "Study of the Effects of Nontraditional Grades or Admission in Graduate Schools and the Awarding of Financial Assistance." *College and University,* 1973, 48 (3), 147–154.

Sgan, M. "Letter Grade Achievement in Pass-Fail Courses." *Journal of Higher Education,* 1970, 1 (8), 636–646.

Smallwood, M. L. *A Historical Study of Examination and Grading Systems in Early American Universities.* Cambridge, Mass.: Harvard University Press, 1935.

This unique book is a study of the history of grading and testing in five colleges—Harvard, Michigan, Mount Holyoke, William and Mary, and Yale— from the time of their founding until early in the twentieth century.

Suslow, S. *A Report on an Interinstitutional Survey of Undergraduate Scholastic Grading, 1960s to 1970s.* Berkeley, Calif.: Office of Institutional Research, University of California, 1976 (mimeographed).

Taylor, H. *How to Change Colleges: Notes on Radical Reform.* New York: Holt, Rinehart and Winston, 1971.

This book is discussed in Chapter 11.

5

Education and Work

The appropriate relationship between education and work has been debated for thousands of years. It is debated hardest, most earnestly, and with strongest emotion in times when employment possibilities are relatively poor. As a result, the current level of concern about education for work is great and curriculum developments are plentiful.

Definition and History

Education for work is alternately called vocational education, occupational education, and career education. The terms are not synonyms, but the differences between them are not obvious. The U.S. government defines vocational education as "organized educational programs which are directly related to the preparation of individuals for paid or unpaid employment, or for additional preparation for a career requiring other than a baccalaureate or advanced degree" (Education Amendments of 1976). In contrast, it defines occupational education as "education, training, or retraining for persons 16 years of age or older who have graduated from or left elementary or secondary school, conducted by an institution authorized to provide post-secondary education . . . which is designed to prepare individuals for gainful employment as semiskilled or skilled workers or technicians or subprofessionals in recognized occupations, or to prepare individuals for enrollment in advanced technical education programs, but excluding any programs . . . considered professional or which require a baccalaureate or advanced degree" (Higher Education Amendments of 1972).

These definitional differences mask the very real traditional differences in the two terms. Vocational education has traditionally been associated with schools rather than colleges. It was originally restricted to the trades, home economics, agriculture, and industrial education for people 14 years of age or older. As a result, vocational education came to be regarded as basic skills and mental training strictly for jobs requiring the "performance of routinized tasks or the performance of tasks that call for more or less complex manipulative operations involving, for the most part, material things or processes" (Goldberg, 1975, p. 309). Occupational education signified something more.

Today this stereotype persists despite significant overlap in the work areas that are labeled vocational and occupational. *Vocational education* has become a charged term. Community college administrators often resent its use to describe their work-related programs, preferring *occupational* instead. Many vocational educators complain that their programs are held in low esteem owing to the connotation of low-level training associated with the term *vocational education*. For this reason neither *vocational education* nor *occupational education* are used in this volume. Instead, college-level training in work subjects is called *professional/technical education*.

The third term, *career education*, popularized by Sidney Marland while U.S. Commissioner of Education, describes education intended to develop the skills necessary to live a full life that revolves about satisfying and meaningful work. In this definition, work includes activities for both earning a living and productive use of leisure time. In this sense, career education represents an attempt to fuse education concerned specifically with work and education concerned with all other facets of life.

Education for work was provided by the earliest American colleges. At least part of the rationale for establishing Harvard and William and Mary, the first two colleges, was that the colonies wanted a learned clergy. During the first half of the eighteenth century, half of all college graduates became clergymen (Brubacher and Rudy, 1976, p. 10).

Education for other professions, such as law and medicine, began outside of college. Students were trained by practitioners in apprenticeships. By the latter half of the eighteenth century, some apprenticeships became group apprenticeships or schools, which competed with one another for students. As a consequence, several schools and practitioners sought affiliation with colleges to attract students and to add to their personal prestige. In 1765, the College of Philadelphia established the first chair in medicine. Fourteen years later, William and Mary College created the first chair in law.

Nonetheless, professional or work education was resisted by many colonial colleges. As noted earlier, the curriculum of the colonial college was a fully prescribed classical general education program. Such an education, in addition to its use for preparing members of the clergy, was also intended to train youth piously in good letters and manners. Professional courses were considered inconsistent with that end. Furthermore, the standards for admission to professional training were much lower than those of colleges and, in later years, even lower than those of college preparatory divisions in many cases. With rare exceptions, professional school standards were not drastically raised until the early twentieth century.

Attempts to introduce work courses other than law, medicine, and divinity were resisted even more strongly. They first made their appearance in new and unorthodox schools or as affiliated— but certainly unequal and unintegrated—branches of established colleges. In 1751, William and Mary College began to offer some instruction in navigation, trade and commerce, zoology, mechanics, and agriculture, but only when the U.S. Military Academy opened half a century later in 1802, did full-scale technical and engineering education commence in American higher education. Between 1821 and 1832, a private establishment in Maine, the Gardiner Lyceum, offered instruction in agriculture and mechanics. In 1824, the Rensselaer Institute was founded in Troy, New York, to train teachers for the children of farmers and mechanics in theoretical and mechanical science.

In the late 1820s and 1830s, manual labor schools, started in Europe, were introduced in America. Schools such as Lafayette College, University of Ohio, Centre College, and Marietta College began farm and mechanic shops in which all students were required to work. It was thought this might encourage poor students to attend college. The economic panic of 1837 temporarily killed the innovation, which was already sickly as farms commonly lost money, students were lazy, and shops were usually underequipped; but as fads manual labor schools in subsequent years were periodically popular.

The pressure to introduce practical or work-related programs was also widely felt in the early decades of the nineteenth century among existing colleges—but not everywhere acceded to. In 1828, the faculty and board of trustees at Yale defended their classical course against Connecticut critics by proclaiming that a classical education was the best preparation for professional study. Their Yale Report (excerpted in Appendix A) held that a classical education was not specific to any one profession but laid a foundation for all professions. It stated further that a college education could only be the start of training for a profession, since specific professions were learned by doing. The report muffled the critics of Yale and permitted it to maintain its classical undergradaute curriculum for much of the nineteenth century with only minor changes—for instance, two agriculture faculty were appointed in 1846.

However, other colleges, many of whose faculty believed the same things as Yale, lacked its enrollments. They were forced to offer practical courses to attract new students. In the 1840s and 1850s, colleges like Brown University, the University of Louisiana, (which created the first business school in 1851), the University of Michigan, and Union College attempted with little success, especially for Brown and Michigan, to mix classical and practical or professional programs. And the following decade brought continuing enrollment declines, which lasted until the end of the Civil War. Finally, the 1862 Morrill Land-Grant Act, reproduced in Appendix A, and the free elective curriculum spurred education for work.

When the Land-Grant Act was passed in 1862, there were six colleges of agriculture, manufacturing, merchandizing, or mechanics in America. The Morrill funds not only supported 69 more (Krug, 1966, p. 85) but also gave the classical colleges enough competition from the land-grant colleges that most of them eventually followed the land-grant lead in combining academic and practical study. The act authorized the sale of federal lands to provide funds for the support of state colleges offering instruction in agriculture and mechanic arts without excluding scientific and classical studies and including military tactics. Every state was given

30,000 acres for each of its senators and congressmen. The proceeds were to be used to establish one or more colleges in whatever manner the state chose. Some states used their land-grant funds to upgrade existing colleges or high schools. Pennsylvania, for instance, turned the Farmer's High School into the Pennsylvania College of Agriculture and Mechanics (A & M). Wisconsin and Minnesota gave the land-grant money to existing state universities to augment their offerings. South Dakota and Washington established new colleges. In 1887, the Morrill legislation was expanded by the Hatch Act, which provided money for agricultural experiment stations. Three years later Congress passed a second Morrill Act providing annual federal appropriations to land-grant colleges and encouragement for similar state support.

Cornell University, offering "any person . . . any study," is often described as the jewel of the land-grant movement. Only partially supported by land-grant funds, it began operation in 1868, the same year the University of Missouri established the initial college of education. Cornell was the first major institution to treat the classical curriculum and work-related programs with complete equality. It emphasized scholarship and a quality faculty, but also had a mechanic shop and emphasized manual labor. It was popular from the start, opening with 400 students—a very large enrollment for its day—after having rejected at least 50 applicants for the first class, a luxury few colleges of that period could afford.

Other land-grant colleges ran the gamut from low-level trade schools to colleges that modeled themselves after eastern liberal arts schools and that paid shorter shrift than Congress had anticipated to agriculture and mechanics. The public attitude to them varied between apathy and hostility. Their students were often academically ill prepared. Most had completed only elementary school, as more advanced public education was rare, and most found the courses too academic and impractical, in part because of limited scientific and technical knowledge in the subjects and in part because of a paucity of textbooks. Nonetheless, historians virtually without exception identify the creation of these new multipurpose colleges as the major turning point in the development of American higher education by offering both liberal and job-related education within a comprehensive institution.

In 1869, soon after the opening of Cornell, the free elective movement was launched with Charles Eliot's inaugural speech as president of Harvard. Letting students choose their own courses resulted in greater integration of traditional academic education and work-related study as students could combine courses from disciplinary departments within the academic college with courses in professional departments and schools. By 1899, for instance, students at conservative Yale were permitted to take law and medical courses as undergraduates. Then in 1902, Eliot induced the Harvard faculty to permit students to complete undergraduate study in three years, making it possible for many students to spend their fourth year in professional school. In 1905, Columbia formally introduced its time-shortened program under the title of the "professional option." Even before that date, 25 percent of its undergraduates had begun professional study on ad hoc basis. Columbia maintained the professional option until 1953, when it required all students to have an undergraduate major.

Changes in society were important factors in the further development of work-related education in the nineteenth and early twentieth centuries. One change involved a growing American business ethic and increased availability of private philanthropic support for colleges. With such support, practical courses of study in journalism, applied sciences, architecture, mechanical drawing, and particularly business grew like Topsy. Another, the rise of public secondary school education, required more and better educated teachers. Beginning in 1839 in Lexington, Massachusetts, normal schools—high schools for the preparation of women teachers— had been established. In subsequent years, some high schools and a few coeducational colleges also engaged in teacher preparation. However, with the development of the public high schools, it became necessary to prepare a better educated corps of teachers. In 1895, Massachusetts took the first step and required that all students admitted to normal schools be high school graduates. By the 1920s, several major universities were accepting transfer credits from normal schools, which were beginning to be upgraded to degree-granting teachers colleges and later to comprehensive colleges. And by then, many private liberal arts colleges had found that preparing secondary school teachers could prove the mainstay of their support.

The first quarter of the twentieth century also saw the development of cooperative education, which alternated on-campus study with work. In 1906, Herman Schneider, an engineering professor at the University of Cincinnati, created a program in which engineering students were divided into two groups which alternately spent one week studying on campus and one week working at engineering jobs off campus. The plan permitted the university to double its engineering enrollments since half of the students were off campus at any one time and allowed students to earn money for their education while acquiring "hands on" experience. The idea was adopted by a number of other technical colleges and, as described in Chapter 12, in 1921 by Antioch, a liberal arts college.

In 1917, Congress passed the Smith-Hughes Act, establishing a Federal Board of Vocational Education. This board was charged with administering funds to be matched by the states for the training and salaries of teachers of agriculture, home economics, trades, and industrial subjects. Although the law specified that the training and teaching had to take place in schools of lower than college grade, it resulted in the introduction of work education in junior colleges. The depression beginning in 1929 supported this development.

In the late 1920s and early 1930s, several progressive liberal arts colleges, including Bennington and Sarah Lawrence, were established. They opposed specialized work training and introduced in its stead a philosophy of "life needs," the functional equivalent of today's career education. Their life-needs curriculum integrated work, life, and learning within the liberal arts mode. Bennington, for instance, made it possible for the students who wanted technical training in secretarial skills to acquire it as part of their liberal education and introduced an off-campus term between Christmas and Washington's birthday for students to gain "real world" experience or additional exposure to their major area.

In 1945, the progressive colleges' concept of "life needs" was reinvented at a U.S. Office of Education conference. The name was changed to "life adjustment education" and aimed at a precollege audience. The Office of Education, by pushing and publicizing the idea, had a greater impact on two-year colleges than the progressive institutions had. In fact, the General College at the University of Minnesota added technical work education in areas such as retailing and selling, practical nursing, commercial arts, and air hostessing to its previously all general education program. The General College no longer felt such courses inconsistent with lower-division liberal education.

The Second World War and the post-war era provided financial incentives for the growth and development of applied technical education, particularly in engineering. In 1963, the Smith-Hughes legislation was expanded by the Vocational Education Act, which increased the list of occupations qualifying for funding to any not requiring professional training or a baccalaureate degree. Associate and certificate programs at four-year colleges were fundable.

In recent years, education for work has continued to expand. Some proprietary schools have begun to award degrees such as the associate in occupational studies for strictly vocational/occupational programs (as illustrated by the Technical Career Institutes described in Chapter 13); business concerns such as American Telephone & Telegraph, International Business Machines, and General Electric have initiated bachelor's degree–granting programs, and colleges have started granting credit for work experience and introduced "upside-down" programs which permit transfer students from proprietary schools or technical institutes to apply their vocational/occupational learning from these institutions against college major and upper-division requirements, as depicted by the General College case study in Chapter 12.

State of Education and Work

College Students and Education for Work

Interviewer: How would you describe the students on this campus?

Dean: They are serious about their work and very career minded.

This recent interchange (Levine, 1976, p. 29) epitomizes education for work today. Such education is more important to current undergraduates than it was to students in the late 1960s. In 1969 and 1976, American undergraduates were asked by the Carnegie Commission and the Carnegie Council how important it was for them to get training and skills for an occupation from their college education. In 1969, 57 percent of college students said it was "essential." In 1976, 67 percent responded in the same fashion. In fact, nearly half (46 percent) of all undergraduates say they would drop out of college if they thought it was not helping their job chances. This opinion is most widely held by students at two-year colleges (51 percent) and least widely shared among those at the most selective liberal arts colleges (24 percent) (Carnegie Surveys, 1975–76).

More than a third of all students (38 percent) would leave college immediately if they could get the same job now as after graduation. Again, community and junior college students (47 percent) express the opinion most frequently while students at selective liberal arts colleges (19 percent) offer it least frequently. Students at comprehensive colleges (37 percent), less selective liberal arts colleges (31 percent), doctorate-granting universities (31 percent), and research universities (28 percent) fall between the extremes (Carnegie Surveys, 1975–76).

Although most undergraduates (85 percent) are attending college with a specific career in mind, many are anxious over their prospects for jobs. Thirty-four percent of them say they worry "quite a lot" or "a great deal" about job prospects. Only 24 percent say they do not worry at all, with these respondents most common at community and junior colleges (32 percent) and least frequent at selective liberal arts colleges (13 percent) (Carnegie Surveys, 1975–76).

Only a bare majority (54 percent) of undergraduates rate current job prospects for students with their majors as "good" or "very good" over the next ten years. The ratings are highest among students at community colleges (67 percent), which have the largest number of work-related courses, and lowest among students at selective liberal arts colleges (43 percent), which offer the fewest work-related courses. Some students (28 percent) fear they may be "overeducated" for the jobs they would find when they finished college. And 11 percent imagine they will be unhappy in the careers available to them (Carnegie Surveys, 1975–76).

However, the picture is not entirely bleak. Twenty percent of undergraduates have added technical or work-related courses to their program with the hope of improving their possible job standing. This is done most often by students at community and junior colleges (31 percent). At all types of four-year institutions, the rate varies from 12 to 15 percent. Though not a palliative, another important consideration is that 90 percent of the undergraduates are interested in their fields regardless of their chances to work in them. This is equally true of undergraduates at all types of colleges (Carnegie Surveys, 1975–76).

Colleges and Education for Work

Colleges offer their students four types of education for work: (1) academic instruction, (2) work experiences, (3) joint industry–higher education programs, and (4) vocational counseling. (Vocational counseling is discussed in Chapter 6.)

ACADEMIC INSTRUCTION

Work-related academic instruction relies upon professional/technical majors, minors, and career courses. Professional/technical majors lead directly to careers in the concentration area. Examples are listed in Table 12, which shows how frequently these programs are found at five different types of colleges and universities.

Professional/technical majors in business and education are offered at a majority of all five types of colleges and universities. Engineering majors are offered at the majority of research universities, doctorate-granting universities, and community and junior colleges. With the exceptions of home economics and medical technology, two-year colleges have the largest number of all of the remaining programs. With the exceptions of secretarial science and law enforcement, liberal arts colleges have the fewest.

Some liberal arts colleges compensate for the absence of professional/technical majors by offering other curricular options. One, the career-oriented liberal arts major, groups liberal arts subjects around work-related themes (such as rural youth leadership at Sterling College) or integrates liberal arts and professional/technical courses of study (such as legal studies at Hampshire College). Another, the student-created major, also makes such concentrations possible. In 1975, for instance, the most popular student-created major at Brown University was biomedical ethics. A third and rarer option is the upside-down program mentioned earlier in this chapter. At The Evergreen State College among others, this

Table 12. Percentage of different types of colleges and universities
with professional/technical majors

Professional/technical majors	Types of institutions				
	Research universities	Doctorate-granting universities	Comprehensive universities & colleges	Liberal arts colleges	Community and junior colleges
Business	70	93	91	75	93
Education	82	88	93	84	67
Engineering	80	64	29	5	55
Health Science	41	50	55	18	63
Forestry	14	10	6	5	27
Home economics	32	52	22	7	32
Auto and aviation repair	5	10	10	2	32
Electronics	7	12	12	0	32
Professional assistant (to doctor, lawyer, or dentist)	7	5	3	2	27
Mortuary science	0	2	3	0	2
Cosmetology	0	0	1	0	12
Law enforcement	11	43	35	13	60
Secretarial science	9	19	32	14	73
Medical technology	25	55	46	23	25

Source: Catalog Study, 1976.

program permits students who have completed two-year technical programs, which are not normally transferable to liberal arts colleges, to substitute those credits at face value as the equivalent of major and upper-division study. These students then take general education at Evergreen to complete the lower-division requirements for the bachelor of arts degree. Some colleges have made contractual arrangements with proprietary or technical schools for this purpose. For instance, Transylvania University has a joint upside-down program with the Northwood Institute in hotel and restaurant management.

Most colleges have not gone this far. De Pauw University, for example, offers students a minor in "Business or Public Service," consisting of several courses in organizational theory and administrative behavior, which can be taken as a supplement to liberal arts majors. St. Louis University has a similar program for which it awards a certificate (Toombs, 1976). A number of colleges offer liberal arts courses aimed at students preparing for certain careers. For example, the University of Michigan's Residential College has a course in the ethics of medicine, and Metropolitan State College in Denver has a course in ecological construction that involves actual outdoor building.

Most of these recent liberal arts career options are too new to evaluate their efficacy. What is clear, however, is that enrollment in professional/technical courses is growing rapidly. (This is discussed further in Chapter 2.)

WORK EXPERIENCES

Student work experiences range from internships and cooperative education to full-time and part-time jobs on and off campus.

Internships. Internships are full- or part-time, credit-bearing, short-term, supervised work experiences. They can be established on or off campus. They can be paid or unpaid. Their supervisor can be a faculty member or an individual on the job charged with monitoring student progress. They may be necessary for professional or occupational certification, as is the case with student teaching; they may be a graduation requirement or recommended program of a college, as at the University of Alabama's New College; or they may be simply a matter of student choice.

Internships are found in 63 percent of four-year arts and sciences colleges and 79 percent of four-year professional/technical colleges. At two-year institutions they are offered by 50 percent of arts and sciences colleges and 82 percent of professional/technical colleges (Catalog Study, 1976). Internships can be divided into three types: (1) service internships, (2) apprenticeships, and (3) general internships.

Service internships are low- or no-pay, community-based learning experiences. The best known are the Peace Corps and VISTA, collectively named ACTION. This organization offers a one-year domestic service program called University-Year-for-Action (UYA) to college students, who receive a full year of college credit, a stipend, and tuition support for working in antipoverty programs. UYA is intended to give students exposure to the real world and to give poor people the benefit of resources of the university. It is administered by individual colleges that recruit students, arrange placement, offer supplementary instruction, and evaluate student performance.

There is much current interest in service internships. A majority of college faculty (54 percent) and more than one-third of college students (36 percent) believe that undergraduate education in America would be improved if students were required to spend a year in community service (Carnegie Surveys, 1975–76). Consonant with the belief, several schools have established regional service-internship resource centers. The University of Kentucky has such a center, funded by ACTION, that serves the states of Alabama, Georgia, Kentucky, Mississippi, North Carolina, South Carolina, and Tennessee. The Kentucky center provides workshops, conferences, consulting services, and an information center for efforts and opportunities relevant to service programs in the region.

Apprenticeships involve on-the-job training for specific types of work. They are far more common at two-year colleges than four-year institutions. Seattle Community College offers aircraft technician and metal fabricator apprenticeships that rely upon the services of a number of aircraft-related industries, and Olympic College in Bremerton, Washington, has shipyard apprenticeships as part of its technical arts curriculum (Heiss, 1973, p. 43). Apprenticeships have strong student appeal. A majority of all undergraduates (57 percent) at all types of colleges and universities would be "extremely" or "somewhat" interested in an apprenticeship program after leaving college in industry, the arts, unions, or service organizations where they would be paid minimum wages while learning skills for a job (Carnegie Surveys, 1975–76).

General internships ordinarily include experiences more academic in orientation, more campus-based, and less targeted toward specific jobs than service internships or apprenticeships. They are the most common form of internships available to students. The business internship at Sterling College, the Undergraduate

Research Opportunities Program at MIT, and the Humanities Internship Program at Scripps College are examples.

Sterling's business internship is equivalent to a single course. In this program, a team of senior business students work as consultants to problem-ridden small businesses under a contract from the U.S. Small Business Administration.

MIT's Undergraduate Research Opportunities Program (UROP) involves the participation of at least 75 percent of the MIT student body. UROP pairs MIT faculty and undergraduates in student-selected, on- and off-campus research opportunities during the academic year and summer. Its available research opportunities now comprise a more than 160-page book, indexed by topic in over 100 areas and containing the names of hundreds of participating faculty members and organizations. Research opportunities are available in all 23 of MIT's academic departments, several science laboratories, a number of administrative offices, and more than 300 off-campus organizations. Off-campus projects require the services of an off-campus supervisor as well as an MIT faculty member. For participating in UROP, students can earn either credit or money but not both. Student and faculty evaluations of UROP, with occasional exceptions, have been enthusiastic and lavish with praise. Students compliment the program for giving them the opportunity to do challenging work in their major area, for the sense of achievement developed in the course of the research project, and for allowing them to meet and work closely with a faculty member.

The Humanities Internship Program at Scripps College is a one-semester, full-time program for students who have completed at least two years of humanities study. Interns are placed with "associates"—professionals employed in an area of the intern's interest. Associates, who work at jobs ranging from pharmaceutical researcher to police officer, receive no stipend, though they may be given the title "adjunct lecturer." The student intern works an average of 20 hours per week and is required to write a contract, specifying the terms and goals for the internship, which must be approved by the internship program director and the associate. By the end of the internship, the student is required to produce a project emphasizing the humanistic implications of the work experience. The internship may serve as a research or apprenticeship setting for the project. Successful completion of the work experience and project counts as the equivalent of two courses. During the internship, students are also required to enroll in two academic courses—an elective and the Humanities Internship Seminar. The seminar is team taught and focuses upon the relationship of work to humanities issues such as individualism, work as worship, work as experience, work as creativity, and community and commitment. The reading list for the course is long and ranges from Homer and Walt Whitman to Studs Terkel and Nora Ephron. Seminars meet one evening a week and a paper based on the reading is required for each class. Another night of the week is reserved for a student "rap session" to discuss ideas, experiences, and projects. For this meeting, students are required to prepare accounts of their observations and problems at work. The program has received rave reviews from all concerned.

Internships of all three types are desired by undergraduates. A majority of undergraduates (52 percent) say they would like to have an apprenticeship, internship, or job for academic credit or to meet graduation requirements. In practice, few students (9 percent) have such experiences. They are most common among students at selective liberal arts colleges (13 percent) and least common among students at the most research-oriented universities (6 percent) and two-year colleges (7 percent) (Carnegie Surveys, 1975–76).

The advantages of internship programs are several: (1) They offer students a chance to integrate work and formal education with expert supervision; (2) they motivate some students to remain in college; (3) they offer students a chance to test career aspirations; (4) they can lead to jobs; (5) they may pay a salary; (6) they may provide students with a general education not available at college; (7) they permit colleges to admit additional students or reduce class size; (8) they enrich the curriculum as students bring back to campus knowledge of the latest practices in the field; (9) they permit faculty members to reduce the amount of applied material in their courses when it can be learned in an internship; and (10) they make students more employable.

The disadvantages of internships are that (1) they are short, one-shot experiences—students may have limited exposure to the work area or form misperceptions on the basis of their experience;

(2) they occasionally involve no more than menial work; (3) they often involve little or no pay, which makes them less available to low-income students; (4) they require that staff be hired to locate internships, arrange placements, and evaluate students; (5) they are often poorly linked with instructional programs as most colleges lack the preparation and return seminars offered by Justin Morrill College; (6) they occasionally permit students to flounder because supervision is lacking; and (7) they often rely upon the services of volunteer internship supervisors who may find it difficult to maintain interest for extended periods of time.

Cooperative Education. Cooperative education joins classroom instruction with work, generally (though not always) in the major area, on an alternating basis. With rare exceptions, the work is off campus. Instruction may be either concurrent with or consecutive to work. In consecutive programs—the most frequent form— periods of full-time work are alternated with periods of full-time study. In concurrent programs, the student works half time and attends classes half time or works full time and attends class part time. Some institutions offer only one of these variations, while others such as the College of San Mateo offer all three.

Cooperative programs of any type are offered by 32 percent of two-year arts and sciences colleges and 51 percent of two-year professional/technical colleges. Twenty-five percent of four-year arts and sciences and professional/technical colleges also have such programs. The programs are mandatory for all students at 4 percent of the institutions, optional at 21 percent of the institutions, and open only to selected students at 75 percent of the institutions (Catalog Study, 1976). (An example of a required program is presented in Chapter 12 in a case study of Antioch College.)

The advantages of cooperative education are that (1) it is not a one-shot experience, so the student can have wide and deep exposure to different career possibilities; (2) it enables theoretical and applied learning to progress hand and hand; (3) it allows students to develop socially, grow personally, learn interpersonal skills, and take charge of their own lives; (4) it provides a salary for most students, which reduces institutional need for financial aid; (5) it encourages some students to remain in college rather than dropping out; (6) it enables employers to obtain staff at low cost; (7) it provides employers with an opportunity to recruit, train, and try out potential employees without making a prior commitment; (8) it results in jobs for many students and greater employability for most; (9) it allows colleges to admit a maximum of twice as many students as capacity since as few as half are on campus at any one time; (10) it results in savings on physical plant and staff for colleges since a large percentage of students are gone each term; (11) it enables faculty members to reduce the applied aspects of major programs if students can learn them on the job; (12) it can improve academic performance—several studies have shown that students in cooperative programs perform better academically than other students (Cross, 1973, p. 18); and (13) it is popular with students and faculty.

The disadvantages of cooperative education are that (1) it frequently lengthens the amount of time required to earn a college degree; for example, the cooperative baccalaureate program at Northeastern University is five years; (2) it is a draining experience to alternate between work and jobs; some students tire of it by their senior year; (3) it cuts courses short because students tend to return from their cooperative experiences late and leave early, especially if the jobs are out of town; (4) it can have a parochializing influence on students, especially if it forces them into a premature decision on major; (5) it is hard to find a sufficient quantity and diversity of cooperative jobs outside of urban areas; (6) it can involve menial jobs and unsupervised experience; (7) it leaves financially needy students with limited options; (8) it often makes integration of work and education the sole responsibility of the student; (9) it is sometimes used by students to be near a boyfriend, girlfriend, or convenient location rather than for its primary educational value; (10) it requires a staff to locate jobs, counsel students, and evaluate students; (11) its staff is often treated as second-class citizens by the academic faculty; (12) it is hard to keep the supply of jobs compatible with changing student interests; and (13) it results in frequent turnover in employees for employers and often an inability of students to pursue work tasks from start to finish.

Full-Time and Part-Time Employment. Internships and cooperative education are not the most common student work experience, however—ordinary jobs are. The majority of undergraduates (54 percent) are employed full or part time. At research universities, 41 percent of the undergraduates have jobs, while at community and junior colleges 63 percent have them (Carnegie Surveys, 1975–76). The most common amount of time devoted to jobs at community and junior colleges is 36 or more hours a week. In contrast, at liberal arts colleges, it is 10 hours or less, as shown in Table 13.

Most student jobs are off campus (Astin, 1975, p. 73). However, one source of on-campus jobs is college work-study, a federal program aimed at financially needy students attending college half time or more. College work-study is usually included as part of the financial aid package that an institution prepares for its students. With the U.S. government paying up to 80 percent of the student's salary and the employer paying the rest, these work-study jobs are very desirable for colleges to maintain for their own use. Furthermore, federal support for off-campus work-study jobs is limited to certain types of nonprofit organizations. As a result 85–90 percent of college work-study jobs are located on campus, and unfortunately few of them are specifically related to student career plans.

The advantages of students holding jobs during college are: (1) They add practical experience to a student's college education; (2) they are a source of income; (3) they reduce student attrition if they are not full time (Astin, 1975, p. 87); (4) they may result in higher student grade-point averages if the student works 20 hours per week or less; (5) they offer experiences that students consider beneficial; (6) they can make students more employable after college and can lead to jobs; and (7) they are creditable at several colleges such as Metropolitan State University.

The disadvantages of jobs are that (1) they reduce the time students have for their studies; (2) they often eliminate opportunities for extracurricular activities; (3) they are generally outside the student's career field and sometimes menial; (4) they increase attrition when they are in the student's planned work area; (5) unlike internships and cooperative education, they are not guided or supervised in an educational sense; (6) they may require students to choose their courses on the basis of what fits around the job; (7) they may be especially detrimental to educationally disadvantaged students who are also frequently poor; (8) they increase student

Table 13. Percentage of students working varying amounts of time at different types of colleges

	Institutional type				
Number of hours per week	Research universities	Doctorate-granting universities	Comprehensive universities	Liberal arts colleges	Community and junior colleges
10 or less	26	23	23	41	9
11–15	25	20	19	18	10
16–20	20	21	17	13	12
21–35	15	16	16	10	19
36 or more	14	20	24	16	51

Source: Carnegie Surveys, 1975–76.

attrition when students work full time or, generally, when the work is off campus (Astin, 1975, p. 87).

JOINT INDUSTRY–HIGHER EDUCATION PROGRAMS

Some colleges offer programs designed specifically for workers. In fact, 43 percent of two-year colleges have such programs and 81 percent would like to have them (American Association of Community and Junior Colleges, 1977). Fitchburg State College in Massachusetts and Raytheon Company have a "learn while you earn" program that enrolls over 700 Raytheon workers. It involves a sequence of courses meeting the college's goals and Raytheon's purposes to help workers in need of upgrading or retraining. Many workers take as long as ten years to complete a degree. The College of New Rochelle in New York has a similar program with a center in Manhattan specially for union members.

Another type of joint program is the faculty-executive exchange. Marymount College brings top business people to campus to teach business and nonbusiness students. The program is designed to bring the work world to students and to inform the work world of the value of a liberal arts education. Both students and their new teachers rate the program highly. In the future, reverse sabbaticals between industrial personnel and faculty are planned. Birmingham Southern College is already engaged in such activity.

A recent grant from the Kellogg Foundation is allowing the college to provide one-month full-time internships for 45 of its faculty in business, labor, and government. In addition, 150 people from the business, labor, and government community are becoming involved in the liberal arts activities of the college.

A number of institutions such as Empire State College in New York award credit for some forms of education offered by industry. In 1975, at least one-eighth of the 32 million employees in the nation's 7,500 largest private firms engaged in some formal education or training under company sponsorship, much of which would not be classified as higher education. Eight out of ten dollars that companies spend on education is spent on internal courses for employees during work hours. This education is said to differ from noncorporate education in three respects: The participants are more highly motivated, the work place is the setting for learning and doing, and the instruction is more pragmatic in orientation (Lusterman, 1977). The current trend toward granting college credit for prior learning will likely result in increased industry-higher education cooperation in developing future company-operated programs.

College Graduates and Education for Work

Ann Bisconti and Lewis Solomon (1977) recently completed a study of 4,138 college graduates who began college in 1961, earned only a bachelor's degree, and were working in 1974–75. Their findings include the following (summarized in "Grads Give Colleges Low Marks for Career Training," 1976, pp. 7–8):

- Less than 5 percent of the sample believed "their college education was sufficient training for their jobs."
- "While 73 percent of the sample said the general knowledge gained from undergraduate study proved 'very useful' in their careers, only 21 percent used the same words to describe the role of college training in the selection of occupational goals. Again 69 percent of the graduates said their education had proved 'very useful' in increasing their chances of finding a job, but a mere 22 percent felt it had an equal effect on the development of leadership ability."

- "Though 43 percent of the graduates . . . gave college high marks in providing the skills necessary to get a job, a full 29 percent said the courses were of no help whatsoever in this respect. About 38 percent said schooling had been very useful for learning skills actually used on the job, but 50 percent claimed it was only 'somewhat useful' in practice."
- "Fewer than half the sample are putting to work what they learned about their major field in college. More than 70 percent reported they use their training in the minor subject infrequently or not at all. . . . More than half of the alums . . . were in a career they did not expect to enter while in college."
- "Most of the graduates indicated that if they had to do it all over again they would be sure to take courses in business administration, English, and psychology. They said these emerged as the most useful in their careers. Other courses recommended most frequently were economics, accounting, and mathematics."
- "Respondents who majored in the humanities and social sciences were only slightly more favorable than other groups in recognizing benefits usually associated with liberal education: increased general knowledge, ability to think clearly, and leadership ability. . . . Graduates in fields generally thought to be vocationally oriented—business, engineering, education—were considerably more favorable than others in their judgments of the career related value of their education."

Concerns and Proposals

Most of the criticisms relevant to education for work are discussed in Chapter 1 on general education, Chapter 2 on concentration, and Chapter 8 on instruction. One additional criticism is examined here.

Criticism: Education for work is inappropriate to an undergraduate education.

This criticism has been voiced by the Yale faculty in 1828, Cardinal Newman in 1853 (1959), Thorsten Veblen in 1918 (1968), Abraham Flexner in 1930 (1968), and many other people. They have all believed that the proper place for work education is on the job. Education for work is said to be externally motivated by financial considerations while the liberal arts are self-motivating. Professional/technical programs are also criticized for being too specialized, nonintellectual, and lacking in the general applicability of liberal arts programs.

The counterargument is offered by Eric Ashby (1966, p. 84):

> The path to culture should be through a man's specialism, not by-passing it. Suppose a student decides to take up the study of brewing; his way to acquire general culture is not by diluting his brewing courses with lectures on architecture, social history, and ethics, but by making brewing the core of his studies. The sine qua non for a man who desires to be cultured is a deep and enduring enthusiasm to do one thing excellently. So there must be an assurance that the student genuinely wants to make beer. From this it is a natural step to the study of biology, microbiology, and chemistry; all subjects which can be studied not as techniques to be practiced but as ideas to be understood. As his studies gain momentum the student could, by skillful teaching, be made interested in the economics of marketing beer, in public houses, in their design, in architecture; or in the history of beer drinking from the time of the early Egyptian inscriptions, and so in social history; or, in the unhappy moral effects of drinking too much, and so in religion and ethics. A student who can weave his technology into the fabric of society can claim to have a liberal education; a student who cannot weave his technology into the fabric of society cannot claim even to be a good technologist.

Education for work has further been advocated on the grounds that liberal arts education is out of touch with the real world, that nonuseful education is a waste of time or elitest because only the rich have the time for it, and that education for work need not be any more specialized than contemporary liberal arts education.

At the present time the national trend, owing to the current economy, is decidely in the direction of adding work education to the college curriculum. The College Placement Council (1975) indicates such programs do improve the chances of students, particularly liberal arts majors, for employment.

Two factors appear to be stopping the immediate expansion of work education. One is that the most selective and traditionally academic colleges, which are historically pacesetters in curriculum development, are making the fewest work-related additions to their curricula. Steady-state conditions that place more emphasis on attracting enrollments than following the pacesetter may result in a new order. In fact, the less highly regarded units of elite institutions, such as Columbia University's School of General Studies and Harvard's Graduate School of Education, are themselves already adopting nontraditional work programs.

The second factor is cost. Work programs are considerably more expensive than academic courses. They require smaller classes, more expensive equipment, and greater student-faculty contact time. Administrators at several schools have indicated that cost is the only thing stopping them from vastly expanding their oversubscribed work offerings. Some programs, in fact, have long waiting lists. If the unpopularity of the liberal arts core grows, that cost differential could be sharply reduced.

Not all colleges are boarding the education-for-work bandwagon. A case in point is St. John's College. Education designed specifically for work would clash with the perennial "great books" philosophy of the school. Many suggestions have been offered to help students at such schools gain work experience. They include (1) assisting students in finding relevant summer jobs (College Placement Council, 1975); (2) establishing easy, tuition-free work leaves from college that can be used to gain college-equivalent learning (Hampshire College); (3) expanding available programs of national service for young people (Carnegie Commission, 1971); (4) developing noncredit or credit career counseling (80 percent of 1973 college students expressed interest in a "career planning year" which would involve career counseling and exposure to many different fields and job opportunities) (Yankelovich, 1974); and (5) creating post–high school and/or post–college work training programs (37 percent of undergraduates responding to the 1976 Carnegie Council undergraduate survey said they would be "extremely" or "somewhat interested" in a technical school program after leaving college that offered certified training for skills needed in industry).

*   *   *

A commentary on education for work can be found in Chapter 12 "Undergraduate Education and the World of Work" in The Carnegie Foundation for the Advancement of Teaching, *Missions of the College Curriculum: A Contemporary Review with Suggestions* (1977).

References

American Association of Community and Junior Colleges. "Over 80 Percent of Community Colleges Would Like to Work with Unions." *Cooperation,* Washington, D.C., May 1977, p. 1.

Ashby, E. *Technology and the Academics: An Essay on Universities and the Scientific Revolution.* New York: St. Mark's Press, 1966.

Astin, A. W. *Preventing Students from Dropping Out.* San Francisco: Jossey-Bass, 1975.

Bisconti, A. S., and Solomon, L. *Job Satisfaction After College: The Graduates Viewpoint.* Bethlehem, Penn.: Career Placement Council Foundation, 1977.

Brubacher, J. S., and Rudy, W. *Higher Education in Transition: A History of American Colleges and Universities, 1636–1976.* (3rd ed.) New York: Harper & Row, 1976.

Carnegie Commission on Higher Education. *Less Time, More Options: Education Beyond the High School.* New York: McGraw-Hill, 1971.

The Carnegie Foundation for the Advancement of Teaching. *Missions of the College Curriculum: A Contemporary Review with Suggestions.* San Francisco: Jossey-Bass, 1977.

This report is discussed in Chapter 11.

Carnegie Surveys, 1975–76.

This project is described in the Preface.

Catalog Study, 1976.

This project is described in the Preface.

Cheit, E. F. *The Useful Arts and the Liberal Tradition.* New York: McGraw-Hill, 1975.

This book examines the evolution and character of education in four professions—agriculture, engineering, business administration, and forestry— advocating that these fields be used as a model in designing programs for liberal education.

College Placement Council, Inc. *Four Year Liberal Arts Graduates: Their Utilization in Business, Industry, and Government—The Problem and Some Solutions.* Bethlehem, Penn., 1975.

This policy statement discusses what an undergraduate can do in college to increase employment options after graduation.

Cross, K. P. *Integration of Learning and Earning: Cooperative Education Nontraditional Study.* Washington, D. C.: American Association for Higher Education, 1973.

Flexner, A. *Universities: American, English, and German.* London: Oxford University Press, 1968.

The educational philosophy of Flexner is discussed in Chapter 10.

Glenny, L. A., Shea, J. R., Ruyle, J. H., and Freschi, K. H. *Presidents Confront Reality: From Edifice Complex to University Without Walls.* San Francisco: Jossey-Bass, 1976.

Goldberg, M. H. "Vocational Training, Career Orientation, and Liberal Education." *Liberal Education,* 1975, 61 (3).

"Grads Give College Low Marks for Career Training." *Higher Education Daily,* Nov. 3, 1976, p. 3.

This article does an excellent job of summarizing the Bisconti-Solomon study of college graduates and job satisfaction.

Heiss, A. *An Inventory of Academic Innovation.* Berkeley, Calif.: Carnegie Commission on Higher Education, 1973.

Keene, R., Adams, F., and King, J. E. *Work and the College Student.* Carbondale, Ill.: Southern Illinois University Press, 1976.

This book contains the proceedings of the first national convention on Work and the College Student at Southern Illinois University on June 4-6, 1976. It contains 60 papers which are divided into seven areas—"The Partnership of Work and Academia," "The Profession Examines Current Work Programs," "Administrators, Former Students, and Businessmen Focus on Programs," "Looking at Problems and Issues," "Focusing on Issues and Possibilities," "Government and and Work," and "Prospects."

Knowles, A., and Associates. *Handbook of Cooperative Education.* San Francisco: Jossey-Bass, 1971.

Krug, E. *Salient Dates in American Education: 1635-1964.* New York: Harper & Row, 1966.

Lazerson, M., and Grubb, W. N. (Eds.) *American Education and Vocationalism.* New York: Teachers College Press, 1974.

Levine, A. "Reflections of an Itinerant Interviewer: A Sketch of Undergraduate Curriculum Trends." A monograph prepared for the Carnegie Council on Policy Studies in Higher Education. Berkeley, Calif., June 1976 (mimeographed).

Levine, A., and Weingart, J. *Reform of Undergraduate Education.* San Francisco: Jossey-Bass, 1973.

Lusterman, S. *Education in Industry.* Paper presented at the 1977 annual meeting of the American Association for Higher Education, Chicago, Ill., March 1977.

Marland, S. *Career Education: A Proposal for Reform.* New York: McGraw-Hill, 1974.

Meyerson, M. "Civilizing Education: Uniting Liberal and Professional Learning." *Daedalus,* Fall 1974, *1,* 173-179.

Newman, J. H. *The Idea of a University.* Garden City, N.Y.: Image Books, 1959. The educational philosophy of Newman is discussed in Chapter 10.

Ross, E. D. *Democracy's College: The Land-Grant Movement in the Formative Stage.* New York: Arno Press, 1969.

This volume offers a history of the land-grant movement—antecedents and consequences—with particular emphasis on the third quarter of the nineteenth century.

Toombs, W. "Career Education and Undergraduate Study." *Research Currents* (ERIC-AAHE), November 1976.

This article discusses the evolution, meaning, and application of the concept of career education in postsecondary education.

Veblen, T. *The Higher Learning in America.* New York: Hill & Wang, 1968.

Yankelovich, D. *The New Morality: A Profile of American Youth in the 70's.* New York: McGraw-Hill, 1974.

6

Advising

Definition and History

Advising refers to counseling available to students or potential students that is directly or indirectly concerned with the undergraduate curriculum. There are four principal types: academic advising, vocational and career advising, personal advising, and special group (for example, minorities and women) advising.

Advising has been a function of colleges in this country since their origin. The presidents and faculty of the colonial colleges were, in effect, the first student affairs officers or advisers. They counseled students regarding their extracurricular activities, moral life, and appropriate intellectual habits. Advising was an integral part of the teachers' job. Presidents and faculty were not only expected to offer instruction but to act in loco parentis—to provide advice and guidance of the kind their students' parents would give if they were available.

In the late 1820s, Kenyon College introduced the first known formal system of advising, when each student was teamed with a faculty member who served as the student's adviser. The innovation was not widely adopted for more than 50 years. When faculty advising did finally spread, it was based on The Johns Hopkins University advising program adopted in 1878 and on basic changes in the character of the American college. These changes involved increases in the number of students enrolled in many colleges, greater diversity in student background and preparation, proliferation of the number of subjects taught in college, introduction of electives into the curriculum, increased faculty specialization, and greater faculty interest in intellectual and research pursuits that reduced their traditional contact with students.

In the late nineteenth century, Harvard led in the expansion of advising. In 1889, it created a special counseling group called the Board of Freshman Advisors to advise the first-year students, and a year later, it established the country's first deanship in student affairs. Similar deanships, some alternatively titled "dean of men" or "dean of women," were established at other colleges in subsequent years.

By the turn of the century, the faculty tea and the "at home," in which students were invited to visit their teachers' houses, were in vogue. Between 1915 and 1926, orientation periods designed to familiarize students with their college blossomed. They ranged from a few days to a full year in length. In 1915–16, ten colleges had formal orientations, and in 1925–26, 82 colleges had them (Brubacher and Rudy, 1976, p. 343). Also in 1925–26, 44 percent of large colleges, 12 percent of medium-sized colleges, and 11 percent of small colleges had placement offices that engaged in vocational advising, finding students jobs to work at while they attended college, and locating jobs for students after graduation (p. 340). The concept of the placement bureau was imported to America in the late nineteenth century from Cambridge and Oxford universities, where bureaus placed students in a very limited number of fields upon graduation.

Psychological testing, supported by the army during World War I, and the development after the war of individualized college curricula—such as the Honors Program at Swarthmore, work-study at Antioch, and tutorials at Harvard—gave additional support to personal and academic advising. Yale University offered the first on-campus psychiatric counseling in 1926. In the late 1920s and early 1930s, colleges that built their programs around intimate faculty involvement in academic and personal advising were founded. Sarah Lawrence College opened in 1929, and three years later Bennington College and the General College at the University of Minnesota admitted their first classes. Both Bennington and the General College (described in Chapter 12) incorporated professional counselors, and Bennington in particular emphasized career advising.

Since the 1930s there have been several additions to student advising worth noting. One is the use of the computer and other technologies to provide information for students. Another developed in the 1960s has been special group advising to provide counseling and group support to nontraditional students. During the 1970s, a third has been recognition of the need for brokerage organizations—off-campus advising services—to reach potential adult students.

State of Advising

Types of Advising

The four major types of advising identified at the beginning of this chapter can be contrasted as follows.

ACADEMIC ADVISING

Academic advising is concerned with the intellective or cognitive components of the curriculum such as course selection, prerequisites, major cognates, requirements, and student performance and progress. It is often divided into two parts—premajor (or general education) advising and major advising. In practice, premajor advising lasts only as long as it takes for a student to decide officially or unofficially upon a major. It is usually the responsibility of a centralized, administratively or professionally staffed advising office, of a selected pool of general education faculty advisers, or most commonly of the faculty in the area in which the student expects to major. Major advising is usually the responsibility of the academic departments, of faculty groupings that offer interdisciplinary or nondisciplinary majors, or for student-created majors, of an adviser or advisory committee chosen by the student.

There are several exceptions. One involves colleges that do not require students to have a major, such as Sarah Lawrence, where the student is either assigned to an adviser or picks one on the basis of compatible interests. A second involves institutions that elaborate upon the usual pattern by adding peer advisers, team advising, community resource people, residence counselors, freshman seminars or orientation courses. A third is the off-campus academic advising available through brokerage organizations.

Most undergraduates seek academic advising. Sixty-nine percent of the undergraduates say they have sought academic advising from their college counseling or advising services or dean's office. Students request such advice most often at the most research-oriented universities (80 percent) and least often at community and junior colleges (61 percent) (Carnegie Surveys, 1975–76).

The majority of students (55 percent) think the academic advice they receive is "adequate." However, more of the remaining students report advice to be "inadequate" than "highly adequate." Twenty-seven percent of the students rate the quality of academic advising as inadequate while only 18 percent rate it as highly adequate. More students (33 percent) at the most research-oriented universities rate it inadequate than those at any other type of institution. Fewest students rate it inadequate at the most selective liberal arts colleges (15 percent) (Carnegie Surveys, 1975–76).

PERSONAL ADVISING

Personal advising deals with affective development and student private life. It may treat concerns including student feelings and emotions, social experience, physical and mental health, finances, and behavior. Like academic advising, personal advising relies upon faculty, administrators, students, and professional staff for counseling. However, the professional staff is generally larger than that associated with academic advising. In fact, some colleges have employed lawyers, medical doctors, psychologists and psychiatrists, financial aid counselors, religious advisers, and draft counselors, as well as other student personnel workers to provide this aid.

Less than one-quarter of students (22 percent) report having sought personal advising other than financial aid counseling. There is often a stigma associated with seeking some forms of personal advising, particularly mental health counseling, certain types of physical health assistance such as sex counseling, and crisis financial aid. Personal advising is used least at research and doctorate-granting universities (19–21 percent) and most at the less selective liberal arts colleges (28 percent). Among students who use personal counseling, 26 percent rate it highly adequate, 48 percent rate it adequate, and 27 percent rate it inadequate. Personal advising receives the highest marks at liberal arts colleges (37 percent highly favorable) and the lowest marks at research universities (22 percent highly favorable) (Carnegie Surveys, 1975–76).

Financial aid counseling is used by more students (36 percent) than other forms of personal advising. It is used most frequently at the less selective liberal arts colleges (54 percent) and least at research universities (27–31 percent). Twenty-two percent of the students categorize their financial aid advising as highly adequate, 49 percent consider it adequate, and 30 percent rate it inadequate. Financial aid advising is rated best at the less selective liberal arts colleges (30 percent highly adequate) and worst at the most research-oriented universities (14 percent highly adequate) (Carnegie Surveys, 1975–76).

Personal advising and the affective elements of the curriculum in general are areas that both faculty and students think should be improved. In fact, 74 percent of undergraduates and 68 percent of faculty believe undergraduate education in America would be improved if more attention were paid to the emotional growth of students (Carnegie Surveys, 1975–76).

CAREER ADVISING

Career advising is concerned with occupational planning, career preparation, and job placement. The principal college agency for career advising is the career planning and placement office. Among the services that may be offered by such offices are the counseling of individual students; the finding and listing of school term (part-time), summer, and postgraduate job opportunities; handling arrangements for the visits of job recruiters on campus; maintaining a library of career-related books and college and university catalogs; testing students for vocational interests and abilities; providing students with information about the skills necessary to find and keep a job; and following up on graduates. Seventy-nine percent of four-year colleges and universities and 76 percent of two-year colleges have career placement offices.[1]

Other sources of on-campus career advising, which are important for students at colleges without career placement offices,

---

[1]Based on a telephone conversation with the College Placement Council, March 1977.

are faculty, administrators, and peers. Off-campus community resource people and brokerage organizations have recently become involved in several locales as supplements to the traditional mix of parents, relatives, and friends.

Some colleges are developing rather innovative career advising programs. For example, in Pennsylvania, Slippery Rock State College's Learning Expectation Approach Projects (LEAP), which began in 1974, is a four-year, noncredit program available to all students. The first year is spent on clarification of student values. The second year is spent on exploring the various careers available to students. The third year is spent on decision making, career skills, and choosing categories of jobs best suited to the individual student. The fourth year is spent examining the life experiences of people in the potential occupational areas selected by the student during the third year. LEAP combines small classes of six to eight students led by a faculty member or student affairs staffperson and a graduate student or upperclassman with psychological and vocational testing for three years. The fourth year is geared more to individualized student efforts. Twenty-five to 30 percent of all Slippery Rock freshmen choose to participate.

Nationally, career advising of all kinds is used by 32 percent of undergraduates. Of the students who use career advising, 17 percent label it highly adequate, 50 percent consider it adequate, and 33 percent view it as inadequate. It is least often inadequate for students at community and junior colleges (29 percent) and most often inadequate for students at research universities (39 percent) (Carnegie Surveys, 1975–76).

SPECIAL GROUP ADVISING

Special group advising, which provides counseling to students with needs that are not shared by students generally, is the most recent of the four types of advising. Examples of special groups receiving counseling include older adults (as at Sacred Heart University, Hartford, Connecticut); women (as at Valencia Community College's Center for Continuing Education for Women, Orlando, Florida); members of ethnic minorities with substandard schooling (as at the University of California, Santa Cruz); veterans and the handicapped (as at California State University, Long Beach); gifted students (as at the University of Pennsylvania's Ben Franklin Program); major-league baseball players (at California State University, Los Angeles); nonstudents (at the Regional Learning Service of Central New York, Syracuse, New York); and low-income students (as at the University of Minnesota's Higher Education for Low-Income People [HELP] Center).

The University of Minnesota's center is a good example of how special group advising works. The university discovered that low-income students needed special assistance to persist in college. For such students, the social environment of the university posed as many problems as the academic requirements. The HELP Center was created to meet the needs of this special group. Funded by private, local, state, and federal money, it provides students with welfare and housing advice, employment and financial counseling, emotional support groups for minorities and women, personal counseling, and academic tutoring. The staff consists of students, professional and community people, graduate students, and faculty members. Approximately 1,000 University of Minnesota students utilize HELP services, with white males making up only 15 percent of the total. Students who use the Center have lower attrition rates and higher grade-point averages than similar students who do not.

Sources of Advising

The sources of advising most frequently available to students include books and pamphlets, college orientation, faculty members, freshman seminars, administrators, professional counselors and counseling centers, students, and team advising. Other forms of advising occasionally available to students include computers and other communication technology, alumni, community resource people, and brokerage organizations.

BOOKS AND PAMPHLETS

Two types of advising literature are produced for students: publications by colleges, and publications by other groups.

College Publications. The best known and most available of college publications is the college catalog, which usually describes a school's academic programs, regulations, requirements, course offerings, faculty, physical plant, admissions procedures, and social environment. College catalogs are often criticized for their trite public relations flavor, their lack of depth in treating curricular issues, and the practice of sometimes listing courses seldom or no longer given.

The Fund for the Improvement of Postsecondary Education (FIPSE) is responding to this catalog problem through its National Project 1, "Better Information for Student Choice." Via this project, FIPSE is supporting a variety of undertakings including the creation of consumer-oriented college catalogs or prospectuses at 11 pilot institutions ranging from the University of California, Los Angeles, to the National Radio Institute, a proprietary school in Washington, D.C. The prospectuses "include such things as current regional and national information on the availability of jobs by career field; accurate educational cost projections; descriptions and explanations of student attrition and retention rates; types of students who are most productive at the institution; current student and faculty perceptions of the quality of the learning processes and student-faculty interactions; the environment of the institution as viewed by various student subcultures; and assessment by graduates of the relationship between their educational experience and job requirements" (FIPSE, 1976, p. 149).

In addition, FIPSE has formed a National Project 1 task force under the auspices of the Education Commission of the States to explore the following issues: "Why better information; which types of information are helpful and why; what information can be provided responsibly and how; what are the process issues in prospectus building; does form of communication make a difference; what are the possibilities for determining the effectiveness of better information and for determining its validity; can better information be provided in order that prospective students might make comparisons among institutions; and what are the varying institutional impacts relative to voluntary versus mandated disclosure of information" (FIPSE, 1976).

This is not to say that college advising publications are wholly inadequate. A wide variety of publications are available that give students a better sense of their campus and how to use it. One example is *Introduction to Penn,* a book about the University of

Pennsylvania prepared by its students. There are also pamphlets for groups with special needs, such as the resource book for older students at the University of Massachusetts, which contains chapters on services available and campus activities and agencies. MIT produces a student-edited *Freshman Handbook* of more than 200 pages intended as a compendium of useful information for freshmen and their advisers with forms to request additional information and chapters such as "Residence/Orientation Week," "People to Talk With," "First Year Planning," and "Petty Bureaucracy." The University of Virginia offers a student handbook that discusses valuable courses to take outside the major and makes suggestions about how to get more out of a college education—such as reading three or four magazines regularly, taking a course in computer programming, buying a ticket to the university drama series, and auditing a course in a different school each term.

Externally Produced Publications. The other type of advising literature is externally produced, some by nonprofit higher education organizations and some by commercial firms. Examples of the former are the Connecticut Commission for Higher Education's guidebook on college transfer, which provides information on how to take courses at more than one school and on the accreditation status, financial aid policies, and admission requirements of the state's public and private colleges, and *The College Handbook,* a guide to two- and four-year colleges published by The College Entrance Examination Board. Examples of volumes produced for commercial consumption include a number of comparative guides to colleges containing information on enrollment, accreditation, location, academic environment, social environment, financial aid, and admissions policies of individual institutions. Barron's Education Service publishes *Barron's Profiles of American Colleges* and *Barron's Guide to Two-Year Colleges* as well as a series of much more detailed profiles of individual colleges. James Cass and Max Birnbaum periodically compile a volume entitled *A Comparative Guide to American Colleges for Students, Parents, and Counselors* describing four-year institutions. And the *Yale Daily News* produces an entirely different type of guide, *The Insiders Guide to the Colleges,* comprised of intimate profiles of fewer than a hundred colleges written with a student's eye toward life inside them.

COLLEGE ORIENTATION

College orientation may be a single-day presentation, at the University of South Florida and many other institutions, or a full-semester, credit-bearing course such as at Sterling College. At Sterling students are assigned to advising groups of 19 members led by a faculty member and two upperclass students who serve as the advisees' residence counselors. These groups seek to diagnose freshmen learning needs and abilities, provide freshmen with realistic expectations of college, give them an opportunity to explore their preconceptions of higher education, and enable them to form a relationship with a faculty member and more advanced students. The groups utilize a common syllabus and meet daily during orientation week and once weekly thereafter for a total of 18 sessions. Their course work is graded pass-fail, and students receive one credit for participation. The rationale for this credit is that Sterling has a nontraditional curriculum that requires serious study to understand, and credit encourages students to take the program seriously.

Innovative programs that require students to perform in unusual ways appear to require more elaborate and extended orientation exercises. This is true at Metropolitan State University, described in Chapter 13, which offers a competency-based, upper-division program for adults. It requires all students to enroll in a six- to ten-week orientation session prior to matriculation. During orientation, its academic program is explained in depth, and students are required to write an educational plan for their work at the university. For this purpose a 243-page textbook was written describing the university's requirements and resources with exercises to test students' comprehension of them.

Innovative academic programs are not the only reason for lengthy orientations, however. Another reason is innovative orientations. For instance, Wheaton College in Illinois recommends a 21-day, outward-bound-style orientation called Vanguard. This rugged wilderness experience is intended to build group solidarity among entering students, test each person's inner strength, encourage self-discovery under stress, and foster personal and religious growth.

FACULTY MEMBERS

Faculty members are formally involved in student advising at 91 percent of four-year arts and sciences colleges and 94 percent of four-year professional/technical colleges (business, education, engineering, health sciences, and trade and technical arts). They serve as formal advisers at 68 percent of two-year arts and sciences colleges and 65 percent of two-year professional/technical colleges (Catalog Study, 1976).

Fifty-three percent of undergraduates report that there are professors at their college whom they feel free to turn to for personal advice; 64 percent report knowing faculty members who take a special interest in their academic progress, and 46 percent say there are professors who greatly influenced their academic careers (Carnegie Surveys, 1975–76). Such relationships are considerably more likely to occur at selective liberal arts colleges than at the most research-oriented universities, however, as Table 14 shows.

At all types of institutions, nonetheless, faculty advising has some problems. Chief among them is its compulsory nature at many schools, which require that student programs and administrative petitions be signed by a faculty adviser and that most faculty

Table 14. Students relationships with faculty at the most selective liberal arts colleges and the most research-oriented universities

Student-faculty relationship	Selective liberal arts colleges	Most research-oriented universities
Student knows a professor he/she can turn to for advice on personal matters	69	39
Student knows a professor who takes a special interest in his/her academic progress	79	50
A professor or professors has had a great influence on student's academic career	58	40

Source: Carnegie Surveys, 1975–76.

members serve as advisers. Levine and Weingart (1973, p. 14) investigated this phenomenon and concluded:

> Compulsory advising evidently does promote greater student-faculty contact; to a lesser extent, the adviser does help to monitor student programs; and for very few students such advising has prevented severe mistakes. However, it simultaneously undermines the advising system. Advising, by virtue of its required administrative role, becomes routinized and transformed into an entirely administrative structure. Many students admitted that they contact their adviser to obtain his signature five minutes before semester programs are due. Others complained of going to their adviser with a problem only to have the adviser reach for a pen and ask "What has to be signed?" Abuses—students forging the signature of an adviser, advisers authorizing secretaries to sign program cards—were occasionally noted as well. On the other hand, a relatively small number of students said that only because of the compulsory consultations had they met their adviser and subsequently developed a good relationship.

Additional problems are symbolized by faculty complaints that student advisees do not come to visit them during office hours reserved for advising (or any other time), and student claims that faculty members are never in their offices (Levine, 1976a, p. 4). There is evidence that both assertions may be warranted. Some faculty (9 percent) have no scheduled office hours, making them virtually inaccessible to students outside of class; yet others (11 percent) hold 21 or more scheduled office hours, providing a good deal of privacy as the pitter-patter of student feet is seldom heard. At one extreme—the most research-oriented universities—the median number of scheduled office hours is three to four per week; at the other—less selective liberal arts colleges—the median number is seven to eight (Carnegie Surveys, 1975–76).

Students also complain that their advisers frequently know little about general education requirements, curricular options, or

faculty outside their departments, while faculty retort that their institutions neither offer rewards for advising, nor measure the
amount of time spent on advising as part of faculty work load
(Levine, 1976b, p. 5). This is especially serious in colleges such as
Hampshire College and Metropolitan State University (both described in Chapter 13) that have individualized student programs
and require a great deal of adviser-advisee interaction.

As institutions grow larger, the quality of advising appears to
decline. The number of staff grows sufficiently large that it becomes increasingly difficult for faculty members to know other
staff outside of their discipline; single departments become the
primary base for faculty operation; and large classes reduce student contact with faculty, particularly for freshmen and sophomores. Surprisingly, however, faculty advising is also criticized,
though not nearly as severely, at small colleges such as Bennington
and Hampshire, where advising is far better than usual. These
schools emphasize faculty advising as a central part of their undergraduate programs, but for students who have exaggerated expectations of advising and have frequently enjoyed a home life in
which they have been the center of attention, and for faculty who
spend more time on advising than teachers at other schools but still
feel they are skimping, negative perceptions are perhaps inevitable.

FRESHMAN SEMINARS

When used as a source of advising, the freshman seminar is a small
class for first-year students in which the instructor serves also as the
student's adviser. Seven percent of four-year arts and sciences colleges and four-year professional/technical colleges have freshman
seminar programs, as do 9 percent of the two-year arts and sciences
colleges and 3 percent of the two-year professional/technical colleges (Catalog Study, 1976). Students and faculty participating in
seminars have very positive attitudes about the advising function.
The advising relationship is perceived as more natural than that
found in traditional faculty advising because it is based on a shared
or common experience. Freshman seminars, however, have many
of the weaknesses of other types of faculty advising, such as the lack
of faculty knowledge about programs outside their field and the
absence of institutional rewards. (Freshmen seminars are also discussed in Chapter 1.)

ADMINISTRATORS

Twenty-five percent of four-year arts and sciences colleges and 17 percent of professional/technical colleges utilize administrators such as the dean of students as formal student advisers. This is also the case at 25 percent of two-year arts and sciences colleges and 13 percent of two-year professional/technical colleges (Catalog Study, 1976). Like faculty counselors, administrative advisers deal with all four types of advising. The primary student criticism of administrative advising is the occasional need to make appointments with busy administrators far in advance of a desired meeting and conflict between the roles student affairs administrators have as advisers and as college disciplinarians.

PROFESSIONAL COUNSELORS AND COUNSELING CENTERS

Most colleges employ professional counselors, people trained in personal advising such as psychologists and clerics, and some colleges house these counselors together in a centralized counseling center. Center services vary from a single type of advising, such as medical-psychological counseling, to all four types of advising. At two-year institutions, 69 percent of arts and sciences colleges and 93 percent of professional/technical colleges have professional counselors and/or professional counseling centers. At four-year institutions, 72 percent of the arts and sciences colleges and 88 percent of the professional/technical colleges have them (Catalog Study, 1976).

Two types of counselors that are not usually thought of when one talks of professionals are the ombudsperson and the residence counselor. *Ombudspersons* investigate campus complaints and make recommendations for their resolution. For example, at the University of California, Berkeley, "the Ombudsperson assists students and academic personnel with problems which may seem insoluble by the usual procedures and agencies" (University of California, Berkeley, 1975, p. 15). The university's two ombudsperson positions are filled by tenured faculty on a rotating basis. Ombudspersons are also employed at Cornell University, Kent State University, University of Pennsylvania, and San Jose State University, to name a few institutions.

Residence counselors are found more frequently than ombudspersons at colleges and universities. The job of the residence counselor, who may be an upper-division student, a graduate student, a faculty member, or simply a responsible adult, varies from informally to formally advising students and keeping order in university dormitories. At Sterling College, as noted earlier, the residence counselor is teamed with faculty in advising small groups of freshmen. At Lehigh College, the upperclass residence counselors are considered the primary resource for general counseling of first-year students and an excellent means for freshmen to learn about specialized counselors when needed. Residence counselors are formal elements in the academic advising systems at 8 pecent of all four-year arts and sciences colleges and at 5 percent of professional/technical schools (Catalog Study, 1976). They are not generally used in this capacity at two-year institutions, most of which are nonresidential.

STUDENT ADVISERS

Students most commonly advise one another through informal conversation, but they may also be involved formally in undergraduate advising. They are used as formal advisers at 4 percent of four-year colleges and universities and 2 percent of two-year arts and sciences colleges, but are not used in two-year professional/technical programs (Catalog Study, 1976). They serve in three primary capacities—as peer advisers, as assistants to faculty advisers, and as student advocates.

Peer advisers are students knowledgeable in some area of undergraduate concern who counsel other students who desire to learn about that area. Justin Morrill College at Michigan State University pays selected upperclass students between $2.35 and $2.75 an hour to advise freshmen and sophomores. Offices are set aside for peer advisers to make them more readily available and each adviser works at least ten hours per week. Justin Morrill students are pleased with the program, and the student advisers feel the program's success is attributable to the advisers' ability to provide information that faculty members are either unaware of or may feel uncomfortable sharing. One weakness of the program is that student advisers cannot make major program decisions, which sometimes prolongs bureaucratic procedure. Another is its cost. A program like Justin Morrill's, with ten advisers working ten hours per school week, would cost at least $7,500 per academic year. But voluntary programs in which peer advisers are not paid tend to have less staying power.

Students as assistants to faculty advisers have been used at Sterling College, as described earlier, and also at Trinity College in Connecticut, Brown University, and Haverford College. Depending upon the college, students may volunteer their time, receive academic credit, or get paid for acting as an assistant. When these programs are good, they can be very, very good, as they combine the strengths of faculty and peer advising while reducing several of the weaknesses. But when they are bad, they can be horrid, as is the case when a faculty member and his assistant each assume the other is doing the counseling.

Student advocacy is counseling designed to protect the student as consumer. At Brown University, for example, students have created, with administrative assistance, a curriculum resource center designed to advise students about possibilities for individual majors and group independent study and about ways to get proposals for them successfully through the appropriate university committees.

TEAM ADVISING

Team advising is counseling by groups of two or more persons who may be students, faculty members, administrators, other college staff, or community resource people. Team advising can involve periodic student meetings with the advising group, as is the case at the University of Alabama's New College, or single sessions with the advising team, as in Haverford College's recent "freshman inquiry." At New College, which requires each student to plan an individualized undergraduate program, students must develop an advising committee consisting in varying proportions of people from the University of Alabama and the surrounding community. The team is supposed to meet with the student at least once each term. In practice it is frequently a difficult and laborious chore for students to find common meeting times for all advising team members. Accordingly, the student is sometimes forced to meet with members individually, which occasionally results in conflicting advice, or to consult primarily with the team chairperson. When the entire team can be brought together, students generally find the experience rich and rewarding.

Haverford's "freshman inquiry" was a one-time advising session at the end of the freshman year for which each freshman was required to write a 1,500-word essay discussing his current intellectual position and future academic plans. The freshman then met with an advising team which consisted of a senior student and three faculty members from the natural sciences, social sciences, and humanities, including the freshman's premajor adviser. The team was charged with approving the freshman's academic plan, recommending changes in the plan, or requiring the inquiry to be repeated at a later date. The vast majority of Haverford faculty and students who participated in the inquiry had very positive feelings about it and thought it a useful extension of faculty advising. The most serious drawback of the inquiry was the amount of time it required of faculty members. Numerous Haverford faculty characterized it as physically draining (Levine and Weingart, 1973, p. 17). For this reason, faculty interest in it waned after only a few years and the program was subsequently ended.

Single-session team advising is far less common than periodic team advising, which tends to be associated with individualized undergraduate curricula. Team advising of both types is found more often in arts and sciences colleges than professional/technical colleges. Three percent of four-year arts and sciences colleges and 2 percent of two-year arts and sciences colleges at two-year institutions use team advising, compared to only 1 percent of four-year professional/technical programs and 0 percent of two-year professional/technical programs (Catalog Study, 1976).

COMPUTERS AND OTHER COMMUNICATIONS TECHNOLOGY

Computers and other communications technology are infrequently used for advising, but current experiments such as the Oregon Career Information System, the Education Testing Service's System of Interactive Guidance and Information (SIGI), and televised advising at the Williamsport Area Community College indicate that the approach has future potential for mass as well as individualized advising.

Oregon's Career Information System is a computerized data bank containing information on common and even some exotic occupational fields, including job descriptions, necessary job skills, required training, places offering training, requirements for admission to training, and manpower projections. Subscribers to the system, including numerous Oregon high schools, libraries, and some colleges, have computer terminals that can be used by students individually or in groups to explore the varied educational and occupational possibilities. The computer language is simple English, and the system is programmed to help students correct errors in communicating with the computer. The system has now been adopted in several locations around the country besides Oregon.

SIGI is also a computerized guidance system, but its purpose is different though complementary to the Oregon system. It involves a six-step procedure that (1) helps students rate occupational values; (2) locates job possibilities consistent with those values; (3) compares occupations of interest; (4) predicts the possibility of getting various grades in occupational preparatory programs; (5) provides lists of local colleges offering programs, sample programs, and sources of financial aid; and (6) explains the risks and rewards of different professions. SIGI, which is significantly more expensive than the Oregon system though popular in field tests, is not being readily adopted by colleges even though ETS is providing the software at very low cost. The reason is money. Student personnel offices generally lack the funds to maintain the system or obtain access to computers even on campuses having extensive computer facilities.

Television advising at Williamsport Community College has involved a 45-minute live TV broadcast giving general information about various types of college financial aid programs. Viewers are given guidelines for state and national aid programs and are encouraged to call in questions during the show.

ALUMNI

Alumni generally make willing advisers, are quite happy to counsel undergraduates without pay, and are flattered to be asked to serve by their alma maters; yet they are rarely used. Stanford University and the University of Cincinnati are exceptions. Stanford established a "paper bank" whereby undergraduates could obtain alumni reactions to their course papers. Such comments are a helpful addition to academic advising. The University of Cincinnati uses alumni for career advising. In March 1977, 560 alumni were available to counsel undergraduates and assist them in exploring 58 different fields in which the alumni were employed. Student reaction to both the Stanford and Cincinnati programs has been extremely positive.

COMMUNITY RESOURCE PEOPLE

Community resource people live or work near a college and are able to contribute to the institution's program by advising part time at low or no cost in their field of expertise. Retired professionals, people active in community affairs and commerce, and individuals who have temporarily or permanently left careers to raise a family are frequent sources for community resource people. Metropolitan State University, described in Chapter 13, is one institution that makes extensive use of such people, currently employing some 290 of them as faculty members and advisers. Money is available for each Metropolitan State student to arrange a one-hour formal advising session with a community resource person of his or her own choosing regarding vocational, academic, and personal concerns. Community resource people also advise Metopolitan State students on internships at their places of work.

BROKERAGE ORGANIZATIONS

Brokerage organizations provide adults who are not attending institutions of higher education with low- or no-cost outreach advising, including education and career information; counseling; assessment of prior experience; referrals to educational institutions, human service agencies, or industrial training programs; and advocacy of the student's case for admission or advanced placement in a desired program. Their basic objective is to aid adults in making decisions based on full and impartial information about whether and how best to seek additional education. The National Center for Educational Brokering listed 200 existing brokerage organizations in 1978, but brokering can be done by independent agencies, consortia of colleges, libraries, labor unions, businesses, education officers of the armed services, special group centers such as women's centers and minorities centers, educational opportunity centers, and possibly even individual colleges. At present, the phenomenon is too new to evaluate. However, a description of one independent brokerage organization, the Capital Higher Education Service of Hartford, Connecticut, appears in Chapter 13.

Concerns and Proposals

Three major criticisms of advising are discussed below. Where appropriate, proposals for improvement are noted.

Criticism 1: There is too much advising in the American college; this serves only to coddle undergraduates and keep them dependent.

The United States is said to have one of the most extensive systems of student advising and counseling in the world (Brubacher and Rudy, 1976, p. 331). However, this is not synonymous with saying that there is too much advising, nor is there any evidence to support the contention that advising coddles undergraduates and retards student independence. In contrast, there is data to suggest that there is a greater need for curricular information by students and potential students today than in previous years. For instance, the number of courses and educational alternatives available to undergraduates is greater than ever before; there are fewer curricular requirements of any kind than in many decades; the job market has not been tighter for college graduates since the depression; undergraduate aptitude test scores are declining; and new students, frequently socially and academically disadvantaged, are entering college in larger numbers than any other time in the history of higher education.

Criticism 2: The quality of academic advising is generally poor.

Levine and Weingart (1973) examined advising at 26 colleges that utilized most of the types and sources of advising discussed in this chapter. They concluded that "advising was . . . uniformly unsuccessful [and] . . . unable to serve the minimal function of providing students with sufficient knowledge to use the resources of the college most advantageously" (p. 18). Faculty advising, which is by far the most popular form of advising, gets the lowest marks.

Suggestions advanced to improve faculty advising include:

- making advising a part of each instructor's course load rather than a tacked on assignment (Metropolitan State University);
- encouraging faculty with strength in counseling to emphasize advising in their course loads (Mayhew and Ford, 1971);
- initiating in-service sessions for faculty to keep them abreast of curricular developments outside their departments (Sterling College);
- adopting faculty reward systems that encourage faculty effort in advising (Sarah Lawrence College);
- and pairing faculty and students with similar expectations of the advising relationships (Levine and Weingart, 1973).

To improve the overall quality of advising, the most successful approach seems to be the use of a combination of advising sources with overlapping strengths and weaknesses.

Criticism 3: Advising divides students into academic, vocational, and personal components and places emphasis largely on the academic, making complete student counseling difficult and in some cases impossible.

This criticism is widely supported. Levine and Weingart (1973, p. 19) have said that the pressure of increased enrollments has forced "the simplification of advising to the point that the affective component has been eliminated in favor of the more easily tended cognitive component." Mayhew and Ford (1971, p. 44) also characterize advising as bifurcated and feel this division makes "the intellectual side of a student . . . of concern to professors, but all other facets of human personality [are] relegated to someone else." They go on to say that "this system replaces the concern with the total student which the colonial college took or pre–World War II liberal arts professor assumed to be his proper job. We now have a cadre of specialists with no one striving for fully integrated development of a maturing adult." Faculty and students concur with this diagnosis. As noted earlier, the vast majority of faculty and students responding to the 1975–76 Carnegie Council surveys said undergraduate education would be improved if more attention were paid to the emotional development of students.

A frequently suggested solution to this problem is that offered by Mayhew and Ford (1971)—a greater integration of advising services. Where it is lacking, more emphasis might also be placed upon personal and vocational advising. This integration has been successfully accomplished in a number of special group advising facilities such as the University of Minnesota General College's HELP Center, which was discussed earlier in this chapter.

References

Bolles, R. N. *What Color Is Your Parachute: A Practical Manual for Job Hunters and Career Changers.* Berkeley, Calif.: Ten Speed Press, 1974.

Brubacher, J. S., and Rudy, W. *Higher Education in Transition: A History of American Colleges and Universities, 1636–1976.* (3rd ed.) New York: Harper & Row, 1976.

Carnegie Surveys, 1975–76.
This project is described in the Preface.

Catalog Study, 1976.
This research is discussed in the Preface.

Fund for the Improvement of Postsecondary Education. *Resources for Change: A Guide to Projects 1976–77.* Washington, D. C.: U.S. Government Printing Office, 1976.

Levine, A. "Reflections of an Itinerant Interviewer: A Sketch of Undergraduate Curriculum Trends." A monograph prepared for the Carnegie Council on Policy Studies in Higher Education. Berkeley, Calif., June 1976a (mimeographed).

Levine, A. *Why Innovation Fails: The Institutionalization and Termination of Innovation in Higher Education.* Unpublished doctoral dissertation. State University of New York, Buffalo, 1976b.

Levine, A., and Weingart, J. *Reform of Undergraduate Education.* San Francisco: Jossey-Bass, 1973.
Chapter 2 of this volume examines five different types of advising at 11 different colleges.

Mayhew, L. B., and Ford, P. J. *Changing the Curriculum.* San Francisco: Jossey-Bass, 1971.

Rudolph, F. *The American College and University: A History.* New York: Knopf, 1962.

University of California, Berkeley. *General Catalog 1975–76.* Berkeley: University of California Press, 1975.

7

Credits and Degrees

Definition and History

The *credit* is a time-based, quantitative measure assigned to courses or course-equivalent learning. It is usually defined as 50 minutes of instruction per week for a term. As terms vary in length, credits are usually referred to as semester or quarter credits. *Unit* and *credit hour* are synonyms for *credit*.

The *degree* may be thought of as a grade or rank that colleges and universities confer upon students for their educational attainments. The bachelor's degree and the associate's degree are the two principal types awarded at the undergraduate level.

Credits and degrees are closely related. When students earn a predetermined number of credits, they are usually rewarded with degrees. It is important to note, however, that all undergraduate degrees are not credit based. The most common alternative requires that students complete a specified number of courses, each of equal weight, to earn a degree. For instance, Amherst College requires that students complete 32 semester courses in order to graduate with a bachelor of arts degree. Other alternatives will be discussed later in the chapter.

History of Degrees

The earliest degrees, doctoral degrees, were awarded at the University of Bologna in the early thirteenth century. The degree, which required six to eight years of study, signified admission into the ranks of the university faculty. Four to five years into the doctoral course, the student became a *baccalaureus*, authorized to tutor or offer informal lectures. In order to achieve this distinction, the student was required to engage in a disputation and pass an oral examination administered by a faculty panel (Spurr, 1970, pp. 9–11).

The baccalaureate was also a feature of the University of Paris and Oxford University curricula. At Paris, students were required to complete a liberal arts program or achieve bachelor's status prior to entering the advanced and more eminent faculties of canon law, theology, and medicine. At Oxford, where English faculty congregated after their expulsion from the University of Paris, the arts curriculum and baccalaureate were emphasized rather than graduate study and the master's degree (which was the equivalent of a Bologna doctoral degree).

The Oxford system was also adopted at Cambridge University, which was established by Oxford faculty and students. And from Cambridge the bachelor of arts (B.A.) degree and master of arts (M.A.) degrees were imported to America.

The first nine bachelor of arts degrees were awarded at Harvard in 1642. To earn a bachelor of arts degree from Harvard, a student was required to attend the college for at least three years and ten months and complete a fully prescribed curriculum. The Harvard master of arts required little more than paying fees for three additional years without getting into trouble—there was not even a residence requirement (Brubacher and Rudy, 1976, p. 20).

New forms of the bachelor's degree were developed in America as early as the second half of the eighteenth century. The University of Pennsylvania introduced the bachelor of medicine (B.M.) degree in 1768, and William and Mary first awarded the bachelor of law (B.L.) in 1793. However, of the 9,144 baccalaureate degrees conferred before 1801, all except 150 were bachelor of arts degrees. The remainder were bachelor of medicine (149) and bachelor of law (1) degrees (Eells, 1965, p. 84).

Other baccalaureate degrees, such as the bachelor of science (B.S.) and bachelor of philosophy (Ph.B.), were created during the nineteenth century. The first bachelor of science degree was awarded in 1851 by Harvard's Lawrence Scientific School for completion of a three-year program. It was preceded in 1835 by the bachelor of natural science degree at Rensselaer Polytechnic Institute. The first bachelor of philosophy was awarded for a modern/ scientific course of studies at Yale in 1852.

Until the nineteenth century, the bachelor's degree was the only earned degree offered by American colleges. Women's degrees, which differed in title as well as content, were a short-lived departure. In 1835, Van Doren College for Young Ladies was empowered to grant the degree of mistress of polite literature. In 1853 Beaver College began awarding the mistress of liberal arts degree. And in 1873 Wheaton College gave students the sister of arts degree.

Earned graduate degrees were awarded for the first time in 1853, when the University of Michigan granted its first academic master's degree. Eight years later Yale conferred the first Ph.D.

Another major development of the nineteenth century was the creation of the two-year associate's degree. The world's first associate's degree, the associate in science, was granted at England's University of Durham in 1873. The University of Chicago awarded the first American associate's degrees in 1898. It offered associate in arts, associate in literature, and associate in science degrees.

Since the nineteenth century the number of college degrees has continued to grow. Degrees are no longer all campus based or even college based. As noted earlier, corporations such as General Electric, IBM, and AT&T now award the baccalaureate degree. In 1970, New York state introduced an even more radical departure from traditional degree practices. It offered bachelor's and associate's degrees through the Regents External Degree program solely by means of examinations and validation of accumulated college-equivalent credits. This external degree program (further discussed in Chapter 9) is not associated with any campus, offers no courses, and employs no faculty.

History of the Credit System

The credit system was not introduced until the 1870s. It was in part a product of the growing practice of allowing students to include elective courses in their undergraduate programs. Colleges needed some mechanism for keeping track of the comparative academic worth of the courses students took and of student progress toward their degrees. It was also an outgrowth of the expansion of public secondary education. Standards became necessary for colleges to evaluate applicant records from a large number of schools offering a variety of programs of varying quality. The credit system responded to both needs.

Dietrich Gerhard (1955) divides the development of the credit system into two phases. During the first or introductory phase, which reached a peak in the 1870s and 1880s, colleges began to measure the teaching of subject matter in course and hour units. During the second or consolidating phase, which started around the turn of the century, high schools as well as colleges assigned credit units of different sorts to their courses and stated their graduation requirements in terms of credits.

Charles W. Eliot symbolically inaugurated phase one in 1869 with his maiden speech as president of Harvard University, in which he proclaimed his commitment to the elective system. In 1870–71, the Harvard catalog stopped listing the studies each of the four classes was required to take and began listing individual courses, each with its own number. By 1884, requirements for the bachelor's degree were stated as 18.4 courses (Gerhard, 1955, p. 653). The University of Michigan established quantitative course accounting even before Harvard. In 1877, it required students to take 24 to 26 full courses to earn a degree, a "full course" being defined as "five exercises a week during a semester, whether in recitations, laboratory work, or lectures" (p. 654). This system, or one like it, was adopted by most colleges with elective curricula before the turn of the century.

The second phase of the credit system's development began in 1892, when Charles W. Eliot encouraged the National Education Association to appoint a Committee of Ten to look into college–high school relations. One of the concerns of this committee, chaired by Eliot, was the lack of standardization in the high school curriculum. To improve this situation, the Committee of Ten recommended that the subjects taught in high schools be taught in the same way to all students enrolled regardless of their educational aspirations and that all subjects be held of equal rank for admission to college (see Appendix A). In this way the committee, composed of well-known and influential educators, hoped to standardize and make uniform the secondary school program. Allowance was not made for differences among schools.

In the 1890s, another approach was taken to the problem— the introduction of a standardized measure of high school studies. In 1895, the New York State Regents proposed the creation of the *count,* which was "ten weeks of work in one of three subjects taken five days a week" (Brubacher and Rudy, 1976, p. 249). In its stead, Eliot in 1897–98 suggested the *point,* defined as approximately a half year's work in one subject consisting of four to five lessons a week in school or a term in college. Eliot recommended 20 points for college admission (Gerhard, 1955, pp. 656–657).

An 1899 report of the Committee on College Entrance Requirements echoed Eliot's sentiments. The committee recommended a list of subjects that should be common to all high school programs and required for college admission. The subjects included four units (four years) of foreign language, two units (two years) of mathematics, one unit (one year) of history, and one unit (one year) of science (Gerhard, 1955, p. 657). The committee's unit was the equivalent of two of Eliot's points.

The recommendation was adopted as policy in 1900 by the newly established College Entrance Examination Board of the Middle Atlantic States and Maryland, which had been created to encourage uniform admissions requirements and provide for a common board to examine students. In 1902, the North Central Association elaborated upon the work of the committee by defining the unit as a course lasting not less than 35 weeks and consisting of four to five meetings a week for not less than 45 minutes each. The unit was firmly established in 1906 by The Carnegie Foundation for the Advancement of Teaching; Eliot was chairman of the board. The Foundation offered college faculty a pension if their institution conformed to certain standards, one of which was "to require 14 'units' of high school credit for admission, each unit signifying five recitations a week throughout the year in one subject" (Rudolph, 1977, p. 222). By 1908, the unit became known as the "Carnegie unit" as a consequence of the pension program and a national conference organized by the Foundation on college entrance requirements. At that time the unit was defined as "any one of four courses carried five days a week during the secondary school year" (Rudolph, 1962, p. 438).

Since the first decade of the century, the credit system has persisted and expanded with little more than procedural changes. During the 1920s and 1930s, a number of curriculum experiments sought to dethrone the system. They included the Honors Program at Swarthmore College (1921), Meiklejohn's Experimental College at the University of Wisconsin (1927), The College of the University of Chicago (1931), and St. John's College (1937). At these institutions the credit system was perceived to undermine undergraduate education. Each adopted a noncredit-based model program that attracted national attention (case studies on each can be found in Chapter 12). Needless to say, these institutions did not restrain the use of the credit system. In recent years the award of credit has even been extended to out-of-class and out-of-college learning, as described in Chapter 9. In 1968, a new form of credit, the "continuing education unit," was created to measure "all significant learning experiences of postsecondary level for which degree credit is not earned" (Kaplan and Veri, 1974, p. 5), primarily to validate these experiences for job advancement purposes. One continuing education unit is awarded for every ten contact hours of continuing or nondegree credit education.

State of Credits and Degrees

Credits

With rare exception all undergraduate degree programs in the United States rely upon the credit system or equally weighted course system. The exceptions are of three basic types. One is the *integrated curriculum,* a completely required undergraduate program which is not broken down into course units. St. John's College's program based on the great books (described in Chapter 12) is of this type.

The second is the *progress by examination curriculum,* in which the degree is earned by passing tests rather than courses. Students can theoretically earn credits by taking courses at such colleges, but these credits are used mainly for transfer purposes in earning a degree at another institution and have no bearing on graduation. Hampshire College has a progress by examination curriculum, which is discussed in Chapter 9.

The third type is the *competency-based curriculum,* in which students must achieve specified learning outcomes in order to earn a degree. Credits are irrelevant to the process, though they can be used in the same way as those earned in a progress by examination curriculum. Alverno College has such a program (see Chapter 9).

The value of the credit varies significantly from college to college. The reason is that the credit is defined on the basis of a term, and terms are variable in length. For example, the semester term averages about 15 weeks while the quarter term averages 10 weeks. As a result, the average semester credit entails 50 percent more class time than the quarter credit.

This is taken into account in formulating degree requirements. Nationally the baccalaureate degree requires an average of 123 semester credit hours or 185 quarter credit hours. An associate's degree requires half that number of credits—an average of 62 semester credit hours or 93 quarter credit hours (Blackburn and others, 1976, p. 10).

Between 1967 and 1974, the number of credits required to earn a degree declined slightly. On the average, the bachelor's degree dropped two credits from 125 semester credit hours to 123, and the associate's degree dropped a single credit from 63 semester credits to 62. However, the specific number of credits required for a degree varies even among colleges using the same calendar. The number is greatest among less selective liberal arts colleges (125 semester credit hours) and least among the most selective liberal arts colleges (119 hours) (Blackburn and others, 1976, pp. 10–11).

Degrees

Hundreds of types of bachelor's and associate's degrees are awarded. There are currently almost 200 different associate's degrees[1] and 650 types of bachelor's degrees, ranging from the bachelor of sacred music to the bachelor of welding engineering (Furniss, 1973).

---

[1]Based on a telephone conversation with American Association of Community and Junior Colleges, March 1977.

BACHELOR'S DEGREES

Despite this diversity, the bachelor of arts (B.A.) and the bachelor of science (B.S.) are the most common of the baccalaureate degrees. Ninty-nine percent of four-year arts and sciences colleges and 25 percent of four-year professional/technical colleges offer the bachelor of arts degree. The bachelor of science is awarded by 82 percent of four-year arts and sciences colleges and 85 percent of professional/technical colleges (Catalog Study, 1976).

No universal differences separate the two degrees. Both consist of general education, a major, electives, and sometimes basic skills components. As Chapter 2 noted, the B.S. is likely to require more courses in the major than the B.A.; the B.S. is awarded significantly more often in the natural sciences than in the humanities; and the B.A. is used four times as often by arts and sciences colleges than professional/technical schools. Beyond this, differences depend on individual college policies, including (1) offering students a choice of degrees with no distinction between them; (2) requiring more advanced courses for the B.S.; (3) offering fewer electives in the B.S. program; (4) requiring a minor for the B.S.; (5) requiring a thesis or project for the B.S.; and (6) having different general education requirements for the B.S. (at such schools, the B.A. program is likely to require slightly more general education) (Catalog Study, 1976).

Another type of baccalaureate degree offered by a number of colleges is the bachelor in general studies, also called the bachelor of liberal arts or bachelor of liberal studies. It is offered by 10 percent of four-year arts and sciences colleges and less than 1 percent of four-year professional/technical schools (Catalog Study, 1976). The general studies degree is characterized by a ceiling on the number of courses students may take in the area of concentration and, in some programs, by an emphasis on general education. The University of Denver, the University of Michigan, and the University of Minnesota are among the institutions awarding such degrees.

ASSOCIATE'S DEGREES

Among associate's degrees, the associate in arts (A.A.), the associate in science (A.S.), and the associate in applied science (A.A.S.) are the most popular types. They are offered at both two- and four-year colleges. At two-year institutions, the associate in arts is offered in 100 percent of the arts and sciences programs and 29 percent of the professional/technical programs; the associate in science is found in 41 percent of the arts and sciences programs and 44 percent of the professional/technical programs; and the associate in applied science is awarded in 7 percent of arts and sciences programs and 41 percent of professional/technical programs. Associate's degrees are not as common at four-year colleges. Among four-year arts and sciences colleges, 20 percent offer the A.A., 9 percent offer the A.S., and 1 percent offer the A.A.S. Among four-year professional/technical colleges, 4 percent award the A.A., 10 percent award the A.S., and 2 percent award the A.A.S. Over three-fourths of four-year arts and sciences colleges (77 percent) and four-year professional/technical colleges (87 percent) offer no associate's degrees (Catalog Study, 1976).

The differences between the three types of associate's degrees are more clear-cut than is the case with the baccalaureate degrees. General education, majors, electives, and basic skills may be part of any of the degrees. However, on the average, the associate in arts degree requires the most general education (a median of 61–70 percent of the course of study) and the associate in applied science requires the least (a median of 21–30 percent). The associate in science fits squarely in the middle (a median of 41–50 percent). With regard to concentration, the degrees are exactly reversed. The median amount of the course of studies required in the major for the A.A.S. is 61–70 percent; for the A.S., 60–61 percent; and for the A.A., 41–50 percent (Catalog Study, 1976).

Associate's degrees also differ by the subject areas in which they are offered. The associate in arts is designed for four-year college transfer and tends to be used more by two-year arts and sciences colleges and four-year institutions than the other two degrees. The associate in applied science is offered primarily in occupational/technical programs and is not usually a transfer degree. The associate in science is used equally in arts and sciences and professional/technical programs, but in arts and sciences programs it is more often awarded in the sciences than in the humanities. The A.S. is sometimes intended for transfer and sometimes not.

Despite the widespread availability of the three associate's degrees, relatively few community college students graduate with them (Monroe, 1972, p. 208). The reasons include early transfer to four-year institutions, enrollment in nondegree programs, taking a job prior to completing the full course of study, and dropping out. As a result, associate's degree requirements tend to be of little concern to community college students. Of more importance to them are the curriculum requirements of transfer institutions and potential employers.

Nondegrees

Not all college programs offer degrees. Some offer certificates and others offer no award. Certificate programs are, for the most part, highly specialized career courses which are usually, though not universally, shorter than degree programs. They are occasionally geared for admission to licensure or career entrance tests, and they are far more common at two-year colleges than four-year colleges and universities. Thirty-one percent of two-year arts and sciences programs and 83 percent of two-year professional/technical programs award certificates. For instance, Monroe Community College in Rochester, New York, has 16 certificate programs in areas such as small business management, broadcast technology, and criminal justice. Among four-year institutions, only 21 percent of arts and sciences colleges and 28 percent of professional/technical colleges offer certificates (Catalog Study, 1976).

Nondegree programs may also consist of activities such as continuing education or community service courses, short-term conferences or workshops, and course attendance by nondegree students. Many institutions, ranging from Harvard University to Miami-Dade Community College, engage in all three. In the fall of 1974, 1,200,283 students were enrolled in nondegree programs offered by institutions of higher education (U.S. National Center for Education Statistics, 1976).

Concerns and Proposals

Criticism 1: The credit system is inappropriate for undergraduate education.

Barbara Burn (1974) has examined the credit system and identifies thirteen weaknesses: (1) The credit system produces fragmented knowledge as a result of breaking education into small pieces; (2) it makes no provision for integrating knowledge, and many students are unable to do this themselves; (3) it denigrates the value of serious scholarly work by assuming that all learning experiences offering the same number of credits are interchangeable and have equal validity; (4) it makes time serving the basic requirement for the degree; (5) it falsely assumes that students learn at the same rate; (6) it falsely assumes that all faculty teaching skills are equal; (7) its focus on a common-time formula gives undue emphasis to form over content; (8) it distorts student motivation by a philosophy that views the purpose of education as the accumulation of course credits rather than learning; (9) its emphasis on contact hours favors teacher-dependent students rather than students who can learn on their own and need only the assistance of a faculty member; (10) its emphasis on classroom learning is inconsistent with new and nontraditional forms of higher education; (11) it is unnecessarily expensive in time and energy; (12) it has no quality standard associated with it; and (13) it emphasizes the certification function of colleges and universities and plays down other functions.

However, Burn also points out twelve strengths: (1) Because the credit system is course based, it allows a student who fails to repeat only a course—not a term or year of work; (2) it makes possible the offering of higher education in a variety of units by assigning varying amounts of credit to different instructional arrangements; (3) it permits a variety of alternative academic calendars; (4) it allows students to work toward their degrees at their own pace by adjusting the number of credits they take; (5) it can reduce the cost of education by incorporating credit by examination and credit for prior learning; (6) it can broaden the learning opportunities available to students if credit is awarded for independent study and nontraditional forms of education; (7) it helps students who select a new major or make other program changes avoid starting all over, since previously accumulated credits can often be applied to the degree; (8) it permits new courses to be initiated more easily than in higher education systems with fixed programs; (9) it allows more individualized and student centered education than a fixed curriculum; (10) it gives teachers a great deal of latitude in determining what and how to teach; (11) it facilitates interinstitutional transfer of credits; and (12) by encouraging the interchangeability of credits among different institutions, it permits colleges autonomy in designing their programs.

One cannot easily conclude that the credit system is educationally inappropriate; it is difficult to know whether the strengths are greater than the weaknesses or vice versa. However, some colleges have created programs designed to maintain the strengths of the credit system while reducing its major weakness of fragmentation. For example, Reed College and New College of the University of South Florida require students to complete a senior thesis, which is designed to decrease course fragmentation, to introduce students to serious scholarship, and to add a dimension to the baccalaureate beyond just "putting in time." Bard and Haverford colleges require students to pass a comprehensive examination intended to offer an integrating experience, to reduce course fragmentation, and to provide a common quality standard for students with different learning abilities. Bowdoin College offers students a general education senior seminar to integrate what may have been a previously fragmented college education. Curriculum requirements in general education and concentration at other institutions serve the same function. In addition, they are a means of stating that all learning is not equivalent.

Criticism 2: Degrees have little meaning.

This criticism is usually raised on the grounds that almost a thousand different baccalaureate and associate's degrees are offered and that there is wide variety in the content of degrees, even those bearing the same name (see Chapters 1 and 2). Individuals unhappy with this situation suggest a number of improvements. They range from Robert Hutchins' proposal (1967) for a uniform system of degree programs and standards (see Chapter 10) to Robert Wolfe's recommendation (1969, pp. 151–153) that degrees be abandoned (see Chapter 11). Less radical proposals include Verne Stadtman's suggestion that degrees be treated simply as certificates of program completion by individual colleges—not as cross-institutional awards of greater significance[2]—and Stephen Spurr's recommendation (1970, p. 183ff) that the number of different degrees awarded be substantially reduced—which would not be difficult, as many degrees are nothing more than a B.A. or B.S. in a specialty area (for example, Bachelor of Science in Engineering). It was the Carnegie Commission's opinion (1973, p. 77) that any lack of common meaning would work itself out because degrees will ultimately become less important than a cumulative record of student educational accomplishment. The Educational Testing Service is putting this concept into action with the creation of the educational passport, a wallet-size microfiche which records the owners' educational and vocational accomplishments.

Criticism 3: The certification or degree-granting function of colleges undermines instruction.

Eighteen percent of students responding to the 1976 Carnegie Council undergraduate survey said that getting a degree was more important to them than the content of their courses. They said it most often at comprehensive colleges and universities (19 percent) and least often at selective liberal arts colleges (9 percent). Under circumstances like this, when ends are more important than means, the result is often circumventive innovation designed to reach the end without having to go through the accepted means for getting there. For higher education, the consequence can be "easy" degrees and low-quality education. Degree mills like Rochdale College, which offered the public a B.A. for $25 with no strings (such as going to class or studying) attached, can thrive in such an environment.

Over the years, a number of experiments have been undertaken to separate teaching from certification. Since 1921, Swarthmore has used external examiners to evaluate its honors students (see case study in Chapter 12). At Chicago during the Hutchins years, the teaching and examining functions were lodged in different parts of the university (see case study in Chapter 12). And

---

[2]Based on a conversation with Verne Stadtman, Carnegie Council on Policy Studies in Higher Education, January 1977.

Harold Hodgkinson (1974) has called for the creation of Regional Examining Institutes, which would engage in credentialing and certification rather than instruction (see Chapter 11).

References

Berg, I. *Education and Jobs: The Great Training Robbery.* Boston: Beacon Press, 1971.

Bird, C. *The Case Against College.* New York: David McKay, 1975.

Blackburn, R., Armstrong, E., Conrad, C., Didham, J., and McKune, T. *Changing Practices in Undergraduate Education.* Berkeley, Calif.: Carnegie Council on Policy Studies in Higher Education, 1976.

Brubacher, J. S., and Rudy, W. *Higher Education in Transition: A History of American Colleges and Universities, 1636–1976.* (3rd ed.) New York: Harper & Row, 1976.

Burn, B. "The American Academic Credit System." *Structure of Studies and Place of Research in Mass Higher Education.* Paris: Organisation for Economic Cooperation and Development, 1974, pp. 113–121.

This paper concisely discusses the origin, evolution, strengths, weakness, and future of the credit system.

Carnegie Commission on Higher Education. *Continuity and Discontinuity: Higher Education and the Schools.* New York: McGraw-Hill, 1973.

Carnegie Surveys, 1975–76.

This research is described in the Preface.

Catalog Study, 1976.

This project is discussed in the Preface.

Eells, W. C. *Degrees in Higher Education.* New York: The Center for Applied Research in Education, Inc., 1965.

This volume provides an introduction to the American degree structure and discusses the evolution and design of seven degrees—research doctorates, professional doctorates, master's degrees, bachelor's degrees, associate's degrees, and other degrees; necessary improvements in the degree structure are also discussed.

Freeman, R. B. *The Over-Educated American.* New York: Academic Press, 1976.

Furniss, W. T. *American Universities and Colleges.* (11th ed.) Washington, D.C.: American Council on Education, 1973.

Gerhard, D. "The Emergence of the Credit System in American Education Considered as a Problem of Social and Intellectual History." *AAUP Bulletin,* Winter 1955, *41,* 647–668.

This is a concise but very detailed history of the credit system in the United States.

Grasso, J. T. *On the Declining Value of Schooling.* Paper presented at the 1977 annual meeting of the American Educational Research Association. New York City, April 4–8, 1977.

Hodgkinson, H. L. "Regional Examining Institutes." In D. W. Vermilye (Ed.). *Lifelong Learners—A New Clientele for Higher Education: Current Issues in Higher Education 1974.* San Francisco: Jossey-Bass, 1974.

This article is discussed in Chapter 11.

Hutchins, R. M. *The Higher Learning in America.* New Haven, Conn.: Yale University Press, 1967.

The educational philosophy of Hutchins is discussed in Chapter 10.

Kapan, A. C., and Veri, C. C. *The Continuing Education Unit.* DeKalb, Ill.: ERIC Clearinghouse in Career Education, 1974.

Levine, A., and Weingart, J. *Reform of Undergraduate Education.* San Francisco: Jossey-Bass, 1973.

Monroe, C. R. *Profile of the Community College: A Handbook.* San Francisco: Jossey-Bass, 1972.

O'Toole, J. "The Reserve Army of Underemployed." *Change,* May 1975, 7 (4), 26–33.

Rudolph, F. *The American College and University: A History.* New York: Knopf, 1962.

Rudolph, F. *Curriculum: A History of the American Undergraduate Course of Study Since 1636.* San Francisco: Jossey-Bass, 1977.

Spurr, S. H. *Academic Degree Structures: Innovative Approaches.* New York: McGraw-Hill, 1970.

This volume is longer and more recent than Eells'. It also covers additional subjects, including "Post-Doctoral Recognition," "Degree Structures in Selected European Countries," "Secondary School–University Articulation," and "The Development and Nomenclature of Academic Degrees."

U.S. National Center for Education Statistics. *Digest of Education Statistics: 1975 Edition.* Washington, D.C.: U.S. Government Printing Office, 1976.

Wolfe, R. P. *The Ideal of the University.* Boston: Beacon Press, 1969.

This volume is discussed in Chapter 11.

8

Methods of Instruction

Definition and History

Until recently, very little was known about learning. The literature on the subject has presented a mass of contradictory theories, several of which have some empirical justification, and many of which have none. As a result, college and university instructors have all but ignored learning and concentrated instead upon the more comprehensible realm of teaching. It is assumed by many educators that quality teaching, whatever that may be, yields quality learning.

Teaching or instruction may be defined as guidance or direction intended to cause learning. In the early American college, it was usually the work of a single individual. At some colleges, the president taught all subjects to all students. At others the president was assisted by tutors—recent graduates who generally led an entire class through the whole undergraduate curriculum. Their primary methods of instruction were the recitation and disputation. For the recitation, they required students to repeat textbook assignments orally and verbatim. The quality of the exercise varied from simple textual regurgitation to Socratic dialogues based on the text. For the disputation, the instructor offered a proposition such as "we sin while we sleep." The student selected to defend or attack the proposition defined the relevant terms and then made his argument by use of Aristolean syllogisms. After he had made his case, other students argued the counterposition and the disputant responded in opposition. The entire procedure was carried out in Latin, the required language both in and out of class.

As late as 1750, the lecture was a rare but occasional supplement to the recitation. At first the lecture was no more than a substitute for textbooks. Teachers read their lectures slowly and students copied them down word for word. In the late eighteenth century, a week of undergraduate study at Yale consisted of 12 to 15 hours of recitation, 3 to 7 hours of disputation, and 2 to 4 hours of lecture (Brubacher and Rudy, 1976, p. 93).

The lecture came to replace recitation and disputation for several reasons. Tutors began to specialize, and more experienced people were hired as professors. Yale began appointing professors in 1755. With few textbooks available, the specialists found the lecture a more useful way to teach students than the other methods of instruction. In the late eighteenth century and early nineteenth century, scientists also found the lecture format more amenable to experimental demonstrations. In addition, students who went to Germany for graduate study returned as critics of the recitation and disputation. They believed the lecture, the predominant mode of German instruction, was a better educational tool. Finally, growth in undergraduate enrollments made it difficult for instructors to call on students often or intensively for recitation and disputation. This growth necessitated dividing instruction into classes. Harvard constructed its first classroom in 1766 and by then the division of studies into courses was well under way.

Recitations and disputations died neither quietly nor quickly. They had many defenders, including the authors of the 1828 Yale Report, who argued that recitations and disputations not only let faculty know if students were working, while lectures did not, but more important, caused students to exercise their "mental faculties." Exercising these faculties was the way students supposedly learned and expanded their capabilities. This theory of learning, called "mental discipline," prevailed until the first decade of the twentieth century, when the early psychological research of Edward Thorndike finally disproved it. Thus as late as 1870, Yale continued to use recitations as a method of instruction.

During the nineteenth century, several other instructional methods appeared. In the 1820s, Rensselaer introduced experiential learning on campus in chemistry and physics laboratory and off campus in surveying. Though the professions such as law and medicine had long trained their practitioners via apprenticeship or experience, Rensselaer was the first college to incorporate this type of study into its formal program. The idea spread quickly. In fact, manual labor programs, in which students were expected to learn from work experience, became quite popular in the 1820s and 1830s.

The blackboard was another product of the 1820s—used for the first time by a teacher at Bowdoin College in about 1823. This decade also saw the first offering of extension courses, at Union College.

Subsequent years witnessed experiments with the seminar, a German import, which at its inception consisted of a small group of students working with a professor in an area of his original research. In 1869, Charles Kendall Adams tried the seminar at the University of Michigan. Seven years later it became a staple in the curriculum at Johns Hopkins University.

In 1893, the correspondence course was tried at the University of Chicago. Study-by-mail programs mushroomed during the remainder of the 1890s.

By 1901, Harvard had 39 courses with over 100 students and 14 with over 200 students (Rudolph, 1977). A discussion class, designed to supplement lecture instruction originally called the "conference quiz section," was created at Harvard in 1904. The quiz section, which dramatically cut graduate student unemployment, was intended to reduce the negative features of large class size.

By 1910, independent study, in which the student learns largely on his or her own with faculty guidance, was available in the University of California's German department (Veysey, 1973, p. 31). In the same year, Harvard introduced a related endeavor, the tutorial, a formal course pairing one student and one faculty member. Within 14 years, independent and guided study of both types were found at 44 colleges and universities (Dressel, 1966, p. 32). Such opportunities were usually reserved for honors students and were accordingly called honors programs.

Since the first decade of this century, new methods of instruction have not been developed; although new methods of delivering instruction have appeared. In 1910, motion pictures were brought into the classroom. In the 1920s, radio was used. In 1959, the computer was employed for the first time. Two years later, Chicago City College began a television-based extension program. Nineteen sixty-one was also the year that S. N. Postlethwait introduced audio-tutorial instruction—programmed instruction based on a tape-recorded study guide supplemented with texts, films, and other learning materials. In 1966, Fred Keller and J. Gilmour Sherman invented the Personalized System of Instruction (PSI), a self-paced program relying on small sequential learning units with well-defined objectives and quick feedback on student performance.

State of Instruction

Instruction at American colleges and universities today relies upon six teaching methods—(1) live courses, (2) mass media, (3) new technologies such as the computer, (4) independent study, (5) experiential education, and (6) libraries.

Live courses

Live courses—which involve two or more students, usually an instructor, and face to face meetings—constitute by far the most common and certainly the most stereotypic form of collegiate instruction. But such courses can vary in many ways including size, duration, type of instructor, and teaching method. The following discussion describes the extent of variation in these characteristics and reports the evidence that exists about their impact on course effectiveness—beginning with perhaps the most controversial, class size.

CLASS SIZE

Forty-eight percent of all undergraduates have taken one or more courses with over 100 students, and fully 8 percent have taken all or most of their courses in large classes of this size. Such courses are most common at the most research-oriented universities, where 94 percent of the students have taken at least one, and 32 percent have taken most or all of their courses in this fashion. Large classes of this size are least common at community and junior colleges and the most selective liberal arts colleges, where only 8 to 9 percent of the students have had at least one and just 1 to 3 percent have had at least 99 classmates in most or all of their courses (Carnegie Surveys, 1975–76).

Fifty-eight percent of all undergraduates have taken at least one class with fewer than 15 students, and 5 percent have taken all or most of their courses in classes as small as this. Small classes are most often available to students at the most selective liberal arts colleges, where 88 percent have had at least one and 22 percent have taken most or all of their courses with fewer than 15 classmates. Students at most other types of colleges and universities have different experiences: Only 55 percent have had at least one small class at research universities, doctorate-granting universities, and community and junior colleges. Only 2 to 3 percent at research universities and doctorate-granting institutions have had all or most of their classes with fewer than 15 students, as is true of 7 percent at two-year colleges (Carnegie Surveys, 1975–76).

Despite arguments to the contrary, class size has not been shown to have a significant effect upon learning. Indicative of the best research in this area is a study by F. G. Macomber, who compared 23 courses, ranging from business to physics to literature, in terms of large, medium, and small enrollments. Macomber found no essential differences in subject matter acquisition among students in classes of different size studying similar subject matters (in Milton, 1972, pp. 22–23).

This does not mean that inherently expensive and seemingly inefficient small classes are without merit. They permit students to meet faculty members and fellow students in a more intimate setting. Their more personal ethos can serve as a source of motivation, offer more individualized attention, and encourage greater in-class participation. In fact, average student evaluations of teaching improve as class size decreases even when other variables known or believed to influence the ratings are held constant (Crittenden and others, 1975). The association of smallness with improved subject matter learning, however, is likely a consequence of the long-standing belief that the best education is a one-to-one relationship between student and teacher—the long-cherished image of Mark Hopkins and his student sharing a log.

DURATION

Courses also differ significantly in amount of time spent in the classroom. The impact of these differences has been tested by the staff of the Antioch Experiment on Independent Study (1958) and by Gruber and Weitman (1962) (in Milton, 1972, p. 22). The Antioch study reduced the amount of time spent in class from between 30 to 80 percent and Gruber and Weitman reduced class time by two-thirds—from three meetings per week to one per week—in subject areas ranging from freshman English to reinforced concrete design. Both studies found that alterations in class time or course length produced no substantial differences in learning.

Another controversial factor in course duration that will be discussed at greater length in Chapter 9 also shows little clear-cut evidence of differential effectiveness: offering several courses concurrently over a standard academic term, such as a quarter or semester, as opposed to offering "intensive" courses one at a time in a shorter period as part of a "block" plan. Advocates of both systems marshal evidence in support of their positions; but so far the evidence is more anecdotal than rigorous. Students who enroll in block plans, however, as at Colorado College, support the plan by large majorities.

INSTRUCTORS

Undergraduate courses are taught by faculty members, graduate students, undergraduates, and other teachers. Instructional effectiveness as judged by students varies widely within and among the groups.

Faculty Members. The qualities of the excellent faculty instructor have been a matter of concern to educational researchers (as well as students) for decades. Early research focused on the qualities needed by the "ideal" teacher. For example, a 1930 study by R. J. Clinton, one of the earliest researchers in this area, asked students to list the qualities of the ideal college professor. The resulting top five were (1) interest in students, (2) fairness, (3) pleasing personality, (4) sense of humor, and (5) subject mastery. Ten years later, a similar study was conducted by W. A. Bousfield, who found a marked change in desired characteristics that has persisted to the present. The big five on his list were (1) fairness, (2) mastery of subject, (3) interest in students and helpfulness, (4) organization of material, and (5) clear exposition (in Knapp, 1962, p. 303).

More recent research has gone beyond obtaining student opinions. For example, Wilson, Gaff, Dienst, Wood, and Bavery

(Wilson and others, 1975) asked both faculty members and students at eight institutions to nominate effective and impactful teachers on their campus; they found substantial agreement in student and faculty choices. And when they examined the differences between frequently nominated and unnominated faculty, they found that effective teachers prefer undergraduate teaching to graduate teaching and research; discuss contemporary issues in their courses; and make use of pedagogy which integrates analogies, stories, or examples from their own experiences into their lessons. Most important, effective teachers interact frequently and well with colleagues and students outside the classroom.

This conclusion is buttressed by student responses to the most recent Carnegie Council undergraduate survey. Fifty-six percent of the undergraduates disagree with the statement "A person can be an effective teacher without personally involving himself with his students." Disagreement is least among students at the most research-oriented universities (51 percent) and greatest among students at less selective liberal arts colleges (65 percent) (Carnegie Surveys, 1975–76).

Of surprise in the study by Wilson and others (1975) are the faculty characteristics that appear to have no impact on faculty teaching effectiveness. No difference in effectiveness is evident among faculty employing different classroom techniques such as the use of highly organized versus highly discursive styles of teaching, specified versus unspecified course objectives, detailed versus nondetailed class notes, wide varieties of differing viewpoints versus narrow range of viewpoints, and single-discipline orientations versus interdisciplinary orientations. In addition, the authors found that age and political orientation varied widely among effective teachers. The insignificance of political orientation is perhaps the most unexpected conclusion, as 42 percent of the undergraduates and 29 percent of the faculty responding to the 1975–76 Carnegie Council surveys believed that a professor's teaching inevitably reflected his or her political values.

No other characteristic of all these studied by Wilson and his colleagues has been the subject of more discussion and concern than faculty preferences for teaching or research—and their possible neglect of teaching in favor of research. Data from recent Carnegie Council surveys should help reassure students and the public on this point in light of the finding that effective and impactful teachers prefer teaching over research. Despite claims to the contrary, college faculty do view teaching rather than research as their primary job. More than three-quarters (76 percent) of them say they are more interested in teaching than research. Faculty are most inclined to this position at community and junior colleges (94 percent) and less selective liberal arts colleges (91 percent). Only at the most research-oriented universities do a majority have greater interest in research (54 percent) (Carnegie Surveys, 1975–76).

In this regard, more than three-fourths of college and university faculty (76 percent) agree that teaching effectiveness, not publications, should be the primary criterion for promotion (Carnegie Surveys, 1975–76). This opinion is shared by the smallest faculty contingent at research universities (48 percent) and the largest at community and junior colleges (96 percent), as Table 15 shows.

Graduate Assistants. Following faculty members, the most common undergraduate instructor is the graduate teaching assistant (TA). Twenty-two percent of college and university faculty members employ TAs in some or most of their undergraduate courses. They are used by a majority of faculty at the most research-oriented universities (51 percent), but by only 3 percent of faculty at less selective liberal arts colleges (Carnegie Surveys, 1975–76).

The teaching assistant has long been maligned. The reasons are several: (1) Most TAs are assigned to teach survey courses during the dissertation or predissertation stage of their education, a

Table 15. Faculty, by institution type, agreeing with the statement "Teaching effectiveness, not publications, should be the primary criterion for promotion of faculty"

Institutional type	Percentage of faculty agreeing
Research universities	48
Doctorate-granting universities	64
Comprehensive colleges and universities	84
Liberal arts colleges	91
Community and junior colleges	96

Source: Carnegie Surveys, 1975–76.

time when their research is generally narrowest and when it is probably least appropriate for them to teach a broad course. As a consequence, the successful teaching of a survey course by a TA requires sacrificing large amounts of time that must be taken from preparation of the dissertation (see Contemporary Civilization case study in Chapter 12). (2) Until a few years ago, teaching assistantships often were reserved for students who lacked sufficient ability to merit fellowships or research assistantships. (3) Teaching assistants are not taken as seriously by undergraduates as are faculty instructors. And (4) most TAs have had little if any training in teaching and teaching has until recently been considered by faculty and graduate students alike a way of earning money to stay in graduate school, not an educational experience. In fact, when J. E. Williams and C. L. Richman asked 200 psychology department chairmen in 1971 whether they agreed or disagreed that "the typical graduate of a conventional Ph.D. program is well prepared to assume his teaching responsibilities," approximately three-fourths of the chairmen disagreed (Milton, 1972, p. 103).

Students or Peer Teachers. A third type of course instructor, the peer teacher or undergraduate, is found in small numbers at 5 percent of four-year and 33 percent of two-year arts and sciences colleges. As a rule they are not found in professional/technical schools (Catalog Study, 1976). Levine and Weingart (1973, pp. 97–99) examined peer-taught courses at six colleges. Such courses, averaging well under a handful in any one term, are usually initiated when a student desiring to teach a course prepares a course outline containing a reading list and means for student and course evaluation. The potential peer instructor is then required to find a faculty adviser and submit the course outline to appropriate college committees for approval. Most of the approved courses are offered pass-fail.

Student teachers find the courses they teach to be difficult but worthwhile. They express disappointment over unanticipated problems and inability to achieve all of the goals they planned for their courses. Students who take peer-taught courses admit they do not work as hard as for a faculty-taught course. They also rate the course as lower in quality than a faculty-taught course, criticizing them for poor structure, the instructor's lack of knowledge, and inadequate classroom leadership. However, peer instructors are praised for their enthusiasm and informality.[1]

Other Instructors. Other types of instructor are community resource persons, professional school faculty members, team teachers, and group participants in leaderless seminars.

Community resource persons, like professional school faculty, possess instructional talents seldom tapped for undergradudate teaching. But 30 percent of the seminars offered in Tufts Experimental College are taught by community resource people and, as noted earlier, Metropolitan State University supplements its core faculty with several hundred community resource people who work full or part time in noncollege jobs in the Saint Paul/ Minneapolis community. In general, the teaching of community resource people is not rated as highly as that of full-time faculty. At least part of the reason is lack of classroom experience (Levine and Weingart, 1973, p. 89–90). Nonetheless, community resource people can be an economical source of instruction. They are usually flattered to be asked to teach and may be willing to accept nonpaying faculty positions or receive a small honorarium. However, to make effective continuing use of them, colleges have found it essential to keep them informed, interested, and active in institutional affairs. Failure to do this has resulted in attrition and curricular gaps, particularly at institutions which have one or more programs relying heavily upon outside assistance.

Professional school faculty, such as those teaching in the freshman seminar program at Stanford University, often find the opportunity to work with undergraduates a welcome and positive experience. For undergraduates, the contact with professional school faculty is rated highly. Moreover, for the institution, professional school faculty members can also be money savers; since their professional school teaching load may be light, they may agree to teach undergraduates occasionally without compensation.

---

[1]Undergraduates play a major educational role as assistants or "proctors" in PSI courses, as discussed later in this chapter; but they serve as surrogates for the course instructor rather than as independent teachers and hence are not included here.

Teaching teams can be composed of administrators, faculty, graduate students, undergraduates, or community resource people. According to the Carnegie Council surveys, 47 percent of undergraduates have taken one or more courses taught by a team of two or more people. Such courses are most common among students at the most selective liberal arts colleges (67 percent) and research universities (62 percent). They are least common among students at community and junior colleges (30 percent) (Carnegie Surveys, 1975–76). When team teaching works well, it is highly rated by students and faculty; however, it usually doesn't work well. Faculty who comprise instructional teams generally are used to working alone, are unfamiliar with subject matter outside their specialty, and tend to treat their teammates' specialty areas as sacrosanct. As a consequence, team teaching is often fragmented, becoming little more than several faculty sharing a common classroom. The larger the team the more often there tends to be discontinuity or lack of integration between individual faculty presentations. Furthermore, when team size increases, faculty attendance tends to drop off and a sense of responsibility for the course decreases. These are not insuperable obstacles but rather problems that must be dealt with in planning team-taught courses.

Leaderless courses form the final variation in instruction. Such classes consist entirely of students, as at Joseph Tussman's Experimental College Program at the University of California, Berkeley. Levine and Weingart (1973, p. 41) examined these classes and found them disappointing owing to "poor attendance and inability of the seminar to make progress without a faculty leader."

TEACHING METHOD

Live courses also differ in teaching method. Two types predominate: lectures, characteristic of the survey course taught by the great person; and discussions, characteristic of the seminar. Some courses depend primarily upon one of these methods; others use both. The most familiar arrangement combining the two is the large lecture with discussion sections.

Dubin and Taveggia (1968, pp. 36–38) examined 108 studies comparing the lecture and discussion methods of teaching and reported no differences in learning between students taught by lectures, discussions, or combinations of the two. McKeachie (1962, pp. 320–324) examined many of the same studies and found systematic differences in the studies that reported one method or the other superior. He concluded that each method of teaching has advantages, with the lecture superior for information learning and discussions superior for achieving higher-level objectives.

Brown and Thornton (1971) have examined the mistakes that instructors make in using lectures and discussions and offer several helpful suggestions on how to improve each. For lectures, they recommend the following (p. 84):

- By all means, remember that teaching is not synonymous with telling or describing. The purposes of the lecture are to summarize, to clarify, to stimulate, to humanize the materials of the course. It should synthesize, evaluate, criticize, and compare ideas and facts with which students have come in contact through out-of-class assignments.
- Introduce the lecture with a brief review of the work preceding. Indicate how the day's lecture fits into the course pattern.
- Narrow the lecture content to essential points that can be treated well rather than make a superficial survey of more than can be grasped in the period.
- As examples and illustrations of lecture points, use items that touch the backgrounds and experiences of the students. Plan use of examples in advance.
- Do not read the lecture. Make it as personal as possible, not obviously filtered through notes. Glance frequently at students in various parts of the room to assess reactions and probable comprehension. Repeat or rephrase obviously confused points. Pace delivery to allow the majority of students to follow.
- Give attention to voice control. Avoid monotonal expression; speak loudly enough to be heard in all parts of the room.
- Communicate enthusiasm for the subject.

- Even when discussion and oral reaction are not feasible or intended, use rhetorical questions to stimulate thinking.
- Summarize at the end of the lecture to review its main points; suggest the nature of the following period's work with suitable transitional comments.

For discussions, Brown and Thornton offer the following hints (p. 102):

- Build upon common experiences and understandings. This may involve a previous reading assignment, or a film used to present the discussion stimulus during the first part of the class period.
- Clarify and restrict the discussion topic or problem so that it is understood and capable of being discussed in the time allotted. Identify assumptions and subproblems. Settle upon an order of discussion.
- Clarify procedures—how the discussion will be conducted, when it will conclude, what it will seek to accomplish.
- Allow the discussion to veer from course when such a step promises to be fruitful. But be ready to come back to the original point when the detour has served its purpose.
- Build a spirit of group cooperation and friendliness rather than allowing sides to be taken on issues. When arguments do arise and cannot be settled, reserve them or treat them as assumptions and continue. But do not hesitate to encourage differing points of view or occasionally to play the "devil's advocate," where this will prove effective.
- Ask questions which elicit facts and opinions, rather than those which can be answered by a yes or no.
- Avoid playing a too dominant role in the discussion; put the responsibility on the students. Throw back questions to the group; ask group members to respond to statements of other students.

- Summarize from time to time to remind the group of its progress, its unfulfilled commitments, and its remaining time budget.
- Restate and clarify contributions, when necessary, to align them with the discussion. Ask students for illustrative examples or restatements so that meanings become clearer.
- Recognize varying opinions with regard to the problem under discussion; help to formulate these as minority views.
- Leave time for a summary. This may be done by the instructor or by one or more students serving as recorder or observers.

A CRITIQUE OF THE LIVE COURSE

Despite the wide variation in characteristics of live courses, there are certain advantages and disadvantages that extend to all. The advantages are that (1) live courses permit face-to-face communication among teacher and students; (2) they encourage personal contacts between student and teacher; (3) they bring students together, thereby reducing the isolation of studying alone and offering the assembled group the opportunity to learn from each other; (4) they have specific start and termination dates; and (5) owing to calendar demands and the possibility of being examined in class, they provide incentives for students to keep up with the work load.

The disadvantages associated with live courses are that (1) they are available at only limited times and locations each day or week; (2) they are spontaneous and frequently lack the polish of prerecorded courses; (3) like all courses, they may be only tangentially connected with student interests, but the live format makes it impossible for the students to speed up or skip over irrelevant concerns; (4) like all courses, they are geared to an average class rather than the individual student, and the members of the class may have to compete with one another for the teacher's attention; and (5) they in no way guarantee two-way communication or actual contact between student and teacher.

Instruction by Mass Media

Radio, television, and newspapers are the primary means of mass media instruction. Mass media need not be an alternative to other modes of instruction. It can also be used in combination with them.

RADIO

This method of instruction is used at a number of institutions, including the open universities at Purdue University and the University of South Florida. Its effectiveness as a means of instruction has been studied in several experiments by Popham and McLuhan (in Jamison and others, 1974, pp. 31–33). Popham divided an introductory course into two sections, one taught by live lecture and discussion, the other by taped lectures (a good proxy for radio) and discussion. At the conclusion of the class, Popham found no differences in learning among the two groups.

McLuhan's experiments were similar. He assigned students in a course on preliterate languages to four groups. Each group studied the same material via the medium of television, radio, live lecture, or print. McLuhan found that students learned more from television and radio than print or lecture. Television proved more effective than radio. However, when McLuhan added visual aids to the radio presentation, radio ranked higher than television. McLuhan attributed the change to the more engaging character of multimedia presentations.

The advantages of instructional radio are (1) it reduces the unit cost of instruction and thereby tuition; (2) it is cheaper than television; (3) it eliminates visual images which distract students and reduce learning in some subject areas; (4) it enables a teacher to reach more people than can be accommodated in a single classroom; (5) it may be a more effective medium for learning than print or lecture (however there is conflicting evidence on this point); and (6) it permits instructional outreach to homes at convenient audience listening times. The disadvantages of radio are that (1) it is not as effective as instruction by television when used alone, particularly in teaching manual tasks but also in subject areas where visual images improve the association process; (2) it does not accommodate student questions and feedback except by phone hookups to the studio or periodic class sessions run by the instructor or section leaders; and (3) it requires a relatively large audience to be cost effective.

TELEVISION

Television is the most common form of mass media instruction. Nine percent of undergraduates have taken courses which use live television lectures and 35 percent have taken courses which use prerecorded televised lectures or demonstrations. Both types of lectures are experienced most frequently by students at research universities (11 percent live and 39 percent prerecorded). They are experienced least by students at selective liberal arts colleges (2 percent live and 15 percent prerecorded) (Carnegie Surveys, 1975–76).

Brown and Thornton (1971, p. 144) report that television is used to instruct undergraduates in seven different ways:

- As a substitute for live faculty lectures on campus.
- As an enlarger of slides, documents, pictures, or even faculty in large lecture rooms.
- As a way to offer instruction off campus, to geographically distant locations, to other colleges, etc.
- As a means of permitting the repeated and convenient observation of an event.
- As a means of encouraging faculty and students to observe their own behavior, e.g., teaching.
- As a means of sharing with many, experiences such as childbirth or field behavior which would not be possible if all attended.
- As a way of videotaping short demonstrations or creating a continuous tape of instructional resources which can be shown at strategic times during class.

The Carnegie Commission (1972) suggested two additional uses:

- As a means of dramatizing or bringing information to life,
- and as a means of making excellent learning opportunities such as "Roots," "Civilization," and "The Ascent of Man" available to audiences across the nation or world.

Research on the effectiveness of television as contrasted with other instructional media has produced findings of little or no difference in student learning. Chu and Schramm examined 202 studies comparing traditional instructional methods with instruction by television at the college level. In all, 150 of the studies reported no difference in student learning, 22 found students learned more with television, and 28 reported greater student learning with traditional instruction (in Jamison and others, 1974, pp. 34–35).

Dubin and Hedley (also in Jamison and others, 1974) performed a similar analysis based on the comparison of 191 college-level studies. They found 102 of the studies to favor television and 89 to support traditional methods of instruction. When Dubin and Hedley tested the results for significance, they found a small but significant difference in favor of traditional methods of instruction. However, this difference disappeared when studies of two-way television (television which puts the audience in contact with the performer) were eliminated from the sample (pp. 35–36).

The advantages of instruction via television are: (1) It permits education to reach large numbers of people who might be unable to attend classes at college. The TV College of Chicago, for example, offers nearly enough courses for students to earn a degree entirely by watching television. And both the Dallas, Texas, County Community College District and the University of Mid-America offer or are planning to offer complete degree programs by television. In Dallas, each television course has a study guide, syllabus, administrative guide, faculty guide, and testing procedure. (2) College students prefer television classes to lecture instruction. (3) Unlike radio, television is employable in all subject matters. (4) The quality of recorded broadcasts is more even than that of live classes. (5) Television broadcasts can be aired repeatedly at locations and times which are convenient to the audience. And (6) TV is a familiar medium associated with recreation rather than work.

The disadvantages of television are: (1) It requires a large audience to be cost effective. Unfortunately enrollment in the University of Mid-America and the Dallas Community College programs have been only a few thousand, far fewer than predicted or hoped for. (2) Radio or tape is an instructional medium superior to television for music. (3) Teachers and students are less fa-

vorable to the use of television in college than in the lower grades
—attitudes are much more positive among those who have experienced the medium. (4) College students prefer small discussion classes to television courses. (5) Television is essentially a one-
way medium, even though it has been adapted to two-way communication via telephones. And (6) college faculty feel threatened
by television.

NEWSPAPERS

In 1973, the first national newspaper course, entitled "America and
the Future of Man," was offered. The course was developed by the
extension division of the University of California, San Diego, and
supported by the National Endowment for the Humanities. The
first newspaper in any city to ask for the course was permitted to
print it free of charge. At least 264 newspapers printed the series,
which consisted of one 1,400-word lecture by a nationally known
scholar each week. The lessons listed the name, address, and telephone numbers of local colleges and universities giving credit for
the course. Each of the 180 participating institutions was required
to appoint an instructor to conduct two in-class sessions. The instructor was also charged with assigning homework, answering
questions, testing students, and grading them. An evaluation of the
program based on random telephone contact with newspaper subscribers in San Diego and Denver found that one in four subscribers read at least one lesson. Five thousand students enrolled for
credit and 11,500 texts and course guides for the course were purchased (Lewis, 1974). By 1976–77, 454 newspapers, 300 colleges,
and an estimated 20 million people were participating in the program. About 30,000 people have received academic credit (Watkins, 1977, p. 7).

There is no known research on the effectiveness of courses by
newspaper at the college level. The advantages of such instruction,
however, are: (1) Courses by newspaper are cheap for sponsors and
may attract students to college who would not otherwise attend; (2)
scheduling is entirely up to the student; (3) the cost to the student is
minimal and there are no start-up costs such as buying a television
set; (4) such courses can provide continuing education as well as
college-level study for people not interested in earning a degree;

and (5) great teachers who could not collectively be brought to a campus or community can teach together. The disadvantages are that (1) relatively short, weekly lectures are not a sufficiently substantial base for an entire course; (2) many of the benefits of convenience and accessibility are lost if newspaper courses are not fully self-contained; (3) the print medium—especially poor-quality newsprint—is of limited value in the study of certain aspects of art, music, and natural science; and (4) the slow pace of such instruction means that it would take an interminable period to earn a degree by newspaper. (Newspaper courses are seldom the only way degree candidates earn credit, however, and degree granting is not their purpose.)

New Instructional Technologies

PROGRAMMED INSTRUCTION

Programmed instruction combines a carefully planned sequence of small-scale learning tasks and evaluation exercises so that students master the skills and knowledge associated with each task before beginning the next. Mastery is assessed via evaluation exercise, and if the student responds incorrectly to the exercise he or she either restudies the previous task (in a linear program) or is assigned a new task based specifically on the weakness demonstrated on the evaluation exercise (in a branching program). In all cases, the student's progress through the program is self-paced.

Programmed instruction, which is based on the principle of mastery learning (see Chapter 4), can be offered by printed programmed texts, teaching machines, computers, or learning modules (short subcourse units organized around a single task or principle). Twenty-nine percent of college and university faculty use self-paced or programmed instruction of all types in some or all of their courses. It is most commonly used by faculty at community and junior colleges (49 percent) and least commonly by faculty at the most research-oriented universities (15 percent) (Carnegie Surveys, 1975–76). Despite this three-to-one difference in faculty use at different types of institutions student exposure to programmed instruction is relatively uniform at all types of institutions. For example, 37 percent of all undergraduates say they have had self-paced instruction with programmed texts or study guides (possibly as part of Keller plan or audio-tutorial courses, which will be discussed later), with students at the most research-oriented universities having had the least experience (30 percent) and students at other research universities having had the most (43 percent). Six percent of all undergraduates report having experienced self-paced instruction with a programmed interacting computer. Here the contact varies from 9 percent at the most research-oriented universities to 3 percent at two-year institutions (Carnegie Surveys, 1975–76).

The advantages of programmed instruction are: (1) It is at least as effective as more traditional methods of instruction. P. C. Lange (in Jamison and others, 1974, pp. 38–40) examined 112 studies which compared programmed instruction with traditional forms of teaching. Forty-nine percent of the comparisons reported no difference, 41 percent favored programmed instruction, and 10 percent favored traditional instruction. (2) Students have greater recall of material taught through programmed instruction than traditional methods. (3) Students master knowledge and skills taught through programmed instruction in less time than traditional instruction. And (4) programmed learning is individualized, so that in branching programs students are able to study areas in which they have demonstrated weakness without forcing an entire class to spend time doing so.

The disadvantages of programmed instruction are that (1) it is expensive—50 to 75 hours of programming are required for each student hour of instruction presented; (2) student boredom is common after the novelty of programmed instruction wears off; (3) programmed instruction has not generally been used to teach higher order skills and knowledge and may not be useful in doing so; (4) programmed instruction offers students little or no opportunity to satisfy their own learning objectives when they differ from those of the course; and (5) learning by programmed instruction can be mechanistic (Cross, 1976, pp. 56–58).

Observing the unique advantages and disadvantages of programmed instruction, Cross (1976, pp. 58–59) has offered several suggestions for using this mode of teaching:

- Programmed instruction is best used for teaching facts and skills.
- Not all students weak in facts and skills achievement are helped by programmed instruction, so instructors need to check regularly with their students to gauge progress and personal reactions to such teaching.
- The effectiveness of programmed instruction depends on the quality of the material used.
- Programmed instruction is most effective in subject areas where learning is sequential, divisible into small units, and for which there are acknowledged "right" answers.
- Programmed instruction should be used only when there are no superior alternatives.

To Cross's list should be added the following three suggestions:

1. Programs with small changes in difficulty and quantity of material in successive units are superior to those covering varying amounts and difficulties of material in each unit.
2. Programs with high probability of success for choosing the correct answer are better for students with low achievement needs. The opposite is true for students with high achievement needs.
3. Immediate feedback or results on tests increases the effectiveness of programmed instruction.

COMPUTER INSTRUCTION

Colleges and universities offer instruction both *about* and *by* computers.

Instruction About Computers. Teaching about computers comes in three forms—specialist courses, service courses, and survey courses (Levien and Mosmann, 1972).

Specialist courses are programs for the training of computer experts—people whose job it is to work with computers. Of the students entering college in fall 1975, 1.8 percent said they planned to major in computer sciences. This is equal to the number of students planning majors in elementary education and greater than the number planning majors in architecture, biology, chemistry, economics, electrical engineering, English, foreign language, history, home economics, journalism, philosophy and religion, physics, sociology, or theater arts ("Fields of Study Chosen by Students," 1975).

Service courses are classes designed to teach students how to use a computer for their work in other areas, such as architecture, chemistry, and sociology. This type of instruction is significantly shorter than the specialist computer courses. In fact, it may be only a portion of a class on research methods or statistics. In any case, service courses are usually offered by disciplinary departments or within subject fields, but they may also be offered on an institutionwide basis.

Survey courses are classes in the genre of "computers and society," which are intended to help students gain an understanding of computers. Such courses are generally single-term classes and deal with topics such as the history, strengths, weaknesses, issues, and future of the computer.

Instruction of all three types about computers is becoming increasingly popular. Twenty-seven percent of undergraduates say they have used their campus computer facility for analyzing data or learning to program (Carnegie Surveys, 1975–76). Such experience is most common among students at the most research-oriented universities (39 percent) and least common among students at community and junior colleges (18 percent).

Instruction By Computer. Twenty-four percent of college and university faculty use instruction by computer. It is most common among faculty at two-year colleges (34 percent) and least common among faculty at selective liberal arts colleges (18 percent) and the most research-oriented universities (17 percent) (Carnegie Surveys, 1975–76). Such instruction comes in two forms—computer-assisted instruction (CAI) and computer-managed instruction (CMI).

Computer-assisted instruction allows students to progress in their studies at their own pace by working individually with a programmed computer. Students usually communicate with the computer by typewriter, electronic pointer, or touch-manipulation board. The computer responds via television, slides, recordings, print, or typewriter. The range of activities possible through computer-assisted instruction includes presenting instructional material, helping students master concepts or perfect skills, facilitating independent study by students, supplementing teacher-led instruction through classroom demonstrations and simulation exercises, monitoring and diagnosing student progress, and prescribing individualized instruction.

The advantages of computer-assisted instruction are that (1) students learn at least as well using computer-assisted instruction as any other method of learning (Cross, 1976, pp. 62–63; Jamison and others, 1974, p. 50); (2) students perform better using computer-assisted instruction alone than by combining it with traditional methods (Jamison and others, 1974, p. 50); (3) learning by computer-assisted instruction is faster than other methods (Cross, 1976, pp. 62–64; Jamison and others, 1974, p. 51); (4) computer-assisted instruction may reduce student attrition (Jamison and others, 1974, p. 54); (5) students study at their own pace with no sense of relative standards of speed or slowness; (6) students receive more personal attention and instructional content time than in a traditional classroom; (7) student reaction is good to enthusiastic (Cross, 1976, pp. 62–64); (8) fewer students perform unsatisfactorily at completion of a course (Jamison and others, 1974, p. 57); (9) in general, students who have not responded well to traditional instruction react positively to computer-assisted instruction; (10) the cost of computer-assisted instruction is dropping quickly—to as low as $.35 per hour per student (Cross, 1976, p. 66); and (11) computers do not scold or embarrass students in public or show personal biases or prejudices.

The disadvantages of computer-assisted instruction are that (1) it is a new method of instruction about which little is known; furthermore many are ignorant about what is known; (2) it can be impersonal; (3) student excitement associated with it may be short-lived; (4) it is generally expensive; (5) currently prepared programs cannot be readily shared because of the wide variety of computer languages in use; and (6) faculty have frequently resisted it.

Computer-managed instruction uses the computer only for testing, diagnosis, prescription, and record keeping. For example, Miami-Dade Community College uses computer-managed instruction in its RSVP (Response System and Variable Prescription) program. RSVP periodically quizzes students using multiple-choice tests. Within a few hours the test is returned with a score, the correct answers, an explanation of ideas missed, a report on relative achievement, and recommendations for future study including television segments, portions of courses, text assignments, homework, and/or sessions with TAs. The program is rated very highly by students for reducing attrition and anxiety, building confidence, and individualizing education. RSVP can be criticized for its limitations, however. It cannot grade essay tests and, owing to the multiple-choice test format, it necessarily offers the same learning prescription to all students who choose the same incorrect answers.

PERSONALIZED SYSTEM OF INSTRUCTION (PSI) OR KELLER PLAN

PSI is a form of self-paced mastery learning developed by the psychologist Fred S. Keller and his associates. It requires the instructor to prepare a detailed course outline, write a set of course objectives, and divide the course into units of about a week's length each. Students taking the PSI course learn by reading traditional texts, newspaper articles, and other printed matter which are keyed to the course outline. Any lectures or demonstrations offered during the course are considered as supplements, used simply to interest students in the subject area. Students progress by taking a mastery test at the end of each unit. When a student believes he or she has learned the material for the unit, the student seeks out a "proctor"—a peer tutor who has previously mastered the content of the course or unit. The proctor administers a short multiple-choice mastery test to the student, grades the test in the student's presence, goes over any incorrect answers with the student, and when needed, also provides additional instruction and study suggestions. For a student to move on to the next unit, the test must be passed with a high score, sometimes as high as 95 percent. Students who achieve lower scores must brush up on the material in the unit and then take other versions of the test from the proctor until they succeed in passing by the required score.

In the decade or so since PSI was developed, it has spread rapidly. According to the Center for Personalized System of Instruction, Georgetown University, it is now used in more than 2,000 courses at more than 700 American colleges. Its advantages are that (1) student performance with PSI is at least as good, if not better, than performance with traditional methods of instruction (Ruskin, 1974, p. 24; Cross, 1976, pp. 94–96); (2) students who study by PSI retain more of what they learn than students who learn by traditional methods (Ruskin, 1974, p. 29); (3) students who study by PSI are more enthusiastic about their courses than students who learn by other means (Cross, 1976, p. 95); (4) PSI can be used for learning "complex academic repertoires" such as application of skills and knowledge (Ruskin, 1974 p. 25); (5) the student failure rate with PSI is less than with traditional methods; (6) PSI incorporates human contact into programmed instruction by using proctors, who may be less threatening to students than a professor or a graduate student; (7) it requires active student participation; (8) PSI students continue to learn after completing the course by serving as proctors; (9) PSI frees faculty from the trivia of instruction to deal with significant educational problems; (10) PSI makes use of familiar, low-cost instructional materials (for example, standard texts); (11) PSI is mastery based and self-paced; and (12) PSI gives students immediate feedback after tests.

The disadvantages of PSI are: (1) Students withdraw from PSI courses at a significantly higher rate than traditional courses (Ruskin, 1974, p. 27). (2) PSI relies upon multiple-choice tests, which require agreed upon right and wrong answers. As a result PSI may be more appropriate for the sciences, introductory courses, and established areas of knowledge than for the social sciences and humanities, advanced courses, and new frontiers. (3) PSI inflates grading. There are few failing grades and it is common practice to give students who master all of the units of a course an A. As a result PSI can be a two-grade system, A or F, and students who are F-bound can withdraw. (4) PSI may be better geared to intellectually excellent students than others (Cross, 1976, p. 95). (5) Procrastination by students is a problem—some students slack off until the end of a term and then rush to complete a course, often unsuccessfully. (6) Proctors are hard to find at community colleges, and even if they are available at other schools they must be trained.

(7) PSI can be mechanistic and generally reduces student contact with the faculty instructor. The instructor, not the proctor, is the expert in the course subject. (8) PSI cannot accommodate student learning desires that differ from the course outlines. (9) Much work is required to set up a PSI course, and deviations from design or other problems can lead to terrific failures.

AUDIO-TUTORIAL INSTRUCTION

Audio-tutorial instruction is another self-paced method of teaching. It blends independent study with in-class meetings. Independent study takes place at an audio-tutorial laboratory booth or carrel. Upon entering the laboratory, students pick up a mimeographed list of behavioral objectives and listen to the tape-recorded programmed course guide at their booths. The tape provides introductory and integrating material and directs the student to other learning resources. The recording may tell the student to stop the tape and read a passage in a book, watch a film, perform an experiment, or look at an exhibit or slide. The materials to be used are in or near the booth. The duration and distribution of time spent in the laboratory are up to the student, as the facilities are open throughout the day and evening.

In-class meetings are of two types. One is a weekly meeting of the entire class, which is used for general information, guest lecturers, examinations, or presentations. Like the lecture in the Personalized System of Instruction, it is a supplementary activity. The other type of class is a quiz section attended by the course instructor and six to ten students. These sessions are essentially show-and-tell classes in which the various items of independent study are discussed. This weekly evaluation requires that each student knows the course material well enough to teach it, provides the personal and social stimulation of discussion groups, offers regular feedback on the course to the instructor, and allows the instructor to diagnose student learning accomplishments (Cross, 1976, p. 85).

One-quarter of American undergraduates have had experience with audio-tutorial instruction during college. Such experience is most common among students in community and junior colleges and comprehensive colleges (27 percent) and least common among students at selective liberal arts colleges (12 percent) (Carnegie Surveys, 1975–76).

The advantages of audio-tutorial instruction are that (1) students learn as well or better using it than by using more traditional methods (Cross, 1976, p. 89); (2) students are enthusiastic about it; (3) it is based on clearly spelled-out learning objectives; (4) it incorporates weekly tests and diagnostic sessions; (5) it uses many media, so the medium best suited to a particular topic can be employed; (6) it integrates practical ("hands-on") instruction with theory, which is not true of most college instruction; (7) it allows the student to regulate the degree of repetition in course materials; (8) the learner is an active participant in the process; (9) students select the time they want to study; (10) booths are generally private, which removes the distractions often associated with the classroom; and (11) human contact is built into the in-class sessions, particularly quiz sections, which have low student-faculty ratios.

The disadvantages of audio-tutorial instruction are that (1) it is time consuming and expensive to initiate; (2) self-pacing is limited because most units of the course are one week long and generally must be completed in time for the weekly quiz section; (3) audio-tutorial instruction may be better geared to the sciences than the social sciences or humanities, which rely upon field exposure that cannot be replicated in the laboratory; (4) tapes are impersonal and can be mechanistic; (5) audio-tutorial instruction is economically infeasible for small classes; (6) results at community and junior colleges are mixed—there are reports of motivational problems among students as well as findings of increased confidence and subsequent enrollments in the same fields (Cross, 1976, p. 89); (7) the audio tutorial model must be followed closely if the program is to work; (8) students are unable to follow individual interests that depart from the course plan; and (9) mastery is generally not emphasized to the degree it is with PSI.

Independent Study

Independent study is out-of-class, student-directed education with varying degrees of faculty guidance or supervision. It can be an individual or group endeavor. Group projects are rare. However, Brown University has a Group Independent Study Program (GISP), which permits cooperative inquiries in which students have the major responsibility for planning and conducting undergraduate courses. Faculty serve only as resource people—advisers and evaluators. GISPs, which must be approved by two academic committees, are initiated informally. When one or more students publicly post a course title and description, other students are invited to join. In fall 1975, 13 group independent study courses, enrolling 86 students, were offered.

The character of independent study varies widely from college to college. Brown and Thornton (1971, pp. 104–105) have identified six types of independent study.

1. The student follows a course syllabus of directed readings with little or no faculty contact, with the possible exception of an introductory meeting and final evaluation.
2. The student follows his or her own intellectual pursuits with the continuing help of an instructor or tutor.
3. The student is excused from a formal course but must—alone or in a group—learn the material that would normally be covered in the course.
4. The student uses programmed materials, audiotutorial instruction, computer assisted instruction, texts, assigned readings, and the like to achieve the same learning as would normally be accomplished in a classroom setting.
5. The student pursues an individual research project or extramural study off campus relying upon field resources.
6. The student, with the aid of one or more faculty members, completes an agreement or contract—a plan of study for a term. The contract may include any or all of the five previous methods of independent study as well as formal courses (see Chapter 9).

Independent study of any of these six types may either be required, optional, or not available on a particular campus. Justin Morrill College of Michigan State University, New College of the University of South Florida, and Princeton University are examples of institutions where independent study is required of all students.

St. John's College is an example of a school where independent study is not available. At most colleges and universities, independent study is optional.

The duration of independent study is also variable. That is, independent study can include a portion of a single course at nearly all schools, an entire year of self-directed work at Yale University or Trinity College (Hartford), or four years of contracts at New College of the University of South Florida.

Institutional policies for permitting independent study differ from college to college as well. In a study of 360 four-year colleges and universities, Dressel and Thompson (1973, p. 18) found that 76 percent of the institutions restricted student participation by ability. The most common criteria for participation were desire (58 percent), recommendations by faculty and administration (55 percent), grade-point average (41 percent), and evidence of creativity (35 percent) (p. 20).

Independent study, with all its attendant variations, is found at 94 percent of four-year arts and sciences colleges and 68 percent of four-year professional/technical schools. At community and junior colleges, it is used in 70 percent of arts and sciences schools and 66 percent of professional/technical programs (Catalog Study, 1976). This represents an enormous expansion of independent study in the past two decades. Less than 25 years ago, it could be found at only 26 percent of American colleges (Dressel and Thompson, 1973, p. 137).

Some colleges not only reserve independent study for honor students but also do little to publicize its availability. Thus despite its wide adoption, only 38 percent of undergraduates have had any experience with it. Even among college seniors, less than half (48 percent) have participated in it. Experience with independent study is least common among students at the most research-oriented universities (32 percent) and doctorate-granting institutions (33 percent). Experience is most common among students at selective liberal arts colleges (48 percent) (Carnegie Surveys, 1975–76).

The advantages of independent study are: (1) It is as effective as traditional methods of instruction. Dubin and Taveggia (1968, pp. 32–44) examined 198 comparisons between independent study and other methods of instruction, and found no differences in learning between students instructed by supervised and unsupervised independent study. More important, they found no significant differences between supervised independent study and face-to-face instruction—lecture instruction, discussion instruction, or combinations of lecture and discussion instruction, and none between unsupervised independent study and face-to-face instruction. (2) Independent study enables students to pursue their own academic interests. (3) It allows students to work at their own pace and learn to the depth they desire. (4) It is a vehicle for expanding the curriculum at small colleges. (5) It provides students with the skills necessary to continue learning throughout life. (6) When successful, it builds confidence among students.

The weaknesses of independent study are: (1) Students have shown relatively little interest in it. This can be attributed in part to the predominantly passive-dependent or teacher-centered style of learning common to most undergraduates (Levine and Weingart, 1973). (2) Colleges frequently impose bureaucratic hurdles, such as forms needing several signatures and required committee approvals, that discourage students from electing independent study. (3) Faculty are not usually supportive of independent study, especially when supervision must be done in addition to their regular teaching load. (4) Independent study gives some students an opportunity to slack off or procrastinate. (5) Learning outcomes vary widely from boondoggles to published books. (6) The monitoring of independent study projects varies considerably from regular tutorials to minimal contact between student and adviser (such as a single postcard from around the world). (7) Independent study is generally in the student's major area and as a result leads to greater specialization in what some consider an already overspecialized undergraduate education. (8) Long-term or intense independent study is lonely for students. (9) Off-campus independent study advising is generally weak. (10) Students rarely receive preparation prior to undertaking independent study. (11) Independent study is frequently restricted to upper-class honors students. (12) Overreliance on independent study is a way for a college to mask an inadequate curriculum and deprives students of the opportunity to study closely with skilled academics. (13) Independent study has a "mickey mouse" image in some quarters.

Experiential Education

Experiential education refers to learning which occurs outside the classroom without benefit of long-term or continuing formal classroom instruction. The source of learning may be recreation, work, self-teaching, travel, or other life activities. Such learning can occur before or during college enrollment. (The mechanics and frequency of awarding credit for experiential education are discussed in Chapter 9).

The advantages of experiential education are that (1) it adds the real-world exposure and hands-on experience absent in most college educations; (2) students tend to be highly motivated (Coleman, 1976, pp. 59–60); (3) student recall of learning is better than with more formal methods of instruction (p. 58); (4) student success with experiential education results in increased confidence and self-assurance (p. 60); and (5) experiential education can produce college-equivalent learning.

The disadvantages of experiential education are that (1) there is little research on it as yet to provide firm bases for action; (2) experience is not education (Hook, 1971) and "doing" is not necessarily "learning"; (3) unguided experiential education and that occurring prior to college is difficult to evaluate; (4) it may be superficial and random; (5) it is more time consuming and less efficient than traditional methods of instruction (Coleman, 1976, p. 54); and (6) unguided experiential education incorporates no methods for moving from the specific to the general or from the practical to the theoretical.

Libraries

Libraries have changed considerably since the nineteenth century. When John Langdon Sibley, the then Harvard librarian, was encountered walking across campus one day and was asked about the condition of the library, he said it was excellent. Only two books were missing from the shelves, and he was on his way to Mr. Agassiz's office to get them back (Brough, 1953, p. 2).

With the rise of the research university, the college library became an important resource center for faculty and students. In this regard the majority of college and university faculty (55 percent) rate their libraries as good to excellent. Faculty rate their libraries as such most often at research universities (88 percent) and least often at doctorate-granting universities (56 percent) (Carnegie Surveys, 1975–76). Students think even better of the library than faculty. Eighty percent of undergraduates say their library is adequate for their needs. This response occurs most often among students at the most research-oriented universities (90 percent) and least among students at liberal arts colleges (65 percent) (Carnegie Surveys, 1975–76).

Despite the positive faculty and student perceptions of the college library as it stands, it is undergoing a revolution in purpose. The library is on its way to becoming the campus learning center. This change is already apparent at Hampshire College, where its library is intended to be "the central meeting place for the campus and a center for communication" (*Hampshire College 1970*). Hampshire has created an information transfer center at its library called INTRAN. The library basement, for instance, houses a television and film studio, a photography studio, graphics studio, experimental classrooms, and a communications network that connects the centrally located library with all parts of the campus, including student rooms. In addition to the usual facilities found at most libraries, Hampshire's building also contains group study facilities, listening carrels, an art gallery, duplication facilities, film screening rooms, a post office, and a bookstore (*Hampshire College 1976–1977*).

John Hostrop (1971) believes that in the future institutions of higher education need to become "library-colleges," institutions that build instruction about the model of a library such that faculty will act principally as resource guides and managers. In such a college, the library will serve as a computer center, media center, and an institutional research center. It will offer prepackaged courses students can use when they choose; instructional research media such as audio-tutorial laboratories, radio, television, computers, video tapes, audiovisual equipment, microfilm and microfiche collections, and programmed materials; classrooms; annotated subject matter bibliographies; comprehensive bibliographies of the holdings of other libraries; directories of community learning resources and resource people; and specialists in information, learning, and media.

Similar changes can also be expected to occur in the community. Already public library systems in Saint Louis and Cleveland, for instance, have begun to transform themselves into adult college-level learning centers with many of the characteristics of the college libraries just described.

The transformation of the library into a learning center will be expensive. Libraries are currently suffering the severe financial crunch of trying to keep up with an ever-increasing number of publications. Reductions in acquisitions are occurring at colleges and universities all over the country. As a consequence, colleges and community libraries will be increasingly required to develop cooperative arrangements simply to remain adequate. In fact, a consortium of major foundations is currently investigating the possibilities for regional and/or national research libraries with electronic and computer communication systems tying them to local branch extensions. Moreover, the American Council of Learned Societies has initiated a "National Enquiry into Scholarly Communication" to analyze and make recommendations on all significant aspects of the total system of communicating scholarly knowledge.

Concerns and Proposals

Criticism 1: The quality of undergraduate teaching is generally poor.

This opinion has been voiced by many (Bell, 1968, p. 102; Wilson, 1972, p. 91; Dearing, 1970, pp. 220–225). The situation is attributed to four factors: lack of rewards for teaching by colleges and universities; lack of graduate student training in teaching; overemphasis by most institutions on research rather than teaching, particularly in hiring faculty with Ph.D.s; and emphasis at many universities on graduate education rather than undergraduate instruction.

Undergraduates, however, dissent from this criticism. Most (72 percent) say they are satisfied or very satisfied with the teaching they have had at college. They are most satisfied at selective liberal arts colleges (85 percent) and least satisfied at research universities (65 percent) (Carnegie Surveys, 1975–76). However, students are equivocal in their satisfaction. Forty percent of them report being bored in class. As might be expected from the above differences, they tend to be bored more often in research universities (43 percent), where they are least satisfied with teaching, and least often in selective liberal arts colleges (30 percent), where they are most satisfied with teaching.

Given this amount of boredom, it seems reasonable to conclude that whether undergraduate instruction is good or bad, it can be improved. In recent years several techniques for doing so have been suggested:

- Developing doctor of arts programs (emphasizing teaching rather than research) at doctorate-granting institutions, and hiring faculty with doctor of arts degrees at undergraduate colleges (Carnegie Commission on Higher Education, 1973).
- Developing systematic student evaluation of courses. Sixty-three percent of faculty and 77 percent of students believe faculty promotions should be based on formal student evaluations of their teachers. This belief is most common among faculty (69 percent) and students (83 percent) at selective liberal arts colleges and least common among faculty (49 percent) and students (71 percent) at community and junior colleges (Carnegie Surveys, 1975–76). The research on student course evaluations indicates that they are statistically highly reliable, but conclusions on validity are mixed (Seldin, 1975, p. 28).
- Creating faculty and instructional development centers. Such centers would be concerned with teaching evaluation and improvement; in-service education and consultation; course evaluation and improvement; the preparation of instructional materials; the dissemination of information about new instructional developments; and other learning-related activities (Gaff, 1975).
- Offering faculty rewards that favor teaching (Mayhew and Ford, 1971, p. 59).

- Hiring excellent secondary school teachers for college instruction and upgrading their subject matter competence (The Carnegie Foundation for the Advancement of Teaching, 1977).
- Providing all graduate students planning to teach extensive experience in the theory and practice of teaching (The Carnegie Foundation for the Advancement of Teaching, 1977).
- Supporting research on the biology of learning—the chemical and brain functions associated with learning, remembering, and forgetting.[2]

Criticism 2: Current undergraduate instruction does not adequately take account of student differences.

When higher education began in this country, it was assumed that uniform types of instruction, such as Latin recitation, would produce uniform results in students, such mental discipline and "furniture of the mind." In recent years the opposite has been found to be true. That is, uniform types of instruction produce widely divergent results in different students. The reason is that students have different cognitive and learning styles. Different types of teacher relationships (peer, subordinate, tutor, tutee, member of a group, and individual) work best for different students. Different modes of symbolizing (listening, talking, doing, graphics, reading, writing, smelling, and touching) are stronger for different students. Different ways of thinking (induction, deduction, analysis, relativism, convergence, comparison, and association) are emphasized by different students. Different ways of storing knowledge (by association, by rote memory, by face, by attributes, by process, by concepts, and by recognition) are prominent among different students. These differences also exist among faculty.

Knowledge about learning styles is new, and undergraduate education has not yet had sufficient opportunity to develop instructional procedures to account for them. Toward this end, K. Patricia Cross (1976, pp. 130–133) has made a series of recommendations:

[2]Based on a conversation with E. Alden Dunham, The Carnegie Foundation for the Advancement of Teaching, January 1977.

1. Teachers and students should be helped to gain some insight into learning and teaching styles.
2. In general, people will probably be happier and more productive if they are studying or teaching via a method compatible with their style.
3. No one method should be regarded as a panacea for all students in all subjects.
4. There are some subjects and some skills that all students need to learn, and we need to be knowledgeable in devising cognitive strategies to teach them.
5. Educators need to be aware of the cognitive styles of students in order to provide appropriate kinds of support, motivation, and reinforcement.
6. Any single school or institution should make certain that the learning program is not systematically biased in favor of a particular cognitive style.
7. More attention needs to be given to the potential of cognitive style for education and vocational guidance.
[8.] Since knowledge about cognitive styles is tentative and incomplete, educators should remain flexible and experimental in their use of the concept.

References

Bell, D. *The Reforming of General Education: The Columbia College Experience in Its National Setting.* Garden City, N.Y.: Anchor Books, 1968.
This volume is discussed in Chapter 11.

Brough, K. J. *Scholar's Workshop: Evolving Conceptions of Library Service.* Urbana: University of Illinois Press, 1953.

Brown, J. W., and Thornton, J. W., Jr. *College Teaching: A Systematic Approach.* (2nd ed.) New York: McGraw-Hill, 1971.
This useful book contains chapters on "College Students and College Teaching," "The College Professor," "A Systematic Approach to College Teaching," "Teaching and Learning Modes," "Instructional Services and Resources," and "Evaluating Instruction."

Brubacher, J. S., and Rudy, W. *Higher Education in Transition: A History of American Colleges and Universities, 1636–1976.* (3rd ed.) New York: Harper & Row, 1976.

Carnegie Commission on Higher Education. *The Fourth Revolution: Instructional Technology in Higher Education.* New York: McGraw-Hill, 1972.
This volume discusses libraries and the information revolution, the penetration of new technology, impact on faculty, impact on students, costs, and future goals.

Carnegie Commission on Higher Education. *Continuity and Discontinuity: Higher Education and the Schools.* New York: McGraw-Hill, 1973.

The Carnegie Foundation for the Advancement of Teaching. *Missions of the College Curriculum: A Contemporary Review with Suggestions.* San Francisco: Jossey-Bass, 1977.

This report is discussed in Chapter 11.

Carnegie Surveys, 1975–76.

This project is discussed in the Preface.

Catalog Study, 1976.

This project is described in the Preface.

Coleman, J. S. "Differences Between Experiential and Classroom Learning." In M. T. Keeton and Associates, *Experiential Learning: Rationale, Characteristics, and Assessment.* San Francisco: Jossey-Bass, 1976.

Crittenden, K. S., Norr, J. L., and LeBailly, R. K. "Size of University Classes and Student Evaluations of Teaching." *Journal of Higher Education,* 1975, 46 (4), 461–470.

Cross, K. P. *Accent on Learning: Improving Instruction and Reshaping the Curriculum.* San Francisco: Jossey-Bass, 1976.

This volume, discussed in Chapter 11, won the American Council on Education Book Award in 1976. It examines new instructional development—such as mastery learning, individualized study, self-paced modules, and cognitive styles— needed for the creation of a new model of undergraduate education.

Dearing, B. "Abuses in Undergraduate Teaching: 1965." In G. K. Smith (Ed.), *Twenty-Five Years: 1945 to 1970.* San Francisco: Jossey-Bass, 1970.

Dressel, P. *The Undergraduate Curriculum in Higher Education.* New York: Center for Applied Research in Education, Inc., 1966.

Dressel, P. L., and Thompson, M. M. *Independent Study: A New Interpretation of Concepts, Practices, and Problems.* San Francisco: Jossey-Bass, 1973.

Dubin, R., and Taveggia, T. C. *The Teaching-Learning Paradox: A Comparative Analysis of College Teaching Methods.* Eugene, Ore.: Center for Advanced Study of Education Administration, University of Oregon, 1968.

This article reexamines 306 previous studies of college teaching that compared independent study, lecture instruction, discussion instruction, and variations of the three. The authors conclude that there are no differences in learning associated with the different methods of teaching.

"Fields of Study Chosen by Students." *The Chronicle of Higher Education,* 1975, 11 (1), 19.

Gaff, J. G. *Toward Faculty Renewal: Advances in Faculty, Instructional, and Organizational Development.* San Francisco: Jossey-Bass, 1975.

Hampshire College 1970. (catalog) Amherst, Mass.

Hampshire College 1976–1977. (catalog) Amherst, Mass.

Hook, S. "John Dewey and His Betrayers." *Change,* Nov. 1971, pp. 22–26.

Hostrop, R. W. "Learning and the Library-College." *The Library-College Journal,* 1971, 4 (2), 35–43.

Jamison, D., Suppes, P., Wells, S. "The Effectiveness of Alternative Instructional Media: A Survey." *Review of Educational Research,* 1974, 44 (1), 1–67.

This article reviews the literature on traditional instructional methods, instructional radio, instructional television, programmed instruction, and computer-assisted instruction.

Knapp, R. "Changing Functions of the College Professor." In N. Sanford (Ed.), *The American College: A Psychological and Social Interpretation of the Higher Learning.* New York: John Wiley & Sons, 1962.

Levien, R. E., and Mosmann, C. "Instructional Uses of Computers." In R. E. Levien, *The Emerging Technology: Instructional Uses of the Computer in Higher Education.* New York: McGraw-Hill, 1972.

Levine, A., and Weingart, J. *Reform of Undergraduate Education.* San Francisco: Jossey-Bass, 1973.

Lewis, C. A. "Courses by Newspaper." In D. W. Vermilye (Ed.), *Lifelong Learners—A New Clientele for Higher Education: Current Issues in Education 1974.* San Francisco: Jossey-Bass, 1974.

McKeachie, W. J. "Procedures and Techniques of Teaching: A Survey of Experimental Studies." In N. Sanford (Ed.), *The American College: A Psychological and Social Interpretation of the Higher Learning.* New York: John Wiley & Sons, 1962.

Mayhew, L. B., and Ford, P. J. *Changing the Curriculum.* San Francisco: Jossey-Bass, 1971.

Milton, O. *Alternatives to the Traditional: How Professors Teach and How Students Learn.* San Francisco: Jossey-Bass, 1972.

Rudolph, F. *Curriculum: A History of the American Undergraduate Course of Study Since 1636.* San Francisco: Jossey-Bass, 1977.

Ruskin, R. S. *The Personalized System of Instruction: An Educational Alternative.* Washington, D. C.: American Association for Higher Education, 1974.

Seldin, P. *How Colleges Evaluate Professors: Current Policies and Practices in Evaluating Classroom Teaching Performance in Liberal. Arts Colleges.* New York: Blythe-Pennington, Ltd., 1975.

Sexton, R. F., and Ungerer, R. A. *Rationales for Experiential Education.* Washington, D. C.: American Association for Higher Education, 1975.

Veysey, L. "Stability and Experiment in the American Undergraduate Curriculum." In C. Kaysen (Ed.), *Content and Context: Essays on College Education.* New York: McGraw-Hill, 1973.

Watkins, B. T. "I'll Start Studying After I Read Peanuts." *The Chronicle of Higher Education.* 1977, 15 (13), 7.

Wilson, L. *Shaping American Higher Education.* Washington, D.C.: American Council on Education, 1972.

Wilson, R. C., et al. *College Professors and Their Impact on Students.* New York: John Wiley & Sons, 1975.

9

The Structure of Academic Time

Definition and History

In this volume, the term *academic time* refers to college calendars and the number of years of study required for students to earn a degree. When Harvard opened in 1636, it adopted the academic time arrangements of Emmanuel College at Cambridge University. These consisted of a four-year degree program and a yearly calendar of four terms which included Michaelmas Term (October 10 to December 16), Hilary or Lent Term (January 13 to the day before Easter), Easter Term (11 days after Easter to the Friday after commencement, which was scheduled for the first Tuesday in July), and Vacation Term (Friday after commencement to October 10). The academic year began with Easter Term, making that term the most common time for students to enroll. In 1639, Harvard closed for a year owing to financial problems. When it reopened, the course of studies took three years to complete. In the late 1650s, the fourth year was reintroduced.

All of the colleges established before the Revolutionary War had four-year degree programs and three academic terms per year (Boyer, 1975). In 1819, however, the University of Virginia attempted a departure from this pattern by introducing the semester system or two-term academic calendar. It proved infeasible because farm students were unable to return home to work at planting and harvesting times.

Several experiments with three-year degrees were tried in the 1840s and 1850s. The Sheffield School at Yale, the Lawrence School at Harvard, and the University of Michigan, for example, established three-year programs in the sciences and other modern subjects leading to degrees such as the bachelor of philosophy and the bachelor of science. In 1850, Francis Wayland, the president of Brown University, proposed an even more radical experiment. He suggested the establishment of three- to four-year undergraduate degree programs, so students could progress at their own pace. His plan, involving three degree programs of differing lengths, was never fully implemented.

The Johns Hopkins University was a bit more successful with the three-year degree. It began with a three-year undergraduate program in 1876. Eventually an optional precollege year was added, and finally in 1907 the program was extended to four years.

Changes in the character and structure of education during the late nineteenth and early twentieth centuries gave impetus to additional reforms. These changes included the proliferation of high schools, the expansion of law school and medical school programs from two and three years to three and four, the desire of professional school faculties that their students possess a college degree before admission, and the growth in the perceived idleness of bright college students (Boyer, 1972, p. 273).

One consequence of high school proliferation was that students were older when they entered college. During Harvard's early years it was not unusual for 12- to 15-year-old students to be admitted. By 1909, the average age had risen to what Harvard president Charles W. Eliot described as the "extravagant limit of 18 years and ten months" (Boyer, 1972, p. 274). Eliot responded to this situation as well as the overriding concern with the unevenness of high school preparation by encouraging the National Education Association to form the previously discussed Committee of Ten. Its 1892 report called for a two-year reduction in the length of primary school education as well as the admission of students into secondary schools two years earlier (see Appendix A). Primary schools were unwilling to reduce their program from eight to six years, but they did eventually begin two years earlier, permitting students to start college at 17 or 18.

William Rainey Harper, president of the University of Chicago, took a different approach from that of Eliot. He suggested that college begin for the average student after the eleventh year of secondary school. Harper put his plan into operation by dividing the University of Chicago into junior and senior colleges. Superior students could theoretically complete the two-year junior college program while they were in high school and enter directly into the senior division. The average student could enter the junior college directly after the eleventh grade. In 1904, more than 12 years after Harper suggested the plan, only six high schools in the nation had programs designed to articulate with that of the junior college (Meinert, 1974, p. 10). However, several colleges were offering advanced placement to quality high school students.

During the Harper administration, the University of Chicago also introduced a four-term, year-round calendar known as the quarter system. It permitted students to accelerate their studies and graduate more quickly than normal.

Another consequence of high school proliferation was that more students could attend college. Unfortunately, many were prohibited from doing so by their need to work. It was for this reason that the City College of New York introduced a new calendar in 1909 that extended college into the evening hours by establishing the first degree-granting night school.

A third consequence of the changes noted by Boyer, particularly the changes in professional education accompanied by the rise of the graduate school, was that students were spending more than four years in college. Charles W. Eliot and President Nicholas Murray Butler of Columbia University initiated programs to counter this trend. As noted in Chapter 5, in 1902 Eliot pushed the Harvard faculty into eliminating the four-year residence requirement for the bachelor's degree on the grounds that students were already completing the academic requirements in less than four years and that lazy students spent their last year primarily on social life. By 1906, 41 percent of Harvard's students graduated in three to three and one-half years (Boyer, 1972, p. 274).

In 1905, the Columbia University faculty, with strong direction from President Butler, approved the "professional option" which permitted students to begin professional school at Columbia after completing two years of college. The law school, which required three years of college, was an exception. The option remained on the books in all Columbia professional schools until 1953.

1928 brought a similar merger between high school and college education. In that year Pasadena High School and Pasadena Junior College merged to form a four-year junior college containing grades 11 through 14.

During the 1930s, 1940s, and early 1950s, when Robert Hutchins was its president and chancellor, the University of Chicago was active in experiments with academic time. Its undergraduate program was made time variable by basing student progress toward graduation on passing examinations rather than on time sitting in courses. To earn a degree, a student had to perform satisfactorily on 14 examinations administered by the Office of the University Examiner, and most students graduated in about three years.

Hutchins admitted students to the University of Chicago undergraduate college after tenth grade. This experiment was more widely supported than Harper's venture. Nonetheless, non–high school graduates never constituted more than a bare majority of the Chicago entering class. (A case study on the University of Chicago can be found in Chapter 12.)

During the 1930s, there was also an important calendar innovation at Hiram College. It was the block calendar, now also called the modular calendar or intensive course calendar, in which students study one course at a time.

During the 1950s, with the support of the Ford Foundation a number of institutions took steps to reduce the amount of time students spend in school. In one such project—responding to the Korean War draft of college-age men—superior students were admitted to college after only three years of high school. Between 1951 and 1955, 1,350 such students entered college early, and most did well academically and socially (Meinert, 1974, p. 13). The program did not catch on, however, in part because the war ended and in part because high school principals opposed it. They said it stripped their schools of their most mature and able students.

In 1951 the Ford Foundation also supported the advanced placement program, whereby students could study college-level courses in high school and be tested after completing the courses for college-level proficiency and college credit. During 1953 this program attracted only 532 students, but by 1960 over 10,000 were participating annually (Meinert, 1974, p. 14).

The 4–1–4 calendar was also a product of the 1950s. It consists of two four-month terms separated by a one-month mini-term which is used for intensive study, special projects, instructional innovation, or off-campus study. The concept was first implemented at Eckerd College in 1961, but had been advocated a few years earlier in the "1958 New College Plan" for Hampshire College.

Most academic time innovations were developed in the 1960s and 1970s. They include time-variable academic programs such as self-paced learning (1966); contract learning (based on pacts between student and teacher regarding the studies to be completed by the student over an agreed upon period of time) implemented first at New College in Sarasota, Florida (1969); test- and college-credit equivalent based degrees such as the New York Regents Degree (1970); and competency-based education (1972). These innovations also include programs designed to reduce the amount of time spent in college by individuals who have acquired the equivalent of college learning outside of college. Exemplary of such programs are the College Level Examination Program, which tests subject proficiency at the undergraduate level and can be used to earn college credits (1967); the assessment of experiential learning or life experience for awarding college credit, in which Brooklyn College's Special Baccalaureate Program for Adults was an early pioneer (1953); a variety of experimental approaches to time-shortened bachelor's degrees at 12 colleges across the country, supported by the Carnegie Corporation (1972); and the California High School Proficiency Examination, which permits students 16 years of age or older who pass it to leave school immediately if they receive parental permission (1975). There have also been new calendar arrangements such as the weekend college that began at Miami-Dade Community College (1965) and terms of differing lengths such as those at the University of Wisconsin, Oshkosh, which has divided its calendar into several patterns resulting in alternating terms of 14 weeks, 8 weeks, 7 weeks, and 3 weeks (1975). An additional innovation is Simon's Rock, an "early college" created in Massachusetts for 16- to 20-year-olds (1965). It eliminates the last two years of high school and awards a bachelor's degree after four years of study as well as lesser degrees for shorter periods of study (see case study in Chapter 13).

State of Academic Time

Bachelor of arts and bachelor of science degrees require four years of full-time study or the equivalent in 98.4 percent of American colleges and universities. Associate's degree programs are almost uniformly two years; 99.6 percent of associate of arts, associate of sciences, and associate of applied science degrees require two years of full-time study (Catalog Study, 1976).

However, only a bare majority of students attain their bachelor's degrees in four years or less. Alexander Astin (1975, p. 12) found that 53.1 percent of the students who entered college in 1968 earned bachelor's degrees by 1972; 12 percent required an additional year or so; and an additional 25 percent expected to complete degrees at a later date. As noted above, more and more curricular options are available to students that permit them either to shorten the amount of time spent in college or to lengthen it. Other curriculum practices are time variable or independent of the clock, resulting either in a shorter or longer program, depending on the individual student. Consider each of these three types of policy in turn.

Time-Shortening Practices

More than one out of five college juniors and seniors (21 percent) responding to the 1976 Carnegie Council undergraduate survey said they plan to earn a bachelor's degree in less than four years. To help them, 16 percent of four-year arts and sciences colleges and 5 percent of four-year professional/technical colleges offer formal time-shortened degree programs, as do 3 percent of two-year colleges (Catalog Study, 1976). Many more permit time short ening informally by making various curriculum options available. This is accomplished by (1) credit by examination, (2) summer term college attendance, (3) course overloads, (4) credit for experiential learning, (5) college courses for high school students, (6) early admission to college, (7) early high school exit and (8) compression of courses and programs.

CREDIT BY EXAMINATION

Credit by examination refers to the practice of granting students college credit for passing tests based on college courses that they have not attended. Thirty percent of undergraduates have earned some credit in this manner. Credit by examination is most common among students at the most research-oriented universities (39 percent) and least common among students at the less selective liberal arts colleges (21 percent) (Carnegie Surveys, 1975–76).

The College Level Examination Program (CLEP), Advanced Placement (AP), and "course challenge" are the three types of test most often used to gain credit by examination.

College Level Examination Program. CLEP, which is administered by the College Entrance Examination Board, was originally intended for adults beginning college or returning after a hiatus who had acquired the equivalent of college learning through experience, work, or self-education. Today at least 40 percent of CLEP takers are recent high school graduates under 19 years of age (Trivett, 1975a, p. 23). Good scores on the CLEP examinations are accepted for credit at most colleges and universities—by 91 percent of four-year colleges and universities and 86 percent of two-year institutions (Catalog Study, 1976).

CLEP includes 34 subject examinations, ranging in topic from Western civilization to immunohemotology, and five general examinations in the areas of English composition, mathematics, natural sciences, humanities, and social sciences–history. Each general test is usually considered the equivalent of a one-year college introductory course. This is so because the examinations are normed or based on the performance of second-semester sophomores. The multiple-choice tests vary in length from one hour to one hour and fifteen minutes each.

In 1975–76, 200,000 general examinations were administered, and the average college awarded credit to 74 percent of the students who submitted scores, according to a 1975 study by the College Board of 535 selected colleges and universities (Grandy and Shea, 1976, p. 9). The ease with which these credits have been earned has been a consistent source of criticism against CLEP. Carl Stecher (1977, p. 36) noted that when Utah State University gave three CLEP general tests to 500 entering freshmen, 61 percent received credit in social science–history, 68 percent received credit in humanities, and 77 percent received credit in the natural sciences. When San Francisco State University administered all five general examinations to two-thirds of its entering freshmen, 38 percent became "instant sophomores," 72 percent received at least one semester of college credit, and 94 percent were granted at least six hours of college credit. As a result, the validity of the CLEP general examinations, the norms upon which they are based, and college policies for awarding credit have all been questioned (Stecher, 1977). Students awarded CLEP credit, however, have been found to earn college grades equivalent to or better than other students at their school (Grandy and Shea, 1976, p. 3). Nonetheless, the College Board has recently introduced several changes in the CLEP format intended to curb some of what Stecher and others have perceived to be sources of abuse.

Advanced Placement Program. Advanced Placement (AP) is another College Entrance Examination Board program. It involves students taking college level courses at their high schools and then taking standardized tests at the completion of the courses to assess whether there has been college-level learning. AP examinations are prepared and graded by committees of high school and college faculty in 13 subject areas. They are graded on a 1-to-5-scale, and colleges commonly require a rating of at least 2.3, or 4 for credit or advanced standing. Ninety-six percent of four-year colleges and universities and 88 percent of community and junior colleges award credit or advanced standing for AP tests (Catalog Study, 1976). Almost 60,000 students take one or more examinations each year, and most of those who receive credit obtain the equivalent of less than one semester of college work (Meinert, 1974, p. 39). They can often parlay this head start into early graduation by combination with other time-saving mechanisms.

Challenge Tests. The "challenge test" is an examination created by an individual college as the equivalent to a course. Students who pass challenge tests are commonly exempted from or given credit for the course counterpart of the examination. Sixty-six percent of two-year colleges and 79 percent of four-year colleges and universities offer such examinations (Catalog Study, 1976).

Other Examinations. Several other tests are also used in awarding college credit. They include examinations prepared by professional societies, College Entrance Examination Board advanced subject area tests, American College Testing Program examinations, state examinations, and College Proficiency Examination Program (CPEP) tests. CPEP is a New York state program now available nationwide through the American College Testing Program. It offers more than 40 examinations in subjects varying from the arts and sciences to education and nursing. Grading on the examination is A to F based on standard scores. Free reading lists, study guides, and content descriptions of the tests are available from ACT. Since CPEP began in 1963, more than 70,000 credits have been awarded ("ACT to Make N.Y. College Proficiency Tests Available Nationwide," 1976, p. 4). A positive reaction to these examinations contributed to the creation of the New York State Regents External Degree Program in 1970. The Regents External Degree is not tied to any college or university or any instructional program. Bachelor's and associate's degrees are awarded by the Regents through the New York State Education Department on the basis of proficiency examinations and/or accumulated college credits. Like the CPEP tests, study guides, reading lists, and examination descriptions are available nationally.

SUMMER SCHOOL ATTENDANCE

Summer school attendance is the most frequent means of earning extra degree credits. Thirty-eight percent of the students responding to the 1976 Carnegie Council undergraduate survey attended one or more summer terms for credit toward their degrees. This practice is most common among students at research and doctorate-granting universities (41 percent) and least common among students at selective liberal arts colleges (22 percent), which not only are less likely to have summer terms but also often impose stringent restrictions on accepting summer school credits from other schools (Carnegie Surveys, 1975–76).

COURSE OVERLOADS

A course overload occurs when a full-time student enrolls in more than the institutionally recommended or prescribed number of courses or credits per term. Fourteen percent of undergraduates have taken an overload in one or more terms in order to graduate early.This occurs most frequently among students at comprehensive universities (16 percent) and least frequently among students at selective liberal arts colleges (7 percent) (Carnegie Surveys, 1975–76). At Antioch College, which has a five-year program, about half of the students are graduating in four years by this method. Early graduation poses an economic hardship to colleges that lose a term's tuition or more for each student opting to leave ahead of schedule. Several colleges are trying to combat the problem by imposing exorbitant transcript fees for extra credits gained through overload if the courses are applied for early graduation or by enacting four-year residence requirements for graduation.

CREDIT FOR EXPERIENTIAL LEARNING

Thirteen percent of undergraduates report receiving credit for experiential learning or work experience outside college (discussed above in Chapter 8). The most research-oriented universities award such credit to only 9 percent of their students in contrast to the less selective liberal arts colleges, which grant credit for experiential learning to 17 percent of their students.

The concept is popular among students. Fifty-five percent would like to be able to earn credit for experiential learning (Carnegie Surveys, 1975–76). Nonetheless, such credit is permitted at only a minority of colleges. It is more common at two-year institutions than four-year colleges and universities. Twenty-two percent of two-year arts and sciences colleges and 37 percent of two-year professional/technical schools offer credit for life experience or prior learning, compared to 17 percent of four-year arts and sciences colleges and 8 percent of four-year professional/technical schools (Catalog Study, 1976).

In recent years two organizations have been concerned with crediting experiential learning: the American Council on Education's Office of Educational Credit (OEC), and the Council for the Advancement of Experiential Learning (CAEL).

Office of Educational Credit, American Council on Education. OEC, which advises about credit for non-college courses, has taken on the job of the former Commission on Accreditation of Service Experience (CASE) of the American Council on Education, which periodically produced a *Guide* for colleges listing armed forces training programs and recommended college credit equivalents. The OEC updated the *Guide* by calling on subject matter specialists to evaluate the military's courses. "Each entry in the [new] *Guide* [now] includes an identification number, course title, military course number and school, location dates and length, course objectives, instructional mode, credit recommendation, and date the course is evaluated" (Trivett, 1975a, p. 37). Two copies of the *Guide* are sent to all institutions listed in the U.S. Office of Education *Education Directory*. OEC and the New York Board of Regents have also produced a pamphlet serving the same purpose for educational programs in noncollegiate organizations, entitled "A Guide for Educational Programs in Noncollegiate Organizations" (1977). OEC, like

CAEL, does not itself grant college credit. Instead, it describes the educational programs of military and other organizations in terms that permit college officials to award appropriate credit for comparable college courses.

Council for the Advancement of Experiential Learning. The other organization seeking to help credit experiential learning is CAEL. Originally a project of the Educational Testing Service and funded by the Carnegie Corporation, the Fund for the Improvement of Postsecondary Education, the Ford Foundation, and the Lilly Endowment, CAEL began as the Cooperative Assessment of Experiential Learning in March 1974. Its purpose was "to develop appropriate concepts, methods, procedures, techniques, and instruments for the assessment of experiential learning and to validate such ideas, processes, and materials through large-scale tryouts on many college campuses" (Cooperative Assessment of Experiential Learning, 1974b). CAEL has since grown into a membership organization of over 300 colleges and universities interested in reviewing, trying out, and validating these assessment procedures and furthering the use and crediting of experiential learning.

In the course of producing assessment materials, CAEL has studied college practices of awarding credit both for learning prior to college admission and for off-campus learning during college. In 1974, it reported that credit for prior experience was awarded most often for work experience, that students receiving such credit were usually older than traditional students and likely to have been out of school for some time, and that colleges were using several models of assessing prior learning to evaluate their knowledge. One was a faculty-based model in which instructional staff attempt to measure what and how much a student knows in order to grant credit generally equivalent to courses offered at the college. A second was a student-based model in which the student is asked to specify what he or she wants to learn and then is required to demonstrate how prior learning contributes to these learning goals. In both models, the student identifies knowledge and skills that appear to be creditable based on institutional rules; solicits or empowers the institution to solicit verification or documentation of previously acquired skills and knowledge; and with assistance from an institutional staff member (or brokerage organization as described in Chapter 6) assembles a portfolio containing a credit request, an explanation of the knowledge and skills previously acquired and their source, and documentation of these skills and knowledge. Institutional evaluation of the portfolio and award of credit follows (Trivett, 1975a, pp. 48–50). Besides the evaluation of portfolios, colleges and universities evaluate both prior and present experiential learning by means of simulations, unobtrusive observation, work samples, case study tests, essay assignments, scores on standardized examinations, panel interviews, oral evaluations, and self-assessment (Trivett, 1975a, p. 50).

(Case studies on Metropolitan State University and the Capital Higher Education Service, two organizations committed to the idea of awarding college credit for noncollege learning, are found in Chapter 13.)

COLLEGE COURSES FOR HIGH SCHOOL STUDENTS

College courses for high school students are found in both high schools and colleges. Seven percent of undergraduates report having taken some college courses for credit while still in high school. The experience was most common among students at selective liberal arts colleges (12 percent) and least common among students at comprehensive colleges (6 percent) (Carnegie Surveys, 1975–76).

High School Offerings of College Courses. The courses in high school are of two types—those in which college-level learning is validated at the completion of the course by a standardized examination (as is the case with Advanced Placement courses discussed earlier) and those in which standardized tests are not used. Illustrative of the latter type, two North Carolina high schools several years ago adopted a general education curriculum produced by Appalachian State University in Boone. During the first year, university faculty commuted from Boone to the high schools to teach the courses with high school teachers as associates. The following summer, the high school teachers taught the same courses at the college level and were given additional instruction. The next year, the high school teachers assumed the instructional burden for the courses in their schools. Fifty-five high school seniors participated and earned 13 or 14 credits per term in the program. When these students entered the university after high school, almost all did so as sophomores. In general, however, graduates of the program have not performed well academically at the university. Moreover, interest in the program by other students has been low, and one of the high schools has dropped out of the program because only ten seniors chose to participate.

Many more New York state high schools cooperate in a Syracuse University program. In 1974–75, over 2,000 students at 40 high schools participated. When a high school student successfully completes a college-level course, it is listed on a Syracuse University transcript. These Syracuse credits have proven widely transferable, and studies of student achievement have shown the courses examined to be equivalent in content and difficulty to comparable college courses.

College Offerings for High School Students. Courses for high school students taught on college campuses by college faculty can involve either concurrent or consecutive attendance.

Concurrent attendance, the more common practice, combines enrollment in high school courses with enrollment in college courses. Students commute between their high school and a nearby college. SUNY College at Fredonia, for example, allows superior high school students who have completed their junior year to take three courses on campus while attending two in high school. Other colleges more commonly limit high school students to one or two of their courses per term. Concurrent programs are offered by 37 percent of two-year arts and sciences colleges, 41 percent of two-year professional/technical colleges, 16 percent of four-year arts and sciences colleges, and 25 percent of four-year professional/technical colleges (Catalog Study, 1976).

Consecutive enrollment involves alternating high school and college courses. The State University of New York College at Buffalo, for instance, permits qualified high school juniors to take two of its courses in the summer before their senior year of high school.

If successful, the students can immediately matriculate as college freshmen without attending their senior year.

EARLY ADMISSION TO COLLEGE

Fewer than 1 percent of undergraduates enter college prior to completing high school or earning a high school equivalency diploma (Carnegie Surveys, 1975–76). But 49 percent of four-year arts and sciences colleges and 48 percent of four-year professional/technical colleges admit some high school students after their tenth or eleventh grade and prior to high school graduation. Thirty-three percent of two-year arts and sciences colleges and 15 percent of two-year professional/technical colleges also have early admission programs (Catalog Study, 1976). Early admission programs are found at institutions ranging from Catholic University of America, Huntington College (Alabama), Shimer College, The Johns Hopkins University, and Appalachian State University to the New School for Social Research, Ursuline College (Ohio), Temple University, University of Minnesota, and Utah State University.

EARLY EXIT FROM HIGH SCHOOL

In 1971, the California legislature voted to allow 16- and 17-year-olds who have their parents' consent to leave high school early with a certificate of proficiency by passing a special High School Proficiency Examination. The examination is designed to test basic educational or survival skills rather than the skills necessary for further academic success, which are tested by Scholastic Aptitude Tests and similar examinations. As a result, the California High School Proficiency Examination emphasizes reading, computation, consumer economics, and mathematics. The first four-hour examination, costing each person examined $10, was administered in December 1975. 670,000 high school students were eligible to take the examination, but only 12,121 did. Nearly 45 percent of those who took the test passed, and approximately half of the students who passed the examinations in the Los Angeles area left school. For students who choose to go on to college, the California Community Colleges have no additional entrance requirements beyond the proficiency certificate. Other qualifications continue to be required, however, by the California State University and Colleges system and the even more selective University of California system.

COMPRESSION OF COURSES AND PROGRAMS

Compressed undergraduate programs involve condensed courses of study. Such programs are effected in four ways: by redistributing time, by waiving requirements, by enriching undergraduate programs, and by changing the curriculum.

Redistribution of time involves mandatory student participation in one or both of two time-shortening procedures discussed earlier: summer session attendance (as in the three-year ceramic sciences B.S. degree at Alfred University) and deliberate course overloads (as in the modular achievement program at Bowling Green State University).

Waiver of requirements is the approach taken by the University of South Alabama's three-year baccalaureate curriculum, where students with at least a B average and a score of 27 or better on the ACT aptitude test are eligible for exemption of up to 48 hours of credit.

Table 16. Institutional use of time-saving techniques in time-shortened
degree programs

Technique	*Percentage of institutional use*
Advanced study based on CLEP or Advanced Placement tests	57
Intensified loads	34
Year-round calender	34
Total revision of curriculum	23
Combining twelfth grade and freshman year of college	21
Admission of twelfth graders to freshman year of college	21
Reduction of degree requirements	15
Credit for work experience	10
High school equivalency credit	3
Challenge examinations	2

Source: Bersi, 1973, p. 12.

Enrichment is illustrated at the University of South Mississippi by its three-year degree program that allows students to earn semester credits for quarter length courses in which the equivalent of a semester's material is covered.

Curriculum revision for compression has been achieved by the University of Illinois at Champaign-Urbana through reducing the overlap of content in lower-division courses and through introducing new methods of instruction. Manhattanville College has revised its program to permit students to complete eight semesters of course work in six semesters through the innovative use of seminars, independent study, field work, and preceptorials. And the University of the Pacific introduced a three-year program at Raymond College that is based on a mentor-preceptor relationship between faculty and students as well as on a shortened interdisciplinary general education program utilizing tutorials, seminars, contracts, and field experiences.

COMBINATIONS

One thing shared by most time-shortened degree programs, and particularly by three-year bachelor's degree programs, is their reliance on more than one of the techniques discussed in the preceding pages. In 1973, Robert Bersi (p. 12) surveyed 62 time-shortened degree programs and found that they used a variety of time-saving techniques, as shown in Table 16. Most frequent is advanced placement from CLEP or AP tests, shared by 57 percent of the programs. A third of the programs employed compression through intensified loads or year-round calendars. But only one or two of the programs reported using challenge examinations or accepting high school classes equivalent to college courses for credit.

Time-Lengthening Practices

Curricular practices that extend the length of an undergraduate education include (1) stopping out, (2) noncredit remedial or compensatory education, (3) repeating courses, (4) part-time attendance, (5) college enrollment beyond the minimum number of credits needed for graduation, and (6) college transfer. None of these practices has been initiated for the purpose of increasing the amount of time students take to earn a degree, but each has this

effect. And each involves at least one-eighth of American undergraduates (Carnegie Surveys, 1975–76).

STOPPING OUT

Stopping out involves leaving college with the intention of returning at a later date. Twenty-seven percent of undergraduates indicate that they have stopped out of college for a quarter or semester
or longer since first enrolling. The stop-out rate is highest at community and junior colleges (31 percent) and lowest at selective liberal arts colleges (10 percent) (Carnegie Surveys, 1975–76). In addition, a substantial but presently unknown number of students
take time off after high school but prior to college. Precollege stop
out is encouraged by institutional policies of deferred enrollments,
which are found at 28 percent of four-year colleges. They allow
admitted students to delay their matriculation to the institution for
an agreed-upon period of time, generally a term or year (Kesselman, 1976a, p. 15).

Among students who stop out after enrolling, 37 percent
leave college for less than one year, 14 percent leave for exactly a
year, and 50 percent leave for longer than a year (Carnegie Surveys, 1975–76). Their reasons for stopping out are varied. C. Hess
Haagen, director of a six-college study on leave taking, identifies 12
rationales: (1) the desire for course work or experiences not available on campus; (2) the need for experiences to place the self and
other personal relationships in perspective; (3) the need for
change; (4) a lack of goals or purpose for being in college; (5) medical or health problems; (6) personal circumstances; (7) recommended or required college leave policies; (8) failure to find
satisfying relationships; (9) lack of interest in college; (10) financial
problems; (11) the irrelevancy of college to student interests; (12)
and poor academic performance.

Another factor in stopping out appears to be student personality and background. For example, Kesselman (1976b, p. 15) reports that stop outs receive less financial aid and are less likely to be
members of disadvantaged minorities than are students who do not
stop out. They are also likely to be more stubborn, assertive, skepti-
cal, theoretically abstract, and independent than students who stay
straight through to graduation.

Kesselman also investigated the impact of stopping out on graduate and professional school admission and employment. With regard to graduate education, she concluded that "a stop out is not necessarily a blemish on your record if you are pursuing an advanced degree in a field other than medicine. In fact, if you've used your time wisely—either to renew motivation, solidify your goals, or obtain experience in your proposed field—the stop out may be . . . 'an incredible plus'" (p. 42). With regard to employment, however, the consequences are more variable, since stopping out may be interpreted by some potential employers as a sign of immaturity and lack of perseverence.

NONCREDIT REMEDIAL OR COMPENSATORY EDUCATION

Approximately 13 percent of undergraduates have taken one or more noncredit compensatory or remedial courses in reading, writing, or arithmetic since entering college. Such courses are most frequently taken by community and junior college students (17 percent) and least frequently by students at research universities (7 percent) (Carnegie Surveys, 1975–76). However, they are offered at a majority of American colleges and universities—53 percent of four-year institutions and 52 percent of community and junior colleges (Catalog Study, 1976). Enrollment in noncredit remedial courses frequently reduces the number of credits a student can take at one time, occasionally delays the student's matriculation into a degree program, and, as a result, lengthens the time required to earn a degree. (Basic skills and compensatory education are discussed more fully in Chapter 3.)

REPEATING COURSES

Twenty-three percent of undergraduates say that they have repeated one or more courses during college. This practice is most common among students at doctorate-granting colleges (26 percent) and least common among students at selective liberal arts colleges (9 percent) (Carnegie Surveys, 1975–76). Repetition results in lengthened degree programs because it involves either a duplication of previously passed courses, for which students are seldom awarded credit, or compensation for repeating previously failed courses for which time was spent but no credit was earned.

PART-TIME ATTENDANCE

In fall 1974, 29 percent of the students enrolled in undergraduate degree programs were attending college part time (U.S. National Center for Education Statistics, 1976). Since the four-year baccalaureate and two-year associate's degrees are predicated upon full-time attendance, part-time attendance either lengthens the course of study or requires that students take overloaded programs for one or more terms to make up for lost time.

ENROLLMENT BEYOND THE MINIMUM NUMBER OF CREDITS NEEDED FOR GRADUATION

Some students do not choose to graduate after obtaining the minimum number of credits required for graduation. In fact, 13 percent of undergraduates indicate that they have decided to stay in school an extra year owing to the state of the economy or job market. A large number of these students are continuing as undergraduates rather than entering graduate programs.

COLLEGE TRANSFER

Thirty-four percent of undergraduates have changed colleges at least once, and 29 percent plan to change before receiving their bachelor's degree. Among students who have already changed or transferred, 70 percent have attended two colleges, 22 percent have attended three, and 7 percent have attended four or more. Past transfers are most common among students currently enrolled in doctorate-granting universities and community and junior colleges (35–36 percent). They are least common among students in selective liberal arts colleges (20 percent). As might be expected, transfer plans are most likely among students attending community or junior colleges, where 58 percent expect to attend another institution. In contrast, students at research universities (8 percent) are least likely to plan to transfer (Carnegie Surveys, 1975–76).

Transfer can lengthen undergraduate education because a new college may not recognize some of a student's previously accumulated credits. A 1973 study of credit loss in the state of Washington found that students lost an average of 5.3 percent of their previous credits when they transferred to a university and 4.1 percent when they transferred to a college (Washington State Council on Higher Education, 1973). Such credit losses create problems for the institutions from which students transfer—most notably community and junior colleges—where faculty and administrators complain that senior college requirements "restrict their right to construct distinctive programs for students who will later transfer" (Trivett, 1974, p. 3). Among the credit barriers that have been imposed by some senior colleges are refusal to accept occupational courses, limitations on the amount of credit that can be earned in certain subject fields, and insistence on exact equivalence of courses from the transfer institution (Kintzer, 1973, p. 27).

Such problems are not universal, however. Some states have negotiated transfer or articulation agreements among their colleges. For example, the Massachusetts Higher Education and Commonwealth Transfer Pact guarantees that graduates of two-year college transfer programs going on to upper-division institutions will receive at least 60 hours of credit toward the bachelor's degree including 33 credit hours toward the completion of general education requirements. The credit loss problem is also abated somewhat by colleges such as American University and Hamline College (Minnesota), which actively recruit transfer students. American University, for example, has written credit transfer agreements with several colleges in the Washington, D.C., area (Trivett, 1974, p. 5).

Time-Variable Practices

Time-variable practices are of four types: (1) progress by examination, (2) self-paced instruction, (3) competency-based education, and (4) contract learning. In each case, time-variable study is a consequence of the program, not necessarily the reason it was created or even adopted by other colleges.

PROGRESS BY EXAMINATION

In a progress-by-examination curriculum, the only requirement to earn a degree is passage of a specified number of tests. As noted earlier, at Hampshire College all students must pass a total of six tests in the areas of general education, the major, and independent study in order to graduate. There are absolutely no time or course requirements. Most students take three courses per term, however.

Since Hampshire began in 1970, its examinations have shifted in form from tests to papers. They may be taken at any time. Students propose examination topics and procedures, and Hampshire faculty serve as advisers as they prepare for the examinations. Committees of two people, only one of whom must be a Hampshire faculty member, evaluate each of the four general education examinations. Committees of two judge the major examinations, but both members must be Hampshire faculty. Committees of three assess the independent study project, and two of the three must be Hampshire faculty members.

This system places the responsibility for passing the examinations and earning the degree squarely on the student. As a result, the examinations are a major source of anxiety for many of the students, while for others, the system presents opportunities to slack off by repeatedly delaying their examinations. Nonetheless, the average Hampshire student graduates in three to three and one-half years. For Hampshire faculty, the joint workload of teaching courses and examining students is enormously heavy. Yet faculty as well as students are both positively inclined toward the progress-by-examination curriculum.

It is still too early to compare the results of the Hampshire curriculum with education elsewhere. However, some outside examiners who have read Hampshire student examinations find them comparable to term papers or term projects at other schools, and others who have been involved in the entire examining committee process regard the results even more favorably (von der Lippe, 1975).

The New York State Regents External Degree program, which was discussed earlier, is another example of progress by examination. Unlike Hampshire, however, the Regents degree has no faculty, courses, or campus associated with it. The Regents tests are also traditional in format: They are prepared by individuals regarded as experts in the area of the test, and in contrast to Hampshire, students have no input in their administration other than being able to register for them and then take them.

SELF-PACED INSTRUCTION

Self-paced instruction is a form of education in which the subject matter is broken down into small, sequential units and in which the speed of a student's progress through the units is determined solely by his or her ability to master them. There is no predetermination of how much material is to be covered in a given period of time, although as a practical matter a term or a year is often the maximum time allowed. (Modes of instruction involving self-pacing, including programmed learning, PSI, and auto-tutorial systems, are discussed in detail in Chapter 8.)

COMPETENCY-BASED EDUCATION

As mentioned earlier, competency-based education places emphasis on educational outcomes rather than the experiences that comprise a curriculum. This means it also emphasizes student attainment rather than time serving. All competency curricula have three features in common: (1) They make explicit statements about the outcomes students must achieve in order to complete the program; (2) they employ learning experiences specifically designed to foster these desired outcomes, and the outcomes can be achieved in any of a number of different ways, including courses, independent study, or experiential education; and (3) they utilize multiple procedures for assessing student attainment of these outcomes—for example, tests, validation by on-campus and off-campus experts, observation, product evaluation, and simulation.

Nine percent of the undergraduates responding to the 1976 Carnegie Council undergraduate survey reported having had competency-based instruction, varying from a single course to an entire four-year program. Competency-based curricula are found at only 3 percent of two-year arts and sciences colleges but at 8 percent of two-year professional/technical colleges, four-year arts and sciences colleges, and four-year professional/technical colleges (Catalog Study, 1976). Among the four-year colleges offering competency-based programs are Alverno College (Wisconsin), Mars Hill College (North Carolina), Sterling College (Kansas), Justin Morrill College at Michigan State University, Metropolitan State University (Minnesota), Florida State University, and Our Lady of the Lake College (Texas). (The programs of Sterling College and Metropolitan State University are discussed in case studies in Chapter 13.)

Alverno College operates one of the first and most interesting competency-based programs. It requires its students to achieve eight competencies in order to graduate:

1. Effective communication ability
2. Analytical capability
3. Problem-solving ability
4. Facility in forming value judgments within the decision-making process
5. Effective social interaction
6. Understanding of individual/environmental relationship
7. Understanding the contemporary world
8. Educated responsiveness to the arts

Each of these competencies has six functional levels. The first four are for generalists and the last two are for specialists. For example, the six levels for the third competency—problem-solving ability— are: (1) learns theoretical frameworks, (2) defines the problem, (3) employs the process, (4) compares approaches, (5) defines and implements an original problem-solving project, and (6) functions as an independent problem solver in a number of different situations. In order to graduate, each student must achieve level four in each of the eight competencies, level six in at least one, and levels five or six in enough of the others to add up to a total of 40 out of the 48 possible competency levels.

The strengths of competency-based education are numerous and appealing: (1) It places the responsibility for an education in the hands of each student and permits students to progress at their own pace; (2) it allows students to choose the method of learning to which they are best suited: (3) it treats equivalent learning from different sources equally; (4) it bases the award of credit on attainment, not exposure; and (5) it focuses on where a student must end up, not the path the student must follow.

As might be expected, there are also problems associated with current competency-based programs. (1) Very little is known about assessment procedures. (2) There is a lack of adequate assessment materials. (3) Assessing the attainment of nonbehavioral outcomes is difficult. (4) The reliability and validity of certain assessment procedures are questionable. (5) There is a lack of evidence that different types of learning are in fact equivalent. (6) The competency-based curriculum demands massive program changes, faculty workload and role changes, and student behavior changes at the institutions adopting it. For instance, faculty must change from course instructors to individual student advisers and evaluators. The new roles require more work. Students must change from passive to active learners. Faculty have found the changes difficult to make and students often remain committed to the tried and true. (7) Competency has been criticized for tying education strictly to degrees and for being a leveling force—that is, seeking to bring all students up to the same achievement level—but providing no way or incentive for the better student to excel.

CONTRACT LEARNING

As defined previously, contract learning fundamentally involves a pact between a student and a faculty member outlining a course of studies to be pursued over an agreed-upon period of time. This program may include formal courses, independent study, and experiential learning. At New College at the University of South Florida (described in Chapter 12), contracts are written on a term-by-term basis, while at Metropolitan State University, they are for the entire two years of upper-division work. Two faculty members must agree on the contract with a student at New College at the University of South Florida, but at the University of Alabama's New College, contracts are agreements between students and a committee that can include University of Alabama faculty, students, administrative staff, and community resource people (see Chapter 6).

Thirty-five percent of undergraduates have used learning contracts in some or all of their courses. Learning contracts were most common among students at less selective liberal arts colleges (43 percent) and least common among students in the most research-oriented universities (25 percent). Among students who have had experience with learning contracts, 9 percent used them for all learning activities, 10 percent used them for most learning activities, 18 percent used them in several courses, and 64 percent used them in only a few courses. They were most likely to be used all of the time by students in selective liberal arts colleges (5.4 percent) (Carnegie Surveys, 1975–76).

Few colleges and universities have undergraduate programs relying entirely upon contracts. Only 5 percent of two-year arts and sciences programs and 8 percent of two-year professional/technical programs are fully contractual (Catalog Study, 1976). Similarly, 8 percent of four-year arts and sciences colleges and 1 percent of four-year professional/technical colleges have such programs. It is interesting to note that with rare exception the contract programs are optional.

Levine and Weingart (1973) studied contract learning at New College at the University of South Florida, which has the oldest contract curriculum in the nation. Their interviews were conducted at a time when New College offered both a contract and noncontract curriculum, and as a result, they were able to note faculty and student attitudes about both approaches. (1973, pp. 107–108):

> Twenty-three percent of the contractual programs were mostly individual projects and research, 44 percent were mostly regularly scheduled seminars, and 33 percent were combinations of seminars and individual work. . . . Faculty involvement with contracts ranged from no sponsorships to four or five a year. All seemed to feel a desire to actively advise the contractors, but some acknowledged that this had been impossible because much of the work the students had done was off campus. Others nevertheless demanded a weekly meeting or some form of written communication. Several said that they did not simply rubber-stamp contracts, but often asked students to revise their proposals and even rejected some.
>
> Most faculty and students agreed with the philosophy of offering contracts, but some faculty were disappointed with the quality of work they had witnessed. However, faculty sponsoring contracts felt they provided a welcome opportunity to get close to students. Some faculty said a contract could be executed with virtually no faculty supervision and that sloppy work often resulted. . . . One of the advantages of the contract system, however, is it allows a student to make use of facilities not present at New College. Thus, one student interviewed was able to obtain an anthropology major

although New College has no anthropology faculty. Another advantage is that students under contract get much individual faculty attention.

The strengths and weaknesses of contracts at New College are typical of those found in contract programs at other schools. An additional comment should be made, however: Contract learning requires extensive faculty work and student energy if it is to be done well. (Case studies dealing with contract learning at the University of Alabama's New College and at Metropolitan State University are found in Chapter 13.)

State of the Academic Calendar

Two facets of the academic calendar warrant particular attention by curriculum planners: (1) the yearly calendar, involving terms of different lengths, and (2) the daily and weekly calendar, involving the scheduling of class meetings.

Yearly Calendar

Currently four academic year calendars dominate American higher education: semester, trimester, 4-1-4, and quarter term; three others have only scattered acceptance: block, variable-term-length, and open entrance.

SEMESTER CALENDAR

The semester calendar is most frequently used by colleges and universities. It is found at 66 percent of two-year arts and sciences colleges, 71 percent of two-year professional/technical colleges, 58 percent of four-year arts and sciences institutions, and 66 percent of four-year professional/technical schools (Catalog Study, 1976).

The semester calendar consists of two terms which average 15 weeks each but which can be as long as 20 weeks. Full-time students take four or five courses per term. Some colleges begin their fall semester before Labor Day and complete the term by Christmas. This "early semester" arrangement originated at Princeton in 1843 *(Commission on Year-Round Integrated Operation Report,* 1961, p. 35) but only within the past decade has become the norm. Until recently, most fall semesters began after Labor Day and ended in the middle of January following Christmas vacation. The January portion of this fall term, sometimes called the "lame duck" session, is reserved primarily for final examinations but frequently for some classes as well. Under either plan, the second semester, or spring term, usually stretches from late January or early February to May. Summer is traditionally a time for vacation.

The advantages of the semester system over other calendars are that (1) it provides the most classroom hours per term; (2) it makes possible a review week at the end of each term; (3) it permits a lengthy, more thorough study of subjects; (4) it encourages a stable college community owing to common vacation and attendance patterns; (5) it enables students to find summer employment at the time when jobs are most available owing to worker vacations and good weather; and (6) it minimizes the number of courses for which faculty must prepare, the number of times students must register for courses, and number of examination periods for which grades must be recorded.

The weaknesses of the semester system are that (1) it allows little flexibility regarding student attendance patterns and faculty teaching schedules; (2) it forces courses into a term or year length regardless of content or purpose; (3) it requires full-time students to study four or five different subjects at a time; (4) it limits students in the number of courses they can take in four years more severely than with any other calendar system; (5) it may unnecessarily stretch subjects that could be covered more quickly in shorter terms; and (6) its three-month summer vacation period is not necessary for all students and faculty.

TRIMESTER CALENDAR

A variation of the semester system is the trimester calendar, which consists of three fifteen-week terms. Full-time students attend either two terms per year and take four courses per term or attend three terms per year and take three courses per term. The latter arrangement is called the 3–3 calendar. It was introduced at Goucher College in the early 1950s, but Dartmouth is generally credited with devising the calendar (Brick and McGrath, 1969, p. 124) and Pittsburgh with increasing its notoriety.

The advantages of the trimester calendar are that (1) it is efficient in using time and facilities because the campus is in full operation all year long and there is no summer hiatus; (2) it allows for acceleration, in that students can take nine or more courses per year versus eight in the semester curriculum; (3) it allows flexibility in student attendance patterns because students can take any of the three terms off; (4) it eliminates the January "lame duck" session; (5) it can be easily adapted from the semester calendar; (6) it provides a longer summer term, beginning in April and ending in August, for students who want or need the time for work; and (7), it enables faculty to earn additional money by teaching during the summer.

Its disadvantages are that (1) it makes transfer from a college on the semester system difficult during the spring, as the trimester term begins earlier than the spring semester; (2) it makes faculty exchange during the spring term difficult for the same reasons; (3) it offers in its 3-3 form less vacation time than many other calendars; (4) it leaves less time for faculty research and course preparation than many other calendars; (5) it entails more registration, bookkeeping, advising, and examination periods than two-term calendars; (6) it is incompatible with several financial aid programs which are based on semester or quarter calendars; (7) it requires a fairly constant year-round enrollment to be economical; and (8) it is fatiguing to faculty and students.

4–1–4 CALENDAR

Another variation on the semester system is the 4–1–4 calendar. It consists of two semesters divided by a one-month term called the interterm, interim term, intersession, mini-term, or January term. The January "lame duck" session is eliminated and the month is used for intensive short courses, independent study, student projects, travel, or fieldwork.

4–1–4 calendars are found at 12 percent of two-year arts and sciences colleges, 10 percent of two-year professional/technical colleges, 21 percent of four-year arts and sciences colleges, and 10 percent of four-year professional/technical institutions (Catalog Study, 1976). The fact that the calendar is so widely used is remarkable when it is considered that the idea is less than 20 years old.

The advantages of the 4–1–4 calendar are (1) it provides a change of pace between semesters, (2) it accommodates an innovative enclave or laboratory for pedagogical experimentation; (3) it breaks down academic compartmentalization through mini-term interdisciplinary teaching and curriculum experimentation; (4) it enables students to accelerate their studies; (5) it allows for new courses without course proliferation; (6) it provides an opportunity for faculty not teaching during the mini-term to pursue research, study, or writing; (7) it eliminates the "lame duck" session; and (8) it increases flexibility for students in undergraduate programs with few electives. The disadvantages of the 4–1–4 calendar are that (1) the mini-term may be little more than a frill; (2) the mini-term costs faculty and students vacation time and results in extra work; and (3) the mini-term adds financial and administrative costs to the regular semester system.

QUARTER CALENDAR

The quarter calendar consists of four ten-week terms. The full-time student takes three courses per quarter and attends three quarters per year. Sixteen percent of two-year and 18 percent of four-year arts and sciences colleges use the quarter calendar; as do 10 percent of professional/technical schools at both two- and four-year institutions (Catalog Study, 1976).

The advantages of the quarter system are that (1) it permits students to take a greater number and variety of courses than is possible with two-term calendars; (2) it enables students to concentrate on a small number of courses per term; (3) it offers students the possibility of acceleration by attending additional terms or by taking four courses; (4) it provides students and faculty flexibility in choosing attendance or vacation patterns; (5) it offers more frequent breaks than the semester system; (6) it allows for courses of three lengths (one quarter, two quarters, three quarters) while the semster system allows for only two; and (7) it is better adjusted to national holidays and traditional work-year breaks, as quarters fit into the spaces between Labor Day, Christmas, and Easter vacation.

The disadvantages of the quarter system are that (1) it makes inefficient use of time as contrasted with the trimester system (40 weeks of instruction versus 45 weeks of instruction per year); (2) it involves twice as much registration and bookkeeping as the semester calendar; (3) it requires more preparation, tests, and grading by faculty; (4) it occasionally results in superficial courses because terms are only ten weeks long; (5) it keeps students on an academic treadmill owing to the need to choose and complete new courses every ten weeks; (6) it makes faculty teaching at the summer session of other colleges difficult; and (7) it makes unavoidable faculty and student absences from class more serious.

OTHER CALENDARS

Five percent of two-year colleges and 3 percent of four-year colleges use calendars other than those discussed above. Among them are the block or intensive course calendar, the variable-term-length calendar, and the open entrance calendar.

Block Calendar. In a block calendar students study one course at a time. Mount Vernon College (Washington, D.C.) and Colorado College have such calendars. At Mount Vernon College, a two-year women's school, the academic year is 30 weeks long and consists of ten three-week blocks. Each block is separated by a two- or three-day break. The college offers three types of courses: three-week intensive courses that constitute a student's full-time load; six-week courses that constitute one-half of a student's full-time load, and 12-week courses that constitute one-quarter of a student's full-time load. At any one time, a student can either be enrolled in one three-week course, two six–week courses, four twelve-week courses, or one six-week and two twelve-week courses. Of all three lengths of course, Mount Vernon students choose the 12-week course least frequently. Faculty teach 24 credits per year, the equivalent of eight full-time courses, but they do so in only 24 weeks rather than the 30 weeks of the semester calendar, thus giving them six free weeks for other activities.

The block calendar at Colorado College, which was introduced in 1970, consists of nine three-and-a-half week terms or blocks which stretch from September 1 to June 1. Each block is separated by a four-and-one-half day break. Students must complete the equivalent of 34 blocks of full-time course work to graduate and faculty teach nine courses a year. Several types of courses are offered: intensive three-week courses, which constitute a full-time course load for students; extended courses, which last seven-and-one-half to ten weeks; adjunct courses, which are late-afternoon, low-credit courses in subjects such as drama, physical education, and instrumental music; and half courses, which constitute a half-time load for full-time students.

The advantages of the block calendar are that (1) studies are deeper and less fragmented than in concurrent course calendars; (2) block-long field trips and field work can be undertaken easily; (3) daily schedules can be left to the discretion of the faculty members and students in terms of the particular nature of the day's studies, (4) prominent scholars who might otherwise be unavailable can be brought to campus to teach for a block (less than one month); (5) students indicate high enthusiasm for the calendar; (6) students reportedly work hard; (7) faculty have to prepare for only one course at a time; (8) acceleration of studies is possible; (9) faculty feel they accomplish more than in conventional calendar systems; and (10) attendance and teaching patterns can be more flexible.

The disadvantages of the block calendar are that (1) more classrooms are necessary; (2) faculty are required to teach more courses per year and become fatigued by the pressure; (3) students are required to work harder; (4) the intensive format is not suited to all courses; (5) classroom friendships are more difficult for students to sustain because classes change every few weeks; (6) the intensive format may discourage students from experimenting with unfamiliar courses; and (7) registration, bookkeeping, and grading occur up to nine or ten times per year.

Variable-Term Length Calendar. The variable-term-length calendar consists of a number of terms, some or all of which differ in length. For example, Western Maryland College has a four-month/one-month/five-month calendar and Pacific University has a calendar consisting of four seven-week terms and two three-week terms.

One of the most interesting calendars of this type is that adopted at the University of Wisconsin at Oshkosh in 1975. It consists of two traditional semesters of 17 weeks each and an eight-week summer session. Each semester can be broken into two seven-week sessions and a three week session, and the summer term can be split into two four-week sessions. Full-time faculty are required to teach 24 credit hours per year, but the calendar permits faculty to teach the equivalent of a 17-week course in two seven-week sessions. The three weeks they save or any other time they free up can be used to teach an additional course toward the 24-credit equivalent, write, study, relax, or engage in research or curriculum development for which a competitive fund has been established. Eighty percent of Oshkosh faculty have utilized the fund. For students the alternative calendar makes possible continuous registration. That is, a student can register at any time and commence undergraduate study immediately. However, 85 percent of the students are on regular schedule and 80 percent of the courses are of the semester variety. It is not yet possible to talk about the strengths or weaknesses of this calendar arrangement because the first comprehensive evaluation is still under way.

Open Entrance Calendar. The open entrance calendar is one in which students can enroll at least weekly. As just noted, this is a feature of the University of Wisconsin at Oshkosh program. Leeward Community College in Honolulu, Hawaii; Central Community College in Hastings, Nebraska; and Platte Community College in Columbus, Nebraska, are among institutions that have also adopted this calendar.

Course Calendar

Colleges and universities in the United States not only offer courses throughout the entire year with the possible exception of Christmas and New Year's week, but they seem to be on the way to offering courses around the clock and around the week. They run courses early in the morning, during the entire day, and in the evening, Monday through Friday; and they offer weekend programs as well.

Very few institutions, of course, offer instruction at all of these times and, as might be expected, day and evening courses during the week are the most common arrangement. Fifty-nine percent of undergraduates take all their courses during the day. This practice occurs most frequently among students in selective liberal arts colleges (73 percent) and research universities (71 percent). It is least frequent among students at community and junior colleges (46 percent) (Carnegie Surveys, 1975–76).

Evening classes are not as popular as day classes. Only 14 percent of undergraduates take all of their classes at night. Those enrolled in community and junior colleges (31 percent) are most likely to attend only at night, while those at research universities (1 percent) and selective liberal arts colleges (.4 percent) are least likely to attend only then (Carnegie Surveys, 1975–76).

Early-morning classes, scheduled to meet before working hours, and weekend colleges are recent phenomena that seem to be gaining in popularity, if a growing number of advertisements in the *New York Times Education Supplement* is any indication. Between 7:00 A.M. and 9:00 A.M., the University of Santa Clara offers what it calls "Early Bird classes" leading to an engineering degree. And Long Island University has a degree in management that includes classes offered to suburbanites on their way to work in New York City by commuter train.

The weekend college provides a way in which students can complete courses and degree programs by attending college primarily or entirely on Friday, Saturday, and Sunday. Long Island University began the C. W. Post Weekend College in 1971. By 1975, 2,500 students were enrolled and 160 courses were being taught per term. This college offers associate's and bachelor's degree programs which range from the liberal arts to nursing. Its credit requirements for degrees are the same as those in non-weekend branches of the university. Three-credit courses are scheduled in several ways: (1) six hours of instruction for six consecutive Saturdays; (2) six hours of instruction for six consecutive Sundays; and (3) 16 hours of instrucion for two separate weekends, six weeks apart. The instructors in the programs are regular Long Island University faculty. They have office hours and telephone contact time for out-of-class consultation by the weekend students, who tend to be older than average college age.

Concerns and Proposals

Criticism 1: Time is an inappropriate commonality in undergraduate degrees.

The time-based degree is defended on the grounds that there is a long tradition behind it. The four-year baccalaureate was imported to America from Cambridge University more than 300 years ago, and alternatives have been tried in this country—beginning as early as 1640—but none have caught on. It is ironic, however, that Cambridge and Oxford universities switched to a three-year degree, which is still the norm today, not long after alumni established the first four-year degree program at Harvard (Boyer, 1975, p. 14). Time-based degrees are also defended for providing quantitative consistency in degrees and for permitting diversity in curriculum.

Critics of time-based degrees frequently argue that undergraduate education should focus on the purpose or desired outcomes of an undergraduate education, not on a common amount of time that students, who vary considerably in ability and background, should be expected to put in (Taylor, 1971; and Milton, 1972). Several time-variable curricular options, such as progress by examination, self-paced instruction, and especially competency-based curricula, rely upon outcomes rather than time.

Criticism 2: Shortening the amount of time required to earn a college degree is unfeasible at this time as student aptitude test scores are declining nationally.

Given the widely reported declines in student aptitude test scores and basic skills proficiency and the influx of academically disadvantaged new students to colleges and universities (see Chapter 3), it does not make sense to talk of a universal policy of time shortening. However, these changes do not mean that time shortening is inappropriate for all students.

There is evidence of significant duplication between high school and college programs. As noted earlier, Blanchard (1971) found an overlap of nearly one-third between the curriculum covered in the last two years of high school and the first two years at liberal arts colleges. Forty-eight percent of the students responding to the 1976 Carnegie Council undergraduate survey also agreed that part of their college education was a wasteful repetition of work covered in high school. Duplication was most often reported by students at comprehensive colleges (41 percent) and least often by students at selective liberal arts colleges (22 percent) (Carnegie Surveys, 1975–76). This problem indicates that articulation between college and secondary school is poor. It also suggests that time in education could be cut for some students without loss of content.

The situation of the underprepared student and the academically advanced student attending the same college is a problem at many schools. To solve this problem, the Carnegie Commission (1971) recommended a policy of time shortening for many undergraduates and more time options for all students. In this regard, the State University of New York College at Geneseo offers both three- and four-year baccalaureate programs to its students. Forty percent of the students elect the three-year program, and Robert Bersi (1973, pp. 31–34) reports that the three-year program is proving a cost-saving device to the college. In addition, California State University at Bakersfield now offers students a variety of time options, including self-paced instruction, credit by examination, and credit for experiential learning. According to Virginia Kemp of Geneseo, the key to successful use of alternative time options is providing accurate information, strong advising, and allowing for self-selection by students.[1]

Criticism 3: General education is weakened by time shortening.

This is not true of all approaches to time shortening and may not be true of any approaches to time shortening. But two approaches —curriculum compression and credit by examination—do reduce the amount of time students devote to general education. For example, John Jay College in New York reduced general education requirements to create a four-year B.A./M.A. program, and the State University of New York College at Geneseo compressed its lower-division program to a single year in the three-year baccalaureate program. With regard to credit by examination, a surprisingly large number of students going directly from high school to college manage to do sufficiently well on the

---

[1]Based on conversation with Virginia Kemp, October 1975.

College Level Examination Program General Tests that they receive exemption from some college general education courses. In 1973, Florida passed legislation requiring all state universities to offer their students general CLEP examinations to satisfy general education requirements.

Several proposals have been advanced on the subject of general education and time shortening. One is to follow the example of those time-shortened general education programs that attempt to deliver better general education courses while eliminating the overlap between the last two years of high school and the first two years of college as well as among lower-division college courses themselves (Giardina and others, 1973, pp. 19–21). Another is to eliminate general education credit "giveaways" (Stecher, 1977, p. 41). A third recommends reducing the amount of time required for specialization. Herbert Lehman College, for example, offers a joint B.A./M.A. which integrates the last year of college and first year of graduate school. In addition, The Carnegie Foundation for the Advancement of Teaching (1977) has suggested reducing the amount of time spent on specialization by reducing the number of student electives.

Criticism 4: Interruption or acceleration of the four-year course of studies results in poorer student performance.

There is evidence to support exactly the opposite conclusion. With regard to interruption, when Judi Kesselman (1976a, p. 13) surveyed over 100 schools about the effects of students' stopping out, the vast majority of deans and admissions officers "expressed the opinion that time out increased motivation and raised grades." Only one dean actively frowned upon the idea. With regard to student achievement in accelerated programs, matched groups of students in three- and four-year degree programs were compared at the State University of New York College at Geneseo. Students in the three-year programs were found to have higher grade-point averages, higher mean scores on the Graduate Record Examination, and greater interest in attending graduate school (Office of Institutional Research, 1975). Accordingly, colleges have been urged to introduce deferred admissions policies (*Report on Higher*

Education, 1971, p. 68) and to support student stop outs (Carnegie Commission, 1971, p. 1).

References

"ACT to Make N.Y. College Proficiency Tests Available Nationwide." *Higher Education Daily,* 1976, 4 (49), 4.

Alverno College Faculty. *Liberal Learning at Alverno College.* Milwaukee, Wis.: Alverno College, 1976.

Astin, A. W. *Preventing Students from Dropping Out.* San Francisco: Jossey-Bass, 1975.

Bersi, R. M. *Restructuring the Baccalaureate: A Focus on Time-Shortened Degree Programs in the United States.* Washington, D.C.: American Association of State Colleges and Universities, 1973.

This slightly dated but still valuable monograph examines the characteristics and costs of seven model time-shortened programs, describes 67 other proposed and operational programs, and provides an alphabetical list of 243 colleges and universities engaged in time shortening.

Berte, N. (Ed.). *New Directions for Higher Education: Individualizing Education by Learning Contracts,* no. 10. San Francisco: Jossey-Bass, 1975a.

This volume contains essays by eight different authors discussing significant experiments with contract learning at five colleges and universities as well as general background readings on the history, theory, strengths, and weaknesses of contract learning.

Berte, N. *Individualizing Education Through Contract Learning.* University: University of Alabama Press, 1975b.

This book expands upon the preceding volume.

Blanchard, B. E. *Curriculum Articulation Between the College of Liberal Arts and the Secondary School: A National Survey.* Chicago: DePaul University, 1971.

Boyer, E. L. "How Much Time for Education?" *Educational Record,* 1972, 53 (4), 271–280.

Boyer, E. L. "Changing Time Requirements." In D. W. Vermilye (Ed.), *Learner-Centered Reform: Current Issues in Higher Education 1975.* San Francisco: Jossey-Bass, 1975.

This essay concisely discusses the history of time use in higher education and probes the new directions that now must be explored.

Brick, M., and McGrath, E. J. *Innovation in Liberal Arts Colleges.* New York: Teachers College Press, 1969.

Brubacher, J. S., and Rudy, W. *Higher Education in Transition: A History of American Colleges and Universtiies, 1636–1976.* (3rd ed.) New York: Harper & Row, 1976.

Carnegie Commission on Higher Education. *Less Time, More Options: Education Beyond the High School.* New York: McGraw-Hill, 1971.

The Carnegie Foundation for the Advancement of Teaching. *Missions of the College Curriculum: A Contemporary Review with Suggestions.* San Francisco: Jossey-Bass, 1977.

This report is discussed in Chapter 11.

Carnegie Surveys, 1975–76.

This study is discussed in the Preface.

Catalog Study, 1976.

This research is described in the Preface.

Commission on Year-Round Integrated Operation Report. Ann Arbor, Mich.: University of Michigan, May 15, 1961.

This report to the University of Michigan on possibilities for year-round operation analyzes the strengths and weaknesses of a variety of calendar arrangements based upon guiding principles generated by the commission.

Cooperative Assessment of Experiential Learning. *A Compendium of Assessment Techniques.* Princeton, N.J.: Educational Testing Service, 1974a.

Cooperative Assessment of Experiential Learning. *CAEL Project Status Report.* Princeton, N.J.: Educational Testing Service, 1974b.

Cooperative Assessment of Experiential Learning. *Current Practices in the Assessment of Experiential Learning.* Princeton, N.J.: Educational Testing Service, 1974c.

Cross, K. P. *Accent on Learning: Improving Instruction and Reshaping the Curriculum.* San Francisco: Jossey-Bass, 1976.

This book is discussed in Chapter 11.

Desmond, R. L. "The Enigmatic Trimester Calendar." *Educational Record,* 1971, 52 (4), 371–376.

Giardina, R. C., Litwin, J. L, and Cappuzello, P. G. *The Dynamics of Baccalaureate Reform.* Bowling Green, Ohio: Bowling Green State University, 1973.

Grandy, J., and Shea, W. M. *The CLEP General Examinations in American Colleges and Universities.* Princeton, N.J.: Educational Testing Service, 1976.

A Guide to Educational Programs in Noncollegiate Organizations: Project on Noncollegiate Sponsored Instruction. Albany, N.Y.: The Regents of the University of the State of New York, 1977.

Hefferlin, J. L. "Intensive Courses—A Research Need." *The Research Reporter,* 1972, 7 (3). Berkeley: Center for Research and Development in Higher Education, University of California, 1972.

Kesselman, J. R. "The Care and Feeding of Stop-outs." *Change,* 1976a, 8 (4), 13–15.

Kesselman, J. R. *Stopping Out.* New York: M. Evans, 1976b.

This book is intended as a guide to leaving college and getting back in. It deals with such practical problems as the effect of stopping out on student futures, timing of stop-outs, planning and financing the stop-outs, and possibility for earning credit during stop outs.

Kintzer, F. C. *Middleman in Higher Education: Improving Articulation Among High School, Community College, and Senior Institutions.* San Francisco: Jossey-Bass, 1973.

Levine, A., and Weingart, J. *Reform of Undergraduate Education.* San Francisco: Jossey-Bass, 1973.

Meinert, C. W. *Time Shortened Degrees.* Washington, D. C.: American Association for Higher Education, 1974.

This book is an excellent review of the literature and an incisive analysis of the subject. It deals with the history, benefits, criticism, approaches, and characteristics of time-shortened degree programs.

Meyer, P. *Awarding College Credit for Non-College Learning: A Guide to Current Practices.* San Francisco: Jossey-Bass, 1975.

This book is intended as a guide or how-to-do-it book on awarding noncollege credit. It is strong on explaining procedure, but weak on making it seem academically palatable.

Milton, O. *Alternatives to the Traditional: How Professors Teach and How Students Learn.* San Francisco: Jossey-Bass, 1972.

Office of Institutional Research. *Research Report: The Second Group of 3-Year Baccalaureate Degree Students Six Semesters Later.* Geneseo, N.Y.: State University College, Sept. 1975.

Report on Higher Education. (Frank Newman, chairman, Task Force.) Washington, D.C.: U.S. Government Printing Office, 1971.

This report is discussed in Chapter 11.

Stecher, C. "CLEP and the Great Credit Giveway." Change, 1977, 9 (3), 36–41.

Taylor, H. *How to Change Colleges: Notes on Radical Reform.* New York: Holt, Rinehart and Winston, 1971.

This book is discussed in Chapter 11.

Trivett, D. A. "New Developments in College Transfer." *Research Currents* (ERIC-AAHE), Sept. 1974.

Trivett, D. A. *Academic Credit for Prior Off-Campus Learning.* Washington, D.C.: American Association for Higher Education, 1975a.

This monograph provides an overview of recent developments in crediting prior off-campus learning such as CLEP and other examinations, CAEL, OEC, and new special degree programs.

Trivett, D. A. *Competency Programs in Higher Education.* Washington, D.C.: American Association for Higher Education, 1975b.

This is a helpful summary of a topic with a ballooning literature.

U.S. National Center for Education Statistics. *Digest of Education Statistics: 1975 Edition.* Washington, D.C.: U.S. Government Printing Office, 1976.

von der Lippe, R. "Progress by Examination." Report no. 2. Amherst, Mass.: Hampshire College, Nov. 1975.

Washington State Council on Higher Education. "Transfer of Credit Among Washington Institutions of Higher Education: Study to Determine How Much Credit Is Lost and What Kinds of Programs Are Accepted." Olympia, Washington, Sept. 1973.

Part Two

A Comparative and Historical Perspective on Undergraduate Curriculum

10

A Comparison of Modern Philosophies of Higher Education

Philosophers have not always seen eye to eye on the purpose or form that undergraduate education should take. In the course of nearly three-and-a-half centuries of undergraduate education in this country, opinion about the purpose of college has evolved from consensus to a current state of wide disagreement. During this period, the college has been variously described as: an institution for educating ministers, raising youth in good letters and manners, and propagating Christianity among Western Indians (Charter of College of William and Mary, 1693); "a place where an extra clever boy may go and still amount to something" (Cooper, in Stone and DeNevi, 1971, p. 17); a preserver of the connection between knowledge, the zest of life, and imagination (Whitehead, 1968, p. 93); an agent for the socialization of the young (Jencks and Riesman, 1968, p. 28); an institution for providing students with the discipline and furniture of the mind (*Yale Report of 1828*); a place to give a man enlarged vision (Cooper, in Stone and DeNevi, 1971, p. 183); a home for teaching, research, and service (Kerr, 1966); an institution for certification, education, and incarceration (Hefferlin, 1975); the one place where liberal education can keep its heart whole (Van Doren, 1959, p. 106); high school with ashtrays (anonymous); a sanctuary of truth, a social service station, a sanctuary of method, and a culture mart (Adelman, 1973, pp. 44–45); an organization primarily engaged in occupational training (Dresch, 1973, p. 12); a repository for universal truths (Hutchins, 1967, p. 66); "a school of probation and introduction to the scholarly life" (Veblen, 1968, p. 209); and "a vast WPA project, which gives promising adolescents work to do while keeping them out of the job market, and also keeping several hundred thousand faculty members off the streets" (Riesman and Jencks, 1962, p. 76).

On the topic of the curriculum best suited for colleges, disagreements have been loud and emotional. For instance, Ezra Cornell answers the question "What subjects should be taught in college?" with two words, "any study" (in Hofstadter and Smith, 1961, p. 55). Robert Hutchins (1967, p. 83) takes a narrower view, limiting the curriculum to universal truths, first principles, reading, writing, thinking, speaking, and mathematics. Daniel Bell (1968, p. 8) takes an entirely different tack, deeming subject matters less important than methods of inquiry or ways of knowing.

On the topic of what subjects should be required in an undergraduate education, Harold Taylor (1971, p. 76) proposes that all subject matter requirements be eliminated, and Robert Hutchins (1967, p. 66) proposes a fully prescribed curriculum that would be required of all students in all colleges all over the world. On the question of how instruction might be delivered, John Dewey (1902, pp. 89–91) recommends the survey course, and Mark Van Doren (1959, p. 117) says "sampling and surveys will not do." On the more fundamental issue of whether the undergraduate curriculum should emphasize breadth or depth, Alfred North Whitehead (1968, p. 25) counsels that "the spirit of generalization should dominate a university," and Abraham Flexner (1968, p. 23) counters that "specialization has brought us to the point we have reached and man's specialized intelligence will alone carry us further." On the role of students in planning their own program, Charles W. Eliot writes that "a young man of 19 or 20 ought to know what he likes best and is most fit for" (in Hofstadter and Smith, 1961, p. 608). Noah Porter does not entirely agree. He states "the majority of undergraduates have neither maturity nor the data which qualify them to judge the value of their studies or their bearing on future employment" (p. 699). On the question of whether colleges should engage in occupational instruction, Thorstein Veblen (1968, p. 140) says vocational training has no connection with higher learning, while Gerald Ford (1974) asks "What good is training if it is not applied to jobs?"

Even what appear to be avenues of agreement have proven to be byways for discord. For instance, both Frank Aydelotte (1927) and Frank Newman's Task Force on Higher Education of the U.S.

Office of Health, Education, and Welfare (*Report on Higher Education*, 1971), diagnose the "lockstep" curriculum to be a major problem in undergraduate education. To remedy the problem, each proposes a contradictory solution. Aydelotte proposes an honors program, making contact between faculty and students more intimate, and the Newman task force proposes off-campus study, reducing student-faculty contact.

Similarly Robert Hutchins has written a book entitled *The Learning Society* (1969) and Charles Benson and Harold Hodgkinson have written one entitled *Implementing the Learning Society* (1974). At first glance these appear to be the ideal blend of theory and practice—but this is not to be. Hutchins recommends limiting higher education to those with an interest in the life of the mind, and Benson and Hodgkinson tell what is required to provide opportunities for higher education to all in the society.

This chapter describes, compares, and contrasts the visions of seven modern philosophers of the university: John Cardinal Newman, John Dewey, Alfred North Whitehead, Thorstein Veblen, Abraham Flexner, Robert Hutchins, and Clark Kerr. Each offers a vision of the modern university that is today still poignant and still widely debated.

Dewey and Whitehead differ from the rest of the group in that their visions focus more upon the process of education than the nature of educational institutions. But all of the philosophers build upon one another. Flexner (1968), for instance, intends his philosophy as a response to Newman, who wrote *The Idea of a University* (1959). Flexner titles the chapter responding to Newman "The Idea of a Modern University." Veblen (1968) and Hutchins (1967) use exactly the same title—*The Higher Learning in America*. In his book, Hutchins specifically takes Dewey and Whitehead to task. Clark Kerr (1966) mentions all except Dewey; and Hutchins (1969) criticizes Kerr's conception.

John Henry Cardinal Newman

Biographical Sketch

1801	Born, London, England
1820	B.A., Trinity College, Oxford

1826–1832	Fellow and tutor, Oriel College, Oxford
1833	Anglican leader in Oxford movement that sought to bring the Church of England and the Roman Catholic Church together
1845	Converted to Roman Catholicism
1847	Became a Roman Catholic priest
1851–1858	Rector of Dublin Catholic University
1853	Nine Newman lectures published under the title *Discourse on University Education*
1858	A second volume of lectures published entitled *Lectures and Essays on University Subjects*
1873	*The Idea of a University* published as a single volume combining revisions of both previous books
1879	Became Cardinal Dean of St. George in Velabro
1890	Died, Birmingham, England

Philosophy of Education

By the time John Henry (later Cardinal) Newman published *The Idea of a University* in 1873, the vision he proffered was no longer attainable. His own Dublin Catholic University had failed some 15 years previously, and colleges in the United States were already inextricably involved with the research and service activities he opposed. Nonetheless, Newman's book has become a classic. It continues to offer a vision of what the university could be, an ideal that has formed the foundation for colleges such as St. John's and Shimer, and for the rest of higher education, a theory and standard for judging any academic practice.

Newman's idea of a university is a community of teachers and students—in his own words "a place of teaching universal knowledge" (p. 7). Research is excluded from the university's mission because Newman believes it to be a distinct and separate function from teaching. Ability in teaching and research is "not commonly united in the same person," and research would be conducted better in isolation or "retirement" than in a university setting (pp. 10, 11).

The community of scholars is an important element in Newman's conception. Given a choice between a university "which dispensed with residence and tutorial superintendence, and gave its degrees to any person who passed an examination in a wide range of subjects [shades of the external degree], and a university which had no professors or examinations at all, but merely brought a number of young men together for three or four years," Newman chooses the latter (p. 165). To him a university is "an alma mater, knowing her children one by one, not a foundry, or a mint, or a treadmill" (p. 165).

Newman's university includes all branches of knowledge. Students learn by contact with peers and teachers.

> This I conceive to be the advantage of a seat of universal learning, considered as a place of education. An assemblage of learned men, zealous for their own sciences, and rivals of each other, are brought, by familar intercourse and for the sake of intellectual peace, to adjust together the claims and relations of their respective subjects of investigation. They learn to respect, to consult, to aid each other. Thus is created a pure and clear atmosphere of thought, which the student also breathes, though in his own case he only pursues a few sciences out of the multitude. He profits by an intellectual tradition, which is independent of particular teachers, which guides him in his choice of subjects, and duly interprets for him those which he chooses. He apprehends the great outlines of knowledge, the principles on which it rests, the scale of its parts, its lights and its shades, its great points and its little [pp. 128–129].

This is for Newman the stuff of which a liberal education is made. The university is an institution concerned wholly with the intellect. Liberal education, philosophy, or universal knowledge is an end in itself and a quantity without specific practical, utilitarian, or work purpose. Law and medicine, for example, are not forms of liberal education; nor is mere accumulation of knowledge liberal education. Liberal education consists "in a comprehensive view of truth in all its branches, of the relations of science to science, of their mutual bearings, and their respective values"—enlargement of the mind (p. 130).

However, Newman fears this method of education will cause overspecialization in faculty. "There can be no doubt that every art is improved by confining the professor of it to that single study. But, although the art itself is advanced by this concentration of mind in its service, the individual who is confined to it goes back. The advantage of the community is nearly in an inverse ratio with his own" (p. 184).

For the student, the consequence of a liberal education is becoming a gentleman—having "a cultivated intellect, a delicate taste, a candid, equitable, dispassionate mind, a noble and courteous bearing in the conduct of life" (p. 144). For the public, a liberal education aims "at purifying the national taste, at supplying true principles to popular enthusiasm and fixed aims to popular aspiration, at giving enlargement and sobriety to the ideas of the age, at facilitating the exercise of political power, and refining the intercourse of private life" (p. 191).

Though acquaintance with the full circle of knowledge is a requisite for a liberal education, Newman thinks literature more important than the sciences. He bases this opinion on the 1,000-year-old tradition of literature, in contrast to the new and uncertain quality of the sciences. But of all subjects, Newman places particular emphasis on religion. It will "see that no doctrines pass under the name of truth, but those which claim it rightfully" (p. 238). Science, "grave, methodical, logical," opposes "reason to reason"; literature, "multiform and versatile," acts to "disclaim and insinuate," to persuade instead of convincing; while religion overarching in its scope, represses neither science nor literature while cultivating the whole (p. 237).

John Dewey

Biographical Sketch

1859	Born, Burlington, Vermont
1879	Graduated from the University of Vermont

1884	Received Ph.D. from The Johns Hopkins University
1884–1888	Philosophy instructor, University of Michigan
1888–1889	Philosophy instructor, University of Minnesota
1889–1894	Chairman, Department of Philosophy, University of Michigan
1894–1904	Professor, Department of Philosophy and Pedagogy, University of Chicago
1897	*My Pedagogic Creed* published
1900	*The School and Society* published
1902–1904	Director, School of Education, University of Chicago. Developed its Laboratory School. Worked with Hull House
1902	*The Child and the Curriculum* and *The Educational Situation* published
1904–1931	Professor, Philosophy Department, Columbia University
1915	Leader in founding American Association of University Professors
1916	*Democracy and Education* published
1919	Lecturer at Tokyo Imperial University, Japan, and National University of Peking and Nanking, China
1920	*Reconstruction in Philosophy* published
1928	Visited Russia
1930–1939	Professor Emeritus, Columbia University
1934	*Art as Experience* published
1937	Chairman, Commission of Inquiry into the Charges Against Trotsky at the Moscow trials
1938	*Experience and Education* published
1952	Died

Philosophy of Education

John Dewey was a prolific writer. His publications spanned a period of 70 years and required 153 pages for a complete listing (Bernstein, 1966, p. 187). A paradox is that very little of his work was targeted at colleges and universities, yet his name and his writing are staples in higher education curricular exposition and debate. The rationale is that Dewey proposes a philosophy of education for a modern industrial society—a philosophy as germane to nursery school as to the most esteemed universities. "It might be said that, if Dewey is recognized as a peculiarly American philospher, it is because he caught the voice, accent and temper of the American tradition and the nature of the special contingencies and choices before it in his own era. He did not, it may be argued, make the tradition, or, for that matter, remake it. The expanding forces of technology, the intervolvement of public and private affairs, the rising tides of the labor movement, the revolt against authoritarianism in religion and in education—all of these play a large part in and color his social philosophy—were, it may be argued, themes he translated into general terms of philosophical analysis; they were *not* consequences of his published ideas" (Erdman, 1955, pp. 21–22).

Dewey's seminal work on education is *Democracy and Education* (1967). The following discussion of his philosophy draws primarily upon this source; any departures from it are noted.

For Dewey, the purpose of education is "to set free and to develop the capacities of human individuals without respect to race, sex, class, or economic status." The method for accomplishing this is "a constant reorganizing and reconstructing of experience" (in Ratner, 1939, pp. 627, 629). This is Dewey's definition of education.

By experience Dewey means the "interaction of [an individual's] native activities with the environment which progressively modifies both the activities and the environment" (Dewey, 1967, p. 79). Experience is partially active and partially passive; it involves trying something and undergoing something. "When we experience something we act upon it, we do something with it; then we suffer or undergo the consequences" (p. 139).

Reconstruction is the process whereby crude and immature experience is refashioned into something intelligible and valuable. Dewey believes life to be "a self-renewing process," characterized by continual change (p. 9). In a complex and changing society, people come into contact with a wide variety of social arrangements—all of which are education. But as a consequence of the many and diverse experiences people undergo and the opportunities available for additional experience, formal education is needed for the purpose of clarification and continued development.

To this end, education has two functions: direction of student learning, and encouragement of student growth. Direction of learning involves taking the "natural or native impulses of the young [which] do not agree with the life-customs of the group into which they are born . . . [and] centering the impulses acting at any one time upon some specific end and in introducing an order of continuity into the sequence of acts" (p. 39). Dewey specifies that the role of the student in this process must be active, not merely that of a passive subject.

On the topic of encouraging growth, Dewey writes: "The criterion of the value of school education is the extent in which it creates a desire for continued growth and supplies means for making the desire effective in fact" (p. 53). He dismisses education intended for preparation of a remote future, for the unfolding of human potentials of one sort or another, or for the recapitulation of the past.

Dewey proposes a method of education based on the principles of problem solving. "They are first that the pupil have a genuine situation of experience—that there be a continuous activity in which he is interested for its own sake; secondly, that a genuine problem develop within this situation as a stimulus to thought; third, that he possess the information and make the observations needed to deal with it; fourth, that suggested solutions occur to him which he shall be responsible for developing in an orderly way; fifth, that he have opportunity and occasion to test his ideas by application, to make their meaning clear and to discover for himself their validity" (p. 163).

According to Dewey, "the subject matter of education [consists] primarily of the meanings that supply content to existing social life" (p. 192):

> The scheme of a curriculum must take account of the
> adaptation of studies to the needs of the existing com-

munity life; it must select with the intention of improving the life we live in common so that the future shall be better than the past. Moreover, the curriculum must be planned with reference to placing essentials first, and refinements second. The things which are socially most fundamental, that is, which have to do with the experiences in which the widest groups share, are the essentials. The things which represent the needs of specialized groups and technical pursuits are secondary. There is truth in the saying that education must first be human and only after that professional. But those who utter the saying frequently have in mind in the term human only a highly specialized class: the class of learned men who preserve the classic traditions of the past. They forget that material is humanized in the degree in which it connects with the common interests of men as men [p. 191].

Dewey prefaces the need for any course of studies on the growing complexity of social life. For continuity in social life, selected and organized forms of past collective experience relevant to contemporary activities must be transmitted to each new generation. However, he cautions, "this very process tends to set up subject matter as something .of value just by itself, apart from its function in promoting the realization of the meanings implied in the present experience of the immature. Especially is the educator exposed to the temptation to conceive his task in terms of the pupil's ability to appropriate and reproduce the subject matter in set statements, irrespective of its organization into his activities as a developing social member" (p. 193).

Dewey recommends a subject matter that begins with "active occupations having a social origin and use"—how-to-do-it activities—for example, managing a machine or riding a bicycle. This he believes to be the knowledge students most deeply incorporate. Next, the curriculum might proceed to subjects such as history and geography, which build upon learning by doing. History, Dewey writes, makes human implications explicit, and geography makes natural connections with the larger world. The third area of the curriculum is science, representing "the fruition of the cognitive factors in experience" (p. 230). In this manner students progress from the concrete to the abstract by "assimilating into their more direct experience the ideas and facts communicated by others who have had a larger experience" (p. 193).

Dewey states that experience-based education requires significant changes in the educational system. For example, he notes that the wholeness of experience is unfortunately unmatched by the compartmentalization of knowledge into academic departments. As a consequence of departmentalism, experience cannot be appropriately reconstructed. Other manifestations of the problem include a split between liberal education (education for pleasure) and utilitarian education (education for work); a split between learning based on doing and learning based on knowing; a split between the sciences and the humanities; a split between individual freedom and common cultural bonds; a split between intellect and morals; a split between work and play; and a split between vocational and nonvocational schools. All these dichotomies, in Dewey's opinion, are conditions inappropriate for education, which seeks to reconstruct experience at large rather than segment and compartmentalize it.

Alfred North Whitehead

Biographical Sketch

1861	Born, Isle of Thanet, Great Britain
1880–1884	Studied at Cambridge University
1885–1911	Lecturer in mathematics, Trinity College, Cambridge University
1910–1913	*Principia Mathematica* (3 volumes) published with coauthor Bertrand Russell
1911–1914	Lecturer in mathematics, University College, University of London
1914–1924	Professor, Imperial College of Science and Technology, University of London
1919	*An Enquiry Concerning the Principles of Natural Knowledge* published
1922	*The Principle of Relativity with Application to Physical Science* published

1924–1936	Professor of Philosophy, Harvard University
1925	*Science and the Modern World* published
1929	*The Aims of Education and Other Essays* published
1933	*Adventures of Ideas* published
1937	Professor Emeritus, Harvard University
1938	*Modes of Thought* published
1947	Died, Cambridge, Massachusetts

Philosophy of Education

It is, in a sense, remarkable that Alfred North Whitehead is thought of as one of the major thinkers in higher education. Whitehead was a mathematician, a man who took only mathematics courses as an undergraduate. When he broadened his field, it was not to education that he moved but to philosophy. His principal writing on education, *The Aims of Education and Other Essays,* was not published until he was 68 years old. For Whitehead, education was no more than an interesting sidelight.

His approach to education is quite different from Dewey's, but there is a kinship in world-view and conclusions of the two writers. Education for each is a thing of the present, to be built around the learner. Whitehead defines education as "the acquisition of the art of the utilisation of knowledge" (p. 4), noting that "education should be useful, whatever your aim in life" (p. 2). In fact, he believes the mission of education is life, but that schools fail to grasp this. "There is only one subject matter for education, and that is life in all its manifestations. Instead of this single unity, we offer children—Algebra, from which nothing follows; Geometry, from which nothing follows; Science, from which nothing follows; History, from which nothing follows; a couple of languages, never mastered; and lastly, most dreary of all, Literature, represented by plays of Shakespeare, with philological notes and short analyses of plot and character to be in substance committed to memory" (pp. 6–7).

Whitehead calls the content of such education removed from life "inert," composed of "ideas that are merely received into the mind without being utilised, or tested, or thrown into fresh combinations" (p. 1). He demands that education deal with the present. "The only use of a knowledge of the past is to equip us for the present. No more deadly harm can be done to young minds than by depreciation of the present. The present contains all that there is. It is holy ground; for it is the past, and it is the future" (p. 3). He also proposes that education inculcate a sense of duty and reverence in students. "Duty arises from our potential control over the course of events. . . . And the foundation of reverence is this perception, that the present holds within itself the complete sum of existence, backwards, and forwards, that whole amplitude of time, which is eternity" (p. 14).

Whitehead's most important contribution to education is his theory of rhythms. He says that "different subjects and modes of study should be undertaken by pupils at fitting times when they have reached the proper stage of mental development" (p. 15). Three stages of development are proposed: romance, precision, and generalization. Romance is the time of first apprehension of a subject matter, in which a student through independent browsing examines unexplored connections and glimpses a topic half concealed by a wealth of material. Precision builds upon romance. Romance discloses "ideas with the possibilities of wide significance" (pp. 18–19). During precision, new facts are acquired "in systematic order which thereby [forms] both a disclosure and an analysis of the general subject matter of the romance" (p. 19). Generalization, the final stage, involves a return to romance—dreaming, exploring, and applying—with the added advantages of ordered ideas and appropriate techniques.

For Whitehead, the process is cyclical. All learning at all ages proceeds via these three stages. At any one time, the individual is learning many different things. Each thing is learned by going through the three stages in succession, but not at the same time. Nonetheless, Whitehead feels that certain ages are dominated more by one stage than any other. From birth to age 13 or 14, life is a period of romance; from 14 to 18, a period of precision; and from 18 to 22, a period of generalization.

In order to be effective, education and curriculum have to be molded to the stages of development through "a continual repetition of such cycles" (p. 19). College is "the great period of generalization" (p. 25):

> At school the boy painfully rises from the particular towards glimpses at general ideas; at the University he should start from general ideas and study their applications to concrete cases. A well-planned University course is a study of the wide sweep of generality. I do not mean that it should be abstract in the sense of divorce from concrete fact, but that concrete fact should be studied as illustrating the scope of general ideas [p. 26].

> The function of a University is to enable you to shed details in favour of principles. . . . A principle which has thoroughly soaked into you is rather a mental habit than a formal statement. It becomes the way the mind reacts to the appropriate stimulus in the form of illustrative circumstances [p. 26].

Whitehead also has definite ideas about the design of the curriculum. He believes that every institution should develop a curriculum based on its own needs and created by its own staff. This curriculum should not and could not embrace all of the subjects that might be valuable for students, as knowledge grows quickly and life remains short. Accordingly, he recommends that a school or college not teach too many subjects, but teach what it does teach thoroughly.

Whitehead proposes, however, that all students receive both general and specialized education. "The general culture is designed to foster an activity of mind; the specialist course utilises this activity" (p. 11). Education for each is the same, though certain general knowledge is a prerequisite for specialization. "There is not one course of study which merely gives general culture, and another which gives special knowledge. The subjects pursued for the sake of a general education are special subjects specially studied; and, on the other hand, one of the ways of encouraging general mental activity is to foster a special devotion. You may not divide the seamless coat of learning" (p. 11).

Whitehead also proposes that "education turn out a pupil with something he knows well and something he can do well, . . . [an] intimate union of practice and theory [which] aids both. . . . Every form of education should give the pupil a technique, a science, an assortment of general ideas, and aesthetic appreciation, and . . . each of these sides of his training should be illuminated by the others" (p. 48). Accordingly, he believes that the three primary curricula—the literary curricula, the scientific curricula, and the technical curricula—should each include the other two fields in their course of study.

As a consequence of these beliefs, Whitehead thinks the justification for a university is that "it [preserves] the connection between knowledge and the zest of life, by uniting the young and the old in the imaginative consideration of learning" (p. 93). He sees nothing inappropriate about professional or technical university studies, such as business administration or medicine, because they are consistent with the mission of the university—"to weld together imagination and experience" (p. 93).

Whitehead thinks the university should engage in education and research. However, he warns against judging faculty productivity on the basis of publications, urging instead that it be measured by the weight of ideas. Some faculty offer their weightiest ideas only when in direct contact with pupils. This fact does not, in Whitehead's opinion, excuse teachers from research or researchers from teaching: "Do you want your teachers to be imaginative? Then encourage them to research. Do you want your researchers to be imaginative? Then bring them into intellectual sympathy with the young at the most eager, imaginative period of life, when intellects are just entering upon their mature discipline. Make your researchers explain themselves to active minds, plastic and with the world before them; make your young students crown their period of intellectual acquisition by some contact with minds gifted with experience of intellectual adventure. Education is discipline for the adventure of life; research is intellectual adventure; and the universities should be homes of adventure shared in common by young and old" (pp. 97–98).

Adventure, imagination, zest for life, utilization of knowledge—Whitehead's vocabulary as well as his philosophy has suited

American preferences for action and achievement more than that of his two contemporaries considered next—Veblen and Flexner.

Thorstein Veblen

Biographical Sketch

1857	Born, Cato, Wisconsin
1880	Graduated from Carleton College
1884	Received his Ph.D. in Philosophy from Yale University after transferring from The Johns Hopkins University
1884–1891	Lived on his family's farm, unable to find a faculty position
1891	Further graduate study at Cornell University in economics
1892–1906	Instructor, finally associate professor of economics, University of Chicago
1899	*The Theory of the Leisure Class* published
1904	*The Theory of Business Enterprise* published
1906–1909	Faculty member, Stanford University
1911–1919	Faculty member, University of Missouri
1914	*Imperial Germany and the Industrial Revolution* published
1918	*The Higher Learning in America* published
1919	*The Vested Interests and the State of the Industrial Arts* published
	Faculty member, New School for Social Research
1923	*Absentee Ownership and Business Enterprise in Recent Times* published
1929	Died, California

Philosophy of Education

The point of departure for Veblen's philosophy of higher education is exactly opposite that of Cardinal Newman's. Where Newman excludes research from the mission of the university, Veblen makes inquiry and scholarship its primary focus. In *The Higher Learning in America* (1968), Veblen writes:

> The conservation and advancement of the higher learning involves two lines of work, distinct but closely bound together: (a) scientific and scholarly inquiry, and (b) the instruction of students. The former of these is primary and indispensable. . . . The work of teaching properly belongs in the university only because and in so far as it incites and facilitates the university man's work of inquiry. . . . The instruction necessarily involved in university work, therefore, is only such as can readily be combined with the work of inquiry, at the same time that it goes directly to further the higher learning in that it trains the incoming generation of scholars and scentists [*sic*] for the further pursuit of knowledge. Training for other purposes is necessarily of a different kind and is best done elsewhere; and it does not become university work by calling it so and imposing its burden on the men and equipment whose only concern should be the higher learning [p. 12].

On these grounds, Veblen feels professional, utilitarian, and undergraduate education to be inappropriate for a university. About professional and technical education, he writes: "In aim and animus the technical and professional schools are 'practical,' in the most thoroughgoing manner; while the pursuit of knowledge that occupies the scientists and scholars is not 'practical' in the slightest degree. The divergent lines of interest to be taken care of by the professional schools and the university, respectively, are as widely out of touch as may well be within the general field of human knowledge. . . . The two are incommensurably at variance so far as regards their purpose, and in great measure also as regards their methods of work, and necessarily so" (pp. 19–20). As a consequence, Veblen urges that the tie between universities and professional/technical schools be severed.

He takes the same stand on utilitarian, vocational, and practical education. "'Vocational training' is training for proficiency in some gainful occupation, and it has no connection with the higher learning" (p. 140). In fact, practical education and higher learning are mutually deleterious when carried out in close proximity:

> Intimate association with these "utilitarians" unavoidably has its corrupting effect on the scientists and scholars, and induces in them also something of the same bias toward "practical" results in their work; so that they no longer pursue the higher learning with undivided interest, but with more or less of an eye to the utilitarian main chance [p. 22].
> [Utilitarians] are, without intending it, placed in a false position, which unavoidably leads them to court a specious appearance of scholarship, and so to invest their technological discipline with a degree of pedantry and sophistication; whereby it is hoped to give these schools and their work some scientific and scholarly prestige, and so lift it to that dignity that is presumed to attach to a non-utilitarian pursuit of learning [p. 23].

Veblen's opinion of the undergraduate college is similar. For him, the college is not a branch of higher learning but rather the "senior member of the secondary school system" (p. 17): "The undergraduate department . . . cannot be rated as an institution of the higher learning. At the best it is now a school for preliminary training, preparatory to entering on the career of learning, or in preparation for the further training required for the professions; but it is also, and chiefly, an establishment designed to give the concluding touches to the education of young men who have no designs on learning, beyond the close of the college curriculum. It aims to afford a rounded discipline to those whose goal is the life of fashion or of affairs" (p. 18).

Veblen criticizes the undergraduate college for substituting "mechanical relations, standards, and tests in the place of personal conference, guidance, and association between teachers and students" (p. 165). He disapproves of credits, grades, the principle of in loco parentis, large-scale education, pupils with an eye on jobs rather than academics, student extracurricular activities, and mediocrity, calling the combination "a system of . . . standardization, gradation, accountancy, classification, credits, and penalties," rapidly taking on the appearance of "a house of correction or a penal settlement" (pp. 162–163).

For Veblen, an institution of undergraduate education should be "a school of probation and introduction to the scholarly life" (p. 209). He argues that the college was on its way to such a mission in the period between the Civil War and Reconstruction, but that it was sidetracked by the free elective curriculum and the take-over of the academy by businessmen in the form of trustees and administrators. The curricular result has been the introduction of more practical courses of study concerned with material success and the encouragement of students to take whatever courses they desire.

Veblen's solution to the problem is "the abolition of the academic executive and of the governing board" (p. 202). With their demise the union of technical schools, undergraduate colleges, and graduate education will dissolve. He hopes that undergraduate education will as a result be purified of "executive megalomania" and revert "in the direction of that simpler scheme of scholarship that prevailed in the days before the coming of electives" (p. 209); to the education of "novices or rather to the untutored probationers . . . whose entrance on a career of scholarship is yet a matter of speculation" (p. 143).

Whether or not this change in undergraduate education occurs, Veblen believes that the graduate school, "having lost the drag of the collegiate division and the vocational schools, should come into action as a shelter where the surviving remnant of scholars and scientists might pursue their several lines of adventure, in teaching and in inquiry, without disturbance to or from the wordly-wise who clamour for the greater glory" (p. 209). This pristine retreat for pure, disinterested study is his ideal of *The Higher Learning in America*.

Abraham Flexner

Biographical Sketch

1866   Born, Louisville, Kentucky

1886	Graduated from The Johns Hopkins University
1886–1890	High school teacher
1890–1905	Started and ran "Mr. Flexner's School"
1906	Received M.A. from Harvard University
1908	*The American College* published
1908–1912	Staff member, The Carnegie Foundation for the Advancement of Teaching
1910	*Medical Education in the United States and Europe* published
1913–1928	Secretary, then Director of the Division of Studies and Medical Education of the Rockefeller Foundation General Education Board
1923	*A Modern College* published
1930	*Universities: American, English, and German* published
1930–1939	Director, Institute for Advanced Studies; Princeton, New Jersey
1959	Died

Philosophy of Education

Abraham Flexner's concept of a university is nearly that of Veblen. The differences, by and large, are more of degree than kind. Like Veblen, Flexner believes the university should be chiefly concerned with scholarship—scholarship in research and scholarship in teaching. Flexner's university would also be an active, but disinterested part of the society. In *Universities: American, English, and German* (1968), he writes: "A modern university would . . . address itself whole-heartedly and unreservedly to the advancement of knowledge, the study of problems, from whatever source they come, and the training of men—all at the highest level of possible effort. The constitution of the stars, the constitution of the atom, the constitutions of Oklahoma, Danzig, or Kenya, what is happening in the stars, in the atom, in Oklahoma, what social and political consequences flow from the fact that the politician is becoming more and more obsolescent while the business man and the idealist are playing a larger part in determining the development of society—all these are important objects to know about. It is not the business of the university to *do* anything about any of them" (p. 24).

From this mission flow the concerns of the scholars and scientists who would populate Flexner's university. Their concerns are four: "the conservation of knowledge and ideas; the interpretation of knowledge and ideas; the search for truth; the training of students who will practise and 'carry on'" (p. 6).

Flexner, like Veblen, complains of how poorly the university has fared in achieving these ends. For Flexner, a genuine university is "an organism characterized by highness and definiteness of aim, unity of spirit and purpose" (pp. 178–179). But what he sees around him is confusion.

> American universities . . . are composed of three parts: they are secondary schools and colleges for boys and girls; graduate and professional schools for advanced students; "service" stations for the general public. The three parts are not distinct: the college is confused with the "service" station and overlaps the graduate school; the graduate school is partly a college, partly a vocational school, and partly an institution of university grade [p. 45].
>
> [Universities] are secondary schools, vocational schools, teacher-training schools, research centres, "uplift" agencies, businesses—these and other things simultaneously [p. 179].

Like Veblen, Flexner is unhappy that so many students attend higher education; that secondary school–level work is offered for the first two years at institutions of higher learning; that students attend college principally "as a means of getting ahead in life" (p. 69); that colleges engage in vocational and practical courses of study; and that courses, grades, tests, and credits are confused with education.

Many of Flexner's criticisms were not previously voiced by Veblen, but he would surely have concurred with them. Flexner opposes the "service" mission when it removes the university from its proper concerns—that is, most of the time. For him, "service" generally means courses inappropriate to a university, such as "juvenile story writing" and "practical advertising"; students of nonuniversity caliber; and self-interested involvement in the society by the university and its staff. Extension and correspondence do not properly belong in a university either. Those functions, Flexner thinks, are better carried out by institutions of adult education.

He believes high school instruction is of poor quality—the substance of education varies from school to school, and learning of widely varying types is treated as equivalent. On this subject, Flexner writes "there is no more sense in counting stenography and bookkeeping toward college matriculation than there would be in counting manicuring, hair-bobbing, or toe-dancing" (p. 59).

Flexner also bemoans the demise of standards in higher education. "Fifty years ago, the degree of Ph.D. had a meaning in the United States; today, it has practically no significance. The same is true of research" (p. 124).

To eliminate these deficiencies, Flexner offers a plan. It is not as radical as the Veblen plan, but a number of the intended consequences are similar. Flexner thinks "the heart of a university" is "the graduate school of arts and sciences, the solidly professional schools (mainly, in America, medicine and law) and certain research institutions" (p. 197). Yet, as noted above, Veblen is quite opposed to building any professional schools, believing them to be too practical and necessarily corrupting of the university.

Flexner's plan to resurrect the desired elements of the university involves splitting the tripartite design of education (secondary school, college, and university) into two parts (secondary school and university). The activities of the college would be split between the secondary school and the university. Activities not appropriate to either would be jettisoned:

> Secondary education includes the present high school and a large part of the college: we are dealing with two divisions (secondary education and university education), not with three (high school, college, and graduate school), a fact that is made clear by the sudden decrease of students at the end of the second college year. The improvement of the university depends therefore upon the improvement of secondary schools, in which, as

rapidly as possible, the system of credits must be abolished, practical or technical subjects must cease to be counted towards university matriculation, and far greater thoroughness and continuity (i.e., higher standards) must be sought.

Within these universities . . . similar reforms could be carried out: majors, minors, units, credits might vanish without more ado. Some of the institutions might discard the first or second year; those that retained the college in whole or part could at least abandon the uniform four-year course, recognize differences of ability and industry, and segregate what is essentially teaching, the instructor's burden, from learning, which is the responsibility of the student. Uniformity is not feasible, perhaps not even desirable. The make-believe professions—journalism, business, library science, domestic science, and optometry—could be discarded: they would not be missed either by the university or society. What becomes of the things thus unloaded is, to be frank, not the university's concern; it is the concern of society to create appropriate organs to perform such of these functions as are really worth performing.

The most formidable "School"—the Harvard Graduate School of Business Administration—could be detached: it is fortunately situated in Boston: what more fitting than a Boston Graduate School of Business? That would leave the university free to attack the problem of professional training for business experimentally. Schools of education might be reformed and put on probation; schools of medicine, law, and engineering could be subjected to searching criticism and such reform as they may require. The entire teaching staff could be put on a full-time basis: no one would have to do "chores" to piece out a livelihood. On the other hand, and for that very reason, a closer and more helpful relation could be established between the university, on the one hand, and business, industry, government, education, and public health, on the other. For, lacking pecuniary interest in affairs, the faculty could treat the modern world as a great clinic. Only thus can the university be modernized . . . and at the same time preserve its intellectual integrity. Extension courses could be restricted, as they are in England, to subjects of university value and to students who are mature. The home study departments would evaporate. With these reforms, the American university would be enormously simplified; advertising would cease; administration would be slight and relatively inexpensive; further developments in the direction of faculty coöperation would in time take place; Harvard, Yale, Columbia, and Chicago would at once stand out as universities. They would need no buildings for years to come; their financial situation would become enormously easier. They would talk in terms of small groups of scholars and teachers. Far higher intellectual standards could be set up. I venture to believe that in less than a generation the influence of universities upon American life would be immensely greater than it is today [pp. 214–216].

Flexner also proposes the creation of a model university with the characteristics of his ideal to stimulate by example the reorganization of secondary schools and higher education:

Progress might be greatly assisted by the outright creation of a school or institute of higher learning, a university in the post-graduate sense of the word. It should be a free society of scholars—free, because mature persons, animated by intellectual purposes, must be left to pursue their own ends in their own way. Administration should be slight and inexpensive. Scholars and scientists should participate in its government; the president should come down from his pedestal. . . . The institution should be open to persons, competent and cultivated, who do not need and would abhor spoon-feeding—be they college graduates or not. It should furnish simple surroundings—books, laboratories, and above all, tranquillity—absence of distraction either by worldly concerns or by parental responsibility for an immature student body. Provision should be made for the amenities of life in the institution and in the private life of the staff. It need not be complete or symmetrical: if a chair could not be admirably filled, it should be left vacant. There exists in America no university in this sense—no institution, no seat of learning devoted to higher teaching and research. Everywhere the pressure of undergraduate and vocational activities hampers the serious objects for which universities exist. Thus science and scholarship suffer; money is wasted; even undergraduate training is less efficient than it might be, if left to itself [pp. 216–218].

Robert Maynard Hutchins

Biographical Sketch

1899	Born, Brooklyn, New York
1915–1917	Attended Oberlin College
1921	Received A.B., Yale University
1922	Received A.M., Yale University
1925	Received LL.B., Yale University
1925–1927	Lecturer, Yale Law School
1927–1929	Professor, Yale Law School
1927–28	Acting Dean, Yale Law School
1928–29	Dean, Yale Law School
1929–1945	President, University of Chicago
1936	*The Higher Learning in America* published
1943	*Education for Freedom* published
1945–1951	Chancellor, University of Chicago
1950	*Morals, Religion, and Higher Education* published
1951–1954	Associate Director, Ford Foundation
1953	*University of Utopia* and *Freedom, Educa-*

	tion, and the Fund published
1954–1975	Chief Executive Office, Fund for the Republic, later Center for the Study of Democratic Institutions
1968	*The Learning Society* published
1977	Died

Philosophy of Education

For Robert Hutchins, the mission of the university is "the pursuit of truth for its own sake" (1967, p. 33). "The object of the university is to see knowledge, life, the world, or truth whole. The aim of the university is to tame the pretensions and excesses of experts and specialists by drawing them into the academic circle and subjecting them to the criticism of other disciplines. Everything in the university is to be seen in the light of everything else. This is not merely for the sake of society or to preserve the unity of the university. It is also for the sake of the specialists and experts, who, without the light shed by others, may find their own studies going down blind alleys" (1969, p. 135).

Hutchins' conception is similar to Newman's, but like Veblen and Flexner, he finds the modern university far off the mark of his ideal: Credits and the mechanical quantification of instruction are inappropriate; too many students go on to higher learning for the wrong reasons; higher education improperly engages in secondary school teaching; vocational and practical subjects are out of place in a university; and the extracurriculum is a poor focus for higher learning. Hutchins also criticizes the university and its populace for anti-intellectualism, for being corrupted in favor of the utilitarian by money, for allowing the isolation of scholar from scholar and discipline from discipline, for substituting empiricism for significant scholarship, for being overly concerned with character and body building, and for being over-professional, which he equates with vocationalism.

Based on these failings, Hutchins offers a concrete plan for restructuring education in the United States. Students would spend six years in elementary school, three or four years in high school, and three or four years in college (1943, p. 77). In this manner they would complete college by the age of 20. Hutchins believes societal conditions dictate how much time students spend in school. It is his opinion that the depression elongated schooling to the equivalent of a junior college education.

More importantly, Hutchins intends his educational rear-rangement to enable colleges to take on a distinct mission of their own and to provide a capstone to the education of most people. This mission and capstone would be liberal education. In this re-spect Hutchins' proposal bears similarity to Cardinal Newman's idea of a university.

Education at the college level would be based on the great books, "books which have through the centuries attained the di-mensions of classics" for being "contemporary in every age" (1967, p. 78). Emphasis would additionally be placed on "the arts of read-ing, writing, thinking, and speaking, together with mathematics, the best example of the process of human reason" (1967, p. 85). The curriculum would be exactly the same for all students. Hutch-ins writes: "Education implies teaching. Teaching implies knowl-edge. Knowledge is truth. The truth is everywhere the same. Hence education should be everywhere the same" (1967, p. 66).

Like Veblen, Hutchins dismisses the free elective curriculum and with it the student-centered approach advocated by Dewey and Whitehead. "If there are permanent studies which every person who wishes to call himself educated should master; if those studies constitute our intellectual inheritance, then those studies should be the center of a general education. They cannot be ignored because they are difficult, or unpleasant, or because they are almost totally missing from our curriculum today. The child-centered school may be attractive to the child, . . . But educators cannot permit the stu-dents to dictate the course of study unless [academics] are prepared to confess that they are nothing but chaperons, supervising an aim-less, trial-and-error process which is chiefly valuable because it keeps young people from doing something worse" (1967, p. 70).

Hutchins believes "all the needs of general education in America . . . to be satisfied by this curriculum" (1967, p. 85): "If our hope has been to frame a curriculum which educes the elements of our common human nature, this program should realize our hope.

If we wish to prepare the young for intelligent action, this course of study should assist us; for they will have learned what has been done in the past, and what the greatest men have thought. They will have learned how to think themselves. If we wish to lay a basis for advanced study, that basis is provided. If we wish to secure true universities, we may look forward to them, because students and professors may acquire through this course of study a common stock of ideas and common methods of dealing with them."

On top of the college, Hutchins builds the university, which deals in "wisdom" and teaches "general principles, the fundamental propositions, the theory of any discipline" (1967, p. 48). Few students would attend or would need to attend the university. In place of the disorder currently characteristic of higher learning, Hutchins proposes a university based on the synoptic of metaphysics or "first principles." There is an almost religious or theological sense to this recommendation, reminiscent of Newman. The design of Hutchins' university is the following:

> The university would consist of the three faculty, metaphysics, social science, and natural science. [Departments would be eliminated.] The professors would be those who were thinking about the fundamental problems in these fields. The teaching would be directed to understanding the ideas in these fields, and would have no vocational aim. The student would study all three subject matters, with emphasis upon one. He would enter upon this program at the beginning of the junior year and continue in it for about three years.
>
> Since it is desirable that the collection of historical and current data should proceed in the vicinity of the university, research institutes in the social and natural sciences may be established in connection with it, though not as part of it. Technical institutes in the same relation to the university may also be created if needed to give practical training for occupations which require a background of special knowledge and facility in special

techniques. Students should in no case be admitted to technical or research institutes until they have completed their general and higher education [1967, p. 116].

Clark Kerr

Biographical Sketch

1911	Born, Stony Creek, Pennsylvania
1932	Received B.A. from Swarthmore College
1933	Received M.A. from Stanford University
1935–36	Instructor in economics, Antioch College
1936	Postgraduate work, London School of Economics
1939	Received Ph.D. from University of California
1939–40	Assistant professor of labor economics, Stanford University
1940–1945	Assistant professor, later associate professor of economics, University of Washington
1945–1952	Associate professor and Director, Institute for Industrial Relations, University of California, Berkeley
1952–1958	Chancellor, University of California, Berkeley
1958–1967	President, University of California
1960	*Unions, Management, and the Public* (with E. Wight Bakke) published
1964	*The Uses of the University* published
1964	*Labor and the Management of Industrial Society* published

1967–1973	Chairman, Carnegie Commission on Higher Education
1968	*Marshall, Marx and Modern Times* published
1974–present	Chairman, Carnegie Council on Policy Studies in Higher Education

Philosophy of Education

Clark Kerr is the philosopher of the modern university. He champions an institution that Newman, Veblen, Flexner, and Hutchins rejected, calling it the *multiversity*. In *The Uses of the University* (1966), Kerr writes:

> It is not one community but several—the community of the undergraduate and the community of the graduate; the community of the humanist, the community of the social scientist, and the community of the scientist; the communities of the professional schools; the community of all the nonacademic personnel; the community of the administrators. Its edges are fuzzy—it reaches out to alumni, legislators, farmers, businessmen, who are all related to one or more of these internal communities. As an institution, it looks far into the past and far into the future, and is often at odds with the present. It serves society almost slavishly—a society it also criticizes, sometimes unmercifully. Devoted to equality of opportunity, it is itself a class society. A community, like the medieval communities of masters and students, should have common interests; in the multiversity, they are quite varied, even conflicting. A community should have a soul, a single animating principle; the multiversity has several [pp. 18–19].

The mission of the multiversity is "the preservation of eternal truths, the creation of new knowledge, the improvement of service whenever truth and knowledge may serve the needs of man" (p. 38). It embodies the teaching university of Newman and Hutchins, the research university of Veblen and Flexner, and the service university that has been condemned by all except Dewey and Whitehead on the grounds that vocational, practical, and objective activities jeopardize the other functions of the institution. Kerr dismisses these claims:

> There are those who fear the further involvement of the university in the life of society. They fear that the university will lose its objectivity and its freedom. But society is more desirous of objectivity and more tolerant of freedom than it used to be. The university can be further ahead of the times and further behind the times, further to the left of the public and further to the right of the public—and still keep its equilibrium—than was ever the case before, although problems in this regard are not yet entirely unknown. There are those who fear that the university will be drawn too far from basic to applied research and from applied research to application itself. But the lines dividing these never have been entirely clear and much new knowledge has been generated at the borders of basic and applied research, and even of applied knowledge and its application [pp. 116–117].

Kerr's concept of the university differs from the others discussed in this chapter in that it is pluralistic—not all of the pieces fit together well, but there is something in it for everyone. Where the others sought to reduce the university's confusion of purpose, Kerr urges that the university be "as confused as possible for the sake of the preservation of the whole uneasy balance" (p. 18).

His conception of what a university should be also differs from the others in that it is not an ideal vision. It is pragmatic. In the existing university, Kerr sees strengths where others saw weakness: "It has few peers in the preservation and dissemination and examination of the eternal truths; no living peers in the search for new knowledge; and no peers in all history among institutions of higher learning in serving so many of the segments of an advancing civilization. Inconsistent internally as an institution, it is consistently productive. Torn by change, it has the stability of freedom. Though it has not a single soul to call its own, its members pay their devotions to truth" (p. 45).

Kerr believes the multiversity poses difficulties for the student, but by and large it rewards him with freedom and opportunity of choice. "The multiversity is a confusing place for the student. He has problems of establishing his identity and sense of security within it. But it offers him a vast range of choices, enough literally to stagger the mind. In this range of choices he encounters the opportunities and the dilemmas of freedom. The casualty rate is high. The walking wounded are many. *Lernfreiheit*–the freedom of the student to pick and choose, to stay or to move on–is triumphant" (p. 42).

For the faculty member, there are advantages and disadvantages as well. The disadvantages include the fact that a professor's life can become "a rat race of business and activity, managing contracts and projects, guiding teams and assistants, bossing crews of technicians, making numerous trips, sitting on committees for government agencies, and engaging in other distractions necessary to keep the whole frenetic business from collapse" (p. 43). But Kerr thinks the compensations many. "'The American professoriate' is no longer, as Flexner once called it, 'a proletariat.' Salaries and status have risen considerably. The faculty member is more a fully participating member of society, rather than a creature on the periphery; some are at the very center of national and world events. Research opportunities have been enormously increased. The faculty member within the big mechanism and with all his opportunities has a new sense of independence from the domination of the administration or his colleagues; much administration has been effectively decentralized to the level of the individual professor. In particular, he has a choice of roles and mixtures of roles to suit his taste as never before. . . . So the professor too has greater freedom. *Lehrfreiheit,* in the old German sense of the freedom of the professor to do as he pleases, . . . is triumphant" (p. 44).

Kerr does point out weaknesses in need of correction. The intellectual world is fragmented into disciplines and specialties which preclude communication, and he wants greater unity. Undergraduate education needs improvement, and he seeks remedies: a means for rewarding teaching as well as research, a curriculum serving both the educational needs of students and the scholarly interests of faculty, avenues for preparing generalists as well as specialists, ways of treating students as unique human beings in an age of mass education, mechanisms for making the university appear small as it grows larger, routes for raising the status of educational policy, and means of individualizing and making more personal university education. But rather than wishing for a different model of higher education—a hypothetical institution that could avoid these problems at least in theory—he advocates improving today's model. Despite its flaws, the American university warrants reform, not replacement.

Newman, Dewey, Whitehead, Veblen, Flexner, Hutchins, Kerr—their philosophies not only illustrate the range of opinion about the aims of higher education in America and about the role of the undergraduate curriculum in achieving these aims; they form the basis for most current arguments in curriculum committees and college task forces about the direction the curriculum should take. Whether perennialist, essentialist, progressive, or reconstructionist, the faculty members of such committees and task forces gravitate toward one or two of these advocates and toward several more recent proponents to be discussed in the next chapter. Out of their dialectic are coming the specific curriculum plans for the 1980s.

References

Adelman, H. *The Holiversity: A Perspective on the Wright Report.* Toronto: New Press, 1973.

Aydelotte, F. "Breaking the Academic Lockstep." *School and Society,* Oct. 1, 1927, *26,* 407–410.

Bell, D. *The Reforming of General Education: The Columbia College Experience in Its National Setting.* Garden City, N.Y.: Anchor Books, 1968.
This book is discussed in Chapter 11.

Benson, C. S., and Hodgkinson, H. L. *Implementing the Learning Society: New Strategies for Financing Social Objectives.* San Francisco: Jossey-Bass, 1974.

Bernstein, R. J. *John Dewey.* New York: Washington Square Press, 1966.

Brubacher, J. S. *On the Philosophy of Higher Education.* San Francisco: Jossey-Bass, 1977.

Charter of the College of William and Mary, 1693.

Dewey, J. *The Educational Situation.* Chicago: University of Chicago Press, 1902.

Dewey, J. *Democracy and Education.* New York: Free Press, 1967.

Dresch, S. P. "Legal Rights and the Rites of Passage: Experience, Education, and the Obsolescence of Adolescence." Unpublished study, Dec. 21, 1973.

Erdman, I. *John Dewey: His Contribution to the American Tradition.* (1st ed.) Indianapolis: Bobbs-Merrill, 1955.

Flexner, A. *Universities: American, English, and German.* London: Oxford University Press, 1968.

Ford, G. Speech given at Ohio State University. Columbus, Ohio, Oct. 1974

Gruber, F. C. *Historical and Contemporary Philosophies of Education.* New York: Crowell, 1973.

Hefferlin, J. L. Concluding speech at Conference on Prediction, Performance, and Promise: Perspective on Time-Shortened Degree Programs. San Francisco, Calif., Oct. 1975.

Hofstadter, R., and Smith, W. *American Higher Education: A Documentary History.* (2 vols.) Chicago: University of Chicago Press, 1961.

Hutchins, R. M. *Education for Freedom.* Baton Rouge: Louisiana State University Press, 1943.

Hutchins, R. M. *The Higher Learning in America.* New Haven, Conn.: Yale University Press, 1967.

'Hutchins, R. M. *The Learning Society.* New York: Mentor, 1969.

Jencks, C., and Riesman, D. *The Academic Revolution.* Garden City, N.Y.: Doubleday, 1968.

Kerr, C. *The Uses of the University.* New York: Harper & Row, 1966.

Newman, J. H. *The Idea of a University.* Garden City, N.Y.: Image Books, 1959.

Ratner, J. (Ed.) *Intelligence in the Modern World: John Dewey's Philosophy.* New York: Random House, 1939.

Report on Higher Education. (Frank Newman, chairman, Task Force.) Washington, D.C.: U.S. Government Printing Office, 1971.

Riesman, D. and Jencks, C. "The Viability of the American College." In N. Sanford (Ed.), *The American College: A Psychological and Social Interpretation of the Higher Learning.* New York: Wiley, 1962.

Schilpp, P. A. (Ed.). *The Philosophy of Alfred North Whitehead.* (2nd ed.) New York: Tudor Publishing, 1951.

Stone, J. C., and DeNevi, D. P. (Eds.). *Portraits of the American University 1890–1910.* San Francisco: Jossey-Bass, 1971.

Taylor, H. *How to Change Colleges: Notes on Radical Reform.* New York: Holt, Rinehart and Winston, 1971.

This volume is discussed in Chapter 11.

Van Doren, M. *Liberal Education.* Boston: Beacon Press, 1959.

Veblen, T. *The Higher Learning in America.* New York: Hill & Wang, 1968.

Whitehead, A. N. *The Aims of Education and Other Essays.* New York: Free Press, 1968.
Yale Report of 1828.
    This report is excerpted in Appendix A.

11

Proposals for Curriculum Change: The Recent, the Radical, and the Rejected

This chapter picks up the theme of the last—curriculum philosophy and theory—and presents the proposals of 21 contemporary authors or groups to change the undergraduate curriculum. These ideas differ from those in Chapter 10 in that they are not referred to as classics. Most are too new, too radical, or too recently rebuffed for this distinction. Their authors are Stephen Bailey, Daniel Bell, the Bressler Commission at Princeton, The Carnegie Foundation for the Advancement of Teaching, Arthur Chickering, K. Patricia Cross, Paulo Freire, Paul Goodman, Harold Hodgkinson, Sidney Hook, Ivan Illich, Erich Jantsch, the Newman Task Force, Philip Phenix, Jean Piaget, Carl Rogers, E. F. Schumacher, B. F. Skinner, Harold Taylor, Alvin Toffler, and Robert Paul Wolfe. The authors disagree about what needs to be changed in undergraduate education, but all agree that significant changes are essential.

Stephen Bailey

In *The Purposes of Education* (1976), Stephen Bailey calls for a curriculum to confront the existential realities of the last decades of the twentieth century. He advocates a life curriculum, a program to respond to the problem of everyday human existence. Bailey divides life into four phases—coping, work, free self, and the enveloping polity. He proposes that undergraduate education be formed and organized around these phases. Coping is concerned with the daily battles that all people fight—cooking, cleaning, shopping, paper work, roles, illnesses, and worries. Education for coping is intended to give people the inner confidence and instrumental skills necessary for problem solving.

Education for work is designed to provide basic skills of language and computation; broad preparation for particular occupations and professions; and help in finding satisfaction in personal relationships, which may be the only redeeming feature in repetitive jobs held by underemployed workers. In addition, Bailey calls for brokerage organizations to encourage lifelong education and continuing education. He also proposes that education for work assist employers in personalizing and deroutinizing the world of work, and teach workers to see the world of jobs in relationship to all other aspects of life.

The free self involves use of time without obligation, a concept closely approximating leisure. Education for the free self has four desired outcomes—creating and appreciating beauty, enhancing satisfaction in physical activity, performing obligations of service, and intensifying intellectual and emotional discovery.

The enveloping polity is concerned with the individual's social and political responsibilities. Education in this area is intended to transmit the abstract and general knowledge needed for informed political participation, and to teach appropriate skills and attitudes, including moral philosophy, syndetic skill (ability to see connections), and negotiation skills (abilities to persuade, to resolve or diffuse conflict, and to bargain).

Daniel Bell

Daniel Bell's 1966 report, *The Reforming of General Education,* is a one-person study of general education at Columbia University that compares the Columbia curriculum with the well-known general education programs at the University of Chicago and Harvard. On the basis of those findings, sociological analysis of the university and society, and theorizing of his own, Bell proposes a new general education curriculum for Columbia. He stresses the terms "conceptualization" and "coherence" in describing the new program. It is intended "to reduce the intellectual provincialism bred by specialization and to demonstrate the philosophical presuppositions and values that underlie all inquiry" (Bell, 1968, p. 296). Emphasis is placed upon the humanities and history.

The structural elements of Bell's general education program include:

1. A one-and-a-half-year course in Contemporary Civilization. The first term would focus on the history of Greece and Rome. The second and third terms, dealing with the period from the Middle Ages to the present, would be organized into three subject areas—economics, political science, and social and intellectual topics. Students would choose one of the three.
2. A one-term course in a social science discipline that would offer major and nonmajor tracks.
3. A one-and-a-half-year humanities sequence paralleling the Contemporary Civilization course but emphasizing literature and philosophy. However, the last term of the course would be concerned with modern and contemporary art.
4. A one-year course in fine arts or music emphasizing new forms of sound in music and visual forms in the arts.
5. No English composition instruction. Students would be required to demonstrate proficiency prior to admission or to bring their writing ability up to proficiency level independently.
6. A two-year sequence in physics-mathematics and biology-mathematics. Science would be included for conceptualization, and mathematics as a tool subject.
7. Third-tier courses designed to generalize the student's experience in the major. Four types of third-tier courses are envisioned: those (a) stressing the historical foundations of related disciplines, (b) applying several disciplines to a common problem, (c) examining the methodological and philosophical presuppositions of related disciplines, and (d) studying comparative culture, particularly non-Western.

Bell's ideas have not been adopted at Columbia (see case study in Chapter 12). Bell chose to play a limited role in advocating them, feeling active participation would make him appear an inflexible proselytizer. In addition, he and the prime mover for the study, Vice President David Truman, were on leave while the report was examined by university committees. As a result, his recommendations faced heated opposition, particularly from natural scientists and students, without strong defenders to do battle. In 1968, Bell's proposals were lost in the shuffle of Columbia's student unrest. But perhaps most important, the elaborate requirements of his plan were by then out of step with the times (Ladd, 1970, pp. 140–143).

Bressler Commission

Nearing the end of his tenure as president of Princeton, Robert F. Goheen established a Commission on the Future of the College with the general mandate to conduct "a major review of undergraduate education at Princeton." The Commission was to study the relationship of undergraduate education to secondary school experience and to post-college careers; the extent to which formal academic instruction should be connected to learning opportunities in the larger society; the appropriate duration of undergraduate programs and desirable potential variations upon the current four-year pattern; and such problems as the size and composition of the student body, methods of instruction, and evaluation of performance. The commission was directed to make recommendations that took stock both of the multiplicity of forces pressing upon undergraduate institutions and also of realistic projections concerning the future financial condition of higher education.

The commission, consisting of three administrators, ten faculty, and six undergraduates, began its deliberations early in 1971. The chairman of the committee was Sociology Department head Marvin Bressler. In November 1971, Bressler produced a report intended only for discussion purposes. The report, which took a holistic view of the curriculum, urged significant changes in the academic program and the use of academic time. Its major recommendations called for:

- The adoption of a three-year undergraduate program with a limited option to pursue a fourth year of study.
- The adoption of a new academic calendar consisting of two eleven-week terms split by a six-week term.
- The retention of the undergraduate program consisting of distribution requirements, electives, major, independent study, and

senior project, but with significant proposals for change. These proposals included (1) introducing two new types of courses—"exploration" courses, which would emphasize gifted teaching, and "discovery" courses, which would emphasize scholarship and research; (2) dividing general education into two areas—sciences and humanities—rather than the usual three or four which include the social sciences and possibly the fine arts; (3) replacing junior year independent study with major courses in research methods; and (4) establishing a senior forum—a cross between a party and a professional society meeting based upon the required senior thesis or project.

The Bressler Report generated campuswide discussion, a good deal of it critical. As a result, all of the major recommendations, with the exception of maintaining the existing curriculum design, were dropped in the final commission report, which is more moderate in tone, more pragmatic in orientation, and more piecemeal in its approach to curriculum design.

The April 1973 Bressler Commission report recommends that:

- Princeton should maintain its four-year undergraduate program and continue existing options for accelerated studies.
- The university should adopt a new academic calendar that would have 12 weeks of instruction per term, with the autumn term beginning earlier in September and ending before Christmas, in order to provide a bigger break between semesters. The second term would begin at the end of January instead of February, and commencement would be moved up a week. (The faculty voted down this recommendation twice.)
- Princeton should retain all the major components of its current program, including general education distribution requirements, electives, concentration or major study, independent work in the junior year, senior comprehensive examinations, and a thesis. But with regard to distribution requirements, only the natural science requirement should remain. (The faculty voted down this recommendation and continued the existing distribution requirement. It did accept some minor changes, however.

These included permitting engineering school courses to fulfill the science requirements, and allowing two courses in different science departments to fill the science requirements rather than the then required two terms in a single department. Whether mathematics courses should be allowed to meet the science requirement and whether the laboratory requirement should be retained are still under consideration.)

- All students should be required to satisfy a one-term requirement in English composition. (This recommendation was approved.)
- Princeton should continue to expand its commitment to interdisciplinary studies. It should review interdisciplinary programs to see which should be phased out and which should be upgraded to become majors, and it should establish a procedure to create interdepartmental programs for short, specified periods of time and then dissolve them if need or interest declines. (In 1973 the faculty at Princeton approved a recommended program in Western Culture and Historical Studies.)
- Princeton should develop an expanded curriculum program in drama with the possibility that such a program might become a major. (A program in theater and dance was approved by the faculty in May 1974.)
- The university should continue to evaluate academic performance by means of letter grades. The limited pass-fail option should be retained, but consideration should be given to various revisions in its use. In addition, the institution should study the problem of grade inflation and consider the adoption of guidelines for establishing a stable grade distribution. (The suggested revisions in pass-fail grading were adopted in May 1974, but a review of the A–F grading system is still under way. This review resulted in the appointment of an ad hoc committee on diagnostic evaluation comprised of students and faculty from each academic division to consider developing standardized instruments for more detailed evaluation of academic performance than can be conveyed through conventional grades. No change in conventional grading is expected, however.)
- Princeton should adopt a policy of equal access in admissions for men and women students. (This was approved unanimously at

the December 1973 meeting of the faculty and approved by the board of trustees at its January 1974 meeting.)

- The size of the college should remain at approximately its present level for the foreseeable future. (Faculty concurred in this decision and the trustees approved it in January 1974.)
- Strong counseling and advising services should be continued and improved. (The faculty approved and implemented a variety of mechanisms to reach this goal.)
- Princeton should permit one semester of advanced standing rather than offering its students one whole year of advanced standing or none at all. (This was approved in a modified form.)

Other recommendations were lost or weakly implemented. They included a proposal that current pedagogical practices be improved by reviewing the mix of teaching designs—such as lectures, precepts, laboratories, and seminars—to determine what constitutes the optimum mix and that the computer serve increasingly as an adjunct to classroom teaching. (This is not happening.) Six-week courses, equivalent to half courses, and student-led seminars were suggested. (Neither are found in the Princeton curriculum.) A recommendation calling for appropriate procedures for evaluating and improving faculty teaching has not, to any appreciable extent, been implemented.

In sum, the Bressler Commission report was a reaffirmation of education at Princeton, and the faculty votes were an even stronger reaffirmation. The most radical proposals of the commission were voted down. The fact of the matter is that Princeton, unlike many colleges, offers a well-articulated and philosophically coherent plan of education for its undergraduates (Bowen, 1977), and most students and faculty are satisfied with this program.

The Carnegie Foundation for the Advancement of Teaching

The 1977 commentary of The Carnegie Foundation for the Advancement of Teaching, entitled *Missions of the College Curriculum: A Contemporary Review with Suggestions,* examines the state of undergraduate education in America. It identifies six general needs: (1) The mission of undergraduate education must be reexamined for the purpose of giving it better definition and renewed vitality; (2) meaning and substance must be restored to general education; (3) the relationships between undergraduate education and work must be strengthened; (4) the cultivation of values must be given a more prominent place in the objectives of the curriculum; (5) the time students are required to spend on degree requirements must be better utilized; and (6) all levels of education must cooperate for the general improvement of basic skills and of the availability to all Americans of lifelong learning.

The Foundation addresses specific action items to governing boards, administrators, and other education policy makers, departments and single-subject colleges, and students, among others. It argues that "governing boards have a responsibility for making the institutional mission an explicit instrument of education policy" (p. 258), and it recommends that governing boards also:

- Have responsibility for making a periodic review of the educational programs of their institutions and determining ways in which the effectiveness of the curriculum and instruction are to be measured.
- With the assistance of the faculty government and academic leadership, adopt a statement of objectives for the general education programs of their institutions, and consider creating a centralized administrative unit to approve new courses and programs proposed for inclusion in general education; periodically review courses and programs offered for that purpose; and allocate funds to departments and academic divisions that provide general education instruction.
- Select academic and administrative leaders who have demonstrated an interest in undergraduate instruction and curricular development (pp. 258–259).

The Foundation's recommendations to administrators and educational policy makers include (pp. 259–260):

- Define and periodically review the institution-wide mission, secure its adoption by governing boards, and encourage academic divisions and departments within the institution to develop statements of educational objectives appropriate to their endeavors.

- Periodically review the educational programs of every academic division or department to discover programs that deserve special support and weaknesses that need correction.
- Identify current and emerging needs of individuals and society for special new educational programs that cannot be easily initiated by single academic divisions or departments, seek financial resources for developing such programs, and coordinate the cooperative efforts that may be required within the college to make the new programs effective.
- Attempt to realize savings of between 1 and 3 percent each year from existing programs to be used as a self-renewal fund for new and expanded undergraduate education programs.
- Once new programs are introduced, give them ample time to prove their effectiveness. Too often, changes are judged ineffective before they have had a chance to prove themselves or adjust to unanticipated conditions.
- Exercise great care in the review of recommendations for faculty appointment and promotion, giving due consideration not only to personnel policies that may be involved in such matters, but also to the effect of personnel decisions on curriculum and educational policy.
- Wherever it is feasible to do so, initiate cooperative efforts between the faculty of their colleges and neighboring high schools that will help to improve the elementary skills of high school graduates and entering college students.
- Explore the feasibility of cooperative arrangements with neighboring educational institutions for the purpose of broadening the availability of skill and occupational training that can be made available to their stu-

dents, either as a supplement or as part of their under-graduate education.

- Make efforts to improve and give greater visibility to career and academic counseling services for under-graduates.
- Seek out opportunities to achieve desired long-term, institutionwide changes in educational policy by en-couraging the efforts of individuals and small groups who can contribute to the realization of such objectives through the successful initiation and development of promising small-scale experiments and changes. On the whole, small incremental efforts may achieve more than large-scale reforms attempted all at once.

The Foundation further urges administrators and academic leaders, "working with faculty senates, councils or other groups with authority and responsibility for educational policy," to (pp. 260–261):

- Encourage the development of a "Bill of Rights and Responsibilities" for all members of the campus com-munity.
- Permit students to petition for exemption from any graduation requirement for which specific objectives and/or educational content cannot be defined explicitly by the faculty.
- Grant exemptions to students who have satisfactorily demonstrated that they have met institutionwide re-quirements for graduation at another institution or through independent study. Where such requirements are normally met in degree-credit courses, exemption should be accompanied with the granting of college credit.
- Minimize time restraints in specifying requirements for graduation and for completion of general educa-tion components of the curriculum.
- Recognize majors created by students themselves with the advice of members of the faculty, and majors that

involve interdisciplinary perspectives. They might particularly encourage interdisciplinary majors that provide a basic foundation for groups of related occupations or professions.

- Systematically encourage improvement of teaching in colleges, and keep faculty members informed of resources available to them for improving teaching skills and helping them to make effective use of new instructional methods and technology.
- Encourage graduate schools to offer doctor of arts or similar degrees for persons who intend to emphasize teaching rather than research during their professional careers and provide positions and opportunities for advancement to persons who hold such degrees.
- Encourage establishment of learning centers that can assist students in the improvement of the foundation skills for college-level learning, and provide opportunities for independent, self-paced learning of the fundamentals of certain subjects that are taught in several different departments (for example, the first principles of statistics).
- Adopt a new form of transcript that indicates not only the courses and grades students receive, but also how courses taken are distributed among the various components of the undergraduate curriculum.
- Provide pass/fail and pass/no credit grading options in addition to letter grades in any course involving the teaching of specific skills and competencies whose mastery can be determined by performance or in courses that students who are not specializing might be afraid to enroll if doing so would involve risking a good academic record.
- Provide on-campus compensatory education for students who need help in overcoming weaknesses in basic skills.
- In the absence of a central administrative division responsible for general education, faculty senates or councils should coordinate development of introduc-

tory courses for nonmajors in each broad subject
field—for example, the social sciences or humanities
Such courses should cover the history, major concerns,
and methods of inquiry that are characteristic of the
subject field.

- Encourage development of broad learning experiences that draw upon more than one discipline as alternatives to some or all discipline-based distribution
  requirements.

To departments and single-subject colleges, the Foundation recommends the following (p. 262):

- Define the objectives of their majors and require
  members of their faculty to specifically define the objectives of their courses.
- In cases where they have approximately equal numbers
  of majors who plan to attend graduate school and
  majors that plan to terminate their formal education at
  the baccalaureate level, develop alternative majors to
  meet the needs of each group.
- Develop introductory courses in their disciplines for
  nonmajors.
- Give adequate recognition to the contributions of
  members of their faculty who engage in general education programs or interdisciplinary instruction, participate in faculty development programs (as masters or
  learners), or develop courses that effectively utilize
  new methods of instruction or instructional technology.
- Resist pressures to include in the majors more courses
  than constitute a reasonable share of the students' total
  undergraduate curriculum.

Its recommendations for students are seven (pp. 262–263).

- Take advantage of resources not only of their own college but also of nearby institutions that can supple-

ment their studies with skill and occupational training or other instruction that may be useful to them after graduation.

› Define and frequently review the personal objectives they hope to reach by going to college.

• Take advantage of increasing opportunities to participate directly in the improvement of undergraduate education as members of committees developing curricular policy and by making contributions to the evaluation of teaching and faculty members at their institutions.

• Consider the advantages of double majors or major-minor combinations (if they are available) when the number of electives offered to them exceed the number they need for sampling the curriculum widely or for developing special personal skills and interests.

• Make greater use than many of them now do of academic, vocational, and personal advising services offered by their institutions.

• Take advantage of opportunities to combine education and work through cooperative education programs or internships.

• Plan off-campus experiences that supplement or enrich classroom instruction.

Arthur Chickering

Arthur Chickering, in a 1976 article entitled "Developmental Change as a Major Outcome," offers a theory of education based on the stages of human growth. It flows from the pioneering efforts of Nevitt Sanford and from work on ego development by Loevinger, moral and ethical development by Kohlberg and Perry, and intellectual development by Bloom and Piaget. Each of these researchers posited a hierarchical stage theory of human development in the sphere he or she studied. Common to all such theories, whether they are concerned with ethics, morals, or intellect, is a belief that people grow by passing through a series of increasingly complex and sophisticated stages, each of which builds on and in-

corporates the previous stages. Movement from stage to stage is
based upon social, environmental, and genetic factors. Bloom, for
example, describes five stages of intellectual development which
begin with simple, concrete skills and progress to abstract and
complex skills: (1) memorization, (2) application, (3) analysis, (4)
synthesis, and (5) evaluation.

Chickering shares the widely held belief that intellectual,
moral, and ethical growth occur in tandem. Separately they are
abstractions, together they are integrated parts of total human development. His educational theory is based on the relationships
that emerge when related stages of ego, intellectual, and moral
development are linked. Chickering proposes four unified stages
of human development. As shown in Table 17, he asserts that each
stage differs from the others in student motives for education, student beliefs about the meaning of knowledge, student uses of
knowledge, student feelings about where knowledge comes from,
student learning processes, appropriate functions of educational
institutions, appropriate teaching practices, appropriate student-
teacher relationships, and appropriate forms of evaluation.

Chickering (1976, p. 92) criticizes most colleges and universities for pitching their programs to only one or two developmental
levels, whereas their students span the entire range. He sums up
the necessary curriculum direction for colleges as follows: "The
basic point . . . is that motives for learning, learning styles, and
orientations toward knowledge are linked to levels of ego development, moral development, and intellectual development. These
motives and orientations, backed by the broader reinforcements of
developmental levels, in turn define appropriate institutional functions or roles. If learning processes and educational practices consistent with them are developed to carry out these institutional
functions, a systematic institutional response can be created that
best serves students at particular levels of development" (pp. 89,
92).

Accordingly, colleges and universities would be expected to
gear their curricula to the developmental level of the student and at
the same time aid the student in reaching higher levels. Minimally,
as shown in Table 17, this would require an individualized curriculum utilizing a diverse and continually changing array of sub-

ject matters, instructional methods, and evaluation techniques to replace what Chickering now views as a uniform curriculum stressing largely cognitive learning and relying entirely upon interchangeable courses bearing equal numbers of credits.

K. Patricia Cross

Since colonial times, higher education has moved from a goal of education for the few to education for the many to education for all. In her book *Accent on Learning* (1976), K. Patricia Cross urges an additional move—education for each. She feels that higher education now develops a very limited range of skills and knowledge, concerned primarily with ideas, and evaluates all students, regardless of their other strengths, on their achievement solely in this area. She proposes (p. 15) that colleges and universities expand their horizons and "gear education to the needs of society by matching the cultivation of individual talents to societal needs in a three-dimensional model patterned after the skills needed in occupations as they are defined in the *Dictionary of Occupational Titles*—work with data, work with people, and work with things." These are skills that are needed by all people, not only for work but also to live in the world.

Cross proposes a new college curriculum consisting of three major programs—excellence with ideas, excellence with people, and excellence with things—and three minor programs—adequacy with ideas, adequacy with people, and adequacy with things. The minimum requirements for college graduation would be excellence in one area and adequacy in the other two. Students planning to be sculptors or auto mechanics, for instance, would achieve excellence in working with things and adequacy in working with people and ideas.

This proposal would radically change the character of higher education. For example, with regard to the concept of remediation, all students would likely be disadvantaged in at least one area. Just as the student who now grows up in a home without books is considered disadvantaged, so the student who grows up in a home with book-covered walls but devoid of mechanical tools would be considered disadvantaged. With such diversity in weaknesses, the term "remedial" would lose its meaning.

Table 17. Arthur Chickering on stages of human development and associated educational practices

	Self-protective Opportunistic	Conformist	Conscientious	Autonomous
Ego Development				
Moral Development	Obedience-punishment oriented	Instrumental egoism and exchange; good-boy, approval oriented	Authority, rule and social-order oriented	Social contracts, legalistic orientation. Moral principle orientation
Intellectual Development	Knowledge (simple recall)	Comprehension Application	Analysis Synthesis	Evaluation
Motive for Education	Instrumental; satisfy immediate needs	Impress significant others; gain social acceptance; obtain credentials and recognition	Achieve competence re competitive or normative standards. Increase capacity to meet social responsibilities	Deepen understanding of self, world, and life cycle; develop increasing capacity to manage own destiny
What is Knowledge?	A *possession* which helps one get desired ends; ritualistic actions which yield solutions	*General information* required for social roles; objective truth given by authority	*Know how:* Personal skills in problem solving; divergent views resolved by rational processes	Personally generated *insight* about self and nature of life; subjective and dialectical; paradox appreciated
What Use is Knowledge?	Education to get: means to concrete ends; used by self to obtain effects in world	Education to be: social approval, appearance, status used by self to achieve according to expectations and standards of significant others	Education to do: competence in work and social role; used to achieve internalized standards of excellence and to serve society	Education to become: self-knowledge; self-development; used to transform self and the world
Where Does Knowledge Come From?	From external authority; from asking how to get things	From external authority; from asking what others expect and how to do it	Personal integration of information based on rational inquiry; from setting goals; from asking what is needed, how things work, and why	Personal experience and reflection; personally generated paradigms, insights, judgments

Learning Processes	*Imitation;* acquire information, competence, as given by authority		*Discover* correct answers through scientific method and logical analyses; multiple views are recognized but congruence and simplicity are sought	*Seek new experiences;* reorganize past conception on the basis of new experiences; develop new paradigms; create new dialectics
Institutional Function	Arouse attention and maintain interest; to show how things should be done	Provide predetermined information and training programs; certify skills and knowledge	Provide structured programs which offer concrete skills and information, opportunities for rational analysis, and practice, which can be evaluated and certified	Ask key questions; pose key dilemmas; confront significant discontinuities and paradoxes; foster personal experience and personally generated insights
Teaching Practice	Lecture-exam	Teacher led; dialogue or discussion Open "leaderless" "learner centered" discussion	Programed learning; correspondence study; televised instruction	Contract learning: 1. Time, objectives, activities, evaluation negotiated between student and teacher at the outset and held throughout Contract learning: 2. Time, objectives, activities, evaluations defined generally by student, modifiable with experience
Student-Teacher Relationships	Teacher is authority, transmitter, judge; student is receiver, judged	Teacher is a "model" for student identification	"Teacher" is an abstraction behind system. Student a recipient	Student defines purposes in collegial relationship with teacher; teacher is resource, contributes to planning and evaluation
Evaluation	By teacher only	By teacher only By teacher and peers	By system	By teacher, peers, system, self; teacher final judge By teacher, peers, system, self; self final judge

Note: Just as each developmental stage incorporates and transforms earlier stages, so also each subsequent learning process and institutional function incorporates and transforms earlier levels.

Source: Chickering, 1976, pp. 90, 91.

In *Accent on Learning,* Cross also discusses the instructional changes that would be necessary to implement her plan in two of the three areas—ideas and people. To achieve competency in working with ideas, she recommends that colleges develop self-paced and mastery-based individualized methods of instruction that take cognizance of differences in faculty teaching styles and student learning styles. To develop competency in working with people, Cross suggests that education for personal development become an integral part of the curriculum rather than continuing to be shunted off to the extracurriculum; that colleges become communities where there is as much interest in student personal development as intellectual development; that teachers be not just disseminators of knowledge, but prods for student analysis and creative thought; that students be given actual experience in relat-,ing to people through small groups emphasizing interpersonal interaction; and that formal classes be offered in interpersonal skill development.

Paulo Freire

Paulo Freire is an educational revolutionary. In *Pedagogy of the Oppressed* (1972, p. 58), he describes current education as being governed by a banking concept: "Students are the depositories and the teacher is the depositor. Instead of communicating the teacher issues communiques and makes deposits which the students patiently receive, memorize, and repeat."

Associated with educational banking are ten properties which Freire calls "mirrors" of our oppressive society (1972, p. 59):

- The teacher teaches and the students are taught;
- the teacher knows everything and the students know nothing;
- the teacher thinks and the students are thought about;
- the teacher talks and the students listen—meekly;
- the teacher disciplines and the students are disciplined;
- the teacher chooses and enforces his choice, and the students comply;
- the teacher acts and the students have the illusion of acting through the action of the teacher;

- the teacher chooses the program content, and the students (who were not consulted) adapt to it;
- the teacher confuses the authority of knowledge with his own professional authority, which he sets in opposition to the freedom of the students;
- the teacher is the Subject of the learning process, while the pupils are mere objects.

Freire proposes a total rejection of the banking concept in favor of the education of liberation—"problem solving education"—which encourages the emergence of consciousness and critical intervention in reality by the oppressed through the examination of the problems of men in their relationship to the world. The student is no longer a docile listener, but a co-investigator in dialogue with the teacher. The teacher continues to present material for students' consideration, but constantly reevaluates his position in light of student reaction. Freire's rationale for this education of freedom is best stated in his own words (1972, pp. 68–69): "Students, as they are increasingly posed with problems relating to themselves in the world and with the world, will feel increasingly challenged and obliged to respond to that challenge. Because they apprehend the challenge as interrelated to other problems within a total context, not as a theoretical question, the resulting comprehension tends to be increasingly critical and thus constantly less alienated. Their response to the challenge evokes new challenges, followed by new understandings; and gradually the students come to regard themselves as committed."

Paul Goodman

Paul Goodman criticizes colleges for losing track of their primary mission—"teaching and learning." He is less than sanguine about the possibilities of change, attributing recalcitrance primarily to administrators. This is shown in the following excerpt from his book *The Community of Scholars* (1962, p. 323):

For the near future the prospect of significant reform in the great majority of schools and especially in the most populous ones, is dim. In the nature of the case the very changes that are needed are the ones the administration must resist, for they curtail administration's reason for being and jeopardize its security. Decentralizing control, splitting up rather than expanding, dispensing with credits, grading, and admissions, de-emphasizing buildings and grounds, being selective about contracting research—all of them make pale the hectic flush. . . . Worse, however, the reforms toward freedom, commitment, criticism, and inevitable social conflict, endanger the Image and indeed nullify the historical role of administration which has been not to protect its community, but to pacify it.

Given this situation, Goodman's solution is to leave the university. He proposes the secession of small groups of approximately five faculty and their students from about 20 American colleges and universities. The five faculty are to team up with five additional professionals knowledgeable about the resources of a local region and set up a small unchartered university, which would be only an association for teaching and learning, a *studium generale*. From 120 to 150 students would be necessary to make the enterprise float. Goodman feels an average class size of 12 to 15 to be ideal—too large for classes to degenerate into group therapy sessions, and too small to become impersonal.

Goodman examines the cost of his dissenting academies and reports that tuition, which is to be the sole source of funding, would be less than that of a good liberal arts college and equal to or perhaps slightly higher than the cost of a state university education. With regard to physical plant and library, Goodman recommends situating colleges in cities or informally associating them with universities. In either case, classroom space and library services could be obtained at low or no cost. With regard to the inability of unchartered colleges to grant degrees, Goodman is pleased. He considers degrees a corrupting influence on students, but pragmatically proposes that, if degrees are needed, either senior students take comprehensives at other institutions that would grant them a degree or else that arrangements be made with graduate and professional schools to accept the students directly from the dissenting academies on their own merits.

Harold Hodgkinson

Harold Hodgkinson (1974) has brought a number of new ideas to the attention of the higher education community. One of the most interesting is his concept of Regional Examining Institutes (REI). It is premised on three needs—(1) people lacking formal education need open access to credentials; (2) teaching needs to be separate from credentialing; and (3) degrees need to be separate from job credentials.

To satisfy these needs, Hodgkinson proposes that colleges remain teaching institutions and continue to award degrees. However, degrees should have no value as job credentials. The award of job credentials would become the function of five Regional Examining Institutes. The REIs would offer no courses or other forms of instruction. Instead they would test for and award job credentials, perform diagnostic and counseling services, and act as a credit bank.

The testing function of REIs would involve development and administration of examinations to qualify people at a variety of competency levels required to earn degrees and certification for specific job skills. Tests would generally be criterion-referenced and techniques such as games, simulations, and in-basket tests would be commonly used.

Their diagnostic and counseling function would involve offering information to people about new jobs, helping them in educational and career planning, and acting as an advocate for them in making cases for jobs, degrees, and credits. They would also aid employers in determining desirable qualifications for workers in a particular job or in developing new testing instruments.

As a credit bank, the REI would act as an equivalency transcript service. Students with college-equivalent learning obtained at many colleges or informally without benefit of college would have the REI evaluate their credits and experiences, make a record of them, and share that record with educational institutions or potential employers.

Were Hodgkinson's REI proposal adopted, colleges and universities could offer curricula and degrees based on institutional and student goals rather than the demands of the work world.

Without stigma, students could attend college anytime in their lives for as long as they want and not even earn a degree if they wish.

Sidney Hook

Sidney Hook is more often associated with governance in higher education than with curriculum. However, he has long proclaimed the need for general education. His 1975 proposal for an ideologically diverse and methodologically centered program is based upon six needs of students (pp. 32–33):

1. Every student has an objective need to be able to communicate clearly and effectively with his fellows, to grasp with comprehension and accuracy the meaning of different types of discourse, and express himself in a literate way. . . .

2. Every student needs to have at least some rudimentary knowledge about his own body and mind, about the world of nature and its determining forces, about evolution and genetics, and allied matters that are central to a rational belief about the place of man in the universe. If he is to have any understanding of these things, he must possess more than the capacity to remember and parrot isolated facts. He must have some grasp of the principles that explain what he observes, some conception of the nature of scientific method. . . .

3. Every student has a need to become intelligently aware of how society functions, of the great historical, economic, and social forces shaping its future, of the alternatives of development still open to us, of the problems, predicaments, and programs he and his fellow citizens must face. . . .

4. Every student needs to be informed, not only of significant facts and theories about nature, society, and the human psyche, but also of the conflict of values and ideals in our time, of the great maps of life, the paths to salvation or damnation, under which human beings are enrolled. He must learn how to uncover the inescapable presence of values in every policy, how to

relate them to their causes and consequences and reasonable value judgments.

5. Every student needs to acquire some methodological sophistication that should sharpen his sense for evidence, relevance, and canons of validity. He should, at least in popular discourse and debate, be able to distinguish between disguised definitions and genuine empirical statements, between resolutions and generalizations, to nail the obvious statistical lie, and acquire an immunity to rhetorical claptrap. This is what I mean when I speak of the centrality of method in the curriculum. Is it expecting too much of effective general education that it develop within students a permanent defense against gullibility?. . . .

6. Finally, every student has a need to be inducted into the cultural legacies of his civilization, its art, literature, and music. His sensibilities should be developed and disciplined because they provide not only an unfailing occasion of delight and enjoyment in the present but also a source of enrichment of experience in the future.

These six needs describe what most educators would like the general education programs at their institution to accomplish, but what Chapter 1 shows they rarely do.

Ivan Illich

Ivan Illich is the apostle of *Deschooling Society*. In that controversial and much-discussed book (1971, p. 1), he urges the disestablishment of schools on the grounds that they distort and mythologize reality: "The pupil is . . . 'schooled' to confuse teaching with learning, grade advancement with education, a diploma with competence, and fluency with the ability to say something new. His imagination is 'schooled' to accept service in place of value. Medical treatment is mistaken for health care, social work for the improvement of community life, police protection for safety, military poise for national security, the rat race for productive work. Health, learning, dignity, independence, and creative endeavor are defined as little more than the performance of institutions which claim to serve these ends." Illich specifically attacks universities for serving as the recruiters of personnel for the consumer society—for certifying some people for bureaucratic service and throwing away others judged unfit for the competitive race.

In place of the labyrinth of oppressive schools, Illich proposes "learning webs"—formal mechanisms for providing all who want to learn with access to learning resources throughout their lives, enabling all who want to share their knowledge to find those who want to learn it, and allowing all who want to address the public the opportunity to do so. A learning web would consist of four education networks:

- *Reference services to education objects.* This network would facilitate student access to formal education—that is, access to things and processes found in museums, libraries, laboratories, theaters, factories, airports, farms, and the like.
- *Skill exchanges.* This network would allow people to list their skills, requirements for sharing them, and addresses where they can be reached.
- *Peer matching.* This network would permit people to describe learning activities they wish to undertake for the purpose of finding a partner for the venture.
- *Reference services for educators-at-large.* This network would provide a listing of professionals, paraprofessionals, and freelancers; the services they can offer; their requirements for offering these services; their addresses; and reactions of former clients.

Learning would be left entirely up to learners. Learners would not be forced "to submit to an obligatory curriculum, or to discrimination based on whether they possess a certificate or diploma" (1971, p. 75). The public would not "be forced to support, through regressive taxation, a huge professional apparatus of educators and buildings which in fact restricts the public's chance for learning to the services the profession is willing to put on the market" (pp. 75–76).

Erich Jantsch

Erich Jantsch's proposal for reform of the university (1969) is a product of the student unrest of the late 1960s, but it differs from most of the other plans of the era in that it is rooted in systems analysis: Jantsch views all of the activities within the university as interrelated and mutually regulating and the activities of the university and the larger society as interrelated and mutually regulating. This pattern of relationships forms a working whole or system.

It is Jantsch's opinion that the primary activities of the university—education, research, and service—are poorly articulated or "blurred." As a consequence, inconsistencies and contradictions are manifested.

Jantsch proposes a new purpose for the university: enhancing society's capability for self-renewal via the activities of education, research, and service. He envisions a university that would allow the pluralism of society to flourish by melding the creative energies of science, technology, and the young; improve societal communication by conveying the fruits of the world of science and technology to the society and the objectives of the society to scientists and technologists; and provide idea leadership and education for future leaders.

To accomplish this, Jantsch proposes a reorientation of the activities of the university. He thinks they might better be organized around the principles of sociotechnical system engineering, which involves the orchestration of relationships between people and their physical environment. Jantsch calls this approach "joint systems" of society and technology. It would deal with the planning and design of society and technology as well as long-range forecasting of changes in their structure and the emergence of new systems.

Tied to such a change would be a university reorganization requiring the elimination of existing academic units and their replacement by three new structures—system laboratories, function-oriented departments, and discipline-oriented departments. The system laboratories would be staffed by sociotechnical system experts who would develop new systems, make long-range forecasts in broad areas such as transportation/communication systems or public health systems, and identify system problems of possible future concern. Function-oriented departments would be staffed by stationary engineers who would develop and introduce alternative technologies into the society in more concrete areas such as urban transportation, housing, and power generation. Discipline-oriented departments would be staffed as they are today by "specialist scientists" who would perform basic research and develop theories of value to the other two units.

All three units would engage in education, research, and service, but there would be marked changes in the character of each of the activities. Education would shift from training to lifelong education and purposeful work, emphasizing engineering of both "stationary" (facilities) systems and "sociotechnical" (facilities and human) systems. Research would be dominated by sociotechnical system engineering and would generally shift from hardware to software research. Service would involve the university in interacting with and leading government and industry in the design and invention of sociotechnical systems and system-related products.

The Newman Task Force

In 1969, Robert Finch, the U.S. Secretary of Health, Education, and Welfare (HEW), proposed the creation of a task force to examine the problems facing the nation's systems of higher education in the next decade. With financing from the Ford Foundation, that task force became a reality. It was chaired by Frank Newman, then of Stanford University, and consisted of eight additional members assembled from the College for Human Services (New York), Harvard, HEW, Stanford, the University of California, Los Angeles, the University of Chicago, and Wesleyan (Connecticut).

The task force issued its findings in 1971 in a volume entitled *Report on Higher Education*. It described the 1970s as "a time of unprecedented crisis for higher education" and "a period of student unrest, public antagonism, and financial uncertainty" (p. 61). As preconditions for a laundry list of needed reforms, the task force cited seven underlying beliefs (pp. 61–62):

- We believe that, without major reforms, simply expanding the present system will not provide meaningful education for the ever-broader spectrum of students gaining entrance.

- We believe public and private institutions are becoming more and more alike. Real diversity will require altogether new educational enterprises, both public and private, that are meaningful for today's students.
- We doubt whether many students have had sufficient exposure outside the educational system to know what a relevant education might be. Both students and faculty need more experience away from the campus.
- We believe our colleges and universities must be less concerned with academic prestige and more concerned with becoming centers of effective learning
- We believe that the drive for coordination is leading toward large, centralized multicampus systems. The identity, integrity, and chance to explore new directions at each campus must be enhanced now before the opportunity for this is hopelessly eroded by growing bureaucracy.
- We believe the academic community must assess how effectively available resources are utilized.
- We believe that community colleges should not be organizations that absorb the leftover problems from the more prestigious segments of higher education, but must develop their own distinctive missions.

On the basis of these beliefs, the task force proposed 13 new directions touching upon the curriculum, each having one or more recommendations associated with it:

Direction 1—New Educational Enterprises.
- The foremost task for public policy should be to create conditions under which new educational enterprises can be founded and endure.
- New enterprises should use education methods other than the predominant classroom–lecture format, different concepts of what constitutes a campus, a diversified faculty, and experiential methods of learning.

Direction 2—Breaking the Pattern of College Attendance.
- Colleges and universities should break the academic lockstep.
- Colleges and universities should consist of individuals of all ages.
- Undergraduate admissions should be changed to favor students with out-of-class experiences.
- Colleges should encourage stopping out and adopt deferred admission plans.
- Cooperative education, work-study programs, and internships in government, industry, and social service should be greatly expanded.

Direction 3—New Resources for Off-Campus Study.
- Educational services such as formal instruction, examinations, library resources, and degrees that are provided as a package by colleges should be offered to the community as separate services so that individuals and groups can use any of them to build their own education.

Direction 4—Regional Examining Universities.
- Equivalency examinations should be developed so that individuals can receive credit for college-level learning acquired outside of school.
- New degree-granting institutions should be established that would both administer equivalency examinations and grant degrees.

Direction 5—Regional Television Colleges.
- Colleges should be developed specifically to offer higher education by television.

Direction 6—Informal Colleges and Tutors.
- Informal colleges, called "college learning clinics," should be created and organized in much the same way as medical clinics.
- Professional tutoring, which would involve the certification

of teachers for small group and individual instruction, should be developed.

Direction 7—Expanding Noncollege Opportunities.
- Opportunities for young people to engage in meaningful tasks outside college should be expanded. These opportunities should include part-time jobs, year-round internship programs, apprenticeship programs, joint work-study scholarships, and social service work.

Direction 8—Diversifying the Faculty.
- Colleges and universities should revise tenure procedures to allow for at least some short-term contracts.
- They should avoid standardized work rules, undifferentiated pay scales, and other practices that reduce the flexibility of institutions to hire faculty and employ varied pedagogies.
- They should try part-time hiring and flexible scheduling that permit faculty to combine teaching and other activities.
- Special chairs should be created that are free of the usual arrangements for recruiting.
- Faculty now teaching should be encouraged to gain experience outside the academy.
- To improve undergraduate teaching, doctor of arts degree programs should be adopted by more universities, and graduate programs should be reduced in length to allow students to obtain other types of experience.

Direction 9—Minority Education.
- Information on the enrollment, persistence rates, and academic performance of minority students should be disseminated widely.
- More data should be collected on the above questions for the purpose of evaluating which programs have been effective and which have not.
- A major national study should be conducted on minority participation and its impact in higher education.

- Community colleges should not be viewed as the sole avenue of entry to higher education for minority students.
- A greater emphasis should be placed upon gearing education to minority students, rather than adapting minority students to conventional colleges as is done now. New kinds of inner-city institutions with special curricula and staff should be created as well as television instruction coupled with neighborhood-based tutoring centers.
- The United States and its leaders should realistically and publicly restate their commitment to broad-based minority education.

Direction 10—Achieving Equality for Women.
- Women should be admitted in all fields and at all levels of academic study on an equal basis with men.
- Requirements for residency, full-time enrollment, credit transfer, and the like should be changed to accommodate the flexible scheduling needs of women.
- Support services such as day care and health services should be established.
- Courses in women's studies should be introduced.

Direction 11—Reviving Institutional Missions.
- Colleges should make a determined effort to strengthen and differentiate their missions.
- On the basis of their missions, colleges should reexamine their academic programs.

Direction 12—Eliminating Peripheral Activities.
- Institutions of higher education should free themselves from responsibilities such as government laboratories, low-cost housing, and publishing companies, which are unrelated to their educational purposes.

Direction 13—New Institutions with Special Missions.
- New types of institutions should be created specifically to undertake scholarly research or to train professionals.

These Newman Task Force recommendations have generated much debate but little substantive action.

Philip Phenix

In *Realms of Meaning* (1964), Philip Phenix proposes a general education program that has the virtues of being comprehensible, logical, coherent, and well integrated. Phenix divides all knowledge into six types or "realms of meaning." The first he calls "symbolics," consisting of ordinary language, mathematics, and other nondiscursive symbolic forms. The second is "empirics"—the physical sciences, biology, psychology, and social science. The third, "esthetics," consists of music, visual arts, the arts of movement, and literature. Realm four, "synnoetics," deals with personal knowledge. The fifth realm, "ethics," is concerned with moral knowledge. And the sixth and final realm, "synoptics," includes history, religion, and philosophy.

The general education curriculum would include a sequential study of all six realms of meaning. Students would begin with symbolics, a prerequisite for learning the other areas. Next they would tackle empirics and esthetics, knowledge necessary to study synnoetics and ethics. Synoptics would come last, to synthesize all the rest. But as much as possible, students would also study the six areas concurrently in order to see the interrelationships among them. Faculty would choose the subject matter for each realm or type of knowledge on the basis of being representative, disclosing the essential nature of the realm, and exemplifying its associated methods of inquiry.

Jean Piaget

Jean Piaget is best known for pioneering research on the intellectual and moral development of children, but he is also associated with university reform. Piaget criticizes instruction and research in higher education for confusing compartmentalization with specialization. Compartmentalization, he believes, is usually the consequence of instruction in areas of disciplinary specialization rather than interdisciplinary specialization. Attempts at reform rarely achieve anything more than multidisciplinarity, which lacks the synthesis and broad view of interdisciplinarity.

To end compartmentalization, Piaget proposes that colleges and universities be divided into mobile interdisciplinary groups consisting, for example, of biologists, psychologists, and linguists. He feels permanent divisions of universities into departments, schools, and centralizing disciplines creates walls where there should be open space, open doors, and open windows.

Piaget calls for new types of faculty, individuals "able to make their students constantly aware of the relations between their special province and the sciences as a whole" (1973, p. 30). To do this, they must train students in new ways, particularly by a close union between training and research. All students should be involved in research from the start of their education, and this research should be supervised by a team of faculty from related fields, rather than a single individual with a single discipline.

Most importantly, to guide education and research, a change in world view is necessary for faculty and students alike. As a new perspective, Piaget recommends structuralism, a school of thought which concentrates on systems or the relationship between phenomena rather than the nature of the phenomena themselves. This is, in his opinion, a perspective which asks the kinds of questions that can break down compartmental walls and in so doing move toward interdisciplinary synthesis.

Carl Rogers

In his book, *Freedom to Learn* (1969, p. 303), Carl Rogers recommends "a tremendous change in the basic direction of education." Noting that knowledge, methods, and skills become obsolete almost as soon as they are learned, he proposes that education aim instead to develop individuals who are open to change.

The means for transforming higher education would be the intensive group experiences. Workshop groups, consisting of a facilitator or leader and 10 to 15 people, would engage in basic encounters for the purpose of helping their members know more about themselves, develop trust and thus overcome self-defeating attitudes, test out more constructive behaviors, and relate better to others in everyday life.

Through such workshops, a college would become "a relationship of persons with common goals rather than a formal hierarchical structure" (p. 307). With enhanced freedom and communication, innovation would seem desirable rather than threatening. These group experiences would initially involve peers—administrators first, followed by faculty, students, and parents. Then vertical groups consisting of people from each of the peer groups would be organized.

Rogers recommends at least nine workshops during the first academic year with one to ten encounter groups at each workshop. The procedure should seek to include hundreds of people, "a sufficient fraction of the total administration, faculty, and student body, so the effects will not be lost" (p. 316). The expected consequences of the workshop experience for each of these three groups would be the following:

1. The administrator:

- will be less protective of his own constructs and beliefs, and hence can listen more accurately to other administrators and to faculty members;
- will find it easier and less threatening to accept innovative ideas;
- will have less need for protection of bureaucratic rules, and hence will decide issues more on the basis of merit;
- will communicate more clearly to supervisors, peers, and subordinates because his communications will be more oriented toward an openly declared purpose, and less toward covert self-protection;
- will be more person-oriented and democratic in staff or faculty meetings; hence
- will draw more widely and deeply on resource potential of his faculty and staff;
- will be more likely to face and openly confront personal emotional frictions which develop between himself and his colleagues, rather than burying the conflict under new "regulations" or avoiding it in other ways;

- will be more able to accept feedback from his staff, both positive and negative, and to use it as constructive insight into himself and his behavior;
- will be more able to communicate realistically with his board of trustees, and thus possibly lay the ground work for altering the organizational *structure* of the educational system (this will be especially true if trustees themselves have been involved in an intensive group experience) [p. 310].

2. The faculty member:

- will show many of the characteristic changes listed for the administrator, and in addition
- will be more able to listen to students, especially to the feelings of students;
- will be able better to accept innovative, challenging, "troublesome," creative ideas which emerge in students, rather than reacting to these threats by insisting on conformity;
- will tend to pay as much attention to his relationship with his students as to the content material of the course;
- will be more likely to work out interpersonal frictions and problems *with* students, rather than dealing with such issues in a disciplinary or punitive manner;
- will develop a more equalitarian atmosphere in the classroom, conducive to spontaneity, to creative thinking, to independent and self-directed work [p. 312].

3. The student:

- will feel more free to express both positive and negative feelings in class—toward other students, toward the teacher, toward content material;
- will tend to work through these feelings toward a realistic relationship, instead of burying them until they are explosive;

- will have more energy to devote to learning, because he will have less fear of continual evaluation and punishment;
- will discover he has a responsibility for his own learning, as he becomes more of a participant in the group learning process;
- will feel free to take off on exciting avenues of learning, with more assurance that his teacher will understand;
- will find both his awe of authority and his rebellion against authority will diminish, as he discovers teachers and administrators to be fallible human beings, relating in imperfect ways to students;
- will find that the learning process enables him to grapple directly and personally with the problem of the meaning of his life [pp. 313–314].

To keep this process alive, Rogers recommends that a plan for continuing change be built into the college which will permit larger and larger fractions of the community to have intensive group experiences.

E. F. Schumacher

Education should be our greatest resource, but it can also be an agent of our destruction, claims E. F. Schumacher in his hotly debated *Small Is Beautiful: A Study of Economics As If People Mattered* (1973). He attacks education for neglecting metaphysical and ethical awareness—our fundamental convictions. As a consequence, "The sciences are taught without any awareness of the presuppositions of science, of the meaning and significance of scientific laws, and of the place occupied by the natural sciences within the whole cosmos of human thought. The result is that the presuppositions of science are normally taken for its findings. Economics is being taught without any awareness of the view of human nature that underlies present day economic theory. In fact, many economists are themselves unaware of the fact that such a view is implicit in their teaching and that nearly all their theories should have to change if that view changed" (p. 94).

Schumacher proposes that education be based on the principle that all subjects, no matter how specialized, derive from a common center—ethics and metaphysics. He asserts further that this center transcends the world of facts, because values and convictions cannot be validated or invalidated. They must, however, be true to reality, for adherence would otherwise inevitably lead to disaster.

Schumacher dismisses solutions to our educational problems relying upon changes in the organization, administration, or financing of schools. He calls proposals advocating more or less specialization in student programs misguided. In their place, he urges education that permits students time to formulate their own convictions, rather than incorporating willy nilly, as they do now, the outmoded and conflicting ideas which float around about them. It is his opinion that "education which fails to clarify our central convictions is mere training or indulgence. For it is our central convictions that are in disorder and, as long as the present anti-metaphysical temper persists, the disorder will grow worse" (p. 101).

B. F. Skinner

Behavioral psychologist B. F. Skinner (1974, p. 196) defines the principal function of education as the transmission of culture and the principal task of students as learning what others already know. He rejects criticisms which characterize this approach as propagandizing, limiting student growth, or undermining student freedom and dignity.

Skinner believes the consequences of the often advanced alternate instructional method of "discovery"—wherein the mission of education is to aid the student in discovering the world for himself—is deleterious. Its effects can include:

1. An exaggerated sense on the part of students of the powers of discovery and how much they have actually learned.
2. The creation of primitive works of arts, music, and literature as a result of dismissing tradition as restrictive and starting all creative efforts from scratch.
3. An inability of students to discover all of the techniques for determining truth or reality that have been accumulated over the

centuries, leading to intellectual defenselessness against bad logic, superstition, mystical nonsense, and demagoguery. As a result, some students make irrationality a virtue, and have difficulty in achieving ethical self-management.

4. A clinging to existentialism, as students lack knowledge of the many cultural practices that have prevailed because they support future directed behavior, which may not be temporally relevant.

To avoid such possibilities, Skinner proposes a departure from not only the punitive curriculum of the past, in which students learned under threat of the rod, but also the relevant curriculum of the present, in which students study what interests them at the moment. Both are plagued by motivational problems and an innate lack of morals and ethics among people.

Skinner's solution is a curriculum based on "our understanding of human behavior" (1974, p. 199). In none of his writings does he advocate a specific subject matter for undergraduate education. He does, however, state that educational policy makers should decide in advance what students should study, as students lack knowledge of what will ultimately be useful. To do otherwise, he writes, is to betray the student (1974, pp. 201–202).

Skinner's proposals for undergraduate education concentrate upon methods of instruction. The crucial change in these methods is the substitution of rewards for punishment. Students should be rewarded for exhibiting desired behavior in order to reinforce this behavior and motivate the student to continue developing it. Beyond this, Skinner recommends that:

- The student should study at his own pace. The student who goes "too fast misses many reinforcing consequences and, indeed, misses more and more of them as he falls further and further behind." Conversely, the student who moves too slowly "is not receiving reinforcements within his range" (p. 200).
- The student should not merely soak up information, but instead should be made to respond.
- Response should be evaluated immediately in order to reinforce correct responses.

- The student should study materials that build upon one another, because signs of increased power or ability are important reinforcers and reinforcement is maximized when the student masters each stage before moving on to the next.

It is Skinner's belief that the personalized system of instruction (see Chapter 8) is an excellent application of these principles and a model for further development.

Harold Taylor

Students Without Teachers: The Crisis in the University (1969), and *How to Change Colleges: Notes on Radical Reforms* (1971)[1] are two volumes by former Sarah Lawrence College president Harold Taylor. The first analyzes the problems of higher education, and the second offers solutions to them.

In *How to Change Colleges,* Taylor summarizes ten things wrong with the university:

1. The university has remained aloof from the moral, political and social issues of contemporary society and has simply acted as the servant of the status quo, selling its services to the highest bidder and ignoring the true interests and needs of the students and the American people.
2. Students have no real part in making education and social policy and are being programmed by others to fit into an unjust, undemocratic, and racist society.
3. Faculty members, who control the curriculum and the teaching system, are concerned with following their own academic careers and not with the education of students.
4. The teaching has therefore been of low quality, dehumanized, mechanized, and organized in a system made to suit the convenience of the faculty.
5. The system consists of: (a) Professors lecturing to students in large classes three times a week, in fifty-minute periods, with one period a week for

---

[1]Quotations in this section are from *How to Change Colleges* by Harold Taylor. Reprinted by permission of Holt, Rinehart and Winston, Publishers.

discussion sections and tests. Most of the lectures are boring and cover ground also covered in assigned textbooks written by other professors who are also boring. (b) Students taking required courses, either as general requirements for the B.A. degree or as special requirements of the subject matter departments, with few other options. The student is locked into whatever courses the faculty decides he must take, and no matter how bad the course and the teacher, the student has no escape and has little chance to plan his own education. This results in low motivation, or at the very least, no encouragement for developing a motivation on the part of those who are already unmotivated. (c) Five courses are to be taken as the regular number each semester in order to graduate in four years, with three units of academic credit for each course. This fragments the student's time and makes it impossible for him to do justice to any one subject, since with fifteen classes a week plus the discussion and test sections, with each class taught in the same way by lectures and reading assignments, there is no time left to think about what is being learned, and not enough is taught about any one thing. (d) An examination and grading apparatus which is used to measure and award credit for the way in which the student meets the expectations of the teacher. This means that the student is constantly and anxiously working to make a good grade rather than learning the subject, while the examinations, sometimes in the form of objective tests administered bi-weekly, measure what he has remembered rather than what he is capable of doing as a thinking person. (e) Departmental majors by which the student must take courses in the junior and senior year which are geared to the academic requirements of graduate school rather than to the development of the student's interests and intellectual ability.

6. The total effect of this system is therefore to divorce

learning from life, to put the student in a passive role, and to force him through the study of materials which are irrelevant to his own interests and to the needs and problems of the society around him.

7. Both the curriculum and the admissions policies are stacked in favor of white middle-income students from suburban or urban high schools where from eighty to ninety-five percent of all seniors go on to college. This means that when intelligent students whose academic preparation has been poor are admitted to college, they find it very hard to keep up in a competitive system which puts its primary emphasis on the skills of academic learning, and in a high proportion of cases are flunked out or drop out through discouragement.

8. The political and social pressures on the students and faculty in the public universities from boards of regents and state legislatures are so great that student and faculty activism is repressed, academic freedom is stifled, and campus dissent is met by police action, tear gas, clubs, and guns.

9. The social restrictions of campus life treat the student as a child rather than as a responsible young adult, and prevent him from enjoying the ordinary privileges of privacy and freedom which he would have if he were not in college.

10. University presidents and administrative officers are crisis managers, fund-raisers, politicians, and bureaucrats, not educators, and they have little knowledge of student realities and little respect for student opinion unless it coincides with their own or unless they are forced to pay attention to students and their views through student confrontations. Since they are responsible to the conservative boards of trustees that appoint them to office, to alumni, to potential donors, and to state legislative bodies, and they are hired to carry out board policy, they seldom take stands on any political or social is-

sues, and are faceless office-holders rather than cultural and educational leaders. They therefore have little influence on student opinion or on the quality of the student's education [1971, pp. 72–74].

Based upon these failings, Taylor offers a cookbook for reform. He urges six major curriculum changes:

1. Remove all subject matter requirements for graduation and arrange instead for each student to choose his own teachers and courses and to plan a year-to-year curriculum of his own [1971, p. 76].
2. Abolish the lecture system as the basic method of teaching and substitute other kinds of student learning [p. 85].
3. Revise drastically the present academic credit system and the class system to which it is tied [p. 91].
4. Eliminate the present grading and testing system and work out new ways of judging student accomplishments [p. 100].
5. Give every student a full opportunity to work in one or more of the creative arts as a normal part of the undergraduate curriculum [p. 120].
6. Reconstruct the departmental system, so each department becomes a study and learning center for students, ... a research and learning institute for students, a place for them to feel at home, a base for them inside the fragmented university [pp. 129, 132].

Alvin Toffler

In *Future Shock* (1971), Alvin Toffler writes about what happens when people are overwhelmed by change. To meet the curriculum needs of the future, he proposes that:

- Nothing should be required in the curriculum unless it can be strongly justified in terms of the future.
- The curriculum should be organized around social problems,

significant technologies, or stages of the life cycle or any of countless alternatives, but not disciplines.

- College admission requirements should be changed as they rigidify the programs of elementary schools and high schools while reflecting no more than "the vocational and social requirements of a vanishing society" (p. 410).
- All-purpose, permanent curricula should be abolished in favor of temporary programs established with procedures for evaluation and renovation.
- Systematic procedures should be established to permit curriculum changes without triggering intramural conflict each time they are attempted.
- "Contingency curricula" should be created for training people to deal with problems that do not currently exist and may not even materialize in the future.
- Greater choice should be permitted among highly diverse esoteric specialties.
- All students should be guided in a common set of skills needed for human communication and social integration. Skills might be organized into three areas—learning, relating, and choosing—that will be crucial given the increasingly transitory nature of information.

Robert Paul Wolfe

Robert Paul Wolfe (1969) proposes a plan for fundamental changes in the character of American undergraduate education as a response to the 1968 Columbia riots. He begins with undergraduate admissions. Pointing out that the admissions race, particularly at elite schools, generates destructive pressure for high school seniors, he recommends that random college admissions by lot be introduced. All students satisfying the requirements would be admissible; all others would be rejected. From the pool of admissible students, a consortium of cooperating schools would select its freshman class and assign the admittees according to their stated preferences. The point of this procedure would be to reduce pressure. After achieving the minimum admission standards, student efforts at upgrading admission test scores and grade point average would make absolutely no difference.

Wolfe also proposes that students complete high school after three years rather than the current four, as 15- and 16-year-olds now possess the social, sexual, and intellectual maturity of 18- and 19-year-olds a generation ago. As a result their senior year in high school is now frequently a waste of time.

Hand in hand with this recommendation go suggestions for substantial change in the nature of the undergraduate curriculum. Wolfe proposes the abolition of grades, credits, and degrees in order to curtail extrinsic motivation on the part of students and the pernicious use of certification by society. He further urges an end to distribution requirements; the use of many methods of instruction including lectures, discussion groups, directed study, and independent study; the offering of a variety of courses; and the establishment of a wide range of colleges of differing character. These changes are designed to encourage student curriculum exploration. None is intended to reduce academic standards. In fact Wolfe thinks standards would increase as students have no reason to attend college other than emotional commitment.

Such commitment would additionally be insured by changes in the relationship between colleges and graduate and professional schools. First, professional schools would be separated from colleges, and no preprofessional courses would be offered at the undergraduate level. Second, admission to graduate and professional schools would be based upon competitive national examinations, making college irrelevant to professional and graduate schools admissions and further reducing the need for undergraduate degrees and grades. As a consequence of the national examinations, the college course of studies could be reduced by a year so that students could, if they desired, spend a fourth year preparing for the tests.

Wolfe's final recommendation is for the elimination of the Ph.D. degree. In its place he proposes a doctor of arts degree requiring three years of course work, independent study, written work, and teaching experience, but no dissertation. For students planning research careers, a fourth year of research support would be available.

References

Bailey, S. K. *The Purposes of Education.* Bloomington, Ind.: Phi Delta Kappa Education Foundation, 1976.

Bell, D. *The Reforming of General Education: The Columbia College Experience in Its National Setting.* Garden City, N.Y.: Anchor Books, 1968.

Bowen, W. G. *Report of the President.* Princeton, N.J.: Princeton University, May 1977.

Bressler, M. *A Report to the Commission on the Future of the College.* Princeton, N.J.: 1971 (mimeographed).

The Carnegie Foundation for the Advancement of Teaching. *Missions of the College Curriculum: A Contemporary Review with Suggestions.* San Francisco: Jossey-Bass, 1977.

Chickering, A. "Developmental Change as a Major Outcome." In M. T. Keeton and Associates, *Experiential Learning: Rationale, Characteristics, and Assessment.* San Francisco: Jossey-Bass, 1976.

Commission on the Future of the College. *The Report of the Commission on the Future of the College.* Princeton, N.J., 1973.

Cross, K. P. *Accent on Learning: Improving Instruction and Reshaping the Curriculum.* San Francisco: Jossey-Bass, 1976.

Freire, P. *Pedagogy of the Oppressed.* New York: Herder and Herder, 1972.

Goodman, P. *The Community of Scholars.* New York: Vintage Books, 1962.

Hodgkinson, H. "Regional Examining Institutions." In D. W. Vermilye (Ed.), *Lifelong Learners—A New Clientele for Higher Education: Current Issues in Higher Education 1974.* San Francisco: Jossey-Bass, 1974.

Hook, S. "General Education: The Minimum Indispensibles." In S. Hook, P. Kurtz, and M. Todorovich (Eds.), *The Philosophy of the Curriculum: The Need for General Education.* Buffalo, N.Y.: Prometheus Books, 1975.

Illich, I. *Deschooling Society.* New York: Harper & Row, 1971.

Jantsch, E. *Integrative Planning for the "Joint Systems" of Science and Technology: The Emerging Role of the University.* May 1969 (unpublished).

Ladd, D. R. *Change in Educational Policy: Self-Studies in Selected Colleges and Universities.* New York: McGraw-Hill, 1970.

Phenix, P. H. *Realms of Meaning.* New York: McGraw-Hill, 1964.

Piaget, J. *To Understand Is to Invent: The Future of Education.* New York: Grossman, 1973.

Report on Higher Education. Frank Newman, chairman, Task Force. Washington, D.C.: U.S. Government Printing Office, 1971.

Rogers, C. R. *Freedom to Learn.* Columbus, Ohio: Charles E. Merrill, 1969.

Sanford, N. *The American College: A Psychological and Social Interpretation of Higher Learning.* New York: John Wiley & Sons, 1962.

Schumacher, E. F. *Small is Beautiful: A Study of Economics as if People Mattered.* New York: Harper & Row, 1973.

Skinner, B. F. "Designing Higher Education." *Daedalus,* Fall 1974, 1, 196–202.

Taylor, H. *Students Without Teachers: The Crisis in the University.* New York: McGraw-Hill, 1969.

Taylor, H. *How to Change Colleges: Notes on Radical Reform.* New York: Holt, Rinehart and Winston, 1971.

Toffler, A. *Future Shock.* New York: Bantam Books, 1971.

Wolfe, R. P. *The Ideal of the University.* Boston: Beacon Press, 1969.

12

Curriculum Highlights of the Past: 1900–1964

Reform, innovation, and change have been characteristics of higher education in this country almost since its beginning. In fact, the second American college, William and Mary, adopted a reformed version of the classical curriculum of the first, Harvard. Since that time change in one form or another has been continuous. Yet there have been highlights in curriculum change—certain high points that are referred to regularly when people discuss undergraduate education. This chapter presents descriptions and life histories of 12 such highlights of the twentieth century through 1964; Chapter 13 continues the cases with 13 highlights since then.

By the start of the twentieth century, the fundamental changes in higher education that had occurred during the nineteenth century—utilitarianism, research, graduate education, and populism, to name but a few—were assimilated and the modern American conception of undergraduate education had emerged (see chapter 16). The period between the turn of the century and the start of World War I found the free elective curriculum waning in popularity. By the time of that war, the undergraduate program was similar to today's blend of free electives, breadth requirements, and concentration. It was also attacked on the same grounds as today's curriculum—for its lockstep approach, overspecialization, eclecticism, and general lack of integrity. The critics suggested four remedies, all called "liberal education." They were, more specifically, general education, collegiate education, experiential or life education, and honors and independent study. Between the end of World War I and the start of World War II, these remedies were most notably realized in the new programs and institutions described on the following pages: the Contemporary Civilization program at Columbia University (1919), work-study at Antioch College (1921), the Honors program at Swarthmore College (1921), the Claremont cluster colleges (1925), the Experimental College at the University of Wisconsin (1927), the undergraduate college at the University of Chicago (1928), Bennington College (1932), the General College at the University of Minnesota (1932), and the Great Books program at St. John's College (1937).

During and after World War II, which made clear the common heritage and bonds among the American people, curriculum change focused more specifically upon general education. With the end of the war, the national solidarity associated with a shared external enemy was threatened, and general education was viewed as a vehicle for reinforcement.[1] Though many colleges wrote reports and adopted new curricula, the most influential and best known curriculum was that adopted at Harvard as a result of a volume entitled *General Education in a Free Society* (1945).

Curriculum change acquired another theme in 1957 with the launching of Sputnik. Many viewed this space breakthrough as a Russian triumph over the intellectual and educational capacity of America. Curriculum reform in succeeding years emphasized intellectual excellence and acceleration of study. Oakland University (1959) in Rochester, Michigan, and New College (1964) of Sarasota, Florida, were founded in that spirit.

Contemporary Civilization
at Columbia University—1919

During World War I, the Student Army Training Corps asked Columbia University to prepare a course on "war issues." Under the leadership of Frederick Woodbridge, dean of the Graduate Faculties, such a course was created and taught at Columbia and all

[1] A general education movement also followed World War I. There was no such movement immediately after the Vietnam war, as it was an unpopular war and failed to foster a sense of national solidarity.

other corps centers. In response, Harry Carmen of the history department and John J. Coss of the philosophy department designed a course to deal with "peace issues." In 1919, "war issues" and "peace issues" were merged to form Contemporary Civilization, the surviving granddaddy of all Western civilization survey courses. Its purpose was to "inform the student of the more outstanding and influential factors of his physical and social environment" (Columbia University, 1919). "CC," as the course is affectionately known, met five days a week at 9, 10, or 11 o'clock and was required of all freshmen. Sections were staffed by faculty from the departments of history, philosophy, economics, and government.

For its first few years, Contemporary Civilization enjoyed a prominent position in Columbia College. The participating faculty were generally senior staff members and included many of Columbia's "greats." Enrollments in the advanced courses of the participating departments increased. Contemporary Civilization was believed by faculty and administrators alike to have given students "better conceptual equipment and better methodological insight." As a result, departments accommodated their offerings to CC. For instance, the history department in 1922 attributed a reorganization of its program to Contemporary Civilization. The Columbia faculty, in fact, voted to eliminate the second year of the college's two-year English requirement because of a widespread feeling that "CC was developing in the student greater articulateness as well as greater intellectual awareness" (Buchler, 1954, pp. 99–112). Given the favorable results, the faculty in 1929 authorized the addition of a second year of CC. The first-year program, called CCA, dealt with the philosophical-historical tradition of Western Europe. The second-year program, called CCB, stressed economics and government, but shifted widely in orientation in later years.

In the 1930s, Columbia created a core program consisting of other survey courses like Contemporary Civilization. In 1934, a two-year sequence—Science A and Science B—was developed in the natural sciences, but it was discontinued in 1941 owing to opposition from science faculty and difficulty in staffing the courses. In 1935, a year-long survey course was created in the humanities dealing with masterpieces in literature and philosophy. Ten years later a second year was added to the humanities course in fine arts and music. The two-year humanities survey is still required of all students.

A turning point in the history of the Contemporary Civilization program came in 1936, however. It was then that Columbia College divided its curriculum into an upper and lower division. In the lower division, students studied a common curriculum, and in the upper division they followed their own interests. A requirement that students have a major was not adopted until 1953. In the interim, the lower-division core program was buffeted by students' increased vocational interests, their competition to enter professional schools, and by departmental desires, particularly in the sciences, to have students begin upper-division study sooner. When major and nonmajor tracks were introduced, the possibility of a common core curriculum ended. Departments became increasingly unwilling to provide senior faculty to teach CC because they felt the faculty could make a greater contribution to their own major programs. Incentives for participation became fewer, and the subject matter of CC, which was interdisciplinary spanning ancient Greece to the present—remained difficult to teach and time consuming to master. The composition of the CC staff shifted from senior and junior faculty predominantly to graduate students—usually those who did not qualify for fellowships, research assistantships, or disciplinary teaching assistantships.

In 1959, a committee chaired by Professor David Truman recommended abolition of the common sophomore-year CCB requirement. Instead, students were given the option of CCB or several departmental introductory courses. This was done because the CCB course lacked structure and cohesion, because social science departments wanted students to begin concentrating earlier, and because it was difficult to get faculty members to teach CCB. In subsequent years, the departmental alternatives were frequently criticized by university review committees for neglecting general education in favor of the major. By the mid-1960s, the history department withdrew from CCB and refused to provide faculty for it. Finally in 1970, with opposition to CCB from students as well, the second-year program was abolished.

Meanwhile, the CCA course was also under attack throughout the 1960s. Radical changes, such as terminating the program, were suggested, but the most famous of the unadopted proposals were those advanced by Daniel Bell in his prize-winning book, *The Reforming of General Education* (1968; see Chapter 11). In 1969, significant, but short-lived structural changes were introduced, including the adoption of smaller classes and a more relevant or contemporary orientation to the course. Today, although still required of all students, CCA is no longer the common general education core course it once was. The course has always been taught in small, discussion-sized classes, but the sections are now more independent. Common examinations have been abandoned, and common readings, which have changed throughout the history of the course from texts to whole original works, have been reduced somewhat. Sixty to 70 percent of the readings are used in all classes.

Lack of success in teaching Contemporary Civilization remains a serious problem, however, and turnover, traditionally one-half each year, now remains about one-third. Moreover, 23 of the 36 instructors teaching in 1975–76 were graduate students. Only one instructor was a tenured faculty member. And of the 24 CC instructors rated in the Columbia-Barnard course evaluation, 15 were graded lower in quality than the average Columbia faculty member.

Nonetheless, new life may be breathed into Contemporary Civilization by its current director and hard financial times, which makes CC attractive to overstaffed departments with little funding for graduate students. In 1977–78, for instance, the number of tenured faculty teaching CC was scheduled to increase to four; the proportion of assistant professors was also expected to rise, and the graduate student teachers, called preceptors, were being systematically screened to improve quality. It may be aided, too, by the wider reexamination of general education within Columbia University at large—including the Graduate Faculties and the College of Physicians and Surgeons—undertaken by its University Committee on General Education, led by professors Robert Belknap and Richard Kuhns, as well as the resurgence of interest in general education nationally. After suffering the vicissitudes of faculty disinterest and student rejections, CC may yet regain some luster of years past.

(For further information, see Belknap and Kuhns, 1977; Bell, 1968; and Buchler, 1954).

Cooperative Education at Antioch—1921[2]

When Arthur E. Morgan, a successful but not formally educated engineer and educator, filled a vacant seat on the Antioch College board of trustees in 1919, the college was on the verge of bankruptcy. Enrollments were few and income was meager. An attempt to give the college to the YMCA had failed. Six weeks after joining the board, Morgan drafted a plan to save the school entitled "Plan of Practical Industrial Education." The board directed Morgan to inaugurate the new program and soon after named him president.

The Morgan plan emphasized general education to be obtained through the alternation of education and work (see Chapter 5). The work experience would enable both the student and the college to be self-supporting. Antioch would obtain additional non-tuition revenues by establishing small, on-campus industries in which the students would work. It was assumed that all student job needs could be fully met by the on-campus jobs and the more than 500 industries within 30 miles of Antioch. The college itself would supplement student work with courses in cultural, vocational, and physical education.

To make his plan work, Morgan made many changes in the college. He encouraged 12 local trustees on the 19-member board to resign and replaced them with people of wealth and prominence in business or public life. He increased enrollment from under 50 to more than 200 in the first year of the program, with many of the new students at the previously all-Ohio college coming from out of state. He replaced nearly two-thirds of the 12-member faculty and increased the number of staff to 25, recruiting people sympathetic to his new program. Finally he directed the attention of the news media to Antioch, raised operating capital, and received some foundation support.

After a few years, Morgan, with the assistance of the reconstructed campus constituencies, established a center for extramural education, now called the Center for Cooperative Education. The center gave the work program a home and physically established its presence on campus. Its role was to locate jobs and place and counsel students. It still performs these functions.

[2]The account relies upon Burton Clark's *The Distinctive College*, 1970.

In operation, Morgan's program differed somewhat from his original plan. The college developed several on-campus industries, including a bronze foundry, a printing shop, and a shoemaking factory, but none brought it the hoped-for revenue.[3] The 500 local off-campus jobs Morgan projected proved less attractive to students than jobs in urban centers like New York and Chicago, and this necessitated a change in Morgan's plan to alternate two weeks of classes with two weeks of work. Work periods gradually increased from 5 weeks or 10 weeks to 8 or 12 weeks and are now 12 or 24 weeks.

In the late 1940s and early 1950s, work-study was attacked by some faculty, who thought students needed further academic studies for graduate education rather than work experience, and by some veterans, who had had a good deal of experiential education prior to college. But the cooperative program accommodated the needs of these students by permitting independent off-campus study and study abroad.

The jobs that students take are also different from those originally envisioned by Morgan. He favored jobs demanding physical labor. There are few such jobs now and, though jobs are forever changing with student interest, most are white collar and preprofessional. The reasons for work are not always those favored by Morgan, sometimes revolving about visiting a girlfriend or boyfriend or desiring to see an exciting city. The standards for awarding credit differ too: There are cases of students receiving credit simply for the experience of looking for a job.

Other problems have cropped up along the way as well. The understaffed Center for Cooperative Education has not yet been fully integrated into the college. Its staff members, who with rare exception lack Ph.D.s, are not accorded the prestige enjoyed by the instructional faculty, while the instructional faculty are uncertain about the center's activities and suspicious of waste in its operation. Differences exist between the center staff and the instructional faculty in their definitions of purpose and their approaches to work.

[3]The tuition paid by students during work periods proved a source of additional funds however. Antioch did not fully capitalize upon this fact until 1961, when it voted to increase enrollment to twice what the campus could accommodate, with one-half of the student body always working off-campus.

The center staff emphasizes affective development more than the faculty. And formal exercises by which students once evaluated and integrated their cooperative learning experiences into the academic program are now few and far between.

Despite these problems, occasional student complaints about placement, and the passage of nearly sixty years since Morgan initiated his plan, there is a firm belief throughout the college that work-study is an essential part of the Antioch curriculum. An enormous number of contributions to students' academic, emotional, and physical development are attributed to it. Faculty acknowledge that the work experiences in the major area, which are common among upperclassmen, bring students back to campus with firsthand knowledge of the newest developments in their fields. This frequently makes it possible for faculty to omit the applied aspects of a subject from their courses. And when graduating seniors are asked to evaluate the strengths and weaknesses of an Antioch education, they invariably rank the work program as its greatest strength. Moreover, many recent problems between the Center for Cooperative Education and Antioch's instructional faculty are being alleviated by its new core general education program, discussed in Chapter 1, which is designed to fuse classroom and experiential education.

In sum, both historically and currently, Antioch offers illustrations of combining work and learning within the undergraduate curriculum for anyone seriously concerned about their integration.

(For further information, see Clark, 1970; and Henderson and Hall, 1946).

The Honors Program at Swarthmore—1921[4]

Swarthmore College was founded in 1864 by members of the Society of Friends (Quakers). Development of the college during its first four decades reflected tension between those who wanted the institution to serve primarily the Society of Friends by preparing the future Quaker teachers, and those who wanted to link Swarthmore with significant movements and trends in higher education in

[4]The Carnegie Council and I are indebted to Theodore Friend III, president of Swarthmore College, for authoring this account of the Swarthmore Honors Program.

the United States. This latter group was itself divided, with interests ranging from the promotion of football and fraternities/sororities to adopting the latest innovations in education.

Joseph Swain, president of the college from 1902 to 1921, and himself a Quaker, established a tenuous balance among the various constituencies. He obtained the transfer of several administrative powers from the board of trustees, so that the president could be an innovator as well as a manager. Swain assembled an excellent faculty, and serious curricular experimentation began. Growth of its endowment placed Swarthmore among the wealthier small colleges, and an expanding applicant pool permitted an increasingly selective admissions policy.

In the Swain era, however, there was not yet consensus that academic standards should be steadily upgraded. Like many colleges throughout the nation in the post–World War I enrollment expansion, Swarthmore had to decide what its real purpose was. Should emphasis be on athletics and extracurricular activities? Should its mission be training for business? Should its energies be directed to training teachers? Should it strive for an intense liberal arts program?

When Frank Aydelotte became president in 1921, he had an opportunity, which many saw as a need, to provide new direction. Aydelotte brought to his new position experience with both American and British education. He had been a Rhodes Scholar at Oxford and was the administrator of the Rhodes program in the United States. He was not alone among American educators in fearing that too much stress on educating large numbers of students could lead to mediocre higher education, but his experience at Oxford provided for him a positive alternative. He sought to introduce at Swarthmore a characterstically British concept of an individualized pursuit of knowledge. He stated his intentions in his inaugural address: "We are educating more students up to a fair average than any country in the world, but we are wastefully allowing the capacity of the average to prevent us from bringing the best up to the standards they could reach. Our most important task at the present is to check this waste. The method of doing it seems clear: to give to those students who are really interested in the intellectual life harder and more independent work than could profitably, be given to those whose devotion to matters of the intellect is less keen, to demand of the former, in the course of their four years work, a standard of attainment for the A.B. degree distinctly higher than we require of them at present."

An "Honors Program" was the result of enthusiastic faculty support of Aydelotte's call to action and their efforts to fulfill the purposes he described. Honors was intended for the "nonaverage" student. Instead of the dilettantism and potpourri of subjects that too often comprised an American college education, Honors provided study in depth and demanded mastery of method. Aydelotte believed that the success of such a program depended on freeing resourceful students from rigid academic structures—what he called "breaking the academic lockstep."

The Honors Program, as distinct from the Course Program, was designed for those juniors and seniors most able to profit from intensive independent study. Each honors student was to design a cohesive program of eight "papers," subjects on which he or she would be evaluated by examiners from outside the college through written and oral examinations at the end of the senior year. A program usually included four examinations in a major field and two each in two minor areas. Examiners conferred and agreed upon a rating for each student of Highest Honors, High Honors, Honors, or no honors. The Swarthmore College faculty had no say in the outcome.

Although a student might choose from a variety of ways to prepare for the examinations, the standard method was through a double-credit seminar consisting of a few students and a professor. The seminar met one day a week for three to five hours, and required an essay of each student every two weeks. The faculty member provided a syllabus, far too long to be completed but broadly illustrative of the field being studied. Discussion centered upon the students' essays. Because the professor did not grade or test students in seminars, the process encouraged a sense of common enterprise among faculty and students. The visiting examiners thus, at least indirectly, evaluated the teachers who had directed the seminars.

Through the Honors Program and admissions policies, Aydelotte very gradually but decisively changed the institution. In an attempt to find students of all-round excellence, Swarthmore recruited a national and diverse student body. In 1922 a scholarship program offering five full four-year scholarships was initiated; 209 students applied for them and even some of the unsuccessful competitors elected to enroll at Swarthmore.

The social orientation of the college was deemphasized. Swarthmore reduced "big-time" stress on intercollegiate sports and began to emphasize participation in athletics. The accent upon parties and social life diminished. Swarthmore women voted to terminate sororities in the early 1930s, and fraternities eventually became less dominant in campus affairs.

Aydelotte's innovations also caused some change in the college's sources of funds. Although some alumni and Quakers protested the new order, foundations more than made up any decline in such support. The eastern press also drew attention to the experiments of Aydelotte's era. The press, the foundations, and the honors examiners who went home with first-hand impressions all helped spread the reputation of Swarthmore. Aydelotte left Swarthmore in 1940 with the national stature of the college prominently established.

The Honors Program has continued to the present. The most significant change in the character of the program was made in 1968 as a result of *Critique of a College,* a comprehensive Swarthmore self-study by faculty, students, and alumni. At that time, the number of honors seminars required of students was reduced to six, and four traditional courses were substituted to replace two double-credit seminars. The structure of the Honors Program was changed to allow course students to participate in honors seminars, and the requirement that a student's entire honors program show a discernible integration was dropped. The resources of the Course Program were enhanced by making more faculty time available to it.

Today the Honors Program is once again being reexamined by Swarthmore's Council on Educational Policy. One reason for the inquiry is that instruction by seminars is expensive. In some departments seminars lack students, and more than half of the seminars enroll fewer than six students whereas eight is considered a desirable number. In addition, the offering of duplicate subjects in the Honors and Course Programs taxes resources, particularly of small departments.

There is an even more basic question: Is there a need for an honors program today? According to some members of the faculty, Swarthmore has a more intellectually homogeneous student body than it did in Aydelotte's day—a change that probably owes a good deal to the Honors Program itself. In fact, some departments permit course students to fill vacancies in honors seminars—a practice some faculty think demonstrates the presumptive homogeneity, but others see as endangering the excellence of honors work. In some fields, particularly the natural sciences, some hold that seminars may not be the best medium for instruction; sequential material is perhaps best learned by means of an established series of courses stressing lectures and laboratory work. The Honors Program has also been criticized for invidious elitism; but the college does offer degrees with distinction outside of honors, and able students who are interested in range of coverage and elect the Course Program receive recognition in that way.

Despite these and other issues—many of them hotly debated in Aydelotte's time and since—a widespread and strong belief in the Honors Program persists at Swarthmore. Many instructors and students still regard their seminars as their most invigorating and rigorous intellectual experiences, and many alumni insist that study under the Honors Program was the most valuable part of their life at Swarthmore.

(For further information, see Aydelotte, 1941; Clark, 1970; Swarthmore College, 1967; and Swarthmore College Faculty, 1941.)

The Cluster College Concept
at the Claremont Colleges—1925

In 1919, the board of trustees of Pomona College, an institution founded 32 years earlier as a "Christian college of the New England type," established an enrollment ceiling of 750 students. The ceiling was a compromise between the desire of the trustees to maintain Pomona as a small liberal arts college and social pressure to provide additional higher education for a rapidly expanding southern California population.

The pressure upon Pomona to grow continued and intensified in subsequent years. Despite the fact that Pomona was financially well endowed, qualified applicants were being rejected in larger numbers each year, and alumni were complaining that their children and friends' children were not being admitted.

In 1923, Pomona's president, James Blaisdell, proposed a solution to the problem. He called it the "group system," but it has since become famous as the "cluster college" concept. Blaisdell called for the creation of several small colleges like Pomona, all clustered in the area around Pomona College. The plan is best explained in Blaisdell's own words: "My own very deep hope is that instead of one great, undifferentiated university, we might have a group of institutions divided into small colleges—somewhat on the Oxford type—around a library and other utilities which they would use in common. In this way I should hope to preserve the inestimable *personal* values of the small college while securing the facilities of the great university" (Clary, 1970, p. 2).

In 1925, Blaisdell's plan was approved by the Pomona trustees, and the new cluster, named Claremont Colleges, was incorporated. The name "Claremont" was taken from the geographical location of the colleges, and the plural "Colleges" was selected to underline the fact that the new institution was a union of colleges, not a single university.

Blaisdell thought of the colleges as separate undergraduate residential accommodations with some shared academic facilities. Each college was to have its own mission, values, and board of trustees but would make an effort to share its facilities to the greatest degree possible without spawning uniformity. A central college was to "serve as a general clearinghouse of the interests of the various other colleges and as an instrument of their mutual service . . . " (Clary, 1970, p. 289). It was charged with offering graduate work, leadership in development of new colleges, summer school activities, community services, possibly undergraduate instruction, and an institutionwide diploma which would be better known than the diplomas of the individual colleges.

Blaisdell was made chief administrative officer of the Claremont Colleges. The graduate school was established in 1925. In 1926, Scripps College, a women's school emphasizing the human-

fine arts, was founded. The depression and World War II stalled further development until 1946, when Claremont Men's College, now coeducational, emphasizing public affairs was created. In 1955, Harvey Mudd, a coeducational institution concerned with science and engineering, was inaugurated. Pitzer College, the most recent of the Claremont schools and originally a women's college, was established in 1963 with an emphasis upon the social and behavioral sciences.

The operation of the Claremont Colleges has not conformed entirely with Blaisdell's plan. The colleges have proved more autonomous and cooperated to a lesser extent than he envisioned. This has been in part an outcome of their independent status: Though the colleges operate under a formal compact, they are legally free to do as they please. In part, it is also a result of the first of the Claremont Colleges being a fully developed liberal arts school. Pomona College never stripped down to the residential and minimum academic facilities that Blaisdell viewed as appropriate and sufficient for a college. In fact, in the 1950s, Pomona, despite dated science facilities, refused to participate in an expanded cooperative science center. Furthermore, because the colleges were created singly, with long spaces of time between the establishment of one and the founding of the next, each was encouraged to be independent and to model itself in this respect after the existing colleges, which meant each was patterned after Pomona. For instance, within three years of its creation, Scripps, the second college, was seeking to match Pomona's program for program and facility for facility—an art department for Pomona's music department, a quadrangle for Pomona's quadrangle, and a playing field for Pomona's field. This has been variously interpreted as manifest destiny on the part of Scripps and a reaction to Pomona's unwillingness to share equally.

The central or coordinating college was not as powerful as Blaisdell imagined either. More often than being regarded as the central government, the coordinating college was regarded as just another one of the states, the state concerned with graduate education. Over the years this difference of opinion has resulted in several governmental reorganizations and name changes for the coordinating college. Today the coordinating college is named

Claremont University Center and administers the graduate school, joint college services, and joint college finances. It neither awards an institutionwide diploma nor offers undergraduate programs.

Despite these deviations from Blaisdell's plan, the result was exactly what he intended. Each Claremont college developed the qualities of a small school and the resources of a major university. Four factors have contributed to this outcome:

First, student cross-registration is permitted between the colleges. This accounts for 10 percent of total Claremont enrollments annually and usually involves no cost to the student's home college, despite the fact that some colleges like Pomona are gross importers of students and others like Harvey Mudd are gross exporters.

Second, the colleges engage in a large number of formal cooperative programs. These range in size from programs involving two colleges, such as the Claremont Men's–Harvey Mudd joint athletic program, to those involving all of the colleges, such as Black Studies and Chicano Studies programs. Many college activities are unaffected by the cooperative arrangement, however. There is significant duplication in staff and courses, particularly at the introductory level and in several subject areas such as the sciences, foreign languages, and history.

Third, the colleges also formally share a large number of services and facilities such as a business office, library, computer, counseling center, and a large auditorium. In fact, Claremont Men's, Harvey Mudd, and Pitzer Colleges could not have been created without joint facilities and services, which were initially provided free of charge by the other colleges.

Fourth and finally, there is both formal and informal cooperation among faculty in similar subject areas. The amount of collaboration (or conflict, for that matter) varies with the discipline.

The cluster arrangement and cooperative services have enabled each college to develop a unique character. Each is of a different size (between 450 and 1,300 students), admits a particular type of student, has a special academic emphasis and curriculum, and, with the exception of Pomona, engages a faculty concentrated in a limited number of fields rather than the whole range of liberal arts. For instance, almost 70 percent of the Harvey Mudd faculty are in the natural sciences, engineering, and mathematics.

The cluster college arrangement is not without costs to the participating colleges, however. An unusually large number of committees have been required to administer the joint and individual activities, so that institutional change is a ponderous process. A more serious problem is that the close proximity of the colleges fosters competition and makes student recruitment and fund raising more work for each. In spite of these difficulties, there is widespread agreement by the participating colleges that the advantages of clustering have far outnumbered the disadvantages. Few other examples of such clustering elsewhere in the country offer as extensive and diverse experience for institutions considering cluster operation and cooperation.

(For further information on the Claremont Colleges, see Clary, 1970. For information on cluster colleges in general, see Gaff, 1970).

Meiklejohn's Experimental College at the University of Wisconsin—1927

The Experimental College of the University of Wisconsin was one of the most ambitious and innovative programs of its time. Its guiding lights were Glenn Frank, who became president of the University of Wisconsin in 1925, and Alexander Meiklejohn, whom Frank brought to the university as a professor of philosophy. Prior to his presidency, Frank had been editor of *Century Magazine,* for which Meiklejohn had written articles on the subject of higher education during his own presidency of Amherst from 1912 to 1924.

Soon after assuming office, Frank appointed a senior faculty and administration committee to review the university's educational program. Both he and Meiklejohn were members. The committee identified three academic problem areas—instruction, advising, and the relationship between colleges and secondary schools. Meiklejohn was directed to draft a proposal to improve the situation. His plan called for a two-year, lower-division experimental college in the letters and science division of the university. The plan was adopted by the university faculty and regents, and Meiklejohn was made chairman of the new college.

In 1927, after a year of planning, Meiklejohn's Experimental College began operation. Eleven university faculty were recruited;

two-thirds of their time was to be spent in the college and one-third in their academic departments in the university. At its peak, the college enrolled 155 students, all of whom were men and residents of the same dormitory.

The curriculum was an integrated program intended to give students a sense of the unity of knowledge and experience. It focused on problems or themes in the creation and conservation of human values in two important cultures—ancient Greece and contemporary America. The first year was spent in the study of the Athenian civilization of the fourth and fifth centuries B.C. Readings included both primary and secondary sources, as well as texts. Particular emphasis was placed on Plato's *Republic*.

In the second year, the "ordered thinking" acquired through the study of Greece was applied to contemporary America. The summer and fall terms were spent on a regional study based on the book *Middletown*. Each student was to choose a city, town, or rural area and produce a major paper on its character and values. The first eight weeks of the fall term were spent on the role of science in the contemporary world. The study of laboratory techniques and evolution were part of the program. Primary sources, secondary sources, and texts continued to be used. *The Education of Henry Adams* was the volume emphasized in the second year, and the final project was an independent study based upon that book.

There were no courses or subject matter divisions in the curriculum, but there were divisions based upon various interrelated phases of culture. Three types of instruction were offered, and each was concerned with the Experimental College topic of the week. First, all of the students met as a group four to five times a week for an informal lecture attended by all of the faculty. The session was led by the faculty member with the most expertise on the topic or by a visiting professor. Questions and informal talks were an integral part of these sessions. Second, each faculty member held individual tutorials or conferences with each of 12 students once a week, lasting one-and-one-half hours or more apiece. These conferences focused on writing and topics of particular interest to the student. After a six-weeks period, the students went on to a different tutor and the tutor went on to a new set of 12 students. The third mode of instruction utilized the small group.

Once a week the 12 students met as a group with the faculty member. The content of the session was determined by the instructor and varied from group to group.

An emphasis upon writing pervaded the curriculum. Each week, students were required to prepare a paper on an assigned topic. For instance, one week they might be expected to write a gubernatorial or presidential address; another, an analysis of a Platonic dialogue. Students were also required to keep a diary detailing their reactions to their readings. Upon the completion of each six-week tutoring session, advisers wrote reports on each student. These reports were given to Meiklejohn, but no grade was given students until the end of the second year. That grade was based upon the regional study project, the final independent study project, and a wide-ranging objective test.

From its earliest days, many problems faced the Experimental College. The joint faculty appointments between the college and the disciplines created conflicting staff loyalties. The two employing units emphasized at least somewhat different standards and qualities of performance, and unfortunately for the college, the disciplines offered the better rewards. Antagonism also developed between the college and other units of the university for reasons ranging from jealousy over the use of facilities (such as new dormitories) and dismay over the college's violation of university rules (such as its award of grades only at the end of two years) to conflicts over the college's use of university funds that might otherwise have gone to other academic units. Furthermore, there were difficulties within the college. Its instructors were never unanimous about what the nature of the college program should be or even about how they should gauge student progress in the college.

Within Wisconsin, there were few applicants for admission because the college had been branded radical both by rumor and the local press. Stories of its imminent demise plagued the college as early as the first year. For these reasons high schools dissuaded their students from applying. As a result most of the Experimental College students were from out of the state, and a large percentage were also Jews. Morale among the students was nonetheless high, and in subsequent years alumni held three major reunions. But state legislators were not pleased by the predominance of out-of-state students, and in 1932, the depression and a coalition of politicians, faculty, and fraternities closed the underenrolled college.

Even though Meiklejohn's college died, his ideas about undergraduate curriculum have persisted and continue to be periodically resurrected in programs like Joseph Tussman's Experimental College Program at Berkeley, which will be discussed in the next chapter.

(For further information, see Meiklejohn, 1932.)

Undergraduate Education at the University of Chicago—1928[5]

In the late 1920s, planning began at the University of Chicago for what would be one of the longest and most far-reaching of U.S. collegiate reforms, the creation of an undergraduate college. The actual change stretched from 1928 to 1947. The impetus for reform came in the 1920s from President Ernest Burton and Dean C. S. Boucher, who acted on the widespread belief that undergraduate education was being neglected at Chicago in preference to graduate instruction. In the 1930s and 1940s, leadership came from President Robert Maynard Hutchins.

There was no point between 1928 and 1947 that might be called the era of the Chicago College Program. The curriculum shifted gradually and continually throughout the period. Several key elements of the program do, however, stand out. These include the admission of students to college after the sophomore or, more often, the junior year of secondary school, a common curriculum, comprehensive examinations, interdisciplinary courses, and a college faculty distinct from that of the graduate school (Bell, 1968).

Admission of non-high school graduates posed several problems. First, high school principals were often reluctant to lose their best students to college and discouraged them from entering Chicago early. Second, the Chicago B.A. was likened to a community college degree because its completion required only two years of post–high school education. Third, the college's admissions policy was predicated on the assumption that few of its students would

[5]The Chicago account has benefited significantly from editing and factual additions by Charles D. O'Connell, Jr., vice president and dean of students at the University of Chicago.

attend graduate school. However, the percentage of students going on to post-college education rose quickly from 20 percent to 80 percent, and a number of graduate and professional schools, including some of Chicago's own, were reluctant to consider students with Chicago degrees. The negative reaction of such schools became increasingly detrimental to the college. After the post–World War II veteran boom, enrollments in the college declined rapidly.

Non-high school graduates never constituted more than a bare majority of the Chicago entering class. In addition, many able high school graduates were discouraged from applying because the college program normally took three years for them to complete, a year more than lower-division programs elsewhere. Differences in educational background between entering students with and without high school diplomas were accommodated by means of placement examinations.

The college curriculum was a common general education core consisting, with variations over the years, of a three-year course in the humanities, a three-year course in the natural sciences, a one-year sequence in mathematics, a three-year course in the social sciences, a one-year course in writing and criticism, a one-year course in philosophy, a one-year course in the history of western civilization, a one-year course in foreign language, and a capstone one-year course called at various times OII (Observation, Interpretation, and Integration) or OMP (Organization, Methods, and Principles of Knowledge). Nonetheless, the curriculum was self-paced. Graduation was determined entirely by comprehensive examinations administered annually by an independent Office of University Examiners. Students were required to pass 14 such examinations, and most succeeded in doing that in about three years.

The courses in the core were interdisciplinary and relied upon original works, although the program could not be accurately described as a "great books" curriculum. The courses differed from survey courses in that they were broader in scope and oriented toward the analysis of texts. Staff-wide planning, team-taught lectures, and faculty-led sections were characteristic of them. Each course met four hours a week—one hour in lecture and three in discussion sections.

The college developed as an enclave that was isolated in many ways from the rest of the university. It emphasized teaching in preference to research and was able to make its own faculty appointments and promotions. Though much of the teaching, particularly in the interdisciplinary courses, was rated highly, college faculty were commonly held in low esteem and accorded second-class status in the university. Some faculty members thought the college blocked their career lines or opportunities for advancement. As the college grew increasingly different from the university, the more traditional faculty left. And a further exodus of faculty occurred when, after World War II, teaching jobs became available at other institutions.

In the 1950s, a radical change in the character of the college stemmed from the serious decline in enrollment, the growing isolation and dogmatism of the college faculty, the opposition of graduate schools that demanded disciplinary training as well as general education of their applicants, and the departure of Hutchins. His replacement, Chancellor Lawrence Kimpton, was not as sympathetic to the "old" college, and in 1953 its charge was reformulated to include both general education and the traditional areas of undergraduate specialization. Attempts by the college to compress the former general education program into two years did not fare well. Between 1953 and 1957, the college began cooperating with graduate departments of the university in creating joint major–general education programs. In 1957–58, the university faculty required that the majority of college appointments be shared with an appropriate graduate department.

Throughout the 1950s and early 1960s various adaptations of the earlier college, in combination with upper-division offerings with departments, were tried. In 1966 the present pattern was established under Provost and Acting Dean of the College Edward Levi. Five collegiate divisions were established—humanities, social science, biological sciences, physical sciences, and a new collegiate division offering an experimental program emphasizing independent study and student research. All five collegiate divisions provide a variety of interdisciplinary courses in addition to traditional majors. And all students at Chicago are required to take four core general education courses as well as a "second quartet" of courses outside their chosen field. In short, the college remains distinct from many of America's undergraduate programs. But because it is more like such programs than it was in the days of Hutchins, it fits more comfortably into the conventional structure of American high schools, colleges, and graduate schools than it did forty years ago, when it sought virtually singlehandedly to rebuild that structure.

(For further information, see Boucher and Brumbaugh, 1940; College of the University of Chicago, 1950; and Severson, 1972.)

Progressive Education at Bennington—1932

Bennington College grew out of the progressive philosophy of education popular in the 1920s and described in Chapter 1. Although the impetus for Bennington came from local townspeople who simply wanted a college nearby, the planning was dominated by consultant William Kilpatrick, a progressive educator at Columbia University's Teachers College. He saw the mission of the new institution as extending progressive education into the college years. At the time, progressive education in secondary schools seemed compromised by college admissions requirements. Bennington would be a laboratory for research in higher education and its program would be the subject of continuous scientific evaluation, in hopes of demonstrating the values of progressivism to other educators.

Like the majority of progressive colleges that developed in the 1920s and 1930s, Bennington admitted only women when it opened its doors in 1932. At that time, wealthy young women were felt to be part of the marriage market rather than the labor market. An experimentally oriented college might have proven an employment liability to job-conscious men after graduation, but Bennington was observed to be an appropriate place to go between "coming out" and marriage.

Bennington sought women with a serious interest and unusual promise in the liberal arts. Based upon research on factors associated with college success at other institutions, Bennington employed previous school records, SAT scores, and personal characteristics in making admission decisions. However, students with poor academic records, but strength in one area were encouraged to apply.

The Bennington Plan of 1929 was the key planning document for the college. According to the plan, the student's first two years of study were to be individually prescribed on the basis of conferences between the student and the staff. An interlocking set of introductory courses was offered in each of four divisions—fine arts, natural science, social studies, and literature. Linked to the introductory courses were trial major sections, which students took in their area of planned concentration. Instruction was available though not required in tool courses such as mathematics and foreign language. These courses were to be taken only by students who planned advanced work that required such knowledge. Oral and written expression, which were thought of as essential tools, were to be part of all courses.

Passage from the lower division to the upper division, which was considered equivalent to honors work at other institutions, was dependent upon a student showing "distinct ability" in one of the four fields. Promotion was independent of grades, credits, time enrolled, or even poor performance outside the major area. Students who were not admitted to the senior division were asked to leave Bennington. Those who were promoted worked on individualized assignments involving extended periods in the library, studio, laboratory, or field, supervised by major area instructors and monitored by informal group conferences or meetings once a week or less. Student concentrations, which could be directed toward vocations, avocations, or both, were not to be limited to a single discipline. Breadth did not mean lack of substance, however. For instance, if a student wanted to prepare for a secretarial career, instruction would be arranged in typing and stenography. In order to receive a B.A., students were required to write a thesis or undertake a project in the major area. Grading, recorded class attendance, and course examinations were felt a detriment to self-motivated learning.

The Bennington program included a nonresident term between Christmas and Washington's Birthday, which was intended to permit junior-division students to experiment in the world outside

Bennington and for senior-division students to use facilities required in the major but not available at Bennington.

The extracurriculum at Bennington was considered a part of the academic program as well. For example, it was an expectation of the 1929 plan that students would learn as much through residential life as in the classroom and that formal elements of the curriculum would emerge from their residential experiences. In fact some faculty members lived in the "Oxbridge"-like student dormitories and participated in noncourse activities such as drama, athletics, publications, and governance.

The whole Bennington program revolved around advising. Professional counselors were hired and faculty recruitment sought individuals with understanding and enthusiasm not only for their specialties but also for undergraduates and progressive education—and not necessarily in that order. There was no tenure provision, and the Ph.D. was thought an irrelevant criterion in hiring.

The original plan for Bennington, as just described, was not fully realized. The depression made it impossible to raise money for systematic institutional research, and thus while Newcomb and Urich studied education at Bennington in later years, its experiment in progressive education was never satisfactorily evaluated.

In addition some elements of the curriculum, such as completely individualized programming, proved to exceed human endurance. Faculty members lacked the energy to advise and prescribe an individualized program for all students, so a more formal array of courses was offered. Core courses came and went, and in 1970 a smorgasbord general education distribution requirement was introduced.

Some elements of the curriculum just did not work as expected. By 1936, academic mitosis struck the four interdisciplinary divisions. At that time, the division of art split into divisions of visual and performing arts. Today there are eight divisions, some of which have informal disciplinary subunits. The trial major was abolished in 1942. Faculty dissatisfaction resulted in a system of presumptive tenure. And in 1969, Bennington's experiment in women's education came to an end as the college became coeducational.

The extracurriculum, the nonresidential term, and residential living have not become as integral to the academic program as envisioned. Residences, for example, are not places where knowledge from the classroom is systematically applied in a living situation. Counseling has weakened under the strain of high attrition and high enrollments of 600 as contrasted with 250 in the 1929 plan. Nonetheless, advising is better at Bennington, which has an approximately 8-to-1 student-to-faculty ratio, than at most other colleges, and administrators are currently working to improve its quality. Today few students are denied admission to the senior division, and the flexibility of the college program has declined as more and more Bennington graduates, now a majority, attend graduate schools where undergraduate prerequisites are specified.

(For further information, see Brockway, 1972, 1974, 1975; and Jones, 1946.)

The General College
at the University of Minnesota—1932

The impetus for change at the University of Minnesota during the 1920s and 1930s came from Lotus Delta Coffman, president from 1920 to 1938. In 1924, Coffman established a dean's committee on administrative reorganization, which, with his enthusiastic support, proposed and established new educational programs throughout the university. Early in the 1930s, the general education experiments at the University of Chicago were receiving much favorable press coverage. Particularly attractive to Coffman and the University of Minnesota reorganization committee was Hutchins' success at making general education an accepted and complete undergraduate program for the average student. For years the University of Minnesota had experienced high attrition among students who were poorly prepared, uncertain about careers, or simply floundering in the college of liberal arts.

The result of Coffman's leadership, Hutchins' influence, and the attrition problem was a recommendation by the reorganization committee for the establishment of an "Institute of Social Intelligence." Renamed the "Junior College" in planning stages and the "General College" after one year of operation, the new unit was a two-year, open-admission, lower-division general education college intended for several groups of students: those not having time to earn a four-year degree, those wanting a broad general education, those desiring courses not available elsewhere in the university, and those not meeting the admission requirements of other units of the university.

Coffman recruited Malcolm McLean to direct the General College. McLean put together a program of broad "overview courses," such as "biology from ovum to grave," which were designed to capture the interest of the most capable students in the university. The courses were rigorously developed and evaluated. They utilized nontraditional forms of instruction, including radio, phonograph, and films. Though their substance has changed over the years, the General College is still committed to them. Today, for example, it offers a ten-credit course entitled "Toward a Good Life," which involves lectures, symposia, seminars, group discussions, readings, films, field projects, and experiences in art, music, and science.

McLean recruited the best teachers in the university to plan the courses and to instruct in the college. All his initial faculty held joint appointments in existing departments. But such appointments dwindled quickly as the faculty tired of teaching General College courses above load, as their other departments made additional demands upon them, and as they realized that rewards were more easily obtained through their department than through the General College. Today the General College has its own staff of approximately 135—100 faculty and 35 graduate assistants—and only a handful of the faculty hold joint appointments. The graduate student ranks have traditionally been used to screen and train for General College faculty positions.

Integration of the original General College curriculum was achieved by a wide-ranging comprehensive examination that students had to pass in order to graduate. The examination, by virtue of the areas tested, served as a de facto distribution requirement. Today few students fail the graduation examination but those who do are given individualized alternatives to get through. Counseling, always an important element of the program, now includes a freshman diagnostic and placement component, which is considered the first step of the comprehensive examination.

Throughout its history, the General College has changed to keep up with the times. In the 1940s, it enlarged its definition of general education to include occupational programs. The specific occupational programs have varied over the years. Another major change involved the introduction of baccalaureate programs in 1970. The General College offers both a bachelor of general studies, which enables a student to take a four-year general education degree, and a bachelor of applied studies, which allows a student to mix technical training and liberal education. Neither program is otherwise available within the university.

A large number of nontraditional programs have also been added to the General College curriculum—credit for prior learning, off-campus and extension education, internships, upward bound, a learning skills center, correspondence education, prisoner education, and a counseling and support center for low-income students. But because of the strong continued commitment of General College faculty to liberal education, many of these new and nontraditional programs are somewhat peripheral to the regular program, and their staff members not fully integrated into the college.

The General College itself occupies a similar position with regard to the rest of the University of Minnesota. It never became a place for the excellent student who was dissatisfied with the university program. Instead, it has attracted students who could not otherwise gain admission to the university. The combination of enrolling such students, being essentially a two-year college, and having a faculty dedicated to interdisciplinary teaching has caused the college to become isolated and, to some extent, looked down upon within the university. Obtaining resources from the university has often involved a struggle. And the foundation funds and the enthusiastic publicity of the early years are now less abundant. Yet the college fills some very important needs for the larger institution. It keeps the university open to all students, provides a second chance for those students who need one, offers a supportive social environment for students who would be dissatisfied elsewhere in the university, acts as a laboratory for curricular experimentation, and allows other units of the university to continue their activities while changing more slowly with time and thought.

In the past, the fortunes of the General College have been closely tied to those of the university. In boom times it has been the first unit to bulge with new enrollments, and in bad times it has been the unit to feel the loss of students hardest. This may be changing. The fortunes of the General College may in the future be tied more closely to forces outside the university than to university trends. When the General College began, there were no community colleges in the Twin Cities. Now there are seven. Many of them have better facilities and some offer a wider choice of programs. There is now also an upper-division college, Metropolitan State University (described in Chapter 13), which competes with the General College for bachelor's degree students. But what the General College has going for it is an excellent general education program, imaginative interdisciplinary courses, a dedicated faculty—and a degree from the University of Minnesota, the most prestigious institution in town.

(For further information, see Gray, 1951.)

Great Books at St. John's—1937

In 1937, St. John's College in Annapolis, an independent men's college, founded in the seventeenth century, had just fired its president for granting a student a degree that the faculty had refused to award. The college was broke, had lost its accreditation, and was fast losing its students. To turn itself around, it hired a new president, Stringfellow Barr, and a new dean, Scott Buchanan.

Barr and Buchanan had been consultants to Robert Hutchins at the University of Chicago and, previously, planners of a Great Books program at the University of Virginia. Together, they introduced a prescribed, four-year undergraduate curriculum for all students based entirely upon a little more than a hundred great books covering the development of civilization from ancient Greece to the present (see Appendix A). The curriculum emphasized the trivium (grammar, rhetoric, and logic) and quadrivium (arithmetic, music, geometry, and astronomy) of classical antiquity. It was shaped by a conviction that students can acquire a truly liberal education only by reading the works of the greatest minds of our civilization.

Barr and Buchanan offered all of the St. John's faculty a one-year trial period with the new curriculum. Most took up the challenge, but only a few stayed at the institution for any length of time. Those who left were replaced by newcomers committed to the Great Books program. Freshmen entering the college in the fall of 1937, only weeks after the announcement of the new program, were given a choice of the new curriculum or the old. Twenty elected the new. In subsequent years all students were required to take the new.

The Great Books program, which attracted much public attention, did away with the standard fare of academic departments and student majors. At its heart was the seminar. Today, seminars, attended by 17 to 21 students and two faculty leaders, meet twice a week from 8 to 10 in the evening to discuss assigned readings in one of the Great Books. Over the four years, readings follow a chronological order from the Greeks to the twentieth century. The seminars are supplemented by group tutorials "designed to cultivate the habits of methodological and careful study" in language, mathematics, and music. Every year, each student attends a mathematics tutorial and a language tutorial with between 12 and 14 other students for one hour four mornings a week. The music tutorial is a second-year requirement that students attend three times a week. Students also enroll in a laboratory each year. Laboratories meet twice a week and consist of 17 to 21 students, a faculty instructor, and advanced student aides. Friday nights are reserved for formal lectures by faculty or by outsiders, which may or may not deal with the great books; discussion follows.

Evaluation of student performance at St. John's also differs from that at most other colleges. During each of the first three years, St. John's students are required to write an essay on some aspect of the liberal arts. Each term, they face the hurdle of the "don rag," a meeting between students and teachers designed to provide diagnosis, advice, and prescription. In their second year, they undergo the "sophomore enabling," an individualized review by the Instruction Committee. If judged unsatisfactory, they cannot enter the junior class. Finally, they are also required to prove proficiency in French, pass a comprehensive examination on a number of books assigned for rereading, and present and defend a senior essay on the liberal arts.

The St. John's program has changed little in the years since its inception. Music was added 30 years ago, and the laboratory program has undergone frequent revision; but the list of books has been altered only slightly. It has expanded a bit, and now places somewhat greater emphasis on the twentieth century than it did forty years ago. Perhaps the most interesting change in the curriculum has been the introduction of preceptorials in 1962—the only elective part of the curriculum. For nine weeks each year, students undertake an in-depth study of a great books-related theme of their own choosing.

In nonprogrammatic ways the college has changed significantly. Though St. John's has offered early admission to high school juniors since the start of the new curriculum, a World War II program to admit high school students after their sophomore year was considered unsuccessful and discontinued. In 1946, Barr and Buchanan left St. John's with the hope of founding a new college in Massachusetts with an identical program. This never happened. After a brief interregnum, Richard D. Weigle assumed the presidency, and brought administrative and financial stability to the college. Women were admitted in 1951. The following year Middle States accreditation was restored. In 1964 a second campus was opened in Santa Fe, New Mexico.

Today, St. John's is no longer the male, regional, open admissions college it was in 1936. Its students, men and women, come from all over the country and its admissions standards are highly selective. There are even substantial numbers of transfer students, despite the fact that they can enter only as freshmen. Student attrition is relatively high, but has been since the start of the program. Faculty positions are scarce, and applications for them are numerous despite the fact that there are no academic ranks, salary is based solely on seniority and age, and every faculty member is expected to learn to teach the whole curriculum from language tutorial to laboratory.

In sum, St. John's proves that an undergraduate curriculum devoted entirely to general education and operating virtually without electives can not only survive the isomorphic tendencies of most colleges and universities, but can even flourish.

(For further information, see Grant and Riesman, 1974; and *The St. John's Program: A Report,* 1955.)

General Education at Harvard—1945

Of the many efforts of colleges to reassess their undergraduate programs during World War II, the best known was that of Harvard College. Late in the 1930s, the Harvard curriculum had been examined by the student government and faculty committees, and some changes had been made in it. But persistent dissatisfaction spurred on by the war led James B. Conant, president of Harvard University, to appoint a faculty committee in 1943 on "The Objectives of a General Education in a Free Society." The committee spent $60,000 and two years in deliberation, travel, and hearings. Its final report, entitled *General Education in a Free Society* and informally called the "Redbook," offered a history of education in America, a theory of general education, and a prescription for the teaching of general education in secondary schools, Harvard College, and in the community (see Appendix A).

According to the "Redbook," general education was distinct from education for specialization. It embraced the humanities, natural sciences, and social sciences, emphasizing their heritage more than their changes. General education helped people "to think effectively, to communicate thoughts, to make relevant judgments, [and] to discriminate among values" (p. 65). It further aimed at developing the whole person, affectively as well as intellectually, while reconciling the needs of the individual and the society. In order to provide such education, which the committee thought should "remain in goal and essential teaching the same for all" (p. 93), the "Redbook" recommended slightly different programs for students of varying ages, abilities, and outlooks.

The "Redbook" dealt briefly with education in the community by recommending more and better adult general education programs and experimentation with new educational media. It offered a far more detailed description of the appropriate subject matters and pedagogy for secondary school general education, however. Recommended high school subjects included humanities, natural science and laboratory, mathematics, and social studies, supplemented by work experiences and general education courses in health, values, and moral character.

With regard to Harvard, the "Redbook" recommended that 6 out of the 16 year-long courses that the college required for graduation be reserved for general education. It recommended further that courses in the humanities and social sciences entitled respectively "Great Texts in Literature" and "Western Thought and Institutions," be required of all students. In the sciences, students would be given an option between two introductory courses in the physical sciences or biological sciences. The remaining three general education courses would be taken, one each, in the humanities, social sciences, and sciences, where advanced survey and interdisciplinary courses such as the heritage of philosophy, music, human relations, and the history of science would be offered. No general education courses were to be permitted to satisfy major or concentration requirements. The committee further recommended changing Harvard's English composition course so that the first term would be a compensatory course and a second term, which was to be tied to the general education courses, would be required of all students. The administration of the general education program, according to the "Redbook's" recommendations, would become a function of a new Committee on General Education chaired by the dean of the faculty. This committee's charge would be to approve student general education programs, administer the general education budget, and establish general education courses.

The "Redbook's" recommendations were in sharp contrast to Harvard's existing general education distribution requirement, under which students took only four year-long courses in four of eight subareas within the humanities, social sciences, and sciences. But in October 1945, the Harvard faculty approved the "Redbook" recommendations in principle, and for four years it experimented with the "Redbook" curriculum. In 1949, it officially approved a compulsory "Redbook"-based program, but the program departed significantly from the document. Instead of required courses in introductory humanities and social sciences, students were given several options; and as alternatives to the advanced general education courses, they could substitute several departmental courses. These changes tightened and provided a rationale for Harvard's existing distribution requirement, but they did not constitute the common core proposed in the "Redbook" and they abrogated its sharp distinction between education for specialization and general education.

In the sciences, the faculty also departed from the "Redbook." Based on the 1949 report of the Committee on Science in General Education, chaired by Professor Jerome Bruner, the faculty permitted students to substitute any one advanced or two intermediate departmental science classes for each natural science general education course. It also concurred with the Bruner Committee's disapproval of the "Redbook's" emphasis on the history and philosophy of science and allowed as general education courses dealing either with the subject matter of a single discipline or with contemporary methods of science—two approaches traditionally used in training majors.

The resulting general education program at Harvard was not without its own problems. Few advanced general education courses were offered, and most students tended to fulfill the general education requirement with departmental courses. The general education courses that were created, although often praised, differed from year to year and instructor to instructor, so that there was little in the way of a common lower-division experience. In fact students who entered Harvard College with a year of advanced study were exempted from two out of the three introductory general education courses. But perhaps most importantly, students (some of whom had already been exposed to rigorous general education programs in prep school) and faculty (some teaching the same course year after year) both grew tired of the general education program. General education courses became difficult to staff, and a new, exciting addition to the curriculum, the freshman seminar (see Chapter 1), threatened to woo faculty and students away from general education. Its small-group discussion format and current research orientation were more attractive to many students and faculty than the large lecture courses in general education.

Criticism of general education became increasingly common, and, in 1962 Harvard created a Special Committee to Review the Present Status of Problems of the General Education Program under the chairmanship of Paul Doty. The committee's 1964 report said of past changes in the general education program: "Almost without exception, they have tended to lessen the impact of the Program on the undergraduate curriculum. It was not just change; it was erosion. What was being eroded was sometimes a technical detail; at other times it was a basic principle or what would have been considered a basic principle by the authors of the *Redbook*. The result, as it seemed to the committee, was that a Program that originated with a strong sense of urgency and direction was becoming increasingly difficult to defend or even understand" (p. 16).

The Doty committee proposed a fundamental reorganization of the general education program, and the Harvard faculty fundamentally rejected the proposal. In its stead, the faculty voted to reduce the amount of general education required and to increase the amount of student course election within general education. Students would henceforth take four year-long general education courses outside of their major area, covering the humanities, social sciences, and sciences. However, natural science majors were excused from general education in the sciences. Three of the four required courses had to be in the general education program.

In 1971, even this requirement was amended to make it possible for students to satisfy all of their general education requirements by substituting two departmental courses for each general education course. The result is that Harvard today has a general education distribution requirement quite similar to that of 1943. General education has less rationale than in previous years, but higher enrollments. It has grown more attractive to departments, especially those with many faculty and fewer enrollments than in previous years. It is still not attractive to junior faculty for whom work in the discipline and research are better rewarded. From the student perspective, the *1975–76 Confidential Guide to Courses at Harvard and Radcliffe* said: "General Education is a mixed bag sometimes reaching sublime peaks of generalized scholarship and often not. . . . Most general education courses are taught at least a little differently from their departmental counterparts, a little less directed to concentration" (p. 11).

In 1975, a task force was created by Dean of Faculty Henry

---

[6]This was one of seven task forces. The others dealt with concentration, educational resources, pedagogical improvement, advising and counseling, composition of the student body, and college life.

Rosovsky to study the possibility of a general education core program at Harvard.[6] In its 1977 report, the task force proposed that students be required to pass semester courses in expository writing, mathematical reasoning and its application, non-Western civilization and culture, political and moral philosophy, and modern social analysis. In addition, a year of study would be required in physical science, biological science, or both combined, and another year would be required in Western art, literature, and thought. In May 1977, the Harvard faculty approved the proposal in principle and established five subject area committees to design needed courses, to assure that needed courses will be available, to propose degree requirements, and to report back to the faculty. Like Columbia, Harvard may be reasserting the importance of general education once again, 30 years after adopting only part of its nationally influential plan.

(For information beyond the "Redbook" itself, see *Report of the Committee on Sciences in General Education*, 1949; *Report of the Special Committee to Review the Status and Problems of the General Education Program*, 1964; and Task Force on the Core Curriculum, 1977.)

Post-Sputnik Pressure at Oakland University—1959[7]

In the mid-1950s, the interest of Americans in higher education was growing, and some major universities were responding to that interest by building branch campuses. It was in that spirit that Mrs. Alfred Wilson, a former trustee of Michigan State University, donated land and money to the university for the construction of a campus in Oakland County. President John Hannah appointed D. B. Varner, the university's vice president for off-campus education, to be chief administrative officer of the new college, originally named Michigan State–Oakland but renamed Oakland University in 1963. Oakland was independent of Michigan State's administration, although governed by its board of trustees until 1970.

The planning of Oakland University began in 1957, the year Sputnik was launched. From a local citizen's advisory board, a

[7]This account relies heavily upon D. Riesman, J. Gusfield, and Z. Gamson, *Academic Values and Mass Education* (1975).

ten-member Program Development Committee, consisting of laymen rather than educators, was created, and a seminar series was initiated. The committee, much in tune with the times, favored a nonvocational liberal arts program. It favored tying even career courses of study such as engineering, business, and teacher education to the liberal arts and basic sciences. The view of education espoused by the committee and emphasized repeatedly in the seminars by outside experts was one that stressed rigor, hard work, and quality. The 23 faculty members recruited for the opening of classes in September 1959 reflected that spirit. Many were products of eastern Ivy League graduate schools, and more than three-fourths were humanities specialists. They shared a commitment to make Oakland an excellent and selective public liberal arts college.

The Oakland curriculum was a product of the desire to offer honors instruction to the average student. There was no remedial education. Students were required to take a substantial general education core which amounted to half the credits necessary to graduate. Among them were a two-year course in Western institutions and Western literature, two-year sequences in social science and in either Russian or French, one-year courses in non-Western studies and in science and mathematics, a one-term course in music or art, and a senior colloquium.

Only one thing had been overlooked in the equation for success at Oakland: the student body. The students who came to Oakland that first year were by and large not honors students. Many were first-generation college students who came from average high schools, and most were in search of jobs and social mobility when they finished college. They chose Oakland because it was the nearest college to their homes and offered easier admission than either the University of Michigan or Michigan State University.

The incongruity between the new college and its students was immediately apparent. More than one-third of the students, including several local high school valedictorians, failed at least one course the first year. Teacher preparation students found the general education curriculum to be so time consuming that they had great difficulty in earning both a bachelor of arts degree and teacher certification in four years—despite the fact that Oakland's Program Development Committee had conceived of the institution, in part, as an answer to the need for more and better trained teachers. Other professional programs suffered similar problems. The result was high attrition (significantly less than half of the 570 students entering in 1959 graduated four years later) and threats and actual attempts by local high school guidance counselors to discourage students from applying to Oakland.

The situation worsened in the second year. The Oakland faculty persisted in using a grading standard they considered appropriate to a highly selective liberal arts college; they reaffirmed the core program and even increased the English requirement by a term, having found students unskilled in writing; they sanctioned a four-and-one-half-year course of study necessary to attain a teaching credential; and they studied the possibility of introducing a comprehensive examination at the end of four years. This curriculum proved untenable, however, and Chancellor Varner overhauled the educational policy making system by introducing a new administrative plan that reduced the autonomy of faculty in educational matters. Among the resulting changes, students were permitted to drop courses as late as the ninth week in the 16-week term in order to decrease the course failure rate. Faculty were given a demographic profile of their students and informed of the negative impact of severe grading on the community and on their students' chances of graduate school admission. And a new course in natural science, more appropriate than the original one for the Oakland student, was introduced.

Some faculty, for whom the reality of Oakland failed to match the dream, left. But as Oakland grew, new faculty, greater in number than the original core and with more accurate perceptions of the student body, were hired. In this manner the curriculum gradually changed and became more consistent with the needs and abilities of Oakland's students.

Today Oakland is an established regional university. Its original general education core has become a distribution requirement owing in part to the early 1960s' reassessment of the curriculum and student needs but even more so to the emphasis in the late 1960s on individualization and student choice in curriculum. Compensatory programs in writing and in mathematics have been introduced.

As a result of the turbulent early years, administrative change, governance concerns, and several other factors, Oakland was one of the first universities in the nation to unionize via the American Associaton of University Professors.

The opening of a local community college in 1964 reduced pressure on Oakland University to accept all students. Oakland established a graduate school in 1965 and a doctoral program in 1971. The engineering, education, and business programs which had a difficult time in the liberal arts college have become separate schools along with nursing and performing arts. An evening division, career programs, and even university sports have been adopted. Courses in areas such as health sciences, journalism, management, and human resource development, and evening instruction are the primary sources of enrollment growth at Oakland which now enrolls 10,000 full-time and part-time students. And in September 1977, an honors program, which sounds surprisingly like a small, selective liberal arts college founded in 1959, began operation.

(For further information see Riesman, Gusfield, and Gamson, 1975.)

Education for Excellence at New College—1964

New College was founded in 1960 by the Board for Homeland Ministries of the United Church of Christ, and the city of Sarasota, Florida, which, for the previous five years, had made a concerted effort to establish a local college. The majority of its board of trustees consisted of Sarasota residents and members of the Board for Homeland Ministries. George Baughman, vice president and treasurer at New York University and a member of that board, was named the first president of the college in 1961.

Baughman's primary job as president was external administration, including fund raising and community relations. These two needs so dominated planning that an academic officer or provost was not appointed until May 1963. He was John Gustad of Alfred University in New York, where he had been known as an innovator and authority on curriculum. It was Gustad who planned the academic program.

The original 20 faculty reported to New College in July 1964, and the college began operation in September of that year. Its program was designed to be completed in three years rather than the customary four. This accelerated curriculum aimed at speeding students on to graduate school, and it was successful in this regard: The charter graduating class won a large number of prestigious fellowships and attended some of the best graduate schools in America. So impressive was their accomplishment that New College received regional accreditation in a record three years, and gained much favorable publicity nationally.

New College students and faculty members spent all but one month per year in residence. The academic calendar was a succession of three 12-week terms, each followed by a four-week period of independent study. To encourage independent learning, compulsory class attendance was eliminated, as was grading, which was felt to be a form of artificial reinforcement. The faculty was organized into broad divisions—humanities, social sciences, and sciences—rather than into departments, and interdisciplinary teaching was stressed. The freshman-year program concentrated on general education. Three core courses, consisting of lectures and discussion groups, were required, one each in the humanities, social sciences, and sciences. Each student also enrolled in one additional course each semester and engaged in a tutorial with a faculty member on a topic of the student's interest. The second year emphasized specialization, but one-third of the student's time that year was spent in studies outside the specialty area. The third and final year involved further work in a specialty area, an integrating senior seminar, and a senior project. In order to graduate, a student also had to satisfy a language requirement (a task commonly stressed in the post-Sputnik era), pass a comprehensive examination after the first year, and succeed in an oral examination based on the senior project at the end of the third year.

New College was forced to begin operation before an adequate financial base could be established, and financial problems developed quickly. In addition, the college recruited an elite national student body, jeopardizing its ties with Sarasota benefactors who

wanted a local school for their children. The intellectually and socially avant garde faculty and students of the college were incompatible with the Sarasota population, further weakening the
"town-gown" relationship. To this extent the college had no financial base as there was no ready-made national group to replace the
lost Sarasota constituency. Moreover tuition income, which is a
primary source of revenue to many private colleges, was diminished because the college offered its students large scholarships
in order to attract them away from established schools such as Yale
and Harvard. After its first year of operation, the money problems,
together with a greater proclivity toward innovation on the part of
Provost Gustad and the faculty than President Baughman and the
board of trustees, caused a vote of no confidence in Baughman by
three-quarters of the faculty. In the end, he was replaced, Gustad
resigned, and numerous faculty and students left the institution.
Fortunately, two large Ford Foundation grants were obtained to
keep the school afloat.

In only four years, the New College's post-Sputnik curriculum gave way to a more student-centered program and greater
student involvement in curriculum governance; both of which were
increasingly common at many colleges in the late 1960s. In 1967,
students were offered the option of a four-year program, which is
today the norm at the college. There were more changes in 1968.
Students considered the core program and senior seminar inconsistent with the spirit of independent study that New College emphasized. Furthermore, faculty proved unable to mount well-
integrated, coherent courses outside the humanities, and the
divisional structure broke down into individually isolated faculty,
each of whom planned his or her own curriculum. As a result, the
core curriculum and senior seminar were both abolished. The
first-year comprehensive also was considered inconsistent with a
self-motivated student body and was terminated. The foreign-
language requirement at New College, like the foreign-language
requirement at many schools during the late 1960s, was removed
by consensus. And the school calendar was reduced to nine months
to permit students a less hectic, more humanely paced lifestyle and
to give faculty an opportunity to engage in research and to rest
from their demanding academic workload.

In 1968, an optional contract system was adopted that gave students a larger role in planning their education. They could either enroll in classes on campus each term or tailor-make a program with the aid of an adviser which stressed the achievement of outcomes through courses, independent study, and off-campus learning. In 1971 this contract system was made mandatory, and graduation requirements were changed to include the completion of nine contracts, four independent study projects, a senior project, and an oral examination based upon the senior project. The general education emphasis of the original program was lost in the process of change.

By the 1970s, New College was low in funding and unable to maintain enrollments. It was a private college in a state with abundant public education and a selective college in an intellectually unattractive region of the country. Thus, in 1974, it merged with the University of South Florida. However, it maintained its autonomy and continues much as it was before the merger. Now its future depends on its ability to attract students and to raise the necessary funding above state formulas to support its low student-faculty ratios.

References

Aydelotte, F. *Breaking the Academic Lockstep.* New York: Harper & Row, 1941.

Belknap, R. L., and Kuhns, R. *Tradition and Innovation: General Education and the Reintegration of the University: A Columbia Report.* New York: Columbia University Press, 1977.

This volume discusses the Contemporary Civilization curriculum as well as the rest of Columbia's general education program with reference to problems, solutions, and future plans.

Bell, D. *The Reforming of General Education: The Columbia College Experience in Its National Setting.* Garden City, N.Y.: Anchor Books, 1968.

This book is discussed in Chapter 11.

Boucher, C. S., and Brumbaugh, A. J. *The Chicago College Plan.* Chicago: University of Chicago Press, 1940.

Brockway, T. "Notes from the Year One." *Quadrille: Bennington College,* Fall 1972, 7 (1), 7–9.

Brockway, T. "Visual Arts at Bennington 1932–1941." *Quadrille: Bennington College,* Spring 1974, 8 (3), 36–43.

Brockway, T. "Music at Bennington, 1932–41." *Quadrille: Bennington College,* Fall 1975, 10 (1), 45–52.

These articles are part of a continuing series which will someday form a book by Brockway, who was at Bennington from its founding.

Buchler, J. "Reconstruction of the Liberal Arts." In D. C. Miner (Ed.), *A History of Columbia College on Morningside.* New York: Columbia University Press, 1954.

Clark, B. R. *The Distinctive College: Antioch, Reed, and Swarthmore.* Chicago: Aldine, 1970.
    Clark's book is a classic organizational study of how three colleges developed and perpetuated innovative missions.

Clary, W. W. *The Claremont Colleges: A History of the Development of the Claremont Group Plan.* Claremont, Calif.: Claremont University Center, 1970.

College of the University of Chicago. *The Idea and Practice of General Education.* Chicago: University of Chicago Press, 1950.

Columbia University. *1919–20 Course Announcement.* New York: Columbia University, 1919.

The Confidential Guide to Courses at Harvard-Radcliffe. Cambridge, Mass.: The Harvard Crimson, 1975.

Gaff, J. G., and Associates. *The Cluster College.* San Francisco: Jossey-Bass, 1970.
    The cluster arrangement is discussed.

Grant, G., and Riesman, D. "St. John's and the Great Books." *Change,* 1974, 6 (4), 28.

Gray, J. *University of Minnesota.* Minneapolis: University of Minnesota Press, 1951.
    This volume contains an account of the creation and growth of the General College.

Harvard Committee. *General Education in a Free Society.* Cambridge, Mass.: Harvard University Press, 1945.

Henderson, A. D., and Hall, D. *Antioch College: Its Design for Liberal Education.* New York: Harper & Row, 1946.

Jones, B. *Bennington College.* New York: Harper & Row, 1946.

Leigh, R. D. *The Educational Plan for Bennington College.* Unpublished manuscript, Bennington College, December 1929. (Mimeograph)

Meiklejohn, A. *Experimental College.* New York: Harper & Row, 1932.

Report of the Committee on Science in General Education. Cambridge, Mass.: Faculty of Arts and Sciences, Harvard University, February 1949.

Report of the Special Committee to Review the Present Status and Problems of the General Education Program. Cambridge, Mass.: Faculty of Arts and Sciences, Harvard University, May 1964.

Riesman, D., Gusfield, J., and Gamson, Z. *Academic Values and Mass Education.* New York: McGraw-Hill, 1975.
    This book describes the early years of Oakland University as well as the now defunct Montieth College at Wayne State University.

The St. John's Program: A Report. Annapolis, Md.: The St. John's College Press, 1955.

Severson, S. *The Defeat of General Education at the University of Chicago: A Case of Collegiate Conflict.* Unpublished master's thesis. University of Chicago, 1972.

Swarthmore College. *Critique of a College.* Swarthmore, Penn., November 1967.

The Swarthmore College Faculty. *An Adventure in Education: Swarthmore College Under Frank Aydelotte.* New York: Macmillan, 1941.

Task Force on the Core Curriculum. *Report of the Task Force on the Core Curriculum.* Cambridge, Mass.: Harvard University, Jan. 24, 1977.

13

Current Curriculum Highlights: 1965 to the Present

The current era of curriculum reform was a by-product of the 1964 Free Speech Movement at the University of California at Berkeley. As at Berkeley, the causes of campus unrest were frequently noncurricular, but the resulting soul searching brought to light student dissatisfaction with the post-Sputnik mentality and curriculum that emphasized the needs of society but failed to consider the needs of the individual student. Experience with the Civil Rights movement and later with the war in Vietnam hastened the student rejection of post-Sputnik education and spread that rejection throughout the campus.

The first curricular fruits of the new era were harvested in Berkeley within a year. They included Joseph Tussman's Experimental College Program, which was conceived before the Free Speech Movement but which sought to overcome the educational problems that were criticized during the protest, and the autonomous Free University of Berkeley, a direct product of the student protest that was emulated on many campuses.

Student activism contributed directly or indirectly to other curricular changes of the late 1960s. The changes emphasized student-centered education and the adoption of new socially relevant courses. A concern for the whole student and affective learning was common. Major curriculum changes conceived or implemented during this period included the establishment of Simon's Rock (1965), the University of California, Santa Cruz (1965), Bensalem College at Fordham University (1967), a new curriculum at Brown University (1969), and Hampshire College (1970).

The nationwide student strike in reaction to the U.S. invasion of Cambodia and the shootings at Kent State and Jackson State universities in spring 1970 closed the 1960s era of campus unrest. Since that time, campus protests have continued, but their causes have more often been bread-and-butter issues such as rising tuition, faculty layoffs, and program cutbacks. The 1970s marked the end to visions of limitless growth for American colleges and universities, now faced with the day-to-day realities of tight budgets and a ceiling or decline in student enrollments.

The impetus for change in the 1970s has come from administrators at institutions suffering from financial or enrollment declines, from public systems responding to perceived new needs, and from organizations not traditionally associated with higher education, such as brokerage organizations and proprietary schools. Some curriculum changes have been primarily procedural, concentrating on more efficient delivery systems and the measurement of educational outputs. Others have tried to attract or respond to a new variety of students—members of minority groups, the academically disadvantaged, adults, and the poor. Still others have involved the development of vocational curricula and community-based educational assistance centers. Some of the outstanding developments of the decade have involved the award of degrees by proprietary schools such as the Technical Career Institutes (1970), the creation of such nontraditional adult colleges as Metropolitan State University (1972), the development of competency-based curricula at Sterling College (1972), and the rise of brokerage organizations like the Capital Higher Education Service (1973).

A number of curriculum changes have traversed the moods of both the 1960s and 1970s. Flathead Valley Community College (1967) is an example of a college created in the 1960s but based on 1970s themes. Economic hardship reached the Flathead Valley in Montana before much of the rest of the country, so that it developed a 1970s-style college before such colleges became fashionable. New College at the University of Alabama (1971) encompassed the moods of the 1960s and 1970s by adopting a curriculum that responded to the concerns of both periods.

The range of results from these current curriculum changes has been wide. Some institutions and programs are flourishing; others are no longer in existence. The following pages describe the substance of these curriculum changes in chronological sequence, examine how each came into being, and observe how each has progressed since then.

Tussman's Experimental College Program at the University of California, Berkeley—1965

In 1964, Joseph Tussman, a professor of philosophy at Berkeley, disgusted with what he perceived to be the incoherence and lack of educational integrity of lower-division study there, sought to reintroduce the experimental college that Alexander Meiklejohn had tried at the University of Wisconsin more than 30 years before (described in Chapter 12). Obtaining permission and resources to start his college was difficult. First Tussman approached Clark Kerr, then president of the University of California system, who reacted favorably. With this go-ahead, Tussman began negotiating the Berkeley administrative labyrinth. He went initially to the dean of the College of Letters and Science, who arranged a meeting with the executive committee of the college and appropriate committee chairpersons. This group referred Tussman's proposal to the letters and science committee on courses, but that committee refused to act because Tussman's college was significantly larger and different than the courses the committee was charged with approving. Tussman returned to the executive committee, which approved the proposal and sent it on to the faculty of letters and science, which also sanctioned it. The next step required approval by the Committee on Courses of the Berkeley Division of the Academic Senate. That committee refused to act until it received more information that could be provided only by the college staff, but the staff could not be hired until the program had been approved. Faced with this "Catch-22" situation, Tussman asked the Committee on Rules and Jurisdiction to intervene. This committee overruled the division Committee on Courses, calling the faculty vote of letters and science sufficient. In subsequent years Tussman came to feel that bypassing the Committee on Courses engendered a lingering, never-to-be-overcome sense of suspicion and criticism within the faculty regarding his experimental college. But at the time, it allowed Acting Berkeley Chancellor Martin Meyerson to give Tussman the necessary financial support to establish his college program.

Five faculty members who had expressed an interest in teaching were recruited from an assortment of academic departments in the sciences, humanities, and social sciences. During the summer of 1965, all aided Tussman in planning, and subsequently taught full-time in the college. A description of the program was sent to the 4,000 freshmen admitted to Berkeley in the fall quarter of 1965. Of these, 325 applied to the college, and 150 were randomly selected.

Tussman's two-year curriculum was very similar to Meiklejohn's, although students did not live together in a common dormitory. Instead they were scattered on and off campus, sharing only a nonresidential building for meetings. Tussman's students studied intensively ancient Greece, seventeenth-century England, the founding of the American constitution, and contemporary society. Unlike the Meiklejohn program, their emphasis was thematic rather than historical. They examined the four periods in order to understand ideas such as war and peace, freedom and authority, the individual and society, acceptance and rebellion, and law and conscience.

Like the Meiklejohn program, the Experimental College Program operated without courses, though students were required to take one class per term elsewhere in the university. The program relied upon a combination of lectures, seminars, conferences, and a short, common reading list of great works. Lectures were scheduled twice a week for an hour-and-a-half each. The format of the lectures varied from individual to group presentations and very real faculty differences emerged in them in the form of bickering and quarrels.

Seminars, too, varied in format, approach, and content with different instructors. They ranged in size from 30 to 8 students at different points in the history of the program, and originally met once but later twice a week. The second meeting was a students-only session which eventually proved unsuccessful owing to poor attendance and the inability of students to work together without a faculty leader.

Conferences, which were bi-weekly meetings between a student and a faculty member, emphasized writing. They often focused on the journal students were required to keep or the five papers they had to write each term.

After the entering class completed the program in spring 1967, Tussman recruited a new staff composed of friends outside the university rather than Berkeley faculty. The first group of faculty lacked a shared educational vision of the college and responded poorly to Tussman's strong direction. They proved to be individualists, unable to collaborate successfully in teaching and planning. This also proved true, but to a far less extent, among the second group. After completing a second two-year program, the experimental college at Berkeley ceased operation in 1969.

In part, the Experimental College Program was a victim of changing times. Conceived before the 1964–65 campus protest at Berkeley, it was not initiated until after it. Thus it offered a program that permitted students little if any involvement in governing the curriculum, though it did permit them freedom in their studies. It also was heavily academic in orientation at a time when students were increasingly emphasizing affective or personal development. Furthermore, it was an all-required curriculum in an age of election.

There were also structural and personal problems beyond lack of cooperation. The faculty work load in the program was so heavy that staff members had to take a virtual two-year leave from their own research and disciplines to fulfill its obligations. Among students, the attrition rate was no lower than that of the university at large, even though Tussman college dropouts more often left for other divisions of the university than leaving the university entirely. Nonetheless, their leaving the integrated curriculum of the program could seldom be compensated for by admitting new students. Thus the per-student cost of the college rose continually. Finally, faculty elsewhere in the university were suspicious of the program despite its rave press notices nationally. And when the university would not expand the program, Tussman decided simply to end it rather than allow it to limp along.

Despite these problems, very few of the program's faculty or alumni can be located who do not highly praise its idea. Moreover, the accomplishments of its graduates in the upper division at Berkeley were impressive. Their grade-point averages were better than normal, and a larger percentage graduated in four years than was true of the general university population.

In sum, the Experimental College Program illustrates the fact that a program may close but need not thereby be considered to have failed. Even though the program ceases operation, it can affect its participants for the better and serve as guidance for the future. This is no small accomplishment for anything experimental.

(For further information, see Suczek, 1972; and Tussman, 1969.)

The Student-Run Free University
in Berkeley—1965

The Free Speech movement began at the University of California, Berkeley, in September 1964 in reaction to a university prohibition on soliciting funds, leafleting, and publicizing political causes in certain areas of the campus. It soon expanded to include protests on issues of educational policy. After it dragged on into the spring term of 1965, a group of graduate students who had been tutoring Free Speech Movement participants having academic difficulties decided to establish an off-campus "Free University" not associated with the University of California. They described it as "a promise and a protest. It promises a new focus for our intellectual concerns. It rejects an education establishment which produces proud cynicism, but sustains neither enthusiasm, nor integrity. The Free University is forged in response to an education both sterile and stultifying; an education which fragments our experience and distorts meaning, which confuses rather than encourages activism, and which provides—behind the pretense of knowledge—escape from ourselves and the problems of our day" (Free University, 1966, p. 1).

The graduate students rented a house not far from the Berkeley campus; disseminated information about the Free University to the college community and the local populace; and held forums, planning sessions, and organizational meetings. By spring 1966, the core participants numbered 170, and 28 noncredit, nongraded courses were offered. These courses were primarily political and theoretical in nature but included topics ranging from political economy and imperialism, radical press, revolutionary thought and action, and nonviolent action, to Afro-music and Beethoven. The courses met in many locations in the Berkeley-Oakland area, including houses, classrooms, the Free University itself (later located in a church), and other available space.

The Free University grew in size from 200 students and 35 courses in fall 1966 to over 200 courses and more than 1,200 enrollees by 1970. It charged students ten dollars for the first course they attended, and four dollars for all additional enrollments. Its faculty were simply people with something to teach. Its governance emphasized community, with many meetings and periodic potluck suppers.

As time passed, the mission of the Free University changed and the percentage of University of California students decreased as the number of local nonuniversity people increased. Course offerings came to embrace affective, craft, skill, and practical political themes more than the earlier theoretical critiques of society. Courses in the late 1960s and early 1970s included astrology, bookkeeping, ceramics, childbirth, credit union, erotic film, gay studies, foreign travel, Free University football, French pastry, housing and real estate, karate, local government, radical psychiatry, Spanish for beginners, and writing novels. The Free University became closely involved with community groups and served as a forum for their educational programs, including a food-stamp protest, the Free Women's school, a community library (not to be confused with the public library), housing and food cooperatives, the Berkeley Free Clinic, a people's medical collective, a drug abuse clinic, and a people's law school.

Survival was touch and go for the Free University from its earliest days. Lack of money was the principal problem. More than half of the enrollees failed to pay the ten-dollar admission fee, since it was waived for people who could not afford it. Salaries for three paid administrators were minuscule, so administrative turnover was high and continuity low. One coordinator left and took a thousand dollars in Free University money with him. Moreover, the quality and size of the Free University community—an important element in its plan—varied considerably, with faculty and students attending or leaving as they wished.

Competition was another problem. The Free University was soon competing for students with several rival free universities within the San Francisco bay area. It also found itself competing with the University of California, which after a few years began to offer courses like those that initially made the Free University unique. Berkeley could offer degrees and credits, commodities that the Free University deliberately and of necessity chose to ignore. For these several reasons, by 1972 the Free University began fading from the Berkeley landscape and subsequently disappeared.

This trajectory from protest to disappearance was not the fate of all free universities, but it does mirror the life of many. For example, the Experimental College at the University of California, Davis, founded soon after the Berkeley Free University, is still thriving. But by and large, the purposes that the free universities served in the 1960s as alternatives to conventional institutionalized education have now been fulfilled elsewhere—on the one hand, by conventional colleges and universities that recognized new areas of student interest at least through non-credit programs if not degree-credit courses; and, on the other, by even more informal educational exchanges and learning networks, as advocated by Friere and Illich, that use supermarket bulletin boards and notices on telephone poles rather than a free university to bring teacher and students together.

(For further information on free universities, see Lichtman, 1973.)

Collegiate Education at the University of California, Santa Cruz—1965

The University of California, Santa Cruz, originated as part of a statewide plan to accommodate high enrollments that were projected in 1957 by a joint committee of the University of California Board of Regents (the university's governing board) and the California State Board of Education. The State Department of Finance also calculated that if another campus of the university were not established in northern California, Berkeley would have to increase its enrollment to 35,000 students by 1975.

In 1961, land for the new campus was acquired in Santa Cruz, south of Berkeley. Dean McHenry was nominated as chancellor or chief executive officer of the new college by Clark Kerr, then president of the University of California, and approved by the regents.

An early decision of McHenry and Kerr was that the new college should reject the Berkeley and UCLA models of mass education. In 1962 an academic plan for the new campus based upon the British conception of collegiate education was adopted. The campus would consist of small residential colleges, each having classrooms, residential facilities, social space, and faculty offices. Four hundred to a thousand students would be associated with each college, whose mission would be to provide general education and about half of their students' courses. At least initially, the university would concentrate on the liberal arts rather than graduate or professional education. For this reason, the campus would operate without academic departments. Instead a tripartite divisional structure of natural sciences, social sciences, and humanities would coordinate disciplinary activities. Small classes and interdisciplinary nonlecture instruction, would be emphasized. In short, Santa Cruz would seek to offer all of the individual attention and human contact associated with a small liberal arts campus within the diversity and array of resources associated with a large university. Rather than allowing the individual colleges of the university to expand indefinitely, a new college would be established nearly every year until there would be perhaps as many as 20, with several professional schools as well.

In 1965, students were admitted to the first college, Cowell, which emphasized the humanities and offered a general education program in Western civilization. The students who came were academically excellent as measured by grade-point averages and scholastic aptitude tests. They were graded pass/fail, required to complete a course of studies that included both general education and a major, and encouraged to enroll in independent study. The first faculty members had doctorates from the most outstanding universities in the country. Each faculty member in the initial cadre was recruited jointly by an academic division and Cowell College. With the exception of the scientists, who required centralized laboratory facilities, the faculty were housed in their college rather than in their divisions. Half of their salaries were paid by the division and half by the college.

After the first year of experimentation, some changes were made in the academic plan. A general education examination in Western civilization at the end of the first year was eliminated after a campus uproar over the high failure rate, but a senior comprehensive or project remains a degree requirement. Also created were "boards of studies"—quasi-departmental units consisting of all of the Santa Cruz faculty in a given discipline and one individual from outside the discipline. (The outside person has gradually disappeared.) The boards were charged with planning undergraduate and graduate major programs, coordinating the comprehensive examinations, and recruiting faculty.

Between 1966 and the present, Santa Cruz has added seven colleges: Stevenson College, which initially emphasized the social sciences and now is a general college of arts and sciences; Crown College, stressing the sciences; Merrill College, focusing on multicultural themes; College V, concerned with the arts; Kresge College, striving for community learning; Oakes College, emphasizing cultural diversity and the minority experience; and College VIII, concerned with adults, especially women, who have had some previous college education. Each college enrolls between 600 and 800 students.

Over the past 10 years, the boards of studies have become increasingly important relative to the colleges. No longer are the colleges coequal with the divisions and boards of studies. The mission of Crown College, for instance, has changed from offering a science general education program to supplementing the offerings of the science boards of studies.

The core general education programs of the older colleges have periodically died and been reborn, usually in a more diluted form. In part, this change has occurred because the disciplines have made competing demands for faculty time and attention and have provided better rewards. This also occurred, however, because the 1960s was a time when requirements of all sorts were under attack. Moreover, the growth of graduate enrollments from ten students in 1965 to 330 in 1976 has reinforced disciplinary education by taking faculty time that might have been spent in the colleges. The newer colleges have failed to adopt core programs in addition because their multidisciplinary and problem-oriented themes are less amenable to a core than those of the early colleges that stressed more familiar subject groupings.

To this extent, the mission of the colleges has evolved primarily into that of supplementing and broadening the offerings of the disciplines. Cowell and Stevenson Colleges, for instance, jointly offer a broader and more integrated lower-division introductory program for science majors than students would traditionally find in a university. In addition, the colleges offer several unique majors or concentrations that supplement disciplinary offerings. These include women's studies, aesthetics studies, arts and crafts, and world civilization. The colleges have also facilitated the development of many interdisciplinary courses by placing faculty from different disciplines in neighboring offices. Perhaps most importantly, however, the colleges have added an affective element to undergraduate education that would otherwise be absent from the curriculum. Because of the collegiate organization, students are not only able to make close friends within the college, receive personalized peer advising, get individual help in compensatory education tutorials, and obtain knowledgeable assistance in field experience and job placement; they also are able to meet senior faculty members as colleagues and friends.

The 1962 plan for as many as 20 colleges and 27,500 students by 1990 has been revised. It is now likely that Santa Cruz will have approximately 7,500 students by 1984–85. This alteration in outlook results both from nationally exaggerated expectations in the 1950s and 1960s of growth for higher education and from the declining popularity of 1960s-style innovations among current college applicants. The result for Santa Cruz has been a sharp decline in the number of students seeking admission; a moderate decline in the average test scores of entering students; and an abrupt reduction in the rate of flow of new resources, causing some imbalances between resources and program commitments. Although Santa Cruz is unlikely to grow as large as its original planners assumed, it is likely to continue to offer a unique blend for a public university of colleagual collegiality and multiversity diversity.

(For further information, see Chancellor's Self Study Accreditation Committee, 1975; Gaff and Associates, 1970; and Members of the Cowell History Workshop, 1970.)

An "Early College" at Simon's Rock—1965

Family illness brought Elizabeth Hall, the former head of The Concord Academy, a prep schools for girls, to her parents' home at Great Barrington, Massachusetts, in the early 1960s. The continued need for her to remain nearby resulted in the establishment of Simon's Rock. Hall's mother offered her a parcel of land from the family estate to build a school. The money to get the project off the ground was also available. So Hall decided to create a very different kind of college: an "early college" that admitted students into collegiate studies after successful completion of the tenth grade in a college preparatory program.

In Hall's opinion, many students were ready for college at age 16. A college for 16- to 20-year-olds would reduce the considerable overlap and repetition in their high school and lower-division college studies, and, in the process, reduce the increasing amount of time they were spending in school. But such a college would do more: There was evidence that 16- to 20-year-olds formed a more natural peer group than those traditionally found either in high school or in college.

In 1964–65, Simon's Rock was incorporated, a board of trustees was formed, and architects were hired to remodel the barns and houses that came with the land as well as to draft plans for additional construction. In 1965–66, students were recruited. There was enthusiasm for the concept of the early college and for Hall's previous accomplishments at The Concord Academy, but parents were reluctant to send their children to Simon's Rock until it had proven itself. They seemed somewhat more willing to send daughters than sons on a new educational venture, however; and as a result, Hall temporarily abandoned her plans for a coeducational college and decided instead to recruit only women initially. Men were not admitted until 1970.

Fifty-six students of mixed quality, some of whom had posed problems at other prep schools, entered Simon's Rock in fall 1966. The initial faculty came primarily from prep schools. Hall thought it easier to upgrade them than to turn Ph.D.s into good teachers. Rather than tenure, she offered faculty a series of appointments of increasing lengths. Throughout the short history of Simon's Rock there has been periodic turbulence over questions of governance, college mission, lifestyle, and financing.

The college was originally limited by the state of Massachusetts to offering a high school equivalency certificate and an associate of arts degree. Students could enter after the tenth grade, earn the equivalency certificate after two years (after only one year, effective in 1976), and earn the A.A. in three years. The two programs, which could also be entered even after completing the eleventh grade, stressed the liberal arts and were traditional in design. Today, an academic and social transitional-year program, designed to ease entrance into college, and extensive personal counseling are integral parts of the curriculum, which now has few requirements other than a minimum number of credits and a short list of required or distribution courses.

In 1972, Simon's Rock took the originally intended but still daring step of initiating a bachelor of arts degree. Students choosing this program enter the institution after finishing the tenth grade and graduate with a B.A. after four years, thus reducing by two years the time normally needed to earn the degree. The rigorous requirements for this degree include English; participation in the transitional-year program; two interdisciplinary modes of academic inquiry and basic skills courses; at least one year of courses in the divisions of science, social science, and humanities; completion of one of seven interdisciplinary majors including American studies, arts and aesthetics, English studies, environmental studies, intercultural studies, premedical studies, and social sciences; a senior interdisciplinary seminar; a senior thesis; and an oral and written examination.

The first students were graduated from the B.A program in 1976. This program has proven essential for the survival of Simon's

Rock. Without it, the college was an expensive private liberal arts junior college at a time when such colleges were closing for lack of students. Nonetheless, the B.A. program has not solved the institution's enrollment problems. Serious problems stem from the combination of hard financial times during which parents would prefer not to pay or even to postpone paying high tuition at a private college to accelerating their children's education; reluctance of students to leave their high schools after spending a year or more building a social niche for themselves; a lack of desire by high school guidance counselors and principals to lose their best students; and high attrition at Simon's Rock, particularly after the second year when some students transfer to other colleges. In 1975–76, for example, when enrollments had been projected for 315 students, Simon's Rock enrolled only 176. Enrollments did increase by 14 percent in 1976–77, however, and today, according to their College Board scores, current Simon's Rock students demonstrate higher academic ability than the average entering college freshman nationally, despite their younger age.

The bachelor's program has resulted in a considerable amount of favorable press and major grants from the Carnegie Corporation and the National Science Foundation, but it has also created additional strains. It has required the development of a complete upper-division undergraduate curriculum that is particularly costly considering the small number of students utilizing it. In addition, increased emphasis has been placed on the Ph.D. as a qualification for faculty hiring, a change considered necessary by many for a quality bachelor's program. And this change has generated greater faculty interest in research and some minor complaints that the faculty who once doted upon extracurricular activities and student personal concerns are no longer quite as involved.

In August 1976, Samuel H. Magill of the Association of American Colleges was appointed president of Simon's Rock. His principal job will be to bring financial stability and increased enrollments to a very unique school: one of the few institutions in the United States to confront head-on the American convention of twelve years of schooling prior to four years of college. So far, this convention has remained so ingrained that despite over a hundred years of criticism, periodic efforts by university presidents (such as Robert Maynard Hutchins) to challenge it, and scattered success at ameliorating its rigidity for some students through early entry programs, no other institution has yet succeeded for long in opposing it.

(For further information, see Martorana and Kuhns, 1975.)

Bensalem College at Fordham University—1967

Bensalem College was the outgrowth of a 1965 luncheon conversation between poet Elizabeth Sewell and Reverend Leo McLaughlin, president of Fordham University. McLaughlin wanted to make Fordham a first-rate university, and Sewell wanted to create a living-learning community. An experimental subunit, they thought, would help each realize his/her dream.

McLaughlin authorized the establishment of the college and, in August 1966, Sewell brought a circle of friends to Fordham to plan and staff the college. The group conceived of the college as a polis and named it Bensalem, after the island home for lost seafarers in Bacon's poem *The New Atlantis*. At Bensalem the faculty and students would live and study together. There were to be no examinations, grades, credits, or requirements—with the very obvious exception that each student would learn the language Urdu. In all other respects, each student would plan his or her own program with the aid of an adviser knowledgeable in the area of the student's interest. The learning activities chosen by the student might occur in the college, in Fordham University, or even in the larger community. After three years of study, including summers, the student would earn a bachelor's degree.

In the summer of 1967, Bensalem opened with 30 students and 6 faculty, living in an old apartment house at the edge of the Fordham campus. The students were bright and had been screened closely before being admitted. The faculty were friends of Bensalem chairperson Sewell, and most were young. The new instructors had decided before the students arrived that the first six to nine months at Bensalem would be spent on general education. After that, students could, if they wished, specialize. The faculty handed out a schedule of planned Bensalem seminars to the students and devoted the first week of instruction to the subject of revolution. The initial instruction was very successful and by the end of the week the students revolted. Their demands for greater intellectual freedom brought an end to the Urdu requirement, to the general education requirement, and to the prearranged seminars. Consensus on the basis of equality between a student's opinion and that of a faculty member was the rule of governance at Bensalem. In subsequent years, however, when disharmony grew, the definition for consensus slipped from unanimity of opinion to 75 percent agreement.

Bensalem, in its first years, was mistakenly thought of as an honors college by many in the university. This impression received added currency when the first graduating class in 1970 received a surprisingly large number of acceptances and fellowships from prestigious graduate schools. But by that time Elizabeth Sewell and Leo McLaughlin had both left Fordham. The departure of the two prime movers deepened the gulf in the already distant relationship between the university and its experimental college. When McLaughlin left the presidency, what remained was a Fordham faculty that had never approved the college. When Elizabeth Sewell left Bensalem, what remained was a group of young faculty unprotected by the mantle of Sewell's academic reputation.

Contact between Fordham and Bensalem had always been meager. None of Bensalem's faculty taught in the university, and few, if any, Fordham faculty taught at Bensalem. The initial Bensalem students had enrolled in a large number of Fordham courses—even graduate courses—and done very well. But in later years, Bensalem students frowned upon taking courses at Fordham—or for that matter at Bensalem itself—so enrollment in Fordham classes plummeted. As a result of this lack of contact, information about Bensalem and Fordham was communicated primarily by rumor. The very positive initial press reports on Bensalem were quickly dispelled at Fordham by stories of illicit drugs, rabid radicalism, rampant sex, and unacademic chicanery. For example, regardless of the quality of a Bensalem student's program or performance, after only three years on the rolls and a faculty signature, the student was entitled to a degree.

The rumors were not entirely fabricated, though they were often overblown. By the late 1960s, the frequent publicity about

Bensalem's educational freedom attracted a new breed of student. Joining the academically oriented students of the first years were affectively oriented and escape-oriented young people (MacDonald, 1973, pp. 22–23). What community and consensus existed in the first few years diminished. The admissions committee, which screened student applicants to Bensalem, became the vehicle through which competing ideological groups sought to attract friends and like-minded people. Little if any attention was paid to academic credentials.

Apathy, alienation, and anger grew. Internal divisions became so serious that for several months two faculty positions remained unfilled because no agreement could be reached on successors. The apartment home of the more than fifty students and between five to seven faculty was uncared for and became increasingly run down. People moved out. Most faculty, unhappy and overworked at Bensalem with little chance of tenure in the university, lasted a single year at the college, and none served more than three years. Student attrition was high.

Bensalem was the subject of numerous internal and external evaluations. At the origin of the college, they were very positive; but they grew increasingly negative into the 1970s. Finally, in 1974, Fordham discontinued the experiment. In the end, though named for Bacon's island home, Bensalem served neither as an island within Fordham nor a home for searching students or faculty. It was a victim of its topography, its location, and its times.

(For further information, see Coyne, 1972; Jerome, 1970; MacDonald, 1973; and Schroth, 1972.)

Comprehensive Community College in the Flathead Valley—1967

As early as 1957, prominent citizens of the Flathead Valley in Montana sought to establish a local college. The valley was an area where the population was poor, much of the work was seasonal, students left to go to college, and few students earned degrees. A hometown college was seen as a way to change this cycle.

In 1965, a summer liberal arts school, Glacier College, was established. But its summer-only sessions were not sufficient to keep students in the valley, and its liberal arts orientation was of little help in preparing students for jobs or attracting industry. In addition, it faced serious problems with regard to accreditation and credit transfer.

As a result, Owen Sowerwine, a retired businessman and member of the local bank's board of directors, toured colleges in the western United States to find something importable to the Flathead Valley. He returned as an apostle of the comprehensive community college and won support for the idea from several community leaders and local civic groups. They launched a campaign to influence voters, stressing the economic returns of establishing a community college, the savings in sending students to a local institution, the open access to all valley residents in contrast to the stringent admissions requirements elsewhere in the state, the low cost of creating a college with a good deal of state and federal support, and the serious need in the valley for vocational/technical preparation as well as cultural education. In April 1967, the voters overwhelmingly approved the establishment of Flathead Valley Community College and a tax levy to support it.

In September of that year, the college began operation in Kalispell, Montana, with 611 students, 12 full-time instructors, and 35 part-time staff. Larry Blake, a Kalispell native with a doctorate from the University of Arizona and considerable experience in community college work, was selected as president by the popularly elected trustees. Most classes met in the late afternoon or evening and utilized the facilities of the local high school and several other community spots. The curriculum emphasized the liberal arts (60 percent) in preference to vocational-technical subjects (40 percent). Blake, who wanted to get as much of the community involved as quickly as possible, weighted the program in this manner because liberal arts courses were much cheaper to run than vocational programs and afforded opportunities to admit a far greater number of students. There were no requirements for the associate degree except satisfactory completion of a minimum number of credits.

Lacking money, Blake expanded the college by growing into the community. He begged, borrowed, and remodeled existing facilities. An art center was created by refurbishing an abandoned railroad station in the center of town; the administration building was formerly an Elks Club and YMCA whose pool was covered over to provide room for a computer; and the biology department was housed in a remodeled garage. The Flathead Valley County library became the college's library. By 1975, the college owned three buildings, rented space at 16 others, including the fairgrounds, a Veterans of Foreign Wars Hall, and a teen center, and offered courses in many locations around the valley, including the Blackfeet Indian reservation.

Blake increased the range of the curriculum offerings as well by emphasizing service to the community. Courses in Blackfeet language for the large Native American population found their way into the curriculum, as did classes in tailoring, sewing with knits, painting, ceramics, video production, knitting, income tax, and bridge. Groups such as the U.S. Forest Service and the local high school asked the college to provide courses for them to meet specific needs, and the college originally did so for groups of 10 or more, later for 15 or more. When the group was too small, a faculty member usually taught the course on his or her own time. Course offerings were extended into daylight hours, but classes were not offered during summer—the lucrative tourist season.

Blake brought national attention and some major grants to his college. Several programs, including Multiple Occupational Programs for the vocational training of the handicapped, and Total Community Education, an outreach program which connects the college with 70 percent of the homes in the valley by television, were established on grant money.

Enrollments reached almost 2,000 students in 1976, and the staff increased to 33 full-time faculty and 41 part-time instructors. By then, 1,000 applications for faculty positions were on file. Many faculty chose the college for its location and were selected because of their ability to teach in more than one subject area. Their salaries were based on degrees completed, and most full-time faculty had completed the master's degree.

In addition to increasing the diversity of the programs, and opening the college to more people, growth brought problems. Blake's aggressive search for favorable national publicity and outside funding took him away from Kalispell frequently. This caused not only organizational difficulties in running the college but also skepticism on the part of townspeople and civic groups about his continued interest in the Flathead Valley. When the projects he brought to campus used up their outside funding, they proved expensive to maintain, especially because most of them generated few enrollments and several had high costs per student. Utilizing catch-as-catch-can buildings and physical facilities around the valley also proved expensive, since at least some of the buildings were outmoded or shoddy, and their remodeling and maintenance costs were high.

The Flathead Valley populace has not been as friendly to the college as its initial vote indicated it might be. With several exceptions, it has voted down college tax levies, owing among other reasons to the recruitment of an all-black basketball team by the college in 1968, the national student unrest of the times (absent at the college, but mistakenly associated with it by some), the attendance at the college of some out-of-towners who affected somewhat unusual garb and behavior, and the economic inflation of recent times.

Making ends meet is now a problem for Flathead Valley Community College. Some of Blake's innovative program have been phased out since he resigned in 1974, and the college is more careful in picking and choosing the grants it applies for. Though there are now more vocational programs thanks to federal assistance than when Flathead Valley Community College began, there are still not as many as were promised when the college started. The physical plant needs to be improved, and some of the newer staff members dream of branch campuses and a new college at the outskirts of Kalispell rather than Blake's institution integrated so completely into the community landscape and culture.

(For further information, see Hall and Associates, 1974.)

Curriculum Reform at Brown University—1969

In 1966, a number of Brown University students who were unhappy with their education got together to seek a collective solution. Many wanted to establish a free university, but put off action pending a study of the field of higher education. They spent an academic year reading, listening to outside speakers, examining curriculum reforms elsewhere, and studying Brown. A summer of continued activity, funded by a grant from the dean of the college, resulted in the more-than-400-page *Draft of a Working Paper for*

Education at Brown University by two of the students—Ira Magaziner and Elliot Maxwell. Their report, which viewed education as an individual process, was a philosophical statement intertwined with recommendations.

Magaziner and Maxwell called first for a radical reconstruction of the freshman year. A new seminar-sized freshman course emphasizing the methods and values of academic inquiry, entitled "Modes of Thought," was proposed. One year of such courses, taught generally by two faculty members, was to be required of each freshman in three areas—the humanities, natural science, and social science. A single semester of formal thought and mathematics was also specified. All other general education requirements were to be eliminated. A writing clinic was suggested for those students whose needs had not been met by "Modes of Thought," and foreign language study was reserved for vacation institutes.

Besides "Modes of Thought," the *Working Paper* suggested several other types of courses—traditional departmental courses, individual and group independent study, and nondisciplinary "third-tier" courses designed to provide breadth for concentrating upperclassmen. Similarly it proposed a variety of major options, including departmental majors, interdisciplinary majors, and student-created majors.

The report also dealt with teaching, examinations, calendar, student leaves, counseling, and institutional self-study, but it gave particular attention to the grading system. Magaziner's and Maxwell's primary recommendation here called for pass/fail grading in the freshman year, in order to ease the transition into college, and a dossier system in subsequent years. The dossier would include student evaluations, instructor evaluations, pieces of student work, letters of recommendation, and a record of extracurricular activities.

In 1967, Brown's president and the faculty chairman of the Educational Policy Committee established a commission to examine the report. When the commission failed to make substantive recommendations, Magaziner resigned as a member and organized the student body to support the report and bring it to the faculty for action. Teams of three students who had been trained in simulations tried to visit every Brown faculty member and wrote reports on their visits, utilizing standardized scales and subjective assessments. Mass meetings, some attended by more than half of Brown's undergraduates, were staged.

By late 1968, this pressure produced another presidential committee, chaired by Associate Provost Paul Maeder. Many members of this committee were favorably inclined toward the *Working Paper*. Despite little external interest in the lengthy committee proceedings, the group kept faculty and students appraised of its progress and not surprisingly issued recommendations in substantial agreement with the proposals for structural changes contained in the Magaziner-Maxwell report. Its only major departure was in the area of grading. Magaziner and the committee were convinced of the infeasibility of dossiers, so a dual system of A/B/C/no credit, and satisfactory–no credit grading was proposed. A faculty member could declare a course satisfactory–no credit, in which case all students would be required to be graded in that manner; but if the faculty member did not so specify, the option would be left to the individual student. Neither failed nor dropped courses would be recorded on the student's transcript.

In the spring of 1969, the Maeder report was the subject of a two-and-one-half-day faculty meeting attended by 350 of Brown's 500 full-time faculty. It was broadcast over the university's radio station and watched over by hundreds of students milling peaceably about the center of the campus. The entire Maeder committtee curriculum package was passed by the faculty with the exceptions of not requiring Modes of Thought courses, or approving group-independent study. All requirements except language and English were abolished, but within a year language and English were out and group-independent studies were in.

The new curriculum was introduced in the fall of 1969. Fifty-two Modes of Thought courses were hurriedly assembled during the summer of 1969, and their number was supposed to be greatly augmented in subsequent years. However, by 1974 the number of courses was still approximately the same as it was in 1969, the distribution of courses was highly skewed in a manner which favored departments with low student-faculty ratios, the number of graduate student instructors had increased significantly while senior faculty participation had declined, and the number of courses taught by two instructors had never risen beyond a very few. In fact, the Modes of Thought program worked out completely differently than Magaziner and Maxwell had imagined. The limited number of courses, the lack of courses in the social sciences, the voluntary character of the program, and the complete abolition of general education requirements encouraged some students to skip over general education entirely and others to minimize it in favor of early specialization.

Like students, many faculty chose not to participate in Modes of Thought. Their reasons included thinking their specialty more interesting, believing their participation would be a negative or neutral factor in gaining promotion and tenure, being discouraged by their departments, feeling they had been coerced into adopting the curriculum, or finding that they could not participate without having to teach above load because resources had not been reallocated to free them from responsibilities in understaffed departments.

Third-tier courses and other elements of the curriculum such as advising and counseling, which also depended upon strong faculty support and increased time commitments to students, fared similarly for much the same reasons. The fate of the programs more dependent on student initiative has varied.

Pass-fail grading has become less popular than in 1969, in part because the Brown student body has changed. In 1971, the Brown admissions office announced that some new students were being attracted by the curriculum—students who were also applying to distinctive colleges like Hampshire, Reed, and Antioch rather than the traditional Ivy League institutions. But such students are no longer applying, and Brown, like many universities, is attracting a more conservative, career-minded student than it did in the 1960s and early 1970s. The change in grading usage had also been brought about by some of Brown's own graduate schools, which reacted negatively to applicants who had taken more than a few undergraduate courses on a satisfactory–no credit basis.

Group-independent study projects and student-created majors were used less frequently after the first couple of years than at the start, but are now increasing in both number and quality. In the fall of 1975, one of Brown's administrative interns—a recent graduate—opened a curriculum resource center with support from many students and the administration. The center has attempted to revive the workable parts of the Magaziner-Maxwell plan. Student volunteers have helped the intern-coordinator of the center counsel undergraduates on the possibilities for independent study and self-created majors. And the center has been aided in its efforts by funds from the dean of the college to support innovative projects. A spring 1976 student-alumni report, entitled *A Report on Institutional and Curriculum Reform at Brown University,* in fact linked the future success of the Brown curriculum to changes in university budgeting, including support such as this. Student leadership in curriculum reform, sporadic as it is, and faculty acceptance of such reform, variable as it is, cannot suffice to assure change without concomitant financial and budgetary aid—aid, as illustrated at Brown, that involves administrative commitment as well.

(For further information, see Ladd, 1970; and Levere, Schoenholtz, ten Kate, and Zall, 1976.)

Experimenting at Hampshire College—1970

The history of cooperation among the four colleges in the Connecticut River Valley of Massachusetts—Amherst College, Mount Holyoke College, Smith College, and the University of Massachusetts at Amherst (formerly the Massachusetts State Agricultural College)—is a rich one. It grew from informal faculty and student exchanges in the 1930s to joint graduate programs, area studies, and faculty appointments by the mid-1950s. In 1958, it resulted in the most widely publicized of their cooperative efforts: the "New College Plan," which proposed the creation of a centrally located experimenting college that would capitalize on and add to the resources of the existing four. This original and innovative plan, which called for freshman seminars and a one-month winter term for fieldwork, influenced the design of several other colleges under development in the late 1950s and early 1960s.

When an Amherst alumnus pledged six million dollars to the venture in 1965, the plan became a reality. The new institution was named Hampshire College. Its goals, purpose, and academic plans were developed by its first president and vice president, Franklin Patterson and Charles Longsworth, in a volume entitled *The Mak-*

ing of a College that was published in 1966. Thus, even before it began operation in September 1970, Hampshire had generated much national excitement and publicity.

The 270 charter students who entered Hampshire in 1970 were selected for their ability to learn independently and proved intellectually capable of holding their own at any of the four other colleges. The charter faculty and staff were young and had a mix of backgrounds that included nonacademic work experience, interdisciplinary training, and, frequently, attendance or teaching at small liberal arts colleges. They were hired with an understanding that they would be expected to emphasize teaching, that their research should involve students, and that Hampshire would not offer them tenure but rather short-term contracts of increasing length.

The Hampshire program emphasized four elements: curricular experimentation, the liberal arts, the needs of the individual student, and cooperation with the other four colleges. For example, Hampshire's course offerings—primarily seminars and small group tutorials—were intended largely to supplement those on the four other campuses; Hampshire students were encouraged to take courses at the other four colleges, and the other students were permitted to take courses at Hampshire.

Hampshire's experimental curriculum was divided into schools and divisions. The schools provided faculty homes and offered academic programs. Originally there were three—natural sciences, social sciences, and humanities and art—organized along broad disciplinary lines; but a fourth school—language and communication—that began as an interdisciplinary program, has since been added. Hampshire originally complemented these schools with three interdisciplinary programs in Caribbean studies, law, and human development; but now there are six such programs, staffed largely by faculty from the schools.

In contrast to the schools, the divisional structure defined a student's course of study at Hampshire. There are three divisions—basic studies, concentration, and advanced study—and students are required to pass six divisional examinations in order to graduate. In the first division, dealing with basic studies or general education, students are required to pass an examination stressing modes of inquiry in each of the four schools. The second division or concentration requires one examination. The third division or advanced study requires completion of an independent study project exhibiting both depth and integration. The first entering class was greeted by a recommended core curriculum in basic studies composed of workshops, lectures, and tutorials, but passage from division to division was then and still is determined solely by examination. Theoretically a student can graduate without taking even one course. All that is required is passage of the six examinations, which were originally scheduled two weeks a year at the end of the spring term.

Other elements of the Hampshire plan include the month-long winter term, an athletic program stressing lifetime recreational skills rather than intercollegiate teams, and dossier transcripts. A dossier can contain student evaluations, faculty evaluations, student work, and anything else a student chooses to put in it. Since its earliest planning documents, Hampshire has also encouraged students to take time off during college. In fact, students are even allowed to defer enrollment at Hampshire after having been accepted for admission.

Today the Hampshire program differs little from the spirit of the initial plan. Between the speedy construction of a full-scale campus and the assemblage of a full complement of faculty and students, however, the curriculum underwent a trial shakedown that did result in some changes. The recommendations for a core curriculum were soon abolished, and divisional examinations shifted in character from a test planned by the student and his or her teachers to a series of papers. Thus students can now be evaluated in divisional examinations at any time during the year.

The dual system of courses and examinations has created some tensions, if not change. The Hampshire faculty is still publicly ambivalent about the place of courses in the curriculum. An explanation of the Hampshire academic program which accompanies every student transcript includes reference to an average course load, and most students do, in fact, take three courses a term. A larger problem, though, is encountered by faculty who are forced to bear a double teaching load; that is, not only offering two courses per semester but also individually advising students and working with them on examinations—in itself a full-time job, especially in the first division. As Hampshire students are not shy about asking for assistance, the amount of effort that most faculty can devote to research is small; and this is a matter of growing concern among some faculty. Moreover, the teaching load leaves little time for curriculum planning and for some faculty even disrupts family life.

Though the teaching load has resulted in some faculty dissatisfaction, it has not caused staff to leave the college. Faculty turnover at Hampshire is low. In fact, the nontenure contract system has worked to the benefit of faculty longevity. Between 1970 and 1975, only 8 out of 75 faculty contracts were not renewed. Such short-term contracts appear to be a temptation for retaining people who might otherwise not be awarded tenure or permanent appointments.

Some elements of the original Hampshire plan have not worked out exactly as expected—among them, a residential living-learning community, an emphasis on educational technology, and an elaborate governance system. The dormitories have not become living-learning communities. To some extent, the individualized character of the Hampshire program works counter to a strong sense of community. Educational technology is not emphasized as there has been little interest or expertise in this area. And the complex campus governance system was recently streamlined in response to declining student interest in governance, which seems to be a nationwide phenomenon. Dossier transcripts vary in quality from student to student and from faculty evaluation to faculty evaluation. And admissions have also brought a few surprises. In particular, the Hampshire program has not attracted older adult students, owing to its absence of predictable systems of grades and credits which complicates their financial planning. This is a particular problem for Hampshire and other innovative colleges of the late 1960s, which are more susceptible to a shrinking admissions pool than longer-established and more diversified institutions. Nonetheless Hampshire has thus far succeeded in its mission of turning a visionary and nearly 20-year-old report into a working reality and of enhancing the programs of its own students as well as those of its four neighbors through comprehensive five-college cooperation.

Awarding Degrees at a Proprietary School:
Technical Career Institutes—1970

Technical Career Institutes, called TCI, began in 1909 as the Marconi Wireless School, which trained shipboard radio operators. In 1919, the school was purchased by a graduate and faculty member, David Sarnoff, as part of his Radio Corporation of America. Under RCA ownership, the school's name was changed to RCA Institutes, and its mission shifted to the teaching of electronics. In 1974, RCA sought to sell or close the school due to rising costs but was blocked by a strong faculty union and threats of student law suits. So RCA gave the school to its faculty, and its name then became Technical Career Institutes.

TCI enrolls about 2,500 students ranging in age from 17 to middle sixties. The majority are members of minority groups; few are women. Recruitment is active and includes advertising by radio, television, and newspapers in Spanish and English as well as traditional high school visits. New York City agencies and social service groups also recommend students to the Institutes. TCI regards itself as a school for second chances and so admits nearly all students who can pay its admission fee. Nonetheless its graduates have a good placement record, particularly those from its most advanced career programs.

TCI offers four technical programs in its day school: (1) Electronic Technology, (2) Electronics Circuits and Systems, (3) Radio-Television and Electronics Servicing, and (4) Airconditioning and Refrigeration Repair, respectively labelled "T-3," "V-7," "V-1," and "V-20."

Electronic Technology, T-3, is a 24-month program accredited by the Engineers Council for Professional Development, which represents the combined engineering societies of America. To enter T-3, students are required to have a high school diploma or its equivalent, including algebra, geometry, trigonometry, and physics. T-3 is a sophisticated electronics program that teaches these students calculus as a foundation skill and that since 1970 has led to the degree of Associate of Occupational Studies. Although the percentage varies from year to year, T-3 tends to enroll about 16 percent of TCI's students.

Electronics Circuits and Systems, V-7, is an 18-month program that is not as theoretical as T-3 and offers no degree, although local colleges award anywhere from 45 to 70 transfer credits to its graduates. It requires two years of high school, including elementary algebra and general science, for admission and is the most popular of TCI's programs—now enrolling around 35 percent of its students.

Radio-Television and Electronics Servicing, V-1, and Airconditioning and Refrigeration Repair, V-20, are both short-term non-degree programs. Both require two years of high school for admission, and together they enroll just under half of TCI's students.

In addition to these four technical day-time programs, TCI offers a nine-month preparatory sequence through which students can complete the two-year high school requirements for V-7, V-1, and V-20, or brush up for T-3. TCI tests all applicants at entrance, and over 70 percent require some preparatory work ranging from three to six to nine months of the sequence. In its night school, TCI offers additional programs, including Digital Computer Electronics, and Communication Electronics and F.C.C. License Preparation.

Full-time day students attend classes from 8:00 A.M. to 1:00 P.M. or from 1:15 P.M. to 6:15 P.M., five days a week. Part-time evening students attend from 6:30 P.M. to 9:50 P.M. Each term consists of 56 days in the day school and 28 nights in the night school, with the last two reserved for finals. Quizzes and in-class examinations are given regularly, and attendance is taken in every class each day. Each term, attrition varies from 13 to 27 percent of the students, depending on the program.

TCI has 110 faculty, about half of whom have a bachelor's degree or higher educational credential and all of whom have had a minimum of two years experience at the journeyman level in their specialty. Their average teaching load is 29 hours a week, including 25 hours of classroom instruction and four hours standing in for an absent teacher or counseling students. They receive no tenure or extended contract, and they have little autonomy as teachers. Classes are regularly observed by TCI's director, academic dean, and faculty peers when an instructor is just employed or when there are complaints about his teaching. Each instructor is required to teach a fixed course outline; course topics, readings on each topic, and the sequence of laboratories are fixed by a curriculum committee; and any duplication or copying of course materials must be approved by the academic dean.

The fact that TCI has become a degree-granting proprietary school puts it in a rather unique position relative to other postsecondary institutions. It has moved out of the league of the proprietary technical and trade schools, but it has not achieved full acceptance by community and junior colleges. It is plagued by the problems of both.

An enormous amount of paper work is perhaps the most obvious of these problems. TCI has a small administrative staff in order to minimize expenses, but degree-granting status means that it is subject to the regulations governing both trade and technical schools and two-year colleges. Compliance with these regulations seems to be assessed via reports and forms, which are occasionally inappropriate for TCI owing to its mixed status.

Though paper work represents an inconvenient and costly problem, it does not affect TCI as substantively as do other pressures placed upon it. For instance, in 1975, the Engineers Council for Professional Development (ECPD) informed TCI that social science and humanities courses, which are normally associated with college and university general education, would be a desirable addition to its program. TCI's short-term programs and lack of general education requirements had always been drawing cards for new students, and TCI administrators believe that their students can acquire a general education later in life when they want it and can better appreciate it. Nonetheless, to retain ECPD accreditation, TCI added four two-hour courses in the humanities to its curriculum. To accomplish this without increasing the length of its programs, comparable cuts were made in technical instruction.

Similarly, New York State's Bureau of Two-Year College Programs has criticized TCI for its high ratio of acceptances to rejections in admissions and has recommended that TCI increase the proportion of its faculty with bachelor's degrees. Because TCI is considering the possibility of upgrading the degree for its T-3 program to an Associate in Science and its non-degree V-7 program to an Associate of Occupational Studies degree program, it is complying at least in part with the bureau's suggestions. TCI administrators feel degrees are useful, if not essential, in competing with New York City's open-admissions community colleges, which are significantly cheaper than TCI and are in increasing numbers offering technical programs in similar subject areas. But compliance with the bureau's request and similar pressures mean significant and expensive changes for TCI that will make it more like the community colleges in character while lessening the competitive advantage of its distinctive mission: fast-paced, career-oriented, specialized technical preparation.

University Reform Through New College at the University of Alabama, Tuscaloosa—1971

In 1968, University of Alabama Executive Vice President F. David Mathews and Academic Vice President Raymond McLain established a committee to consider the creation of a new unit at their Tuscaloosa campus. Their charge to the committee was to plan "a new undergraduate division for the University that would have as its sole responsibility the development of programs to improve the quality of learning and would not be bound to any existing admission standards, major-minor programs, or degree requirements. The new division would admit students, work on a very individual basis to devise programs of study for these students, utilize existing courses to fit these programs wherever possible, and when appropriate, devise new instructional courses or experiences" (Palmer, 1975, p. 13).

The committee met for two years, traveled to five college campuses, and then with strong enthusiasm and guidance from its chairman, Raymond McLain, proposed the creation of New College.

The faculty senate of the College of Arts and Sciences responded quickly to the committee recommendation: By a large majority, it voted to table the New College plan. Many faculty felt the college would usurp arts and sciences prerogatives and feared its cost would be excessive. Only a few years before, an honors college had been created within arts and sciences, but administrative funding had been much less than the faculty had wished, and the new venture might cut into this funding still further.

Within one month after the faculty vote, however, David Mathews, who was by now president of the university, announced the creation of New College. For its dean, he appointed Neal Berte, assistant to the president at Ottawa University and former consultant to the McLain committee.

Berte's initial job was one of public relations. In addition to faculty opposition, negative public reaction carried over from a previous student-run experimental college. Berte and his staff sought the support of Alabama's newspapers and spoke at civic clubs, television studios, radio stations, and high schools across the state. To win the support of the university faculty, he met with opponents, explained the college to them, solicited their advice, and invited them to participate in New College as advisers, guest lecturers, and as members of review committees. Most significantly, he sought to minimize the threats that New College posed to existing programs within the university. Initial plans had called for the New College to admit the top 10 percent of the Tuscaloosa student body, but that conception had been scrapped during the McLain committee deliberations in order to make sure New College innovations would be transferable to the rest of the university. To emphasize this point, Berte secured Mathews' support for increased funding of the existing honors college. He limited New College enrollment to 200 students, rather than the projected 500 students, so there would be little danger of New College draining off the most interesting students in the university. In fact, New College was structured such that its students would take two-thirds to three-fourths of their work in the rest of the university.

Berte also encouraged faculty who came to him with proposals for innovation to try them in their own departments rather than concentrating all new programs in New College. As a result, New College would not be the lone attraction to university students who might be excited by the glitter of innovation. In addition, he limited the life of New College, explaining that it would phase itself out when the university adopted the programs that made it unique. Finally, with the aid of Mathews, he built an endowment for New College and obtained large foundation grants, including a $250,000 Venture Fund grant from the Ford Foundation, that were targeted for the whole university and not just New College alone.

New College opened in January 1971 as a nonresidential college and admitted its first 20 students on the basis of motivation rather than academic achievement. Enrollment has since climbed to the anticipated 200 students and now includes a cross-section of students with regard to age, sex, ability, and interest. Fully 10 percent of the students even lack the academic qualification for entering any other division of the university.

New College has sought faculty who are personable, expert in more than one discipline, and experienced in interdisciplinary teaching. Its faculty appointments have been of two types: either full-time appointments in New College itself or joint appointments with other departments in the university. The full-time appointments appear to maintain continuity within New College while the joint appointments keep the college from becoming isolated from the rest of the university. To date, the joint appointments have not proven to be a serious barrier to tenure or promotion in the other departments involved.

The New College program emphasizes contract learning. Each semester, every student plans his or her own program with the assistance of an advising committee composed in varying degree of New College faculty and students, university faculty and administrators, and off-campus resource people. This agreed-upon program becomes a contract between New College and the student for that semester. In order to graduate, each student is required to take six interdisciplinary New College problem-oriented seminars, two each in the humanities, social sciences, and natural sciences; develop a major or depth study of his or her own design; and satisfactorily complete 128 credits. A credit-bearing, out-of-class learning experience, which might involve independent study and/or an internship is recommended to every student. New College has served and continues to serve principally as an administrative unit, organizing the contracts, providing core seminars, and offering a variety of independent study and nonclassroom learning experiences. All of the rest of a student's program can be taken in the university. In this environment, some students flourish, a few flounder, and a small number slide through. However, 100 percent of the New College graduates who have applied to graduate and professional school have been accepted.

Since 1971, New College has expanded its experiments in undergraduate education. Credit for prior learning and a variety of instructional innovations have always been part of its bill of fare, but more recently programs have been introduced in basic skills, women's studies, and career explorations, and an external degree program now enrolls 150 off-campus students.

In 1975 David Mathews took a leave of absence from the university presidency to become Secretary of Health, Education, and Welfare, and in 1976 Neal Berte left New College to become president of Birmingham-Southern College. New College has continued its momentum, however, with Bernie Sloan, a long-time New College staffer, as dean and with Mathews having returned in 1977 as president. Over the years, acceptance of New College by university faculty has grown, and programs originated in the college have diffused throughout the university. Departments such as physics and schools such as business and commerce, for example, now offer students individualized programs and attribute them to New College. In addition, the College of Arts and Sciences has adopted the student-designed major, the School of Business and Commerce has introduced internships, and the School of Education has hired a New College student to act as a consultant in the development of a program based upon her independently constructed major. To some New College faculty, the price for this acceptance has been the growth of self-censorship, designed to prevent the college from appearing too way out, that some New College faculty view as an occasional source of undesired conservatism within the college. But in comparison with other innovative units created at other institutions both before and after, New College has had more influence in overcoming conservatism and stimulating experimentation, both within the University of Alabama and elsewhere, despite its controversial beginnings, than virtually any other.

(For further information, see Palmer, 1975.)

Nontraditional Education
at Metropolitan State University—1972

In 1968, the state of Minnesota had a five-tier system of higher education consisting of the University of Minnesota, six state colleges, 17 public junior colleges, 27 state and local vocational/technical schools, and 22 private institutions, most of them four-year colleges. Statewide coordination of this system was provided by the Higher Education Coordinating Commission, composed of representatives from the five tiers and gubernatorial appointees approved by the legislature.

In spring of 1968, G. Theodore Mitau became chancellor of one of these five systems: the state colleges. In August of that year he proposed the creation of an upper-division state college in the Minneapolis–St Paul area. His proposal had two purposes. On one hand, Mitau sought to establish a public college for Twin City graduates of two-year colleges who were unable to gain transfer admission to the University of Minnesota or who lacked the resources to go to a private college after completing their two-year programs. On the other hand, he was attempting to extend the size and reach of the state college system by gaining a foothold in population-rich Minneapolis–St. Paul, dominated as it was by the University of Minnesota.

The community colleges supported Mitau's idea of the new college; the vocational/technical schools remained outside the debate; the private colleges were publicly neutral; and a University of Minnesota task force, not surprisingly, opposed it. In 1970, a consultant called in by the Higher Education Coordinating Commission concluded that probable future declines in higher education enrollments indicated a need for the expansion of the University of Minnesota rather than creation of a new institution, and the executive director of the commission concurred. Yet polls showed that Twin Cities residents favored a new college, and Chancellor Mitau, with support from an influential civic group, pushed the Minnesota legislature into narrowly approving the upper-division college. The legislature authorized $300,000 for planning and operation of a state college center in Minneapolis–St. Paul. However, Minnesota's governor, in a dispute with the legislature, threatened to veto all education appropriations. Mitau realized that college enrollments were declining nationally and that if the legislation were not signed into law during that legislative session, it was likely to be killed forever. He therefore called upon old friends, U.S. senators Humphrey and Mondale, to persuade the governor to sign the legislation, and the governor acquiesced.

Mitau chose David Sweet, his state college vice chancellor for academic affairs, as the president of the new nontraditional college. Sweet was immediately faced with two problems. First, the budget for the college from 1973 to 1975 would be set by the legislature in the fall of 1972, which meant that he would have to have the college operating by the spring of 1972 so that there would be three to four months of experience before budgeting time. Second, $300,000 dollars was a very small sum with which to plan and operate a college, and hence Sweet obtained additional outside funds—from the U.S. Office of Education, the Carnegie Corporation, and two local philanthropies, the Hill Family and Bush foundations.

In the end, the limited funds and public sentiment dictated a campusless format for the college. Today, Metropolitan State University, or "Metro," as it is frequently called, operates out of two office building malls located in Minneapolis and St. Paul. Space for meetings and classes are provided by YMCAs, libraries, and churches all over the Twin Cities as well as in the Northern State Power Company building.

Metro admitted its first 47 students in February 1972, and during the first year enrollments grew at a rate of 50 students a month. These students and their successors have on the average been in their mid-thirties, with ages ranging from the early twenties to the seventies and eighties. Metro students include some people who have dropped out of college or are transferring from community colleges or vocational/technical schools, others who have equivalent of two years of college study through experience, and still others who have unique educational objectives that other institutions cannot satisfy. Many simply need a college degree for job purposes.

By 1976, 1,400 students were in attendance. In that year Metro had minority enrollments of 9 percent, which was greater than either Minnesota's or the Twin Cities' proportion of minorities. However, attracting such students was and continues to be difficult, requiring intensive recruitment.

The total number of students who have enrolled has been less than the thousands optimistically anticipated, and approximately 100 less than projected. Like Metro, many nontraditional colleges began with unrealistic expectations that their gates would be flooded with students who could not satisfy their needs at existing schools. The fact of the matter is that older students are frequently frightened about returning to school—especially a nontraditional one—often lack financial and emotional support for returning to school, and choose Metro or a similar nontraditional school in order to earn a degree rapidly rather than to take a few courses periodically, which significantly limits potential enrollment.

Metro's entering students are offered an individualized, competency-based curriculum. Each student is required to plan a program stressing the outcomes that he or she desires in five specific areas designated by the college—basic learning skills, personal growth and development, civic skills, vocational skills, and cultural and recreational skills. Half of the students emphasize vocational skills, though they must study all five areas. In practice, the student, with the aid of a faculty adviser, writes a plan of study called a degree plan, specifying the competencies to be achieved and the means for obtaining them—including group learning opportunities (courses), independent study, internships, and prior learning. Prior learning and group learning opportunities have become the most popular of all these options. Students are also encouraged to make use of community resources such as local colleges, libraries, museums, industry training programs, and people working in the area with expertise in topics of interest. In fact, Metro has tried to limit its own staff and facilities to those subjects and resources not otherwise available in the Twin Cities community.

Since the first harried days of the college, change based on experience with the curriculum and designed to improve or refine the program has been continual. For instance, 1974 saw the creation of a six- to ten-week prematriculation orientation and degree plan development course, complete with a 243-page Metro-manufactured text on the college and its resources. It was a response to very heavy faculty advising loads, inefficiency in the advising system, weaknesses in the quality and design of student degree plans, and attrition resulting from lack of peer contact and student confusion about the nontraditional curriculum. Similarly, vagueness in the original conception of the Metro B.A. has been ameliorated by making more uniform the number of competencies that students are expected to pursue at any one time (three per full-time term) and the form of the competency statements they are expected to write (all statements take the form of knowing, applying, or evaluating information and skills). There have also been changes to improve the reliability of assessment procedures, and research is continuing on the establishment of valid assessment measures.

Metro has developed a nontraditional staff to match its non-traditional program. It began with seven full-time faculty, two of whom were on loan from other state colleges. In 1972, 18 community resource people were added to the staff. These were primarily part-time faculty holding full-time jobs in the Twin Cities and with expertise in an area of interest to Metro students. By 1976, there were 290 community resource people and 29 permanent faculty working for Metro.

Workloads for permanent faculty are excessively heavy because of both the innovative nature of Metro and its individualized student program. The community faculty, who are currently being evaluated individually, vary greatly in quality and interest in the college. Communication and cooperative planning have at times been serious problems for both faculty and students, stemming not only from the "burn-out" effect of the heavy work load of the permanent faculty and the large number of community faculty with primary involvements outside Metro but also from the nonresidential student body, the lack of a campus, and high administrative turnover.

Metro has now entered a period of consolidation. The past frenzied activity, waves of visitors, and glare of the national spotlight are subsiding, permitting the possibility of more time to plan. And the frequent changes which have caused friction between faculty and administration are ending. There is even some talk of starting a graduate program.

In this consolidation period, Metro faces two tensions that have been with it from the start. The first is avoiding both the adoption of innovation simply for the sake of staying new and the preservation of innovations simply because they make Metro different. The second is avoiding the tempting drift toward the traditional, which comes even from strong supporters of Metro's mission. This pressure toward convention arises everywhere—from Metro's own students, who desire a curriculum like that with which they have had previous experience; from its permanent faculty, who frequently want to be teachers rather than advisers or curriculum resource managers; from graduate and professional schools that are unfamiliar with or bothered by the college's competency-based transcript; and from local community colleges that offer programs not well articulated with Metro's own. All of these groups have already caused Metro to make minor compromises with its educational plan. If Metro can avoid major compromises, it will succeed in offering a viable but radical alternative to traditional campus-bound state colleges if not a model for their emulation.

(For further information, see Martorana and Kuhns, 1975; and Medsker, Edelstein, Kreplin, Ruyle, and Shea, 1975.)

Competency-Based Education
at Sterling College—1972

In 1969, a student, faculty, and administration committee was established at Sterling College at the behest of its board of trustees and president to study the future curricular needs of the college. On the basis of its findings, the committee was to propose a "curriculum model" for the 500-student, rural, Presbyterian liberal arts college located 80 miles west of Wichita. The committee, at a loss about how even to begin its assignment, engaged a consultant, L. Richard Meeth, a professor of higher education at State University of New York, Buffalo, and a former Presbyterian minister who had administered and studied liberal arts colleges.

Meeth assigned the committee background reading on the undergraduate curriculum—a literature with which they were unfamiliar—and summer projects on three topics: the relationship of Sterling to the community, the liberal arts and the church, and the resources of the college. Meeth himself did research on the opinions of Sterling's alumni and attrition of its students.

In the fall of 1970, the committee turned its attention to the desired outcomes of a Sterling education. By Christmas, that, along with information from Meeth about new curriculum developments elsewhere, tipped the members in favor of an outcome- or competency-based curriculum. Faculty on the committee from each of Sterling's three academic divisions—humanities, science, and social science—wrote statements of desired outcomes or competencies that their students should be expected to achieve. With Meeth's help and extensive faculty input, a list of 20 to 30 such competencies was in the end boiled down to the following nine:

1. Comprehension of Christian heritage and its relevance to the student's life and community.
2. Demonstration of awareness of the student's values and commitments, of others' values, and of the alternatives.
3. Demonstration of how to acquire knowledge and how to use it.
4. Comprehension of the artistic and aesthetic dimensions of culture.
5. Comprehension of the relationship of man to his physical and social environment.
6. Demonstration of proficiency in at least one discipline in depth.
7. Demonstration of competency in verbal communication.
8. Demonstration of physical skill and knowledge in one or more recreational activities.
9. Demonstration of ability to work in groups studying, analyzing, and formulating solutions to problems and acting on them.

Satisfaction of the nine competencies would require both knowledge and action components. Knowledge was to be demonstrated either by passing courses, satisfactorily completing independent study, or passing an examination in the competency area. The action component would involve nonclassroom or field experiences and/or applied courses.

Throughout its deliberations, the committee worked closely with faculty; students, except for those on the committee, remained outside the discussions. All of the committee's meetings were open, and all faculty were invited to attend, particularly dissident groups. Minutes and periodic position papers were circulated widely. And at least once a semester the entire faculty was asked to vote on whether the committee should continue operation.

In the winter of 1971, the faculty in a secret ballot overwhelmingly approved the new curriculum. After this vote, committees composed of students, faculty, administrators, and community resource people were established for each competency. At first, participation was voluntary, now all Sterling faculty are required to sit on one such committee. The nine committees were charged with creating appropriate field experiences or action components and mechanisms to assess competency in each competency area. The appropriate courses or knowledge components were chosen by the original planning commission. That function, however, was subsequently given to the competency committee as well.

Prior to implementing the new curriculum, additional consultants were brought in and workshops were held for faculty and staff on such subjects as the nature of a competency curriculum, instruction for competence, and the writing of competency statements. These aids were financed by a grant from the Kellogg Foundation, and many other extras necessary for implementing the curriculum, such as release time for faculty, additional consultant aid, and support for subsequent curricular embellishment and refinement were possible only because of other outside grants.

The curriculum was formally introduced in the fall of 1972. The accent in its implementation was on gradual change and flexibility. For instance, it was initially decided that all entering students and already-enrolled sophomores would be required to study under the new curriculum, but when some sophomores became upset, the program was made voluntary for them. (One-third eventually opted for it, however.) Similarly, when faculty expressed concern over giving students academic credit for field experiences, a compromise was effected that decreased the number of credits to be awarded and increased the amount of time necessary to earn them. Moreover, faculty and planners alike agreed that credit was not to be awarded for field experience alone but for analyzing and synthesizing this experience in an academic fashion.

Particularly sensitive elements of the old curriculum were maintained. Thus the divisional structure that faculty felt strongly about was merely supplemented by the competency committees rather than being replaced by them. At first, majors were not required to be competency-based because faculty would have resisted that, although in 1976 the college began seeking outside funds to support the creation of such majors. The academic credit system and minimum credit requirements for graduation were also continued because both students interested in transfer and faculty afraid of complete dependence on competency would have opposed their disappearance. And traditional noncompetency-based transcripts were maintained for fear of negative reaction by graduate schools and employers.

There were, however, fundamental changes at Sterling with the launching of the new curriculum. A new credit-bearing orientation and advising system, organized around small groups of students led by faculty and older peers, was created to acquaint students who might otherwise have been confused or worried by the unusual curriculum. A learning skills center and a grading system lacking the designation "failure" were introduced as necessary supports for the curriculum. And all courses were fitted to the specification of the nine competencies. In the process, 20 courses were eliminated, new syllabi were developed for others, and new applied and interdisciplinary courses, such as "Dynamics of Human Communications," Methods of Inquiry," and "Values, Society, and the Individual," were created to satisfy certain competencies.

Since implementing the new curriculum, Sterling has continued its development. The high administrative turnover which characterized the planning period is now over. Carol Gene Brownlee, a member of the original committee and staunch advocate of the new curriculum, became dean of the college in 1972. Support for growth has also come from outside the institution. The Fund for the Improvement of Postsecondary Education gave Sterling a grant for the creation of competency-based career programs, and the Kellogg Foundation provided additional funds for institutionalizing the new curriculum. While the nontraditional demands of the curriculum resulted at first in gross faculty workload increases and imbalances, work is being done to correct these problems. And college staff and consultants have been working on the creation of valid and reliable measures of competency attainment and experiential learning, which were originally lacking.

Currently, two obstacles impede future curriculum development. One is the Sterling faculty. In some cases, their disciplinary orientation has proved inconsistent with interdisciplinary competencies; they have dragged their feet on introducing competency-based majors; and they have supported the preservation of the divisional structure. The second is the Sterling students. They more often choose Sterling for its Christian orientation than for its innovative curriculum; they tend to choose courses and other well-known activities in preference to less traditional options for satisfying competency requirements; and many fail to see or take advantage of the flexibility of the curriculum and its potential for satisfying their individual needs and interests. However, there is evidence to suggest that student behavior is beginning to change and hope that faculty attitudes will follow suit. Even as is, Sterling represents one of only a handful of pioneering institutions that have committed themselves to defining and developing specific learning outcomes for all their undergraduates and basing their entire curriculum on these outcomes.

Educational Brokering at the
Capital Higher Education Service, Inc.—1973

After a summer of riots in 1968, a group of Hartford, Connecticut, industrial and business leaders created Greater Hartford Process, Inc. as a nonprofit long-range planning and development agency to spur the social and economic resurgence of their city. Education became a serious concern for "Process." Higher education opportunities were far superior in the suburbs surrounding Hartford than in the city proper, and although there was an abundance of small private colleges in Hartford, there were no public upper-division institutions.

Beginning in 1968, Process sought to establish a public university in Hartford. Until 1973, the state legislature refused to authorize such a university, but in that year it went part way by creating a Board of State Academic Awards (BSAA), which had the power to grant academic credits. Process went to the Fund for the

Improvement of Postsecondary Education (FIPSE) to obtain start-up money to get the BSAA going. FIPSE suggested that a private agency also be created to advise, counsel, and give information to students on available educational opportunities. That was the start of the Capital Higher Education Service, Inc., called CHES. Process hoped that the state might someday adopt CHES as part of the Board of State Academic Awards, but FIPSE unfortunately chose to fund CHES and not the BSAA.

CHES began operation in June 1973. It was described as "a freestanding, facilitating agency for adult nontraditional learners ... who seek more postsecondary education as a means to self-improvement. As an independent, not-for-profit, client-oriented, postsecondary educational initiator, catalyst, interpreter, communicator (broker), and operational bridge between its clients, colleges, business, and other institutions and organizations . . . " (Capital Higher Education Service, Inc., 1975).

CHES's first director was Fred Pinkham, former president of Ripon College and early executive at the National Commission on Accrediting. He was succeeded in 1974 by Donald Barnes, former president of the Institute for Educational Development. Unlike many organizations similar to CHES, Pinkham opted for a more expensive professional counseling staff in order to gain the respect and cooperation of the local colleges. To discover the services learners most wanted from the counselors, Pinkham immediately opened the doors of CHES to the public. These early interactions between CHES and the public did an excellent job of shaping CHES's mission to learner needs and identified the services learners most wanted. But the lack of planning that preceded the early public contacts had its costs in confusion because counselors were inventing models for service while trying to serve inquiring clients.

The basic activity at CHES was the interview. Each learner, called a client, worked with one of seven counselors, called program advisers, in an individual or group situation. After contacting CHES, a client was given an orientation to the goals, services, and nominal fees of the organization. An interview was then arranged with a program adviser. During this interview, the student decided on how to proceed, based upon the need that originally brought him or her to CHES and information on CHES's services as described in the orientation and elaborated upon during the course of the interview.

CHES's services for clients were of three general types: (1) helping the client develop an appropriate educational plan, which ranged from no further education to enrollment in degree programs, assorted courses in several colleges, or training programs in business or other agencies; (2) helping the client put together an educational plan, which frequently involved contacting a college to place the would-be student in a course or speaking to a department chairperson to negotiate credit for previous schooling; and (3) helping the client prepare for assessment of learning from prior experiences, which involved assisting him or her to recognize and communicate past learning as it related to degree or program requirements in a particular organization. The final product of these three services was a portfolio, consisting of the client's written and documented case for institutional recognition.

CHES also offered a variety of services for institutions, including (1) support counseling for adults already enrolled in higher education locally or in external degree programs at far away colleges, (2) training in competence assessment to students and staff at local colleges, and (3) offering seminars on educational opportunities for employees at large business concerns.

In 30 months of operation, 368 people used CHES's advisory services at a cost of $430,000, or an average of over $1,000 per person. Their combined fees came to only about $1,900 or approximately two-thirds of 1 percent of CHES's gross expenses. CHES consumed its three-year FIPSE grant in less than two-and-one-half years, and the state of Connecticut did not pick up its operation as had been hoped. So on November 30, 1975, the Capital Higher Education Service, Inc. closed. As of 1977, two of CHES's program advisers were still continuing to provide some of its services on a private basis.

Though CHES was expensive, it was not without strengths. From its experience, the body of knowledge on the needs of nontraditional learners was expanded. Its activities made the Hartford area more receptive to nontraditional students. Several new programs, such as a competency-based A.A. general studies program at Manchester Community College, were developed at institutions cooperating with it. CHES also helped to make local industries and agencies aware of the educational needs of their employees or constituents. In addition, it experimented with or developed a variety of mechanisms for meeting the needs of nontraditional learners— including seminars for industrial workers on career and educational planning, and easily accessible education information systems in several high public-use locations around the city.

(For more information, see Capital Higher Education Service, Inc., 1975).

*   *   *

As evidenced by the cases in this and the previous chapter, curricular experimentation has been widely divergent and varied in American colleges and universities during this century and especially since World War II. Complaints about curricular stagnation and somnambulance may apply to some institutions; but curricular innovation has been more widespread than commonly recognized. College curriculum committees and task forces, of course, require restraint in recommending the adoption of particular policies and practices from other institutions, but as illustrated here, they do not lack for examples of possible changes or of the strategies that faculty, students, and administrators can use to accomplish these changes.

References

Capital Higher Education Service, Inc. *Final Report to Fund for the Improvement of Postsecondary Education.* Hartford, Conn., Dec. 10, 1975.

Chancellor's Self-Study Accreditation Commission. *Academic Quality at Santa Cruz.* University of California, Santa Cruz, 1975.

Coyne, J. "Bensalem: When the Dream Died." *Change,* 1972, 4 (8), 39–44.

Free University. *Free University Catalog.* Berkeley, Calif., 1966.

Gaff, J. G., and Associates. *The Cluster College.* San Francisco: Jossey-Bass, 1970. The University of California, Santa Cruz, is discussed intermittantly throughout this book.

Hall, L., and Associates. *New Colleges for New Students.* San Francisco: Jossey-Bass, 1974. This volume includes two essays on Flathead Valley Community College.

Jerome, J. *Culture Out of Anarchy: The Reconstruction of American Higher Learning.* New York: Herder and Herder, 1970. This book discusses the early and middle years of Bensalem College.

Ladd, D. R. *Change in Educational Policy: Self-Studies in Selected Colleges and Universities.* New York: McGraw-Hill, 1970. This volume includes a case study on the 1969 curriculum reform at Brown University.

Levere, A., Schoenholtz, K., ten Kate, C., and Zall, R. *A Report on Institutional and Curricular Reform at Brown University.* Brown University, Jan. 1976.

Lichtman, J. *Bring Your Own Bag: A Report on Free Universities.* Washington, D.C.: American Association for Higher Education, 1973.

MacDonald, G. B. (Ed.) *Five Experimental Colleges: Bensalem, Antioch-Putney, Franconia, Old Westbury, Fairhaven.* New York: Harper Colophon, 1973.

Magaziner, I., and Maxwell, E. *Draft of a Working Paper for Education at Brown University.* An unpublished report, Brown University, 1966.

Martorana, S. V., and Kuhns, E. *Managing Academic Change: Interactive Forces and Leadership in Higher Education.* San Francisco: Jossey-Bass, 1975.

This volume includes essays on Simon's Rock and Metropolitan State University.

Medsker, L., Edelstein, S., Kreplin, H., Ruyle, J., and Shea, J. *Extending Opportunities for a College Degree: Practices, Problems, and Potentials.* Berkeley, Calif.: UC Center for Research and Development in Higher Education, 1975.

Metropolitan State University is one of the colleges examined in this book.

Members of the Cowell History Workshop 144G, University of California at Santa Cruz. *Solomon's House: A Self-Conscious History of Cowell College.* Felton, Calif.: Big Trees Press, 1970.

This book describes the first year at Santa Cruz by a group who lived through it.

Palmer, S. "Strategies for Change and Innovation: New College." An unpublished report, New College, University of Alabama, 1975.

Patterson, F., and Longsworth, C. R. *The Making of a College: Plans for a New Departure in Higher Education.* Cambridge, Mass.: M.I.T. Press, 1966.

Schroth, R. A. "College as Camelot." *Saturday Review,* Sept. 11, 1972, pp. 52–57.

This article gives a blow-by-blow description of what killed Bensalem College.

Suczek, R. F. *The Best Laid Plans: A Study of Student Development in an Experimental College Program.* San Francisco: Jossey-Bass, 1972.

This book is concerned with the Tussman College at Berkeley and more specifically with differences in the development of students in the experimental college and the regular university.

Tussman, J. *Experiment at Berkeley.* London: Oxford University Press, 1969.

14

Characteristics
of Curriculum Change

Change implies something new and something different. The degree of newness and differentness is relative; a change may be new and different only at the college at which it has been adopted. In fact, much of the prominent change in higher education might better be classified as renovation of older ideas than as innovation. For example, the Santa Cruz cluster college concept was borrowed from the Claremont Colleges, which adopted the idea from Oxford and Cambridge in England. Similarly Joseph Tussman's college at Berkeley was modeled on Alexander Meiklejohn's college at Wisconsin. Whether renovation or innovation, academic change exhibits several consistent patterns or characteristics in terms of strategy, stages, participants, and elements. This chapter reviews these characteristics, using as illustrations the institutions described in the past two chapters.

Strategies for Curriculum Change

At least five different strategies for change are commonly used in American higher education. They include (1) the establishment of new colleges, (2) the development of innovative enclaves within existing colleges, (3) holistic change within existing colleges, (4) piecemeal change within existing colleges, and (5) peripheral change outside existing colleges.

The establishment of new colleges. Organizing a totally new college or university was the strategy used in the creation of such distinctive institutions as Bennington College, Oakland University, Hampshire College, and Metropolitan State University. A new college is the easiest way to establish a nontraditional institutional mission or curriculum. For example, Bennington College was a product of the desire to extend progressive education into the college years, and Metropolitan State University was designed to develop a nontraditional program for nontraditional students. The establishment of these two programs as new colleges avoided the expenditure of enormous amounts of time and effort that would have been required to transform an established institution and reorient its staff and students. Creating a new college, however, is by no means a guarantee of success for a nontraditional mission. New schools rarely fulfill all of the expectations of their founders, as illustrated most vividly by Oakland University during its first years. If the new institution is innovative, it is subject as well to pressures to revert to the tried and true. Metropolitan State, among others, is feeling pressure of this type from government agencies, faculty, students, graduate schools, and local colleges. Creating a new college is also expensive, and during a buyer's market when many existing institutions of higher education have unused capacity from lack of students—as is the case today—it is a high-risk and inefficient strategy for change.

The development of innovative enclaves within existing institutions. This second strategy involves setting aside a specific place in the curriculum for experimentation. The enclave may be an experimental subunit, such as Meiklejohn's Experimental College at the University of Wisconsin or the General College at the University of Minnesota; an experimental period in the calendar, such as the nonresidential term at Bennington College; or any other innovation separate from the mainstream of traditional campus activities. Innovative enclaves are relatively inexpensive and easy to implement. They can serve as institutional laboratories for curriculum experimentation and as sources of institutional self-renewal if they either diffuse through the campus or involve large numbers of faculty and students who participate in both the enclave and the rest of the institution. New College at the University of Alabama is an excellent example of such an influential enclave. The disadvantages of enclaves are that they can become appendages isolated from the rest of the campus, sanctuaries for dissatisfied faculty and students, and means for protecting an institution from making needed campuswide changes. Bensalem College had several of these qualities. It was isolated from the rest of Fordham University and served as a sanctuary for nonconventional students.

Holistic change within existing colleges. This third strategy involves the adoption of a major institutionwide curriculum change characterized by a unifying and coherent philosophy of education. It is exemplified by such extensive curricular reforms as the adoption of the Great Books program at St. John's College, the reorganization of undergraduate education at Brown University, and the introduction of the competency curriculum at Sterling College. Of all forms of change, holistic reform is the most educationally defensible when major change is necessary; the most efficient, since it involves substitution rather than addition of new curricula; the most difficult to get adopted; the least likely to succeed, particularly at large universities; and thus the least common. It is risky because it involves already established institutions with built-in resources, habits, and staff—and a staff, at that, usually lacking any consensus about educational philosophy. But it is particularly risky because it replaces the old curriculum: If the change does not succeed, there is nothing else left. St. John's 1937 curriculum reform is an example of successful holistic change, while Brown University's 1969 reform is an example of a less successful one.

Piecemeal change within existing colleges. This fourth strategy involves the adoption of minor curriculum changes such as the elimination of language requirements, the adoption of internship and field-study programs, and the mounting of new courses. It is the most common form of curriculum change, the easiest to implement, and a series of such changes can in sum produce holistic change; but it sometimes relies more on political negotiation than on educational philosophy (Levine and Weingart, 1973, p. x). The initiation of the

Contemporary Civilization course at Columbia University is an example of piecemeal change.

Peripheral change outside existing colleges. This fifth and last strategy involves the establishment of institutions or changes within institutions not traditionally associated with higher education, but which have an effect on the activities of existing colleges and universities. As Sir Nevill Mott said, "the infallible recipe for stirring up a university is to set up a rival" (in Hefferlin, 1969, p. 3). The autonomous Free University of Berkeley; the freestanding Capital Higher Education Service brokerage organization; and Technical Career Institutes, a degree-granting vocational/technical proprietary school, are all examples of peripheral changes. Such changes can inform existing colleges of new student needs and desires as well as potentially profitable curriculum additions. For instance, the Capital Higher Education Service alerted Hartford area colleges of the needs of adult learners, and that information resulted in the adoption of new curricula by several of the colleges. Negatively, peripheral change can compete with colleges and draw away their students. Peripheral institutions are just as likely to change colleges as colleges are to change them. Technical Career Institutes, for example, is becoming more like the community colleges around it, especially in awarding associate's degrees and offering general education instruction.

Stages of Change

The process of curriculum change involves four stages—recognition of need, planning and formulation of a solution, initiation and implementation of the plan, and institutionalization of the change.

Recognition of need. This first stage involves a realization that some individual, group, institutional, or larger social need is not being satisfied. The realization may be that of an individual, as was the case with Joseph Tussman at Berkeley, or of a group, as when the board of trustees and president at Sterling College decided to reexamine the curriculum. The realization may not even come from within a college. The need to create a college in Montana's

Flathead Valley, for example, was realized by local community leaders, and the need for the Capital Higher Education Service, an external brokerage organization, was recognized by Greater Hartford Process, Inc., a private community organization.

The development of need is a matter of perception. When an existing college is experiencing difficulties, the realization of need may be immediate; otherwise it may not occur until there has been extensive self-study or external examination, or it may never occur. But colleges that continually fail to recognize needs are likely candidates for extinction.

Planning and formulating a solution. During this second stage, a plan is formulated to satisfy the need identified in the first stage. The planning and formulation, like the realization of need, can be an individual or group endeavor. The plan formulated may involve any of the five types of change discussed previously—or possibly no change at all, if the need is thought of as inappropriate or inconsequential.

Initiation and implementation of the plan. The plan formulated in stage two is put into operation on a trial basis in stage three. During this stage, the change is tested as a solution to the unsatisfied need. If the change has been approved through appropriate channels, such as the state legislature in the case of Metropolitan State University or the faculty in the curriculum reform at Brown, those responsible for the innovation are likely to be granted substantial autonomy in working out unresolved questions and unanticipated problems, and in general setting up house. A change that is not so approved lacks legitimacy and is subject to more immediate scrutiny, as occurred at New College of the University of Alabama, which was initiated by President Mathews despite the faculty vote to table the idea.

Institutionalization of the change. After a change has been initiated and implemented, it either is institutionalized or it dies. Groups with a sense of ownership or interest in change, such as accrediting agencies at Technical Career Institutes, the faculty at the University of Chicago, and the public at Oakland University, begin to send cues to the innovation staff about how the innovation should adapt to its environment—either the larger institution, if it was initiated in one as an enclave, holistic change, or piecemeal change; or the environment of existing institutions, if it is a new college or a peripheral change. The cues and the institutionalization stage in general are designed to make the change just a routine part of the existing college or the world of higher education. Cues are usually more abundant for changes within existing institutions than for peripheral changes or new colleges, which are more independent in obtaining finances and seeking students.

During the period of institutionalization, the change may diffuse through an institution or to other colleges; it may remain or become an isolated enclave; it may be reconstructed; or it may be terminated. The outcome depends upon how well it meets the need for which it was established and how well it fits in with what preceded it. New College at the University of Alabama is an example of a change that has not only survived but also resulted in the diffusion of new curricula through its university. The undergraduate college at the University of Chicago was in its early years an example of an isolated enclave and later in its history an illustration of reconstructed change. And at the other extreme, Bensalem College and the Capital Higher Education Service exemplify changes that failed to be institutionalized and were terminated. In other words, institutionalization continues throughout the life-span of a curriculum change. And during this life-span, the change continues to be subject to cues, pressure, and movement between the poles of diffusion and termination.

Participants in Change

The making of educational policy involves and is influenced by many different participants. They include individuals, groups, and organizations. Within existing colleges, educational policy involves trustees, faculty, students, and administrators.

Trustees. Though trustees are the legal governors of their institutions, their role in curriculum change has been small. Most often they have been involved in formally approving or vetoing change and in encouraging or discouraging change by the appointment of

key personnel, as in the case of the appointment of Stringfellow
Barr and Scott Buchanan as president and dean at St. John's. Occasionally trustees have recognized the need for change and initiated curriculum change, as in the formation of the curriculum
committee at Sterling. Less often they have actually formulated a
curriculum, as Arthur Morgan did at Antioch.

Faculty. Educational policy is considered the bailiwick of the faculty.
Faculty have been involved in identifying curriculum needs, as
Joseph Tussman did at Berkeley; in planning and formulating curriculum, as the "Redbook" committee did at Harvard; in initiating
and implementing new curricula, as the faculty did at Sterling College; and in institutionalizing and terminating curriculum, as the
Fordham faculty did with Bensalem.

The major role of the faculty in curriculum change was first
formally stated in the 1915 American Association of University
Professors' "General Declaration of Principles." Today the faculty
are clearly the dominant force in the last two stages of curriculum
change—initiation and implementation of the plan, and institutionalization of the innovation. Not only are they responsible for
the operation of most new curricula as teachers, but they are also
the prime movers in the hiring and promotion of instructional staff
and their consent is usually obtained before implementing or terminating academic programs. New College at the University of
Alabama and Bensalem College were both established without faculty approval, and in both instances very negative faculty reactions
were the consequence. At New College, extensive public relations
work by the first dean was necessary to assuage faculty resentment;
but at Bensalem, faculty reaction was so negative that it contributed
to the closing of the college.

With regard to influencing educational policy, faculty feel
they have more impact on their departments than on their colleges
as a whole. The latest Carnegie Council faculty study found that 65
percent of faculty feel they have a great deal or quite a bit of opportunity to influence departmental policy. In contrast only 18 percent of them feel they have such opportunities in institutionwide
policies.

It is also important to note that not all faculty are equally involved in educational policy. Forty-three percent of the faculty in-

dicate that a small group of senior professors has disproportionate power in decision making, and 77 percent feel that junior faculty have too little say in the running of their departments.

Finally, a paradox about faculty and curriculum change should be noted. Forty-four percent of American faculty believe that the undergraduate curriculum at their college or university is in *serious* need of reform (Carnegie Surveys, 1975–76). Table 18 shows that opinions vary at different types of institutions, ranging from a high in comprehensive universities and colleges II to a low in selective liberal arts colleges, but that more than one-third of faculty at all types of colleges and universities concur about the need for reform. At the same time, faculty are usually singled out as the primary retardant of change. John Corson (1975) attributes faculty resistance to three factors: (1) "The bulk of all professors are more concerned with substantive issues of the discipline in which they have been trained, with the concerns of the 'guilds' of which they are members, than with the whole curriculum imposed on the undergraduate" (pp. 98–99); (2) faculty are "deeply divided . . . on virtually all important matters . . . confused and uncertain . . . as to their roles and responsibilities in the vastly altered setting in which they find themselves," so that concensus on educational policy is prevented (p. 99); and (3) departments dominate the college, making any undergraduate reforms which threaten them unacceptable. Perhaps the explanation of the paradox is that "no priesthood . . . ever institutes its own reforms" (Hefferlin, 1969, p. 150).

Table 18. Percentage of faculty by Carnegie type agreeing that the undergraduate curriculum at their institution is in serious need of reform

Research universities I	40
Research universities II	47
Doctorate-granting universities I	45
Doctorate-granting universities II	50
Comprehensive universities and colleges I	48
Comprehensive universities and colleges II	52
Liberal arts colleges I	36
Liberal arts colleges II	43
Two-year colleges	40

Source: Carnegie Surveys, 1975–76.

Students. Student involvement in educational policy making has historically been informal and indirect. However, in response to campus protests during the 1960s and early 1970s, many colleges established mechanisms to involve students in college governance. According to Gross and Grambsch (1974, p. 134), the resulting changes in student power to affect educational policy were slight. By 1975, a time when student interest in campus governance had declined, 70 percent of the faculty responding to the Carnegie Faculty Survey reported that in the provision or content of courses students were only informally consulted or had little or no role. With regard to bachelor's degree requirements, 68 percent of the faculty responded in the same manner, in contrast to only 15 percent who said that students had control, voting power on committees, or a formal consultative role.

Nonetheless, students have been active in all stages of curriculum change. Student-perceived needs were identified through the protests of the 1960s. Planning and formulating solutions, and initiating and planning curriculum changes have seldom been as dramatic as that led by Magaziner and Maxwell at Brown. More often they involve students on committees, student government, student demonstrations, and student-supported peripheral changes such as free universities and experimental colleges. Nonetheless, students strongly influence the institutionalization stage of change, as well as the previous three stages, by their enrollment patterns—where they choose to go to school and which programs they choose to study. Indeed a general decline in student interest in 1960s-style innovation has had an impact on the number of applications for admission and the quality of applicants at institutions like Santa Cruz and Hampshire. Student attrition was also one of the important rationales for changing the curriculum at Oakland University. And the unwillingness of men to enroll at Simon's Rock initially turned it into a women's college.

Administration. Different times result in different types of administrators. When resources are plentiful, as from the end of World War II to the late 1960s, growth and change are the order of the day; and such periods of prosperity call forth the visionary administrator or innovator. During such times, change occurs by adding to what already exists. It also encourages administrators to give faculty members significant autonomy in educational policy making.

Hard times, like those since the late 1960s, however, demand the services of a consolidating administrator or integrator. When resources are meager, retrenchment is required. A need arises to integrate the mass of new activities added in prosperous times, with the programs comprising the older core. More importantly, a decline in resources means that some things have to be eliminated. Innovation is accepted largely for survival and is accomplished only via substitution. For example, Glenny et al. (1976, p. 29) found that 50 percent of a sample of 1,227 institutions of higher education had engaged in consolidation or elimination of undergraduate courses between 1968 and 1974. Forty-one percent of the institutions indicated similar changes in whole undergraduate programs.

In response to the poor financial state of higher education, today's administrator, sometimes struggling to keep his or her institution financially afloat, is becoming increasingly involved in all stages of change and educational policy making, particularly faculty hiring and program development. Faculty frequently regard such administrative interest and activity as an incursion into their prerogatives. The result has been an increase in faculty-administration conflicts, a rise in faculty unionism, and an increase in faculty votes of no confidence in their chief academic officers.

Educational policy is also influenced by a large number of groups and organizations external to colleges. Among them are government; the courts; the public; accrediting and professional associations; mass media; high schools; graduate and professional schools and employers; foundations and donors; and other colleges.

Government. The government—at federal, state, and local levels— has become the primary source of funding for higher education. With this increasing financial burden has come a greater involvement of government in setting educational policy. For example, the study by Glenny et al. (1976, p. 75) showed that between 35 percent and 45 percent of college presidents perceived a shift in decision making away from colleges and their governing boards toward the state legislature or governor between 1968 and 1974. Government, as shown in the Metropolitan State University case study, is involved in all stages of the change process. State government involvement, for instance, has varied from substantive controls, such as budget and limits on program development at Metropolitan State University, to procedural controls, such as follow-up reporting at Technical Career Institutes and budget formulas at Metropolitan State University, to the creation of statewide governing or coordinating boards, such as the Higher Education Coordinating Commission in Minnesota.

Courts. The role of the courts in higher education has been expanding quickly. Courts are now rendering decisions in areas of education policy ranging from admission requirements to faculty hiring and firing criteria.

The public. The public influences educational policy by its votes on educational revenues, by its choice of public servants, and by its attendance patterns at institutions of higher learning.

Professional, licensing, and accrediting associations. These organizations are involved in all of the phases of curriculum change. Some professional societies, such as the Association of American Geographers, are active in identifying curricular needs and in assisting with the planning and formulation of programs by providing small amounts of funding and occasional forums for curriculum development. Licensing organizations in areas such as nursing and cosmetology and some professional societies such as the Engineers Council for Professional Development, which set content and quality standards for practitioners, also affect the planning and formulation of curriculum as well as the manner in which it is implemented. Accrediting associations are primarily involved with reviewing curriculum change after it has been implemented. All such orgnaizations affect the institutionalization of change by setting minimum standards of quality for academic programs based in varying degree on college goals. These standards have been criticized, on one hand, for being meaningless or lacking rigor and, on the other, for being too rigorous, capricious, and seeking to foster needless conformity at the cost of useful innovation.

Mass media. The news media have significantly affected the success of curriculum changes. Positive press reports enabled Swarthmore to increase enrollments and attract foundation support. Negative press reports accelerated the closing of Bensalem College.

High schools. High schools change colleges by means of the educational programs they offer and by way of the guidance and counseling they provide. For instance, contemporary high school curricular changes—such as increasing the number of electives available to students, decreasing the number of basic skills courses required, and introducing college-level instruction—have changed the character of the freshmen entering college. With regard to guidance and counseling, high school counselors and principals have deterred the development of college early-admission programs, as was illustrated at Simon's Rock. Counselors also discouraged students from attending Meiklejohn's Experimental College at Wisconsin and from applying to Oakland University. This contributed to the failure of the Experimental College and precipitated a curriculum review at Oakland. In contrast, favorable responses by high school counselors encouraged the institutionalization of New College at Alabama.

Graduate schools, professional schools, and employers. The desire for further education or work by college graduates has an enormous impact on college educational policy. Graduate schools, professional schools, and employers influence colleges by setting quality standards and course or subject prerequisites for admission. Accordingly, schools like Sterling College, with nontraditional or innovative programs, continue to use traditional transcripts for fear that, if they do not, their graduates will be rejected by post-college institutions and employers. (Such fears are grounded in fact, as Chapter 4 notes.) The need of students to satisfy course prerequisites for admission to graduate and professional schools also reduces the flexibility of colleges to offer nontraditional or innovative programs. This is shown in the case studies of Bennington College and the University of Chicago. Community colleges feel similar pressures from the four-year colleges where their students transfer.

With regard to employers, job prospects for college graduates are not as good as they once were (Trivett, 1975). Unemployment and underemployment have been particularly high among students majoring in the liberal arts (College Placement Council, 1975). The result in 67 percent of the institutions in the Glenny study (1976, p. 26) has been a sharp increase between 1968 and 1974 in student enrollments in the more employable vocational and professional areas. This is to say that employers leave a discernible mark upon the curriculum and student programming.

However, the most profound impact upon colleges comes from the graduate and professional schools that socialize and train their future faculty. The socialization and training in most cases emphasize one discipline and research rather than teaching. A 1975 Carnegie Council survey of graduate students indicated that more than ten times as many were studying for the research-oriented Ph.D. than the teaching-oriented doctor of arts.

Foundations and donors. Foundations and donors have provided the money to support educational changes that would not otherwise be possible—such as innovative upper-division Metropolitan State University, the competency curriculum at Sterling College, and early admission at Simon's Rock. However, such grants have been criticized for encouraging colleges to start programs they do not need, and for creating programs that institutions cannot sustain when foundation support is severed. This was considered a problem at both the General College at the University of Minnesota in its early years and Flathead Valley Community College in more recent years.

Other colleges. Colleges generally adopt programs which have been tried at other institutions. Traditionally, they look to more prestigious institutions for curricular guidance and as models for emulation. In the case of the community college, for instance, emulation is frequently based on student need to be accepted for transfer at a four-year institution.

This pattern of colleges following more prestigious colleges prompted David Riesman (1956, pp. 14–15) to describe higher education as a snake-like academic procession with the most elite schools in the country at the head of the serpent. Current steady-state conditions may change the beast, however. Colleges and subunits within large universities, experiencing financial reversals, are turning their attention to institutions like themselves or even less fortunate ones that have developed financially attractive curricula. To this extent, the snake may in the future be spending more time in contemplation of its tail than its head.

Elements of Successful Change

Success for a curriculum change means that the change achieves the purposes for which it was intended and continues without being prematurely cut down. Utilizing this definition, the establishment of New College at the University of Alabama can be regarded as a successful change and the creation of Bensalem College at Fordham University must be regarded as an unsuccessful change, despite its impact on its students.

Success or failure in curriculum change is a product of three factors—the environment targeted for change, the characteristics of the change, and the process by which the change is introduced.

THE ENVIRONMENT

Successful curriculum change is most likely in either an unstable or particularly supportive environment. Marvin Bressler of the Princeton University sociology department has noted five states of the environment that support change.[1] The first is when there is a crisis in the environment. It was under such circumstances that the Great Books program was adopted at St. John's and the work-study program was established at Antioch. The second state is when people have a shared self-interest in change, as was the case in the adoption of a baccalaureate program at Simon's Rock and the creation of Flathead Valley Community College by local residents. A third state is when there is a power imbalance, as at Brown University when students forced the faculty to adopt a new curriculum, and at Bennington where progressive educators who dominated the original planning committee altered the intended mission of the college. The fourth state is when there is structural change in the environment. For example, the establishment of the Capital Higher Education Service caused several Hartford area colleges to

[1]Based on a conversation with Marvin Bressler, December 1975.

change their undergraduate programs, and the creations of New College caused a number of other University of Alabama colleges to adopt new curricula. The fifth and final state is when it is consistent with the *Zeitgeist,* or spirit of time. The "Redbook" at Harvard and several similar reports of the period captured well the spirit of World War II and post–World War II America.

The importance of an unstable environment as noted by Bressler has been observed as well by JB Hefferlin (1969) in a study of the conditions specifically supportive of curriculum change in existing colleges. He found that colleges without graduate programs—and thus more chance for instability or change—had a greater rate of change than universities. Academic reform was also most prevalent at colleges and universities with changing faculty owing to expansion and turnover, low rates of tenure, junior staff members influential in educational policy making, rotating department chairpersons, and trustees and educational leaders oriented more toward change than stability. Student-centered institutions—that is, colleges and universities financially dependent on attracting students and their tuition money—and those located in metropolitan areas also exhibited a proclivity for change, due, as were the other factors, to greater instability.

CHARACTER OF THE CHANGE

Successful curriculum change is most likely when an innovation is consistent with the norms, values, and traditions of the environment in which it is being introduced. Levine (1976b) identified two attributes of change that favor innovation success. One is compatibility—the degree to which an innovation is like the environment into which it has been introduced. Since change represents a departure from the practices of any environment, it is by definition always somewhat different or incongruent with the environment into which it is introduced. All environments, whether they are existing colleges or larger social systems, are status quo oriented— seeking to maintain a pattern of constancy and stability. They attempt to minimize disruption and deviance. That is, they react negatively to incompatibility and positively to compatibility.

This can be seen in a comparison of the histories of Bensalem College and New College at the University of Alabama. Bensalem, which was terminated by Fordham University after only a few years of operation, was grossly incompatible with its environment in terms of academic practices, standards, curriculum goals, the character of its students, the nature of its faculty, and the facilities it occupied. In contrast, New College at the University of Alabama, which deviated from the university with regard to program goals and practices, was remarkably like the university in staff, students, facilities, and standards. In fact, New College's dean made a concerted effort to minimize its perceived incompatibility with the university environment, and the result has been growth and diffusion of its programs through the university.

Successful curriculum change is also most likely when people think they are directly or indirectly getting something valuable out of it. The second attribute identified by Levine is profitability—the degree to which a change satisfies environmental or personal needs. The greater the profitability, the greater the likelihood of successful change. Again this can be illustrated by comparing Bensalem and Alabama's New College. Bensalem was unprofitable because it was costly, brought the university negative press in its later years, suffered high attrition, was thought by some administrators and faculty to have encouraged campus disruption and immorality, and did nothing after its first two years to enlarge the academic reputation of the university, the reason for which it was created. Alabama's New College, on the other hand, brought its university positive press; attracted large grants, some of which were applicable to other units of the university; and reflected exactly the needs for which it was created.

THE PROCESS

The way in which a change is introduced influences people's attitudes, acceptance, and participation in the change. Five areas of the process are especially critical. They include (1) communication and publicity, (2) leadership from administrators, (3) wide-based support, (4) rewards and resources, and (5) appropriate forms of innovation management and organization.

Communication and Publicity. Successful curriculum change is most likely when the change is clearly defined, widely publicized, and well communicated. For success, the need for change and the purpose of the specific change or changes envisioned should be clearly articulated, as was done in the adoption of the Great Books program at St. John's. In contrast, at Brown the curriculum proposals of the Magaziner and Maxwell report were separated from the educational philosophy upon which they were based. Accordingly, the Brown faculty passed the proposals but ignored their philosophy. The resulting diffuse and often inconsistent interpretations of the goals of the new curriculum created much subsequent dissatisfaction.

During all stages of change, communication should be two-way, informative, frequent, and aimed at a wide audience if the change is to be successful. Workshops and orientation sessions are particularly useful in getting students and faculty ready to participate in change. These forms of communication were utilized by the curriculum committee at Sterling College and the original staff at Alabama's New College. Frequent, information-rich, large-audience communication can counter the misrepresentation of fact, rumor mongering, and misperceived threats such as those that closed Meiklejohn's Experimental College. It also tends to reduce self-selection of new curricula by students and faculty for inappropriate reasons, as occured at Bensalem. Two-way communication is necessary to discover the arguments of opponents and be able to respond to them. It is additionally useful in keeping graduate schools, professional schools, and employers aware of change and providing feedback on their reaction. Brown University's failure to solicit the opinions of its own graduate and professional schools regarding a grading change resulted in the rejection of some qualified applicants for postgraduate study at Brown itself and encouraged the development of an educationally unprincipled defensive strategy for using the optional grading system by some students. Widespread communication or publicity is valuable in that it may encourage the use of new curricula. For instance, student-created majors, though available for 20 years at Brown, were not used significantly until they were publicized after being reapproved as part of the 1969 curriculum reform.

Leadership from Administrators. Successful curriculum change is most likely with strong presidential and administrative support. Administrative support has been described by Lewis Mayhew (1976, p. 8) as "the most important condition necessary for innovation and change in American higher education." This was confirmed to some extent by Gross and Grambsch (1974, p. 128), who found the chief academic administrator or president to be the most powerful person in both public and private universities. They also found that administrators occupy six of the eight most powerful positions in private universities and five of the eight most powerful positions in public institutions.

The power of the administration with regard to curricular change stems from its ability to encourage, if not initiate, and fund desired academic programs and to kill or discourage and financially starve undesired programs. The benefits of administrative support are apparent in President Mathews' establishment of New College one month after a resounding faculty "no" vote and the complete transformation of the St. John's curriculum only a few weeks after the arrival of President Barr and Dean Buchanan. The costs of nonsupport can be seen at Brown University, where it took two years for a faculty vote on the Magaziner and Maxwell report when there was only lukewarm administrative support and not even opposition.

Wide-Based Support. Successful curriculum change is most likely when its base of support is wide. Such support is necessary so that a curriculum change is not forced to rely wholly upon a small number of powerful people for continuance. At Fordham University, Bensalem College relied almost entirely upon the power of Father McLaughlin, the university president, and the prestige of Elizabeth Sewell, its director. When they left Fordham, so did the college's principal base of support. A large following is also necessary to get sufficient faculty to participate in a curriculum change after it has been initiated, especially if participation is above load. For example, though student leadership did an excellent job of eliminating faculty opposition to the Brown curriculum reform, it did not build faculty support. As a consequence, only a small proportion of faculty chose to teach in the voluntary parts of the new curriculum. Incidentally, the support must also come from students or the new curriculum will be lacking in enrollments, as is the case at Simon's Rock. Another virtue of a wide base of support is that it produces a sense of ownership among supporters. Such a feeling is more difficult to turn into opposition than is an uncommitted or passive attitude, and generally results in greater autonomy of operation for the new curriculum.

Rewards and Resources. Successful curriculum change is most likely when a change is buttressed by a supportive system of rewards and reallocation of resources. The importance of rewards can be seen in an examination of the Contemporary Civilization program at Columbia University. Contemporary Civilization suffers from involuntary participation by some staff, high turnover in instructors, few senior faculty, and negative teaching evaluations. These conditions stem from several facts involving faculty rewards: First, faculty background and training do not prepare them well for broad, cooperative, interdisciplinary teaching in courses like Contemporary Civilization, and little incentive exists for faculty to develop these skills. Second, teaching in Contemporary Civilization is frequently a negative factor in promotion and tenure consideration because it involves service outside the instructor's discipline and demands a disproportionate amount of faculty time that could be used for more positively perceived activities such as publication and departmental service. Third, departments use the course as a dumping ground for their least-qualified graduate students, most junior faculty, and underenrolled professors with esoteric specialties. The only reward offered Columbia instructors for participation in Contemporary Civilization is a sabbatical after three years of teaching that has encouraged some departments to donate faculty for a limit of no more than two and one-half years. In any case, the lack of rewards associated with Contemporary Civilization for both faculty and departments encourages the poor quality of the course that has continued from year to year.

The need for resource reallocation is highlighted in the case of the Modes of Thought or freshman seminar program at Brown University. This program, which was to have been the primary focus of the freshman year, now offers a grossly inadequate number of courses that overrepresents the foreign languages and includes few classes in the social sciences. The reason is that sufficient resources have not been allocated to support the program. The departments participating in Modes of Thought are those with the lightest teaching loads; some of the smaller departments with heavy loads provide no faculty at all for the program. Small departments with high student-to-faculty ratios are simply unable to release faculty for Modes of Thought teaching without replacement, while large departments with relatively few students, such as the foreign languages, flock to Modes of Thought to attract students.

Appropriate Forms of Innovation Management and Organization. Finally, successful curriculum change is most likely when a change is organized or managed by means of the appropriate form of administration. The environment within existing colleges and universities is the primary determinant of the appropriate form of administration and organization for any change. Antagonistic, neutral, and supportive environments require different types of administrative arrangements, different types of leadership, different modes of implementing change, and different types of change. This is shown in Table 19.

In an *antagonistic environment*, change can be introduced only by the imposition of high administrators, powerful faculty, and occasionally determined students. This limits the possible types of change to small changes (enclave, piecemeal) or external changes (new institutions, peripheral). The nature of the organization for such innovations must be a protective cushion, which isolates and protects the change from its environment. It often involves the establishment of a separate faculty, student body, physical plant, or administration. This was attempted in creating the college at the University of Chicago and the Free University of Berkeley. The chief operating officer, often bearing a title such as provost, should be an individual perceived to be competent and respectable in the antagonistic environment. The person must be a good politician who publicizes the positive aspects of the change and defuses the negative and threatening aspects. He or she should be a charismatic leader to maintain confidence among people associated with the change in order to counteract the negative environment. Neal Berte of Alabama's New College was such an individual.

In a *neutral environment,* successful changes is best introduced by building a coalition of supportive campus opinion leaders (faculty, students, administrators, and others). This was the tack taken by the planning committee at Sterling College. The process of introducing change in such an environment varies from negotiation, as at Brown, to wheedling, as in the recruitment of students to Simon's Rock. In such an environment, all types of change are possible. Purists, frustrated by indifference, may seek external change (peripheral change and new colleges) and optimists, predicting a bright future, may try holistic change, but the changes most likely to be successful are small ones (enclaves and piecemeal changes), owing to the lack of threat from the environment and lack of support within it. The leadership for the change will be strongest if it comes from the campus coalition and an efficient, but low-profile

Table 19. Environment, administration, and organization of change

Environment	Nature of administration and organization	Nature of leadership	Tactic of implementing change	Likely strategy or type of change
Antagonistic	Protective cushion	Competent, political, personally charismatic director, with strong administration backing	Imposition	New institution, enclave, piecemeal change, or peripheral change—but *not* holistic change
Neutral	Participative coalition	Opinion leaders and efficient, low-profile coordinator	Range from wheedling to negotiation	New institution, enclave, holistic change, piecemeal change, or peripheral change
Supportive	Traditional or existing forms	Deans, department chairpersons, or counterparts	Consensus	Holistic change or piecemeal change

coordinator, who can get things done without stirring up a hornet's nest. The freshman seminar program at Harvard is directed via such an arrangement.

In a *supportive environment,* change is much desired. Such an environment might be a university that offers the master's degree, and is given permission to award the Ph.D. A supportive environment is a prerequisite for successful holistic change and a good bet for successful piecemeal change or an innovative enclave. External change is unlikely and unnecessary given support for change within existing institutions. The best means of organizing for successful change in this environment is by traditional or established mechanisms, since consensus in favor of the change already exists. Accordingly, the operating leadership will likely be deans, department chairmen, or their counterparts.

Some cynics claim that academic change is impossible, while less sardonic observers of higher education claim it is merely unpredictable. Yet enough is known about the dynamics of organizations, both academic and nonacademic, to be able to hazard guesses with better than an even chance of success about the likely fate of curricular reforms such as those discussed in earlier chapters. Prediction is imperfect, of course, but any curriculum committee or advocate of curricular change will do well to take the factors reviewed in this chapter into account if they hope for successful change.

References

Baldridge, J. V. *Power and Conflict in the University.* New York: Wiley, 1971.
This book presents a political model of change and examines its correctness in a case study of New York University.

Bennis, W. *The Leaning Ivory Tower.* San Francisco: Jossey-Bass, 1973.
This book by an eminent organizational theorist generates new theories and explains how some old ones went awry.

Bennis, W., Benne, K. D., and Chin, R. *The Planning of Change.* New York: Holt, Rinehart and Winston, 1969.
This volume contains 43 essays—some old, some new, and many excellent—by well-known specialists on the subject of change. The human relations approach is stressed.

Berte, N. *Innovations in Undergraduate Education.* Report of a conference sponsored by New College and the Natural Science Foundation. University, Alabama, Jan. 1972.

Carnegie Surveys, 1975–76.
  This study is discussed in the Preface.
Clark, B. R. *The Distinctive College: Antioch, Reed, & Swarthmore.* Chicago: Aldine, 1970.
  This book discusses what it took to make organizational and educational innovation work at three colleges. It is must reading for those interested in organizations and academic change.
College Placement Council, Inc. *Four-Year Liberal Arts Graduates: Their Utilization in Business, Industry, and Government–The Problem and Some Solutions.* Bethlehem, Penn., 1975.
Corson, J. *The Governance of Colleges and Universities.* New York: McGraw-Hill, 1975.
Gaff, J. G., and Associates, *The Cluster College.* San Francisco: Jossey-Bass, 1970.
Glenny, L. A., Shea, J. R., Ruyle, J. H., and Freschi, K. H. *Presidents Confront Reality: From Edifice Complex to University Without Walls.* San Francisco: Jossey-Bass, 1976.
Gross, E., and Grambsch, P. V. *Changes in University Organization, 1964–1971.* New York: McGraw-Hill, 1974.
  This study of 68 universities examines changes in goals as ranked by faculty and administrators.
Hage J., and Aiken, M. *Social Change in Complex Organizations.* New York: Random House, 1970.
  This volume provides a useful introductory synopsis of existing theory on organizational change combined with fresh insights of the authors.
Havelock, R. G. *Planning for Innovation through Dissemination and Utilization of Knowledge.* Ann Arbor, Mich.: University of Michigan Institute for Social Research, July 1969.
Hefferlin, J. L. *Dynamics of Academic Reform.* San Francisco: Jossey-Bass, 1969.
  This is the classic study of change in higher education. Based on historical analysis, site studies, and surveys of 110 representative colleges, it discusses the problems of reform, the process of reform, changes in curriculum, agents of change, and correlates of reform.
Ladd, D. R. *Change in Educational Policy: Self-Studies in Selected Colleges and Universities.* New York: McGraw-Hill, 1970.
Levine, A. *Reflections of an Itinerant Interviewer: A Sketch of Undergraduate Curriculum Trends.* A technical monograph prepared for the Carnegie Council on Policy Studies in Higher Education. Berkeley, Calif., June 1976a (mimeographed).
Levine, A. *Why Innovation Fails: The Institutionalization and Termination of Innovation in Higher Education.* Unpublished doctoral dissertation. State University of New York, Buffalo, 1976b.
  This volume presents and tests a model of the post-implementation life of change in a study of 14 experimental colleges at the State University of New York at Buffalo.
Levine A., and Weingart, J. *Reform of Undergraduate Education.* San Francisco: Jossey-Bass, 1973.
  Concerned in large measure with the substance of the college curriculum, this study of 26 colleges and universities also examines the dynamics behind their programs.
Lippit, R., Watson, J., Westley, B. *The Dynamics of Planned Change.* New York: Harcourt Brace Jovanovich, 1958.

Martorana, S. V., and Kuhns, E. *Managing Academic Change: Interactive Forces and Leadership in Higher Education.* San Francisco: Jossey-Bass, 1975.

Mayhew, L. B. *How Colleges Change: Approaches to Academic Reform.* Stanford, Calif.: ERIC Clearinghouse on Information Resources, Stanford Center for Research and Development in Teaching, 1976.

This monograph offers useful and interesting prescriptions for academic change based on personal observation and wide acquaintance with the literature.

Mayhew, L. B., and Ford, P. J. *Changing the Curriculum.* San Francisco: Jossey-Bass, 1971.

The authors discuss the issues involved in change, the curriculum practices of the late 1960s and early 1970s, the college student, and the needs and mechanisms for curriculum change.

Riesman, D. *Constraint and Variety in American Education.* Lincoln: University of Nebraska Press, 1956.

Rogers, E., and Shoemaker, F. *Communication of Innovations.* New York: Free Press, 1971.

There is no better or more comprehensive book on the topic of innovation

Sarason, S. B. *The Creation of Settings and the Future Societies.* San Francisco: Jossey-Bass, 1972.

Schein, E. H. *Professional Education: Some New Directions.* New York: McGraw-Hill, 1972.

Trivett, D. A. "Jobs and College Graduates." *Research Currents* (ERIC-AAHE), November 1975.

15

The Undergraduate
Curriculum
Around the World

In order to put the American undergraduate curriculum in perspective, this chapter looks at the character of undergraduate education in seven nations—The People's Republic of China, France, the Federal Republic of Germany, Great Britain, Japan, Sweden, and the Union of Soviet Socialist Republics. All of these countries are facing or have faced the same two problems that confront the United States—increasing demands for access to higher education and the need for better articulation of the university with the needs of society. These problems have serious curriculum implications, and the seven countries have chosen to deal with them in a variety of different ways. In five of the seven—all but Great Britain and the Soviet Union—the result has been a major curriculum change in the past ten years.

Undergraduate Education
in the People's Republic of China

Education in China is a story of change still in progress—two revolutions in less than 30 years and reforms before and after. The first revolution, which ended in 1949 with the victory of Mao Tse-tung's communists over Chiang Kai-shek's nationalists, resulted in a complete reformulation of Chinese education. The second revolution, the Cultural Revolution, closed most of China's universities from 1966 to 1970. When the universities reopened, they did so with new missions—middle-class privilege was to be eliminated in favor of egalitarian socialism, education was to be articulated with Chinese socioeconomic needs, cultural ideology was to be aligned with the nation's economics base, and theory was to be melded with practice. To accomplish these ends, the government took six major steps: (1) Secondary school graduates were assigned to work in the countryside for two or more years before being permitted to apply for higher education; (2) university selection criteria were changed to favor achievement in nonacademic activities; (3) university education placed emphasis upon practical experience outside the classroom in lieu of classroom study; (4) the length of university study was reduced significantly; (5) nonprofessional teachers were brought into the universities; and (6) after completing university study, students were assigned to work in factories and communes.

Since the death of Mao, the prime supporter of Cultural Revolution reforms, a more conservative national leadership has taken power, and many of these changes are being reversed. Radical Maoist disciples, led by the "Gang of Four" who favored further politicization of the university, have been purged; radical university administrators have been removed; and a new government plan for higher education has been adopted that emphasizes traditional notions of academic excellence rather than the previously stressed nonintellective accomplishments.

Types of Institutions

Chinese undergraduate institutions can be divided into six types:

1. Comprehensive universities, of which Peking University, with 17 departments, 60 specialty areas, 2,000 faculty members, at least 10 factories of its own, and linkages with 60 industrial plants, is the preeminent institution. Postgraduate education at these universities is resuming for the first time since the Cultural Revolution.
2. Polytechnic colleges, which specialize in science and technical courses. Tsinghua University is considered the best of these. It is

structured much like Peking University except that it emphasizes science and engineering.

3. Specialized technical and engineering colleges operated by factories. Typical of these largely part-time institutions is the July
   21 University at the Shanghai Machine Tool Plant. Employees
   of the plant who are selected by fellow workers take political and
   technical courses at the factory college and return to productive
   work when their studies are completed.

4. Agricultural colleges.

5. Medical colleges.

6. Specialized institutions in areas such as physical education,
   teacher training, and fine arts.

In 1974, China had 330 colleges and universities. The
number is growing.

Students

Today fewer than 600,000 students are enrolled in higher
education—less than three-quarters of the number in attendance
before the Cultural Revolution. This number represents approximately one out of every 150 secondary school graduates eligible to
enroll in institutions of higher education and one out of every three
students who apply to them.

Following the Cultural Revolution, admissions favored factory workers, children of peasant families, soldiers from the
People's Liberation Army, students from rural areas, and minority
groups. Space was also found for very bright students and students
from influential families. Nonetheless, the criteria for admission
were four: (1) good socialist consciousness; (2) completion of secondary school and two years of work experience—although the
work experience requirement was waived in a few high-demand
specialty areas; (3) good health; and generally, (4) being 21 to 24
years old and unmarried.

This practice is changing. Newly announced policies favor
"admission of the excellent." Special consideration is no longer
given to children of working-class or peasant families. Highly qualified applicants are admitted directly from secondary school without two years of work experience, particularly in the fields of lan-

guage, science, fine arts, and sports. Work experience is being waived for approximately 30 percent of this year's entering students, and enriched high schools are being established for gifted students.

Entrance examinations existed prior to the Cultural Revolution, but were abolished in its aftermath. They were reinstated in 1973, but primarily for placement purposes or to supplement other applicant information. The failure rate was low and university admissions generally emphasized other types of nonacademic achievement. At present the examinations are used to screen for the most able students. As a result, rural and minority students are at a disadvantage in passing the tests, owing to the poorer quality and shorter duration of their prior schooling. At least ten million students will take the highly competitive admissions examinations this year for 200,000 freshman places. The general examinations, which most students can take only once or twice, test basic knowledge and problem-solving ability in Chinese language, mathematics, and politics. Supplementary examinations are required in certain fields. For example, students applying for science and engineering programs will also be tested in physics and chemistry; those applying for art and literature will be examined in history and geography; and applicants for foreign language will be tested in the language they studied in secondary school.

With this change in the testing procedures, the admissions process is also being reformed. In the past, available places in the universities were allocated by regional revolutionary committees to communes and factories. Candidates wrote applications which had to be supported by fellow workers, and peer recommendations carried a great deal of weight. Completed applications required approval by the regional revolutionary committee as well as subsequent action by the university. This process is being retained principally for admission to less academic workers' schools and some forms of part-time instruction.

Faculty

During the Cultural Revolution many faculty were subjected to "intellectual remodeling," which involved working with their hands and living among workers and peasants for varying periods. When they returned to the university, they again found peasants and workers who were engaged as part-time teachers. (Differences in the conception of faculty in China and the United States make an estimate of the number of Chinese faculty in American terms impossible.) Periodic sessions were added to the academic year for student evaluation of teaching and the curriculum; theory courses were eliminated in a number of disciplines; syllabi and research proposals were required to be approved by local community groups; and most research was moved out of the university to 30-odd research institutes, while that remaining was limited to practical and applied studies. Future plans call for more basic research, a decrease in the number of nonprofessional faculty, and greater emphasis on research in general.

Curriculum

The length of higher education is variable in China. Short programs range from a month to two years in specialty areas such as radio announcing and textile machinery design. More traditional university programs, such as education and medicine, averaged three years or less until recent times, having been reduced from five or six years during the Cultural Revolution by increasing specialization, lessening breadth, and offering more practical programs geared to work needs. However, dissatisfaction with the quality of graduates has resulted in the length of higher education being extended again. In fact, some recent graduates are being called back for further instruction.

Another innovation of the Cultural Revolution scheduled for change is the current tripartite course design. Approximately 70 percent of all courses have been reserved for academic study, 20 percent for political work, and 10 percent for production. Both students and faculty have been required to spend a portion of every year working in factories or fields, and after graduation, students have been expected to work in the countryside rather than in the more desirable urban areas. This field and factory work was designed to serve three purposes—(1) disseminate current knowledge into the community, (2) keep the intelligentsia from becoming aloof from the masses, and (3) bar institutions of higher education from becoming "ivory towers." But in practice, work experience also served to lessen the amount of time students and faculty spent on academic studies, reduce the number of needed specialists that could be educated, sometimes slow down production, and occasionally alienate workers from ideologically zealous students. As a consequence, the government is planning to reduce student and faculty participation in production work as well as cut back the amount of time spent on political study.

Evaluation of student performance in universities can be expected to change in a manner consistent with the new admissions policy. At present, institutions of higher education offer no degrees or titles, though they award certificates. After the Cultural Revolution, surprise tests were prohibited. Instead, open-book examinations with preannounced questions and student cooperation in answering were encouraged. Tests were intended to help students review and to check on the effectiveness of teaching. As another aid to students, lecture notes were distributed in advance of class at Peking University.

Curriculum Innovations

Outside of the traditional pattern of higher education in China, there have been several developments. One is "spare-time schools." These are off-campus, conveniently available institutions offering courses in subjects such as basic literacy, industrial technology, politics, and agricultural technology. Students do exactly what the school name suggests—they take courses they desire in their spare time. Such schools are located all over the country.

Two other innovations are radio courses and mobile teaching teams, both intended to provide instruction in areas low in population.

Tensions and Future Directions

Chinese higher education has entered a period of uncertainty. The Cultural Revolution left a number of questions unanswered, and many of the questions it answered are currently being reasked. These questions include:

1. Can applied research be sustained with minimal commitment to basic research?

2. Is a university system that admits only one out of every 50 applicants consistent with the goals of a socialist state?

3. Can a university premised on equality of access also incorporate quality, particularly given the serious complaints about declining student performance following the Cultural Revolution?

4. What should be done about unequal student entrance skills?

5. Is it possible to transform the elite functions of university education in a manner consistent with the socialist aims of the Chinese state and the Cultural Revolution without destroying the essential mission of higher education?

6. Do peasant and worker teachers make a contribution to the university or simply bog it down?

7. What is the appropriate balance between politics, academic study, and production?

8. Is some production experience for students and faculty so important that it is worth interrupting production schedules and lengthening the education of needed specialists?

9. Does production experience have educational value in all subject areas?

10. Is anything lost by reducing the breadth of the curriculum?

11. Can a higher education system wracked by ideological strife and a concomitant state of continual change produce quality education for large numbers of students?

The answers to these questions will greatly affect the future direction of Chinese undergraduate education.

Undergraduate Education in France

Higher education in France began in the twelfth century with the rise of the University of Paris. French universities were battered during the Reformation and closed by the French Revolution in 1793. Under Napoleon I, the universities were reorganized into a single institution directly administered by the national government. It was not until 1896 that the system was again broken down into individual universities. From World War II until the late 1960s, French higher education could be characterized as "frequently reformed but little changed." Massive protests in 1968 resulted in the Orientation Act of Higher Education designed to better articulate university activities with societal needs; reduce student dissatisfaction with the poor job market and university crowding; and foster greater university autonomy, increased interdisciplinary instruction, and more democratic university governance. Subsequent reforms with similar goals were proposed in 1969, 1972, and 1976. The 1976 proposal by Junior Minister Alice Saunier-Seite, which provoked national university protests, attempted to gear university education more closely to the job market.

Types of Institutions

There are four general types of higher education institutions in France.

1. *Grandes écoles,* elite professional training institutions that admit only the best French students. Following secondary school, the most outstanding students are selected for a two-year preparatory course, culminating in the *concours,* a competitive entrance examination for the *grandes écoles.* These schools offer specialized courses leading to senior staff positions in government, commerce, industry, and engineering. They emphasize teaching and engage in little research. Several hundred such schools throughout the country enroll about 80,000 students or between 10 and 15 percent of the students in French higher education.

2. *Public universities,* open to any student with a *baccalauréat,* a certificate of secondary school completion requiring a higher level of achievement than the United State counterpart. France's 75 public universities offer general education leading to a wide range of jobs. They are actively engaged in research but are far less concerned about teaching than the *grandes écoles.* They are sometimes described as primarily testing and certifying organizations. As a consequence of their open access policies, public universities enroll most of Frances' undergraduates who accordingly are not as excellent as those of the *grandes écoles.*

3. *Private universities,* consisting of seven Protestant or Catholic institutions, which account for under 3 percent of higher educa-

tion enrollments. In recent years these school have become increasingly secular; however they have long mirrored the public universities because degree tests and diploma requirements are administered by the state.

4. *Specialized institutes* in the fine arts and technical subjects, including a variety of technological universities, called Instituts de Technologie Universitaires (IUTs), started in 1967.

Students

Open access, which is dependent on screening in primary and secondary schools, has been the souce of much of France's recent higher education reform. The number of students completing secondary school and aspiring to higher education has increased rapidly during this century. By 1973, 81.1 percent of the students with *baccalauréats* were continuing their schooling. In 1975, French institutions of higher education enrolled almost 20 percent of the 18- to 23-year-old age group—942,774 students—which is 80 percent more than nine years earlier. This growth has meant overcrowding in classes, growing numbers of low-socioeconomic-status students, and decreasing opportunity for good jobs and social mobility. Forty-five percent of the university students drop out or are flunked out after the first year, which is a sharp contrast with the 95 percent completion rate at the *grandes écoles.*

The tight job market encourages students to enter the brightest professional fields rather than the liberal arts. However, they find the disciplines of choice to be oversubscribed and free access limited, de facto, to colleges of law, letters, and sciences. The first formal limitation on access was not imposed until 1971, and that was only in medicine.

Open access is currently being rethought. In 1975, France's Parliament voted for a series of changes in elementary and secondary education called the Haby Reforms after their author, Minister of National Education René Haby. Under this controversial new plan, the secondary school program would consist of three two-year cycles. The first two cycles would be common basic courses taken by all students. The third cycle would be specialized. Upon completion of the third cycle, students would take a standardized examination for the *baccalauréat de base*. Those hoping to go on to higher education would then spend a foundation year on studies related to their planned area of university concentration in preparation for a university entrance examination. The universities would then accept or reject students on the basis of their examination score and school record, with particular emphasis on the foundation year. A modified version of this plan went into effect in fall 1977, and other portions are still being debated prior to action.

Faculty

All of France's 42,000 faculty are civil servants. Until 1968, universities were organized around a small number of full professors who occupied chairs and assembled junior staff around them. The arrangement bore a certain similarity to the feudal system and was criticized for breeding conformity, homogeneity, and a lack of concern for social needs. The Orientation Act attempted to reduce the preeminence of chairs and gave voting franchise to junior faculty. However, senior staff continue to dominate decision making.

Curriculum

Until 1968, all of France's 23 universities then in existence consisted of the same five faculties—medicine, law, letters, science, and pharmacy; used the same methods of instruction, the *cours magistral* or large lecture; taught the same subjects; had the same requirements for degrees; made no adaptations to local needs, engaged in little curricular innovation; and were governed by the Ministry for National Education.

The Orientation Act replaced the faculties with *unites de enseignement et de recherche* (UERs), education and research units. Each UER consists of the professors, other teaching staff, and students in a discipline (such as physics or history), a faculty (such as medicine) or an interdisciplinary field (such as theater arts). More than 720 UERs have been formed nationally. Each is governed by a council composed of faculty, students, technical and service personnel, and people from the community if desired. The councils are responsible for establishing curriculum, means of evaluating students, teaching methods, budget preparation, and other governance chores.

The Orientation Act proposed that UERs merge in varying combinations to form new and autonomous universities. This was intended to break down the entrenched boundaries between disciplines in the old universities and to replace the uniform system of French higher education. Seventy-five universities have been created. Most of the combinations are either less interdisciplinary than the old system or simply aggregations designed to reinstate the five faculties. Only a relatively small number of the new universities have achieved the desired end of the Orientation Act.

The course of studies at French universities is divided into three cycles. Each cycle is intended to be a coherent program at the end of which a student can leave the university with a nationally recognized degree. The first cycle is two years long and consists of basic training courses for all students in broad subject fields. It is criticized in the same manner as lower division study in this country, and the benefits of establishing colleges solely for first cycle are currently being debated. The second cycle, with emphasis on specialization, is one or two years long and leads to the *licence,* a degree commonly associated with teaching, and the *maîtrise,* associated with research. The third cycle, varying from one to three years, leads to three types of doctoral degrees.

The Orientation Act proposed that universities begin to award their own individual degrees, but student and faculty have tenaciously resisted the possibility, feeling that degrees from some universities would be of less worth than others, that degrees earned previously at lesser schools would be devalued, and that standards would disappear. As a consequence, common national degrees and degree tests continue to thrive.

Curriculum Innovations

Two current innovations stand out in French higher education. One seeks by several means to reduce differences between the universities and the elite *grandes écoles.* For this purpose, several new universities have been established. Université de Haut-Rhin, for example, offers an unusual curriculum combining literature and science and has attached to it two *grandes écoles* in chemistry and textile production. The Université de Campiegne is another, having been modeled after the Massachusetts Institute of Technology and designed to compete with the *écoles*. Taking another tack, some universities have developed joint programs with *écoles*. Thus the Université de Paris-Sud and the École Superieure d'Électricité have several common courses and are engaged in joint research activities.

The other innovation is the Université de Vincennes. It is more like an American institution than a traditional French university. It aims at offering higher education to working people by providing part-time instruction. Its staff members interview prospective students to determine motivation, experience, and other qualifications rather than relying on the *baccalauréat* as a test of admissibility. It makes use of semester credits, departments, interdisciplinary studies, small classes, evening and weekend classes, considerable audiovisual instruction, and grading based on a combination of class participation and written work. As a result, it has been and continues to be highly controversial.

Tensions and Future Directions

The primary tension confronting higher education in France today is democratization versus modernization. Demands for democratization are heard most loudly from France's new students who want continued open access to the university, the curriculum that past students studied, standard national tests, degrees that everyone who graduated before them obtained, and improved social mobility. Those favoring modernization, such as Minister Saunier-Seite and her supporters, want a university system that will serve society. This requires diverse programs geared to the work needs of society, institutional degrees to reflect diverse programs, eventual limitations on open access, periodic review of university programs by France's principal sectors of economic, social, and cultural activity, decentralization of university governance, and diversity among universities in quality and program.

The modernization-democratization debate raises a number of serious questions:

1. Are democratization (open access) and modernization (responding to social needs) entirely inconsistent goals for the university?

2. Does open access to the university have any meaning when students are screened so rigorously in elementary and secondary school?

3. Is there actually open access when admission to the best institutions, the *grandes écoles,* is so strictly limited?

4. Would diverse degrees and degree programs assure continued quality now associated with standardized degree tests and degree programs?

5. Can diversity in degree programs and degrees be achieved given the failure of reaggregation, the dominance of traditional senior staff, and the academic conservatism of new French students?

6. Should academics, the public, or some mix of the two plan and evaluate university programs?

7. Is centralized national governance of higher education compatible with plans for decentralization and increasing curricular diversity?

8. Can standard academic programs, degrees, and degree tests meet changing social needs, satisfy student needs and interests, keep up with changing bodies of knowledge, and provide for quality education in subspecialty areas?

9. Should the university cater to the public demands that would result in dissatisfaction over the job market and increased costs for education or respond to labor market conditions that would limit student access?

10. Should undergraduate education stress general education or preparation for work?

For France, the future will likely bear similarity to present cycles: proposals for curriculum reform, protest, and compromise.

Undergraduate Education in the Federal Republic of Germany

German higher education is in the throes of change—the directions are many, and the outcomes have been diverse and uneven. What is certain is that the concept of the pure German research university, which inspired nineteenth-century American academics, is gone. That university ideal, first established with the rise of the national state and guided by von Humboldt toward a mission of scholarship and training of professionals for state service, was already being reshaped in the years following the 1848 Revolutions. The post-revolutionary universities emphasized cultural subjects, while applied science and technology found refuge elsewhere—in technical institutes that later became separate universities themselves and in schools of engineering. Less than a century later, Nazism rocked the universities. Research was perverted, especially outside the hard sciences. Faculty were isolated; they were forced to take ideological positions in their research; and communication between specialties was restricted. In the decades following World War II, the elite German system of higher education has had to make accommodation to the masses who have demanded entry.

Types of Institutions

West German institutions of higher education are of two principal types—universities, which offer the doctoral degree, and colleges, which do not award the doctorate and tend to have shorter, less prestigious programs in a narrower range of subjects, such as theology, teaching, or music. In 1976, there were 55 state universities, which accounted for 80 percent of all enrollments, and 47 colleges, which enrolled the remaining 20 percent. In recent years, new types of higher educational institutions have developed that will be discussed later under the heading "Curriculum Innovations."

Students

Between 1945 and 1975, enrollments in German higher education increased eightfold to a total enrollment of 840,757. By 1973, 20 percent of university-age students were attending some form of higher education. Like France, Germany has a system of open admissions that enables any student with an *Abitur* (test-based secondary school completion certificate) to attend university-level institutions. Almost 90 percent of *Abitur* holders currently go on to the university. Some variation in student entrance skills exists, however, since the high school examinations are developed on a local basis.

The consequences of enrollment growth have been the same in Germany as in France—overcrowded classes, poor faculty-student ratios, and high drop-out rates (25 to 50 percent). But the West German solution has differed from France's. Germany has ended open admissions by imposing a *numerus clausus* or enrollment quota in the fields of medicine, psychology, and several other sciences, although not in the arts or other social sciences. The *numerus clausus* is intended to postpone rather than eliminate student choice, yet in practice it has resulted in selection from among applicants who are all theoretically qualified for admission in the field of their choice and entitled by the constitution to enroll. Consequently court appeals against the quotas are resulting.

Faculty

West German faculty are divided into three ranks—full professors, *Dozenten* (the equivalent of an associate professor), and assistants (the equivalent of an assistant professor). Full professors and *Dozenten* have the *Habilitation* degree, which is proof of continued and successful research entitling one to give lectures and seminars at the university. This degree generally is completed five years after the doctorate and requires a second dissertation. In 1965, the city of Berlin added a fourth rank, *Tutor,* which is the equivalent of a graduate teaching assistant in this country. In 1973, there were 93,841 faculty of all types.

The organization of German faculty has traditionally been hierarchical and autocratic. Full professors occupied chairs around which institutes were built. The direction of these institutes was determined entirely by their chairholders, who controlled administration, research, teaching, curriculum, and examinations. Professors controlled or at least had a good deal of influence on the academic careers of young faculty, who had little input into institute affairs.

In the 1960s, protests by junior faculty, who outnumbered senior staff, and students, who complained of too little contact with senior faculty and inadequacies in the curriculum, resulted in national laws to democratize higher education decision making and to introduce departments in lieu of institutes and other existing academic divisions. A policy of *Drittelparität,* calling for joint decision making by students, faculty, and service personnel, was adopted in varying degree by the German states. This democratization, which gave students, junior faculty, and nonacademic personnel voting franchise, has been cited as a major cause of the politicization and polarization of German universities. Some units of the Free University of Berlin, for example, have been criticized for sacrificing scholarship to ensure a Marxist line in hiring, teaching, and examining. There have also been complaints by faculty that democratization in some radically controlled departments has resulted in cooperative examinations, which fail to distinguish the contribution of different students and to produce unrealistically low failure rates on degree examinations.

Curriculum

Colleges and universities have historically been divided into *Fakultäten,* divisions such as arts and letters, science, economics and social science, medicine, theology, and law. Larger institutions have had as many as seven divisions.

Higher education tends to be very specialized. There has traditionally been no separation between undergraduate and graduate instruction. University students, particularly in the social sciences and humanities, have until recently been allowed to study freely without credits, grades, time limits, prescribed sequences of classes, or course examinations, until they complete their programs and must pass state and institutional examinations to earn a degree. Freedom is more narrowly prescribed in the colleges.

As the numbers of students attending higher education has increased, these curriculum arrangements have resulted in unnecessary student fumbling due to a lack of professorial contact and an average time to earn a first degree of six to eight years rather than the anticipated four to six years. Examinations were criticized for being arbitrary and for being poorly articulated with courses. In fact, the course work needed to pass examinations was sometimes not even offered. Many of the courses that were offered were criticized for being impractical. This problem stemmed, in part, from a curriculum geared more toward faculty research than social needs or student concerns.

In the past decade, however, curriculum reformers have sought many improvements: shortening the course of studies, defining programs more clearly, introducing more formal syllabi and course patterns, initiating examinations after two years, increasing the percentage of students earning degrees, encouraging more interdisciplinary activity, and developing more work-related curricula.

Curriculum Innovations

Higher education reform has resulted in a variety of new and controversial developments, all of which serve to increase diversity in German education. Opponents characterize them as political expedients, damaging to quality, superficial, and hopefully transitory. They include:

The creation of new universities. Exemplary of these new institutions is the controversial University of Bremen, established in 1971. Bremen organizes teaching around interdisciplinary research projects that are agreed upon by faculty and students and that focus on social problems and occupations.

The establishment of comprehensive universities. Germany is in the process of forming comprehensive universities called *Gesamthochschule*, which combine different levels and types of higher education, including vocational education, colleges of education, and traditional universities, all under one roof. However, serious problems remain concerning questions of institutional status, appropriate pay scales, academic quality, differing state licensure requirements, and negative faculty attitudes toward colleagues teaching less esoteric and more utilitarian subjects.

The development of alternatives to higher education. The percentage of secondary school students seeking the *Abitur* jumped from 12 percent in 1972 to 23 percent in 1975, and it has been anticipated that between 1975 and 1978 at least 128,700 applicants would be rejected by colleges and universities. As a result, the government and industry are developing correspondence programs, practical short courses, extension instruction and "sandwich" courses that combine work and short-term vocational education. However, neither these nor *Fernuniversität*, the German counterpart of the British Open University, offer university-level credentials.

The founding of Fachhochschulen. Fachhochschulen are intended as another alternative to the traditional university for *Abitur* holders. They are institutions of higher education that upgrade the previously lower-level engineering and technical schools to university level and provide needed middle-level management and technical personnel for industry and commerce. The *Fachhochschule* in Berlin offers courses in 14 areas such as food technology, data processing, architecture, and electrical engineering. Candidates for admission must have an *Abitur* or equivalent and six months of practical work experience. Courses of study are six semesters in contrast to the university minimum of eight. Students take a preliminary examination after the fourth semester and a state examination after the sixth. On passing the state examination, they receive the degree of *Ingenieur-grad* rather than the more advanced degree of the existing technical universities. *Fachhochschulen* graduates are eligible for entrance into the universities, and almost one-third of them have chosen to go on with their schooling rather than entering the labor market as they were expected to do. Though a problem, this situation is not surprising, as federal regulations ensure higher salaries to university graduates than to those of the *Fachhochschulen* or other institutions.

Tensions and Future Directions

The future of West German higher education will in large measure be determined by the way the Federal Republic answers a number of questions, including the following:

1. How should the university choose between, or balance, its two now-antagonistic historical characteristics—the commitment to open access and elite education?
2. What should take precedence—university traditions (*Lehrfreiheit* and *Lernfreiheit*) or social needs?
3. Should university education be faculty or student centered?
4. Has the adoption of *Drittelparität* replaced one form of autocratic governance (governance by the senior faculty) with another?
5. Can academic freedom and scholarship survive in a politicized university?
6. How can university autonomy and social accountability best be balanced?

7. Is the current pattern of rapid ad hoc university change superior to slower planned change?

8. Would a uniform national higher education policy be superior to the plethora of diverse, sometimes antagonistic, state and local policies?

Undergraduate Education in Great Britain

British higher education dates back to the twelfth century and the establishment of the Oxford and Cambridge colleges, which were emulated by the first American colleges. Since that time, higher education in Britain has changed greatly, although it still retains an elite character. The strategies of change have been those of the United States: New universities have developed, new missions have been added to existing universities by accretion, and activities deemed inappropriate for the universities have found a home in a diverse array of other postsecondary institutions.

Types of Institutions

Higher education in the United Kingdom is described as a binary system consisting on the one hand of universities and on the other of all other postsecondary institutions, including polytechnics, colleges of education, colleges of further and higher education, technical colleges, and specialized colleges of art, music, and the like. There are 44 universities (plus the Open University) that are autonomous degree-granting institutions. They include the most elite, Oxford and Cambridge Universities; the University of London, with some 40 colleges, institutes, and medical and dental schools, enrolling the largest number of students and offering an external degree program; the Open University, offering a program combining correspondence, television and radio, summer residential sessions, and tutorial meetings for adults lacking normal university admission qualifications; provincial universities known as the civic or "Redbrick" universities, such as Birmingham and Leeds; the new postwar universities conceived to develop interdisciplinary studies and other innovations; the former colleges of advanced technology which became universities in the early 1960s; and the universities in Scotland, Wales, and Northern Ireland.

The other postsecondary institutions are considered public institutions and do not grant degrees. Thirty of them are polytechnics, most of which prior to 1971 had been regional colleges, offering degree, sub-degree, and postgraduate part-time and full-time courses, with more applied emphases than the universities. The colleges of education numbered 160 a few years ago, but most of them will be transformed beyond recognition by 1980, some being eliminated, others combined with universities, with polytechnics, or in some cases with each other. A dozen Sixth Form and Tertiary Colleges combine all courses for postsecondary as well as secondary levels. Several hundred further education institutions offer a mix of secondary and postsecondary, degree and nondegree, vocational and academic courses, both part time and full time. The award of degrees for these public institutions is done to a large extent by the Council for National Academic Awards (CNAA), an autonomous degree-granting body established in 1964, which offers university-level degrees and other certification up to and including the Ph.D. Degrees offered through the public sector (especially those in teacher training) are also "validated" by the universities and by professional and accrediting bodies for specific professional fields such as business and nursing.

Adult education is offered mostly outside the universities in courses provided by local education authorities and voluntary organizations, the former mainly the colleges of further education, in schools in the evening, and in schools specifically designed for adult education. The leading voluntary agency in adult education is the Workers' Educational Association (WEA) which pioneered adult education in Britain. As a result of a recent study called the Russell Report, adult education may receive more priority in the future. Cooperative arrangements between adult education and the Open University may also enhance the priority.

Of these several levels and types of higher education in Great Britain, only university and university-equivalent education will be discussed in the following pages.

Students

In 1974, 633,571 students were enrolled in British universities. This constituted approximately 80 percent of the qualified applicant pool. Students entering the universities are usually about 18 years old and, like their counterparts in most other countries, generally middle class or higher. University entry is competitive and based upon school-leaving examinations administered by regional boards as well as upon interviews, principals' letters of recommendation, and school records, particularly in the major school subjects. British secondary schools place far more emphasis on concentration or specialization than American colleges. Students applying to a university in the sciences must have three high school advanced specialty subjects, and students seeking admission in the arts need two. Once admitted to the university, their drop-out rate is low— under 20 percent.

Pressure to enter the universities mounted after World War II. Between 1963, when Lord Robbins' investigative committee urged the rapid expansion of British higher education, and 1975, the percentage of the college-age group in the university sector rose from 4.5 percent to nearly 20 percent. The creation of polytechnics, the expansion of other postsecondary education opportunities, and a tight job market have resulted in a slight decline in pressures on the university sector in recent years. This trend is likely to continue owing to declines in birthrate and reductions in salary differential for university and nonuniversity educated persons.

Faculty

As in the United States, faculty advancement is based upon experience, publications, and academic attainment. In contrast with America, however, there tends to be somewhat less emphasis upon publication, much less emphasis on service, and much greater stress on teaching. The academic ranks are different from those in this country. Young faculty progress from a two- or three-year probationary period to the rank of lecturer, which leads either to the post of senior lecturer or to reader (for those with a research bent). Professor is the rank at the top of the hierarchy. Professorships are not found outside of the university, and polytechnics are the only other postsecondary institutions with readerships. In general, faculty-student ratios are significantly lower in British universities (1:10) than in American institutions, which encourages a personalized British university environment comparable to that of small liberal arts colleges in the United States.

Curriculum

In Great Britain, study for the first degree or bachelor's degree is generally three years in length, but there are exceptions: Some programs such as modern language (four years) and medicine (five to six years) are longer; at Scottish universities, the first degree with honors—master of arts—requires an average of four years; and certain innovative programs as at the University of Keele, which will be described later, are also four years long. Short nondegree programs of one or two years in length that lead to diplomas and certificates are of course also available.

There are two types of curricula in English and Welsh universities. One involves intensive specialization in one or two subjects and leads to a degree with honors. The other allows students to spread their studies over a wider field and leads to an ordinary or general degree. High examination scores can result in a general degree with honors. Eighty percent of students choose the specialized pattern of study for honors.

Scottish universities offer several variations on the British theme. These involve either (1) study of one subject for three years and two related subjects for one year each, (2) study of three subjects for three years, or (3) study of three subjects for two years with emphasis upon one of the three in the third year. The Scottish curriculum is less specialized than that of the English and Welsh universities. Its first year is reserved for general education rather than launching students immediately into concentration.

Progress at the British universities is based upon passing examinations at the end of each academic year rather than accumulating credits. In order to graduate, students must pass between 6 and 13 examinations depending upon their area of study and their university. Sequences of lectures, discussions, and practical classes are geared to each examination, and the combination of classes and examinations is called a course.

Curriculum Innovations

Britain is engaged in a number of interesting undergraduate curriculum practices, but three stand out: the Open University, the new postwar universities, and alternatives to full-time attendance.

The Open University. The Open University is a national nontraditional institution allowing British students to study at home. It has no campus, no terms, and no classroom lectures. Course materials are sent by mail and homework is returned in the same manner. The university makes use of radio and television instruction, and its experimental science kits permit students to conduct laboratory work at home. It operates regional centers throughout Britain, staffed by part-time faculty and counselors and offering supplementary tutorial instruction and required week-long summer programs. The Open University is above all open in admission. Most of its students are adults in their twenties through sixties. They work at their own pace in preparation for examinations, which are given each November. Unlike other British universities, the Open University works on the credit system. Each of its credits is equivalent to 350 hours of study, and its students must accumulate six credits for an ordinary degree or eight credits for an honors degree. They can transfer these credits to other universities if they wish.

The New Universities. These institutions were all founded after World War II. The first, the University of Keele, established in 1949, was based on the Scottish conception of higher education and requires every student to study sciences, humanities, and social science in what is called a foundation course. This addition necessitated a four-year program in order to maintain the specialized three-year course associated with the traditional honors degree. Seven other universities—Sussex, York, East Anglia, Essex, Lancaster, Kent, and Warwick—established after 1960 created even more innovative programs that involve foundation courses and breadth study through the undergraduate years, alternatives to examinations such as papers, organization of departments into interdisciplinary schools (Sussex), service-oriented departments such as operations research and new subject areas such as linguistics (Lancaster), major-minor combinations, and honors programs based on multiple majors rather than on a single specialty.

Alternatives to Full-Time Attendance. Three options are most common: (1) sandwich courses, most frequently found in technically oriented universities and polytechnics, which alternate attendance there with work or on-the-job training on a three- or six-month basis; (2) part-time attendance, wherein students attend a college or university one day a week and night sessions as needed; and (3) block release, in which workers study full time for a short period of six to twleve weeks during any single work year. Expansion of these programs has been handicapped in recent years by high un-employment.

Tensions and Future Directions

Unlike Germany, France, and China, the undergraduate cur-riculum in Great Britain is not in the midst of major change, but some change may be in the offing as several important questions are currently being debated. Of these, the first one listed below is, in fact, being hotly debated and is likely to have the most immediate effects.

1. Should new school-leaving examinations be created and the ad-vanced secondary school course of studies be broadened from three to five subjects, owing not only to significant increases in student attendance at comprehensive secondary schools (now 77 percent) and at non-university-level postsecondary institutions, but also to the trend toward more general and less specialized secondary school curricula, as well as to the possibility of declin-ing student interest in higher education?
2. Is a short course of studies at the university level which em-phasizes depth, but possibly isolates scientists from humanists, more desirable than a longer, more costly course of studies which would add additional breadth and possibly integrate the sciences and humanities?
3. Are highly competitive university admissions standards appro-priate to a country committed to educational equity and mass access?
4. Is a binary system of higher education which purports to sepa-rate utilitarian from nonutilitarian studies and elite from non-elite institutions preferable to a unitary system of higher educa-tion which would integrate them?
5. Should the policy of maintaining institutions with overlapping

missions between the sectors in the binary system be continued from the sake of equity when efficiency demands distinct definitions?

Undergraduate Education in Japan

Twice since the end of World War II, Japanese higher education has undergone major change. Once the change was externally induced and once it was internally induced.

The external change occurred as the result of the postwar occupation of Japan. During that period, the number of institutions of higher education increased more than fourfold and the educational system was restructured. The time allocated for elementary and secondary school was reduced from 14 to 12 years, and higher education was increased from three to four years. An assortment of postsecondary institutions, consisting of universities, vocational schools, technical colleges, and normal schools, was turned into a higher education system. And the Japanese universities, based on the continental model, were "Americanized." For instance, general education was introduced and specialization was scaled down. Most of these occupation-induced reforms proved to be unstable, however, owing to a lack of financial commitment as well as a lack of cultural or social commitment.

The internal changes were caused by nationwide student unrest during 1968–69. The results were a parliamentary reform law entitled "Provisional Measures for University Management," a 1971 government higher education reorganization report, and a series of administrative and curriculum changes at individual institutions. Observers differ in their analysis of the efficacy of these reforms.

Types of Institutions

Japan has four types of higher education institutions—universities, junior colleges, technical colleges, and graduate schools and research centers.

Universities. The number of Japanese universities has grown from 46 in 1948 to 413 in 1974. Universities engage in general education, vocational education, teacher training, technical education, disciplinary education, and correspondence instruction. Their curricula can be divided into three types—(1) a comprehensive general curriculum providing knowledge and skills for careers, such as public administration, which are not particularly specialized; (2) an academic curriculum, which is disciplinary based, and (3) an occupational curriculum, which prepares students for professional occupations such as medicine and law. The universities are hierarchically ordered and include former imperial universities, national universities, municipal universities, and private universities. The imperial universities, particularly Tokyo and Kyota, are the most elite of all.

Junior Colleges. Japanese junior colleges number 506 and offer two- to three-year programs. Like universities, they require 12 years of elementary and secondary education for admission. They offer two types of program—a general education curriculum and an occupational curriculum preparing students for lower-status jobs than the university. As there is no transfer program between the junior colleges and the universities, only 8 percent of junior college graduates go on to the universities.

Technical Colleges. There are 65 technical colleges, which offer five-year programs and require only nine years of elementary and secondary schooling for admission. Technical college programs prepare students for mid-level positions in areas such as the mercantile fields and engineering.

Graduate Schools and Research Centers. These schools and centers are associated with universities. There are 199 of them. Graduate schools tend to offer instruction up to the master's level, while research centers usually offer the doctorate. Most Japanese undergraduate programs are terminal, however, so relatively few students pursue graduate work.

Students

The demand for higher education by Japanese youth has expanded rapidly since World War II. Although 38 percent of the age group are currently enrolled in some form of higher education (2,020,000 students in 1975), the supply of higher education is inadequate to meet the demand. For example, Nihon University enrolls over 100,000 students and has a student-faculty ratio of 57:1.

Admission, which is highly competitive, is based upon examinations. Each institution has its own tests, lasting several days. Groups of institutions are beginning to work on common examinations, some private colleges admit students from their own preparatory schools without examinations, and admission of highly rated students without tests is being explored. Nonetheless, the testing period and preparation for it are referred to as "examination hell."

The problem is particualrly acute at the few elite universities, which admit as few as 10 to 15 percent of their applicants. These institutions, such as Tokyo and Kyoto Universities, are much more closely tied to social class status and good jobs than are the most prestigious universities in the United States. For instance, it is quite common for industry and even government agencies to recruit from only a handful of all the universities.

Each year, 20 percent of the students taking the admission tests are repeaters who failed to pass the examination for an institution to which they sought admission one or more times previously. They are called *Rōnin*, after the unemployed Samurai of the feudal age. The consequences of the intense competition and restricted access at the top include a high suicide rate, mental and physical breakdown, a well developed preparatory school and tutoring industry, achievement-motivated parents who begin to push their children toward the "right" university as soon as they can locate the "right" kindergarten, and the continuing growth of the private higher education sector.

Faculty

Japanese colleges and universities are divided into faculties, such as humanities, law, and social science; and the faculties are divided into chairs, consisting of a senior faculty occupant and his staff. The Japanese government is trying to break down this organization but has been successful only at some institutions.

There were 108,400 faculty in 1975. Faculty mobility is low and institutional loyalty is high. The majority of faculty teach at the same institution where they did their graduate work. At Tokyo and Kyoto Universities, this is true of 90 percent of the faculty. However, salaries are so low that three out of four faculty teach at a second institution to supplement their income.

Average teaching loads vary between 8 and 20 hours a week. At private institutions they tend to be about twice as heavy as at public institutions. Demands on faculty have traditionally been light, however. Japanese society places more emphasis on the role of higher education in screening for admission and certification than its role in education, and as a consequence students have made few demands on faculty and faculty have made few demands on students, permitting faculty to concentrate more on research or on money-making activities than on teaching. This now appears to be changing, owing to swelling numbers of students, the protests of the 1960s, and 1969 legislation which permits the minister of education to suspend faculty who have been justifiably criticized by students but have shown no improvement within the succeeding nine months.

The quality of faculty, like that of students, is quite variable. That is particularly the case at the less selective institutions, since the enormous growth of Japanese higher education has necessitated a very quick expansion in the faculty complement.

Curriculum

The undergraduate program at Japanese colleges and universities consists of general education and specialized study. At universities, which frequently require a thesis for graduation, 30 percent of the program is general education, 62 percent is specialized in the major, and the remaining 8 percent varies. At junior colleges 20 percent is general education, 40 percent is major study, and 40 percent is variable. At technical colleges 28 percent is general education, 55 percent is major study, and 17 percent varies.

General education is confined to lower-division instruction and usually consists of distribution requirements. Lectures are most common in the lower division, while seminars are reserved for upper-division instruction. Integration of lower- and upper-division instruction is poor.

Universities and junior colleges operate on the credit system. Seventy-two to 93 credits are required for junior college graduation, and 124 credits are needed for a university degree. Technical colleges base student progress on accumulated hours of instruction, with 6,545 hours required for graduation.

Eighty percent or more of the undergraduates finish their programs on time, the failure rate is quite low, and transfer between institutions is rare. Students tend to drop out for personal or financial reasons rather than academic reasons.

Curriculum Innovations

Three recent innovations stand out. They are the establishment of Tskuba University, the founding of the United Nations University, and the creation of the University of the Air.

Tskuba University. This new institution has been founded on the principles of the government's 1971 reorganization report. It differs from established institutions by separating education activities from research activities, by eliminating faculties in favor of disciplinary and interdisciplinary units, by integrating general education more completely with specialized study, and by formally soliciting outside opinions on university administration and research activities. Yet many question whether Tskuba remains as innovative in practice as in its design.

The United Nations University. This unique university, founded under the auspices of the United Nations and headquartered in Tokyo, has received a $100 million endowment from Japan and small grants from other countries. Consisting of an international network of research and training centers, it seeks to identify and find solutions to pressing world problems such as war and peace, hunger, human rights, population, and development. To this end, it has rejected traditional academic departments in favor of a problem-oriented organization, allowing multidisciplinary, mission-oriented, practical applications of knowledge.

The University of the Air. Modeled after the British Open University, the University of the Air offers instruction leading to a baccalaureate degree and is designed for people who have previously been denied access to higher education, including working youths, housewives, and older adults. Forty-five-minute lessons are broadcast on television or radio twice each day, seven days a week, at convenient times. They are supplemented with texts, other printed materials, and local centers for face-to-face contact. The courses are interdisciplinary in nature and fall into four subject areas—nature and humanities, science of living, social and international relations, and science and engineering. All high school graduates or the equivalent can enroll, but fees are higher than those charged by regular universities.

Tensions and Future Directions

The tensions in Japanese higher education come primarily from two sources—the forced but unintegrated remodeling after World War II and the rapid expansion of demand for higher education. As a consequence of these tensions the following questions arise:

1. What should be the mission of Japanese higher education?
2. How can access be increased, quality be maintained, and diversity be encouraged?
3. How can restricted access to elite public institutions and a brutal entrance examination system be ameliorated in a society that places so much emphasis upon credentials?
4. How should the curriculum be organized to eliminate the currently poor articulation between lower- and upper-division study?
5. How can transfer arrangements and interconnections between institutions of higher education be established in a closed higher education system?
6. How should faculty be organized to produce the best possible type of education?
7. How can plans for reform be effectively initiated when they are met with widespread criticism?

Undergraduate Education in Sweden

On July 1, 1977, Swedish higher education was radically transformed. The change had taken more than nine years of planning and debate to implement, however. It began in 1968, when the minister of education charged a special commission (the "U68" Commission) with developing a plan for postsecondary education in Sweden. The plan took five years to draft and was followed by four years of national debate, culminating in the passage of a much-modified reform law by the Swedish Parliament. The law placed emphasis upon enrolling mature students, building stronger bonds between education and work, establishing short-term study, and ensuring geographically accessible higher education.

Types of Institutions

Prior to the reforms, Sweden had a binary system of higher education consisting of six universities and 25 other postsecondary institutions, including professional and vocational colleges in such areas as the arts, agriculture, and teacher training. The U68 legislation has created a university system divided into six regions based on the existing universities. Each region is governed by a 21-member board. Two-thirds of the members represent the "public interest" and one-third are chosen by the constituents of the university. At present, new colleges and universities are being built to provide higher education in the nation's largest cities and regionally in low population areas.

Students

Between 1950 and 1973, enrollment in Swedish higher education shot up from 17,000 (less than 4 percent of the college-age group) to 110,000 (more than 21 percent of this group). This growth necessitated admission restrictions or a *numerous clausus* in certain fields—medicine, teaching, technology, business and economics, dentistry, and pharmacy.

U68 legislation has retained these restrictions with parliamentary-determined ceilings. It has also introduced new criteria for entrance into higher education. To be admitted, applicants must have completed at least two years of secondary school (secondary school courses vary from two to four years) or be over 25 years old and have at least four years of work experience, including housework or military service. All admittees are also required to have the equivalent of two years of secondary school study in Swedish and English.

In the restricted or closed admissions areas, an elaborate selection process has been introduced. Applicants are divided into four groups: (1) those with three or four years of secondary education, (2) those with two years of secondary education, (3) those with other qualifications such as work experience, and (4) those with foreign qualifications. The groups are evaluated on differing criteria. The first two are evaluated on the basis of school marks and vocational experience; the third is assessed on the basis of vocational background and voluntary aptitude tests; and the fourth is assessed variably. The proportion of each of the first three groups admitted to higher education is equivalent to the percentage of applications received from that group relative to the total. Foreign applications are limited to a maximum of 10 percent of each entering class.

Faculty

There are approximately 7,500 full-time-equivalent faculty in Sweden. Under U68, curriculum management has been placed in the hands of a board rather than the faculty. One board was created for each major area consisting of equal numbers of faculty, students, and work-world representatives as well as one spokesperson for university technical and administrative staff. Boards are charged with planning course content and curriculum design.

Curriculum

U68 established four types of undergraduate curricula—general, local, individual, and special. Ninety percent of students are expected to opt for *general* programs, now 80 in number, begun and organized at the national level around five vocational areas—(1) technology; (2) administration, economics, and social science; (3) welfare and medicine; (4) teaching; and (5) culture and information work. *Local* programs are similar to the general ones, but are initiated by the individual higher education regions to meet local vocational needs. *Individual* programs of study are student-designed. And *special* programs are short-term courses lasting a term or two. To go on to graduate school or research training, 60 credits of the 120 required for the first degree must be earned in the subject matter in which the student plans to do research.

Most programs offered under U68 are interdisciplinary and clearly vocational. Many are designed to give students basic education, allowing them to go to work and obtain continuing education later. Journalism, for instance, provides students with a practical placement half-way through the three-and-one-half-year course.

Decisions about the nature of some curricular elements still have to be made. Examinations, degree designations, and evaluation are still up in the air. However, a three-point pass-fail grading system—high pass, pass, and fail—appears quite likely to be adopted.

Tensions and Future Directions

It is much too early to even guess at the consequences of the U68 legislation. Certain curricular tensions are, however, apparent as they were voiced loudly during the debate over the reform proposals:

1. Should the curriculum be molded as closely as it is now to vocational needs, which are ephemeral and rely upon constantly changing knowledge?
2. Will quality be sacrificed by the stress upon the democratization of higher education and the admission of nontraditional students?
3. Is democratization consistent with restricted admissions in many of the most desirable fields?
4. Can informed decisions on academic matters be made by governing boards dominated by nonfaculty?
5. Will regionalism result in wide diversity in quality and standards?

Undergraduate Education in the Union of Soviet Socialist Republics

Like the other six nations examined thus far, the Soviet Union has experienced an enormous increase in the number of students completing secondary school who aspire to attend college. But like only Britain, in contrast to the other countries, the Soviet Union has not undergone an educational upheaval in the past decade. The twin purposes of Soviet higher education remain education for specialists to meet societal needs and education for ideology.

Types of Institutions

There are more than 800 institutions of higher education in the Soviet Union, which can be divided into three types—universities, polytechnics, and specialized institutes.

Universities. There are 63 universities that enroll 10 percent of the students in higher education. Each is divided into traditional university subject areas, called faculties, such as physics, history, and philosophy. The faculties are in turn divided into departments. The faculty of philosophy, for example, consists of departments of Marxism-Leninism, logic and ethics, scientific communism, history of philosophy, and esthetics.

Polytechnics. Sixty-eight polytechnics train students in a number of technical specialties. Leningrad Polytechnic, for instance, has ten faculties and offers instruction in 48 specialty areas.

Specialized Institutes. Specialized institutes could be called "monotechnics," as they generally offer instruction in single subject areas such as teacher training, agriculture, engineering, art, or medicine. There are more than 700 such schools.

Students

Enrollments in higher education rose from 1.2 million in 1950 to 4.6 million in 1973. In the latter year, this amounted to 17 percent of the 18- to 21-year-old age group and 26 percent of 20- to 24-year-olds.

Before students can apply for admission to higher education, they must complete 10 to 11 years of primary and secondary school, which is comparable to 12 years of education in this country. Applicants to full-time day programs cannot be over the age of 35.

Competition for admission is fierce. Sixty to 90 percent of secondary school graduates would like to attend college, but less than one-third can. At institutions such as Moscow State University, there are 10 to 20 applications for each vacancy. Admission is tied to an examination, which generates an enormous amount of tension and long-term cramming on the part of college applicants. In some ways the pressure rivals that of the Japanese system, because students can usually apply to only one institution and to only one faculty within that institution. However, once students are admitted the failure rate is low; nearly 80 percent of all admittees graduate on schedule.

Faculty

Teaching and research are organized around chairs occupied by senior professors who hold the doctorate degree. The degree is a sign of research eminence, unlike the American union card, and is not generally obtained until a person is 40 to 50 years of age. Chairholders exert significant influence over junior faculty (senior lecturers and assistant lecturers), but they are not as powerful as their counterparts in France, Germany, and Japan because the Soviet government determines the subjects taught, the number of lectures per course, the content of courses, the texts used, and the number of students admitted.

The average teaching load is about ten hours per week and the average student-faculty ratio is 18:1. Both differ widely from institution to institution, however.

Curriculum

Undergraduate programs vary from four to five and one-half years in length, with in-class and end-of-term examinations each year. The formal course load decreases for students from year to year. The first year, it averages approximately 36 hours of lectures, seminars, and laboratories per week. The second year course load averages 32 hours, the third year averages 30, the fourth averages 24, and the fifth year is spent largely on a diploma project. Soviet colleges and universities award diplomas rather than degrees. The diploma project is comparable to a senior thesis or senior project in the United States. Each student's project must be approved by his or her department chairman, presented to the university community, and defended before a board.

The undergraduate curriculum is more specialized than that found in the United States. There is no concept of general education, though all students are required to take a foreign language and five year-long political education courses entitled History of the Communist Party of the Soviet Union, Dialectical Materialism, Historical Materialism, The Stages of Capitalism and Socialism, and The Basis of Scientific Communism.

Most of the undergraduate course of study is in the major. There are very few electives. Twenty-two majors with 300 specialty areas corresponding to job specialization are offered. Annual government quotas for admission to each specialty are based on manpower needs, and upon graduation students are assigned by the government to jobs for three years. Majors in the sciences, which have the heaviest enrollments, consist of two parts or cycles. The first cycle involves the general study of the major area; the second consists of specialization within the major. In chemistry, for instance, the first cycle consists of courses in mathematics, physics, organic chemistry, inorganic chemistry, qualitative and quantitative analysis, physical chemistry, and the like; while the second involves study of a specialty such as radio chemistry or polymer chemistry.

Once enrolled, it is extremely hard for students to change their major. It is equally difficult to transfer from one college to another or from one type of instructional program to another. Many institutions offer three programs—full-time day courses (enrolling 47 percent of all students), part-time evening courses (enrolling 15 percent), and correspondence courses (enrolling 38 percent). The Soviet government is attempting to raise enrollment in full-time day courses to 60 percent.

Curriculum Innovations

Two Soviet adult education programs are particularly outstanding: (1) "Universities of culture" are study groups sponsored by workers' clubs, factory clubs, and the government. The students enrolled in these voluntary courses decide on the subject matter and length of their class. There are no examinations and tuition is nominal. (2) "Parents' universities," located in schools or workers' clubs, offer a series of lectures on children and education, such as individual growth and development, child psychology, and school organization.

Tensions and Future Directions

Undergraduate education in the Soviet Union is currently being evaluated in light of the experience of other countries. At least three questions are being asked:

1. Can mass access be accommodated in a higher education system in which quotas are based on manpower needs?
2. Is the existing highly specialized vocational undergraduate curriculum superior to a broader, more generally applicable, less job-specific curriculum?
3. Does Soviet society gain more from centralized educational planning and ideological biases in curriculum design than it would from a policy more supportive of *Lernfreiheit* and *Lehrfreiheit*?

Conclusion

Undergraduate curriculum is not created in a vacuum. It is a product of the higher education traditions and character of a society. As a consequence, the curricula of the seven countries reviewed here vary considerably, and all of them differ from those of the United States, which has the largest system of higher education in the world, embracing 43.6 percent of the college-age group as of 1973 and 11,185,000 students and 687,000 faculty as of 1975.

The experience of the seven nations shows, too, that any curriculum is necessarily a product of many considerations which are not strictly programmatic. These were expressed earlier as "tensions," and they are common to all or most of the nations, including the United States, despite their curriculum differences. They include the following:

1. Who should receive higher education?
2. Should access to higher education be available to all or to only a select few?
3. Should access be based on academic ability or other criteria such as ideology or socioeconomic status?
4. Should higher education respond to social and labor-market conditions or student interest?

5. Are high-quality education and high-quantity attendance incompatible?
6. Who should teach?
7. Who should plan and evaluate education—the public? the faculty? the government?
8. Should education, evaluation, and certification be standardized or diverse?
9. Should undergraduate education be firmly rooted in a particular ideology or attempt, so far as possible, to be value neutral with emphasis on the academic freedoms?
10. Should undergraduate education include breadth studies and take longer to complete, or should it be specialized and take a shorter time to complete?
11. What should be the relationship between a college education and the world of work?
12. What should be done about uneven student entrance skills?
13. Where should students live while in college?

The answers to such questions are the prerequisite for planning an undergraduate curriculum. Unfortunately, program planning in terms of simply designing courses and requirements is too often thought of as the be-all and end-all of curriculum planning. As a result, these necessary prior questions are never asked, and most curricula fail to address them coherently—thus remaining assortments of courses and requirements without much unity or rationale.

References

THE PEOPLE'S REPUBLIC OF CHINA

Brown, G. "Contradictions Remain at Peking University." *Times Higher Education Supplement,* Oct. 24, 1975, p. 27.

Butterfield, F. "China Revives Test to Enter College; Some Students to Skip Farm Work." *New York Times,* Oct. 22, 1977.

Chambers, D. I. "The 1975–1976 Debate Over Higher Education in the People's Republic of China." *Comparative Education,* 1977, 13 (1), 3–14.
This article reviews the state and the tensions of higher education in The People's Republic of China. The article is particularly important because of uncertainty about the future directions in the post-Mao era.

Cleverly, J. "China's Succession Battle Stirs Higher Education Debate." *Change,* 1976, 8 (5), 15–17.

Cleverly, J. "Deflowering the Cultural Revolution: Letter from China." *Change,* 1977, 9 (5), 31–37.
This article discusses the likely consequences of Mao's death and the purge of the Shanghai Four on Chinese education. Cleverly suggests a reversal of many of the changes resulting from the Cultural Revolution.

Hunt, R. C. "Change in Higher Education in the People's Republic of China." *Higher Education,* 1975, 4 (1), 45–60.
This is a concise summary of the evolution of education in China since the 1949 Revolution with accent on the consequences of the Cultural Revolution.

Mauger, P., Mauger, S., Edmonds, W., Berger, R., Daly, P., and Marett, V. *Education in China.* London: Anglo-Chinese Educational Institute, 1974.
This book provides a concise description of the entire Chinese formal education system.

Munro, J. W. "A Major Turn Around in China." *The Chronicle of Higher Education,* 1977, 15 (10), 1.

"A New Elitism in China?" *The Chronicle of Higher Education,* 1977, 15 (13), 3.
These articles offer the best and most up-to-date picture of higher education in post-Mao China.

Pincus, F. L. *Education in the People's Republic of China.* Baltimore, Md.: Research Group One, 1975.
In 33 pages, this booklet gives a nutshell view of Chinese education.

Seybolt, P. J. "Higher Education in China." *Higher Education,* 1974, 3 (3), 265–284.
This article provides a short, though slightly dated, description of higher education in China.

Taylor, R. *Education and University Enrollment Policies in China 1949–1971.* Canberra, Australia: Australian National University Press, 1973.

FRANCE

Arra, S. "Protest Dwindling After French Government Compromise." *Higher Education Daily,* May 5, 1976, pp. 4–6.
This article summarizes the proposals of French Junior Minister Alice Saunier-Seite and the reactions to them.

Bourricaud, F. "The French University as a 'Fixed Society' or, the Futility of the 1968 'Reform.'" In P. Seabury (Ed.), *Universities in the Western World.* New York: Free Press, 1975.

Burn, B. "Higher Education in France." In *Higher Education in Nine Countries: A Comparative Study of Colleges and Universities Abroad.* New York: McGraw-Hill, 1971.

Fomerand, J. "The French University: What Happened After the Revolution?" *Higher Education,* 1977, 6 (1), 93–116.
This is one of the most recent accounts of contemporary French higher education and the impact of the 1968 Orientation Act.

Hecquet, I., Verniers, C., Cerych, L. *Recent Student Flows in Higher Education.* New York: International Council for Educational Development, 1976.

Organisation of Economic Co-operation and Development. *France: Reviews of National Policies for Education.* Paris, 1971.

Patterson, M. "French University Reform: Renaissance or Restoration?" In P. G. Altbach (Ed.), *University Reform.* Cambridge, Mass.: Schenkman, 1974.

THE FEDERAL REPUBLIC OF GERMANY

Berens, E. "States and Industry Provide Training for Rejected Students." *The German Tribune*, Nov. 16, 1975 (710), 13.

Bergdoll, U. "Work-and-Train Course for Abitur Holders." *The German Tribune*, Nov. 8, 1973 (604), 13.

Burn, B. "Higher Education in the Federal Republic of Germany." In *Higher Education in Nine Countries: A Comparative Study of Colleges and Universities Abroad*. New York: McGraw-Hill, 1971.

Catudal, H. M. "University Reform in the Federal Republic: The Experiment in Democratization at the Free University of Berlin." *Comparative Education*, 1976, 12 (3), 231–242.

Domes, J., and Frank, A. P. "The Tribulations of the Free University of Berlin." *Minerva*, 1975, 13 (2), 183–197.

Hecquet, I., Verniers, C., Cerych, L. *Recent Student Flows in Higher Education*. New York: International Council for Educational Development, 1976.

Knauer, G. N. "The Academic Consequences of Disorder in the German Universities." *Minerva*, 1974, 12 (4), 510–514.
This is a translation of Professor Knauer's letter of resignation from the Free University of Berlin.

Krueger, M., and Wallisch-Prinz, B. "The Current Debate in West Germany." In P. G. Altbach (Ed.), *University Reform*. Cambridge, Mass.: Schenkman, 1974.
This essay is a revealing but dated analysis of German higher education early in the 1970s.

Nipperdey, T. "The German University in Crisis." In P. Seabury (Ed.), *Universities in the Western World*. New York: Free Press, 1975.
This is the most detailed discussion of the pre- and post-reform German universities, but the description is somewhat colored by the author's feelings.

Organisation of Economic Co-operation and Development. *Germany: Reviews of National Policies for Education*. Paris, 1972.

Schlicht, U. "German Universities Too Politicized Says Report." *The German Tribune*, July 10, 1977, (795) 11–12.

Smart, K. F. "Vocational Education in the Federal Republic of Germany: Current Trends and Problems." *Comparative Education*, 1975, 11 (2), 153–164.

von Dohnanyi, K. "Dilemmas in Access: The German Situation." In B. Burn (Ed.), *Access, Systems, Youth and Employment*. New York: International Council for Educational Development, 1977.

GREAT BRITAIN

Burn, B. "Higher Education in Great Britain." In *Higher Education in Nine Countries: A Comparative Study of Colleges and Universities Abroad*. New York: McGraw-Hill, 1971.
This chapter provides a concise overview, but the data are seven years old.

Christopherson, D. G. "Current Trends in the United Kingdom." *Higher Education*, 1975, 4 (2), 133–147.
This article discusses the developments following a 1972 government white paper on higher education.

Driver, C. "Higher Education in Britain." In P. G. Altbach (Ed.), *University Reform*. Cambridge, Mass.: Schenkman, 1974.

This is an account of post–Robbins Commission reforms in British higher education and points out some directions of future change.

Hajnal, J. *The Student Trap: A Critique of University and Sixth-Form Curricula.* Harmondsworth, England: Penguin, 1972.

This book critiques university and secondary education in Britain.

Hecquet, I., Verniers, C., Cerych, L. *Recent Student Flows in Higher Education.* New York: International Council on Higher Educational Development, 1976.

Layard, R., King, J., and Moser, C. *The Impact of Robbins.* Harmondsworth, England: Penguin, 1969.

This book discusses the consequences of the 1963 government committee chaired by Lord Robbins, which studied the British universities.

Niblett, W. R., and Butts, R. F. (Eds.). *Universities Facing the Future: An International Perspective.* San Francisco: Jossey-Bass, 1972.

Perry, W. *The Open University: History and Evaluation of a Dynamic Innovation in Higher Education.* San Francisco: Jossey-Bass, 1977.

This volume is the most detailed and nonjournalistic account of Britain's Open University popularly available.

JAPAN

Agency for Cultural Affairs, Government of Japan. *Outline of Education in Japan.* July 1972.

This pamphlet gives facts and figures on higher education in Japan.

Burn, B. "Higher Education in Japan." In *Higher Education in Nine Countries: A Comparative Study of Colleges and Universities Abroad.* New York: McGraw-Hill, 1971.

This chapter offers a concise but slightly dated summary of higher education in Japan.

Central Council for Education of Japan. "The Reform of Japanese Higher Education." *Minerva,* 1973, 11 (3), 387–414.

This article consists of the excerpts of the minister of education's 1971 committee to reform Japanese education. It is must reading for those interested in the state of Japanese higher education.

Cummings, W. K., and Amano, I. "Japanese Higher Education." In P. G. Altbach (Ed.), *Comparative Higher Education Abroad: Bibliography and Analysis.* New York: Praeger, 1976.

This article provides a useful updating on changes and continuities in Japan's colleges and universities.

Kato, I. "Japanese Universities: Student Revolt and Reform Plans." In P. Seabury (Ed.), *Universities in the Western World.* New York: Free Press, 1975.

Kida, H. "Higher Education in Japan." *Higher Education,* 1975, 4 (3), 261–272.

Kitamura, K. *Japanese Mass Higher Education.* Paper read at the International Seminar on Higher Education. Tokyo, June 1976.

Kitamura, K., and Cummings, W. K. "The 'Big Bang' Theory and Japanese University Reform." In P. G. Altbach (Ed.), *University Reform.* Cambridge, Mass.: Schenkman, 1974.

This article discusses the reforms flowing from the 1969 student unrest with reference to the nation's previous history.

Nagai, M. *Higher Education in Japan: Its Take-Off and Crash.* Tokyo: University of Tokyo Press, 1971.

Organisation for Economic Co-operation and Development. *Japan: Reviews of National Policies for Education.* Paris, 1971.

This volume offers an assessment of Japanese education by international experts.

SWEDEN

Anderson, C. A. "Sweden Re-examines Higher Education: A Critique of the U68 Report." *Comparative Education,* 1974, 10 (3), 167–180.

Bonham, G. W. "Editorial: Sweden Tests the Future." *Change,* 1977, 9 (8), 10–13.

Duckenfield, M. "U68: Decentralized Decisions and an End to Binary System." *Times Higher Education Supplement,* May 13, 1977, p. 15.

This article is a concise and easily understandable description of the complicated higher education reforms initiated in July 1977.

U68–Higher Education: Proposals by the Swedish 1968 Educational Commission. Stockholm, 1973.

This volume is an English translation of the U68 Commission report.

UNION OF SOVIET SOCIALIST REPUBLICS

Burn, B. "Higher Education in the Soviet Union." In *Higher Education in Nine Countries: A Comparative Study of Colleges and Universities Abroad.* New York: McGraw-Hill, 1971.

This chapter offers an accurate but dated portrait of Soviet higher education.

Smith, H. *The Russians.* New York: Ballantine Book, 1976.

This book gives the flavor of Soviet higher education based on the author's four years in Russia as *New York Times* bureau chief.

Tomiak, J. J. *The Soviet Union.* Hamden, Conn.: Shoe String Press, 1972.

One chapter in this volume briefly sketches the design of higher education in the U.S.S.R.

U.S. Department of Health, Education, and Welfare. *Education in the U.S.S.R.: Recent Legislation and Statistics.* Washington, D.C.: U.S. Government Printing Office, 1975.

U.S.S.R. Ministry of Education. *Public Education in the U.S.S.R.: 1971–1973.* Moscow, 1973.

16

A Chronological History of Undergraduate Education: From Ancient Greece to the Present

The current pattern of American undergraduate education is a result of almost 2,500 years of historical evolution. The first formal schools of higher learning or advanced education existed in fifth-century B.C. Athens. Education flourished in Greece to such an extent that Rome imported the Greek system of higher learning, Greek language instruction and all. Throughout its history, Rome followed closely the model of higher education in the earlier Hellenic culture. The primary difference was that Roman higher education was more closely tied to the state than Greek higher education, which was generally a private enterprise.

With the decline of the Roman Empire in the fifth century A.D., scholarship in western Europe was eclipsed until the end of the ninth century. Much of the literature of antiquity was lost to the West either through neglect or barbarian destruction. The center of intellectual activity shifted to Constantinople and the Arab world. It was not until the twelfth century that the scholarship of the Byzantines and Moslems—and many of the lost classics that had found repository in the universities of Constantinople and the Arab world—made their way to western Europe through Spain and southern Italy.

During this period of decline in western Europe, its principal institutions for higher learning were the monasteries and the schools associated with cathedrals. In A.D. 789, the growth and development of cathedral schools and monasteries were spurred by Charlemagne, who decreed that every Frankish cathedral and monastery should establish a school for the education of both clergy and laymen. In northern Europe cathedral schools became the intellectual centers, and in southern Europe private schools served this function. Students gathered around cathedral schools and great teachers, attracting additional teachers and more students. Out of these groupings, called *studium generale,* the first universities developed during the renaissance of the twelfth century.

Bologna and Paris were the most famous of the early medieval universities. Both emphasized advanced degree preparation, notably in law and theology, respectively. In England, Oxford University was modeled on Paris, which had been established seven decades earlier, but it placed greater emphasis on the arts or bachelor's curriculum than either Paris or Bologna. A second English university founded at Cambridge by Oxford faculty and students, continued this undergraduate emphasis. By the thirteenth century, many of the major features of contemporary higher education had emerged, including degrees, faculties, colleges, courses, examinations, and commencement, although there were no endowments in the current sense, no laboratories, and, with rare exception, no university libraries or university-owned buildings. By the seventeenth century, and the colonization of North America, most of the countries of Europe had established universities on this medieval model.

The first American college was founded in 1636 by the General Court of Massachusetts. It was modeled after Emmanuel College, one of the many collegiate units at Cambridge University, but it was by no means a replica of that institution. By the time of the American Revolutionary War, more than 15 colleges had been founded, nine of which survive.

The colonial college was a teaching institution. It sought to impart to students a basic body of classical knowledge and useful intellectual skills. The students were by and large the elite of colonial society. When they finished college, they had learned the culture of their class, had been taught the morality of the Christian world, were prepared to assume socially prestigious vocations, often as clergyman, and would as a result enjoy the fruits of colonial life. Many elements of undergraduate education of that period can be found in present-day colleges, including the bachelor of arts and master's degrees, a four-year course of study, general education, prescribed programs of study, dormitory living and residential education, a concern for character, and a commitment to the principle of in loco parentis, which is now waning.

Countries other than England also had major influences on American higher education. The Scottish impact was first felt early in the eighteenth century, as Scottish doctors and scientists emigrated to the colonies and as Americans studied medicine at the University of Edinburgh. Scottish contacts encouraged American colleges to offer instruction in more practical subjects such as medicine, to expand existing courses and programs of study in the natural sciences, and to experiment further with laboratory research and inductive logic.

From France, the Enlightenment came to America in all its glory. France touched a sympathetic chord in the United States not only for being an ally in the American Revolution but also with its own revolutionary war 13 years later. The French added to the Scottish contribution in science, research, and professional education. They pioneered in the study of modern language and teacher education. France also influenced America with its literature on political theory and its revolutionary war–based, antireligious spirit, which was at least briefly popular among college students in the United States. The concepts of the French philosophers influenced Thomas Jefferson's proposal for the radical experiment in university education introduced at the University of Virginia.

A fourth country influencing higher education in America was Germany. Early in the nineteenth century, Americans began to go to Germany for advanced study. Upon completion of their studies, they usually returned to the United States to seek college faculty positions. The major German contribution to American higher education thus involved accelerating the development of graduate education and cementing the role of research in the university. But other features of contemporary American higher education that originated in Germany are the organization of the faculty and the curriculum according to academic disciplines, the major or concentration, academic freedom, wide latitude for students in choosing courses, scholarly library collections, theses, laboratory courses, and seminar instruction.

Once fully integrated into the American college by the late nineteenth century, the blend of British, Scottish, French, and German influences combined with America's own Jeffersonian democratic ideals to produce in the twentieth century a new conception of college education based upon meritocratic standards. Students were less frequently admitted to college simply because they were the socially elite of their society but more often because they represented the intellectually most capable of the society. The college student learned a basic body of knowledge, but it was no longer the classical colonial curriculum, nor was it thought to be an all-inclusive body of knowledge. More emphasis was placed on the development of intellectual skills so that college graduates would be able to keep up with an expanding body of information and facts. Moral training and education for personal growth became less prominent in the college. After graduation, the student was still able to obtain a good job, usually outside the clergy, that would enable him or her to enjoy the good life of the society.

Another important element in the development of the American college was a commitment to serve the needs of the public. Historians disagree about how well the earliest American college fulfilled this need and even about whether the college was a popular institution, but it is known that when Andrew Jackson assumed the presidency in 1828, popular feeling about higher education and the value of its program was declining. By the 1850s enrollments were decreasing not only in proportion to the population but in absolute numbers. The rationale generally offered for these declines, which lasted until the end of the Civil War, is that the colleges were failing to meet the public need for utilitarian instruction. Since that time a number of events, including the 1862 Morrill Land-Grant Act, the birth of the Wisconsin Idea in 1904, and the 1947 Report of the President' Commission on Higher Education (all described or excerpted in Appendix A), as well as the Higher

Education Act of 1965, have made public service a central mission of American higher education. As a result of that mission, contemporary colleges and universities engage in field study and experimentation; offer extension, correspondence, and off-campus study; provide technical, vocational, and recreational courses; maintain a close relationship with business and government; and undertake research on social problems.

One outcome of this collegiate commitment to serve public needs, in combination with free secondary education and compulsory high school attendance laws, has been a growth in the proportion of the American population attending college. With this development has come an acceptance of mass access to higher education and a movement toward universal access, making admission to colleges and universities now potentially available to all in the society who desire it. As a result, the notion that there is a single body of knowledge which all educated people must possess has become untenable in the face of the large number of services higher education now offers and the diversity of learner needs and interests. Moreover, the kinds of skills taught vary from student to student, and from the three R's (reading, writing, and arithmetic), to practical technical and vocational skills, to more abstract research skills. Interest in personal development has increased in importance. However, the growth in the proportion of college graduates in society throughout the twentieth century has meant that the graduates must compete harder for a relatively smaller pool of good jobs and are consequently not assured of the good life merely by a college degree.

In sum, over the past 350 years, higher education in the United States has developed through a process of addition or accretion. The Scottish, French, and German influences and the American commitment to service and utilitarianism have supplemented the functions of the colonial English college rather than replacing them. New functions, new subjects, new modes of instruction, new courses and settings, and new clienteles have been added to the old, resulting in the most comprehensive and diverse educational institutions yet developed: multiversities and multiple purpose colleges rather than the unitary institutions of old.

This chapter will highlight in a chronological fashion specific events that have contributed to the situation just sketched. The chonology is in two parts. The first concerns the antecedents of American higher education; the second chronicles the history of higher learning in this country. Asterisks beside events indicate that they are discussed more fully in Chapters 12 and 13, or excerpted in Appendix A.

Antecedents of American Higher Education

532–500 B.C. Pythagoras teaches philosophy to a group of disciples organized as a quasi-religious community. The disciples are admitted on a probationary status and are required to observe a silence varying from two to five years. Diet and clothing are also restricted. The Pythagoreans become active in public affairs in what is now southern Italy. The Pythagorean philosophy is not particularly popular in Athens, and the Pythagorean school dies out in the fourth century B.C.

460 B.C. Hippocrates is born on the Greek island of Cos. During his lifetime, he writes more than 70 books on medicine, and Cos becomes one of the earliest centers for medical training, which is carried on in an apprenticeship fashion.

445 B.C. Protagoras becomes one of the first Sophists. The Sophists are commercial Athenian philosophers who train students in the two practical skills needed for politics—dialectic (persuasion) and rhetoric (oratory). They are credited with originating the public lecture. The Sophists are criticized by Plato, Isocrates, and Socrates for their cynical, pragmatic approach to life. Other well-known Sophists include Gorgias and Prodicus.

425 B.C. Socrates (470–399 B.C.), considered a gadfly about Athens, preaches a philosophy that virtue is knowledge, utilizing a question-and-answer pedagogy which has since come to be called the Socratic method. Socrates has no school, accepts no student fees, and offers no classes. Instead he engages in daily public discussions with any who will respond to his questioning. In 399 B.C. he is condemned by an Athenian jury and executed for impiety and corrupting the young.

390 B.C. Isocrates establishes a school of higher learning. The curriculum is five to six years in length and includes gymnastics, music, literature, history, philosophy, and, in a student's final years of study, rhetoric. The program is more academic than that of the sophists and more practical than that of Plato, whose teaching is described below. Isocrates accepts any student who can pay the tuition. His students come from Athens as well as abroad.

387 B.C. Plato, a student of Socrates, establishes the Academy near Athens. The Academy, a religious association dedicated to the Muses, consists of a small piece of land containing a garden, a home for Plato, and small huts constructed by students. The Academy offers instruction in gymnastics, music, poetry, literature, mathematics, and philosophy. The curriculum is based on Plato's philosophy of society as described in *The Republic*, in which Plato identified three primary classes in Athenian society—artisans, soldiers, and philosophers. Higher education—that is, education for those 17 years of age and older—is concerned with the training of both soldiers and men of public affairs. Ages 17 to 20 are spent on military instruction. Mathematics is studied from ages 20 to 30. Ages 30 to 35 are spent in the study of philosophy. Each more advanced subject is used to screen out those unfit for further study. It is expected that the individuals ultimately studying philosophy will be few in number, and those performing best would ideally be the rulers of the society. The Academy ceases operation in A.D. 529.

335 B.C. Aristotle, the teacher of Alexander the Great, establishes the Lyceum near Athens. The Lyceum is more empirical than Plato's Academy. Aristotle divides education into three life stages. From birth through pubescence, education focuses on physical development. From puberty to 17, the student studies music, mathematics, grammar, literature, and geography. This combination of mathematics and literature is referred to as *enkuklios paideia,* a general education preparatory for the study of philosophy. Education from 17 on includes military training and study of the biological and physical sciences, ethics, rhetoric, and philosophy. In the mornings Aristotle lectures to a small, select group in advanced problems of philosophy. In the afternoons he instructs larger groups on more popular topics in the subject of rhetoric. Aristotle popularizes a technique used earlier by Protagoras—presenting a thesis and arguing each side in turn. Under Aristotle's leadership, the Lyceum also engages in scientific and historical research. The school continues operation until approximately A.D. 200.

330–314 B.C. Xenocrates, the director of Plato's Academy, requires that students complete the *enkuklios paideia* prior to entrance.

308 B.C. Zeno develops the stoic philosophy. The name is taken from the place where he customarily lectures—the *stoa pokile* or painted colonnade. The stoic philosophy emphasizes peace of mind and moral worth, both of which, according to Zeno, require avoidance of excesses.

306 B.C. Epicurus establishes a small school called the Kepos, or garden. The school is based upon a philosophy called epicureanism, which emphasizes simple pleasures, relaxation, and friendship.

c. 280 B.C. The Museum, an institute for advanced studies, is founded in Alexandria, Egypt, by Ptolemy I or Ptolemy II. Though not intended as a school, the Museum's scholars in philosophy, rhetoric, medicine, and literature attract disciples. The scholars are free from taxes and receive free meals at a common table. Associated with the Museum is the largest library in the world which, at its peak, contains at least 200,000 volumes. The Museum endures for over five centuries, failing sometime before A.D. 300.

200–100 B.C. The Ephebia, Athenian institutions for compulsory military training for men between the ages of 18 and 20, are transformed into finishing schools for the wealthy. Literary and scientific studies enter the curriculum. Foreigners are admitted.

First century B.C. Dionysus of Halicarnassus complains that Greek higher education fosters premature specialization. Some students begin to specialize in rhetoric even before completing the *enkuklios paideia* or general education.

92 B.C. Platus Gallus establishes a Latin school of rhetoric in Rome. Until this time, rhetoric, considered the most prestigious of subjects, was generally taught in the Greek language by Greeks. When expansion brought Rome into contact with Greece, Rome imported the teachers, pedagogies, and forms of education of the richer Hellenic culture. Rhetoric continued to be taught in Greek because much of the literature had not been translated into Latin, because Greek was considered an international language, and because knowledge of Greek was a sign of culture in Rome. In fact, few Roman Latin-language schools were even established in less popular subjects such as medicine, science, and philosophy.

55–46 B.C. Cicero is active in shaping Roman higher education. Among his accomplishments are three classic works on oratory—*De Oratore, Brutus,* and *Orator*—in which he surveys oratorical principles and practices. Cicero, who studied academic, epicurean, and stoic philosophy, also serves as a conduit in transmitting Greek philosophy to Rome. As a result, he is credited with bringing to Rome the rudimentary vocabulary of philosophy.

50–25 B.C. Varro, a Roman scholar, describes the *disciplinae liberae* (liberal arts) as grammar, rhetoric, and dialectic (the trivium); arithmetic, music, geometry, and astronomy (the quadrivium); and medicine and architecture. The *disciplinae liberae* is the Roman formulation of the *enkuklios paideia* adopted from Greece.

A.D. **51** Paul, the apostle of Jesus, lectures throughout the Mediterranean on the philosophy of Christianity.

69–79 Roman Emperor Vespasian establishes the equivalent of endowed chairs in rhetoric in both Greek and Latin at the University of Athens. Throughout this century numerous schools of rhetoric are founded in Rome. Perhaps the most famous is Quintilian's school, which teaches geometry, arithmetic, astronomy, and music. The last three to four years at the school are spent in the study of rhetoric.

100 Two law schools are established in Rome. The schools of law, which had no Greek precursor, grow out of apprenticeships to which Cicero is credited with adding theoretical expositions.

177–138 Emperor Hadrian establishes the University of Rome.

179 Pantaenus becomes head of the Catechetical School of Alexandria. Catechetical schools offer instruction culminating in baptism, which is necessary for admission into the church. The catechetical schools resemble the Pythagorean school. For example, the Alexandria School, which is the most advanced of its kind, offers a program based on the Greek curriculum which includes philosophy and the *enkuklios paideia*.

224–651 The Academy of Gōndēshāpūr is established in Persia. It is considered the most advanced seat of learning in the world. The Academy's curriculum includes philosophy, astronomy, ethics, theology, law, finance, religion, medicine, and government. It is through this institution that a number of the Greek classics in science and mathematics reach the Arab world and subsequently are transmitted to Western scholars. Byzantine scholars are credited with preserving the majority of the classics.

300–400 Medical education is first available in Latin.

328–373 Athanasius brings monastacism to Rome. Monasteries permit groups of people to follow the ascetic life by isolating themselves from temporal concerns and devoting themselves to religion. Christian monasteries have some of the same characteristics as the philosophical schools of Greece. In fact, early Christians refer to their beliefs as philosophy, and words like *secta, haeresis,* and *cathedra* or *thronos* are adopted from the vocabulary of the Greek philosophical schools.

334 Emperor Constantine requires that students of architecture be at least 18 years old and have completed the study of the liberal arts.

354 The catechetical schools are first governed by common rules or canons.

361 Julian forbids Christians to teach in schools of rhetoric and grammar because they do not honor the gods of the men whose writings are being taught.

410–427 Martianus Capella writes *The Marriage of Philosophy and Mercury,* in which he summarizes the state of knowledge of his age.

Capella offers what is considered an all-inclusive treatment of the seven liberal arts, which consist of the trivium and quadrivium. His book is a popular medieval text. At the time Capella writes, western European scholarship has already entered a four-century eclipse. During this period, much of the literature of antiquity is lost either through neglect or barbarian destruction. Centers of advanced intellectual activity are found in Constantinople, Persia, and the Arab world.

425 Theodosius II creates the University of Constantinople. The university has 31 faculty members in grammar, rhetoric, philosophy, and law. Grammar and rhetoric are taught in both Latin and Greek. The university operates with lapses until 1453.

460 Lawyers must pass an examination in law before they can practice in Roman courts.

493–526 Theodoric encourages a brief revival of education in Italy. There are law schools in Rome and schools of grammar and rhetoric in Milan. Boethius becomes famous as a teacher of logic, metaphysics, and ethics.

500–599 Children bound for the priesthood are required by the church to go to schools under the control of a bishop. As a result, the catechetical schools are replaced by schools with larger teaching staffs, greater physical plants, and direct bishop's control. They are called cathedral schools, and are one of two primary sources of education during the period of scholarly decline following the fall of Rome. The other is the monastery.

529 Benedict, a senator, leaves Rome in the wake of a scandal to seek a solitary, penitent life. His spiritual example attracts others and leads to the creation of the Benedictine order. Benedictines devote seven hours each day to labor—generally manual labor, though literary work is possible. Another two to five hours each day are spent in reading. As a result monasteries founded by the Benedictine order and other monasteries like them become the principal agencies for the training of scholars, for copying and preserving literature, for disseminating new manuscripts, and for collecting libraries. Most monasteries, however, emphasize study as a means of discipline, not as an end in itself; the scholarship of monks is concerned almost entirely with the scriptures and theological writing; many monks are uneducated; and many monasteries pay little or no attention to learning.

750–1100 For approximately 350 years Muslims build universities which are considered the most outstanding institutions for advanced studies of their day. They include Niẓāmīyah and Mustansiriyah in Baghdad and Cordoba, Toledo, and Granada universities in Spain. The schools offer both vocational and professional programs.

789 Charlemagne decrees that all Frankish monasteries and cathedrals should have schools for the education of clergy and orders that education also be provided for laymen. This results in the expansion of the number of educational institutions and improvement in the quality of the existing schools. The cathedral schools—which are more often located in urban areas, more willing to admit nonclerics, and more inclined to expand the curriculum beyond the narrowly ascetic subjects—become the centers of scholarly ferment leading to the formation of universities.

980 Gerbert of Aurillac (c. 945–1003), considered the greatest teacher of his time, is an instructor at the cathedral school at Rheims. He is credited with reviving the study of mathematics. The curriculum at Rheims consists of grammar, followed by dialectic and rhetoric, and then the quadrivium. Cathedral schools like Rheims are built around great scholars who teach with the approval of (or, more correctly, a license from) the local bishop. There are few cathedral schools in southern Europe, and as a result non-church schools develop in the south.

c. 1000 Bishop Fulbert (c. 960–1028) establishes the cathedral school at Chartres. He is appointed by Gerbert, now Pope Sylvester II. Fulbert's field of study is medicine, an area in which Chartres already has a considerable reputation. With the possible exception of the cathedral school in Orleans, Chartres is credited with offering the most complete and thorough program of classical studies of all of the cathedral schools during the early twelfth century. The curriculum at Chartres expands upon the classical trivium and quadrivium, utilizes previously proscribed works of the pagan Greeks and Romans, and provides no instruction in theology as a field of study. Bernard and Therry are among the best known of the Chartres teachers of this era.

1053–1080 Guibert of Nogents, an unhappy student, complains of the paucity of grammar instructors in the larger cities. The number of teachers is few and their quality poor. By the early 1100s, the subject flourishes and schools are so numerous that anyone with money can study grammar if he chooses.

1099 Abélard starts a school near Paris. His reputation as a teacher and his great differences in philosophy from William of Champeaux of the Paris cathedral school make Paris an intellectual center for students. Abélard attracts thousands of students. In fact, estimates (which are probably exaggerated) indicate that he draws as many as 30,000 students. The presence of large numbers of students draws additional teachers to Paris as well. The combination results in the creation of the University of Paris in the mid-twelfth century. The cathedral school of Chartres, only 50 miles away, pales as an intellectual center as Paris grows in stature.

1100 The University of Salerno is well known across Europe. Its fame is spread by knights returning from the crusades. Salerno has been a medical center for at least 300 years, but it is credited with becoming the first western European university when a school for the teaching of medicine is specifically created. The staff is composed of monks, and the curriculum consists of the surviving classic works in medicine, including those of Galen, Hippocrates, and Isaac Judeus.

c.1100 The University of Bologna is the first formally organized university. Its prior history is much like that of Paris. The great educational repute of Bologna as a city attracted large numbers of students, causing an influx of instructors to teach them. The University of Bologna emphasizes the study of civil and canon law. Irnerius (1067–1138) is credited with establishing the law school. Bologna also has a lesser arts curriculum concentrating upon the trivium. Grammar and rhetoric are cognate subjects that must be mastered before a student can study the law. Forty-eight months of study are required to earn the bachelor's or first arts degree. Late in the thirteenth century, Bologna adds a faculty in medicine. Theology, the other common faculty in medieval universities, is never established. Unlike other universities of this period, Bologna is largely controlled by its adult-aged students, not its faculty. Students determine even matters of lecture organization. Faculty are charged fines for violating student-created rules of classroom discipline, including being absent and giving a lecture attended by five or fewer students. Control of graduation and admission standards is left to faculty, however. Beginning in the early thirteenth century, successive popes wrest control of the university governance from both faculty and students.

1150 The great University of Paris, built from three cathedral schools, is formally organized. Paris develops faculties in canon law, theology, and arts. The pope prohibits the study of civil law, common at other schools, viewing Paris as a religious institution. In fact, Paris is best known for its school of theology. An arts curriculum is a prerequisite for study in theology, canon law, and medicine. A student can enter the arts faculty at age 12 as long as he is able to read, write, and speak Latin. The average age of entrance is 15 or 16, however. Six years of study are required to earn the first arts degree—master of arts. During these six years a student studies under several scholars, defends a thesis, becomes a bachelor or apprentice teacher, continues his studies under a master, and passes a public examination. The basic arts curriculum emphasizes Latin, logic, and grammar. There is no science or laboratory study, nor is the whole of the classical trivium and quadrivium found at Paris. Few books are available for study. There are three primary forms of instruction—lectures by licensed teachers or masters, informal lectures by bachelors and other nonlicensed teachers, and reviews in student lodgings.

1167 English scholars forced to leave France for political reasons congregate in Oxford, a small school town near London. The original Oxford program is a copy of the Paris program. In time the quadrivium and modern French are adopted. The undergraduate or arts faculty is preeminent rather than the graduate faculty.

1180 The first recorded residence officially associated with a university is established by Josse de Lordes of Paris to serve as lodging for 18 poor scholars. The creation of this "College de Dix-Huit" marks the beginning of collegiate education that links the living situation with learning. By 1500 there are 68 colleges.

1209 Three thousand students are in attendance at Oxford, but following the hanging of three students by local townspeople, there is a mass exodus to Cambridge. As the early medieval university has no buildings of its own, such moves or threats thereof are frequent. Classrooms are usually located in a teacher's home or in rented halls.

1214 At the demand of the pope, who views universities as church colonies, King John decrees that the town of Oxford atone financially and physically for the Oxford hangings. The itinerant scholars, no longer fearing local headhunters, return.

1215 The first fully prescribed arts curriculum is required at Paris.

1231 Frederick II forbids the practice or teaching of medicine anywhere within his empire by anyone without a license from the University of Salerno. He specifies a minimum period of study and an arts course prior to medical study.

1260 Sir John de Balliol, as a penance required by the church, establishes the first Oxford residential college.

1264 Walter de Merton establishes the first college at Oxford not intended solely as housing for indigent students. He grants it large landholdings, scholarship aid, and an administrative staff.

1266 Roger Bacon, a Franciscan monk and one of the best-known teachers of the Middle Ages, lectures at Oxford. He rejects the methodology of scholasticism, the principal way of discovering the truth during the Middle Ages. Scholasticism is characterized by employment of the dialectic, a form of logic which involves disputation or discrimination of truth from error in matters of opinion. Bacon favors a precursor of modern scientific method, emphasizing experimentation and observation. He also applauds the study of modern language. For these departures from tradition, Bacon is subsequently jailed for 12 years despite his devotion to Christian principles.

1300 European traffic in scholarly Moslem works ceases as political conditions bring a decline in Islamic scholarship. For more than 100 years prior to this time, Moslem scholarship has been an important source of new books and knowledge for western European scholars.

1353 King Charles IV establishes the University of Prague, the first university in central Europe.

1413 The Scottish University of Saint Andrews is founded. Its curriculum is a mix of Bologna and Paris programs.

1538 The University of St. Thomas Aquinas, the first in the New World, is founded in Santo Domingo.

1560 The first scientific academy, the Academia Secretorum Naturae, is founded in Naples. Scientific academies are a response to the absence of—and even opposition to—scientific study in the universities.

1575 Calvinists establish the University of Leiden.

1582 Calvinists found the University of Edinburgh.

1694 The University of Halle is established in Germany. Lectures are given in the vernacular rather than Latin, and scholasticism is attacked.

1737 The University of Göttingen is founded. Göttingen separates the faculties of theology and philosophy for the first time.

The American Experience

1636*¹ Harvard College, a Puritan institution and the first American college, is founded by the General Court of Massachusetts. The new college is patterned after Emmanuel College at Cambridge University in England. Students are required to pass an oral examination and write an essay in Latin to be admitted to the col-

¹Asterisked events are described more fully in other chapters or Appendix A as noted.

lege. The students are in their mid-teens. The original fully-prescribed curriculum is based on the classical trivium and quadrivium and consists of logic, Greek, rhetoric, astronomy, Aramaic, Hebrew, Syriac, ethics and politics, mathematics, history, botany, and catechism (see Appendix A for details). All of the later colonial colleges will have similar academic programs and be controlled by Protestant religious sects.

1636 The first college preparatory school is started in Charlestown, Massachusetts, to prepare students for the first year of college.

1642 Harvard awards the first nine bachelor's degrees in America. A master of arts degree is awarded after completing three years of further study beyond the bachelor's degree.

1647 The Massachusetts legislature directs towns of over 100 households to establish a school to prepare students for college. Towns half that size are required only to teach reading and writing.

1692 A second American college, William and Mary, is established. It is influenced by the Scottish conception of higher education. Greater emphasis is placed on mathematics, history, and science than at Harvard. By the time of the Revolutionary War, William and Mary is experimenting with curricular election and an honors code.

1728 Harvard establishes a professorship in mathematics and natural science.

1745 Knowledge of arithmetic is made a requirement for college entrance at Yale College.

1756 The College of Philadelphia introduces a more utilitarian curriculum than the other colonial colleges. Three years is required to earn a degree. Equal portions of the curriculum are devoted to classical languages; mathematics and science; and logic, metaphysics, and ethics. New subjects, such as political science, history, chemistry, navigation, trade and commerce, zoology, mechanics, and agriculture, are added to the curriculum.

1765 The College of Philadelphia establishes the first chair in medicine in the colonies.

1770 Two literary societies are created at Princeton. The extracurricular literary societies quickly become popular at other colleges as well. They are essentially debating clubs designed to provide the intellectual stimulation lacking in the formal college curriculum, which is dominated by recitation. The literary societies are controlled and financed by students. Until the Civil War they remain a center of student interest, rivaling and occasionally undermining a college's undergraduate program.

1776 Phi Beta Kappa is started at William and Mary College.

1779 William and Mary College establishes the first chair in law in the United States and allows a small amount of curricular election.

1783 Yale rejects an otherwise fully qualified woman applicant for admission because of her sex.

1785 President Ezra Stiles of Yale adopts one of the first grading systems in the colonies. It is a four-point grading system which contains the following categories: *optimi,* second *optimi, inferiores (boni),* and *pejores.*

1785 The first state college, the University of Georgia, is chartered.

1789 The first Catholic college, Georgetown, is established.

1802 The U.S. Military Academy, which emphasizes technical education, is founded. It is the first college to offer formal instruction in engineering.

1815 Three American students—Edward Everett, Edward Cogswell, and George Ticknor—seek further education in Germany—the first of some 10,000 over the next century.

1819 Based upon his German experiences, George Ticknor, now a Harvard professor, criticizes the American college for the poor quality of its libraries, the exclusion of modern languages from the curriculum, and the lack of specialized departments.

1821 Emma Willard starts an institution of higher learning for women in Troy, New York.

c. 1823 The blackboard is used by an instructor at Bowdoin College for the first time.

1824* The University of Virginia opens. Students are offered eight possible fields of study ranging from anatomy and medicine to ancient languages. Degree programs within each field are completely prescribed. However, nondegree programs that allow students to choose whatever courses they please are also offered. Award of degrees is based entirely upon the passage of general examinations within each field of study. There is no universitywide degree (see Appendix A).

1824 Rensselaer Polytechnic Institute, the first entirely technical school, is founded to instruct children of farmers and mechanics in theoretical and mechanical sciences. Rensselaer becomes the first college to offer extension courses and laboratory instruction.

1825 Miami University in Ohio permits the substitution of modern languages, practical mathematics, and political economy for certain subjects in the traditional or classical curriculum.

1825 President Philip Lindsley of the University of Nashville adopts a curriculum accenting utilitarian, vocational, and research concerns.

1825 Major changes are made in the Harvard curriculum as a result of the first institutional self-study. The changes include (1) departmentalization of faculty and curriculum, (2) permitting juniors and seniors a small number of elective courses, (3) establishment of partial courses, which allow nondegree students to study only selected parts of the curriculum, particularly modern languages, and (4) introduction of some self-pacing of the curriculum.

1825 The first Greek letter social fraternity, Kappa Alpha, is created at Union College.

1826 Union College introduces a scientific curriculum, which includes modern languages, mathematics, and sciences, as an alternative to the classical program. The *parallel* course, as it is called, is a nondegree program.

1828* The faculty at Yale responds to the growing criticism of the American college. The purpose of college, according to the Yale Report (see Appendix A for excerpts), is to provide "the discipline and furniture of the mind." *Discipline* refers to the need to expand the powers of the mental faculties; and *furniture* speaks to the need to fill the mind with knowledge. The Yale faculty indicates that each of the subjects in its classical curriculum has a special role in providing discipline and knowledge. Their report is a rebuff to critics and institutions offering technical or partial courses of study. The most important subject in the Yale curriculum is said to be the classical languages, which provide "the most effectual discipline of mental faculties." Modern languages are dismissed as being of lesser educational value. The report affirms the use of lecture and recitation modes of instruction while rejecting the study of professional subjects in college. Breadth of learning gained in classical study is seen as the best preparation for any profession. The mission of the college is sharply defined. The faculty feel that institutions other than colleges should provide the popular studies that are being demanded of institutions such as Yale.

c. 1828 Kenyon College introduces faculty advising. Each student is teamed with one member of the Kenyon faculty.

1830 Columbia University adopts a program which includes both science and modern languages.

1831 Ohio University establishes a program to prepare public school teachers.

1833 Oberlin College is the first college to admit women to a formerly all-male institution.

1835 Rensselaer Institute awards the first engineering degree.

1836 The first degree-granting women's college, Wesleyan Female College of Macon, Georgia, is founded.

1837 The People's College is established in New York state to provide science and technical education to craftsmen.

1839 The first normal school for the preparation of teachers is established in Lexington, Massachusetts. It later relocates to Framingham, Massachusetts.

1845 Union College becomes the first liberal arts college to inaugurate an engineering program.

1846 Yale makes two faculty appointments in agriculture.

1847 The tuition-free Academy of New York City, later City College of New York, is chartered by the New York state legislature.

1847 Yale takes the first tentative steps toward the creation of a graduate school.

1847 Harvard creates the Lawrence Scientific School, which emphasizes the study of geology and zoology. Instruction does not initially lead to a bachelor's degree. The educational requirements for admission are considerably less than those of Harvard College. Students are required only to have had a good common school or elementary school education.

1849 Avery College for blacks begins in Pennsylvania.

1850 Under the leadership of President Francis Wayland, Brown University adopts a curriculum including a nondegree partial course, variable student loads, an increased number of science courses, a modified extension program, a greater number of free electives, and a new degree to be awarded for nonclassical study — the Ph.B. Insufficient funding, declining quality in students, and a lack of public support end the program four years later.

1851 A business school is established at the University of Louisiana.

1851 Harvard awards the first bachelor of science degrees to students who complete programs in the sciences. The standards for admission in B.S. programs are lower than B.A. courses.

1852 In his inaugural address as president of the University of Michigan, Henry Tappan proposes that the university develop extensive programs in the fine arts, natural sciences, and utilitarian subjects; that students be permitted elective courses; that the degree of bachelor of science be awarded in science programs; and that graduate work be added to the activities of the university. Tappan's 11-year tenure also includes experimentation with an experimental college comparable to today's junior colleges.

1852 Yale and Harvard engage in the first intercollegiate sports contest, a boat race.

1853 The University of Michigan offers the first earned master's degree—that is, a degree based upon completing a particular program rather than simply putting in a specified number of years beyond the bachelor's degree.

1854 Yale establishes what will be called the Sheffield Scientific School in 1861; a unit separate from the rest of the college like the Lawrence Scientific School at Harvard. It offers a two-year course of study that emphasizes applied chemistry.

1854 The American Missionary Society is formed to bring higher education to blacks. Within six years it establishes six black colleges.

1855 The first state agricultural college, Michigan State University, is established.

1861 Yale University awards the first Ph.D. degree.

1862* Congress passes the Morrill Land-Grant Act (see Appendix A), which authorizes the sale of federal lands to provide funds for the support of colleges offering instruction in "agriculture and mechanic arts without excluding other scientific and classical studies and including military tactics."

1868* Cornell University opens its doors. The motto of the new college is "any person . . . any study" (see Appendix A). Science is made an integral part of the curriculum. Students are given a wide choice in subjects for study as well as manual labor experiences. The group system, which offers students a choice of internally coherent courses of study, is adopted.

1868 The University of Missouri creates a school of education.

1869 President Charles W. Eliot, in his inaugural address at Harvard, proclaims his belief in the elective system (for excerpts, see Appendix A). Within six years, most of the required courses in the Harvard curriculum are relegated to the freshman year.

1869 Charles Kendall Adams emphasizes seminar instruction in an experimental program at the University of Michigan.

1870 The variable quality of candidates for admission causes the University of Michigan to begin periodically to visit and inspect local high schools.

1870 The Harvard catalog begins to list courses by subject rather than by the student class for which they are intended.

1870 College enrollments equal 1.7 percent of the 18- to 21-year-old population.

1876* The Johns Hopkins University, the first American research university, is established in Baltimore. The new school, emphasizing graduate education, is modeled after the German research university. At Johns Hopkins, an undergraduate education is three years long. Laboratories and seminars are popular modes of instruction (for background, see Appendix A).

1878 The Johns Hopkins catalog of 1877–78 makes the first known reference to the terms *major* and *minor*.

1878 New York state establishes a system of uniform high school examinations, called Regents Examinations.

1881 Harvard begins to offer term-length courses, called *half courses*.

1885 The first regional accrediting association, the New England Association of Colleges and Secondary Schools, is established.

1886 Chapel attendance is made voluntary at Harvard.

1888 Clark University, an institution specializing in graduate education, is established. Its first president is G. Stanley Hall, a Johns Hopkins–trained psychologist.

1890 A second Morrill Land-Grant Act is passed by Congress. The legislation provides for an annual federal appropriation to land-grant colleges and encouragement for similar state support.

1890 President Eliot merges the graduate and undergraduate faculties at Harvard.

1890 Harvard establishes the Board of Freshman Advisers, a body specifically concerned with counseling new students.

1891 The Educational Exchange of Greater Boston, a free-standing brokerage organization, is created to advise and counsel adult students.

1892* The National Education Association appoints a Committee of Ten on college and school relations to help standardize the high school curriculum (for excerpts from the committee report, see Appendix A).

1892 With money from John D. Rockefeller and leadership from William Rainey Harper, the University of Chicago is created. Many of the curricular innovations of the waning century find a home at Chicago. The university develops high-quality graduate and research programs, a residential undergraduate college like that of Oxford and Cambridge, and programs of service to society.

1896 The lower-division program at the University of Chicago is designated the "Junior College." After two years of experience with this program, the university awards associate's degrees.

1898 The first professional school of forestry is created at Cornell University.

1899 Yale permits undergraduates to include law and medical courses in their programs.

1900 College enrollments equal 4 percent of the 18- to 21-year-old population.

1901 The first College Entrance Examination Board tests are administered.

1901 The first public junior college is established in Joliet, Illinois.

1902 Charles W. Eliot persuades the Harvard faculty to abandon the four-year requirement for the B.A. By 1906, 41 percent of Harvard's students graduate in three to three and one half years.

1904* Charles Van Hise, president of the University of Wisconsin, proposes the "Wisconsin Idea" (see Appendix A). The state of Wisconsin is to be regarded as the campus of the university. Faculty expertise is applied to state problems. The University becomes involved with the state legislature, local government, civic groups, and the office of the governor. Higher education is expanded throughout the state as the university offers extension and correspondence courses on popular topics and technical subjects.

1904 City College of New York requires all new faculty to hold a Ph.D.

1905 The Columbia University faculty, under the leadership of Nicholas Murray Butler, adopts the "professional option" plan, which allows students to enroll jointly in professional school programs and the undergraduate college with a time savings in earning both degrees.

1906 The University of Cincinnati establishes the first cooperative work-study program in its school of engineering.

1906 The Carnegie Foundation for the Advancement of Teaching establishes minimum institutional criteria to qualify institutions for a faculty pension program. These include having six full-time faculty, department chairmen with Ph.Ds, a four-year liberal arts program, a secondary school completion requirement for admission, and a nondenominational orientation.

1908 The Carnegie Foundation for the Advancement of Teaching develops the "Carnegie Unit" as a standard measure of time exposure by students to high school subjects.

1909 City College of New York inaugurates the first night-school program leading to a bachelor's degree.

1909 President A. Lawrence Lowell introduces a system of concentration or majors and general education distribution requirements at Harvard. Students are required to take six year-long courses in three fields outside the major area.

1910 Reed College, stressing independent study and scholarship, is founded. Students are required to pass a comprehensive examination and write a senior thesis before graduating.

1910 President Lowell of Harvard introduces a comprehensive examination in the major. Students who do well on the examination graduate with honors. The Harvard tutorial system is instituted to help students prepare for the examination.

1913 A committee of the National Education Association recommends reducing the common breadth component of undergraduate education by at least two years.

1914 During the presidency of Alexander Meiklejohn, the first survey course, Social and Economic Institutions, is created at Amherst College.

1919* A general education core course, "Contemporary Civilization," is adopted at Columbia (see case study in Chapter 12).

1920 Reserve Officer Training Corps (ROTC) is established by the National Defense Act.

1920 College enrollments equal 8 percent of the 18- to 21-year-old population.

1921* Arthur E. Morgan introduces work-study or cooperative education at a liberal arts college, Antioch College (case study in Chapter 12).

1921* President Frank Aydelotte develops an honors program at Swarthmore College (case study in Chapter 12).

1925* The Oxbridge cluster college concept is put into operation in the establishment of the Claremont Colleges (case study in Chapter 12).

1927* Alexander Meiklejohn establishes an experimental college at the University of Wisconsin (case study in Chapter 12).

1928 The Harvard Houses, residential academic units, are created.

1928* Many years of undergraduate reform begin at the University of Chicago (case study in Chapter 12).

1928 Pasadena High School and Pasadena Junior College merge to form a four-year institution containing grades 11 to 14.

1929 Sarah Lawrence College, one of the earliest progressive schools, is founded (for a discussion of progressivism, see Chapter 1).

1930 College enrollments equal 12 percent of the 18- to 21-year-old population.

1932* Bennington College begins operation with a curriculum emphasizing the progressive philosophy of education (case study in Chapter 12).

1932* The General College, a two-year general education division, is established at the University of Minnesota (case study in Chapter 12).

1933 Black Mountain College, an experimental arts college, is founded.

1935 Framingham Teachers College, the first normal school, offers the bachelor of science degree in education.

1937* Stringfellow Barr and Scott Buchanan introduce the Great Books curriculum at St. John's College in Annapolis, Maryland (for case study, see Chapter 12; for the list of current Great Books, see Appendix A).

1941 College enrollments equal 18 percent of the 18- to 21-year-old population.

1944 The G.I. Bill, Serviceman's Readjustment Act, is passed by Congress. This legislation, providing direct financial assistance for returning soldiers to attend college, enables 2.25 million veterans to enroll at 2,000 different colleges.

1945* The Committee on the Objectives of a General Education in a Free Society produces the "Redbook" at Harvard (for case study, see Chapter 12; for excerpts, see Appendix A).

1947* The President's Commission on Higher Education for Democracy issues its report. The report calls for tuition-free education for all youth through the first two years of college; financial assistance for needy but competent students in tenth through fourteenth grades; lower tuition charges in upper-division, graduate, and professional schools; expansion of adult education; elimination of barriers to equal access in higher education; development of community colleges; and rededication of the curriculum to general education (for excerpts, see Appendix A).

1951 Advanced placement or advanced study programs begin at 12 colleges and secondary schools under Ford Foundation auspices.

1951 Early admission programs that admit students to college after the junior year of secondary school are initiated by 12 colleges with Ford Foundation support.

1957 The Soviet Union launches Sputnik. This Russian space achievement spurs the development of accelerated science and language instruction in the United States.

1958 The National Defense Education Act provides for undergraduate loans, graduate fellowships, institutional aid for teacher education, and broad support for education in the sciences, mathematics, and foreign languages.

1958* The 4–1–4 calendar, with its credit-bearing winter miniterm for intensive study or field study is proposed in the 1958 Hampshire College Plan. In 1960 it is adopted at Eckerd College (see case study of Hampshire in Chapter 13).

1959–60* In the aftermath of Sputnik, two colleges offering rigorous honors programs—Oakland University (Michigan) and New College (Florida)—are established (see case studies in Chapter 12).

1960 Framingham Teachers College, the first normal school, becomes Framingham State College. It is authorized to offer a range of B.A. and B.S. degrees and within a year is permitted to award master's degrees.

1963 College Board scores begin to decline nationally.

1964 Massive student disorder at the University of California, Berkeley, brings campus unrest of the 1960s to national attention.

1964 College enrollments equal 40 percent of the 18- to 21-year-old population.

1965 Upward Bound, a program to prepare students with academic potential but lacking in motivation or academic skills for college, is developed by the Carnegie Corporation and the Office of Economic Opportunity.

1965 The Higher Education Act of 1965 provides institutional aid to private and public colleges as well as individual students. Included in the bill is money for research, libraries, recruitment of disadvantaged students, educational facilities, developing colleges, community colleges, occupational education, and improvement of undergraduate education. Student aid programs include educational opportunity grants for those with low income, guaranteed student loans, work-study assistance, and fellowship grants.

1965* The Experimental College (Tussman College), modeled on the Meiklejohn College at Wisconsin, begins four years of operation at the University of California, Berkeley (see case study in Chapter 13).

1965* The first free university, a student-organized and student-run experimental college, is created in Berkeley (see case study in Chapter 13).

1965* The University of California, Santa Cruz, combining a collegiate structure and disciplinary organization, is founded (see case study in Chapter 13).

1966 New York state approves the SEEK (Search for Education, Elevation, and Knowledge) program, providing for academic, psychological, and financial assistance at senior colleges at the City University of New York to students from designated poverty areas with high school diplomas but lacking in qualifications for university entrance.

1966 The Keller Plan for self-paced learning is developed.

1967 The College Level Examination Program, which tests subject proficiency at college standards, is established.

1967 The Carnegie Commission on Higher Education is formed to study the structure, functions, financing, and future of higher education.

1968 Executive Order 11375 requires that organizations with federal contracts agree not to discriminate against employees or applicants for employment on the basis of sex, race, color, religion, or place of national origins. The Department of Labor is charged with issuing rules and regulations and ensuring compliance, which leads to the establishment of affirmative action regulations.

1968 A program of "Special Services for Disadvantaged Students," including remedial instruction, counseling, and support services, is created by the Higher Education Amendments of 1968.

1968* An "early college," Simon's Rock, in Great Barrington, Massachusetts, offers a college education to 16- to 20-year-olds (see case study in Chapter 13).

1969* At the urging of students, Brown University radically alters its undergraduate program (see case study in Chapter 13).

1970 The Regents External degree, awarded entirely on the basis of examinations and college-equivalent credit, is created by New York state.

1970* Hampshire College, a cooperative endeavor on the part of four neighboring colleges in the Connecticut River Valley, admits its first class. Graduation is based exclusively upon passing six comprehensive examinations (see case study in Chapter 13).

1970 City University of New York abandons selective admissions in favor of open admissions. All high school graduates are guaranteed admission to some branch of the university no matter what their previous academic performance may have been.

1970 Forty-eight percent of the 18- to 21-year-old population is enrolled in college.

1971 An HEW task force directed by Frank Newman urges an expansion of noncollege educational opportunities, a break with the four-year lockstep pattern of college education, off-campus programs, diversification of college faculty, commitment to minority education, equality for women, new educational enterprises, greater college autonomy, and revival of college missions (see excerpts in Chapter 11).

1971* Metropolitan State University, a noncampus, external degree college, is established by the Minnesota legislature (see case study in Chapter 13).

1972 The Fund for the Improvement of Postsecondary Education and the National Institute of Education are established by the Education Amendments of 1972.

1972* Sterling College, a liberal arts institution in Sterling, Kansas, introduces a competency-based undergraduate curriculum (see case study in Chapter 13).

1973* The Capital Higher Education Service, Inc., a free standing educational brokerage organization, is created in Hartford, Connecticut (see case study in Chapter 13).

1974 The U.S. Supreme Court declares moot the case of *De Funis* v. *Odegaard,* which challenges the right of institutions of higher education to utilize different standards for affirmative action minority admissions.

1975 California administers a statewide proficiency examination to allow students to leave high school early.

1976 The Virginia Board of Education votes that, beginning in 1978, high school students be required to achieve minimum proficiency levels in reading, writing, speaking, computational skills, and U.S. history and culture in order to graduate.

1976 In *Bakke* v. *The Regents of the University of California,* the California Supreme Court rules that affirmative action admissions at the University of California, Davis, medical school violate the equal protection clause of the Fourteenth Amendment of the United States Constitution. The Regents appeal the decision to the U.S. Supreme Court.

1977 The Carnegie Foundation for the Advancement of Teaching issues recommendations about undergraduate education in *Missions of the College Curriculum: A Contemporary Review with Suggestions,* for which Frederick Rudolph's book, *Curriculum: A History of the American Undergraduate Course of Study Since 1636,* and the present handbook are companions (see Chapter 11).

References

Adelman, H. *The Holiversity: A Perspective on the Wright Report.* Toronto: New Press, 1973.

Aries, P. *Centuries of Childhood: A Social History of Family Life.* New York: Random House, 1962.

Brubacher, J. S., and Rudy, W. *Higher Education in Transition: A History of American Colleges and Universities, 1636–1976.* (3rd ed.) New York: Harper & Row, 1976. This book offers a comprehensive general history and contemporary retrospective on higher education in the United States.

Butts, R. F. *Education of the West: A Formative Chapter in the History of Civilization.* (Revised ed.) New York: McGraw-Hill, 1973.

Carnegie Foundation for the Advancement of Teaching. *Missions of the College Curriculum: A Contemporary Review with Suggestions.* San Francisco: Jossey-Bass, 1977.

Cheit, E. F. *The Useful Arts and the Liberal Tradition.* New York: McGraw-Hill, 1975.

Clarke, M. L. *Higher Education in the Ancient World.* London: Routledge and Kegan Paul, 1971. This volume describes the development of higher education from Greece to the beginning of the Middle Ages.

Dressel, P. *The Undergraduate Curriculum in Higher Education*. New York: Center for Applied Research in Education, Inc., 1966.

Haskins, C. H. *The Rise of Universities*. Ithaca, N.Y.: Cornell University Press, 1967.
This brief book (104 pages) provides a sketch of university life during the Middle Ages.

Hofstadter, R., and Smith, W. *American Higher Education: A Documentary History*. (2 vols.) Chicago: University of Chicago Press, 1961.
These volumes contain most of the critical documents in the history of U.S. higher education, or excerpts thereof, accompanied with background glosses.

Rashdall, H. *The Universities of Europe in the Middle Ages*. (3 vols.) Oxford, England: Clarendon Press, 1936.
Rashdall is the standard reference on higher education in the Middle Ages.

Rudolph, F. *The American College and University: A History*. New York: Knopf, 1962.
This volume offers a very readable and entertaining general history of American higher education.

Rudolph, F. *Curriculum: A History of the American Undergraduate Course of Study Since 1636*. San Francisco: Jossey-Bass, 1977.
Written in the same enjoyable style as his earlier book, this volume concentrates on the history of undergraduate curriculum in America.

Rudy, W. *The Evolving Liberal Arts Curriculum*. New York: Teachers College Press, 1960.
Rudy discusses United States curriculum trends between 1825 and 1955 and institutional and regional differences.

Schachner, N. *The Medieval Universities*. (Perpetua ed.) New York: A. S. Barnes, 1962.
This volume is much longer than Haskins and much shorter than Rashdall, permitting a combination of history and flavor.

Sloan, D. *The Scottish Enlightenment and the American College Ideal*. New York: Teachers College Press, 1971.

Thwing, C. F. *A History of Higher Education in America*. Englewood Cliffs, N.J.: Prentice Hall, 1906.
This is an excellent but little-used history of the early American colleges.

Veysey, L. R. *The Emergence of the American University*. Chicago: University of Chicago Press, 1965.
This book describes and analyzes the period in which the modern American university emerged, 1870–1910.

Wieruszowski, H. *The Medieval University: Masters, Students, Learning*. Princeton, N.J.: Nos Reinhold, 1966.

"The Yale Report of 1828." In R. Hofstadter and W. Smith. *American Higher Education Documentary History*. Vol. 1. Chicago: University of Chicago Press, 1961.

Glossary

Abitur is the test-based secondary-school completion certificate of the Federal Republic of Germany (West Germany).

Absolute grading involves evaluating all students by means of common, fixed standards or specified criteria.

Academic advising is guidance or counseling concerned with the intellective or cognitive components of the curriculum, such as course selection, prerequisites, major cognates, requirements, and student performance and progress.

Academic time refers to college calendars and the number of years of study required for a student to earn a college degree.

Achievement tests seek to measure actual student accomplishment or attainment in one or more subject areas, such as mathematics or foreign language.

Advanced disciplinary courses are specialized courses within a discipline above the introductory level, such as effects of early environmental deprivation (psychology) or endocrine physiology (biology).

Advanced learning skills are the abilities a student needs to sustain college-level study and continued learning throughout life. These skills, which require a firm foundation in the three R's and other basic skills, include mathematics through geometry and second-year algebra, foreign language, English composition, and proficiency in some physical activities.

Advanced Placement Program is a College Entrance Examination Board endeavor that allows high school students to earn college credits. It involves college-level courses in high school and standardized tests at the completion of each course to assess whether there has been college-level learning. The examinations are prepared and graded by committees of high school and college faculty in 13 subject areas.

Advising refers to counseling available to students or potential students, directly or indirectly concerned with the undergraduate curriculum.

Affective learning is learning associated with emotions and feelings.

American College Testing Program is a college aptitude examination covering English, mathematics, science, and social science, taken by 51 percent of 1976 college freshmen.

Apprenticeships involve on-the-job training for specific types of work under the tutelage of skilled workers.

Aptitude tests seek to measure readiness for or disposition toward a particular form of learning, such as a specified vocation or college study.

Arts and sciences colleges refer to institutions or units within larger institutions that offer programs in the fine arts, humanities, natural sciences, and social sciences.

Audio-tutorial instruction is a form of programmed education utilizing a tape-recorded study guide supplemented with texts, films, and other learning materials. This mode of instruction, which blends independent study with in-class meetings, was created by S. N. Postlethwait in 1961.

Baccalauréat de base is a certificate of secondary-school completion in France.

Basic skills and knowledge refers to the information and skills a student needs to commence college study.

Binary system refers to a two-level higher education system composed of a closed group of elite universities and a more open group of lower-status postsecondary institutions.

Blanket grading is the practice of giving all students in a class the same grade.

Block calendar, also called the modular calendar or intensive course calendar, is an arrangement whereby students study one course at a time.

Block release is a means of attending higher education part time in Great Britain, in which students study full time for a period of six to twelve weeks during the work year.

Brokerage organizations provide people who are not attending institutions of higher education with low- or no-cost outreach advising consisting of education and career information; counseling; referrals to higher education, proprietary schools, human service agencies and industrial education programs; assessment of prior experience; and advocacy of a student's case for admission or advanced standing in a desired program. Their basic objective is to aid people in making decisions based on full and impartial information about whether and how best to seek additional education.

Career advising is guidance or counseling concerned with career planning, occupational preparation, and job placement.

Career education is education intended to develop the skills necessary to live a full life that revolves about satisfying and meaningful work.

Career-oriented liberal arts majors are concentrations which group liberal arts subjects around work-related themes or integrate liberal arts and professional/technical courses of study. Examples of such majors include energy studies, sociology of business, and human services.

Carnegie unit was developed in 1908 by The Carnegie Foundation for the Advancement of Teaching as one way of standardizing the secondary school curriculum. It was defined as "any one of four courses carried five days a week during the secondary school year."

Catechetical schools were Catholic schools started during the second century A.D. to offer instruction culminating in baptism.

Certificate programs are college courses of study that do not lead to degrees and are generally, though not universally, shorter than degree courses. They are usually highly specialized career programs, and they are occasionally geared for admission to licensure or career entrance tests.

Challenge tests are examinations created by an individual college covering subject matter equivalent to that offered in a course. Students who pass challenge tests are commonly exempted from or given credit for the course counterpart of the examination.

Closed-book tests seek to discover exactly what students have learned. Textbooks, notebooks, and other forms of assistance cannot be used during the test.

Cluster colleges are institutions clustered geographically about one

another that work together cooperatively as a group. The six
Claremont Colleges are an example of such an arrangement.

Cognates are related courses outside of a particular discipline needed
for work in that discipline, for example, mathematics for
physics.

Cognitive learning is associated with the intellect as opposed to the
emotions or psychomotor facilities.

College refers to both freestanding undergraduate institutions and
undergraduate schools within large universities.

College Level Examination Program (CLEP) is a form of credit by
examination administered by the College Entrance Examination Board, intended originally for adults beginning college
or resuming college study after a hiatus, who acquired the
equivalent of college learning through experience, work, or
self-education. Today 40 percent of CLEP takers are 19 years
old or younger.

College Proficiency Examination is a New York state program, now
available nationwide through the American College Testing
Program, that offers more than 40 examinations in college-
equivalent subjects varying from arts and sciences to education and nursing.

Common school was the name used for public elementary schools
until early in this century.

Community and junior colleges are two-year institutions offering a variety of programs that might include credit-free instruction,
liberal arts courses, professional/technical courses, degree
and nondegree programs, and adult and continuing education. They are also referred to as "two-year colleges" in this
book.

Community resource people live or work in the immediate area surrounding a college and have the expertise to engage in student teaching or advising. They include community professionals, business and civic leaders, retired professionals, and
faculty spouses.

Compensatory education attempts to enhance students' skills, knowledge, and attitudes—not necessarily to qualify them for more
advanced academic programs but simply to build basic new
strengths.

Competency-based education places emphasis on learning outcomes and student attainment of them rather than on the experiences (courses) that comprise a curriculum or on a prespecified amount of seat time that students must put in to earn a degree. In competency programs, students ideally earn a degree whenever and however they achieve the learning outcomes required for graduation. Sterling and Alverno Colleges are examples of institutions with such programs.

Comprehensive examinations test students in broad areas such as general education or major studies. They are written and/or oral examinations covering material taught in more than one course and usually administered to all the members of one college class.

Comprehensive universities and colleges include both comprehensive universities and colleges I and comprehensive universities and colleges II (see below).

Comprehensive universities and colleges I are institutions that offer a liberal arts program as well as several other professional/technical programs. Many offer master's degrees; none offer doctorates. All had at least two professional programs and 2,000 students in 1970.

Comprehensive universities and colleges II are institutions that offer liberal arts programs and at least one professional or occupational program. All had at least 1,000 students in 1970.

Compression of undergraduate programs is a mechanism for reducing the time necessary to earn a bachelor's degree by one or more years by compacting the course of study.

Computer-assisted instruction allows students to progress in their studies at their own pace by working individually with a programmed computer.

Computer-managed instruction involves the use of a computer for testing, diagnosis, and prescription purposes, but not for actual instruction.

Concentration. See *major.*

Concurrent high school–college enrollment occurs when high school students attend class at both high school and college during one or more terms.

Consecutive high school–college enrollment involves alternating high school and college attendance.

Continuing education unit was created in 1968 to measure "all significant learning experiences of postsecondary level for which degree credit is not earned." One continuing education unit is awarded for every ten hours of continuing or nondegree credit education. It is intended primarily as a work credential.

Contract learning involves a pact between a student and one or more faculty members outlining a course of studies to be pursued over an agreed-upon period of time. The course of studies may include formal courses, independent study, and experiential learning.

Cooperative education joins classroom instruction with work, generally, though not always, in the student's major area, on a continuing and alternating basis. Work, which is with rare exception off campus, and education may be concurrent or consecutive. In consecutive programs, the most frequent type of cooperative education, periods of full-time work are alternated with periods of full-time study. In concurrent programs, the student works part time or full time while attending classes part time.

Core general education programs are tightly knit, yet broad and often interdisciplinary, series of courses, usually required of all students.

Course overload occurs when a full-time student enrolls in more than the institutionally recommended or prescribed number of courses or credits per term.

Covert grading involves evaluating students but not informing them of their grades.

Credit is a time-based quantitative measure assigned to courses or course-equivalent learning. A credit can be defined as 50 minutes of instruction per week for a term. As terms vary in length, credits are usually referred to as semester or quarter credits. *Unit* and *credit hour* are synonyms for *credit*.

Credit by examination refers to the practice of granting students college credit for passing tests based on the subject matter of college courses they have not attended.

Cultural Revolution was a period of ideological and social upheaval in the People's Republic of China from 1966 to 1970.

Curriculum is the body of courses and formally established learning experiences presenting the knowledge, principles, values, and skills that are the intended consequences of the formal education offered by a college.

Deferred electives are college electives reserved for use later in life rather than all electives being required in a block for college graduation.

Degrees are grades or ranks which colleges and universities confer upon students for their educational attainments.

Developmental education. See *compensatory education.*

Diploma project is the commonly required Russian equivalent of the senior thesis in the United States.

Diplôme d'Etudes Universitaires Generales (DEUG) is the first French university degree, obtained after two years of study.

Disciplinarum libri (liberal arts) consisted of grammar, rhetoric, and dialectic (the trivium); arithmetic, music, geometry, and astronomy (the quadrivium); and medicine and architecture. It was the Roman formulation of the *enkuklios paideia.*

Disciplinary major, the most common form of major, is a concentration in an area having a unique body of knowledge and method of inquiry. Biology, English, and sociology are examples of disciplinary majors.

Discipline refers to a discrete body of knowledge with a characteristic regimen for investigation and analysis, such as history, English, and biology.

Disputation was a form of instruction popular in the colonial college. The instructor offered a propostion, and a student was selected to defend or attack it. The student defined the relevant terms and made an argument by use of Aristotelean syllogisms, and then other students argued the counter position and the disputant responded in opposition.

Distribution general education requirements are designed to ensure that each student takes a minimum number of courses or credits in specified subject areas. There are four forms of distribution requirements—prescribed distribution requirements, minimally prescribed or "smorgasbord" distribution requirements, recommended distribution guidelines, and a small group of programs which can be described only as miscellaneous.

Doctorate-granting universities include both doctorate-granting universities I and doctorate-granting universities II (see below).

Doctorate-granting universities I awarded 40 or more Ph.D.s in 1969–70 or received at least $3 million in total federal financial support in 1969–70 or 1970–71.

Doctorate-granting universities II are institutions awarding at least ten Ph.D.s, with the exception of several embryonic institutions.

Dossier is a nongraded transcript listing student educational activities and containing faculty and student evaluations and examples of student work.

Double major simply involves completing the requirements of two majors.

Dropping out is leaving college on one's own volition without receiving a degree and without returning at a later date.

Early admission refers to the practice of enrolling students in college prior to completing high school.

Elective general education curriculum exists when no general education program is prescribed by a college. The student can create a general education based on whatever courses he or she selects or may simply neglect general education.

Enkuklios paideia was a general education curriculum in mathematics and philosophy developed in Greece and also employed in Rome. It was considered preparatory for the study of philosophy. See *disciplinarum libri*.

Essay test is an examination in which one or more questions must be answered with a descriptive, analytic, or interpretive composition.

Essentialism is a philosophy that holds that education should be based upon an "essential" or prescribed body of knowledge dealing with the heritage of humankind. The subject matter tends to be abstract or conceptual rather than applied or practical. There is no one essentialist curriculum; however, all essentialist curricula are teacher centered, utilize tried-and-true forms of pedagogy, and are premised on the assumption that learning is hard work which is often done unwillingly by students.

Experiential learning refers to learning acquired outside the college classroom. The source of learning may be noncollege courses,

work, self-teaching, travel, or other life activities. Such learning can occur before or during college enrollment.

Experimental college is a college established as a laboratory for testing
nontraditional curricular ideas.

External degree programs are courses of study leading to degrees that
are pursued largely or fully off campus.

Extracurriculum consists of the noncredit and nonclassroom activities available to students through recreational, social, and
cultural activities sponsored by colleges or by college-related
organizations.

Fachhochschulen are new institutions of higher education in West
Germany which upgrade engineering and technical schools to
university level and admit students with high school graduation certificates and at least six months of work experience.

Factory universities are a type of Chinese higher education in which
factories operate colleges. Employees selected by fellow workers take political and technical courses at the factory university and return to productive work when their studies are
completed.

Fakultäten are academic divisions—such as arts and letters,
economics and social science, science, and theology—in West
German institutions of higher education.

Field distribution subjects involve no specified courses but only require that students take courses or credits in one or more of
three broad areas—humanities, natural science, and social
science.

Field majors are broad-based concentrations composed of several
disciplines in related areas. Natural sciences, social science,
fine arts, and humanities are examples of such concentrations.

Fill-in tests consist of a number of items in which the test taker is
required to complete one or more blanks in a statement.

Formative evaluation is a nonfinal assessment designed to identify
strengths and weaknesses in student performance. The emphasis is upon improvement of student achievement.

4–1–4 calendar consists of two four-month terms separated by a
one-month mini-term which is used for intensive study, special projects, instructional innovation, or off-campus study.

Free elective system in its purest form requires of students no pre-scribed courses; every student can freely elect whatever courses he or she desires.

Freshman inquiry, introduced at Haverford College, is a one-time group advising session at the end of the freshman year.

Freshman seminar is a pedagogical technique introduced by Nathan Pusey at Lawrence College in 1945. It is basically a small class concerned with general education and writing for freshmen. Intimate faculty-student contact is emphasized.

Full-time equivalent is a summary measure of full-time and part-time staff or students at an institution of higher education ex-pressed in terms of their comparable full-time number. For example, one full-time student and two half-time students equal two full-time equivalent students.

General education is the breadth component of the undergraduate curriculum, defined on an institutionwide or collegewide basis. It usually involves study in several subject areas and frequently seeks to provide a common undergraduate ex-perience for all students at a particular institution. See *liberal education.*

General understanding courses are intended to give students a broad and basic undergraduate learning experience.

Gesamthochschule is an innovation in German higher education that combines different levels and types of instruction, including vocational education, teacher education, and university edu-cation under one roof.

Grade inflation is the artificial raising of student grade-point aver-ages.

Grades are a valuation of student performance that may be based strictly on test results or include other factors as well.

Grandes écoles are elite French professional training institutions which admit only the very best French students. They offer specialized courses leading to senior staff positions in gov-ernment, commerce, industry, and engineering.

Great Books refers to slightly more than 100 books intended to em-body the heritage of Western civilization, ranging from Homer to Einstein. They form the basis of the St. John's Col-lege curriculum.

Habilitation is a West German degree indicating continued and successful research and entitling one to give lectures and seminars at universities in Germany. It normally is completed five years after the doctorate and requires a second dissertation.

Haby reforms are a series of changes in French elementary and secondary education recommended by National Education Minister Haby and approved by the French Parliament in 1975.

Hidden curriculum consists of learning that is informally and sometimes inadvertently acquired by students in interactions with fellow students and faculty members and inferred from the rules and traditions of the institution.

Higher education refers strictly to college and university education.

Holistic change is major curriculum change characterized by a unifying and coherent philosophy of education.

Honors programs are courses of study reserved for excellent students.

In loco parentis is the principle that the college governs student behavior, functioning in place of parents.

Independent study is out-of-class, self-directed education with varying degrees of faculty guidance or supervision. It can be an individual or group endeavor.

Innovative enclave refers to a specific place in the curriculum, such as an experimental college or mini-term, set aside for experimentation.

Instruction is guidance or direction intended to cause learning.

Integrated curriculum is an undergraduate program which is not broken down into course units such as the St. John's Great Books curriculum.

Intellectual remodeling refers to a form of faculty development in the People's Republic of China in which faculty were forced to spend varying periods working with their hands and living among workers and peasants.

Interdisciplinary courses are courses that combine two or more disciplines.

Interdisciplinary major (also called the interdepartmental major) is any formally established or institutionalized concentration linking two or more disciplines. *Field majors* and *joint majors* are forms of the interdisciplinary major.

Internships are full- or part-time, credit-bearing, short-term, supervised work experiences. They can be on or off campus, paid or unpaid. The supervisor can be a faculty member or an individual on the job who monitors student progress.

Introductory courses are the most common element in general education programs. They are overview courses such as "Introduction to Physics" or "Introduction to Sociology."

Joint major involves student construction of a concentration with the participation and consent of two departments. The student generally fulfills most of the requirements of both departments.

Junior colleges. See *community colleges.*

Learning is the acquisition of knowledge, skills, and attitudes.

Learning centers are walk-in, frequently individualized, basic skills resource centers for students.

Learning modules are short subcourse units organized around a single theme or principle. For instance, a statistics course might have modules on regression analysis, analysis of variance, and chi square.

Lecture-section courses combine a large lecture which all students in the course attend and small discussion-sized classes.

Lehrfreiheit is freedom of inquiry, teaching, and publication for faculty members.

Lernfreiheit is freedom for the student to move from university to university and to take whatever courses he or she chooses.

Letter grades come in two forms—traditional letter grades, the familiar A, B, C, D, F, with or without pluses and minuses; and modified letter grades, which include variations such as no F or no D grade.

Liberal arts colleges include both liberal arts colleges I and liberal arts colleges II (see below).

Liberal arts colleges I are institutions that scored five or above on Astin's selectivity index or were included among the 200 leading baccalaureate-granting institutions in terms of number of graduates receiving Ph.D.s at 40 leading doctorate-granting institutions from 1920 to 1966. They are also referred to in this volume as "selective" and "the most selective" liberal arts colleges.

Liberal arts colleges II include all liberal arts colleges not meeting the criterion for liberal arts I. They are also referred to in this book as "less selective" liberal arts colleges.

Liberal education is perhaps the most commonly used synonym for *general education*. The Carnegie Council defines it very specifically as "education rooted in the concerns of civilization and our common heritage," but others use the term more generally to refer to any education that liberates the learner in spirit and mind.

Library colleges are institutions that build instruction around the model of a library, such that faculty act principally as resource guides and managers. At such colleges the library serves as a computer center, learning resource center, media center, and institutional research center.

License is a second university degree in France, commonly associated with teaching.

Literary societies were essentially eighteenth- to nineteenth-century debating clubs designed by students to provide the intellectual stimulation lacking in the college curriculum of the time.

Maîtrise is a second university degree in France associated with research.

Major (or concentration), which usually consists of a number of courses in one field or in two or more related fields, is the depth component of the undergraduate curriculum.

Major-minor involves completing one major and a shorter-term concentration in another area. The shorter-term concentration, or minor, generally involves a course of study equivalent to about one-half of a major.

Mastery learning is associated with criteria- or objective-based learning, which requires an instructor to develop an explicit set of course objectives. The objectives are translated into a sequence of short learning units called modules. The instructor designates specific levels of achievement or mastery that students must attain in each module, and students are required to master the skills and knowledge in that module in order to go on to the next.

Minor, an abbreviated concentration, generally consisting of half as many courses as a major.

Modified pass-fail grading is of two principal types—three-point pass-fail and four-point pass-fail. Three-point pass-fail grading systems rate students honors, pass, or fail. Four-point pass-fail adds a second pass or honors designation, resulting in honors, high pass, pass, fail; or high honors, honors, pass, fail.

Multiple-choice tests consist of a series of questions and several possible answers to each question. The test taker is asked to select the correct answer from among the fixed alternatives.

Multiversity refers to the contemporary university—a densely populated, multimillion-dollar, multifaceted institution actively involved in teaching, research, and service.

Nondegree programs consist of activities such as continuing education or community service courses, short-term conferences or workshops, and course attendance by nondegree students.

Nonstandardized tests are noncommercially prepared, generally teacher-produced examinations, lacking normative scores from representative populations.

Nontraditional describes students (such as minorities, women, adults) and curricula (such as external degree program, credit for prior experience) which were not integral parts of the American college in the past.

Normal schools were high schools initiated in 1839 for the preparation of women teachers.

Numerical grading generally relies upon a 1-to-100 scale.

Numerus clausus is the practice of restricting college enrollments or imposing admissions ceilings.

Occupational education is "education, training, or retraining for persons 16 years of age or older who have graduated from or left elementary or secondary school, conducted by an institution authorized to provide post-secondary education . . . which is designed to prepare individuals for gainful employment as semi-skilled or skilled workers or technicians or subprofessionals in recognized occupations, or to prepare individuals for enrollment in advanced technical education programs, but excluding any programs . . . considered professional or which require a baccalaureate or advanced degree" (*Education Amendments* of 1972).

Ombudspersons assist students and academic personnel with problems that may seem insoluble by the usual procedures and agencies. It is the ombudsperson's job to investigate complaints and make recommendations for their resolution.

Open-book tests allow students to use resource materials such as textbooks and notebooks during examinations.

Open-entrance calendar permits students to enroll in college when they wish without waiting any longer than a week.

Open University is a nontraditional external degree program designed primarily for adults in Great Britain.

Oral evaluations are formal, face-to-face assessments of student performance.

Oral test is generally a face-to-face, question-and-answer session between a student and his or her teacher, though it can involve a student and a panel of faculty members.

Pass-fail grading consists of only two grades, which may be called credit–no credit, satisfactory-unsatisfactory, pass–no credit, or pass-fail.

Peer advisers are students knowledgeable in some area of undergraduate concern who counsel other students desiring to learn about that area.

Peer grading involves evaluation of each student by the other members of the class.

Peer teaching involves students teaching one another.

Perennialism is a philosophy of education founded on the assumption that the substance of education is perennial or everlasting. Perennialists view the ability to reason as the characteristic that distinguishes human beings from other animals and believe that education should be concerned principally with training the rational faculties. Perennialists also believe that people are everywhere alike and that education should be the same for everyone. As a result, perennialist education, or the training of the rational faculties, is based upon the study of immutable and universal truths, which are thought best acquired by study of the Great Books.

Performance tests are used primarily in skill subjects such as student teaching, performing arts, and laboratories. The student is asked to put on a demonstration of his or her abilities before one or more experts. Performance tests differ from simulation examinations in that they do not allow for role playing or the use of a fabricated setting.

Peripheral change involves the establishment of institutions or changes within institutions not traditionally associated with higher education but that affect the activities of existing colleges and universities. Examples of such institutions are *proprietary schools* and *brokerage organizations*.

Personal advising deals with affective development and student private life. It may treat concerns including student feelings and emotions, social experience, physical and mental health, finances, and behavior.

Personalized system of instruction, created by Fred Keller and J. Gilmour Sherman in 1966, is a form of self-paced mastery learning relying upon short sequential units with well-defined objectives and immediate feedback on student performance.

Piecemeal change refers to minor curriculum changes which lack the unifying and coherent philosophy of *holistic change*.

Polytechnics are universities or postsecondary institutions that specialize in science and technical courses, often for the purpose of preparing students for mid-level technical jobs.

Postsecondary education refers to all types of education beyond high school.

Prerequisites are courses specified as requirements for taking more advanced courses.

Prescribed distribution requirements involve combinations of specified courses, student course options from short preselected lists, and a limited number of electives in designated areas.

Proctor is a peer tutor in the *personalized system of instruction* who has previously mastered the content of the course or unit.

Professional option plan allows students to enroll jointly in professional school programs and the undergraduate college with a time savings in earning both degrees.

Professional/technical education is college-level training in work subjects. In the Catalog Study referred to in this volume, professional/technical education is a composite of five fields—

business, education, engineering, health science, and technical arts.

Professional/technical majors are constructed around occupations or
vocations, and are intended to lead directly to careers in the
concentration area.

Programmed instruction combines a sequence of learning tasks and
evaluation exercises in which students are required to master
the skills and knowledge associated with each task in order to
begin the next. Mastery is assessed via evaluation exercises.
Students who respond incorrectly to the exercises restudy the
previous task in linear programs or are assigned a new task
based specifically on the weaknesses they demonstrated in
branching programs.

Progress by examination curriculum involves earning a college degree
by passing tests rather than courses.

Progressivism is a philosophy of education based on life experience.
The practical progressive philosophy is student centered,
which is to say that student interest is the primary determinant of the direction of education. The instructor is viewed as
an expert and adviser whose job is to guide the student. The
progressive curriculum is problem-oriented rather than subject matter based. Progressives believe that the methods of
critical thought are life-long skills while bodies of knowledge
are continually changing.

Proprietary schools are profit-seeking educational institutions.

Psychomotor learning is learning associated with the body.

Public universities are French open-admission institutions which any
student with a *baccalauréat* (a certificate of secondary school
completion) can attend.

Quarter calendar consists of four ten-week terms. The full-time student takes three courses per quarter and attends three quarters per year.

Recitation was a popular instructional method in the colonial college. Students were required to repeat textbook assignments
orally and verbatim.

Recommended distribution guidelines are generally the same as *smorgasbord distribution* requirements except that they are not re-

quired. The student is given the option of satisfying the requirements or ignoring them.

Reconstructionism is a philosophy of education that accepts the progressive design of education but adds an additional ingredient—an emphasis on reconstructing society.

Redbook was the 1945 report of the Harvard Committee on General Education in a Free Society, formally entitled *General Education in a Free Society.*

Regents External Degree Program is a New York state program without an instructional component that offers bachelor's and associate's degrees on the basis of a proficiency examination and/or accumulated credits.

Relative grading relies upon sliding standards such as the performance of a class on an examination (normative grading or grading on a curve) or student academic potential.

Remedial education is instruction designed to bring students up to required basic skills or knowledge levels in order for them to attend a program for which they were previously ineligible. Its purpose is to correct weaknesses.

Research universities include both research universities I and research universities II (see below).

Research universities I are the 50 leading universities in terms of federal financial support of academic science in at least two of the three years 1968–69 to 1970–71, and awarded at least 50 Ph.D.s in 1969–70. They are also referred to in this volume as the "most research-oriented" universities.

Research universities II are among the 100 leading institutions in terms of federal support in at least two of the years from 1968–69 to 1970–71 and awarded at least 50 Ph.D.s in 1969–70 or were among the 50 leading institutions in total number of Ph.D.s awarded from 1960–61 to 1969–70.

Residence counselors may be upper-division students, graduate students, faculty members, or simply responsible adults whose job varies from informally to formally advising students and keeping order in university dormitories.

Rōnin are Japanese students taking university admission examinations for at least the second time. The word was originally used to describe out-of-work samurai during the feudal age.

ROTC is an abbreviation for Reserve Officer Training Corps, which was established by the National Defense Act of 1920.

Sandwich courses alternate college or university attendance with work or on-the-job training on a three- or six-month basis.

Scholastic Aptitude Test (SAT) is a college aptitude test in verbal and mathematical skills taken by 71 percent of 1976 college freshmen.

Scholasticism, characterized by employment of the dialectic—a form of logic which involves disputation or discrimination of truth from error in matters of opinion,—was the principal means of discovering truth during the Middle Ages.

Section is a small discussion-sized class accompanying a large lecture or one of several classes offered during a term under a single course title, such as "Introduction to Humanities" or "Intermediate French."

Self-evaluation is assessment by the learner.

Self-paced instruction is a form of education in which the subject matter to be covered is broken down into short, sequential units. The student progresses through the units at his or her own pace, with the speed of progress determined solely by the student's ability to master the material.

Semester calendar consists of two terms which average 15 weeks each, but can be as long as 20 weeks. Full-time students take four or five courses per term.

Seminar is generally a small class consisting of advanced students and a faculty member investigating a field of the faculty member's research. There are a variety of exceptions, including the freshman seminar.

Senior seminar is a course designed to cap the general education experience by assembling in one class students with differing majors for the purpose of solving a common problem.

Senior thesis or project is an undergraduate creation produced by upper-division students, generally in an area related to the major.

Sequencing involves courses that build upon one another and must as a result be taken in a particular order.

Service internships are low or nonpaying community-based learning experiences.

Simulation tests recreate real life situations in an artificial environment and are used to measure applied skills and knowledge.

Smorgasbord distributions are general education requirements, wherein few if any particular courses are specified. Rather, students are required to take courses in broad areas such as language, social science, science, fine arts, and humanities.

Socratic method is a pedagogical technique utilizing a question-and-answer format which is said to have been developed by Socrates.

Sophists were fifth century B.C. commercial Athenian philosophers who trained students in the two practical skills needed for politics—dialectic (persuasion) and rhetoric (the art of speaking).

Spare-time schools, located throughout the People's Republic of China, are off-campus, conveniently available courses and schools in subjects such as basic literacy, industrial technology, politics, and agricultural technology. Students take courses they desire in their spare time.

Special group advising provides counseling to students with needs that are not shared by more traditional students and is available on many campuses for such groups as women, racial minorities, ethnic minorities, and veterans.

Standardized tests are prepared examinations with explicit instructions for administration and scoring and information about normative scores of representative populations of test takers.

Stopping out is leaving college with the intention of returning at a later date.

Student advocacy is counseling designed to protect the student as consumer.

Student-created major is a concentration constructed by the student with approval of a designated university officer or committee.

Studium generale was the name given to the masses of students and teachers who gathered together, often about cathedral schools, during the late Middle Ages. Out of these groupings came the first universities.

Subject field refers to an aggregation of disciplines such as humanities, social science, or natural science.

Summative evaluation is terminal assessment intended to provide a final or overall judgment of student performance. The emphasis of summative grading is upon describing how well the student succeeded.

Survey course is a synoptic in a broad academic field. Over the years the realm of the survey course has been expanded to include overview and introductory courses in academic departments or disciplines such as sociology, biology, and art.

Teaching. See *instruction.*

Team advising (or team teaching) is counseling (or teaching) by groups of two or more students, faculty members, administrators, other college staff, or community resource people.

Team teaching. See *team advising.*

Tests are means of measuring student ability or attainment.

Three Rs are reading, writing, and arithmetic.

Transfer refers either to a student who changes colleges or to the process of changing colleges.

Trimester calendar is a variation of the semester system consisting of three 15-week terms.Full-time students attend two terms per year and take four courses per term or attend three terms per year and take three courses per term. The latter arrangement is called the 3–3 calendar.

Tripartite design as used in this volume refers to the practice in the People's Republic of China, of reserving 70 percent of each course for academic study, 20 percent for political work, and 10 percent for production.

Trivium and quadrivium. See *Disciplinarium Libri.*

True-false tests consist of declarative sentences, which the test taker must rate as true or false. A variation on this format requires the test taker to state why false statements are incorrect.

Tutorial is a formal course pairing one student and one faculty member.

U68 was a commission formed in 1967 to develop a plan for post-secondary education in Sweden. Its recommendations were implemented in modified form in July 1977.

Undergraduate education refers to learning opportunities available to students at the pre-baccalaureate level.

Unit. See *credit.*

Unites de enseignement et de recherche (UER) are disciplinary-based education and research units created in France by the 1968 Orientation Act.

Upside-down programs permit students to transfer vocational/occupational programs from community and junior colleges, proprietary schools, and technical institutions to satisfy major and upper-division requirements. During their junior and senior years of college, such students take primarily general education. These programs are called upside-down because they invert the traditional pattern of study.

Variable term-length calendar consists of a number of terms, some or all of which differ in length.

Vocational education is defined as the "organized educational programs which are directly related to the preparation of individuals for paid or unpaid employment, or for additional preparation for a career requiring other than a baccalaureate or advanced degree" (Education Amendments of 1976).

Weekend colleges provide a way for students to complete courses and degree programs by attending college primarily or entirely on Friday, Saturday, and Sunday.

Written evaluations, which vary from unstructured instruments to check-box assessments of student performance, are generally used as supplements to other forms of grading, particularly to pass-fail grading, which is low in information content.

APPENDIX A

A Documentary History of the Undergraduate Curriculum: 12 Salient Events

Of all the momentous events in the history of the American undergraduate curriculum that have been noted in previous chapters and discussed by Frederick Rudolph in his companion volume, *Curriculum: A History of the American Undergraduate Course of Study Since 1636* (1977), twelve that have been recorded warrant documentation here. They begin with (1) the formation of the Harvard College curriculum as of 1642, and continue with (2) the founding of the University of Virginia in 1824, (3) the Yale Report of 1828, (4) the Morrill Land-Grant Act of 1862, (5) the creation of Cornell University in 1868, (6) the inauguration of Charles William Eliot as president of Harvard in 1869, (7) the establishment of The Johns Hopkins University in 1876, (8) the report of the "Committee of Ten" in 1893, (9) the launching of the "Wisconsin Idea" in 1904, (10) the Great Books curriculum at St. John's College in 1937, (11) the Harvard "Redbook" on *General Education in a Free Society* in 1945, and (12) the report of the President's Commission on Higher Education in 1947.

Event 1: The Creation of the First Undergraduate Program—1642

By 1642, the Harvard curriculum was firmly established. President Dunster taught all students all of the subjects. The first year, students studied logic, Greek, Hebrew, rhetoric, divinity catechetical, history, and the nature of plants. The second year they studied ethics and politics, Greek, rhetoric, Aramaic, and divinity catechetical. The third and final year, they studied arithmetic, astronomy, Greek, rhetoric, Syriac, and divinity catechetical.

Students generally studied one subject a day from 8:00 in the morning until 5:00 at night Monday through Friday, and a half day on Saturday. Dunster taught each class individually one to two hours each day, except rhetoric and divinity catechetical, which were taught to all students at once. He weekly engaged each class in disputation and declamation. Students spent the rest of the academic week in supervised, required study or recitation.

This process is described in the following excerpt from a 26-page 1643 promotional pamphlet entitled "New Englands First Fruits." The authorship of the document is unknown. The only known surviving copy is part of the collection of the New York–based Pierpoint Morgan Library. The following excerpt was taken from S. E. Morison's *The Founding of Harvard College* (pp. 432–436):

New Englands First Fruits:
1. In respect of the Colledge, and the proceedings of Learning *therein.*

1. After God had carried us safe to *New England*, and wee had builded our houses, provided necessaries for our liveli-hood, rear'd convenient places for Gods worship, and setled the Civill Government: One of the next things we longed for, and looked after was to advance *Learning* and perpetuate it to Posterity; dreading to leave an illiterate Ministery to the Churches, when our present Ministers shall lie in the Dust. And as wee were thinking and consulting how to effect this great Work; it pleased God to stir up the heart of one Mr. *Harvard* (a godly Gentleman, and a lover of Learning, there living amongst us) to give the one halfe of his Estate (it being in all about 1700. 1.) towards the erecting of a Colledge: and all his Library: after him another gave 300. 1. others after them cast in more, and the publique hand of the State added the rest: the Colledge was, by common consent, appointed to be at *Cambridge*, (a place very pleasant and accommodate) and is called (according to the name of the first founder) *Harvard Colledge.*

The Edifice is very faire and comely within and without, having in it a spacious Hall; (where they daily meet at Commons, Lectures) Exercises, and a large Library with some Bookes to it, the gifts of diverse of our friends, their Chambers and studies also fitted for, and possessed by the Students, and all other roomes of Office necessary and convenient, with all needfull Offices thereto belonging: And by the side of the Colledge a faire *Grammar* Schoole, for the training up of young Schollars, and fitting of them for *Academicall Learning,* that still as they are judged ripe, they may be received into the Colledge of this Schoole: Master *Corlet* is the Mr., who hath very well approved himselfe for his abilities, dexterity and painfulnesse in teaching and education of the youth under him.

Over the Colledge is master *Dunster* placed, as President, a learned conscionable and industrious man, who hath so trained up, his Pupills in the tongues and Arts, and so seasoned them with the principles of Divinity and Christianity, that we have to our great comfort, (and in truth) beyond our hopes, beheld their progresse in Learning and godlinesse also; the former of these hath appeared in their publique declamations in *Latine* and *Greeke,* and Disputations Logicall and Philosophicall, which they have beene wonted (besides their ordinary Exercises in the Colledge-Hall) in the audience of the Magistrates, Ministers, and other Schollars, for the probation of their growth in Learning, upon set dayes, constantly once every moneth to make and uphold: The latter hath been manifested in sundry of them, by the savoury breathings of their Spirits in their godly conversation. Insomuch that we are confident, it these early blossomes may be cherished and warmed with the influence of the friends of Learning, and lovers of this pious worke, they will by the help of God, come to happy maturity in a short time.

Over the Colledge are twelve Overseers chosen by the generall Court, six of them are of the Magistrates, the other six of the Ministers, who are to promote the best good of it and (having a power of influence into all persons in it) are to see that every one be diligent and proficient in his proper place.

2. *Rules, and Precepts that are observed in the Colledge.*

1. When any Schollar is able to understand *Tully,* or such like classicall Latine Author *extempore,* and make and speake true Latine in Verse and Prose, *suo ut aiunt Marte;* And decline perfectly the Paradigm's of *Nounes* and *Verbes* in the Greek tongue: Let him then and not before be capable of admission into the Colledge.

2. Let every Student be plainly instructed, and earnestly pressed to consider well, the maine end of his life and studies is, *to know God and Jesus Christ which is eternall life,* Joh. 17.3. and therefore to lay *Christ* in the bottome, as the only foundation of all found knowledge and Learning.

And seeing the Lord only giveth wisedome, Let every one seriously set himselfe by prayer in secret to seeke it of him *Prov* 2, 3.

3. Every one shall so exercise himselfe in reading the Scriptures twice a day, that he shall be ready to give such an account of his proficiency therein, both in *Theoretticall* observations of the Language, and *Logick,* and in *Practicall* and spirituall truths, as his Tutor shall require, according to his ability; seeing *the entrance of the word giveth light, it giveth understanding to the simple,* Psalm 119.130.

4. That they eshewing all profanation of Gods Name, Attributes, Word, Ordinances, and times of Worship, doe studie with good conscience, carefully to retaine God, and the love of his truth in their mindes, else let them know, that (notwithstanding their Learning) God may give them up *to strong delusions,* and in the end *to a reprobate minde,* 2.Thes. 2.11, 12. Rom. 1.28.

5. That they studiously redeeme the time; observe the generall houres appointed for all the Students, and the speciall houres for their owne Classes: and then diligently attend the Lectures, without any disturbance by word or gesture. And if in any thing they doubt, they shall enquire, as of their fellowes, so, (in case of *Non satisfaction)* modestly of their Tutors.

6. None shall under any pretence whatsoever, frequent the company and society of such men as lead an unfit, and dissolute life.

Nor shall any without his Tutors leave, or (in his absence) the call of Parents or Guardians, goe abroad to other Townes.

7. Every Schollar shall be present in his Tutors chamber at the 7th. houre in the morning, immediately after the sound of the Bell at his opening the Scripture and prayer, so also at the 5th. houre at night, and then give account of his owne private reading, as aforesaid in Particular the third, and constantly attend Lectures in the Hall at the houres appointed? But if any (without necessary impediment) shall absent himself from prayer or Lectures, he shall bee lyable to Admonition, if he offend above once a weeke.

8. If any Schollar shall be found to transgresse any of the Lawes of God, or the Schoole, after twice Admonition, he shall be lyable, if not *adultus,* to correction, if *adultus,* his name shall be given up to the Overseers of the Colledge, that he may bee admonished at the publick monethly Act.

3. The times and order of their Studies,
unlesse experience shall shew cause to alter.

The second and third day of the weeke, read Lectures, as followeth.

To the first yeare at 8th. of the clock in the morning *Logick,* the first three quarters, *Physicks* the last quarter.

To the second yeare, at the 9th. houre, *Ethicks* and *Politicks,* at convenient distances of time.

To the third yeare at the 10th. *Arithmetick* and *Geometry,* the three first quarters. *Astronomy* the last.

Afternoone.

The first yeare disputes at the second houre.

The 2d. yeare at the 3d. houre.

The 3d. yeare at the 4th. every one in his Art.

The 4th. day reads Greeke.

To the first yeare the *Etymologie* and *Syntax* at the eigth houre.

To the 2d. at the 9th. houre, *Prosodia* and *Dialects.*
Afternoone.

The first yeare at 2d. houre practice the precepts of *Grammar* in such Authors as have variety of words.

The 2d. yeare at 3d. houre practice in *Poësy, Nonnus, Duport,* or the like.

The 3d. yeare perfect their *Theory* before noone, and exercise *Style, Composition, Imitation, Epitome,* both in Prose and Verse, afternoone.

The fift day reads Hebrew, and the Easterne Tongues.

Grammar to the first yeare houre the 8th.

To the 2d. *Chaldee* at the 9th. houre.

To the 3d. *Syriack* at the 10th. houre.

Afternoone.

The first yeare practice in the Bible at the 2d. houre.

The 2d. in *Ezra* and *Danel* at the 3d. houre.

The 3d. at the 4th. houre in *Trostius* New Testament.

The 6th. day reads Rhetorick to all at the 8th. houre.

Declamations at the 9th. So ordered that every Scholler may declaime once a moneth. The rest of the day *vacat Rhetoricis studiis.*

The 7th. day reads Divinity Catecheticall at the 8th. houre,
Common places at the 9th. houre.

Afternoone.

The first houre reads history in the Winter,

The nature of plants in the Summer

The summe of every Lecture shall be examined, before the new Lecture be read.

Every Schollar, that on proofe is found able to read the Originalls of the *Old* and *New Testament* into the Latine tongue, and to resolve them *Logically;* withall being of godly life and conversation; And at any publick Act hath the Approbation of the Overseers and Master of the Colledge, is fit to be dignified with his first Degree.

Every Schollar that giveth up in writing a *System,* or *Synopsis,* or summe of *Logick,* Naturall and Morall *Philosophy, Arithmetick, Geometry* and *Astronomy:* and is ready to defend his *Theses* or positions: withall skilled in the Originalls as abovesaid: and of godly life & conversation: and so approved by the Overseers and Master of the Colledge, at any publique *Act,* is fit to be dignified with his 2d. Degree.

Event 2: The Founding of the University of Virginia—1824

The curriculum at the new University of Virginia created by Thomas Jefferson, departed radically from the practices of its day. Students were offered a choice of eight prescribed courses of study, and provision was made for attendance by nondegree students.

The plan of studies for the university is described in the April 7, 1824 minutes of the Board of Visitors to the university during the rectorship of Jefferson. This excerpt is taken from Richard Hofstadter and Wilson Smith's *American Higher Education: A Documentary History*, Volume 1, pages 230–231.

Wednesday, April 7, 1824

In the University of Virginia shall be instituted eight professorships, to wit: 1st, of ancient languages; 2d, modern languages; 3d, mathematics; 4th, natural philosophy; 5th, natural history; 6th, anatomy and medicine; 7th, moral philosophy; 8th, law.

In the school of ancient languages shall be taught the higher grade of the Latin and Greek languages, the Hebrew, rhetoric, belles-lettres, ancient history and ancient geography.

In the school of modern languages shall be taught French, Spanish, Italian, German and the English language in its Anglo-Saxon form; also modern history and modern geography.

In the school of mathematics shall be taught mathematics generally, including the high branches of numerical arithmetic, algebra, trigonometry, plane and spherical geometry, mensuration, navigation, conic sections, fluxions or differentials, military and civil architecture.

In the school of natural philosophy shall be taught the laws and properties of bodies generally, including mechanics, statics, hydrostatics, hydraulics, pneumatics, acoustics, optics and astronomy.

In the school of natural history shall be taught botany, zoology, mineralogy, chemistry, geology and rural economy.

In the school of anatomy and medicine shall be taught anatomy, surgery, the history of the progress and theories of medicine, physiology, pathology, materia medica and pharmacy.

In the school of moral philosophy shall be taught mental science generally, including ideology, general grammar, logic and ethics.

In the school of law shall be taught the common and statute law, that of the chancery, the laws feudal, civil, mercatorial, maritime and of nature and nations; and also the principles of government and political economy.

This arrangement, however, shall not be understood as forbidding occasional transpositions of a particular branch of science from one school to another in accommodation of the particular qualifications of different professors.

In each of these schools instruction shall be communicated by lessons or lectures, examinations and exercises, as shall be best adapted to the nature of the science, and number of the school; and exercises shall be prescribed to employ the vacant days and hours.

The professors shall be permitted to occupy, rent free, a pavilion each, with the grounds appropriated to it. They shall also receive from the funds of the University such compensation as shall have been stipulated by the agent or fixed by the Board; and from each student attending them tuition fees as hereinafter declared.

The professors shall permit no waste to be committed in their tenements, and shall maintain the internal of their pavilions, and also the windows, doors and locks external during their occupation, in as good repair and condition as they shall have received them.

The collegiate duties of a professor, if discharged conscientiously, with industry and zeal, being sufficient to engross all his hours of business, he shall engage in no other pursuits of emolument unconnected with the service of the University without the consent of the Visitors. . . .

TH. JEFFERSON, *Rector*

Event 3: The Yale Report of 1828

As attacks on the classical curriculum escalated, the Yale faculty issued a spirited defense in the form of the Yale Report of 1828. It was the first formal statement of an educational philosophy in the history of American higher education. A version of that report follows, as edited by Hofstadter and Smith (1961, Volume 1, pp. 277–291).

Report of the Faculty, Part I

We are decidedly of the opinion, that our present plan of education admits of improvement. We are aware that the system is imperfect: and we cherish the hope, that some of its defects may ere long be remedied. We believe that changes may, from time to time be made with advantage, to meet the varying demands of the community, to accommodate the course of instruction to the rapid advance of the country, in population, refinement, and opulence. We have no doubt that important improvements may be suggested, by attentive observation of the literary institutions in Europe; and by the earnest spirit of inquiry which is now so prevalent, on the subject of education.

The guardians of the college appear to have ever acted upon the principle, that it ought not to be stationary, but continually advancing. Some alteration has accordingly been proposed, almost every year, from its first establishment. . . .

Not only the course of studies, and the modes of instruction, have been greatly varied; but whole sciences have, for the first time, been introduced; chemistry, mineralogy, geology, political economy, &c. By raising the qualifications for admission, the standard of attainment has been elevated. Alterations so extensive and frequent, satisfactorily prove, that if those who are intrusted with the superintendence of the institution, still firmly adhere to some of its original features, it is from a higher principle, than a blind opposition to salutary reform. Improvements, we trust, will continue to be made, as rapidly as they can be, without hazarding the loss of what has been already attained.

But perhaps the time has come, when we ought to pause, and inquire, whether it will be sufficient to make *gradual* changes, as heretofore; and whether the whole system is not rather to be broken up, and a better one substituted in its stead. From different quarters, we have heard the suggestion, that our colleges must be *new-modelled;* that they are not adapted to the spirit and wants of the age; that they will soon be deserted, unless they are better accommodated to the business character of the nation. As this point may have an important bearing upon the question immediately before the committee, we would ask their indulgence, while we attempt to explain, at some length, the nature and object of the present plan of education at the college. . . .

What then is the appropriate object of a college? It is not necessary here to determine what it is which, in every case, entitles an institution to the *name* of a college. But if we have not greatly misapprehended the design of the patrons and guardians of this college, its object is to *lay the foundation* of a *superior education:* and this is to be done, at a period of life when a substitute must be provided for *parental superintendence.* The ground work of a thorough education, must be broad, and deep, and solid. For a partial or superficial education, the support may be of looser materials, and more hastily laid.

The two great points to be gained in intellectual culture, are the *discipline* and the *furniture* of the mind; expanding its powers, and storing it with knowledge. The former of these is, perhaps, the more important of the two. A commanding object, therefore, in a collegiate course, should be, to call into daily and vigorous exercise the faculties of the student. Those branches of study should be prescribed, and those modes of instruction adopted, which are best calculated to teach the art of fixing the attention, directing the train of thought, analyzing a subject proposed for investigation; following, with accurate discrimination, the course of argument; balancing nicely the evidence presented to the judgment; awakening, elevating, and controlling the imagination; arranging, with skill, the treasures which memory gathers; rousing and guiding the powers of genius. All this is not to be effected by a light and hasty course of study; by reading a few books, hearing a few lectures, and spending some months at a literary institution. The habits of thinking are to be formed, by long continued and close application. The mines of science must be penetrated far below the surface, before they will disclose their treasures. If a dexterous performance of the manual operations, in many of the mechanical arts, requires an apprenticeship, with diligent attention for years; much more does the training of the powers of the mind demand vigorous, and steady, and systematic effort.

In laying the foundation of a thorough education, it is necessary that *all* the important mental faculties be brought into exercise.... In the course of instruction in this college, it has been an object to maintain such a proportion between the different branches of literature and science, as to form in the student a proper *balance* of character. From the pure mathematics, he learns the art of demonstrative reasoning. In attending to the physical sciences, he becomes familiar with facts, with the process of induction, and the varieties of probable evidence. In ancient literature, he finds some of the most finished models of taste. By English reading, he learns the powers of the language in which he is to speak and write. By logic and mental philosophy, he is taught the art of thinking; by rhetoric and oratory, the art of speaking. By frequent exercise on written composition, he acquires copiousness and accuracy of expression. By extemporaneous discussion, he becomes prompt, and fluent, and animated. It is a point of high importance, that eloquence and solid learning should go together; that he who has accumulated the richest treasures of thought, should possess the highest powers of oratory. To what purpose has a man become deeply learned, if he has no faculty of communicating his knowledge? And of what use is a display of rhetorical elegance, from one who knows little or nothing which is worth communicating? ...

No one feature in a system of intellectual education, is of greater moment than such an arrangement of duties and motives, as will most effectually throw the student upon the *resources of his own mind.* Without this, the whole apparatus of libraries, and instruments, and specimens, and lectures, and teachers, will be insufficient to secure distinguished excellence. The scholar must form himself, by his own exertions. The advantages furnished by a residence at a college, can do little more than stimulate and aid his personal efforts. The *inventive* powers are especially to be called into vigorous exercise. ...

In our arrangements for the communication of knowledge, as well as in intellectual discipline, such branches are to be taught as will produce a proper symmetry and balance of character. We doubt whether the powers of the mind can be developed, in their fairest proportions, by studying languages alone, or mathematics alone, or natural or political science alone. As the bodily frame is brought to its highest perfection, not by one simple and uniform motion, but by a variety of exercises; so the mental faculties are expanded, and invigorated, and adapted to each other, by familiarity with different departments of science.

A most important feature in the colleges of this country is, that the students are generally of an age which requires, that a substitute be provided for *parental superintendence.* When removed from under the roof of their parents, and exposed to the untried scenes of temptation, it is necessary that some faithful and affectionate guardian take them by the hand,

and guide their steps. This consideration determines the *kind* of government which ought to be maintained in our colleges. As it is a substitute for the regulations of a family, it should approach as near to the character of parental control as the circumstances of the case will admit. It should be founded on mutual affection and confidence. It should aim to effect its purpose, principally by kind and persuasive influence; not wholly or chiefly by restraint and terror. Still, punishment may sometimes be necessary. There may be perverse members of a college, as well as of a family. There may be those whom nothing but the arm of law can reach. . . .

Having now stated what we understand to be the proper *object* of an education at this college, viz. to lay a solid *foundation* in literature and science; we would ask permission to add a few observations on the *means* which are employed to effect this object.

In giving the course of instruction, it is intended that a due proportion be observed between *lectures,* and the exercises which are familiarly termed *recitations;* that is, examinations in a text book. The great advantage of lectures is, that while they call forth the highest efforts of the lecturer, and accelerate his advance to professional eminence; they give that light and spirit to the subject, which awaken the interest and ardor of the student. . . . Still it is important, that the student should have opportunities of retiring by himself, and giving a more commanding direction to his thoughts, than when listening to oral instruction. To secure his steady and earnest efforts, is the great object of the daily examinations or recitations. In these exercises, a text-book is commonly the guide. . . . When he comes to be engaged in the study of his *profession,* he may find his way through the maze, and firmly establish his own opinions, by taking days or weeks for the examination of each separate point. Text-books are, therefore, not as necessary in this advanced stage of education, as in the course at college, where the time allotted to each branch is rarely more than sufficient for the learner to become familiar with its elementary principles. . . .

We deem it to be indispensable to a proper adjustment of our collegiate system, that there should be in it both Professors and Tutors. There is wanted, on the one hand, the experience of those who have been long resident at the institution, and on the other, the fresh and minute information of those who, having more recently mingled with the students, have a distinct recollection of their peculiar feelings, prejudices, and habits of thinking. At the head of each great division of science, it is necessary that there should be a Professor, to superintend the department, to arrange the plan of instruction, to regulate the mode of conducting it, and to teach the more important and difficult parts of the subject. But students in a college, who have just entered on the first elements of science, are not principally occupied with the more abstruse and disputable points. Their attention ought not to be solely or mainly directed to the latest discoveries. They have first to learn the principles which have been in a course of investigation, through the successive ages; and have now become simplified and settled. Before arriving at regions hitherto unexplored, they must pass over the intervening cultivated ground. The Professor at the head of a department may, therefore, be greatly aided, in some parts of the course of instruction, by those who are not as deeply versed as himself in all the intricacies of the science. Indeed we doubt, whether elementary principles are always taught to the best advantage, by those whose researches have carried them so far beyond these simpler truths, that they come back to them with reluctance and distaste. . . .

In the internal police of the institution, as the students are gathered into one family, it is deemed an essential provision, that some of the officers should constitute a portion of this family; being always present with them, not only at their meals, and during the business of the day; but in the hours allotted to rest. The arrangement is such, that in our college buildings, there is no room occupied by students, which is not near to the chamber of one of the officers.

But the feature in our system which renders a considerable number of tutors indispensable, is the subdivision of our classes, and the assignment of each portion to the particular charge of one man. . . .

The course of instruction which is given to the undergraduates in the college, is not designed to include *professional* studies. Our object is not to teach that which is peculiar to any one of the professions; but to lay the foundation which is common to them all. There are separate schools for medicine, law, and theology, connected with the college, as well as in various parts of the country; which are open for the reception of all who are prepared to enter upon the appropriate studies of their several professions. With these, the academical course is not intended to interfere.

But why, it may be asked, should a student waste his time upon studies which have no immediate connection with his future profession? . . . In answer to this, it may be observed, that there is no science which does not contribute its aid to professional skill. "Every thing throws light upon every thing." The great object of a collegiate education, preparatory to the study of a profession, is to give that expansion and balance of the mental powers, those liberal and comprehensive views, and those fine proportions of character, which are not to be found in him whose ideas are always confined to one particular channel. When a man has entered upon the practice of his profession, the energies of his mind must be given, principally, to its appropriate duties. But if his thoughts never range on other subjects, if he never looks abroad on the ample domains of literature and science, there will be a narrowness in his habits of thinking, a peculiarity of character, which will be sure to mark him as a man of limited views and attainments. Should he be distinguished in his profession, his ignorance on other subjects, and the defects of his education, will be the more exposed to public observation. On the other hand, he who is not only eminent in professional life, but has also a mind richly stored with general knowledge, has an elevation and dignity of character, which gives him a commanding influence in society, and a widely extended sphere of usefulness. His situation enables him to diffuse the light of science among all classes of the community. Is a man to have no other object, than to obtain a *living* by professional pursuits? Has he not duties to perform to his family, to his fellow citizens, to his country; duties which require various and extensive intellectual furniture? . . .

As our course of instruction is not intended to complete an education, in theological, medical, or legal science; neither does it include all the minute details of *mercantile, mechanical,* or *agricultural* concerns. These can never be effectually learned except in the very circumstances in which they are to be practised. The young merchant must be trained in the counting room, the mechanic, in the workshop, the farmer, in the field. But we have, on our premises, no experimental farm or retail shop; no cotton or iron manufactory; no hatter's, or silver-smith's, or coach-maker's establishment. For what purpose, then, it will be asked, are young men who are destined to these occupations, ever sent to a college? They should not be sent, as we think, with an expectation of *finishing* their education at the college; but with a view of laying a thorough foundation in the principles of science, preparatory to the study of the practical arts. . . .

We are far from believing that theory *alone,* should be taught in a college. It cannot be effectually taught, except in connection with practical illustrations. . . . To bring down the principles of science to their practical application by the laboring classes, is the office of men of superior education. It is the separation of theory and practice, which has brought reproach upon both. Their union alone can elevate them to their true dignity and value. The man of science is often disposed to assume an air of superiority, when he looks upon the narrow and partial views of the mere artisan. The latter in return laughs at the practical blunders of the former. The defects in the education of both classes would be remedied, by giving them a knowledge of scientific principles, preparatory to practice.

We are aware that a thorough education is not within the reach of all. Many, for want of time and pecuniary resources, must be content with a partial course. A defective education is better than none. If a youth can afford to devote only two or three years, to a scientific and professional education, it will be proper for him to make a selection of a few of the most important branches, and give his attention exclusively to these. But this is an imperfection, arising from the necessity of the case. A partial course of study, must inevitably give a partial education. . . .

A partial education is often expedient; a superficial one, never. . . .

But why, it is asked, should *all* the students in a college be required to tread in the *same steps?* Why should not each one be allowed to select those branches of study which are most to his taste, which are best adapted to his peculiar talents, and which are most nearly connected with his intended profession? To this we answer, that our prescribed course contains those subjects only which ought to be understood, as we think, by every one who aims at a thorough education. They are not the peculiarities of any profession or art. These are to be learned in the professional and practical schools. But the principles of sciences, are the common foundation of all high intellectual attainments. As in our primary schools, reading, writing, and arithmetic are taught to all, however different their prospects; so in a college, all should be instructed in those branches of knowledge, of which no one destined to the higher walks of life ought to be ignorant. What subject which is now studied here, could be set aside, without evidently marring the system[?] Not to speak particularly, in this place, of the ancient languages; who that aims at a well proportioned and superior education will remain ignorant of the elements of the various branches of the mathematics, or of history and antiquities, or of rhetoric and oratory, or natural philosophy, or astronomy, or chemistry, or mineralogy, or geology, or political economy, or mental and moral philosophy?

It is sometimes thought that a student ought not to be urged to the study of that for which he has *no taste or capacity*. But how is he to know, whether he has a taste or capacity for a science, before he has even entered upon its elementary truths? If he is really destitute of talent sufficient for these common departments of education, he is destined for some narrow sphere of action. But we are well persuaded, that our students are not so deficient in intellectual powers, as they sometimes profess to be; though they are easily made to believe, that they have no capacity for the study of that which they are told is almost wholly useless.

When a class have become familiar with the common elements of the several sciences, then is the proper time for them to *divide off* to their favorite studies. They can then make their choice from actual trial. This is now done here, to some extent, in our Junior year. The division might be commenced at an earlier period, and extended farther, provided the qualifications for admission into the college, were brought to a higher standard.

If the view which we have thus far taken of the subject is correct, it will be seen, that the object of the system of instruction at this college, is not to give a *partial* education, consisting of a few branches only; nor, on the other hand, to give a *superficial* education, containing a smattering of almost every thing; nor to *finish* the details of either a professional or practical education; but to *commence* a *thorough* course, and to carry it as far as the time of residence here will allow. It is intended to occupy, to the best advantage, the four years immediately preceding the study of a profession, or of the operations which are peculiar to the higher mercantile, manufacturing, or agricultural establishments. . . .

Our institution is not modelled exactly after the pattern of *European* universities. Difference of circumstances has rendered a different arrangement expedient. It has been the policy of most monarchical governments, to concentrate the advantages of a superior education in a few privileged places. In England, for instance, each of the ancient universities of Oxford and Cambridge, is not so much a single institution, as a large number of distinct, though contiguous colleges. But in this country, our republican habits and feelings will never allow a monopoly of literature in any one place. There must be, in the union, as many colleges, at least, as states. Nor would we complain of this arrangement as inexpedient, provided that starvation is not the consequence of a patronage so minutely divided. We anticipate no disastrous results from the multiplication of colleges, if they can only be adequately endowed. We are not without apprehensions, however, that a feeble and stinted growth of our national literature, will be the consequence of the very scanty supply of means to most of our public seminaries. . . .

Although we do not consider the literary institutions of Europe as faultless models, to be exactly copied by our American colleges; yet we would be far from condemning every feature, in systems of instruction which have had an origin more ancient than our republican seminaries. We do not suppose that the world has learned absolutely nothing, by the experience of ages; that a branch of science, or a mode of teaching, is to be abandoned, precisely because it has stood its ground, after a trial by various nations, and through successive centuries. We believe that our colleges may derive important improvements from the universities and schools in Europe; not by blindly adopting all their measures without discrimination; but by cautiously introducing, with proper modifications, such parts of their plans as are suited to our peculiar situation and character. The first and great improvement which we wish to see made, is an elevation in the standard of attainment for admission. Until this is effected, we shall only expose ourselves to inevitable failure and ridicule, by attempting a general imitation of foreign universities. . . .

It is said that the public now demand, that the doors should be thrown open to all; that education ought to be so modified, and varied, as to adapt it to the exigencies of the country, and the prospects of different individuals; that the instruction given to those who are destined to be merchants, or manufacturers, or agriculturalists, should have a special reference to their respective professional pursuits.

The public are undoubtedly right, in demanding that there should be appropriate courses of education, accessible to all classes of youth. And we rejoice at the prospect of ample provision for this purpose, in the improvement of our academies, and the establishment of commercial high-schools, gymnasia, lycea, agricultural seminars, &c. But do the public insist, that every college shall become a high-school, gymnasium, lyceum, and academy? Why should we interfere with these valuable institutions? Why wish to take their business out of their hands? The college has its appropriate object, and they have theirs. . . . What is the characteristic difference between a college and an academy? Not that the former teaches more branches than the latter. There are many academies in the country, whose scheme of studies, at least upon paper, is more various than that of the colleges. But while an academy teaches a little of every thing, the college, by directing its efforts to one uniform course, aims at doing its work with greater precision, and economy of time; just as the merchant who deals in a single class of commodities, or a manufacturer who produces but one kind of fabrics, executes his business more perfectly, than he whose attention and skill are divided among a multitude of objects. . . .

But might we not, by making the college more accessible to different descriptions of persons, enlarge our *numbers,* and in that way, increase our income? This might be the operation of the measure, for a very short time, while a degree from the college should retain its present value in public estimation; a value depending entirely upon the character of the education which we give. But the moment it is understood that the institution has descended to an inferior standard of attainment, its reputation will sink to a corresponding level. After we shall have become a college in *name only,* and in reality nothing more than an academy; or half college, and half academy; what will induce parents in various and distant parts of the country, to send us their sons, when they have academies enough in their own neighborhood? There is no magical influence in an act of incorporation, to give celebrity to a literary institution, which does not command respect for itself, by the elevated rank of its education. When the college has lost its hold on the public confidence, by depressing its standard of merit, by substituting a partial, for a thorough education, we may expect that it will be deserted by that class of persons who have hitherto been drawn here by high expectations and purposes. Even if we should *not* immediately suffer in point of *numbers,* yet we shall exchange the best portion of our students, for others of inferior aims and attainments.

As long as we can maintain an elevated character, we need be under no apprehension with respect to numbers. Without character, it will be in vain to think of retaining them. It is a hazardous experiment, to act upon the plan of gaining numbers first, and character afterwards. . . .

The difficulties with which we are now struggling, we fear would be increased, rather than diminished, by attempting to unite different plans of education. It is far from being our intention to dictate to *other* colleges a system to be adopted by them. There may be good and sufficient reasons why some of them should introduce a partial course of instruction. We are not sure, that the demand for thorough education is, at present, sufficient to fill all the colleges in the United States, with students who will be satisfied with nothing short of high and solid attainments. But it is to be hoped that, at no very distant period, they will be able to come up to this elevated ground, and leave the business of second-rate education to the inferior seminaries.

The competition of colleges may advance the interests of literature: if it is a competition for *excellence,* rather than for numbers; if each aims to surpass the others, not in an imposing display, but in the substantial value of its education. . . .

Our republican form of government renders it highly important, that great numbers should enjoy the advantage of a thorough education.

On the Eastern continent, the *few* who are destined to particular departments in political life, may be educated for the purpose; while the mass of
the people are left in comparative ignorance. But in this country, where
offices are accessible to all who are qualified for them, superior intellectual
attainments ought not to be confined to any description of persons. *Merchants, manufacturers,* and *farmers,* as well as professional gentlemen, take
their places in our public councils. A thorough education ought therefore
to be extended to all these classes. It is not sufficient that they be men of
sound judgment, who can decide correctly, and give a silent vote, on great
national questions. Their influence upon the minds of others is needed; an
influence to be produced by extent of knowledge, and the force of eloquence. Ought the speaking in our deliberate assemblies to be confined to
a single profession? If it is knowledge, which gives us the command of
physical agents and instruments, much more is it that which enables us to
control the combinations of moral and political machinery. . . .

Can merchants, manufacturers, and agriculturists, derive no benefit
from high intellectual culture? They are the very classes which, from their
situation and business, have the best opportunities for reducing the principles of science to their practical applications. The large estates which the
tide of prosperity in our country is so rapidly accumulating, will fall mostly
into their hands. Is it not desirable that they should be men of superior
education, of large and liberal views, of those solid and elegant attainments, which will raise them to a higher distinction, than the mere posses-
sion of property; which will not allow them to hoard their treasures, or
waste them in senseless extravagance; which will enable them to adorn
society by their learning, to move in the more intelligent circles with dignity, and to make such an application of their wealth, as will be most hon-
orable to themselves, and most beneficial to their country?

The active, enterprising character of our population, renders it
highly important, that this bustle and energy should be directed by sound
intelligence, the result of deep thought and early discipline. The greater
the impulse to action, the greater is the need of wise and skilful guidance.
When nearly all the ship's crew are aloft, setting the topsails, and catching
the breezes, it is necessary there should be a steady hand at helm. Light
and moderate learning is but poorly fitted to direct the energies of a nation, so widely extended, so intelligent, so powerful in resources, so rapidly
advancing in population, strength, and opulence. Where a free government gives full liberty to the human intellect to expand and operate, education should be proportionably liberal and ample. When even our moun-
tains, and rivers, and lakes, are upon a scale which seems to denote, that we
are destined to be a great and mighty nation, shall our literature be feeble,
and scanty, and superficial?

Report of the Faculty, Part II

. . . The subject of inquiry now presented, is, whether the plan of instruction pursued in Yale College, is sufficiently accommodated to the present

state of literature and science; and, especially, whether such a change is demanded as would leave out of this plan the study of the Greek and Roman classics, and make an acquaintance with ancient literature no longer necessary for a degree in the liberal arts. . . .

Whoever . . . without a preparation in classical literature, engages in any literary investigation, or undertakes to discuss any literary topic, or associates with those who in any country of Europe, or in this country, are acknowledged to be men of liberal acquirements, immediately feels a deficiency in his education, and is convinced that he is destitute of an important part of practical learning. If scholars, then, are to be prepared to act in the literary world as it in fact exists, classical literature, from considerations purely practical, should form an important part of their early discipline.

But the claims of classical learning are not limited to this single view. It may be defended not only as a necessary branch of education, in the present state of the world, but on the ground of its distinct and independent merits. Familiarity with the Greek and Roman writers is especially adapted to form the taste, and to discipline the mind, both in thought and diction, to the relish of what is elevated, chaste, and simple. . . .

But the study of the classics is useful, not only as it lays the foundations of a correct taste, and furnishes the student with those elementary ideas which are found in the literature of modern times, and which he no where so well acquires as in their original sources;—but also as the study itself forms the most effectual discipline of the mental faculties. This is a topic so often insisted on, that little need to be said of it here. It must be obvious to the most cursory observer, that the classics afford materials to exercise talent of every degree, from the first opening of the youthful intellect to the period of its highest maturity. The range of classical study extends from the elements of language, to the most difficult questions arising from literary research and criticism. Every faculty of the mind is employed; not only the memory, judgment, and reasoning powers, but the taste and fancy are occupied and improved.

Classical discipline, likewise, forms the best preparation for professional study. The interpretation of language, and its correct use, are no where more important, than in the professions of divinity and law. . . .

In the profession of medicine, the knowledge of the Greek and Latin languages is less necessary now than formerly; but even at the present time it may be doubted, whether the facilities which classical learning affords for understanding and rendering familiar the terms of science, do not more than counterbalance the time and labor requisite for obtaining this learning. . . .

To acquire the knowledge of any of the modern languages of Europe, is chiefly an effort of memory. The general structure of these languages is much the same as that of our own. The few idiomatical differences, are made familiar with little labor; nor is there the same necessity of accurate comparison and discrimination, as in studying the classic writers of Greece and Rome. To establish this truth, let a page of Voltaire be compared with a page of Tacitus. . . .

Modern languages, with most of our students, are studied, and will continue to be studied, as an accomplishment, rather than as a necessary acquisition. . . . To suppose the modern languages more practical than the ancient, to the great body of our students, because the former are now spoken in some parts of the world, is an obvious fallacy. The proper question is,—what course of discipline affords the best mental culture, leads to the most thorough knowledge of our own literature, and lays the best foundation for professional study. The ancient languages have here a decided advantage. If the elements of modern languages are acquired by our students in connection with the established collegiate course, and abundant facilities for this purpose, have for a long time, been afforded, further acquisitions will be easily made, where circumstances render them important and useful. From the graduates of this college, who have visited Europe, complaints have sometimes been heard, that their classical attainments were too small for the literature of the old world; but none are recollected to have expressed regret, that they had cultivated ancient learning while here, however much time they might have devoted to this subject. On the contrary, those who have excelled in classical literature, and have likewise acquired a competent knowledge of some one modern European language besides the English, have found themselves the best qualified to make a full use of their new advantages. Deficiencies in modern literature are easily and rapidly supplied, where the mind has had a proper previous discipline; deficiencies in ancient literature are supplied tardily, and in most instances, imperfectly. . . .

Such, then, being the value of ancient literature, both as respects the general estimation in which it is held in the literary world, and its intrinsic merits,—if the college should confer degrees upon students for their attainments in modern literature only, it would be to declare *that* to be a liberal education, which the world will not acknowledge to deserve the name;—and which those who shall receive degrees in this way, will soon find, is not what it is called. A liberal education, whatever course the college should adopt, would without doubt continue to be, what it long has been. Ancient literature is too deeply inwrought into the whole system of the modern literature of Europe to be so easily laid aside. The college ought not to presume upon its influence, nor to set itself up in any manner as a dictator. If it should pursue a course very different from that which the present state of literature demands; it it should confer its honors according to a rule which is not sanctioned by literary men, the faculty see nothing to expect for favoring such innovations, but that they will be considered visionaries in education, ignorant of its true design and objects, and unfit for their places. The ultimate consequence, it is not difficult to predict. The college would be distrusted by the public, and its reputation would be irrecoverably lost. . . .

No question has engaged the attention of the faculty more constantly, than how the course of education in the college might be improved, and rendered more practically useful. Free communications have at all times been held between the faculty and the corporation, on subjects connected with the instruction of the college. When the aid of the corporation has been thought necessary, it has been asked; and by this course of proceeding, the interests of the institution have been regularly advanced. No remark is more frequently made by those, who visit the college after the absence of some years, than that changes have been made for the better; and those who make the fullest investigation, are the most ready to approve what they find. The charge, therefore, that the college is stationary, that no efforts are made to accommodate it to the wants of the age, that all exertions are for the purpose of perpetuating abuses, and that the college is much the same as it was at the time of its foundation, are wholly gratuitous. The changes in the country, during the last century, have not been greater than the changes in the college. These remarks have been limited to Yale College, as its history is here best known; no doubt, other colleges alluded to in the above quotations, might defend themselves with equal success.

Event 4: The Morrill Land-Grant Act—1862

The Morrill Land-Grant Act of 1862 resulted in the expansion of public education, increased access of non-elites to higher education, the spread of practical utilitarian higher education, and the growth of Western higher education. This important piece of legislation follows.

Land-Grant Colleges

First Morrill Act

An Act Donating public lands to the several States and Territories which may provide colleges for the benefit of agriculture and the mechanic arts

Be it enacted by the Senate and House of Representatives of the United States of America in Congress assembled, That there be granted to the several States, for the purposes hereinafter mentioned, an amount of public land, to be apportioned to each State a quantity equal to thirty thousand acres for each Senator and Representative in Congress to which the States are respectively entitled by the apportionment under the census of 1860: *Provided,* That no mineral lands shall be selected or purchased under the provisions of this act.

(7 U.S.C. 301) Enacted July 2, 1862, ch. 130, sec. 1, 12 Stat. 503.

SEC. 2. *And be it further enacted,* That the land aforesaid, after being surveyed, shall be apportioned to the several States in sections or subdivisions of sections, not less than one-quarter of a section; and wherever there are public lands in a State, subject to sale at private entry at one dollar and twenty-five cents per acre, the quantity to which said State shall be entitled shall be selected from such lands, within the limits of such State; and the Secretary of Interior is hereby directed to issue to each of the States, in which there is not the quantity of public lands subject to sale at private entry, at one dollar and twenty-five cents per acre, to which said State may be entitled under the provisions of this act, land script to the amount in acres for the deficiency of its distributive share; said script to be sold by said States and the proceeds thereof applied to the uses and purposes prescribed in this act, and for no other purposes whatsoever: *Provided,* That in no case shall any State to which land script may thus be issued be allowed to locate the same within the limits of any other State, or of any territory of the United States; but their assignees may thus locate said land script upon any of the unappropriated lands of the United States subject to sale at private entry, at one dollar and twenty-five cents, or less, an acre: *And provided further,* That not more than one million acres shall be located by such assignees in any one of the States: *And provided further,* That no such location shall be made before one year from the passage of this act.

(7 U.S.C. 302) Enacted July 2, 1862, ch. 130, sec. 2, 12 Stat. 503.

SEC. 3. *And be it further enacted,* That all the expenses of management, superintendence, and taxes from date of selection of said lands, previous to their sales, and all expenses incurred in the management and disbursement of moneys which may be received therefrom, shall be paid by the States to which they may belong, out of the treasury of said States, so that the entire proceeds of the sale of said lands shall be applied, without any diminution whatever, to the purposes hereinafter mentioned.

(7 U.S.C. 303) Enacted July 2, 1862, ch. 130, sec. 3, 12 Stat. 504.

SEC. 4. That all moneys derived from the sale of lands aforesaid by the States to which lands are apportioned and from the sale of land scrip hereinbefore provided for shall be invested in bonds of the United States or of the States or some other safe bonds; or the same may be invested by the States having no State bonds in any manner after the legislatures of such States shall have assented thereto and engaged that such funds shall yield a fair and reasonable rate of return, to be fixed by the State legislatures, and that the principal thereof shall forever remain unimpaired: *Provided,* That the moneys so invested or loaned shall constitute a perpetual fund, the capital of which shall remain forever undiminished (except so far as may be provided in section 5 of this act), and the interest of which shall be inviolably appropriated, by each State which may take and claim the benefit of this act, to the endowment, support, and maintenance of at least one college where the leading object shall be, without excluding other scientific and classical studies and including military tactics, to teach such branches of learning as are related to agriculture and the mechanic arts, in such manner as the legislatures of the States may respectively prescribe, in order to promote the liberal and practical education of the industrial classes in the several pursuits and professions in life.

(7 U.S.C. 304) Enacted July 2, 1862, ch. 130; sec. 4, 12 Stat. 504; amended Mar. 3, 1883, ch. 102, 22 Stat. 484; amended Apr. 13, 1926, P.L. 113, 69th Cong., 44 Stat. 247.

SEC. 5. *And be it further enacted,* That the grant of land and land scrip hereby authorized shall be made on the following conditions, to which, as well as the provisions hereinbefore contained, the previous assent of the several States shall be signified by legislative acts:

First. If any portion of the fund invested, as provided by the foregoing section, or any portion of the interest thereon, shall, by any action or contingency, be diminished or lost, it shall be repalced by the State to which it belongs, so that the capital of the fund shall remain forever undiminished; and the annual interest shall be regularly applied without diminution to the purposes mentioned in the fourth section of this act, except that a sum, not exceeding 10 per centum upon the amount received by any State under the provisions of this act, may be expended for the purchase of lands for sites or experimental farms, whenever authorized by the respective legislatures of said States;

Second. No portion of said fund, nor the interest thereon, shall be applied, directly or indirectly, under any pretense whatsoever, to the purchase, erection, preservation, or repair of any building or buildings;

Third. Any State which may take and claim the benefit of the provisions of this act shall provide, within five years, at least not less than one college, as prescribed in the fourth section of this act, or the grant to such State shall cease; and said State shall be bound to pay the United States the amount received of any lands previously sold, and that the title to purchasers under the State shall be valid;

Fourth. An annual report shall be made regarding the progress of each college, recording any improvements and experiments made, with their costs and results, and such other matters, including State industrial and economical statistics, as may be supposed useful; one copy of which shall be transmitted by mail free, by each, to all the other colleges which may be endowed under the provisions of this act, and also one copy to the Secretary of the Interior;

Fifth. When lands shall be selected from those which have been raised to double the minimum price in consequence of railroad grants, they shall be computed to the States at the maximum price, and the number of acres proportionately diminished;

Sixth. No State, while in a condition of rebellion or insurrection against the Government of the United States, shall be entitled to the benefit of this act;

Seventh. No State shall be entitled to the benefits of this act unless it shall express acceptance thereof by its legislature within three years from

July 23, 1866: *Provided,* That when any Territory shall become a State and be admitted to the Union such new State shall be entitled to the benefits of the said act of July second, eighteen hundred and sixty-two, by expressing the acceptance therein required within three years from the date of its admission into the Union, and providing the college or colleges within five years after such acceptance, as prescribed in this act.

(7 U.S.C. 305) Enacted July 2, 1862, ch. 130, sec. 5, 12 Stat. 504; amended Mar. 3, 1873, ch. 231, sec. 3, 17 Stat. 559.

Sec. 6. * * *
(7 U.S.C. 306) Enacted July 2, 1862, ch. 130, sec. 6, 12 Stat. 505; repealed Dec. 16, 1930, P.L. 547, 71st Cong., sec. 1, 46 Stat. 1028.

Sec. 7. *And be it further enacted,* That land officers shall receive the same fees for locating land scrip issued under the provisions of this act as is now allowed for the location of military bounty land warrants under existing laws; *Provided,* That their maximum compensation shall not be thereby increased.

(7 U.S.C. 307) Enacted July 2, 1862, ch. 130, sec. 7, 12 Stat. 505.

Sec. 8. *And be it further enacted,* That the governors of the several States to which scrip shall be issued under this act shall be required to report annually to Congress all sales made of such scrip until the whole shall be disposed of, the amount received for the same, and what appropriation has been made of the proceeds.

(7 U.S.C. 308) Enacted July 2, 1862, ch. 130, sec. 8, 12 Stat. 505.

Event 5: The Creation of Cornell University—1868

Cornell was the jewel of the land-grant movement. It was a leader in opening college to the poor, in accepting the sciences and practical arts as coequal in the curriculum with the liberal arts, in establishing curricular options for students, and in adopting coeducation.

The following is the charter day address by Ezra Cornell. In this short speech, Cornell spoke his now famous mission for the new college. It would be "a place where any person can find instruction in any study." This speech was printed in the Cornell University *Register,* 1869–70 (pp. 16–17).

Mr. chairman, citizens, and friends:—I fear that many of you have visited

Ithaca at this time to meet with disappointment. If you came as did a friend recently from Pennsylvania, "expecting to find a finished institution," you will look around, be disappointed with what you see, and report, on your return to your homes, as he did, "I did not find one single thing finished."

Such, my friends, is not the entertainment we invited you to. We did not expect to have a "single thing finished," we did not desire it, and we have not directed our energies to that end. It is the commencement that we have now in hand. We did expect to have commenced an institution of learning which will mature in the future to a great degree of usefulness, which will place at the disposal of the industrial and productive classes of society the best facilities for the acquirement of practical knowledge and mental culture, on such terms as the limited means of the most humble can command.

I hope we have laid the foundation of an institution which shall combine practical with liberal education, which shall fit the youth of our country for the professions, the farms, the mines, the manufactories, for the investigations of science, and for mastering all the practical questions of life with success and honor.

I believe that we have made the beginning of an institution which will prove highly beneficial to the poor young men and the poor young women of our country. This is one thing which we have not finished, but in the course of time we hope to reach such a state of perfection as will enable any one by honest efforts and earnest labor to secure a thorough, practical, scientific or classical education. The individual is better, society is better, and the state is better, for the culture of the citizen; therefore we desire to extend the means for the culture of all.

I trust that we have made the beginning of an institution which shall bring science more directly to the aid of agriculture, and other branches of productive labor. Chemistry has the same great stores of wealth in reserve for agriculture that it has lavished so profusely upon the arts. We must instruct the young farmer how to avail himself of this hidden treasure.

The veterinarian will shield him against many of the losses which are frequent in his flocks and herds, losses which are now submitted to as matters of course by the uneducated farmer, and which, in the aggregate, amount to millions of dollars every year in our own State alone.

The entomologist must arm him for more successful warfare in defence of his growing crops, as the ravages of insects upon both grain and fruit have become enormous, resulting, also, in the loss of many millions of dollars each year.

Thus, in whatever direction we turn, we find ample opportunity for the applications of science in aid of the toiling millions. May we not hope that we have made the beginning of an institution which will strengthen the arm of the mechanic and multiply his powers of production through the agency of a better cultivated brain? Any person who visits our Patent Office at Washington, and contemplates the long halls stored with rejected models, will realize that our mechanics have great need of this aid.

The farmer is also enriched by increasing the knowledge and power of the mechanic. Mechanism, as applied to agriculture, was the great motive power which enabled the American farmers to feed the nation while it was struggling for existence against the late wicked rebellion, and it will enable them to pay the vast debts incurred by the nation while crushing that rebellion. This is an inviting field in which we must labor most earnestly. The mechanic should cease the fruitless effort "to bore an auger hole with a gimlet."

I desire that this shall prove to be the beginning of an institution, which shall furnish better means for the culture of all men of every calling, of every aim; which shall make men more truthful, more honest, more virtuous, more noble, more manly; which shall give them higher purpose, and more lofty aims, qualifying them to serve their fellow men better, preparing them to serve society better, training them to be more useful in their relations to the state, and to better comprehend their higher and holier relations to their families and their God. It shall be our aim, and our constant effort to make true Christian men, without dwarfing or paring them down to fit the narrow gauge of any sect.

Finally, I trust we have laid the foundation of an University—"an institution where any person can find instruction in any study."

Such have been our purposes. In that direction we have put forth our efforts, and on the future of such an institution we rest our hopes. If we have been successful in our beginning, to that extent and no further may we hope to be encouraged by the award of your approval. We have purposed that the finishing shall be the work of the future, and we ask that its approval or condemnation shall rest upon the quality of its maturing fruit.

To take the leadership of this great work we have selected a gentleman and a scholar, who, though young in years, we present before you to-day for inauguration, with entire confidence that the "right man is in the right place."

We have also selected a Faculty which I trust will very soon convince you that we have not thus early in the enterprise commenced blundering. They are in the main young men, and they are quite content to be judged by their works.

Invoking the blessing of Heaven upon our undertaking, we commend our cause to the scrutiny and the judgment of the American people.

Event 6: The Inauguration of Charles William Eliot as President of Harvard—1869

Charles William Eliot's 40-year presidency of Harvard marked a period of enormous change for the institution, including the adoption of the elective system and the transformation of Harvard from a college to a university. Even more importantly, Eliot changed the

face of higher education nationally by advocating the standardization of the high school curriculum, a uniform course credit system,
a three-year baccalaureate education, and an end to the required
classical curriculum.

The following is a portion of Eliot's 1869 inaugural address,
which was published by Harvard University under the apt title "A
Turning Point in Higher Education" (1969). In this now-classic
speech, Eliot called for major reforms in undergraduate education,
including the introduction of the elective system. The excerpt,
which consists of the first 21 pages of the 30-page speech, contains
all parts of the address germane to the college curriculum.

The endless controversies whether language, philosophy, mathematics, or
science supplies the best mental training, whether general education
should be chiefly literary or chiefly scientific, have no practical lesson for us
to-day. This University recognizes no real antagonism between literature
and science, and consents to no such narrow alternatives as mathematics or
classics, science or metaphysics. We would have them all, and at their best.
To observe keenly, to reason soundly, and to imagine vividly are operations as essential as that of clear and forcible expression; and to develop
one of these faculties, it is not necessary to repress and dwarf the others. A
university is not closely concerned with the applications of knowledge,
until its general education branches into professional. Poetry and
philosophy and science do indeed conspire to promote the material welfare of mankind; but science no more than poetry finds its best warrant in
its utility. Truth and right are above utility in all realms of thought and
action.

It were a bitter mockery to suggest that any subject whatever should
be taught less than it now is in American colleges. The only conceivable
aim of a college government in our day is to broaden, deepen, and invigo-
rate American teaching in all branches of learning. It will be generations
before the best of American institutions of education will get growth
enough to bear pruning. The descendants of the Pilgrim Fathers are still
very thankful for the parched corn of learning.

Recent discussions have added pitifully little to the world's stock of
wisdom about the staple of education. Who blows to-day such a ringing
trumpet-call to the study of language as Luther blew? Hardly a significant
word has been added in two centuries to Milton's description of the unprofitable way to study languages. Would any young American learn how
to profit by travel, that foolish beginning but excellent sequel to education,
he can find no apter advice than Bacon's. The practice of England and
America is literally centuries behind the precept of the best thinkers upon
education. A striking illustration may be found in the prevailing neglect of

the systematic study of the English language. How lamentably true to-day are these words of Locke: "If any one among us have a facility or purity more than ordinary in his mother-tongue, it is owing to chance, or his genius, or anything rather than to his education or any care of his teacher."

The best result of the discussion which has raged so long about the relative educational value of the main branches of learning is the conviction that there is room for them all in a sound scheme, provided that right methods of teaching be employed. It is not because of the limitation of their faculties that boys of eighteen come to college, having mastered nothing but a few score pages of Latin and Greek, and the bare elements of mathematics. Not nature, but an unintelligent system of instruction from the primary school through the college, is responsible for the fact that many college graduates have so inadequate a conception of what is meant by scientific observation, reasoning, and proof. It is possible for the young to get actual experience of all the principal methods of thought. There is a method of thought in language, and a method in mathematics, and another of natural and physical science, and another of faith. With wise direction, even a child would drink at all these springs. The actual problem to be solved is not what to teach, but how to teach. The revolutions accomplished in other fields of labor have a lesson for teachers. New England could not cut her hay with scythes, or the West her wheat with sickles. When millions are to be fed where formerly there were but scores, the single fish-line must be replaced by seines and trawls, the human shoulders by steam-elevators, and the wooden-axled ox-cart on a corduroy road by the smooth-running freight-train. In education, there is a great hungry multitude to be fed. The great well at Orvieto, up whose spiral paths files of donkeys painfully brought the sweet water in kegs, was an admirable construction in its day; but now we tap Fresh Pond in our chambers. The Orvieto well might remind some persons of educational methods not yet extinct. With good methods, we may confidently hope to give young men of twenty to twenty-five an accurate general knowledge of all the main subjects of human interest, besides a minute and thorough knowledge of the one subject which each may select as his principal occupation in life. To think this impossible is to despair of mankind; for unless a general acquaintance with many branches of knowledge, good so far as it goes, be attainable by great numbers of men, there can be no such thing as an intelligent public opinion; and in the modern world the intelligence of public opinion is the one indispensable condition of social progress.

What has been said of needed reformation in methods of teaching the subjects which have already been nominally admitted to the American curriculum applies not only to the university, but to the preparatory schools of every grade down to the primary. The American college is obliged to supplement the American school. Whatever elementary instruction the schools fail to give, the college must supply. The improvement of the schools has of late years permitted the college to advance the grade of its teaching, and adapt the methods of its later years to men instead of boys. This improvement of the college reacts upon the schools to their advantage; and this action and reaction will be continuous. A university is not built in the air, but on social and literary foundations which preceding generations have bequeathed. If the whole structure needs rebuilding, it must be rebuilt from the foundation. Hence, sudden reconstruction is impossible in our high places of education. Such inducements as the College can offer for enriching and enlarging the course of study pursued in preparatory schools, the Faculty has recently decided to give. The requirements in Latin and Greek grammar are to be set at a thorough knowledge of forms and general principles; the lists of classical authors accepted as equivalents for the regular standards are to be enlarged; an acquaintance with physical geography is to be required; the study of elementary mechanics is to be recommended, and prizes are to be offered for reading aloud, and for the critical analysis of passages from English authors. At the same time the University will take to heart the counsel which it gives to others.

In every department of learning the University would search out by trial and reflection the best methods of instruction. The University believes in the thorough study of language. It contends for all languages— Oriental, Greek, Latin, Romance, German, and especially for the mother-tongue; seeing in them all one institution, one history, one means of discipline, one department of learning. In teaching languages, it is for this American generation to invent, or to accept from abroad, better tools than the old; to devise, or to transplant from Europe, prompter and more comprehensive methods than the prevailing; and to command more intelligent labor, in order to gather rapidly and surely the best fruit of that culture and have time for other harvests.

The University recognizes the natural and physical sciences as indispensable branches of education, and has long acted upon this opinion; but it would have science taught in a rational way, objects and instruments in hand—not from books merely, not through the memory chiefly, but by the seeing eye and the informing fingers. Some of the scientific scoffers at gerund grinding and nonsense verses might well look at home; the prevailing methods of teaching science, the world over, are, on the whole, less intelligent than the methods of teaching language. The University would have scientific studies in school and college and professional school develop and discipline those powers of the mind by which science has been created and is daily nourished—the powers of observation, the inductive faculty, the sober imagination, the sincere and proportionate judgment. A student in the elements gets no such training by studying even a good text-book, though he really master it, nor yet by sitting at the feet of the most admirable lecturer.

If there be any subject which seems fixed and settled in its educational aspects, it is the mathematics; yet there is no department of the Uni-

versity which has been, during the last fifteen years, in such a state of vigorous experiment upon methods and appliances of teaching as the
mathematical department. It would be well if the primary schools had as
much faith in the possibility of improving their way of teaching multiplication.

The important place which history, and mental, moral, and political
philosophy, should hold in any broad scheme of education is recognized of
all; but none know so well how crude are the prevailing methods of teaching these subjects as those who teach them best. They cannot be taught
from books alone, but must be vivified and illustrated by teachers of active,
comprehensive, and judicial mind. To learn by rote a list of dates is not to
study history. Mr. Emerson says that history is biography. In a deep sense
this is true. Certainly, the best way to impart the facts of history to the
young is through the quick interest they take in the lives of the men and
women who fill great historical scenes or epitomize epochs. From the centers so established, their interest may be spread over great areas. For the
young especially, it is better to enter with intense sympathy into the great
moments of history, than to stretch a thin attention through its weary centuries.

Philosophical subjects should never be taught with authority. They
are not established sciences; they are full of disputed matters, open questions, and bottomless speculations. It is not the function of the teacher to
settle philosophical and political controversies for the pupil, or even to
recommend to him any one set of opinions as better than another. Exposition, not imposition, of opinions is the professor's part. The student should
be made acquainted with all sides of these controversies, with the salient
points of each system; he should be shown what is still in force of institutions or philosophies mainly outgrown, and what is new in those now in
vogue. The very word "education" is a standing protest against dogmatic
teaching. The notion that education consists in the authoritative inculcation of what the teacher deems true may be logical and appropriate in a
convent, or a seminary for priests, but it is intolerable in universities and
public schools, from primary to professional. The worthy fruit of academic
culture is an open mind, trained to careful thinking, instructed in the
methods of philosophic investigation, acquainted in a general way with the
accumulated thought of past generations, and penetrated with humility. It
is thus that the university in our day serves Christ and the church.

The increasing weight, range, and thoroughness of the examination
for admission to college may strike some observers with dismay. The increase of real requisitions is hardly perceptible from year to year; but on
looking back ten or twenty years, the changes are marked, and all in one
direction. The dignity and importance of this examination have been
steadily rising, and this rise measures the improvement of the preparatory
schools. When the gradual improvement of American schools has lifted

them to a level with the German gymnasia, we may expect to see the American college bearing a nearer resemblance to the German faculties of philosophy than it now does. The actual admission examination may best be compared with the first examination of the University of France. This examination, which comes at the end of a French boy's school life, is for the degree of Bachelor of Arts or of Sciences. The degree is given to young men who come fresh from school and have never been under university teachers; a large part of the recipients never enter the university. The young men who come to our examination for admission to college are older than the average of French Bachelors of Arts. The examination tests not only the capacity of the candidates, but also the quality of their school instruction; it is a great event in their lives, though not, as in France, marked by any degree. The examination is conducted by college professors and tutors who have never had any relations whatever with those examined. It would be a great gain if all subsequent college examinations could be as impartially conducted by competent examiners brought from without the college and paid for their services. When the teacher examines his class, there is no effective examination of the teacher. If the examinations for the scientific, theological, medical, and dental degrees were conducted by independent boards of examiners, appointed by professional bodies of dignity and influence, the significance of these degrees would be greatly enhanced. The same might be said of the degree of Bachelor of Laws, were it not that this degree is, at present, earned by attendance alone, and not by attendance and examination. The American practice of allowing the teaching body to examine for degrees has been partly dictated by the scarcity of men outside the faculties who are at once thoroughly acquainted with the subjects of examination, and sufficiently versed in teaching to know what may fairly be expected of both students and instructors. This difficulty could now be overcome. The chief reason, however, for the existence of this practice is that the faculties were the only bodies that could confer degrees intelligently, when degrees were obtained by passing through a prescribed course of study without serious checks, and completing a certain term of residence without disgrace. The change in the manner of earning the University degrees ought, by right, to have brought into being an examining body distinct from the teaching body. So far as the College proper is concerned, the Board of Overseers have, during the past year, taken a step which tends in this direction.

The rigorous examination for admission has one good effect throughout the college course: it prevents a waste of instruction upon incompetent persons. A school with a low standard for admission and a high standard of graduation, like West Point, is obliged to dismiss a large proportion of its students by the way. Hence much individual distress, and a great waste of resources, both public and private. But, on the other hand, it must not be supposed that every student who enters Harvard College necessarily graduates. Strict annual examinations are to be passed. More than a fourth of those who enter the College fail to take their degree.

Only a few years ago, all students who graduated at this College passed through one uniform curriculum. Every man studied the same subjects in the same proportions, without regard to his natural bent or preference. The individual student had no choice of either subjects or teachers. This system is still the prevailing system among American colleges, and finds vigorous defenders. It has the merit of simplicity. So had the school methods of our grandfathers—one primer, one catechism, one rod for all children. On the whole, a single common course of studies, tolerably well selected to meet the average needs, seems to most Americans a very proper and natural thing, even for grown men.

As a people, we do not apply to mental activities the principle of division of labor; and we have but a halting faith in special training for high professional employments. The vulgar conceit that a Yankee can turn his hand to anything we insensibly carry into high places, where it is preposterous and criminal. We are accustomed to seeing men leap from farm or shop to court-room or pulpit, and we half believe that common men can safely use the seven-league boots of genius. What amount of knowledge and experience do we habitually demand of our lawgivers? What special training do we ordinarily think necessary for our diplomatists?—although in great emergencies the nation has known where to turn. Only after years of the bitterest experience did we come to believe the professional training of a soldier to be of value in war. This lack of faith in the prophecy of a natural bent, and in the value of a discipline concentrated upon a single object, amounts to a national danger.

In education, the individual traits of different minds have not been sufficiently attended to. Through all the period of boyhood the school studies should be representative; all the main fields of knowledge should be entered upon. But the young man of nineteen or twenty ought to know what he likes best and is most fit for. If his previous training has been sufficiently wide, he will know by that time whether he is most apt at language or philosophy or natural science or mathematics. If he feels no loves, he will at least have his hates. At that age the teacher may wisely abandon the school-dame's practice of giving a copy of nothing but zeros to the child who alleges that he cannot make that figure. When the revelation of his own peculiar taste and capacity comes to a young man, let him reverently give it welcome, thank God, and take courage. Thereafter he knows his way to happy, enthusiastic work, and, God willing, to usefulness and success. The civilization of a people may be inferred from the variety of its tools. There are thousands of years between the stone hatchet and the machine-shop. As tools multiply, each is more ingeniously adapted to its own exclusive purpose. So with the men that make the State. For the individual, concentration, and the highest development of his own peculiar faculty, is the only prudence. But for the State, it is variety, not uniformity, of intellectual product, which is needful.

These principles are the justification of the system of elective studies which has been gradually developed in this College during the past forty years. At present the Freshman year is the only one in which there is a fixed course prescribed for all. In the other three years, more than half the time allotted to study is filled with subjects chosen by each student from lists which comprise six studies in the Sophomore year, nine in the Junior year, and eleven in the Senior year. The range of elective studies is large, though there are some striking deficiencies. The liberty of choice of subject is wide, but yet has very rigid limits. There is a certain framework which must be filled; and about half the material of the filling is prescribed. The choice offered to the student does not lie between liberal studies and professional or utilitarian studies. All the studies which are open to him are liberal and disciplinary, not narrow or special. Under this system the College does not demand, it is true, one invariable set of studies of every candidate for the first degree in Arts; but its requisitions for this degree are nevertheless high and inflexible, being nothing less than four years devoted to liberal culture.

It has been alleged that the elective system must weaken the bond which unites members of the same class. This is true; but in view of another much more efficient cause of the diminution of class intimacy, the point is not very significant. The increased size of the college classes inevitably works a great change in this respect. One hundred and fifty young men cannot be so intimate with each other as fifty used to be. This increase is progressive. Taken in connection with the rising average age of the students, it would compel the adoption of methods of instruction different from the old, if there were no better motive for such change. The elective system fosters scholarship, because it gives free play to natural preferences and inborn aptitudes, makes possible enthusiasm for a chosen work, relieves the professor and the ardent disciple of the presence of a body of students who are compelled to an unwelcome task, and enlarges instruction by substituting many and various lessons given to small, lively classes, for a few lessons many times repeated to different sections of a numerous class. The College therefore proposes to persevere in its efforts to establish, improve, and extend the elective system. Its administrative difficulties, which seem formidable at first, vanish before a brief experience.

There has been much discussion about the comparative merits of lectures and recitations. Both are useful—lectures, for inspiration, guidance, and the comprehensive methodizing which only one who has a view of the whole field can rightly contrive; recitations, for securing and testifying a thorough mastery on the part of the pupil of the treatise or author in hand, for conversational comment and amplification, for emulation and competition. Recitations alone readily degenerate into dusty repetitions, and lectures alone are too often a useless expenditure of force. The lecturer pumps laboriously into sieves. The water may be wholesome, but it runs through. A mind must work to grow. Just as far, however, as the student can be relied on to master and appreciate his author without the aid of frequent questioning and repetitions, so far is it possible to dispense with recitations. Accordingly, in the later College years there is a decided tendency to diminish the number of recitations, the faithfulness of the student being tested by periodical examinations. This tendency is in a right direction, if prudently controlled.

The discussion about lectures and recitations has brought out some strong opinions about text-books and their use. Impatience with text-books and manuals is very natural in both teachers and taught. These books are indeed, for the most part, very imperfect, and stand in constant need of correction by the well-informed teacher. Stereotyping, in its present undeveloped condition, is in part to blame for their most exasperating defects. To make the metal plates keep pace with the progress of learning is costly. The manifest deficiencies of text-books must not, however, drive us into a too sweeping condemnation of their use. It is a rare teacher who is superior to all manuals in his subject. Scientific manuals are, as a rule, much worse than those upon language, literature, or philosophy; yet the main improvement in medical education in this country during the last twenty years has been the addition of systematic recitations from text-books to the lectures which were formerly the principal means of theoretical instruction. The training of a medical student, inadequate as it is, offers the best example we have of the methods and fruits of an education mainly scientific. The transformation which the average student of a good medical school undergoes in three years is strong testimony to the efficiency of the training he receives.

There are certain common misapprehensions about colleges in general, and this College in particular, to which I wish to devote a few moments' attention. And, first, in spite of the familiar picture of the moral dangers which environ the student, there is no place so safe as a good college during the critical passage from boyhood to manhood. The security of the college commonwealth is largely due to its exuberant activity. Its public opinion, though easily led astray, is still high in the main. Its scholarly tastes and habits, its eager friendships and quick hatreds, its keen debates, its frank discussions of character and of deep political and religious questions, all are safeguards against sloth, vulgarity, and depravity. Its society and, not less, its solitudes are full of teaching. Shams, conceit, and fictitious distinctions get no mercy. There is nothing but ridicule for bombast and sentimentality. Repression of genuine sentiment and emotion is indeed, in this College, carried too far. Reserve is more respectable than any undiscerning communicativeness; but neither Yankee shamefacedness nor English stolidity is admirable. This point especially touches you, young men, who are still undergraduates. When you feel a true admiration for a teacher, a glow of enthusiasm for work, a thrill of pleasure at some excellent saying, give it expression. Do not be ashamed of these emotions. Cherish the natural sentiment of personal devotion to the teacher who calls out your better powers. It is a great delight to serve an intellectual master. We Americans are but too apt to lose this happiness. German and French students get it. If ever in after years you come to smile at the youthful reverence you paid, believe me, it will be with tears in your eyes.

Many excellent persons see great offense in any system of college rank; but why should we expect more of young men than we do of their elders? How many men and women perform their daily tasks from the highest motives alone—for the glory of God and the relief of man's estate? Most people work for bare bread, a few for cake. The college rank-list reinforces higher motives. In the campaign for character, no auxiliaries are to be refused. Next to despising the enemy, it is dangerous to reject allies. To devise a suitable method of estimating the fidelity and attainments of college students is, however, a problem which has long been under discussion, and has not yet received a satisfactory solution. The worst of rank as a stimulus is the self-reference it implies in the aspirants. The less a young man thinks about the cultivation of his mind, about his own mental progress,—about himself, in short,—the better.

The petty discipline of colleges attracts altogether too much attention from both friends and foes. It is to be remembered that the rules concerning decorum, however necessary to maintain the high standard of manners and conduct which characterizes this College, are nevertheless justly described as petty. What is technically called a quiet term cannot be accepted as the acme of university success. This success is not to be measured by the frequency or rarity of college punishments. The criteria of success or failure in a high place of learning are not the boyish escapades of an insignificant minority, nor the exceptional cases of ruinous vice. Each year must be judged by the added opportunities of instruction, by the prevailing enthusiasm in learning, and by the gathered wealth of culture and character. The best way to put boyishness to shame is to foster scholarship and manliness. The manners of a community cannot be improved by main force any more than its morals. The Statutes of the University need some amendment and reduction in the chapters on crimes and misdemeanors. But let us render to our fathers the justice we shall need from our sons. What is too minute or precise for our use was doubtless wise and proper in its day. It was to inculcate a reverent bearing and due consideration for things sacred that the regulations prescribed a black dress on Sunday. Black is not the only decorous wear in these days; but we must not seem, in ceasing from this particular mode of good manners, to think less of the gentle breeding of which only the outward signs, and not the substance, have been changed.

Harvard College has always attracted and still attracts students in all conditions of life. From the city trader or professional man, who may be careless how much his son spends at Cambridge, to the farmer or mechanic, who finds it a hard sacrifice to give his boy his time early enough to enable him to prepare for college, all sorts and conditions of men have wished and still wish to send their sons hither. There are always scores of young men in this University who earn or borrow every dollar they spend here. Every year many young men enter this College without any resources whatever. If they prove themselves men of capacity and character, they never go away for lack of money. More than twenty thousand dollars a year is now devoted to aiding students of narrow means to compass their education, besides all the remitted fees and the numerous private benefactions. These latter are unfailing. Taken in connection with the proceeds of the funds applicable to the aid of poor students, they enable the Corporation to say that no good student need ever stay away from Cambridge or leave college simply because he is poor. There is one uniform condition, however, on which help is given: the recipient must be of promising ability and the best character. The community does not owe superior education to all children, but only to the élite—to those who, having the capacity, prove by hard work that they have also the necessary perseverance and endurance. The process of preparing to enter college under the difficulties which poverty entails is just such a test of worthiness as is needed. At this moment there is no college in the country more eligible for a poor student than Harvard on the mere ground of economy. The scholarship funds are mainly the fruit of the last fifteen years. The future will take care of itself; for it is to be expected that the men who in this generation have had the benefit of these funds, and who succeed in after life, will pay manyfold to their successors in need the debt which they owe, not to the college, but to benefactors whom they cannot even thank, save in heaven. No wonder that scholarships are founded. What greater privilege than this of giving young men of promise the coveted means of intellectual growth and freedom? The angels of heaven might envy mortals so fine a luxury. The happiness which the winning of a scholarship gives is not the recipient's alone: it flashes back to the home whence he came, and gladdens anxious hearts there. The good which it does is not his alone, but descends, multiplying at every step, through generations. Thanks to the beneficent mysteries of hereditary transmission, no capital earns such interest as personal culture. The poorest and the richest students are equally welcome here, provided that with their poverty or their wealth they bring capacity, ambition, and purity. The poverty of scholars is of inestimable worth in this money-getting nation. It maintains the true standards of virtue and honor. The poor friars, not the bishops, saved the church. The poor scholars and preachers of duty defend the modern community against its own material prosperity. Luxury and learning are ill bedfellows. Nevertheless, this College owes much of its distinctive character to those who, bringing hither from refined homes good breeding, gentle tastes, and a manly delicacy, add to them openness and activity of mind, intellectual interests, and a sense of public duty. It is as high a privilege for a rich man's son as for a poor man's to resort to these academic halls, and so to take his proper place among cultivated and intellectual men. To lose altogether the presence of those who in early life have enjoyed the domestic and social advantages of wealth would be as great a blow to the College as to lose the sons of the poor. The interests of the College and the country are identical in this regard. The country suffers when the rich are ignorant and unrefined. Inherited wealth is an unmitigated curse when divorced from culture. Harvard College is sometimes reproached with being aristocratic. If by aristocracy be meant a stupid and pretentious caste, founded on wealth, and birth, and an affectation of European manners, no charge could be more preposterous: the College is intensely American in affection, and intensely democratic in temper. But there is an aristocracy to which the sons of Harvard have belonged, and, let us hope, will ever aspire to belong—the aristocracy which excels in manly sports, carries off the honors and prizes of the learned professions, and bears itself with distinction in all fields of intellectual labor and combat; the aristocracy which in peace stands firmest for the public honor and renown, and in war rides first into the murderous thickets.

The attitude of the University in the prevailing discussions touching the education and fit employments of women demands brief explanation. America is the natural arena for these debates; for here the female sex has a better past and a better present than elsewhere. Americans, as a rule, hate disabilities of all sorts, whether religious, political, or social. Equality between the sexes, without privilege or oppression on either side, is the happy custom of American homes. While this great discussion is going on, it is the duty of the University to maintain a cautious and expectant policy. The Corporation will not receive women as students into the College proper, nor into any school whose discipline requires residence near the school. The difficulties involved in a common residence of hundreds of young men and women of immature character and marriageable age are very grave. The necessary police regulations are exceedingly burdensome. The Corporation are not influenced to this decision, however, by any crude notions about the innate capacities of women. The world knows next to nothing about the natural mental capacities of the female sex. Only after generations of civil freedom and social equality will it be possible to obtain the data necessary for an adequate discussion of woman's natural tendencies, tastes, and capabilities. Again, the Corporation do not find it necessary to entertain a confident opinion upon the fitness or unfitness of women for professional pursuits. It is not the business of the University to decide this mooted point. In this country the University does not undertake to protect the community against incompetent lawyers, ministers, or doctors. The community must protect itself by refusing to employ such. Practical, not theoretical, considerations determine the policy of the University. Upon a matter concerning which prejudices are deep, and opinion inflammable, and experience scanty, only one course is prudent or justifiable when such great interests are at stake—that of cautious and well-considered experiment. The practical problem is to devise a safe, promising, and instructive experiment. Such an experiment the Corporation have meant to try in opening the newly established University Courses of Instruction to competent women. In these courses the University offers to young women who have been to good schools as many years as they wish of liberal culture in studies which have no direct professional value, to be sure, but which enrich and enlarge both intellect and character. The University hopes thus to contribute to the intellectual emancipation of women. It hopes to prepare some women better than they would otherwise have been prepared for the profession of teaching, the one learned profession to which women have already acquired a clear title. It hopes that the proffer of this higher instruction will have some reflex influence upon schools for girls—to discourage superficiality, and to promote substantial education.

The governing bodies of the University are the Faculties, the Board of Overseers, and the Corporation. The University as a place of study and instruction is, at any moment, what the Faculties make it. The professors, lecturers, and tutors of the University are the living sources of learning and enthusiasm. They personally represent the possibilities of instruction. They are united in several distinct bodies, the academic and professional Faculties, each of which practically determines its own processes and rules. The discussion of methods of instruction is the principal business of these bodies. As a fact, progress comes mainly from the Faculties. This has been conspicuously the case with the Academic and Medical Faculties during the last fifteen or twenty years. The undergraduates used to have a notion that the time of the Academic Faculty was mainly devoted to petty discipline. Nothing could be further from the truth. The Academic Faculty is the most active, vigilant, and devoted body connected with the University. It indeed is constantly obliged to discuss minute details, which might appear trivial to an inexperienced observer. But, in education, technical details tell. Whether German be studied by the Juniors once a week as an extra study, or twice a week as an elective, seems, perhaps, an unimportant matter; but, twenty years hence, it makes all the difference between a generation of Alumni who know German and a generation who do not. The Faculty renews its youth, through the frequent appointments of tutors and assistant professors, better and oftener than any other organization within the University. Two kinds of men make good teachers—young men and men who never grow old. The incessant discussions of the Academic Faculty have borne much fruit: witness the transformation of the University since the beginning of President Walker's administration. And it never tires. New men take up the old debates, and one year's progress is not less than another's. The divisions within the Faculty are never between the old and the young officers. There are always old radicals and young conservatives.

The Medical Faculty affords another illustration of the same principle—that for real university progress we must look principally to the teaching bodies. The Medical School to-day is almost three times as strong as it was fifteen years ago. Its teaching power is greatly increased, and its methods have been much improved. This gain is the work of the Faculty of the School.

If then the Faculties be so important, it is a vital question how the quality of these bodies can be maintained and improved. It is very hard to find competent professors for the University. Very few Americans of eminent ability are attracted to this profession. The pay has been too low, and there has been no gradual rise out of drudgery, such as may reasonably be expected in other learned callings. The law of supply and demand, or the commercial principle that the quality as well as the price of goods is best regulated by the natural contest between producers and consumers, never has worked well in the province of high education. And in spite of the high standing of some of its advocates, it is well-nigh certain that the so-called law never can work well in such a field. The reason is that the demand for instructors of the highest class on the part of parents and trustees is an ignorant demand, and the supply of highly educated teachers is so limited that the consumer has not sufficient opportunities of informing himself concerning the real qualities of the article he seeks. Originally a bad judge, he remains a bad judge, because the supply is not sufficiently abundant and various to instruct him. Moreover, a need is not necessarily a demand. Everybody knows that the supposed law affords a very imperfect protection against short weight, adulteration, and sham, even in the case of those commodities which are most abundant in the market and most familiar to buyers. The most intelligent community is defenseless enough in buying clothes and groceries. When it comes to hiring learning and inspiration and personal weight, the law of supply and demand breaks down altogether. A university cannot be managed like a railroad or a cotton-mill.

There are, however, two practicable improvements in the position of college professors which will be of very good effect. Their regular stipend must and will be increased, and the repetitions which now harass them must be diminished in number. It is a strong point of the elective system that, by reducing the size of classes or divisions, and increasing the variety of subjects, it makes the professors' labors more agreeable.

Experience teaches that the strongest and most devoted professors will contribute something to the patrimony of knowledge; or if they invent little themselves, they will do something toward defending, interpreting, or diffusing the contributions of others. Nevertheless, the prime business of American professors in this generation must be regular and assiduous class teaching. With the exception of the endowments of the Observatory, the University does not hold a single fund primarily intended to secure to men of learning the leisure and means to prosecute original researches. . . .

Event 7: The Establishment of
The Johns Hopkins University—1876

The Johns Hopkins University was America's first research university and gradaute school. This excerpt from "The Launching of a University," by Johns Hopkins' first president, Daniel Coit Gilman, tells how this unusual institution evolved and how it differed from the other colleges of its day.

When the announcement was made to the public, at the end of 1873, that a wealthy merchant of Baltimore had provided by his will for the establishment of a new university, a good deal of latent regret was felt because the country seemed to have already more higher seminaries than it could supply with teachers, students, or funds. Another "college" was expected to join the crowded column, and impoverish its neighbors by its superior attractions. Fortunately, the founder was wise as well as generous. He used the simplest phrases to express his wishes; and he did not define the distinguished name that he bestowed upon his child, nor embarrass its future by needless conditions. Details were left to a sagacious body of trustees whom he charged with the duty of supervision. They travelled east and west, brought to Baltimore experienced advisers, Eliot, Angell, and White, and procured many of the latest books that discussed the problem of education. By and by they chose a president, and accepted his suggestion that they should give emphasis to the word "university" and should endeavor to build up an institution quite different from a college, thus making an addition to American education, not introducing a rival. Young men who had already gone through that period of mental discipline which commonly leads to the baccalaureate degree, were invited to come and pursue those advanced studies for which they might have been prepared, and to accept the inspiration and guidance of professors selected because of acknowledged distinction or of special aptitudes. Among the phrases that were employed to indicate the project were many which then were novel, although they are now the commonplaces of catalogues and speeches.

Opportunities for advanced, not professional, studies, were then scanty in this country. In the older colleges certain graduate courses were attended by a small number of followers—but the teachers were for the most part absorbed with undergraduate instruction, and could give but little time to the few who sought their guidance.

Event 8: Report of the Committee of Ten—1893

In 1892, the National Education Association appointed a Committee of Ten, chaired by President Eliot of Harvard, to examine the diversity and lack of commonality in secondary school curriculum and the state of articulation between secondary schools and colleges. The resulting 1893 report represented the first national attempt to standardize the high school curriculum and to coordinate secondary and postsecondary education. The following excerpt is from the National Educational Association's "Report of the Committee of Ten" (U.S. Bureau of Education, 1893, pp. 3–4, 5, 6–7, 11, 16–17, 44–53).

To the National Council of Education:

The Committee of Ten appointed at the meeting of the National Educational Association at Saratoga on the 9th of July, 1892, have the honor to present the following report: —

At the meeting of the National Council of Education in 1891, a Committee appointed at a previous meeting made a valuable report through their Chairman, Mr. James H. Baker, then Principal of the Denver High School, on the general subject of uniformity in school programmes and in requirements for admission to college. The Committee was continued, and was authorized to procure a Conference on the subject of uniformity during the meeting of the National Council in 1892, the Conference to consist of representatives of leading colleges and secondary schools in different parts of the country. This Conference was duly summoned, and held meetings at Saratoga on July 7th, 8th, and 9th, 1892. There were present between twenty and thirty delegates. Their discussions took a wide range, but resulted in the following specific recommendations, which the Conference sent to the National Council of Education then in session.

1. That it is expedient to hold a conference of school and college teachers of each principal subject which enters into the programmes of secondary schools in the United States and into the requirements for admission to college—as, for example, of Latin, of geometry, or of American history—each conference to consider the proper limits of its subject, the best methods of instruction, the most desirable allotment of time for the subject, and the best methods of testing the pupils' attainments therein, and each conference to represent fairly the different parts of the country.

2. That a Committee be appointed with authority to select the members of these conferences and to arrange their meetings, the results of all the conferences to be reported to this Committee for such action as it may deem appropriate, and to form the basis of a report to be presented to the Council by this Committee.

3. That this Committee consist of the following gentlemen: Charles W.

Eliot, President of Harvard University, Cambridge, Mass., *Chairman*, William T. Harris, Commissioner of Education, Washington, D.C., James B. Angell, President of the University of Michigan, Ann Arbor, Mich., John Tetlow, Head Master of the Girls' High School and the Girls' Latin School, Boston, Mass., James M. Taylor, President of Vassar College, Poughkeepsie, N.Y., Oscar D. Robinson, Principal of the High School, Albany, N.Y., James H. Baker, President of the University of Colorado, Boulder, Colo., Richard H. Jesse, President of the University of Missouri, Columbia, Mo., James C. Mackenzie, Head Master of the Lawrenceville School, Lawrenceville, N.J., and Henry C. King, Professor in Oberlin College, Oberlin, Ohio.

These recommendations of the Conference were adopted by the National Council of Education on the 9th of July; and the Council communicated the recommendations to the Directors of the National Educational Association....

The Committee of Ten, after a preliminary discussion on November 9th, decided on November 10th to organize conferences on the following subjects:—1. Latin; 2. Greek; 3. English; 4. Other Modern Languages; 5. Mathematics; 6. Physics, Astronomy, and Chemistry; 7. Natural History (Biology, including Botany, Zoölogy, and Physiology); 8. History, Civil Government, and Political Economy; 9. Geography (Physical Geography, Geology, and Meteorology). They also decided that each Conference should consist of ten members....

The Committee next adopted the following list of questions as a guide for the discussion of all the Conferences, and directed that the Conferences be called together on the 28th of December:—

1. In the school course of study extending approximately from the age of six years to eighteen years—a course including the periods of both elementary and secondary instruction—at what age should the study which is the subject of the Conference be first introduced?
2. After it is introduced, how many hours a week for how many years should be devoted to it?
3. How many hours a week for how many years should be devoted to it during the last four years of the complete course; that is, during the ordinary high school period?
4. What topics, or parts, of the subject may reasonably be covered during the whole course?
5. What topics, or parts, of the subject may best be reserved for the last four years?
6. In what form and to what extent should the subject enter into college requirements for admission? Such questions as the sufficiency of translation at sight as a test of knowledge of a language, or the superiority of a laboratory examination in a scientific subject to a written examina-

tion on a text-book, are intended to be suggested under this head by the phrase "in what form "

7. Should the subject be treated differently for pupils who are going to college, for those who are going to a scientific school, and for those who, presumably, are going to neither?
8. At what stage should this differentiation begin, if any be recommended?
9. Can any description be given of the best method of teaching this subject throughout the school course?
10. Can any description be given of the best mode of testing attainments in this subject at college admission examinations?
11. For those cases in which colleges and universities permit a division of the admission examination into a preliminary and a final examination, separated by at least a year, can the best limit between the preliminary and final examinations be approximately defined? . . .

On one very important question of general policy which affects profoundly the preparation of all school programmes, the Committee of Ten and all the Conferences are absolutely unanimous. Among the questions suggested for discussion in each Conference were the following:

7. Should the subject be treated differently for pupils who are going to college, for those who are going to a scientific school, and for those who, presumably, are going to neither?
8. At what age should this differentiation begin, if any be recommended?

The 7th question is answered unanimously in the negative by the Conferences, and the 8th therefore needs no answer. The Committee of Ten unanimously agree with the Conferences. Ninety-eight teachers, intimately concerned either with the actual work of American secondary schools, or with the results of that work as they appear in students who come to college, unanimously declare that every subject which is taught at all in a secondary school should be taught in the same way and to the same extent to every pupil so long as he pursues it, no matter what the probable destination of the pupil may be, or at what point his education is to cease. Thus, for all pupils who study Latin, or history, or algebra, for example, the allotment of time and the method of instruction in a given school should be the same year by year. Not that all the pupils should pursue every subject for the same number of years; but so long as they do pursue it, they should all be treated alike. It has been a very general custom in American high schools and academies to make up separate courses of study for pupils of supposed different destinations, the proportions of the several studies in the different courses being various. The principle laid down by the Conferences will, if logically carried out, make a great simplification in secondary school programmes. It will lead to each subject's being treated by the school in the same way by the year for all pupils, and this, whether the individual pupil be required to choose between courses which run through several years, or be allowed some choice among subjects year by year. . . .

As samples of school programmes constructed within the schedules of Table III., the Committee present the following working programmes, which they recommend for trial wherever the secondary school period is limited to four years. All four combined might, of course, be tabulated as one programme with options by subject.

These four programmes taken together use all the subjects mentioned in Table III., and usually, but not always, to about the amounts there indicated. History and English suffer serious contraction in the Classical programme. All four programmes conform to the general recommendations of the Conferences, that is,—they treat each subject in the same way for all pupils with trifling exceptions; they give time enough to each subject to win from it the kind of mental training it is fitted to supply; they put the different principal subjects on an approximate equality so far as time-allotment is concerned; they omit all short information courses; and they make sufficiently continuous the instruction in each of the main lines, namely, language, science, history and mathematics. With slight modifications, they would prepare the pupils for admission to appropriate courses in any American college or university on the existing requirements; and they would also meet the new college requirements which are suggested below.

In preparing these programmes, the Committee were perfectly aware that it is impossible to make a satisfactory secondary school programme, limited to a period of four years, and founded on the present elementary school subjects and methods. In the opinion of the Committee, several subjects now reserved for high schools,—such as algebra, geometry, natural science, and foreign languages,—should be begun earlier than now, and therefore within the schools classified as elementary; or, as an alternative, the secondary school period should be made to begin two years earlier than at present, leaving six years instead of eight for the elementary school period. Under the present organization, elementary subjects and elementary methods are, in the judgment of the Committee, kept in use too long.

The most striking differences in the four programmes will be found, as is intimated in the headings, in the relative amounts of time given to foreign languages. In the Classical programme the foreign languages get a large share of time; in the English programme a small share. In compensation, English and history are more developed in the English programme than in the Classical.

Many teachers will say, at first sight, that physics comes too early in these programmes and Greek too late. One member of the Committee is firmly of the opinion that Greek comes too late. The explanation of the positions assigned to these subjects is that the Committee of Ten attached great importance to two general principles in programme making:—In

Table A-1

Year	Classical. Three foreign languages (one modern).	
	Latin	5 p.
	English	4 p.
I.	Algebra	4 p.
	History	4 p.
	Physical Geography	3 p.
		20 p
	Latin	5 p.
	English	2 p.
II.	*German [or French] begun	4 p.
	Geometry	3 p.
	Physics	3 p.
	History	3 p.
		20 p.
	Latin	4 p.
	*Greek	5 p.
III.	English	3 p.
	German [or French]	4 p.
	Mathematics $\left\{\begin{array}{l}\text{Algebra 2}\\\text{Geometry 2}\end{array}\right\}$	4 p.
		20 p.
	Latin	4 p.
	Greek	5 p.
	English	2 p.
	German [or French]	3 p.
	Chemistry	3 p.
IV.	Trigonometry & Higher Algebra $\left.\begin{array}{l}\\\quad or\\\text{History}\end{array}\right\}$	3 p.
		20 p.

*In any school in which Greek can be better taught than a modern language, or in which local public opinion or the history of the school makes it desirable to teach Greek in an ample way, Greek may be substituted for German or French in the second year of the Classical programme.

Table A-1 (continued)

Latin-Scientific. *Two foreign languages (one modern).*	
Latin	5 p.
English	4 p.
Algebra	4 p.
History	4 p.
Physical Geography	3 p.
	20 p
Latin	5 p.
English	2 p.
German [*or* French] begun	4 p.
Geometry	3 p.
Physics	3 p.
Botany or Zoölogy	3 p.
	20 p.
Latin	4 p.
English	3 p.
German [*or* French]	4 p.
Mathematics $\left\{\begin{array}{l}\text{Algebra 2}\\\text{Geometry 2}\end{array}\right\}$	4 p.
Astronomy ½ yr. & Meteorology ½ yr.	3 p.
History	2 p.
	20 p.
Latin	4 p.
English $\left\{\begin{array}{ll}\text{as in Classical} & 2\\\text{additional} & 2\end{array}\right\}$	4 p.
German [*or* French]	3 p.
Chemistry	3 p.
Trigonometry & Higher Algebra $\left.\begin{array}{l}\\ or \\ \end{array}\right\}$ History	3 p.
Geology or Physiography ½ yr. and Anatomy, Physiology, & Hygiene ½ yr. $\left.\begin{array}{l}\\ \\ \end{array}\right\}$	3 p.
	20 p.

Table A-1 (continued)

Year	Modern Languages. Two foreign languages (both modern).	
I.	French [or German] begun	5 p.
	English	4 p.
	Algebra	4 p.
	History	4 p.
	Physical Geography	3 p.
		20 p.
II.	French [or German]	4 p.
	English	2 p.
	German [or French] begun	5 p.
	Geometry	3 p.
	Physics	3 p.
	Botany or Zoölogy	3 p.
		20 p.
III.	French [or German]	4 p.
	English	3 p.
	German [or French]	4 p.
	Mathematics $\left\{\begin{array}{ll}\text{Algebra} & 2\\ \text{Geometry} & 2\end{array}\right\}$	4 p.
	Astronomy ½ yr. & Meteorology ½ yr.	3 p.
	History	2 p.
		20 p.
IV.	French [or German]	3 p.
	English $\left\{\begin{array}{ll}\text{as in Classical} & 2\\ \text{additional} & 2\end{array}\right\}$	4 p.
	German [or French]	4 p.
	Chemistry	3 p.
	Trigonometry & Higher Algebra 3 $\left.\begin{array}{l} \\ or \\ \\ \end{array}\right\}$ History	3 p.
	Geology or Physiography ½ yr. and Anatomy, Physiology, & Hygiene ½ yr. $\left.\begin{array}{l} \\ \\ \\ \end{array}\right\}$	3 p.
		20 p.

Table A-1 (continued)

English.
One foreign language (ancient or modern).

Latin, or German, or French	5 p.
English	4 p.
Algebra	4 p.
History	4 p.
Physical Geography	3 p.
	20 p.

Latin, or German, or French	5 or 4 p.
English	3 or 4 p.
Geometry	3 p.
Physics	3 p.
History	3 p.
Botany or Zoölogy	3 p.
	20 p.

Latin, or German, or French	4 p.
English { as in others 3 / additional 2 }	5 p.
Mathematics { Algebra 2 / Geometry 2 }	4 p.
Astronomy ½ yr. & Meteorology ½ yr.	3 p.
History { as in the Latin-Scientific 2 / additional 2 }	4 p.
	20 p.

Latin, or German, or French	4 p.
English { as in Classical 2 / additional 2 }	4 p.
Chemistry	3 p.
Trigonometry & Higher Algebra	3 p.
History	3 p.
Geology or Physiography ½ yr. and Anatomy, Physiology, & Hygiene ½ yr.	3 p.
	20 p.

the first place they endeavored to postpone till the third year the grave
choice between the Classical course and the Latin-Scientific. They believed
that this bifurcation should occur as late as possible, since the choice between these two roads often determines for life the youth's career.
Moreover, they believed that it is possible to make this important decision
for a boy on good grounds, only when he has had opportunity to exhibit
his quality and discover his tastes by making excursions into all the principal fields of knowledge. The youth who has never studied any but his native language cannot know his own capacity for linguistic acquisition; and
the youth who has never made a chemical or physical experiment cannot
know whether or not he has a taste for exact science. The wisest teacher, or
the most observant parent, can hardly predict with confidence a boy's gift
for a subject which he has never touched. In these considerations the
Committee found strong reasons for postponing bifurcation, and making
the subjects of the first two years as truly representative as possible. Secondly, inasmuch as many boys and girls who begin the secondary school
course do not stay in school more than two years, the Committee thought it
important to select the studies of the first two years in such a way that
linguistic, historical, mathematical, and scientific subjects should all be
properly represented. Natural history being represented by physical geography, the Committee wished physics to represent the inorganic sciences of
precision. The first two years of any one of the four programmes presented above will, in the judgment of the Committee, be highly profitable
by themselves to children who can go no farther.

Although the Committee thought it expedient to include among the
four programmes, one which included neither Latin nor Greek, and one
which included only one foreign language (which might be either ancient
or modern), they desired to affirm explicitly their unanimous opinion that,
under existing conditions in the United States as to the training of teachers
and the provision of necessary means of instruction, the two programmes
called respectively Modern Languages and English must in practice be distinctly inferior to the other two.

In the construction of the sample programmes the Committee
adopted twenty as the maximum number of weekly periods, but with two
qualifications, namely, that at least five of the twenty periods should be
given to unprepared work, and that laboratory subjects should have double periods whenever that prolongation should be possible.

The omission of music, drawing, and elocution from the programmes offered by the Committee was not intended to imply that these subjects
ought to receive no systematic attention. It was merely thought best to leave
it to local school authorities to determine, without suggestions from the
Committee, how these subjects should be introduced into the programmes
in addition to the subjects reported on by the Conferences.

The Committee were governed in the construction of the first three
programmes by the rule laid down by the language Conferences, namely,

that two foreign languages should not be begun at the same time. To obey this rule is to accept strict limitations in the construction of a four years' Classical programme. A five years' or six years' programme can be made much more easily under this restriction. The Committee were anxious to give five weekly periods to every foreign language in the year when it was first attacked; but did not find it possible to do so in every case.

The four programmes can be carried out economically in a single school; because, with a few inevitable exceptions, the several subjects occur simultaneously in at least three programmes and with the same number of weekly periods.

Numerous possible transpositions of subjects will occur to every experienced teacher who examines these specimen programmes. Thus, in some localities it would be better to transpose French and German; the selection and order of science subjects might be varied considerably to suit the needs or circumstances of different schools; and the selection and order of historical subjects admit of large variety.

Many subjects now familiar in secondary school courses of study do not appear in Table III. or in the specimen programmes given above; but it must not be supposed that the omitted subjects are necessarily to be neglected. If the recommendations of the Conference were carried out, some of the omitted subjects would be better dealt with under any one of the above programmes than they are now under familiar high school and academy programmes in which they figure as separate subjects. Thus, drawing does not appear as a separate subject in the specimen programmes; but the careful reader of the Conference reports will notice that drawing, both mechanical and free-hand, is to be used in the study of history, botany, zoölogy, astronomy, meteorology, physics, geography, and physiography, and that the kind of drawing recommended by the Conferences is the most useful kind,—namely, that which is applied to recording, describing, and discussing observations. This abundant use of drawing might not prevent the need of some special instruction in drawing, but it ought to diminish the number of periods devoted exclusively to drawing. Again, neither ethics nor economics, neither metaphysics nor aesthetics appear in the programmes; but in the large number of periods devoted to English and history there would be some time for incidental instruction in the elements of these subjects. It is through the reading and writing required of pupils, or recommended to them, that the fundamental ideas on these important topics are to be inculcated. Again, the industrial and commercial subjects do not appear in these programmes; but book-keeping and commercial arithmetic are provided for by the option for algebra designated in Table III.; and if it were desired to provide more amply for subjects thought to have practical importance in trade or the useful arts, it would be easy to provide options in such subjects for some of the science contained in the third and fourth years of the "English" programme.

The Committee of Ten think much would be gained if, in addition to the usual programme hours, a portion of Saturday morning should be regularly used for laboratory work in the scientific subjects. Laboratory work requires more consecutive time than the ordinary period of recitation affords; so that an hour and a half is about the shortest advantageous period for a laboratory exercise. The Committee venture to suggest further that, in addition to the regular school sessions in the morning, one afternoon in every week should be used for out-of-door instruction in geography, botany, zoölogy, and geology, these afternoon and Saturday morning exercises being counted as regular work for the teachers who conduct them. In all laboratory and field work, the Committee believe that it will be found profitable to employ as assistants to the regular teachers,—particularly at the beginning of laboratory and field work in each subject,—recent graduates of the secondary schools who have themselves followed the laboratory and field courses; for at the beginning the pupil will need a large amount of individual instruction in the manipulation of specimens, the use of instruments, and the prompt recording of observations. One teacher without assistants cannot supervise effectively the work of thirty or forty pupils, either in the laboratory or in the field. The laboratory work on Saturday mornings could be maintained throughout the school year; the afternoon excursions would of course be difficult, or impossible, for perhaps a third of the school year.

In general, the Committee of Ten have endeavored to emphasize the principles which should govern all secondary school programmes, and to show how the main recommendations of the several Conferences may be carried out in a variety of feasible programmes.

One of the subjects which the Committee of Ten were directed to consider was requirements for admission to college; and particularly they were expected to report on uniform requirements for admission to colleges, as well as on a uniform secondary school programme. Almost all the Conferences have something to say about the best mode of testing the attainments of candidates at college admission examinations and some of them, notably the Conferences on History and Geography, make very explicit declarations concerning the nature of college examinations. The improvements desired in the mode of testing the attainments of pupils who have pursued in the secondary schools the various subjects which enter into the course will be found clearly described under each subject in the several Conference reports; but there is a general principle concerning the relation of the secondary schools to colleges which the Committee of Ten, inspired and guided by the Conferences, feel it their duty to set forth with all possible distinctness.

The secondary schools of the United States, taken as a whole, do not exist for the purpose of preparing boys and girls for colleges. Only an insignificant percentage of the graduates of these schools go to colleges or scientific schools. Their main function is to prepare for the duties of life that small proportion of all the children in the country—a proportion small in number, but very important to the welfare of the nation—who show themselves able to profit by an education prolonged to the eighteenth year, and whose parents are able to support them while they remain so long at school. There are, to be sure, a few private or endowed secondary schools in the country, which make it their principal object to prepare students for the colleges and universities; but the number of these schools is relatively small. A secondary school programme intended for national use must therefore be made for those children whose education is not to be pursued beyond the secondary school. The preparation of a few pupils for college or scientific school should in the ordinary secondary school be the incidental, and not the principal object. At the same time, it is obviously desirable that the colleges and scientific schools should be accessible to all boys or girls who have completed creditably the secondary school course. Their parents often do not decide for them, four years before the college age, that they shall go to college, and they themselves may not, perhaps, feel the desire to continue their education until near the end of their school course. In order that any successful graduate of a good secondary school should be free to present himself at the gates of the college or scientific school of his choice, it is necessary that the colleges and scientific schools of the country should accept for admission to appropriate courses of their instruction the attainments of any youth who has passed creditably through a good secondary school course, no matter to what group of subjects he may have mainly devoted himself in the secondary school. As secondary school courses are now too often arranged, this is not a reasonable request to prefer to the colleges and scientific schools; because the pupil may now go through a secondary school course of a very feeble and scrappy nature—studying a little of many subjects and not much of any one, getting, perhaps, a little information in a variety of fields, but nothing which can be called a thorough training. Now the recommendations of the nine Conferences, if well carried out, might fairly be held to make all the main subjects taught in the secondary schools of equal rank for the purposes of admission to college or scientific school. They would all be taught consecutively and thoroughly, and would all be carried on in the same spirit; they would all be used for training the powers of observation, memory, expression, and reasoning; and they would all be good to that end, although differing among themselves in quality and substance. In preparing the programmes of Table IV. [see Table A-1.], the Committee had in mind that the requirements for admission to colleges might, for schools which adopted a programme derived from that table, be simplified to a considerable extent, though not reduced. A college might say,—We will accept for admission any groups of studies taken from the secondary school programme, provided that the sum of the studies in each of the four years amounts to sixteen, or eighteen, or twenty periods a week,—as may be thought best,—and provided, further, that in each year at least four of the subjects presented shall have been pursued at least three periods a week, and that at least three of the subjects shall have been pursued three years or more. For the purposes of this reckoning, natural history, geography, meteorology, and astronomy might be grouped together as one subject. Every youth who entered college would have spent four years in studying a few subjects thoroughly; and, on the theory that all the subjects are to be considered equivalent in educational rank for the purposes of admission to college, it would make no difference which subjects he had chosen from the programme—he would have had four years of strong and effective mental training. The Conferences on Geography and Modern Languages make the most explicit statement to the effect that college requirements for admission should coincide with high-school requirements for graduation. The Conference on English is of opinion "that no student should be admitted to college who shows in his English examination and his other examinations that he is very deficient in ability to write good English." This recommendation suggests that an ample English course in the secondary school should be required of all persons who intend to enter college. It would of course be possible for any college to require for admission any one subject, or any group of subjects, in the table, and the requirements of different colleges, while all kept within the table might differ in many respects; but the Committee are of opinion that the satisfactory completion of any one of the four years' courses of study embodied in the foregoing programmes should admit to corresponding courses in colleges and scientific schools. They believe that this close articulation between the secondary schools and the higher institutions would be advantageous alike for the schools, the colleges, and the country. . . .

Event 9: Launching the "Wisconsin Idea"—1904

The "Wisconsin Idea" of service to society was a product of the presidency of Charles R. Van Hise at the University of Wisconsin. It embodied two functions—university assistance to state government, and university assistance to the public through extension and correspondence education in a wide variety of subjects all over the state. Charles McCarthy, a University of Wisconsin faculty member, was credited with originating the term, "Wisconsin Idea." The following description of the idea is from Lincoln Steffen's 1909 article "Sending a State to College" in which he popularized the university's unique mission (from *American Magazine*, February 1909).

It is related of a professor at the University of Wisconsin that one day when he was coming through the grounds, carrying under one arm a copy of

Geiger's "Humanismus" and under the other a cheese purchased at the College of Agriculture, he stopped a couple of his colleagues to ask, with humorous nods at his burdens, if he "didn't illustrate pretty well that this was a university." He didn't; but another man did. This other man may be described as the Milwaukee drummer for the university at Madison. He led me out to one of the great machine shops of Milwaukee, where, in a room and "in time" set aside by the firm for "the school," he showed me a class of mechanics taking and paying for the regular correspondence course in "shop mathematics" under the direction of the faculty of the state university.

Cheeses and Prize Pigs

The learned professor with his Latin book and his college-bred cheese only illustrated pretty well the realization at Madison of the old ideal of a university: "a place where anybody may learn anything." And a more striking illustration would be a farmer's family of which I heard. The son was on one of the varsity teams, the daughter was in the College of Letters and Science, and the mother and father came to Madison in the winter, the one to attend the "Housekeepers' Conference" in the College of Agriculture, the other the Farmers' Course: ten days in which the professors come into the ring with their horses, cows, pigs, pumpkins and apparatus to show and, as one of them put it, "rub in" to the ever-increasing hundreds of "old farmers" who come there, the results of the year's scientific experimentation in grain and cattle breeding and feeding, etc., and in the chemistry of dairying—of which the professor's cheese was a mere commercial by-product.

Madison is indeed a place where anybody who can go there, may learn anything. And between five and six thousand people do go there; all sorts of people, young and old, rich and poor, men and women from everywhere; and among them they do learn almost everything. Which sounds universal. But it isn't, of course. The population of Wisconsin alone is two and a quarter millions. The great majority cannot go to Madison, ever, even for ten days. They all contribute to the support of this state university; they all need, and many of them want to learn something—as the fortunes made by the private correspondence schools prove. The University of Wisconsin is reaching for these people. It has organized a public correspondence school and the Milwaukee class in shop mathematics is but one of many such "schools" by means of which the university is mailing instruction out to the homes, farms and shops of the people who cannot go to Madison.

Breaking thus the bounds of Madison, the university is breaking also the bounds of that old definition of a university and setting up a new ideal for education. The University of Wisconsin is offering to teach anybody—anything—anywhere. . . .

Professors in Public Office

What the brain is to a man's hands, feet and eyes, this university is to the people of the state: the instinctive recourse for information, light and guidance. And the state itself, responding to the general feeling of confidence, draws constantly upon the faculty. The legislature summons professors not only to hearings, but to working membership on committees; and governors and heads of departments, not only consult, they appoint them to office. There are forty-one professors in public office; some of these do two or more services; President Van Hise, as geologist and head of the university, performs five distinct functions under the government, city and state; and counting all the regular and no honorary services rendered by all the professors, the total is sixty-six.

Some of these services are crucial. Professor Meyer, for example, is on the Railroad Commission and, since he and other professors were called in by La Follette to draw the Wisconsin bill to regulate rates, the law is comprehensive. The Wisconsin Commission can regulate; it can regulate the rates and the financing of railroads; and not only railroads, but practically all the public service corporations in the state, including those in cities; and not only that, it "shall" and it is laboring now to put a value upon all those businesses and their plants. And even the railroad men admit, grudgingly, that this commission is doing this delicate work well "so far."

But the most remarkable example of state service by the university, is the bureau of legislation. Dr. Charles McCarthy, the Irish football coach who investigated the correspondence schools for President Van Hise, established, with diplomatic skill and native political sense, an office in which he gets bills drawn right. His theory is that legislation is expert work, and that laws enacted break down in the courts partly because they are badly drawn by inexpert men. Now La Follette's "radical" legislation all stood up in court, and one reason was that he had it written by professors and other men who knew. With his university backing him, McCarthy proposed that all legislators should have all their bills drawn by him and his staff of voluntary and other experts and, following Madison methods, he not only offered to do this work; he went forth and "blarneyed" elected legislators into accepting his offer. And why not? He explained that he would take the rough draft of an intention, any intention, and , looking up all previous legislation along the same line anywhere in the world, would follow it through the courts and, with the help of professors and attorneys, draw and deliver, in confidence, a bill which, containing all experience, correcting all discovered defects and meeting all court and other objections, would probably sustain the test of debate, judicial scrutiny and actual practice. Also, McCarthy would furnish arguments to beat said law.

President Van Hise keeps in the faculty the professors who take public office; he insists upon it; they are better teachers, he says. And anybody can see that they must be. When I asked a question of a Madison professor, his answer was more often a fact from "the little town of Caribeau" than an academic reason from a book. These teachers come into the classrooms of Madison, like the Short Horns, with "dung on their boots," the dung of the farm, of commerce and of politics. Think of Dr. Charles McCarthy, lobbyist-in-chief to the legislature, as a "lecturer on political science" and of Railroad Commissioner Balthasar Henry Meyer as he is: Professor of Political Economy, lecturing, and so reaching also the boys and girls. And meanwhile he and McCarthy are teaching men, busy people who don't know they are being taught. McCarthy has heart-to-heart talks with legislators and leaders and he furnishes the latest references for speeches and debates all over Wisconsin. And Meyer and his Railroad Board, called upon constantly to arrange differences between shippers and the railroads, and between towns and public service corporations, apply university methods. First they send out young experts, usually university-bred, to get the cold facts; then they might decide; but they don't. They go down there with blackboards and lantern slides and, calling a mass meeting, explain the whole thing; explain it, too, in its relation to other business, to the state and to the life and progress of the human species; and having explained this, and settled a row, they leave behind them not merely peace, but light; not merely the right of a wrong, but a sense of the use, of a university and of the state.

One way of stating what is going on all about us today, is to say that communities—cities and counties, states and nations, are becoming conscious. Like man himself, human society is rising out of the instructive into an intelligent state of being. A common sense is developing of the relations of individuals and institutions to one another and to the whole. This means mind; a public mind distinct from the minds of any or even of all the individuals in the community. And this public mind, conscious of a common purpose, is co-ordinating all the resources, efforts and powers of states and their people to the service of the welfare of all. Some European countries, notably Denmark and Belgium, are approaching complete co-operation. Wisconsin is a leading example of the drift in America. President Van Hise has entered his university into an agreement with Beloit and the other lesser colleges of the state, dividing their functions and merging their uses. His great university library is but one of the public libraries which are co-operating to such an extent that you can send to any one of them for any book; it will be drawn for you from the library that has it. It is merger and custom everywhere in Wisconsin; and what is the result? Most of us think of the state and a university as great institutions, above, beyond and separate from us and our daily lives. In Wisconsin the university is as close to the intelligent farmer as his pig-pen or his tool-house; the university laboratories are part of the alert manufacturer's plant; to the worker, the university is drawing nearer than the school around the corner and is as much his as his union is his or his favorite saloon. Creeping into the minds of the children with pure seed, into the debates of youth with pure facts, into the opinions of voters with impersonal, expert knowledge, the state university is coming to be a part of the citizen's own mind, just as the state is becoming a part of his will. And that's what this whole story means: the University of Wisconsin is a highly conscious lobe of the common community's mind of the state of the people of Wisconsin.

Event 10: Establishing a Great Books Curriculum—1937

In 1937, St. John's College introduced an undergraduate program based upon slightly more than 100 books that were to be read by all students over a four-year period (see Chapter 12). The books, ranging from the *Iliad* (Homer) to *Walden* (Thoreau), were selected for their richness of thought and their contribution to knowledge. Supporters of the concept, including Scott Buchanan, Stringfellow Barr, Mortimer Adler, and Robert Hutchins, felt the great books the best possible education short of studying with each of the authors because they conveyed the wisdom of the ages.

Since 1937, a few of the books have changed (Einstein's theory of relativity, for instance, has been added to the list); a number of colleges have adopted great books programs, and almost every college has at one time or another debated the merit of the approach. The following is the current list of great books studied at St. John's *(St. John's College: Statement of the St. John's Program 1975–76)*.

Freshman Year

Homer:	*Iliad, Odyssey*
Aeschylus:	*Agamemnon, Choephoroe, Eumenides, Prometheus Bound*
Sophocles:	*Oedipus Rex, Oedipus at Colonus, Antigone*
Thucydides:	*Peloponnesian War*
Euripides:	*Hippolytus, Medea, Bacchae*
Herodotus:	*History*[*][1]
Aristophanes:	*Clouds, Birds*
Plato:	*Ion, Meno, Gorgias, Republic, Apology, Crito, Phaedo, Symposium, Parmenides, Theaetetus,*

[1]Books read only in part marked by asterisks.

	Sophist, Timaeus, Phaedrus
Aristotle:	Poetics, Physics,* Metaphysics,* Ethics,*
	On Generation and Corruption,* The Politico
Euclid:	Elements*
Lucretius:	On the Nature of Things
Plutarch:	Pericles, Alcibiades
Marcus Aurelius:	Meditations*
Nicomachus:	Arithmetic*
Lavoisier:	Elements of Chemistry*
Essays by:	Archimedes, Toricelli, Pascal, Fahrenheit, Black,
	Avogadro, Dalton, Wollaston, Gay-Lussac,
	Cannizzaro, Mach, Bridgman, Couper, Morveau,
	Proust, Berthollet, Richter, T. Thomson, Whewell,
	Berzelius, Dulong, Mendeleev

Sophomore Year

	The Bible*
Aristotle:	De Anima, On Interpretation,* Posterior Analytics,*
	Categories,* Parts of Animals,* Generation of
	Animals*
Apollonius:	Conics*
Virgil:	Aeneid
Plutarch:	Caesar, Antony, Brutus, Cato the Younger, Pompey,
	Cicero
Epictetus:	Discourses, Manual
Tacitus:	Annals
Ptolemy:	Almagest*
Galen:	On the Natural Faculties
Plotinus:	Fifth Ennead*
Diophantus:	Arithmetic*
Augustine:	Confessions, City of God*
St. Anselm:	Proslogium
Maimonides:	Eight Chapters on Ethics
Aquinas:	Summa Theologica,* Summa Contra Gentiles*
Dante:	Divine Comedy
	Song of Roland
Chaucer:	Canterbury Tales*
Machiavelli:	The Prince, Discourses*
Copernicus:	On the Revolution of the Spheres*
Luther:	The Freedom of a Christian, Secular Authority
Rabelais:	Gargantua and Pantagruel*
Calvin:	Institutes*
Palestrina:	Missa Papae Marcelli

Montaigne:	*Essays**
Viéte:	*Introduction to the Analytical Art*
Bacon:	*Novum Organum**
Shakespeare:	*Richard II, Henry IV, Henry V, The Tempest, As You Like It, Hamlet, Othello, Macbeth, King Lear, Coriolanus, Sonnets**
Kepler:	*Epitome IV*
Harvey:	*Motion of the Heart and Blood*
Descartes:	*Geometry**
Pascal:	*Generation of Conic Section*
Bach:	*St. Matthew Passion, Inventions*
Haydn:	*Quartets**
Lamarck:	*Philosophical Zoology*
Mozart:	*Operas**
Beethoven:	*Sonatas**
Schubert:	*Songs**
Darwin:	*Origin of Species*
Verdi:	*Otello*
Mendel:	*Experiments in Plant Hybridization*
Stravinsky:	*Symphony of Psalms*
Des Prez:	*Mass*
Poems by:	*Marvell, Donne, and other 17th-century poets*
Essays by:	*Bernard, Weismann, John Maynard Smith, Dreisch, Boveri, Teilhard de Chardin*

Junior Year

Cervantes:	*Don Quixote*
Galileo:	*Two New Sciences*
Hobbes:	*Leviathan*
Descartes:	*Discourse on Method, Meditations, Rules for the Direction of the Mind*
Milton:	*Paradise Lost, Samson Agonistes*
La Rochefoucauld:	*Maximes**
La Fontaine:	*Fables**
Pascal:	*Pensées**
Huygens:	*Treatise on Light,* On the Movement of Bodies by Impact*
Spinoza:	*Theologico-Political Treatise*
Locke:	*Second Treatise of Government*
Racine:	*Phèdre*
Newton:	*Principia**
Leibniz:	*Monadology, Discourse on Metaphysics, Principles of Nature and Grace Founded on Reason, Essay on Dynamics*

Swift:	*Gulliver's Travels*
Berkeley:	*Principles of Human Knowledge*
Fielding:	*Tom Jones*
Hume:	*Treatise of Human Nature,* Dialogues Concerning Natural Religion, Enquiry Concerning Human Understanding*
Rousseau:	*Social Contract*
Adam Smith:	*Wealth of Nations*
Kant:	*Critique of Pure Reason,* Fundamental Principles of Metaphysics of Morals*
Mozart:	*Don Giovanni*
Jane Austen:	*Pride and Prejudice*
Hamilton, Jay, and Madison:	*The Federalist*
Melville:	*Billy Budd, Benito Cereno, Moby Dick*
Dedekind:	*Essay on the Theory of Numbers*
Essays by:	*Boscovich, Thomas Young*

Senior Year

Shakespeare:	*Antony and Cleopatra*
Moliere:	*The Misanthrope, Tartuffe*
Goethe:	*Faust*
Hegel:	*Introduction to the History of Philosophy, Preface to the Phenomenology, Logic (from the Encyclopedia), Philosophy of History,* Philosophy of Right,* Philosophy of Spirit**
Lobachevsky:	*Theory of Parallels**
Tocqueville:	*Democracy in America**
Lincoln:	*Speeches**
Kierkegaard:	*Philosophical Fragments, Fear and Trembling*
Wagner:	*Tristan and Isolde*
Thoreau:	*Walden*
Marx:	*Communist Manifesto, Capital,* Political and Economic Manuscripts of 1844**
Dostoevski:	*Brothers Karamazov, The Possessed*
Tolstoy:	*War and Peace*
Lewis Carroll:	*Alice in Wonderland*
Mark Twain:	*The Adventures of Huckleberry Finn*
William James:	*Psychology, Briefer Course*
Nietzsche:	*Birth of Tragedy, Thus Spake Zarathustra,* Beyond Good and Evil**
Freud:	*General Introduction to Psychoanalysis, Civilization and Its Discontents, Beyond the Pleasure Principle*
Valéry:	*Poems**

Jung:	*Two Essays in Analytic Psychology**
Mann:	*Death in Venice*
Kafka:	*The Trial*
Heidegger:	*What is Philosophy?*
Heisenberg:	*The Physical Principles of the Quantum Theory**
	*Supreme Court Opinions**
Millikan:	*The Electron**
Poems by:	*Yeats, T. S. Eliot, Wallace Stevens, Baudelaire,*
	Rimbaud, and others
Essays by:	*Faraday, Lorenz, J. J. Thomson, Whitehead,*
	Minkowski, Rutherford, Einstein, Davisson, Bohr,
	Schrödinger, Maxwell

Event 11: The Harvard "Redbook"—1945

In 1945, the Harvard Committee on the Objectives of General Education in a Free Society issued its report, informally known as the "Redbook," but titled *General Education in a Free Society.* Its recommendations were only partly adopted at Harvard, although they were implemented elsewhere. Their effect on the national higher education community was tremendous and remains a legend. The following excerpt from the "Redbook" (pp. 42–58) is the theory of general education which undergirded the committee's recommendations. (See Chapter 12 for further discussion of the committee, its specific recommendations, and their fate.)

Heritage and Change

We have tried so far to sketch in broad outline the growth of American education and to indicate the factors which have determined this growth. The very momentum of its development, like that which has marked American life generally, left a legacy of disturbance and maladjustment undreamed of in simpler times. A passage from Machiavelli's *Discourses* comes to mind in which, after asking why the Roman Republic showed signs of confusion in the period of its fastest growth, he observes that such confusion was inevitable in so vigorous a state. "Had the Roman Commonwealth," he concludes, "grown to be more tranquil, this inconvenience would have resulted that it must at the same time have grown weaker, since the road would have been closed to that greatness to which it came. For in removing the causes of her tumults, Rome must have interfered with the causes of her growth." Just so in the United States, the most ideally planned educational system would have found itself in conflict with the unforeseen forces set loose by the growth and development of the country.

But this very growth, the source of the gravest problems to education, is at the same time the index of its strength and promise.

In order to pass judgment on the actualities of education and to make reasonable proposals for revising the present system, it is necessary to have an insight, however tentative, into the ideal aims of education in our society. The present chapter will accordingly consider what can, perhaps overformally, be called a philosophy of American education, and especially that part of it which is general education.

It was remarked at the end of the previous chapter that a supreme need of American education is for a unifying purpose and idea. As recently as a century ago, no doubt existed about such a purpose: it was to train the Christian citizen. Nor was there doubt how this training was to be accomplished. The student's logical powers were to be formed by mathematics, his taste by the Greek and Latin classics, his speech by rhetoric, and his ideals by Christian ethics. College catalogues commonly began with a specific statement about the influence of such a training on the mind and character. The reasons why this enviable certainty both of goal and of means has largely disappeared have already been set forth. For some decades the mere excitement of enlarging the curriculum and making place for new subjects, new methods, and masses of new students seems quite pardonably to have absorbed the energies of schools and colleges. It is fashionable now to criticize the leading figures of that expansive time for failing to replace, or even to see the need of replacing, the unity which they destroyed. But such criticisms, if just in themselves, are hardly just historically. A great and necessary task of modernizing and broadening education waited to be done, and there is credit enough in its accomplishment. In recent times, however, the question of unity has become insistent. We are faced with a diversity of education which, if it has many virtues, nevertheless works against the good of society by helping to destroy the common ground of training and outlook on which any society depends.

It seems that a common ground between some, though not all, of the ideas underlying our educational practice is the sense of heritage. The word heritage is not here taken to mean mere retrospection. The purpose of all education is to help students live their own lives. The appeal to heritage is partly to the authority, partly to the clarification of the past about what is important in the present. All Catholic and many Protestant institutions thus appeal to the Christian view of man and history as providing both final meaning and immediate standards for life. As observed at the outset, it is less than a century since such was the common practice of American education generally, and certainly this impulse to mold students to a pattern sanctioned by the past can, in one form or another, never be absent from education. If it were, society would become discontinuous.

In this concern for heritage lies a close similarity between religious education and education in the great classic books. Exponents of the latter have, to be sure, described it as primarily a process of intellectual discipline in the joint arts of word and number, the so-called *trivium* (grammar, logic, rhetoric) and *quadrivium* (arithmetic, geometry, astronomy, music). But, since the very idea of this discipline goes back to antiquity and since the actual books by which it is carried out are in fact the great books of the Western tradition, it seems fairer, without denying the disciplinary value of such a curriculum, to think of it as primarily a process of opening before students the intellectual forces that have shaped the Western mind. There is a sense in which education in the great books can be looked at as a secular continuation of the spirit of Protestantism. As early Protestantism, rejecting the authority and philosophy of the medieval church, placed reliance on each man's personal reading of the Scriptures, so this present movement, rejecting the unique authority of the Scriptures, places reliance on the reading of those books which are taken to represent the fullest revelation of the Western mind. But be this as it may, it is certain that, like religious education, education in the great books is essentially an introduction of students to their heritage.

Nor is the sense of heritage less important, though it may be less obvious, a part of education for modern democratic life. To the degree that the implications of democracy are drawn forth and expounded, to that degree the long-standing impulse of education toward shaping students to a received ideal is still pursued. Consider the teaching of American history and of modern democratic life. However ostensibly factual such teaching may be, it commonly carries with it a presupposition which is not subject to scientific proof: namely, the presupposition that democracy is meaningful and right. Moreover, since contemporary life is itself a product of history, to study it is to tread unconsciously, in the words of the hymn, where the saints have trod. To know modern democracy is to know something at least of Jefferson, though you have not read him; to learn to respect freedom of speech or the rights of the private conscience is not to be wholly ignorant of the *Areopagitica* or the *Antigone*, though you know nothing about them. Whether, as philosophers of history argue, being conditioned by the present we inevitably judge the past by what we know in the present (since otherwise the past would be unintelligible) or whether human motives and choices do not in reality greatly change with time, the fact remains that the past and the present are parts of the same unrolling scene and, whether you enter early or late, you see for the most part the still-unfinished progress of the same issues.

Here, then, in so far as our culture is adequately reflected in current ideas on education, one point about it is clear: it depends in part on an inherited view of man and society which it is the function, though not the only function, of education to pass on. It is not and cannot be true that all possible choices are open to us individually or collectively. We are part of an organic process, which is the American and, more broadly, the Western evolution. Our standards of judgment, ways of life, and form of government all bear the marks of this evolution, which would accordingly influence us, though confusedly, even if it were not understood. Ideally it should be understood at several degrees of depth which complement rather than exclude each other. To study the American present is to discern at best the aims and purposes of a free society animating its imperfections. To study the past is immensely to enrich the meaning of the present and at the same time to clarify it by the simplification of the writings and the issues which have been winnowed from history. To study either past or present is to confront, in some form or another, the philosophic and religious fact of man in history and to recognize the huge continuing influence alike on past and present of the stream of Jewish and Greek thought in Christianity. There is doubtless a sense in which religious education, education in the great books, and education in modern democracy may be mutually exclusive. But there is a far more important sense in which they work together to the same end, which is belief in the idea of man and society that we inherit, adapt, and pass on.

This idea is described in many ways, perhaps most commonly in recent times, as that of the dignity of man. To the belief in man's dignity must be added the recognition of his duty to his fellow men. Dignity does not rest on any man as a being separate from all other beings, which he in any case cannot be, but springs from his common humanity and exists positively as he makes the common good his own. This concept is essentially that of the Western tradition: the view of man as free and not as slave, an end in himself and not a means. It may have what many believe to be the limitations of humanism, which are those of pride and arise from making man the measure of all things. But it need not have these limitations, since it is equally compatible with a religious view of life. Thus it is similar to the position described at the end of the last chapter as coöperation without uniformity, agreement on the good of man at the level of performance without the necessity of agreement on ultimates. But two points have now been added. First, thus stated, the goal of education is not in conflict with but largely includes the goals of religious education, education in the Western tradition, and education in modern democracy. For these in turn have been seen to involve necessary elements in our common tradition, each to a great extent implied in the others as levels at which it can be understood. Certainly no fruitful way of stating the belief in the dignity and mutual obligation of man can present it as other than, at one and the same time, effective in the present, emerging from the past, and partaking of the nature not of fact but of faith. Second, it has become clear that the common ground between these various views—namely, the impulse to rear students to a received idea of the good—is in fact necessary to education. It is impossible to escape the realization that our society, like any society, rests on common beliefs and that a major task of education is to perpetuate them.

This conclusion raises one of the most fundamental problems of education, indeed of society itself: how to reconcile this necessity for common belief with the equally obvious necessity for new and independent insights leading to change. We approach here the one previously mentioned concept of education which was not included under the idea of heritage: namely, the views associated with the names of James and Dewey and having to do with science, the scientific attitude, and pragmatism. This is hardly the place to try to summarize this body of thought or even to set forth in detail its application by Mr. Dewey to education. To do so would be virtually to retrace the educational controversies of the last forty years. But, at the risk of some injustice to Mr. Dewey's thought as a whole, a few points can be made about it. It puts trust in the scientific method of thought, the method which demands that you reach conclusions from tested data only, but that, since the data may be enlarged or the conclusions themselves combined with still other conclusions, you must hold them only tentatively. It emphasizes that full truth is not known and that we must be forever led by facts to revise our approximations of it. As a feeling of commitment and of allegiance marks the sense of heritage, so a tone of tough-mindedness and curiosity and a readiness for change mark this pragmatic attitude.

Here, then, is a concept of education, founded on obedience to fact and well disposed, even hospitable, to change, which appears at first sight the antithesis of any view based on the importance of heritage. Such hostility to tradition well reflects one side of the modern mind. It is impossible to contemplate the changes even of the last decades, much less the major groundswell of change since the Renaissance, without feeling that we face largely new conditions which call for new qualities of mind and outlook. Moreover, it is obviously no accident that this pragmatic philosophy has been worked out most fully in the United States. Yet, in spite of its seeming conflict with views of education based on heritage, strong doubt exists. whether the questioning, innovating, experimental attitude of pragmatism is in fact something alien to the Western heritage or whether it is not, in the broadest sense of the word, a part of it.

The rest of the present volume would hardly suffice for this sweeping subject. But it can be observed even here that we look back on antiquity not simply out of curiosity but because ancient thought is sympathetic to us. The Greek idea of an orderly universe, of political freedom under rationally constructed laws, and of the inner life itself as subject to the sway of reason, was certainly not achieved without skepticism, observation, or the test of experience. The ancient atomists and medical writers and, to a large extent, Socrates himself relied precisely on induction from observed facts. Socrates, the teacher and the gadfly of the Athenian city, impressed on his pupils and the public at large the duty of man to reflect on his beliefs and to criticize his presuppositions. Socrates was an individualist proclaiming that man should form his opinions by his own reasoning and not receive them by social indoctrination. And yet, it was this same Socrates who died in obedience to the judgment of the state, even though he believed this judgment to be wrong. Again, historical Christianity has been expressly and consistently concerned with the importance of this life on earth. The doctrine of the Incarnation, that God took the form of man and inhabited the earth, declares this concern. While perhaps for Greek thought, only the timeless realm had importance, in Christian thought the process of history is vested with absolute significance. If the ideal of democracy was rightly described above in the interwoven ideas of the dignity of man (that is, his existence as an independent moral agent) and his duty to his fellow men (that is, his testing by outward performance), the debt of these two ideas to the similarly interwoven commandments of the love of God and the love of neighbor is obvious.

These evidences of a consistent and characteristic appeal throughout Western history to the test of reason and experience are not adduced for the purpose of minimizing the huge creativeness of the modern scientific age or of glozing over its actual break from the past. In the well-known opening chapters of his *Science and the Modern World* in which he inquires into the origin of modern science, Mr. Whitehead pictures it as inspired by a revolt against abstract reasoning and a respect for unique fact. So considered, the first impulse of modern science was antirational or, better, antitheoretical, in the sense that it was a reaction against the most towering intellectual system which the West has known, namely, scholasticism. But be this question of origin as it may, there is no doubt that the modern mind received one of its characteristic bents in the empiricism, the passion for observation, and the distrust of abstract reasoning which have attended the origin and growth of science.

But there also seems no doubt that what happened was a shift, perhaps to some degree a restoration, of emphasis within the Western tradition itself rather than a complete change in its nature. It is a mistake to identify the older Western culture with traditionalism. Classical antiquity handed on a working system of truth which relied on both reason and experience and was designed to provide a norm for civilized life. Its import was heightened and vastly intensified by its confluence with Christanity. But when, in its rigid systematization in the late Middle Ages, it lost touch with experience and individual inquiry, it violated its own nature and provoked the modernist revolt. The seeming opposition that resulted between traditionalism and modernism has been a tragedy for Western thought. Modernism rightly affirms the importance of inquiry and of relevance to experience. But as scholasticism ran the danger of becoming a system without vitality, so modernism runs the danger of achieving vitality without pattern.

While, then, there are discontinuities between the classical and the modern components of our Western culture, there are also continuities. For instance, it would be wrong to construe the scientific outlook as inimical to human values. Even if it were true that science is concerned with means only, it would not follow that science ignores the intrinsic worth of man. For the values of human life cannot be achieved within a physical vacuum; they require for their fulfillment the existence of material conditions. To the extent that classical civilization failed to mitigate the evils of poverty, disease, squalor, and a generally low level of living among the masses, to that extent it failed to liberate man. Conversely, to the extent that science, especially in its medical and technological applications, has succeeded in dealing with these evils, it has contributed to the realization of human values. Thus science has implemented the humanism which classicism and Christianity have proclaimed.

Science has done more than provide the material basis of the good life; it has directly fostered the spiritual values of humanism. To explain, science is both the outcome and the source of the habit of forming objective, disinterested judgment based upon exact evidence. Such a habit is of particular value in the formation of citizens for a free society. It opposes to the arbitrariness of authority and "first principles" the direct and continuing appeal to things as they are. Thus it develops the qualities of the free man. It is no accident that John Locke, who set forth the political doctrine of the natural rights of man against established authority, should have been also the man who rejected the authority of innate ideas.

Students of antiquity and of the Middle Ages can therefore rightly affirm that decisive truths about the human mind and its relation to the world were laid hold of then, and yet agree that, when new application of these truths was made through a more scrupulous attention to fact, their whole implication and meaning were immensely enlarged. Modern civilization has seen this enlargement of meaning and possibility; yet it is not a new civilization but the organic development of an earlier civilization. The true task of education is therefore so to reconcile the sense of pattern and direction deriving from heritage with the sense of experiment and innovation deriving from science that they may exist fruitfully together, as in varying degrees they have never ceased to do throughout Western history.

Belief in the dignity and mutual obligation of man is the common ground between these contrasting but mutually necessary forces in our culture. As was pointed out earlier, this belief is the fruit at once of religion, of the Western tradition, and of the American tradition. It equally inspires the faith in human reason which is the basis for trust in the future of democracy. And if it is not, strictly speaking, implied in all statements of the scientific method, there is no doubt that science has become its powerful instrument. In this tension between the opposite forces of heritage and change poised only in the faith in man, lies something like the old philosophic problem of the knowledge of the good. If you know the good, why do you seek it? If you are ignorant of the good, how do you recognize it when you find it? You must evidently at one and the same time both know it and be ignorant of it. Just so, the tradition which has come down to us regarding the nature of man and the good society must inevitably provide our standard of good. Yet an axiom of that tradition itself is the belief that no current form of the received ideal is final but that every generation, indeed every individual, must discover it in a fresh form. Education can therefore be wholly devoted neither to tradition nor to experiment, neither to the belief that the ideal in itself is enough nor to the view that means are valuable apart from the ideal. It must uphold at the same time tradition and experiment, the ideal and the means, subserving, like our culture itself, change within commitment.

General and Special Education

In the previous section we have attempted to outline the unifying elements of our culture and therefore of American education as well. In the present section we shall take the next step of indicating in what ways these cultural strands may be woven into the fabric of education. Education is broadly divided into general and special education; our topic now is the difference and the relationship between the two. The term, general education, is somewhat vague and colorless; it does not mean some airy education in knowledge in general (if there be such knowledge), nor does it mean education for all in the sense of universal education. It is used to indicate that part of a student's whole education which looks first of all to his life as a responsible human being and citizen; while the term, special education, indicates that part which looks to the student's competence in some occupation. These two sides of life are not entirely separable, and it would be false to imagine education for the one as quite distinct from education for the other—more will be said on this point presently. Clearly, general education has somewhat the meaning of liberal education, except that, by applying to high school as well as to college, it envisages immensely greater numbers of students and thus escapes the invidium which, rightly or wrongly, attaches to liberal education in the minds of some people. But if one clings to the root meaning of liberal as that which befits or helps to make free men, then general and liberal education have identical goals. The one may be thought of as an earlier stage of the other, similar in nature but less advanced in degree.

The opposition to liberal education—both to the phrase and to the fact—stems largely from historical causes. The concept of liberal education first appeared in a slave-owning society, like that of Athens, in which the community was divided into freemen and slaves, rulers and subjects. While the slaves carried on the specialized occupations of menial work, the freemen were primarily concerned with the rights and duties of citizenship. The training of the former was purely vocational; but as the freemen were not only a ruling but also a leisure class, their education was exclusively in the liberal arts, without any utilitarian tinge. The freemen were trained in the reflective pursuit of the good life; their education was unspecialized as well as unvocational; its aim was to produce a rounded person with a full understanding of himself and of his place in society and in the cosmos.

Modern democratic society clearly does not regard labor as odious or disgraceful; on the contrary, in this country at least, it regards leisure with suspicion and expects its "gentlemen" to engage in work. Thus we attach no odium to vocational instruction. Moreover, in so far as we surely reject the idea of freemen who are free in so far as they have slaves or subjects, we are apt strongly to deprecate the liberal education which went with the structure of the aristocratic ideal. Herein our society runs the risk of committing a serious fallacy. Democracy is the view that not only the few but that all are free, in that everyone governs his own life and shares in the responsibility for the management of the community. This being the case, it follows that all human beings stand in need of an ampler and rounded education. The task of modern democracy is to preserve the ancient ideal of liberal education and to extend it as far as possible to all the members of the community. In short, we have been apt to confuse accidental with fundamental factors, in our suspicion of the classical ideal. To believe in the equality of human beings is to believe that the good life, and the education which trains the citizen for the good life, are equally the privilege of all. And these are the touchstones of the liberated man: first, is he free; that is to say, is he able to judge and plan for himself, so that he can truly govern himself? In order to do this, his must be a mind capable of self-criticism; he must lead that self-examined life which according to Socrates is alone worthy of a free man. Thus he will possess inner freedom, as well as social freedom. Second, is he universal in his motives and sympathies? For the civilized man is a citizen of the entire universe; he has overcome provincialism, he is objective, and is a "spectator of all time and all existence." Surely these two are the very aims of democracy itself.

But the opposition to general education does not stem from causes located in the past alone. We are living in an age of specialism, in which the avenue to success for the student often lies in his choice of a specialized career, whether as a chemist, or an engineer, or a doctor, or a specialist in some form of business or of manual or technical work. Each of these specialties makes an increasing demand on the time and on the interest of the student. Specialism is the means for advancement in our mobile social structure; yet we must envisage the fact that a society controlled wholly by specialists is not a wisely ordered society. We cannot, however, turn away from specialism. The problem is how to save general education and its values within a system where specialism is necessary.

The very prevalence and power of the demand for special training makes doubly clear the need for a concurrent, balancing force in general education. Specialism enhances the centrifugal forces in society. The business of providing for the needs of society breeds a great diversity of special occupations; and a given specialist does not speak the language of the other specialists. In order to discharge his duties as a citizen adequately, a person must somehow be able to grasp the complexities of life as a whole. Even from the point of view of economic success, specialism has its peculiar limitations. Specializing in a vocation makes for inflexibility in a world of fluid possibilities. Business demands minds capable of adjusting themselves to varying situations and of managing complex human institutions. Given the pace of economic progress, techniques alter speedily; and even the work in which the student has been trained may no longer be useful when he is ready to earn a living or soon after. Our conclusion, then, is that the aim of education should be to prepare an individual to become an expert both in some particular vocation or art and in the general art of the free man and the citizen. Thus the two kinds of education once given separately to different social classes must be given together to all alike.

In this epoch in which almost all of us must be experts in some field in order to make a living, general education therefore assumes a peculiar importance. Since no one can become an expert in all fields, everyone is compelled to trust the judgment of other people pretty thoroughly in most areas of activity. I must trust the advice of my doctor, my plumber, my lawyer, my radio repairman, and so on. Therefore I am in peculiar need of a kind of sagacity by which to distinguish the expert from the quack, and the better from the worse expert. From this point of view, the aim of general education may be defined as that of providing the broad critical sense by which to recognize competence in any field. William James said that an educated person knows a good man when he sees one. There are standards and a style for every type of activity—manual, athletic, intellectual, or artistic; and the educated man should be one who can tell sound from shoddy work in a field outside his own. General education is especially required in a democracy where the public elects its leaders and officials; the ordinary citizen must be discerning enough so that he will not be deceived by appearances and will elect the candidate who is wise in his field.

Both kinds of education—special as well as general—contribute to the task of implementing the pervasive forces of our culture. Here we revert to what was said at the start of this chapter on the aims of education in our society. It was argued there that two complementary forces are at the root of our culture: on the one hand, an ideal of man and society distilled from the past but at the same time transcending the past as a standard of judgment valid in itself, and, on the other hand, the belief that no existent expressions of this ideal are final but that all alike call for perpetual scrutiny and change in the light of new knowledge. Specialism is usually the vehicle of this second force. It fosters the open-mindedness and love of investigation which are the wellspring of change, and it devotes itself to the means by which change is brought about. The fact may not always be obvious. There is a sterile specialism which hugs accepted knowledge and ends in the bleakest conservatism. Modern life also calls for many skills which, though specialized, are repetitive and certainly do not conduce to inquiry. These minister to change but unconsciously. Nevertheless, the previous statement is true in the sense that specialism is concerned primarily with knowledge in action, as it advances into new fields and into further applications.

Special education comprises a wider field than vocationalism; and correspondingly, general education extends beyond the limits of merely literary preoccupation. An example will make our point clearer. A scholar—let us say a scientist (whether student or teacher)—will, in the laudable aim of saving himself from narrowness, take a course in English literature, or perhaps read poetry and novels, or perhaps listen to good music and generally occupy himself with the fine arts. All this, while eminently fine and good, reveals a misapprehension. In his altogether unjustified humility, the scientist wrongly interprets the distinction between liberal and illiberal in terms of the distinction between the humanities and the sciences. Plato and Cicero would have been very much surprised to hear that geometry, astronomy, and the sciences of nature in general, are excluded from the humanities. There is also implied a more serious contempt for the liberal arts, harking back to the fallacy which identifies liberal education with the aristocratic ideal. The implication is that liberal education is something only genteel. A similar error is evident in the student's attitude toward his required courses outside his major field as something to "get over with," so that he may engage in the business of serious education, identified in his mind with the field of concentration.

Now, a general education is distinguished from special education, not by subject matter, but in terms of method and outlook, no matter what the field. Literature, when studied in a technical fashion, gives rise to the special science of philology; there is also the highly specialized historical approach to painting. Specialism is interchangeable, not with natural science, but with the method of science, the method which abstracts material from its context and handles it in complete isolation. The reward of scientific method is the utmost degree of precision and exactness. But, as we have seen, specialism as an educational force has its own limitations; it does not usually provide an insight into general relationships.

A further point is worth noting. The impact of specialism has been felt not only in those phases of education which are necessarily and rightly specialistic; it has affected also the whole structure of higher and even of secondary education. Teachers, themselves products of highly technical disciplines, tend to reproduce their knowledge in class. The result is that each subject, being taught by an expert, tends to be so presented as to attract potential experts. This complaint is perhaps more keenly felt in colleges and universities, which naturally look to scholarship. The undergraduate in a college receives his teaching from professors who, in their turn, have been trained in graduate schools. And the latter are dominated by the ideal of specialization. Learning now is diversified and parceled into a myriad of specialties. Correspondingly, colleges and universities are divided into large numbers of departments, with further specialization within the departments. As a result, a student in search of a general course is commonly frustrated. Even an elementary course is devised as an introduction to a specialism within a department; it is significant only as the beginning of a series of courses of advancing complexity. In short, such introductory courses are planned for the specialist, not for the student seeking a general education. The young chemist in the course in literature and the young writer in the course in chemistry find themselves in thoroughly uncomfortable positions so long as the purpose of these courses is primarily to train experts who will go on to higher courses rather than to give some basic understanding of science as it is revealed in chemistry or of the arts as they are revealed in literature.

It is most unfortunate if we envisage general education as something formless—that is to say, the taking of one course after another; and as something negative, namely, the study of what is not in a field of concentration. Just as we regard the courses in concentration as having definite relations to one another, so should we envisage general education as an organic whole whose parts join in expounding a ruling idea and in serving a common aim. And to do so means to abandon the view that all fields and all departments are equally valuable vehicles of general education. It also implies some prescription. At the least it means abandoning the usual attitude of regarding "distribution" as a sphere in which the student exercises a virtually untrammeled freedom of choice. It may be objected that we are proposing to limit the liberty of the student in the very name of liberal education. Such an objection would only indicate an ambiguity in the conception of liberal education. We must distinguish between liberalism in education and education in liberalism. The former, based as it is on the doctrine of individualism, expresses the view that the student should be free in his choice of courses. But education in liberalism is an altogether different matter; it is education which has a pattern of its own, namely, the pattern associated with the liberal outlook. In this view, there are truths which none can be free to ignore, if one is to have that wisdom through which life can become useful. These are the truths concerning the structure of the good life and concerning the factual conditions by which it may be achieved, truths comprising the goals of the free society.

Finally, the problem of general education is one of combining fixity of aim with diversity in application. It is not a question of providing a

general education which will be uniform through the same classes of all
schools and colleges all over the country, even were such a thing possible in
our decentralized system. It is rather to adapt general education to the
needs and intentions of different groups and, so far as possible, to carry its
spirit into special education. The effectiveness of teaching has always
largely depended on this willingness to adapt a central unvarying purpose
to varying outlooks. Such adaptation is as much in the interest of the quick
as of the slow, of the bookish as of the unbookish, and is the necessary
protection of each. What is wanted, then, is a general education capable at
once of taking on many different forms and yet of representing in all its
forms the common knowledge and the common values on which a free
society depends.

Event 12: The President's Commission
on Higher Education—1947

With its report, *Higher Education for Democracy,* President Truman's
Commission on Higher Education ushered in the modern era of
undergraduate education. Among its recommendations of curricular improvement were proposals for the development and expansion of community colleges; the end of curricular, economic, religious, and racial barriers to higher education; mass access to
college; the availability of a minimum of two years of college for all
capable Americans; the initiation of a strong general education
component in the curriculum; and the mixing of general education
with education for work.

The following selection is an edited version of volume 1 of the
report, entitled "Establishing Goals" (pp. 1–3, 5–8, 25–29, 32,
36–39, 47–74). Five other volumes were titled: "Equalizing and
Expanding Individual Opportunity," "Organizing Higher Education," "Staffing Higher Education," "Financing Higher Education,"
and "Resource Data."

The President's Commission on Higher Education has been charged with
the task of defining the responsibilities of colleges and universities in
American democracy and in international affairs—and, more specifically,
with reexamining the objectives, methods, and facilities of higher education in the United States in the light of the social role it has to play.

The colleges and universities themselves had begun this process of
reexamination and reappraisal before the outbreak of World War II. For
many years they had been healthily dissatisfied with their own ac-

complishments, significant though these have been. Educational leaders were troubled by an uneasy sense of shortcoming. They felt that somehow the colleges had not kept pace with changing social conditions, that the programs of higher education would have to be repatterned if they were to prepare youth to live satisfyingly and effectively in contemporary society.

One factor contributing to this sense of inadequacy has been the steadily increasing number of young people who seek a college education. As the national economy became industrialized and more complex, as production increased and national resources multiplied, the American people came in ever greater numbers to feel the need of higher education for their children. More and more American youth attended colleges and universities, but resources and equipment and curriculum did not keep pace with the growing enrollment or with the increasing diversity of needs and interests among the students.

World War II brought a temporary falling off in enrollment, but with the war's end and the enactment of Public Laws 16 and 346, the "Veterans' Rehabilitation Act," and "The G.I. Bill of Rights," the acceleration has resumed. The increase in numbers is far beyond the capacity of higher education in teachers, in buildings, and in equipment. Moreover, the number of veterans availing themselves of veterans' educational benefits falls short of the numbers that records of military personnel show could benefit from higher education. Statistics reveal that a doubling of the 1947–48 enrollment in colleges and universities will be entirely possible within 10 to 15 years, if facilities and financial means are provided.

This tendency of the American people to seek higher education in ever greater numbers has grown concurrently with an increasingly critical need for such education. To this need several developments have contributed:

(a) Science and invention have diversified natural resources, have multiplied new devices and techniques of production. These have altered in radical ways the interpersonal and intergroup relations of Americans in their work, in their play, and in their duties as citizens. As a consequence, new skills and greater maturity are required of youth as they enter upon their adult roles. And the increasing complexity that technological progress has brought to our society has made a broader understanding of social processes and problems essential for effective living.

(b) The people of America are drawn from the peoples of the entire world. They live in contrasting regions. They are of different occupations, diverse faiths, divergent cultural backgrounds, and varied interests. The American Nation is not only a union of 48 different States; it is also a union of an indefinite number of diverse groups of varying size. Of and among these diversities our free society seeks to create a dynamic unity. Where there is economic, cultural, or religious tension, we undertake to effect democratic reconciliation, so as to make of the national life one continuous process of interpersonal, intervocational, and intercultural cooperation.

(c) With World War II and its conclusion has come a fundamental shift in the orientation of American foreign policy. Owing to the inescapable pressure of events, the Nation's traditional isolationism has been displaced by a new sense of responsibility in world affairs. The need for maintaining our democracy at peace with the rest of the world has compelled our initiative in the formation of the United Nations, and America's role in this and other agencies of international cooperation requires of our citizens a knowledge of other peoples—of their political and economic systems, their social and cultural institutions—such as has not hitherto been so urgent.

(d) The coming of the atomic age, with its ambivalent promise of tremendous good or tremendous evil for mankind, has intensified the uncertainties of the future. It has deepened and broadened the responsibilities of higher education for anticipating and preparing for the social and economic changes that will come with the application of atomic energy to industrial uses. At the same time it has underscored the need for education and research for the self-protection of our democracy, for demonstrating the merits of our way of life to other peoples.

Thus American colleges and universities face the need both for improving the performance of their traditional tasks and for assuming the new tasks created for them by the new internal conditions and external relations under which the American people are striving to live and to grow as a free people.

The Role of Education

It is a commonplace of the democratic faith that education is indispensable to the maintenance and growth of freedom of thought, faith, enterprise, and association. Thus the social role of education in a democratic society is at once to insure equal liberty and equal opportunity to differing individuals and groups, and to enable the citizens to understand, appraise, and redirect forces, men, and events as these tend to strengthen or to weaken their liberties.

In performing this role, education will necessarily vary its means and methods to fit the diversity of its constituency, but it will achieve its ends more successfully if its programs and policies grow out of and are relevant to the characteristics and needs of contemporary society. Effective democratic education will deal directly with current problems.

This is not to say that education should neglect the past—only that it should not get lost in the past. No one would deny that a study of man's history can contribute immeasurably to understanding and managing the present. But to assume that all we need do is apply to present and future problems "eternal" truths revealed in earlier ages is likely to stifle creative imagination and intellectual daring. Such an assumption may blind us to new problems and the possible need for new solutions. It is wisdom in education to use the past selectively and critically, in order to illumine the pressing problems of the present.

At the same time education is the making of the future. Its role in a democratic society is that of critic and leader as well as servant; its task is not merely to meet the demands of the present but to alter those demands if necessary, so as to keep them always suited to democratic ideals. Perhaps its most important role is to serve as an instrument of social transition, and its responsibilities are defined in terms of the kind of civilization society hopes to build. If its adjustments to present needs are not to be mere fortuitous improvisations, those who formulate its policies and programs must have a vision of the Nation and the world we want—to give a sense of direction to their choices among alternatives.

What America needs today, then, is "a schooling better aware of its aims." Our colleges need to see clearly what it is they are trying to accomplish. The efforts of individual institutions, local communities, the several States, the educational foundations and associations, and the Federal Government will all be more effective if they are directed toward the same general ends.

In the future as in the past, American higher education will embody the principle of diversity in unity: each institution, State, or other agency will continue to make its own contribution in its own way. But educational leaders should try to agree on certain common objectives that can serve as a stimulus and guide to individual decision and action.

A Time of Crisis

It is essential today that education come decisively to grips with the world-wide crisis of mankind. This is no careless or uncritical use of words. No thinking person doubts that we are living in a decisive moment of human history.

Atomic scientists are doing their utmost to make us realize how easily and quickly a world catastrophe may come. They know the fearful power for destruction possessed by the weapons their knowledge and skill have fashioned. They know that the scientific principles on which these weapons are based are no secret to the scientists of other nations, and that America's monopoly of the engineering processes involved in the manufacture of atom bombs is not likely to last many years. And to the horror of atomic weapons, biological and chemical instruments of destruction are now being added.

But disaster is not inevitable. The release of atomic energy that has brought man within sight of world devastation has just as truly brought him the promise of a brighter future. The potentialities of atomic power are as great for human betterment as for human annihilation. Man can choose which he will have.

The possibility of this choice is the supreme fact of our day, and it will necessarily influence the ordering of educational priorities. We have a big job of reeducation to do. Nothing less than a complete reorientation of our thinking will suffice if mankind is to survive and move on to higher levels.

In a real sense the future of our civilization depends on the direction education takes, not just in the distant future, but in the days immediately ahead.

This crisis is admittedly world-wide. All nations need reeducation to meet it. But this fact does not lessen the obligation of colleges and universities to undertake the task in the United States. On the contrary, our new position in international affairs increases the obligation. We can do something about the problem in our own country and in occupied areas, and hope that by so doing we will win the friendly cooperation of other nations.

The fundamental goal of the United States in its administration of occupied areas must be the reeducation of the populations to the individual responsibilities of democracy. Such reeducation calls for the immediate removal of authoritarian barriers to democratic education, and inculcation of democratic ideals and principles through the guidance, example, and wisdom of United States occupation forces. The primacy of the objective of reeducation, however, appears too often to have been lost sight of in the press of day-to-day administrative problems. Yet every contact by Americans with Germans or Japanese either strengthens or retards the achievement of the goal. Evidence reaching this Commission indicates that while many specific existing barriers to democratic reform have been removed, new obstacles are being created daily by inadequacies of educational personnel and policy. Cognizant of the great responsibility of American education to promote democratic ideals in occupied areas, the Commission recommends the formation of a special committee to appraise progress and offer advice to the Departments of State and National Defense on educational policy and administration in occupied areas.

The schools and colleges are not solely or even mainly to blame for the situation in which we find ourselves, or that the responsibility for resolving the crisis is not or can not be entirely theirs [*sic*]. But the scientific knowledge and technical skills that have made atomic and bacteriological warfare possible are the products of education and research, and higher education must share proportionately in the task of forging social and political defenses against obliteration. The indirect way toward some longer view and superficial curricular tinkering can no longer serve. The measures higher education takes will have to match in boldness and vision the magnitude of the problem.

In the light of this situation, the President's Commission on Higher Education has attempted to select, from among the principal goals for higher education, those which should come first in our time. They are to bring to all the people of the Nation:

Education for a fuller realization of democracy in every phase of living.

Education directly and explicitly for international understanding and cooperation.

Education for the application of creative imagination and trained intelligence to the solution of social problems and to the administration of public affairs.

Education is by far the biggest and the most hopeful of the Nation's enterprises. Long ago our people recognized that education for all is not only democracy's obligation but its necessity. Education is the foundation of democratic liberties. Without an educated citizenry alert to preserve and extend freedom, it would not long endure.

Accepting this truth, the United States has devoted many of its best minds and billions of its wealth to the development and maintenance of an extensive system of free public schools, and through the years the level of schooling attained by more and more of our people has steadily risen.

Record of Growth

The expansion of the American education enterprise since the turn of the century has been phenomenal. The 700,000 enrollment in high schools in the school year 1900 was equal to only 11 percent of the youth of usual high-school age, 14 through 17 years old. This increased in 1940 to over 7,000,000 students representing 73 percent of the youth.

Almost as spectacular has been the increase in college attendance. In 1900 fewer than 250,000 students, only 4 percent of the population 18 through 21 years of age, were enrolled in institutions of higher education. By 1940 the enrollment had risen to 1,500,000 students, equal to a little less than 16 percent of the 18–21-year-olds. In 1947, enrollments jumped to the theretofore unprecedented peak of 2,354,000 although approximately 1,000,000 of the students were veterans, older than the usual college age because World War II had deferred their education. The situation in the fall of 1947 gives every indication that the school year 1948 will witness even larger enrollments. (See Chart I, "Growth of College Population.")

This record of growth is encouraging, but we are forced to admit nonetheless that the educational attainments of the American people are still substantially below what is necessary, either for effective individual living or for the welfare of our society.

According to the U.S. Bureau of the Census, almost 17,000,000 men and women over 19 years of age in 1947 had stopped their schooling at the sixth grade or less. Of these, 9,000,000 had never attended school or had stopped their schooling before completing the fifth grade. In 1947, about 1,600,000 or 19 percent of our high-school-age boys and girls were not attending any kind of school, and over two-thirds of the 18- and 19-year-old youths were not in school.

These are disturbing facts. They represent a sobering failure to reach the educational goals implicit in the democratic creed, and they are indefensible in a society so richly endowed with material resources as our own. We cannot allow so many of our people to remain so ill equipped either as human beings or as citizens of a democracy.

Great as the total American expenditure for education may seem, we have not been devoting any really appreciable part of our vast wealth to higher education. As table I shows, even though in the last 15 years our annual budget for education has risen in number of dollars, it has actually declined in relation to our increasing economic productivity.

The $1,000,000,000 we have put into our colleges and universities in 1947 was less than one-half of 1 percent of the gross national product, which is the market value of all the goods and services produced in the country in that year.

Barriers to Equal Opportunity

One of the gravest charges to which American society is subject is that of failing to provide a reasonable equality of educational opportunity for its youth. For the great majority of our boys and girls, the kind and amount of education they may hope to attain depends, not on their own abilities, but on the family or community into which they happened to be born or, worse still, on the color of their skin or the religion of their parents.

Economic Barriers

The old, comfortable idea that "any boy can get a college education who has it in him" simply is not true. Low family income, together with the rising costs of education, constitutes an almost impassable barrier to college education for many young people. For some, in fact, the barrier is raised so early in life that it prevents them from attending high school even when free public high schools exist near their homes.

Table A-2. Direct cost of higher education and its relation to the gross national product

Fiscal year	Amount (in millions)[a]	Proportion of gross national product (percent)[b]
1932	$ 421	0.63
1940	522	.55
1947	1,005	.46

[a] Source: General and educational expenditures, not including capital expansion, as reported by U.S. Office of Education.
[b] Source of gross national product: U.S. Bureau of Foreign and Domestic Commerce.

Despite the upward trend in average per capita income for the past century and more, the earnings of a large part of our population are still too low to provide anything but the barest necessities of physical life. It is a distressing fact that in 1945, when the total national income was far greater than in any previous period in our history, half of the children under 18 were growing up in families which had a cash income of $2,530 or less. The educational significance of these facts is heightened by the relationship that exists between income and birth rate. Fertility is highest in the families with lowest incomes.

In the elementary and secondary schools the effects of these economic conditions are overcome to a considerable extent, though not entirely, by the fact that education is free and at certain ages is compulsory. But this does not hold true at the college level. For a number of years the tendency has been for the college student to bear an increasing share of the cost of his own education. Even in State-supported institutions we have been moving away from the principle of free education to a much greater degree than is commonly supposed.

Under the pressure of rising costs and of a relative lessening of public support, the colleges and universities are having to depend more and more on tuition fees to meet their budgets. As a result, on the average, tuition rates rose about 30 percent from 1939 to 1947.

Nor are tuition costs the whole of it. There are not enough colleges and universities in the country, and they are not distributed evenly enough to bring them within reach of all young people. Relatively few students can attend college in their home communities. So to the expense of a college education for most youth must be added transportation and living costs—by no means a small item.

This economic factor explains in large part why the father's occupation has been found in many studies to rank so high as a determining factor in a young person's college expectancy. A farm laborer earns less than a banker or a doctor, for instance, and so is less able to afford the costs of higher education for his children. The children, moreover, have less inducement to seek a college education because of their family background. In some social circles a college education is often considered a luxury which can be done without, something desirable perhaps, "but not for the likes of us."

The importance of economic barriers to post-high school education lies in the fact that there is little if any relationship between the ability to benefit from a college education and the ability to pay for it. Studies discussed in the volume of this Commission's report, "Equalizing and Expanding Individual Opportunity," show that among children of equally high ability those with fathers in higher-income occupations had greater probability of attending college.

By allowing the opportunity for higher education to depend so largely on the individual's economic status, we are not only denying to millions of young people the chance in life to which they are entitled; we are also depriving the Nation of a vast amount of potential leadership and potential social competence which it sorely needs.

Barrier of a Restricted Curriculum

We shall be denying educational opportunity to many young people as long as we maintain the present orientation of higher education toward verbal skills and intellectual interests. Many young people have abilities of a different kind, and they cannot receive "education commensurate with their native capacities" in colleges and universities that recognize only one kind of educable intelligence.

Traditionally the colleges have sifted out as their special clientele persons possessing verbal aptitudes and a capacity for grasping abstractions. But many other aptitudes—such as social sensitivity and versatility, artistic ability, motor skill and dexterity, and mechanical aptitude and ingenuity—also should be cultivated in a society depending, as ours does, on the minute division of labor and at the same time upon the orchestration of an enormous variety of talents.

If the colleges are to educate the great body of American youth, they must provide programs for the development of other abilities than those involved in academic aptitude, and they cannot continue to concentrate on students with one type of intelligence to the neglect of youth with other talents.

Racial and Religious Barriers

The outstanding example of these barriers to equal opportunity, of course, is the disadvantages suffered by our Negro citizens. The low educational attainments of Negro adults reflect the cumulative effects of a long period of unequal opportunity. In 1940 the schooling of the Negro was significantly below that of whites at every level from the first grade through college. At the college level, the difference is marked; 11 percent of the white population 20 years of age and over had completed at least 1 year of college and almost 5 percent had finished 4 years; whereas for the non-whites (over 95 percent of whom are Negroes) only a little more than 3 percent had completed at least 1 year of college and less than 1½ percent had completed a full course.

The Quota System. At the college level a different form of discrimination is commonly practiced. *Many colleges and universities, especially in their professional schools, maintain a selective quota system for admission, under which the chance to learn, and thereby to become more useful citizens, is denied to certain minorities, particularly to Negroes and Jews. . . .*

The Need for General Education

Present college programs are not contributing adequately to the quality of students' adult lives either as workers or as citizens. This is true in large part because the unity of liberal education has been splintered by overspecialization.

For half a century and more the curriculum of the liberal arts college has been expanding and disintegrating to an astounding degree. The number of courses has so multiplied that no student could take all of them, or even a majority of them, in a lifetime. In one small midwestern college, for example, the number of courses offered increased from 67 in 1900 to 296 in 1930. During the same period the liberal arts college of one of the great private universities lengthened its list of courses from 960 to 1,897.

This tendency to diversify the content of what was once an integrated liberal education is in part the consequence of the expansion of the boundaries of knowledge. New advances in every direction have added more and more subjects to the liberal arts curriculum and have at the same time limited the area of knowledge a single course could cover. This development is at once the parent and the child of specialization.

Specialization is a hallmark of our society, and its advantages to mankind have been remarkable. But in the educational program it has become a source both of strength and of weakness. Filtering downward from the graduate and professional school levels, it has taken over the undergraduate years, too, and in the more extreme instances it has made of the liberal arts college little more than another vocational school, in which the aim of teaching is almost exclusively preparation for advanced study in one or another specialty.

This tendency has been fostered, if not produced, by the training of college teachers in the graduate school, where they are imbued with the single ideal of an ever-narrowing specialism.

The trend toward specialization has been reenforced by the movement toward democratization of higher education. The young people appearing in growing numbers on college campuses have brought with them widely diverse purposes, interests, capacities, and academic backgrounds. Some expect to enter one of the old-line professions; others want training in one of the numerous branches of agriculture, industry or commerce. Some consider college education a natural sequel to high school; others seek it as a road to higher social status.

The net result of the situation is that the college student is faced with a bewildering array of intensive courses from which to make up his individual program. To secure a reasonably comprehensive grasp of his major field, he must in some cases spend as much as half or more of his time in that one department. The other half he scatters among courses in other departments which, designed for future specialists in those fields, are so restricted in scope that the student can gain from them only a fragmentary view of the subject. He, therefore, leaves college unacquainted with some of the fundamental areas of human knowledge and without the integrated view of human experience that is essential both for personal balance and for social wisdom.

Today's college graduate may have gained technical or professional training in one field of work or another, but is only incidentally, if at all, made ready for performing his duties as a man, a parent, and a citizen. Too often he is "educated" in that he has acquired competence in some particular occupation, yet falls short of that human wholeness and civic conscience which the cooperative activities of citizenship require.

The failure to provide any core of unity in the essential diversity of higher education is a cause for grave concern. A society whose members lack a body of common experience and common knowledge is a society without a fundamental culture; it tends to disintegrate into a mere aggregation of individuals. Some community of values, ideas, and attitudes is essential as a cohesive force in this age of minute division of labor and intense conflict of special interests.

The crucial task of higher education today, therefore, is to provide a unified general education for American youth. Colleges must find the right relationship between specialized training on the one hand, aiming at a thousand different careers, and the transmission of a common cultural heritage toward a common citizenship on the other.

There have already been many efforts to define this relationship. Attempts to reach conclusions about the ends and means of general education have been a major part of debate and experimentation in higher education for at least two decades.

"General education" is the term that has come to be accepted for those phases of nonspecialized and nonvocational learning which should be the common experience of all educated men and women.

General education should give to the student the values, attitudes, knowledge, and skills that will equip him to live rightly and well in a free society. It should enable him to identify, interpret, select, and build into his own life those components of his cultural heritage that contribute richly to understanding and appreciation of the world in which he lives. It should therefore embrace ethical values, scientific generalizations, and aesthetic conceptions, as well as an understanding of the purposes and character of the political, economic and social institutions that men have devised.

But the knowledge and understanding which general education aims to secure whether drawn from the past or from a living present, are not to be regarded as ends in themselves. They are means to a more abundant personal life and a stronger, freer social order.

Thus conceived, general education is not sharply distinguished from liberal education; the two differ mainly in degree, not in kind. General education undertakes to redefine liberal education in terms of life's problems as men face them, to give it human orientation and social direction, to invest it with content that is directly relevant to the demands of contemporary society. General education is liberal education with its matter and method shifted from its original aristocratic intent to the service of democracy. General education seeks to extend to all men the benefits of an education that liberates.

This purpose calls for a unity in the program of studies that a uniform system of courses cannot supply. The unity must come, instead, from a consistency of aim that will infuse and harmonize all teaching and all campus activities.

Objectives of General Education

The purposes of general education should be understood in terms of performance, of behavior, not in terms of mastering particular bodies of knowledge. It is the task of general education to provide the kinds of learning and experience that will enable the student to attain certain basic outcomes, among them the following:

1. To develop for the regulation of one's personal and civic life a code of behavior based on ethical principles consistent with democratic ideals. . . .
2. To participate actively as an informed and responsible citizen in solving the social, economic, and political problems of one's community, State, and Nation.
3. To recognize the interdependence of the different peoples of the world and one's personal responsibility for fostering international understanding and peace. . . .
4. To understand the common phenomena in one's physical environment, to apply habits of scientific thought to both personal and civic problems, and to appreciate the implications of scientific discoveries for human welfare. . . .
5. To understand the ideas of others and to express one's own effectively. . . .
6. To attain a satisfactory emotional and social adjustment. . . .
7. To maintain and improve his own health and to cooperate actively and intelligently in solving community health problems. . . .
8. To understand and enjoy literature, art, music, and other cultural activities as expressions of personal and social experience, and to participate to some extent in some form of creative activity. . . .
9. To acquire the knowledge and attitudes basic to a satisfying family life. . . .
10. To choose a socially useful and personally satisfying vocation that will permit one to use to the full his particular interests and abilities. . . .
11. To acquire and use the skills and habits involved in critical and constructive thinking. . . .

Methods of General Education

The objectives of general education are not to be achieved by prescribing any single pattern of courses for all students. Seeking to gain common goals for all, general education nonetheless approaches these goals through different avenues of subject matter and experience. These avenues must be as numerous and varied as the wide differences among students.

If all students are to attain common goals, much experimentation with new types of courses and teaching materials will be required. Only as these are developed, appraised, and modified to meet the widely varied abilities and needs of students in a democracy can all attain common objectives. . . .

The effectiveness of any general education program will depend on the quality and attitudes of those who administer and teach it. Its success will be commensurate with the faculty members' recognition of the importance of such instruction to society and their willingness to assume initiative and responsibility in reorganizing instruction and rearranging the life of the institution to accomplish its objective. . . .

Campus Activities

Formal courses are not the only sources of general education, however. There are a great variety of extra classroom resources in the university community that should be used for educational purposes. . . .

Interrelationship of General and Vocational Education

Although general education, as the term is currently used, is concerned with the nonspecialized activities of living, it is by no means antagonistic to vocational education. Rightly conceived, the two are complementary. General education should contribute to vocational competence by providing the breadth of view and perspective that make the individual a more effective worker and a more intelligent member of a society of freemen.

It is urgently important in American education today that the age-old distinction between education for living and education for making a living be discarded. . . .

The Importance of Counseling

One of the most important instruments for accomplishing the purposes of higher education outlined in this report is an effective guidance and counseling program. In mass education, counseling provides the most likely means for adapting instruction to the individual student. . . .

Education Adjusted To Needs

To make sure of its own health and strength a democratic society must provide free and equal access to education for its youth, and at the same time it must recognize their differences in capacity and purpose. Higher education in America should include a variety of institutional forms and educational programs, so that at whatever point any student leaves school, he will be fitted, within the limits of his mental capacity and educational level, for an abundant and productive life as a person, as a worker, and as a citizen.

The Community College

As one means of achieving the expansion of educational opportunity and the diversification of educational offerings it considers necessary, this Commission recommends that the number of community colleges be increased and that their activities be multiplied.

Community colleges in the future may be either publicly or privately controlled and supported, but most of them, obviously, will be under public auspices. They will be mainly local or regional in scope and should be locally controlled, though they should be carefully planned to fit into a comprehensive State-wide system of higher education. They will derive much of their support from the local community, supplemented by aid from State funds.

Some community colleges may offer a full four years of college work, but most of them probably will stop at the end of the fourteenth grade, the sophomore year of the traditional college. In the latter case they should be closely articulated with the high school.

Whatever form the community college takes, its purpose is educational service to the entire community, and this purpose requires of it a variety of functions and programs. It will provide college education for the youth of the community certainly, so as to remove geographic and economic barriers to educational opportunity and discover and develop individual talents at low cost and easy access. But in addition, the community college will serve as an active center of adult education. It will attempt to meet the total post–high school needs of its community.

TERMINAL AND SEMIPROFESSIONAL EDUCATION

In the past the junior college has most commonly sought to provide within the local community the freshman and sophomore courses of the traditional college curriculum. With notable exceptions, it has concentrated on preparing students for further study in the junior and senior years of liberal arts colleges or professional schools.

But preparatory programs looking to the more advanced courses of the senior college are not complete and rounded in themselves, and they usually do not serve well the purpose of those who must terminate their schooling at the end of the fourteenth grade. Half the young people who go to college find themselves unable to complete the full 4-year course, and for a long time to come more students will end their formal education in the junior college years than will prolong it into the senior college. These 2-year graduates would gain more from a terminal program planned specifically to meet their needs than from the first half of a 4-year curriculum.

For this reason, the Commission recommends that the community college emphasize programs of terminal education.

These terminal programs should include both general and vocational training. They should be designed both for young people who want to secure as good a general education as possible by the end of the fourteenth grade and for those who wish to fit themselves for semiprofessional occupations.

Semiprofessional training, properly conceived and organized, can make a significant contribution to education for society's occupational requirements. In not providing this sort of training anywhere in existing programs, the educational system is out of step with the demands of the twentieth century American economy.

Because of advancing technology, the occupational center of our economic sytem is shifting away from the major producing industries. The proportion of the working population engaged in these industries has decreased, while the proportion in the distributive and service trades has increased. In 1880, for instance, about one-half of all workers were engaged in agriculture; in 1947, less than one-seventh of the workers were so engaged.

One result of this development is a new and rapidly growing need for trained semiprofessional workers in these distributive and service occupations. To meet the needs of the economy our schools must train many more young people for employment as medical secretaries, recreational leaders, hotel and restaurant managers, aviators, salesmen in fields like life insurance and real estate, photographers, automotive and electrical technicians, and so on through a long list of positions in the business and professional world.

Education on the technician level—that is, the training of medical technicians, dental hygienists, nurses' aides, laboratory technicians—offers one practical solution for the acute shortage of professional personnel in medicine, dentistry, and nursing. An adequate staff of well-trained assistants can substantially increase the number of patients one doctor, dentist, or nurse can handle.

For these semiprofessional occupations a full 4 years of college training is not necessary. It is estimated that in many fields of work there are *five* jobs requiring 2 years of college preparation for every *one* that requires 4 years. Training for these more numerous jobs is the kind the community college should provide.

If the semiprofessional curriculum is to accomplish its purpose, however, it must not be crowded with vocational and technical courses to the exclusion of general education. It must aim at developing a combination of social understanding and technical competence. Semiprofessional education should mix a goodly amount of general education for personal and social development with technical education that is intensive, accurate, and comprehensive enough to give the student command of marketable abilities.

COMMUNITY CENTER OF LEARNING

Post-high school education for youth is only one of the functions to be performed by the community college. One such college has been known to have a daytime junior college enrollment of 3,000 but an adult enrollment in the late afternoon and evening of 25,000.

The community college seeks to become a center of learning for the entire community, with or without the restrictions that surround formal course work in traditional institutions of higher education. It gears its programs and services to the needs and wishes of the people it serves, and its offerings may range from workshops in painting or singing or play writing for fun to refresher courses in journalism or child psychology.

If the health of the community can be improved by teaching restaurant managers something about the bacteriology of food, the community college sets up such a course and seeks to enroll as many of those employed in food service as it can muster. If the community happens to be a center for travelers from Latin America, the college provides classes in Spanish for salespeople, waitresses, bellboys, and taxicab drivers.

The potential effects of the community college in keeping intellectual curiosity alive in out-of-school citizens, of stimulating their zest for learning, of improving the quality of their lives as individuals and as citizens are limited only by the vision, the energy, and the ingenuity of the college staff—and by the size of the college budget. But the people will take care of the budget if the staff provides them with vital and worthwhile educationl services.

IN RELATION TO THE LIBERAL ARTS COLLEGE

The Commission does not intend to suggest that the expansion of educational opportunity at the freshman-sophomore level should be limited to the community college. Part of the needed expansion can be achieved through existing 4-year colleges, part of it through the lower divisions of the universities.

Some of the established colleges may wish to institute terminal curriculums and contribute to the development of semiprofessional training. Others will prefer to concentrate on general education for students who plan to complete a 4-year course. Still others, especially the liberal arts colleges of universities, may welcome the opportunity to focus their energies on senior college programs.

In any case, the liberal arts college is so well established in the American educational tradition that it need not fear community colleges will weaken its own appeal. It should encourage the development of the community college, not oppose it. Experience indicates that these community institutions awaken intellectual curiosity and ambition in many youth who would not otherwise seek college education at all, and in many cases these students will be stimulated to continue their college careers if the 4-year colleges will meet them halfway with liberal admission policies.

There is little danger of lowered standards in this. We know now that ability to complete successfully the work of the last 2 years of college depends more upon the quality of mind and the mental habits a student brings to his work than upon the nature of the subject matter he has already covered. There is no reason to believe that community colleges, if they are adequately staffed, cannot do as good a job as the lower divisions of 4-year colleges in preparing students for advanced work in liberal and professional education.

While it favors the growth of community colleges, the Commission emphasizes that they must be soundly established with respect to financial support and student attendance. This calls for careful planning on a State-wide basis in determining location of the colleges and the curriculums to be offered. Simply to create more small, inadequately financed institutions would only retard the development of a sound program of post–high school education.

The Senior Liberal Arts College

Essential as programs of general education at high school and junior college levels are, they do not alone meet the need for education for responsible living. Many college students deserve and society urgently needs more liberal education than these lower levels can provide.

We cannot terminate liberal education at the end of the conventional sophomore year and turn the colleges and universities over thereafter to academic specialization and professional education.

Our society is desperately in need of men and women capable of giving wise leadership—the kind of leadership that can come only from those who have read with insight the record of human experience, who know the nature, career, and consequences of human values, who sense the meaning of the social forces operating in the world today, who comprehend the complexities and intricacies of social processes, and who command the methods of rigorous critical thinking.

Advanced courses in liberal education are necessary to force the student to grapple with intellectual tasks of difficulty and complexity. He must have depth as well as breadth in his educational experience if he is to acquire the capacity for intellectual independence. He needs to cut his teeth on solid intellectual matter, reach a higher level of critical thinking, and attain some facility in the methods of scientific investigation.

EXCESSIVE SPECIALIZATION

To put the case for advanced courses in liberal studies, however, is not to sanction present curricular practices in the senior college. It should be possible to provide an education in depth without losing the breadth that is the essence of liberal education. It should be possible to steer a sensible course between overgeneralization and overspecialization.

The elective system was introduced in American colleges in protest against a rigidly prescribed curriculum that, however much it made for a common background among educated men, was too inflexible to meet changing social conditions. Then, when it seemed that too many students were taking advantage of the elective system to keep their college education as elementary as possible, the principle of concentration on a "major" subject was adopted, to make sure that every student's college experience would include a measure of intellectual discipline. But today in many undergraduate colleges, particularly in the large universities, concentration has proceeded so far that it has almost destroyed the historic values of liberal education. It has led to an unwarranted degree of specialization at the undergraduate level.

In one liberal arts college, for instance, an analysis of the programs of students graduating in 1939 and 1940 revealed that some of these graduates had taken as much as half their college work in a single department. Those who majored in English literature took an average of 73 quarter hours in that department, plus an average of 16 hours in composition. Majors in political science took an average of only 52 hours in their own department but concentrated a total of 106 hours in the social sciences. Majors in the physical sciences took on the average 95 hours in that field—more than half of the number required for baccalaureate degree.

Such a degree of specialization amounts to vocationalism in liberal education. When the liberal arts college allows its students to specialize in one field of study so early and so intensively that other areas of knowledge are ignored or barely touched upon, it gives up its liberal birthright and becomes in fact a professional school.

The influence of graduate education and the specialized scholarly interests of a graduate faculty are largely responsible for excessive and narrow specialization in the liberal arts college.

Since often there are not enough students in the graduate school to justify giving all the specialities the graduate faculty wishes to offer, these highly specialized courses, dealing intensively with small pieces of a given subject, are opened to undergraduates. The result is that many undergraduate programs are little more than a collection of unrelated fragments of knowledge or a sequence of courses in an extremely narrow field.

The imposition of the narrow specialization of the graduate school on undergraduate education is unfortunate because the purpose of the senior college is basically different. Specialization at the graduate level is organized to train a few highly selected persons for careers in research and scholarship. Programs of concentration in the senior college, however, need to be built around a much wider range of intellectual and occupational objectives to serve a much larger and less selected body of students.

Furthermore, too much concentration too early is bad even for future specialists. The competent expert should be able to view his specialty in the whole context of knowledge, within as well as without the division of studies of which it is a part. The historian should certainly know something of science and the scientist something of history. But so should the physicist be acquainted with the fundamentals of the biological sciences, and the sociologist with the fundamentals of political science.

Specialization is a great good. It has its place in any culture that has risen above the primitive level and in ours it occupies a place of primary importance. Nothing said in this report is to be interpreted as in any way discounting the tremendous gains that have grown out of the efforts of specialists to penetrate ever more deeply into the secrets of nature and the motives and processes of human and social behavior.

The point made here is twofold: that not all college students will become specialists and therefore should not be educated as such, and that the specialist himself will be more effective if he can see how the smaller problem of his special concern is related to larger issues and values.

BROADER FIELDS OF CONCENTRATION

Most colleges have long had in effect certain rules of distribution which are intended to keep concentration from getting out of hand. But distribution cannot counteract the splintering of the curriculum. Even when a student distributes a reasonable proportion of his credit hours among a number of departments, the individual courses remain fragmentary and the sequences narrow.

Today many institutions are experimenting with plans for broadening the fields of major concentration, and this trend should be encouraged and accelerated. The plans are of various kinds—topical majors, divisional majors, area studies, functional majors—but they are all interdepartmental and some of them cut across divisional boundaries as well.

The aim in all of them is to avoid both the sterility of overspecialization and the superficiality of hasty synthesis; to combine depth with breadth, the advantage of intensive study with the more inclusive view.

The divisional major that seems to have taken hold most widely is that in the humanities. The major is usually made up of a sequence of courses that are themselves divisional in scope, drawing their materials and instructors from the history, literature, philosophy, and fine arts departments. The courses are not, or should not be, surveys organized to give a hurried introduction to the subject, but instead should be integrated around some central theme.

Of the interdivisional plans the most common are the increasingly popular majors in American studies or similar programs centered on the culture of some foreign area or people: Scandinavian studies, Far Eastern studies, Russian studies, and so on.

As these area curriculums develop they should take on an increasing degree of integration. They should do more than bring together a collection of already available courses from various departments. There should be a definite attempt to present in a sound and comprehensive synthesis the geographic, historical, cultural, social, political, and economic elements of a contemporary foreign culture.

In most cases these area programs are both cultural and professional in purpose. They offer an excellent opportunity to students interested mainly in a liberal education, and they also constitute an invaluable preparation for many types of professional service abroad. They can also make an invaluable contribution to the international understanding so needed in our time.

The functional major has been described as "a sequence of courses and other educational activities leading to the attainment of a clearly defined educational or vocational goal." The student, with faculty advice and approval, draws up his own plan of study, selecting subjects that are related to each other and to a well-defined objective and arranging them in a systematic program.

This kind of major is perhaps the most far reaching of the attempts to revitalize the senior college curriculum. Not only does it permit greater flexibility than the conventional departmental major, but it emphasizes purpose and unity in the individual's educational experience. It provides the integration that the modern college has so often failed to achieve and the purpose that liberal arts programs have so often lacked.

The purposes that govern functional majors may be either broadly vocational or cultural. There is no reason to be scornful of vocationl motives in liberal arts education. Historically the B.A. degree has had a vocational aim as preparation for the learned professions. It is not out of keeping with the traditional purpose of liberal education to extend it to serve other vocational interests.

However, vocational offerings in the liberal arts college should be built around and based on liberal studies. They should be broader in scope than those in the more specialized colleges and should be of a kind that requires relatively few specific skills—journalism, for example, or general business, or library science.

Liberal education can be thoroughly useful when its relevance to life is brought sharply into focus by a vocational purpose that gives point and direction to the student's program. The danger of futility lies in an unfocused, aimless study of liberal subjects. For this reason the traditional segregation of liberal education in one period of a person's college career and of professional education in another has not served the best interests of either.

The aim should be to integrate liberal and vocational education, letting them proceed simultaneously though in varying proportions throughout the student's college life, each enriching and giving meaning to the other.

General Education in the Senior College

The emphasis to be placed on more intensive study in the senior college does not mean there is no place for general education beyond the sophomore level. On the contrary, general education should be continued throughout the 4-year program.

There is no logical reason why a student majoring say, in one of the sciences should not be able to take a general course, fitted to his level of maturity, in the humanities or the social sciences in his junior or senior year. A number of institutions are beginning to provide such general courses at the senior college level, and this development is to be commended.

All these plans for revision and reform in the senior college curriculum are still in the trial stage, and the work of experimentation should be carried on as continuously, vigorously, and speedily as possible.

Whatever the methods developed, the purpose is clear: to provide a well-rounded education that will fit men and women to understand the broad cultural foundations, the significant accomplishments, and the unfinished business of their society; to participate intelligently in community life and public affairs; to build a set of values that will constitute a design for living; and to take a socially responsible and productive part in the world of work.

References

Cornell, E. "Address of Mr. Cornell." *Register,* (Cornell University) 1869–70, pp. 16–18.

Eliot, C. W. *A Turning Point in Higher Education: The Inaugural Address of Charles William Eliot as President of Harvard College, October 19, 1869.* Cambridge, Mass.: Harvard University Press, 1969.

Gilman, D. C. "The Launching of a University." (March 1902) In J. C. Stone and D. P. DeNevi (Eds.), *Portrait of the American University 1890–1910.* San Francisco: Jossey-Bass, 1971.

Harvard Committee. *General Education in a Free Society.* Cambridge, Mass.: Harvard University Press, 1945.

Hofstadter, R., and Smith, W. *American Higher Education: A Documentary History.* 2 vols. Chicago: University of Chicago Press, 1961.

Morison, S. E. *The Founding of Harvard College.* Cambridge, Mass.: Harvard University Press, 1935.

The President's Commission on Higher Education. *Higher Education for American Democracy: A Report of The President's Commission on Higher Education.* New York: Harper & Row, 1947.

Rudolph, F. *Curriculum: A History of the American Undergraduate Course of Study Since 1636.* San Francisco: Jossey-Bass, 1977.

St. John's College: Statement of the St. John's Program 1975–76. (Catalog) Annapolis, Md.

Steffens, L. "Sending a State to College." *American Magazine,* Feb. 1909, 68.

U.S. Bureau of Education. "Report of the Committee of Ten." *Report of the Committee on Secondary School Studies Appointed at the Meeting of the National Educational Association, July 9, 1892, with the Reports of the Conferences Arranged by this Committee and Held December 28–30, 1892.* Washington, D.C.: U.S. Government Printing Office, 1893.

Appendix B

Institutions Included
in the Catalog Study
by Carnegie Type

Research Universities I

PUBLIC

Ohio State University, Main Campus (Ohio)
Purdue University, Main Campus (Indiana)
University of California, San Diego (California)
University of Florida (Florida)
University of Georgia (Georgia)
University of Hawaii at Manoa (Hawaii)
University of Illinois, Urbana Campus (Illinois)
University of Iowa (Iowa)
University of North Carolina at Chapel Hill (North Carolina)
University of Utah (Utah)

PRIVATE

California Institute of Technology (California)
Columbia University (New York)
Cornell University (New York)
Duke University (North Carolina)
The Johns Hopkins University (Maryland)

Note: It should be noted that there is an overabundance of some types of institutions, such as private community and junior colleges, relative to the entire sample in order to ensure adequate representativeness within the group. Another group, which might be titled "most selective liberal arts colleges" (public), was omitted as an irrelevant class because its population consists solely of two institutions.

Northwestern University (Illinois)
University of Pennsylvania (Pennsylvania)
University of Rochester (New York)
University of Southern California (California)
Vanderbilt University (Tennessee)
Washington University (Missouri)
Yeshiva University (New York)

Research Universities II

PUBLIC

Auburn University, Main Campus (Alabama)
Colorado State University (Colorado)
Florida State University (Florida)
Indiana University at Bloomington (Indiana)
Iowa State University of Science and Technology (Iowa)
Oregon State University (Oregon)
Temple University (Pennsylvania)
University of Cincinnati, Main Campus (Ohio)
University of Nebraska, Lincoln (Nebraska)
University of Oklahoma, Norman Campus (Oklahoma)
University of Oregon, Main Campus (Oregon)

PRIVATE

Boston University (Massachusetts)
Brandeis University (Massachusetts)
Brown University (Rhode Island)
Catholic University of America (District of Columbia)
Emory University (Georgia)
George Washington University (District of Columbia)
Illinois Institute of Technology (Illinois)
Rice University (Texas)
Syracuse University, Main Campus (New York)
Tufts University (Massachusetts)
Tulane University of Louisiana (Louisiana)

Doctorate-Granting Universities I

PUBLIC

Kent State University, Main Campus (Ohio)

North Dakota State University, Main Campus (North Dakota)
Ohio University, Main Campus (Ohio)
The University of Alabama (Alabama)
University of Delaware (Delaware)
University of Idaho (Idaho)
University of Maine at Orono (Maine)
University of Missouri, Kansas City (Missouri)
University of North Dakota, Main Campus (North Dakota)
University of South Carolina, Main Campus (South Carolina)
University of Southern Mississippi (Mississippi)
University of Vermont and State Agricultural College (Vermont)

PRIVATE

American University (District of Columbia)
Brigham Young University, Main Campus (Utah)
Dartmouth College (New Hampshire)
Fordham University (New York)
Georgetown University (District of Columbia)
Howard University (District of Columbia)
Lehigh University (Pennsylvania)
Marquette University (Wisconsin)
Northeastern University (Massachusetts)
University of Denver (Colorado)
University of Notre Dame (Indiana)

Doctorate-Granting Universities II

PUBLIC

Bowling Green State University, Main Campus (Ohio)
East Texas State University (Texas)
Illinois State University (Illinois)
Memphis State University (Tennessee)
North Texas State University (Texas)
Northern Illinois University (Illinois)
Texas Tech University (Texas)
University of Akron, Main Campus (Ohio)
University of Nevada at Reno (Nevada)
University of Wisconsin, Milwaukee (Wisconsin)
Western Michigan University (Michigan)

PRIVATE

Adelphi University (New York)
Baylor University (Texas)
Clark University (Massachusetts)
Duquesne University (Pennsylvania)
Southern Methodist University (Texas)
Texas Christian University (Texas)
University of the Pacific (California)
University of Portland (Oregon)
University of Tulsa (Oklahoma)

Comprehensive Universities and Colleges I

PUBLIC

Alcorn State University (Mississippi)
Appalachian State University (North Carolina)
Armstrong State College (Georgia)
California Polytechnic State University, San Luis Obispo (California)
California State University, Chico (California)
Central Michigan University (Michigan)
College of William and Mary, Main Campus (Virginia)
Eastern New Mexico University, Main Campus (New Mexico)
Fort Hays Kansas State College (Kansas)
Framingham State College (Massachusetts)
Georgia Southwestern College (Georgia)
Idaho State University (Idaho)
Kansas State College at Pittsburg (Kansas)
Kearney State College (Nebraska)
Louisiana Tech University (Louisiana)
McNeese State University (Louisiana)
Minot State College (North Dakota)
Morgan State University (Maryland)
Nicholls State University (Louisiana)
North Carolina Agricultural and Technical State University (North Carolina)
Northeast Louisiana University (Louisiana)
Prairie View A & M University (Texas)

Rutgers, The State University of New Jersey, Camden Campus (New Jersey)
State University of New York College at Cortland (New York)
Tarleton State University (Texas)
University of North Carolina at Charlotte (North Carolina)
University of Northern Iowa (Iowa)
University of South Florida (Florida)
University of Tennessee at Chattanooga (Tennessee)
University of Wisconsin, Whitewater (Wisconsin)
Virginia State College (Virginia)
West Georgia College (Georgia)
Winona State University (Minnesota)

PRIVATE

Elmira College (New York)
Fairfield University (Connecticut)
Fairleigh Dickinson University (New Jersey)
Manhattan College (New York)
Russell Sage College, Main Campus (New York)
Seattle Pacific College (Washington)
Seattle University (Washington)
Simmons College (Massachusetts)
Suffolk University (Massachusetts)
University of Hartford (Connecticut)
University of San Francisco (California)
Valparaiso University (Indiana)

Comprehensive Universities and Colleges II

PUBLIC

Boston State College (Massachusetts)
California State College, Stanislaus (California)
Central Washington State College (Washington)
Eastern Oregon State College (Oregon)
Glassboro State College (New Jersey)
Kutztown State College (Pennsylvania)
Lake Superior State College (Michigan)
State University of New York College at Fredonia (New York)

University of Arkansas at Pine Bluff (Arkansas)
Wayne State College (Nebraska)
Western New Mexico University (New Mexico)
Worcester State College (Massachusetts)

PRIVATE

Concordia Teachers College (Nebraska)
Grove City College (Pennsylvania)
Hardin-Simmons University (Texas)
Illinois Wesleyan University (Illinois)
Jacksonville University (Florida)
King's College (Pennsylvania)
Oklahoma Baptist University (Oklahoma)
Saint Lawrence University (New York)
Saint Norbert College (Wisconsin)
Saint Olaf College (Minnesota)
Saint Peter's College (New Jersey)
West Virginia Wesleyan College (West Virginia)

Liberal Arts Colleges I

PRIVATE

Agnes Scott College (Georgia)
Albertus Magnus College (Connecticut)
Central University of Iowa (Iowa)
College of New Rochelle (New York)
Davidson College (North Carolina)
Goddard College (Vermont)
Hamilton College (New York)
Hampden-Sydney College (Virginia)
Hartwick College (New York)
Hobart-William Smith Colleges (New York)
Hollins College (Virginia)
Manhattanville College (New York)
Marymount College (New York)
Muhlenberg College (Pennsylvania)
Ripon College (Wisconsin)
Southwestern at Memphis (Tennessee)

Sweet Briar College (Virginia)
University of Redlands (California)
Washington Jefferson College (Pennsylvania)
Wilson College (Pennsylvania)

Liberal Arts Colleges II

PUBLIC

Johnson State College (Vermont)
Lander College (South Carolina)
Lyndon State College (Vermont)
University of Maine at Machias (Maine)
University of Maryland, Baltimore County Campus (Maryland)
University of North Carolina at Asheville (North Carolina)

PRIVATE

Alma College (Michigan)
Aquinas College (Michigan)
Bethel College (Tennessee)
Bloomfield College (New Jersey)
Brescia College (Kentucky)
Briarcliff College (Iowa)
Central Wesleyan College (South Carolina)
Concordia College, Saint Paul (Minnesota)
Findlay College (Ohio)
Friends World College (New York)
Georgetown College (Kentucky)
Huron College (South Dakota)
Jarvis Christian College (Texas)
King's College (New York)
Lake Erie College (Ohio)
Lone Mountain College (California)
Lycoming College (Pennsylvania)
Marietta College (Ohio)
Mount Union College (Ohio)
Queens College (North Carolina)
Saint John Fisher College (New York)
Southwestern University (Texas)
Spertus College of Judaica (Illinois)

Spring Arbor College (Michigan)
Wayland Baptist College (Texas)
Wheeling College (West Virginia)
Whittier College (California)
Wilmington College (Ohio)

Two-Year Colleges

PUBLIC

American River College (California)
Arizona Western College (Arizona)
Bellevue Community College (Washington)
Blue Mountain Community College (Oregon)
Brevard Community College (Florida)
Bucks County Community College (Pennsylvania)
Cape Cod Community College (Massachusetts)
Charles County Community College (Maryland)
Clackamas Community College (Oregon)
Connors State College (Oklahoma)
Cowley County Community Junior College (Kansas)
Diablo Valley College (California)
Dixie College (Utah)
Eastern Shore Community College (Virginia)
Grand Rapids Junior College (Michigan)
Hagerstown Junior College (Maryland)
Highline Community College (Washington)
Hutchinson Community Junior College (Kansas)
Iowa Lakes Community College (Iowa)
Los Angeles City College (California)
Manatee Junior College (Florida)
Metropolitan Community College (Minnesota)
Miami-Dade Community College (Florida)
Middlesex Community College (Connecticut)
Modesto Junior College (California)
Monroe Community College (New York)
Orange Coast College (California)
Porterville College (California)
Riverside City College (California)

Rockland Community College (New York)
Santa Fe Community College (Florida)
Schoolcraft College (Michigan)
Suffolk County Community College (New York)
Tacoma Community College (Washington)
Trinidad State Junior College (Colorado)
University of Minnesota Technical Institute at Crookston (Minnesota)
Westchester Community College (New York)
Worthington Community College (Minnesota)

PRIVATE

Bay Path Junior College (Massachusetts)
Birdwood Junior College (Georgia)
Central Y. M. C. A. Community College (Illinois)
Cullman College (Alabama)
Dean Junior College (Massachusetts)
Grand View College (Iowa)
Green Mountain College (Vermont)
Immaculata College of Washington (District of Columbia)
Keystone Junior College (Pennsylvania)
Lees-McRae College (North Carolina)
Marion Institute (Alabama)
Mary Holmes College (Mississippi)
Montreat-Anderson College (North Carolina)
Ohio Valley College (West Virginia)
Paul Smith's College of Arts and Sciences (New York)
Presentation College (South Dakota)
Southwestern Christian College (Texas)
Suomi College (Michigan)
Truett-McConnell College (Georgia)
Union College (New Jersey)
Villa Maria College of Buffalo (New York)
Wesley College (Delaware)

Appendix C

Acknowledgments

Hundreds of people assisted in the preparation of this volume by talking about undergraduate education at their college, by discussing a program they directed or created, by commenting on drafts of this book or its companion volume, *Missions of the College Curriculum: a Contemporary Review with Suggestions,* by assisting in the research or writing of this book, or by arranging site visits to their campus. Space permits us to mention only a relatively few, but I am grateful to each and every one of the generous people who helped me.

We extend a special thank you to:

Margie Abbot, Office of the Dean of the College, Brown University

Dorothy Abrahamse, History Department, California State University, Long Beach

Walter Agard, formerly of Meiklejohn College, University of Wisconsin

Philip Altbach, Director, Comparative Education Center, Faculty of Educational Studies, State University of New York at Buffalo

Thomas Amara, Student, University of California, Berkeley

Richard Bailey, Dean of the General College, University of Minnesota

Donald Barnes, former Director, Capital Higher Education Service, Hartford, Connecticut

Alison Bernstein, Program Officer, Fund for the Improvement of Postsecondary Education, Washington, D.C.

Carl D. Biggs, Vice President for Academic Affairs, University of South Florida

Merle Borrowman, Dean of the School of Education, University of California, Berkeley

Paul E. Bragdon, President, Reed College

Marvin Bressler, Professor of Sociology, Princeton University

May Brodbeck, Vice President of Academic Affairs, University of Iowa

E. Howard Brooks, Provost, Claremont Colleges

Carol Gene Brownlee, Dean of the College, Sterling College

Nathan Buch, Director, Technical Career Institutes

Charles Bunting, Deputy Director, Fund for the Improvement of Postsecondary Education, Washington, D.C.

Barbara Burn, Director of International Programs, University of Massachusetts, Amherst

John H. Chandler, President, Scripps College

Earl F. Cheit, Dean of the Graduate School of Business Administration, University of California, Berkeley

Arthur M. Cohen, President, Center for the Study of Community Colleges, University of California, Los Angeles

J. Prescott Cole, Dean of Academic Affairs, Coe College

Arnold Collery, Dean of the College, Columbia University

Martin Corry, NEXUS, American Association for Higher Education, Washington, D.C.

Joseph P. Cosand, Professor, Center for Higher Education, University of Michigan

K. Patricia Cross, Distinguished Research Scientist, Educational Testing Service, Berkeley

Eugene E. Dawson, President, University of Redlands

A. Robert DeHart, President, DeAnza College

Paul Doty, Mallinckrodt Professor of Biochemistry, Harvard University

Stewart Edelstein, Assistant Provost for Social and Behavioral Sciences, University of Maryland

Edward B. Fedder, Executive Officer, Budget Planning, College of Letters and Science, University of California, Berkeley

William B. Fretter, Chairman, Academic Senate, University of California, Berkeley.

Theodore E. Friend, President, Swarthmore College

Marian Gade, Carnegie Council on Policy Studies in Higher Education, Berkeley, California

Zelda Gamson, Co-Director, Residential College, University of Michigan

Donald Gerth, President, California State College, Dominguez Hills

Virgil W. Gillenwater, Executive Vice President, Northern Arizona University

John W. Gillis, Academic Vice President, Chapman College

Richard Gilman, President, Occidental College

Emily Hannah, Vice Chancellor for Academic Affairs, Minnesota State College System

JB Lon Hefferlin, Editor, Higher Education Series, Jossey-Bass, Inc., Publishers

Richard Hendrix, Program Officer, Fund for the Improvement of Postsecondary Education, Washington, D.C.

Richard L. Hoffman, Vice President of Academic Affairs, Mars Hill College

Meg Holmberg, Graduate Student, University of California, Berkeley

Stephen Horn, President, California State College, Long Beach

Bruce Johnson, Dean of Instruction, Flathead Valley Community College

David Justice, Program Officer, Fund for the Improvement of Postsecondary Education, Washington, D.C.

Helen Kelly, President, Immaculate Heart College

J. Terrence Kelly, Dean of Administration and Open College, Miami-Dade Community College

John Laster, NEXUS, American Association for Higher Education, Washington, D.C.

R. Jan Lecroy, Vice Chancellor for Academic Affairs, Dallas County Community College District

Jane Lichtman, NEXUS, American Association for Higher Education, Washington, D.C.

Janet Lieberman, Assistant Dean of Faculty, LaGuardia Community College

R. A. Lombardi, President, Saddleback Community College

T. R. McConnell, School of Education, University of California, Berkeley

Dean McHenry, Chancellor Emeritus, University of California, Santa Cruz

Jeanne Marengo, Carnegie Council on Policy Studies in Higher Education, Berkeley, California

Martin Moed, Dean of Faculty, LaGuardia Community College

Frederick W. Ness, President, Association of American Colleges

Charles D. O'Connell, Vice President and Dean of Students, University of Chicago

Frederick Obear, Vice President for Academic Affairs, Oakland University

Paul Olscamp, President, Western Washington State College

Charles Oxnard, Dean of the College, University of Chicago

Roderic Park, Provost, University of California, Berkeley

Robert Parker, Director, Cooperative Program, Antioch College

Tom Parker, formerly of Bennington College

Gertrude K. Patch, President, Lone Mountain College

Francis Pipkin, Associate Dean of Faculty, Harvard College

Joseph Platt, President, Claremont University Center

Eugene Rice, Director of Contemporary Civilization Program, Columbia University

Richard Richardson, Jr., Director of the Center for Higher Education and Adult Education, Arizona State University

David Riesman, Henry Ford II Professor of Social Sciences, Harvard University

Henry Rosovsky, Dean of the Faculty of Arts and Sciences, Harvard University

Marc Ross, Director, Residential College, University of Michigan

Sheldon Rothblatt, Professor, University of California, Berkeley

Neil Rudenstine, Provost, Princeton University

Frederick Rudolph, Mark Hopkins Professor of History, Williams College

Arman Sarafian, President, La Verne College

Michael Scriven, Professor of Philosophy and Education, University of California, Berkeley

Neil Smelser, Professor of Sociology, University of California, Berkeley

Virginia Smith, President, Vassar College

James Sours, President, Southern Oregon State College

Verne A. Stadtman, Carnegie Council on Policy Studies in Higher

Education, Berkeley, California

David Sweet, President, Rhode Island College

Edwin Taylor, Editor, *American Journal of Physics,* Division of Study and Research in Education, Massachusetts Institute of Technology

Martin Trow, Director, Center for Studies in Higher Education, University of California, Berkeley

Barbara Turlington, Executive Assistant to the President, American Association of Universities

Barbara White, President, Mills College

Claudia White, Carnegie Council on Policy Studies in Higher Education, Berkeley, California

A. Perry Whitmore, formerly of Simon's Rock

Edward Wilcox, Director of the General Education Program and Freshman Seminars, Harvard University

James Q. Wilson, Professor of Government, Harvard University

Mitchell Zeftel, Graduate Student, University of California, Berkeley

Index

C

DATE DUE